THE FIFTH FREEDOM

PRINCETON STUDIES IN AMERICAN POLITICS
HISTORICAL, INTERNATIONAL, AND COMPARATIVE PERSPECTIVES

SERIES EDITORS

IRA KATZNELSON, MARTIN SHEFTER, AND THEDA SKOCPOL

A list of titles in this series appears at the back of the book

THE FIFTH FREEDOM

JOBS, POLITICS, AND CIVIL RIGHTS IN THE UNITED STATES, 1941–1972

Anthony S. Chen

PRINCETON UNIVERSITY PRESS   PRINCETON AND OXFORD

Library of Congress Cataloging-in-Publication Data

Chen, Anthony S., 1972–
The fifth freedom : jobs, politics, and civil rights in the
United States, 1941–1972 / Anthony S. Chen.
p.   cm. — (Princeton studies in American politics : historical, international,
and comparative perspectives)
Includes bibliographical references and index.
ISBN 978-0-691-13457-4 (cloth : alk. paper)
ISBN 978-0-691-13953-1 (pbk. : alk. paper)
1. Affirmative action programs—United States—History—20th century.
2. Discrimination in employment—Government policy—United States—
History—20th century. 3. African Americans—Employment—History—
20th century. I. Title.
HF5549.5.A34C486 2009
331.13'3097309045—dc22   2009003503

British Library Cataloging-in-Publication Data is available

This book has been composed in Sabon

Printed on acid-free paper. ∞

press.princeton.edu

Printed in the United States of America

10 9 8 7 6 5 4 3 2 1

To my mom, dad, and sister

Contents

Illustrations

Tables

Preface and Acknowledgments _____

The debate about affirmative action remains one of the most contentious and impassioned in American politics. Is affirmative action the grossest betrayal or highest embodiment of American values? Has the policy had beneficial effects, or has it merely exacerbated the problems it was meant to alleviate? Is it constitutional, or does it fundamentally violate the Equal Protection Clause of the Fourteenth Amendment? These are important questions, and I will not pretend that I have no opinions concerning them. My opinions on these questions are expressed elsewhere.

This book is motivated by a different set of questions. What explains the advent of affirmative action in employment? More precisely, what accounts for the *unusual character* of the policy regime governing the regulation of job discrimination in the United States? Why did a significant part of it center on monitoring compliance with government regulations (or demonstrating compliance with self-regulation) rather than on the enforcement of the law by administrative agencies? How did enforcement become anchored in the federal courts? What explains the emergence of a small but controversial set of racially attentive policies under the aegis of "affirmative action"? These are the questions that I explore in the following pages.

I am not the first scholar to wonder where affirmative action came from. Others, too, have found the policy curious and sought to track down its origins. This book is distinctive because it frames the puzzle differently, and it analyzes a uniquely rich array of untapped evidence to support a novel explanation. In particular, it makes the case for the critical but overlooked role played by a conservative bloc of political actors whose dogged resistance to the regulatory ideal of "fair employment practices" (FEP) paved the way for the emergence of affirmative action instead. Business groups, northern whites, and the conservative Republicans who represented them were among the most significant opponents of FEP, but they had no idea that the long-term success of their opposition would fuel the rise of a policy that many of their ideological heirs would, ironically, find even more objectionable. I would not be the first writer to note that the history of affirmative action is shot through with irony, but the story I tell suggests that the greatest ironies have remained poorly understood and largely hidden from view.

Claiming the mantle of scholarship, of course, does not shield me or anyone else from the charge of playing politics with history. C. Vann

Woodward has remarked that the recent past is the "favorite breeding place of mythology," and his observation seems especially pertinent for someone writing on the social and political history of civil rights in the United States. When the historical landscape is staked out with so many strongly held political convictions, not the least your own, it can become quite easy to lose your way. This is not to say that scholars can or must abjure all sense of political commitment in their work. The closeness of the recent past makes it only all the more important to assess historical evidence with as much detachment, fairness, and honesty as one can humanly muster. These ascetic values form the basis of objectivity in Thomas L. Haskell's thoughtful formulation. I agree with him that asceticism is within mortal reach, and I have tried as best I can to show my appreciation and understanding of alternative perspectives, even as I register my disagreement with them. But making and supporting a "powerful argument," as he terms such a process, is a difficult enterprise, and I am no less fallible or limited than anyone else whose work has been guided by the same ideal. I leave it to others to determine how close I have come to hitting the mark.[1]

"A book is made with one's own flesh and blood of years," wrote novelist Willa Cather. "It is cremated youth. It is all yours—no one gave it to you." Anyone who has written a book cannot fail to recognize the tiniest sliver of truth in her observation. I cannot count the times I have rued how long it has taken me to write mine. A great deal of life has rushed past me, it seems, since the project initially came to mind. While everybody else seemed to be getting on with their life, I was sitting at a desk somewhere in Berkeley, Ann Arbor, or San Francisco, hunched over a computer screen, trying to think straight and come up with the right words. I sometimes enjoy writing, but the process is always agonizingly slow. All of the time and energy that I have put into the book make it tempting for me to give into the authorial conceit that Cather described. This book is my cremated youth. It is all mine. Nobody gave it to me.

Such self-serving feelings, however, are ultimately fleeting and minor. Anybody who has written a book also recognizes that a whole universe of supportive and generous people helped along the way. Without them, nothing would have been possible. This recognition is the largest part of the truth, and it is the most abiding as well. *The Fifth Freedom* is certainly not without flaw or defect, but whatever strengths or merits may be ascribed to it stem from the aid, consideration, generosity, and company of the many people whom I now have the pleasure of acknowledging in print. I apologize to anyone whom I may have inadvertently overlooked.

This book began in the Department of Sociology at the University of California, Berkeley, where it first took shape as a doctoral dissertation supervised by Jerome Karabel and Margaret Weir. I am immensely grateful to both of them for the time and attention they invested in me. On the many occasions when I lost my way, Jerry was always ready with a discerning observation or clarifying question. Margaret read what I wrote in a timely fashion, sometimes several times, and she furnished me with many pages and hours of instructive commentary. I can never full repay either of them, except to promise that I will try my best to emulate their remarkable example when I myself begin to advise my own students. Other faculty at Berkeley gave generously of their time as well. As the other members of my dissertation committee, Sam Lucas and Michael Omi shared many critical insights with me. Trond Peterson was not formally on my committee, but he deserves special mention for patiently helping me puzzle out my regression results.

I completed the book at the University of Michigan. There are few institutions of higher education where the senior faculty are more supportive of their junior colleagues and still fewer where so many accomplished people are so utterly lacking in pretension. For taking time out of their own busy schedules to discuss portions of the manuscript with me, I would like to thank Barbara Anderson, Becky Blank, John Chamberlin, Susan Collins, Mary Corcoran, Sheldon Danziger, John DiNardo, Kevin Gaines, Rick Hall, Howard Kimeldorf, Karyn Lacy, Matthew Lassiter, Jim Levinsohn, Ann Lin, Mark Mizruchi, Jeff Morenoff, Pam Smock, David Thacher, Maris Vinovskis, Yu Xie, Dean Yang, and Al Young. My friends among the junior faculty—Jake Bowers, Justin McCrary, Rob Mickey, Rob Van Houweling, Jason Owen-Smith, Cara Wong, and Dean Yang—helped me solidify more aspects of the analysis than I am able to remember. Working with Rob Mickey and Rob Van Houweling on our collaborative research into Proposition 11 was a tremendous experience. It was not only edifying to work with them on developing our ideas about racial politics and partisan alignment, but also I learned more from them about American politics than I could have from any class or monograph. Rob Mickey gets credit for coming up with the title of the book.

Other friends and colleagues from all around the country found the time to share their helpful reactions to different parts of the manuscript. I am grateful to Brian Balogh, Henry Brady, Clem Brooks, Dan Carpenter, Kerwin Charles, Ken Chay, Jack Citrin, Don Critchlow, Frank Dobbin, Tom Guglielmo, Victoria Hattam, Greg Huber, David Kirp, Dan Kryder, Taeku Lee, William Leuchtenberg, Nelson Lichtenstein, Rob Lieberman, Clarence Lo, Nancy MacLean, Jordan Matsudaira, Jeff Manza, Suzanne Mettler, Sid Milkis, Alice O'Connor, Chris Parker, Paul Pierson, Jill Quadagno, Chris Rhomberg, Daryl Scott, Eric Shickler, Theda Skocpol, Art Stinchcombe, Melissa Wilde, Dean Yang, and Julian Zelizer. Audiences at Berkeley, Yale, Mount Holyoke, Northwestern, NYU, Oregon, UC Irvine, and UC Santa Cruz gave me challenging and helpful comments. At my undergraduate alma mater, Elizabeth Long and Angela Valenzuela set me on the road to a doctorate, and Chandler Davidson never failed to offer his encouragement. Though his formal connection to the project was exceedingly slim, Tom Sugrue graciously agreed to read and comment on my dissertation. When it came time for me to wade into the cold waters of the academic job market, he supported me and cheered me on from afar. I cannot thank him enough for having faith in a young, unknown sociologist. I want to thank Paul Frymer, Robert Lieberman, and John D. Skrentny as well for their supportive and constructive engagement with my work over the years. My friends Isaac Martin and Melissa Wilde deserve special mention for inviting me to join their book-writing group. While working on their own books—which have now deservedly taken their respective fields by storm—they managed to offer me feedback and comments that were essential as I began the process of revision. Over the years, Nick Adams, David Glisch-Sánchez, Don Mathanga, Robin Phinney, Larisa Shambaugh, and Elias Walsh provided excellent research assistance, and I look forward to seeing their own work come to fruition one day soon.

Through the good offices of the Robert Wood Johnson Scholars in Health Policy Research Program, I had the opportunity to spend a good part of two years revising the manuscript while launching a new project on the politics of health care reform in the American states. My thanks go to John Ellwood, Neil Smelser, Jonah Levy, and Bob Anderson for organizing and leading a program that proved so conducive to getting work done. For his moral and intellectual support, I am grateful to Mark Peterson of the National Advisory Council. As part of the program, I profited tremendously from conversations with Margaret Weir and Paul Pierson. For their friendship, collegiality, intellect, and healthy sense of irreverence, I want to extend special thanks to the RWJ scholars at the Berkeley site: Karen Albright, Michael Anderson, Seema Jayachandran, Sandra Kalev, Jordan Matsudaira, Rob Mickey, Naomi Murakowa, Aaron Panofsky, Chris Parker, Michael Schwartz, and Rob Van Houweling. Chris was the ideal officemate for two years, and I learned a tremendous amount about race and American politics from numerous conversations with him.

Like everyone else who conducts archival research, I am particularly indebted to the dozens of archivists whose assistance enabled me to navigate the immense treasure trove of historical documents under their watch. All of them handled of my requests—no matter how arcane or unreasonable—with proficiency and grace, and I am sorry that space does not permit me to name them individually. I simply could not have conceived the project, let alone completed it, without the help of the sure-footed professionals at the Archives and Special Collections, University of Nebraska; Bancroft Library, University of California, Berkeley; Benson Latin American Collection, University of Texas; Bentley Historical Library, University of Michigan; California State Archives; California State Library; Catherwood Library, Cornell University; Chicago Historical Society; Department of Rare Books, Special Collections, and Preservation, University of Rochester; Carl Albert Center, University of Oklahoma; Dirksen Center; Franklin Delano Roosevelt Presidential Library and Museum; Grenander Department of Special Collections and Archives, SUNY- Albany; Hagley Museum and Library; Harvard Law School Library; Illinois Historical State Library; John F. Kennedy Presidential Library and Museum; Knight Library, University of Oregon; Kroch Library, Cornell University; Library of Congress; Lyndon Baines Johnson Library; Manuscripts and Archives, Yale University; Minnesota Historical Society; New York Public Library; New York State Archives; New York State Library; Ohio Historical Society; Rare Books, Special Collections, and Preservation, University of Rochester; Russell Library, University of Georgia; Schlesinger Library, Harvard University; Schomburg Center for the Study of Black Culture; Special Collections and University Archives, Rutgers University Library; Swarthmore Peace Collection, Swarthmore College Library; W.E.B. Du Bois Library, University of Massachusetts; Taggart Law Library, Ohio Northern University Law School; Urban Archives, Temple University; Western Reserve Historical Society; Young Research Library, University of California, Los Angeles. My thanks go as well to the many librarians at Berkeley and Michigan, who almost always made it a snap to retrieve and borrow even the most obscure materials, sometimes at other campuses. JoAnn Dione at Michigan deserves special mention for helping me locate and process old Gallup Poll data for my analysis.

For housing me on research trips out of town, I would like to thank Julie Chen and Scott Burton; Andy, Dave, and Heather Kuhlken; John J. McCoy and Daniel Moore; Alan and Anne Morrison; Steve Rodrigues; Corinne Ulmann; and Margaret Weir and Nick Ziegler. Victoria Johnson generously housed me for three weeks in August as I worked feverishly on the copyediting.

A special word of thanks goes to Chuck Myers, my editor at Princeton University Press. Chuck has been strongly supportive of me and my work from the beginning. His good judgment and consummate skill made the editorial process extremely rewarding, and he showed me more patience than I deserved as I finished up the manuscript. Thanks as well to Jill Harris, Linda Truilo, and the entire production team at Princeton for all of their hard and expert work in preparing the manuscript for publication. I am grateful to them for their patience as well.

Portions of chapters 3 and 6 appeared in earlier form in Anthony S. Chen, "'The Hitlerian Rule of Quotas': Racial Conservatism and the Politics of Fair Employment Legislation in New York State, 1941–1945," *Journal of American History* 92 (2006): 1238–64. Portions of chapters 4 and 6 appeared in earlier form in Anthony S. Chen, "The Party of Lincoln and the Politics of State Fair Employment Legislation in the North, 1945–1964," *American Journal of Sociology* 112 (2007): 1713–774. Portions of chapters 4 and 6 draw on ideas and material presented earlier in Anthony S. Chen, Robert W. Mickey, and Robert P. Van Houweling, "Explaining the Contemporary Alignment of Race and Party: Evidence from California's 1946 Ballot Initiative on Fair Employment," *Studies in American Political Development* 22 (2008): 204–28.

Over the years, I have been fortunate to receive many forms of financial aid in support of my research and writing. I gratefully acknowledge the support of a Graduate Opportunity Program and the Mentored Research Program at Berkeley; a Doctoral Fellowship from the Institute for Labor and Employment at the University of California; and a Miller Center Fellowship in Public Affairs from the University of Virginia. I am particularly thankful for three years of support from a Soros Fellowship for New Americans. Paul and Daisy Soros have left a remarkable bequest to posterity, and the fellowship program bearing their name continues to be ably led by Warren Ilchman, Carmel Geraghty, Stan Heginbotham, and Jeffrey Soros. Thanks finally to the American Bar Foundation and its director, Robert L. Nelson, for sponsoring me as a Visiting Scholar and providing me with the ideal setting in which to wrap up the project. Research grants were generously provided by the Graduate Division at Berkeley; the National Science Foundation [SES-0000244]; the Hagley Museum; and the Rackham School of Graduate Studies; and the Office for the Vice President of Research at the University of Michigan.

My friends sustained me throughout the book project. They were invariably there when I needed to talk through some part of it, but they were also there to bolster my confidence and distract me from the manuscript when I needed it the most. Thanks to Emily Beller, Jake Bowers, Sarah Burgard, Kristen Carey, Michael Chang, Kerwin Charles, Carolyn Chen, Jennifer Chen, Amander Clarke, Victor Fannuchi, Peter Hall, Caroline Hanley, Bill Hayes, Linus Huang, Victoria Johnson, Sandra Kalev, Tally Katz-Gerro, Sun Kim, Matt Lassiter, Greg Levine, Alex Li, Justin

McCrary, Isaac Martin, Jordan Matsudaira, Rob Mickey, Jeff Morenoff, Stephanie Mudge, Andrew Noymer, Lisa Nuszkowski, Kristin Seefeldt, Lisa Stulberg, David Thacher, Jill Thacher, Harold Toro, Rob Van Houweling, Susana Wappenstein, Melissa Wilde, Jaeyoun Won, Cara Wong, Mayling Wu, and Kathy Yep. David Thacher's dry humor and effortless brilliance kept me sane over the final, challenging weeks of the summer. Thanks as well to the "Yangs": Jerry Chen, Jean Cheng, Eric Chou, Akiko Hall, Alan Kuo, Karen Liao, Ray Lin, Jiannbin Shiao, Erwin Tan, and Kathy Yep. A special shout should go out to my college buddies from the fourth-floor study lobby, including Booth Babcock and Mako Tokushida; Shawn "Gimpy" Brooks and Jenn Brooks; "Big John" and Calli Doherty; Michael "Tex" Duncan and Marty Beard-Duncan; Kristin Field; Angela, Gregory, and Sylvia Foster-Rice; Kyle Gupton; Oren, Julie, and Avi Hayon; John "Sparkles" Koshy; Dave, Heather, Andy, and Ethan Kuhlken; Mike Lannutti and Holly Shirk; John McCoy and Dan Moore; Tapish, Emily, Maya, and Phoebe Palit; Ajit George and Keith Rozendal.

My deepest gratitude goes to my family. It is to them that I dedicate *The Fifth Freedom*. My sister Julie has been a never-ending source of encouragement, levity, and support. How many times did laughing on the phone with her help to lift the weight that one often feels when writing? How often did she make time for me, no matter how busy she may have been? In the years it has taken me to complete the book, she has grown into a brilliant, self-confident woman whose career has taken off. I could not be more elated that she and her fiancé found each other. Scott is a remarkable man, and I wish them every happiness in their life together.

My sister and I have enjoyed so many opportunities over the years because of the diligent labor and immeasurable sacrifice of our parents. We never cease to marvel at their uncommon strength. As immigrants from the island nation of Taiwan, they gave up the certain modesty of their lives at home for the indeterminate prospect of building better lives for themselves and their children in America. They should rest assured that they have now made it. A well-deserved and pleasant retirement is just on the horizon, more than forty years after my father worked in the cafeteria and laundry room at the University of Oklahoma to put himself through graduate school. The journey along the way was far from easy. With only the benefit of their pluck and good sense, they learned a difficult new language, made friends, launched careers, started a family, maintained a home, raised two kids, and sent them to college, somehow making sure that each of them graduated debt-free. They even managed to save every extra penny, in no small part because of my mother's astounding fiscal discipline. America may well be the land of immigrants—and I know there is nowhere else in the world that they would rather be—but making it here still takes a tenacity and toughness that perhaps only immigrants themselves will ever fully grasp. Dedicating this long-awaited book to my parents is a small gesture by which I hope to show them that the depth and meaning of their sacrifice is not altogether lost on their son, who loves and admires them beyond all else.

Ann Arbor, Michigan
August 2008

Abbreviations

ACLU	American Civil Liberties Union
ADA	Americans for Democratic Action
ADL	Anti-Defamation League of B'Nai B'rith
AINYS	Associated Industries of New York State
AJC	American Jewish Congress
AFL	American Federation of Labor
AFL-CIO	American Federation of Labor and Congress of Industrial Organizations
BSCP	Brotherhood of Sleeping Car Porters
CACI	Chicago Association of Commerce and Industry
CCC	California Chamber of Commerce
CCEEO	Colorado Committee for Equal Employment Opportunities
CCFEP	California Committee for Fair Employment Practices
CDE	Committee on Discrimination in Employment (New York)
CGEP	Committee on Government Employment Policy (Eisenhower)
CIC	Catholic Interracial Council
CIO	Congress of Industrial Organizations
CORE	Congress on Racial Equality
CSC	Civil Service Commission
DOJ	Department of Justice
DOL	Department of Labor
EEOC	Equal Employment Opportunity Commission
FCC	Federal Council of Churches
FCNL	Friends Committee on National Legislation
FEP	Fair Employment Practices
FEPC	Fair Employment Practices Committee
FTC	Federal Trade Commission
IFEPC	Illinois Fair Employment Practice Committee
ILGWU	International Ladies' Garment Workers' Union
IMA	Illinois Manufacturers' Association
ISCC	Illinois State Chamber of Commerce
JACL	Japanese American Citizens League
LCCR	Leadership Conference on Civil Rights
MCFEM	Minnesota Council for Fair Employment on Merit
MEA	Minnesota Employers' Association

MOWM	March on Washington Movement
NAACP	National Association for the Advancement of Colored People
NAM	National Association of Manufacturers
NC	National Council for a Permanent FEPC
NCC	National Council of Churches
NLRB	National Labor Relations Board
NUL	National Urban League
NYSCAD	New York State Commission against Discrimination
OCC	Ohio Chamber of Commerce
OCFEP	Ohio Committee for Fair Employment Practices
OFCC	Office of Federal Contract Compliance
OMA	Ohio Manufacturers' Association
OPM	Office of Production Management
PCEEO	President's Committee on Equal Employment Opportunity
PfP	Plans for Progress
SCLC	Southern Christian Leadership Conference
SNCC	Student Nonviolent Coordinating Committee
TCAD	Temporary Commission against Discrimination (New York)
UAW	United Automobile Workers
UPWA	United Packinghouse Workers of America
USCC	U.S. Chamber of Commerce
USCRC	U.S. Civil Rights Commission
WMC	War Manpower Commission

THE FIFTH FREEDOM

1

On the Origins of Affirmative Action:
Puzzles and Perspectives

The years after the Second World War were a time of optimism and confidence for most Americans. Before the breakout of armed hostilities, President Franklin Delano Roosevelt had characterized America's growing involvement in the conflict overseas as a valiant defense of "four essential human freedoms"—freedom of speech and freedom of religion, freedom from fear and freedom from want. Now the war had come and gone, and the Allies had prevailed. Democracy had triumphed over fascism, freedom over fear. To be sure, success had come at a terrible cost. Over a million military personnel died or sustained injury during the war. Many more sacrifices remained quietly untold, never making it into the official record. But the country had rallied together as never before, and it finally pulled through the darkness. Better days were ahead. Millions of servicemen were returning home from their assignments abroad, ready to resume their lives as civilians with the generous assistance of the G.I. Bill. Old couples reunited. New romances began. There was a baby boom. A steady flow of defense dollars had righted the once-listing economy, and jobs were growing plentiful. For men without a college degree, some of the best jobs belonged to workers at big companies in the manufacturing and industrial sector—companies like General Motors and U.S. Steel. There, strong unions won collective bargaining agreements that meant steady employment, high wages, and generous fringe benefits such as retirement pensions and private health care insurance. Hundreds of thousands of Americans suddenly had the financial wherewithal to become homeowners for the first time, often with the help of federally backed mortgage guarantees. Flush with cash and credit, they went on a buying spree to fill their new homes with washers and dryers, couches and sofas, television sets and every other conceivable sort of household and consumer good. Shiny new cars practically rolled off assembly lines in Detroit and right into the driveways and garages of new homeowners. Life was good, and there was a widespread sense that it would only get better. As the historian James T. Patterson would later write, many Americans were developing "grand expectations" about the road ahead.[1]

Everyone understood that jobs were the key to unlocking America's newfound prosperity. "Never underestimate the value of a job," wrote one typical observer. "It may mean the difference between security and insecurity." But not all Americans with hopes for the future were able to find jobs so easily. Jobs and the security they conferred proved painfully elusive. In 1947, a resident of Richmond, Calif., wrote to Republican Governor Earl Warren to tell him about her frustrating experience on the job market. For some time now, Mrs. F. L. Osborne had been trying without success to find work as a secretary or retail clerk in northern California. It should not have been so hard. Her credentials seemed impressive enough. A high school graduate, she had excelled at San Francisco Junior College and won a coveted transfer to the prestigious University of California, Berkeley. Finding employment, though, had been strangely and impossibly difficult. Although she was perfectly qualified for the positions to which she had applied, one company had flatly turned her down in San Francisco, and two others in Berkeley had "coldly and abruptly" rejected her. Osborne could hardly hide her disappointment. Her husband had served overseas in the war against fascism and totalitarianism. Things were supposed to get better for them afterward. The whole experience led her to question the sacrifices that they had made for their country. Did the United States not fight the Axis menace so that all Americans might speak and worship freely, so that all Americans might live their lives free from fear and want? If she and her husband could not fully partake of the "four freedoms" for which America went to war, then "why have our men died and for what cause?" Osborne and her husband were black.[2]

Thousands of other African Americans would have listened to Osborne's story with a sense of knowing familiarity. The same question surely stood out in their minds as well. But it was less a debilitating doubt than a spur to further action. After the Second World War, growing numbers of African Americans refused to bury quietly their hopes and dreams. Instead, they fought back, staging acts of resistance—big and small, quiet and noisy—all across the country. The most visible and gripping stories emerged in the South, which furnished the plotline, setting, and *dramatis personae* for the now-celebrated campaign of direct action against Jim Crow segregation. A quarter century later, African Americans and their allies could look back with some satisfaction at the accomplishments of what Americans had begun to call the civil rights movement—particularly its southern-led, church-based branch. There was a vibrant movement for civil rights in the North as well, but it was the southern branch that garnered the lion's share of the attention from the press and the public. Personified by the Rev. Martin Luther King, Jr., it had succeeded in toppling the legal edifice of segregation and won federal legislation that proclaimed formal equality in public accommodations, education, voting, employment, and housing. The scope of freedom had grown ineluctably wider.[3]

Yet the politics of civil rights had also become more complicated. The political shifts that took place over the course of the 1960s are easy to exaggerate with the luxury of hindsight, and some authors have made the point in the extreme, arguing that a categorical discontinuity divides the decade. Such claims seem overstated. Nonetheless, it is hard to deny that a change of some sort had begun to occur by the mid-1960s. By all appearances, the fire next time had come. A riot had consumed Watts, and then Detroit and Newark. The most charismatic leader of the civil rights movement was viciously gunned down on the balcony of his Memphis hotel room. A profusion of younger leaders rose in his stead, and their militant rhetoric and revolutionary pronouncements made for sensational headlines and garnered easy publicity. Equally puzzlingly, political discourse was rapidly becoming polarized around a new, unfamiliar policy that required or encouraged employers and contractors to develop written "goals and timetables" for the racial integration of their work force. The policy had attracted precious little attention before it gained the force of law. It had certainly inspired no one to march in the streets. But it quickly touched off a fire storm of controversy. Critics castigated it as nothing less than racial quotas and preferential treatment, while proponents viewed the policy as a clear and necessary extension of the egalitarian ideals that had motivated the civil rights movement. Nobody had foreseen it in the early years after the war, no matter how grand their expectations for the future. Yet a policy called affirmative action had somehow managed to become a major focal point of the national conflict over civil rights. This book represents a new effort to rethink how and why such a policy emerged.[4]

Affirmative action remains one of the most politically and ideologically freighted issues in American politics. Even though it first surfaced more than forty years ago, few policies continue to inspire as much soul-searching about the content of our national character. Still fewer have provoked such harsh bromides or forceful defenses. Where did affirmative action come from? How did something so controversial ever come into existence?

Not so long ago it was difficult to find a book or study that offered more than polemic, but now serious answers are plentiful. The most important accounts focus on the tumultuous period of American history that spanned the Kennedy and Nixon presidencies. The central actors and institutions are familiar by now. According to one influential perspective, identified with Hugh Davis Graham, affirmative action was essentially the handiwork of a radicalized civil rights lobby, which "captured" federal executive agencies and courts and led them to subvert the color-blind intent of the Civil Rights Act. In the view of Jill S. Quadagno, Thomas J.

Sugrue, Nancy MacLean, and Martha Biondi, civil rights activism played the most crucial role. The intransigent exclusion of African Americans from the most desirable sectors of employment in the postwar economy, along with the manifest inadequacy of state and federal laws against discrimination, led to a burst of grass-roots protests that all but necessitated federal adoption of affirmative action programs. A third view, advanced by John D. Skrentny, Robin Stryker, and Nicholas Pedriana, focuses on shifts in political culture and partisan politics. At a time when the riots of the late 1960s conferred a new, if momentary, legitimacy to color-conscious policies, affirmative action emerged as a politically opportunistic gambit by the Nixon administration to drive a racial wedge between working-class whites and African Americans. The work of Paul Frymer, Robert Lieberman, and Paul D. Moreno represents a final line of research, one that strongly highlights the critical role of American political and legal institutions. The decentralized and fragmented policy-making institutions in the United States—including the federal courts—presented political opportunities that made the emergence of affirmative action possible.[5]

There is clearly no consensus on the origins of affirmative action, but recent scholarship has identified many of the key actors and storylines. With only a few exceptions, however, existing accounts do not acknowledge the full dimensions of earlier struggles and miss the numerous ways in which they contributed to the emergence of affirmative action. Long before affirmative action became a target of ideological contention and a badge of partisan loyalty, there had been a vital campaign to make it the responsibility of the government to protect Americans from the ravages of job discrimination. The campaign unfolded over the entire federal system, not just the national government, and it drew in a far wider spectrum of social and political actors than generally appreciated. Nor does recent scholarship properly specify the actual set of alternatives over which policymakers repeatedly and fiercely clashed throughout the postwar period. The court-based regulatory system in place today—of which affirmative action forms a small but controversial part—was never the sole historical possibility. Years ago, key numbers of policymakers sought statutory authority for a very different form of government involvement in which the equal treatment of individuals in the labor market—and nothing more than equal treatment—would be enforced through an administrative process based in the executive branch, with the courts playing only a supporting rather than primary role. Yet no major account seriously grapples with these critical developments. What is missing from current debates is a sufficiently broad perspective on history and politics. What is missing is a sense of the road not taken.[6]

This book sets out to fill in the gaps; it looks farther back in time and casts a wider gaze over history, politics, and society than do previous accounts.[7] The story I tell does not begin in the 1960s with the Kennedy administration. In fact, it begins two full decades earlier. In line with a recent turn in historical scholarship on civil rights, exemplified in the work of Risa Goluboff, Martha Biondi, Ira Katznelson, Denton Watson, Robert Korstad, Nelson Lichtenstein, and others, I begin with the 1940s, a period that Richard Dalfiume has rightly called the "forgotten years" of the black freedom struggle. Nor does the book focus, as others have, on intrigue in the federal bureaucracy or activism in the federal courts. Rather, it shifts the focus from the executive and judicial branches to the legislative branch, and it devotes special attention to tracing the interplay of state and national politics. Lastly, it does not rehearse the familiar struggles that have essentially become set pieces in the standard history of civil rights. The stories in the following pages are not staged primarily in the South. Few pages are devoted to the dramatic and critical confrontations that took place in Birmingham, Little Rock, Greensboro, or Selma, and the characters driving the plot are not Rosa Parks, Martin Luther King, Jr., and Fannie Lou Hamer—or Orval Faubus, "Bull" Connor, and George Wallace for that matter. This book instead chronicles less-known events and developments that unfolded in northern states and cities. Its main characters include northerners such as A. Philip Randolph, Will Maslow, Irving M. Ives, Frieda S. Miller, Helen G. Douglas, and Augustus F. Hawkins—but also Robert A. Taft, Otto Christenson, and thousands of rural and suburban whites. Many of these events and characters are not closely associated with the standard history of civil rights in the United States, but examining their struggles is absolutely crucial to clarifying the precise origins of affirmative action policies in employment.[8]

When a sufficiently broad perspective is taken, it becomes possible to see in full something that has been forgotten or only glimpsed in part: From the 1940s to the 1970s, there was a vibrant campaign for job equality in the United States. Decades before the phrases "affirmative action" or "equal employment opportunity" entered legal parlance, tens of thousands of Americans—mostly liberal in their political persuasion—made common cause under a different banner, that of "fair employment practices" (FEP). The storied March on Washington took place in 1963, but some Americans during the 1940s and 1950s were already staging marches on Albany and Sacramento, all in the name of winning "fair employment practices" legislation. Theirs was far more than a pet cause of a vocal minority. It was certainly more than the eschatological fantasy of a tiny vanguard. The campaign for FEP enjoyed wide support throughout the populous, industrial cities of the North, Midwest, and West. It drew in the involvement of not only the high and mighty of American politics—elected officials, party strategists, and professional lobbyists—but also ordinary voters hailing from all walks of life and representing every racial, ethnic, and religious background. Everyone had his or her own personal motives for participating, but what most of them had in common was a commitment to the idea that the government should take serious steps to make sure that jobs—and the measure of economic security that they conferred—were not denied to anyone on account of race, religion, or national orientation. The history of FEP has not been entirely absent from accounts of the civil rights movement, but it has yet to receive the serious attention it deserves. When the fierce, protracted battle over FEP is placed at the center of the story, it becomes the missing link between the "forgotten years" of the civil rights movement and the puzzling rise of affirmative action years later.[9]

The campaign for FEP pressed for legislation wherever legislation could be made, including northern statehouses and city halls. Its highest hopes, however, centered on Capitol Hill, where advocates sought a federal law that would have mandated nondiscrimination in most phases of public and private employment. Central to their vision was a regulatory model in which the authority to enforce equal treatment would be lodged primarily in the hands of a federal agency with administrative powers in the mold of the National Labor Relations Board (NLRB), whose design epitomized the regulatory ambitions of the early New Deal. The antidiscrimination agency would have two specific types of authority to enforce equal treatment. First, it could order offending employers and unions to cease and desist from their discriminatory behavior. Equally significantly, it could order offenders to take "affirmative action" to compensate victims of discrimination for the economic harms that they had suffered as individuals. The passage of FEP legislation would not have outright eliminated the pervasive pattern of racial and ethnic inequality in the labor market, but it would have undoubtedly made "fair employment practices" more than a slogan for millions of Americans.[10]

The campaign for FEP legislation was far from a quixotic mission. It was certainly no errand in the political wilderness. On several occasions in the postwar years, those who banded together to press for FEP legislation were not without real prospect of success. Beginning in 1945, they achieved a number of important political and legislative victories, including the passage of laws in most industrial states; the issuance of executive orders by presidents of both parties; and the eventual inclusion of a job discrimination provision (Title VII) in the Civil Rights Act of 1964. Their best-laid plans, however, were only imperfectly realized over the years. By the early months of 1972, job discrimination had come to be regulated by a set of policies that would have appeared unrecognizable to anyone with clear memories of the original struggle for FEP. In particular, public policy had evolved into a bewildering labyrinth of federal and state statutes, administrative regulations, and executive orders. At the federal level alone, responsibility for monitoring job discrimination was fragmented across numerous departments and agencies. Furthermore, enforcement did not occur through a streamlined administrative process. Aggrieved individuals were left to their own devices. Either they could pursue a civil lawsuit in federal court or they could appeal to a contracting agency for whatever action it deemed most constructive.[11]

The most striking difference involved the legal and political significance of the term "affirmative action" itself. In the heady ferment of the postwar years, the term originally referred to administrative orders requiring employers or unions to hire, reinstate, or promote individual workers who were the proven victims of discriminatory behavior. Now it referred to written plans for racial integration that all federal contractors were mandated to file as part of their bid for federal contracts, irrespective of what lawyers would later call a "factual predicate" of discrimination. The plans did not merely describe the steps that employers or unions would proactively take to guarantee the equal treatment of individuals. Instead, the instructions set "goals and timetables" for increasing the representation of selected racial groups over time. Numerous private companies were also voluntarily adopting similar plans, motivated by the hope of reducing the pressure for legal and legislative action. The entire regulatory system was a far cry from what had been envisaged in the heady years after the Second World War, and the emergence of "affirmative action" was the most puzzling and controversial development of them all.[12]

This book traces the story of the remarkable journey from FEP to affirmative action. In so doing, it examines the politics behind the gradual eclipse of one model of social regulation and the unexpected rise and institutionalization of another. This critical but unnoticed transformation in public policy frames the puzzle motivating the analysis in the following pages.

The puzzle may be expressed in a series of interrelated questions. Why did liberals never successfully establish a strong, centralized system for regulating job discrimination, one anchored by a Fair Employment Practices Committee (FEPC) with enforcement authority along the lines of the NLRB? Why did a different regulatory system—of which affirmative action formed a small but controversial part—arise instead? More specifically, why did federal jurisdiction over job discrimination become so fragmented? Why did regulatory authority become so decentralized? How did enforcement become the responsibility of the federal courts rather than a full-fledged federal agency? Why did the policy regime develop primarily through administrative regulations and judicial rulings rather than statutory law? Lastly, what explains the emergence of a small cluster of policies—some mandatory, some voluntary—that led companies to monitor and strive to increase the representation of racial minorities in their work force? Simply put, what explains the advent of affirmative action in employment?

Such questions have no easy answers, but any answer must begin with the simple recognition that liberals were the motive force of the campaign for job equality. At every level of the political process, liberally minded men and women could be found insisting on strong government action against discrimination. Working together, liberals formed a coherent political bloc that represented the main source of momentum for policy change. To be sure, they were a heterogeneous lot, reflecting in part the underlying complexity of their beliefs. American liberalism after the New Deal was a continuously shifting constellation of ideas that exhibited competing, even contradictory, ideological tendencies. As Alan Brinkley has written, some liberals merely wished to rein in what they saw as the inherent proclivity of capitalism toward monopoly; others extolled the virtues of central planning; still others argued for a kind of corporatist or quasi-corporatist arrangement between business, labor, and government. Nevertheless, liberals at mid-century shared a common core of beliefs about whether and how the government should regulate social and economic life. Indeed, most of them were emphatically convinced that government could not simply stand aside and let private interests do as they pleased. What made these men and women liberals—particularly in matters of civil rights—was their unwavering support of the idea that government *could* and *should* regulate discrimination. Precisely how discriminatory behavior should be regulated was a matter of some disagreement, but it was widely agreed that regulation was the responsibility of neither the private sector nor civil society. Instead, it was the rightful responsibility of government to guarantee the equal treatment of individuals, even if it meant wielding strong sanctions. Nowhere was the responsibility more serious than in the case of jobs, which the vast majority of Americans used to build the foundations of their economic security. The fight for FEP was thus more than a simple matter of ensuring equal treatment in the labor market. For liberals, particularly those inspired by Roosevelt's prewar rhetoric, it symbolized a kind of fifth freedom—"freedom from discrimination"—that would make the promise of the Four Freedoms a meaningful reality for all Americans.[13]

To be sure, many liberals accepted Gunnar Myrdal's argument that the racial inequality in the United States stemmed fundamentally from the prejudicial beliefs and moral failings of individual Americans. In his widely read treatise, *An American Dilemma*, Myrdal argued that the "Negro problem" reflected a "problem in the heart of the American." "It is there," he wrote in the study that would garner him the Nobel Prize, "that the decisive struggle goes on." But liberals did not jump from

Myrdal's individualistic diagnosis of racial inequality to the conclusion that the prejudicial beliefs of individual Americans were the only legitimate targets of the assault on racial inequality. On the contrary, liberals considered prejudice far beyond the reach of any public or private intervention. How could any external force truly change a person's innermost thoughts and feelings? Even if it were possible, how could anyone else on the outside know that the change was genuine? The only reasonable hope lay in addressing the behavior that stemmed from prejudice. Discrimination and prejudice were bound up with each other in a vicious cycle, but only discrimination was directly observable and therefore amenable to regulation. Of course, private entities could not be counted on to regulate themselves. Even if it were carried out in good faith, voluntary action by employers and unions could only go so far. For liberals, safeguarding the fifth freedom was a responsibility that could only be entrusted to the government.[14]

Liberals formed a discernible bloc in postwar American politics, one that was defined by their shared beliefs about government regulation. But the liberal bloc was both socially and politically diverse. Its most stalwart members were almost certainly African Americans. They experienced the harshest and most ruinous forms of segregation and discrimination, no matter where in the country they lived. Historically, black Americans had been a people of the rural South. Until the eve of the war, more than three-quarters still resided in southern states, and a majority of these men and women lived in rural areas. American participation in the Second World War—and the corresponding renaissance of northern industry—redrew the geography of African American life, spurring a Second Great Migration that would send large numbers of them northward. By 1970, millions of enterprising African Americans had left their southern homes, pushed out by technological advances in agricultural production and beckoned by the promise of economic opportunity. More than ten million African Americans lived outside the South—out of twenty-two million in the United States overall—and all but a slender fraction of them made their homes in big cities. Unfortunately, few of the migrants to northern cities found what they had truly hoped for. If the "North" figured in the black imagination as a kind of Canaan, a mythic place where they might live out the true meaning of the American creed, reality proved manifestly different. Osborne's story of her discouraging experience in northern California was not a contrived tale meant to prod a hesitant official into action. Job discrimination was an all-too-common experience for African Americans—for those who left Dixie behind no less than for those who remained. The historical record is crammed with thousands of letters, diaries, stories, and reports recounting the heartbreaking multitude of ways that they were shut out unfairly from the booming postwar labor market.[15]

All of the individual stories eventually added up, one by one, and the result was a grim litany of statistics that scarcely hinted at the depth of human frustrations that surely lay beneath them (table A.1). Perhaps the most striking figure of all was the unemployment rate, particularly for black men. Black women had long been employed at a higher rate than white women, but male unemployment began to diverge along racial lines in the postwar years. By the 1950s, black men were unemployed at nearly twice the rate as white men, a disparity that would endure for decades. Even when the most persistent of them succeeded in finding work, they nevertheless earned less than comparable non-Hispanic white men. The best estimates are admittedly rough, but it appears that a black high school graduate in 1940 earned about sixty cents for every dollar earned by a white high school graduate. The differential narrowed to roughly eighty cents on the dollar by 1970, but it was still a considerable gap. It is impossible, of course, to attribute all of the differences in employment and earnings to crude acts of racial discrimination at the hiring gate. By migrating to the urban North, African Americans were moving to regions of the country that tended to feature higher average rates of unemployment than the South. Moreover, African Americans were on average a less-educated population than whites, and the educational deficit was greatest for southern migrants. Nevertheless, racial inequalities existed at every level of educational attainment, and blacks received a smaller return to their educational attainment than did whites. For most of the postwar period, black men received a twenty percent smaller premium for obtaining a college degree than their white counterparts. Racial discrimination was thus a pervasive presence in the lives of African Americans, wherever they chose to live. The point was certainly not lost on African Americans themselves. "Employment discrimination is not confined to any one section of this country," said a speaker at the 1947 conference of the Alabama branch of the National Association for the Advancement of Colored People (NAACP). "When it comes to getting a skilled or white-collar job, the bars of race prejudice are raised just about as high in the North and West as they are in the South."[16]

But blacks were not the only Americans to experience the sharp sting of job discrimination. Nor were they the only ones to take political action as a result. Mexican Americans faced serious job discrimination as well, particularly in the Southwest, where most of them resided. According to a rough wartime estimate by federal official Carlos E. Castañeda, more than two million "Latin Americans" lived in Texas, New Mexico, Colorado, Arizona, and California. Of these, four-fifths were "American-born citizens," and the remainder had already been living in the region before it became part of the United States. Job discrimination against Mexican Americans assumed myriad forms, but it was perhaps most visible in the racial segregation of the occupational structure. Workers of Mexican background were concentrated in the ranks of unskilled labor, while "Anglos" or people of Western European origin tended to hold skilled or supervisory positions. "Throughout the Southwest [Mexican Americans] are refused employment on an equal basis with other workers," Castañeda wrote. "When employment is given to them it is restricted to the dirtiest, most undesirable and most exacting jobs. Regardless of previous training, natural ability or aptitude, seniority, or any other consideration, they are generally denied opportunities for advancement." A similar pattern of occupational segregation held true elsewhere in the country. For instance, in the meatpacking plants of wartime Chicago, "Spanish American" workers at many plants were limited to the sweet pickle, green meat, or hide cellar departments—all extremely unpleasant places to work. The political life of Mexican Americans was less formally organized than other ethnic groups, particularly at mid-century, but cities such as Los Angeles and Chicago nevertheless witnessed bursts of political activity against discrimination during the war itself. In the years thereafter, Mexican American legislators in New Mexico would prove instrumental in launching a campaign for state legislation that would ultimately bear fruit in 1949. "We need. . . [a law against discrimination] here," wrote one of them to U.S. Sen. Dennis Chavez (D-NM), "and I hope that it will pass so that the discrimination against our people will be stopped."[17]

Though smaller in number, Japanese Americans also formed a definite part of the liberal bloc. As they began to emerge from internment immediately after the war, many Japanese Americans were not particularly inclined toward politics. They were focused on more practical issues, like finding a safe place to live and eking out a living in the face of lingering prejudices. Internment had shattered their former lives, and most of them did not think of turning to the federal government for protection from the new problems they faced. If they took an interest in politics at all, what concerned them the most was securing the equal right to naturalization for the Issei (first-generation Japanese Americans). Nevertheless, when it came to offering support on Capitol Hill, Japanese Americans were reliable members of the liberal bloc. In particular, Mike Masaoka of the Japanese American Citizens League (JACL) testified numerous times before Congress on the importance of taking legislative action against job discrimination.[18]

Turning to the political arena in much more significant numbers were various immigrant groups who traced their ancestry to Southern and Eastern Europe and now lived in the same northern cities that were magnets for African Americans. The raw, unbridled nativism that led Congress to impose national-origin restrictions on immigration during the 1920s had subsided by mid-century, but there was a still a discernible bias in the labor market against the foreign born and, to a lesser extent, their children. The bias certainly fluctuated from city to city, no less than it did from firm to firm or job to job. As the postwar period wore on, much of it gradually declined. The most recent and sophisticated evidence actually suggests that the "new" immigrants had more than leveled the economic playing field by the 1940s. To the extent that white ethnics succeeded in carving out niches for themselves in certain jobs or occupation, their background could actually favor them. But ethnic prejudice was definite, even if many "new" immigrants and their children succeeded admirably in overcoming it. Combined with age-old religious antipathies, ethnic prejudice put white ethnics on distinctly unequal footing. Thousands of Italian and Polish Catholics along with Russian and Polish Jews found that they had to try much harder than their native, Protestant peers to achieve the same levels of economic success. For a time during the postwar era, white ethnics insisted on protection from discrimination as well.[19]

The grass-roots membership of the liberal bloc was hence robustly interracial and interfaith. Blacks and Jews made up the most active members of the liberal bloc, but it also included thousands of white Protestants and Catholics, and more limited numbers of Mexican Americans and Japanese Americans. It was never the most cohesive assortment of people, but their shared experience of employment discrimination—combined with the fact that northern blacks could vote—furnished a common and powerful basis for collective action. Almost everyone in the liberal bloc grasped the idea that they wielded more political clout together than they did by themselves. Indeed, it was the political behavior and collective action of these ordinary men and women that set the policy-making process in forward motion, even if their presence is fully visible in the historical record only at certain moments. When these men and women wrote letters, formed delegations, and appeared en masse at legislative hearings, elected officials could not help but pay attention, even when such collective mobilization did not always achieve its intended effect. If direct action was the weapon of choice in the struggle to dismantle Jim Crow, northern liberals of all racial backgrounds and religious faiths worked for social change—perhaps less visibly but no less ardently—through the normal channels of electoral politics.[20]

Of course, grass-roots participation was not wholly spontaneous. Much of it was conjured into existence by interest groups that had a stake of one sort or another in seeing the passage of FEP legislation. Among the most important and active of these groups were those with members who clearly stood to benefit from the protection of such legislation, including race groups like the NAACP, the National Urban League (NUL),

JACL, and the League of United Latin American Citizens (LULAC); religious groups like the American Jewish Congress (AJC), Catholic Interracial Council (CIC), National Council of Churches (NCC), and American Friends Service Committee (AFSC); industrial unions like the United Automobile Workers (UAW), United Steelworkers of America (USWA), and other international unions that together formed the Congress of Industrial Organizations (CIO); and liberal lobbies like the American Civil Liberties Union (ACLU) and Americans for Democratic Action (ADA). The sheer number of interest groups involved obviously posed a problem of coordination, which liberals surmounted with varying degrees of success. While no single, federated organization ever arose to preside over the entire campaign, umbrella organizations sprung up at various levels of the federal system. The push for Congressional legislation was guided in the 1940s by the National Council for a Permanent FEPC (NC), which found itself supplanted in the early 1950s by the newly formed Leadership Conference on Civil Rights (LCCR). Indeed, it was partly a desire to revitalize the campaign for FEP legislation that led to the establishment of the LCCR. Umbrella organizations were also formed in many states outside the South, where liberals rallied under the banner of groups with names like the Ohio Committee for Fair Employment Practices (OCFEP) and the Minnesota Council for Fair Employment on Merit (MCFEM).[21]

The liberal bloc did not always and everywhere act with complete unity. Its political strength and capacity for collective action was diminished from time to time by internecine conflicts and organizational rivalries, which were inevitable in a bloc of such size and diversity. Among the most enduring and significant divisions was the one that separated African Americans from the white, working-class ethnics with whom they vied for jobs and housing. The two groups had formed the northern core of Roosevelt's electoral bloc since the Great Depression, but tension between them mounted as the Second Great Migration brought ever-increasing numbers of African Americans into northern factories and neighborhoods. Though violence at work was known to break out, conflicts over housing often led to the most explosive confrontations. In 1953, when black families began moving into the Trumbell Park Homes in South Deering, a neighborhood in southeast Chicago, white homeowners unleashed a program of terror and intimidation, detonating "aerial bombs" outside of black apartments and threatening economic and physical retaliation against anyone who transacted business with African Americans. South Deering was no exception. As vividly related by Thomas J. Sugrue, Detroit was the home base of the powerful UAW along with many of the most racially progressive locals in the country, but it too was convulsed by "hidden" waves of violence when African Americans began to move into all-white neighborhoods.[22]

A color bar similarly divided blacks and whites at work, where jobs followed a discernible racial hierarchy. In most northern industries, skilled and semiskilled positions belonged to whites, while African Americans were relegated to unskilled and temporary positions. Compared to their white counterparts, blacks were the "last hired, first fired," relegated as they were to the least secure, most taxing, and poorest paying jobs. These discriminatory arrangements still flourished not only because of employer discrimination but also because of union discrimination. This was particularly difficult to eradicate because local unions enjoyed considerable autonomy from their internationals. Even when strong leaders like the UAW's Walter Reuther sought to eliminate racial discrimination from local unions and threw their weight behind the liberal campaign for FEP legislation, their efforts met with varying enthusiasm—and sometimes open defiance—from their white rank and file. For their part, African Americans harbored suspicions that union pieties about racial equality were meant only to buoy public relations. The tensions between the two groups simmered steadily throughout the postwar period, and occasionally they boiled over.[23]

If postwar liberals found themselves at odds with one another in the workplace and neighborhood, they nevertheless found the occasion to act on their mutual interests in the political arena. When the time came to inject their convictions into the policy-making process, they enjoyed the advantage of having allies on both sides of the aisle. A liberal faction existed in each of the major parties for much of the period, and neither party turned a wholly deaf ear to calls for fair employment practices. The bipartisanship, however, was decidedly lopsided. The overall pattern was fairly difficult to discern in Congress, but it was no less real. In the postwar House, a modest majority of the Democratic delegation usually represented jurisdictions outside the states of the former Confederacy, and these "northern" Democrats were by far the strongest supporters of FEP, particularly representatives who were themselves religious or racial minorities. The most prominent Democrats on the issue included men and women such as Emanuel Celler (D-NY), Helen Gahagan Douglas (D-CA), Augustus Hawkins (D-CA), Mary Y. Norton (D-NJ), and Adam Clayton Powell (D-NY). Each of them represented a liberal, urban district where the demand for protection from discrimination ran the highest. The campaign in the Senate was spearheaded in the early years by Dennis Chavez (D-NM), and he was joined by his co-partisans from states with large, diverse, industrial cities—such as Herbert H. Lehman (D-NY) or Hubert H. Humphrey (D-MN). By comparison, support among Republicans in Congress was more inconsistent and uneven, quite in contrast to their enduring reputation as the "Party of Lincoln." The national GOP in the postwar period was sharply divided between a liberal and conservative wing, but liberal Republicans—most of whom represented competitive districts in or near urban areas—were more a harried and fading minority than a rising power. Admittedly, certain Republicans, among them senators like Irving M. Ives (R-NY) or Wayne Morse (R-OR), assumed a prominent role in the politics of fair employment, just as their Democratic peers did. This tended to be the case only for senators, however. Support for FEP was far more uncommon among Republicans in the House, where most GOP lawmakers hailed from conservative, rural areas. The partisan imbalance was even more pronounced in the Oval Office. Although they never offered unqualified backing, Democrats like Harry S. Truman and John F. Kennedy were far friendlier to FEP legislation than Republicans Dwight D. Eisenhower or Richard Nixon, who went on record opposing exactly the kind of enforceable legislation that liberals sought.[24]

The same uneven pattern of bipartisanship was also present in state politics, where it was more pronounced and visible than it was nationally. In both chambers of most legislatures, it was urban Democrats like Berkeley-Oakland's W. Byron Rumford who were the most consistent backers of FEP legislation. A handful of Democrats who represented predominantly rural districts were decidedly less enthusiastic about fair employment than their urban co-partisans, but the former tended to cast their votes almost as regularly for FEP proposals as the latter. By contrast, support for FEP among GOP legislators was far more variable. It was not entirely missing, but much of the liberalism among Republicans came from lawmakers in hotly contested districts—or from Republicans who either held or coveted statewide office. There is even some evidence that in the rare instances when GOP lawmakers cast their votes for FEP, many did so out of electoral considerations, over and against their own personal preferences and ideological commitments. Genuine esteem for liberal-style FEP legislation was restricted for the most part to Republican governors. The most successful among them, New York's Thomas E. Dewey, used his popularity and clout in 1945 to push through the first state FEP law in the United States. Other liberal Republican governors tried to emulate his example, but for every Earl Warren (CA), Luther Youngdahl (MN), or C. Elmer Anderson (MN), there seemed to be a Goodwin Knight (CA) or C. William O'Neill (OH) standing on the other side of the issue. Far more consistent in their support were Democratic governors, among them Edmund G. Brown (CA), G. Mennen Williams (MI), George M. Leader (PA), Frank Lausche (OH), Adlai Stevenson (IL), and Otto Kerner (IL).

For a time after the war, it appeared that the liberal bloc might well succeed. The state campaign was flourishing. A slew of early laws passed in northeastern states like New York, New Jersey, Connecticut, and Massachusetts, making "freedom from discrimination" more than a mere rallying cry for millions of Americans. The breakthroughs gave liberals genuine hope that other legislative successes would soon follow, particularly in the populous states of the industrial Midwest and West. Not everyone thrilled to the thought, however. On the Left, radical critics reacted with scorn. They regarded state laws as "dead-letter" legislation. On the Right, conservatives reacted with dismay. They feared that early success would enable liberals not only to win the passage of additional state laws but also to build momentum to extract a federal law from Congress. This was indeed the liberal strategy, and it was neither far-fetched nor unrealistic. The states had long served as a testing ground for new ideas and new policies, well before Justice Louis Brandeis likened them memorably to the laboratories of American democracy. As recently as the New Deal, states had led the way on historic social legislation. Many of the central provisions of the Social Security Act began as state laws. Not unreasonably, liberals hoped to set off the same chain reaction with FEP. Though they did not fully realize it at the time, their best chance came during the first half of Truman's second term, when FEP legislation became the "storm center" of a titanic fight over civil rights in Congress. In 1949 and then again in 1950, liberals came within a razor's edge of gaining the upper hand. The entire episode validated their strategic blueprint.[25]

But the experiment with FEP stalled. Conservatives, not liberals, prevailed at the turn of the decade. With the election of Eisenhower and the Republican takeover of Congress in 1952, political momentum for Congressional legislation dissipated for years. Several more states passed laws, but the most electorally significant states—California, Ohio, and Illinois among them—were severely delayed in passing FEP legislation. By the mid-1950s, state laws had become a substitute for, rather than a spur to, national action. As for Congress, it waited until 1964 to address employment discrimination. Even then, it passed a law that was little more than a dim shadow of what liberals had hoped to achieve. The provision covering job discrimination, Title VII, was mediocre at best, establishing the Equal Employment Opportunity Commission (EEOC) but giving it only a sliver of jurisdiction over job discrimination and leaving it without any independent authority to enforce the law. The EEOC could attempt to reconcile aggrieved parties informally, and it could hold public hearings in the hope of embarrassing employers or unions into changing their behavior. If reconciliation proved impossible, however, it could do nothing more. Victims wanting enforcement action would have to file, finance, and win a federal lawsuit on their own. In 1972, when Congress revisited the issue under liberal pressure, it once again contemplated a wide range of regulatory alternatives, including a proposal to make the EEOC a full-fledged administrative agency in the mold of the NLRB. This moment presented the last, best hope for the liberal vision of FEP. What resulted instead, however, was the Equal Employment Opportunity Enforcement Act, which essentially ratified the court-based system that had taken root in 1964 and left intact the handful of affirmative action policies that had emerged through executive, administrative, and judicial action.

The gradual eclipse of the liberal vision laid the basis for the rise of a new court-based regulatory system, one that became a controversial hybrid of color-blind and color-conscious policies. This chimerical regime was not fated to be. However much affirmative action appears the inevitable outgrowth of regulatory capture, grassroots protest, or shifts in political culture during the Johnson and Nixon years, it might have looked differently if liberals had ever gotten their way. Had liberals successfully convinced Congress to provide for administrative enforcement of the law, particularly before the southern-based civil rights movement crested in the mid-1960s, subsequent disagreements might have taken a vastly different path. There would have been a bona fide regulatory agency on the scene, and policymakers might have focused on a different set of issues, instead of becoming mired in bitter quarrels over racial quotas and group rights. Politics and partisanship would have surely remained part of the equation, but the disputes would have centered on questions of regulatory design. Was the law, as it was written, adequate for the task of ensuring the equal treatment of individuals in the labor market, or was new legislation required? Should the agency be given the authority to initiate investigations without first waiting for a complaint? What constitutes evidence of discrimination, and should the threshold be set higher or lower? Once the agency makes a factual determination about discrimination, how much deference should federal courts give it under review? The most intriguing possibility is that the meaning "affirmative action" might not have taken a color-conscious turn. Instead, it could have acquired a strictly color-blind meaning, referring to the administrative orders requiring employers or unions to compensate individual victims of discrimination for the harms that they had demonstrably suffered—just as liberals had long hoped. The road not taken did not make all the difference, but it made a rather substantial one.

If the seeds that liberals sowed never fully bloomed, it was partially a consequence of their own making. Myriad failures of will and judgment plagued them along the way. The gradual acquiescence of the American labor movement to a two-party political system; a debilitating surge of antiradicalism among labor liberals; the systematic purge of Left-led unions from the CIO and the subsequent decline of interracial unionism— all of these problems or missteps probably weakened and distracted the potential bloc that might have been mobilized behind the FEP campaign. Over time, such problems changed the meaning of liberalism itself.[26]

Nevertheless, the potential to develop a Left-led, interracial labor movement existed only on a handful of occasions in a limited number of places. To be sure, Left-led unions were absolutely instrumental in advancing the cause of racial equality in certain international and local unions, as numerous authors have powerfully documented. The settings of their stories range remarkably far and wide. During the Great Depression and well into the postwar years, industrial democracy and civil rights went hand in hand for autoworkers in Detroit, public workers in New York City, tobacco workers in Winston-Salem, shipyard workers in wartime Miami, steelworkers in Pittsburgh and Birmingham, and meat packers in Chicago. Moreover, it is impossible to deny that the anticommunist crusades of the McCarthy era—at times led by Cold War liberals—had a chilling effect on these and other inspiring episodes of interracial unity in the American working class. It nevertheless seems difficult to imagine how a "black-labor-Left" bloc, in the phrasing of one historian, would have ever become a major force for policy change in either *state* or *national* politics. Such a bloc was only imaginable, much less possible, in a limited number of localities or municipalities—and rarely higher in the federal system. Even if fratricide had been averted and a black-labor-Left bloc had sprung into existence at the state or national level; even if such a bloc had been led by "independent leftists" rather than members of the Communist Party; even if it had been strong enough to win major concessions from large employers in key industries; even then, it would have been faced with the necessary task of forming and sustaining a viable third party, or else deal with the risk of being captured and domesticated by one of other two. This task may have been slightly easier in state politics than national politics, but it would have been daunting in either venue. Ultimately, it is hard to see how such a bloc could have done more than simply serve as a font of contrapuntal ideas. The formation of a durable third party in American politics is a challenging prospect under the most favorable political circumstances, but the involvement of communists, real or imagined, during the Cold War would have proven a fatal liability on Capitol Hill or any number of northern statehouses. A black-labor-Left bloc would have faced more dangers than opportunities in the campaign for national or state legislation.[27]

More damaging to the political fortunes of the FEP legislation than liberal anticommunism was the checkered liberalism of southern Democrats and the political and economic interests that they represented. Along with northern workers and African Americans, southern planters and their grass-roots allies were a core constituency of Roosevelt's unusual electoral bloc—one that Ira Katznelson has memorably likened to a cross between Sweden and South Africa. On a wide range of issues that came before Congress, particularly policies that involved regional redistribution of economic resources, southern Democrats were among the most stalwart supporters of the New Deal. Their support, however, stopped abruptly at civil rights and industrial relations. It should thus come as no surprise that nothing unleashed their oratorical talents and penchant for demagoguery more effectively than the question of FEP, which stood at the intersection of the two issues—politics and jobs—that posed the gravest threat to the "racial order" and distinctive political economy of the South. Countless examples of southern Democratic opposition existed, but among the most vehement and outspoken congressional critics were Mississippi's John E. Rankin in the House and Georgia's Richard Russell in the Senate. Of course, not all southern Democrats assumed the same reactionary posture. Representative L. Brook Hays of Arkansas and other southern moderates sought to articulate a compromise position. The vast majority of southern Democrats, however, seldom hesitated to denounce FEP legislation, often in the most hyperbolic terms. If southern Democrats had been a powerless minority, then their views would not have mattered. But the institutional features of Congress—particularly the Senate filibuster—essentially gave them "veto" power over any civil rights proposal, including FEP legislation. Hence the initial barrier faced by the campaign for FEP legislation was the studied obstructionism of southern Democrats and the agrarian and business elites whom they represented.[28]

But the politics of FEP were not fractal. The contours of political conflict over the issue did not look the same in northern statehouses as they did on Capitol Hill, and for a very simple reason. There were no southern Democrats in the North. If northern states passed FEP laws at radically different times during the postwar era, it simply could not have been on account of fire-breathing, southern demagogues hoping to preserve white supremacy. Indeed, when a close accounting of the North is taken, it becomes clear that the major sources of political opposition to "freedom from discrimination" were strikingly different there than they were in the country as a whole. It also becomes increasingly evident that the political travails of liberalism were not only, or even primarily, self-made.

A major but continually overlooked source of opposition to FEP legislation did not come from within the actual or potential ranks of the New Deal bloc. It hailed from without. This opposition took the form of a powerful though loosely organized bloc of conservatives—voters, interest groups, and office-holders—who were committed in varying degrees to the principle of equal treatment but united in their antipathy to government intervention in social and economic life. The liberal campaign for freedom from discrimination occasioned a "massive political resistance" among conservatives in industrial states outside the South, and they mobilized to fight against FEP legislation at every level of the federal system. Few legislative proposals sparked their ire as readily. Wary of the social-democratic resonance of the Four Freedoms and resentful of the New Deal, conservatives balked at the notion of extending government authority, not just federal authority, any further into the industrial relations system. In response to liberal demands for fair employment practices, conservatives juxtaposed a different ideal, one they considered equally "sacred and fundamental." Instead of "freedom from discrimination," they defended something they called "freedom of enterprise." This was *their* fifth freedom.[29]

The conservative bloc rarely found it necessary to organize itself formally, quite in contrast to the liberal bloc. Instead, it depended on the strength of overlapping preferences and sought to exert influence away from the glare of publicity. There was no organization analogous to the ACLU or the ADA, and there was certainly no organization analogous to the National Council for a Permanent FEPC. Nevertheless, the conservative bloc exerted a powerful, collective force in American politics. What united it more than anything else was the shared belief that government could not and should not regulate human behavior. Social change could come only after voluntary reflection and personal introspection, which themselves could be prompted only by steady education and gentle persuasion. "Mandatory" or "compulsory" legislation would only backfire and harden the attitudes that it was meant to liberalize.

At the forefront of conservative opposition was American business, which considered FEP legislation a rank infringement on traditional managerial prerogatives over hiring, promotion, and firing. During the Great Depression, businessmen had fallen in popularity among large segments of the electorate, and they saw the postwar years as a valuable opportunity to defend their remaining privileges, shore up their public image, and restore legitimacy to the "free enterprise" system. At the top of their political agenda—running second only to limiting unionization through legislation like Taft-Hartley and right-to-work laws—was the campaign against FEP legislation. The business community was no grim monolith, but it was remarkably united in opposing the passage of FEP laws. Indeed, companies of all kinds lobbied frequently, if at times quietly, against FEP proposals. It did not seem to matter whether a firm was big or small, domestically or internationally oriented, capital- or labor-intensive. Nor was there much variation by industry. Banking, finance, retail, manufacturing, and agricultural firms all stood firmly against the FEP at one time or another. Equally noteworthy is the fact that opposition to FEPC was not spontaneously fomented by a handful of ideological mavericks. To the contrary, it was widespread and organized. Throughout the postwar period, scores of business associations all across the country voted repeatedly to oppose FEP legislation. In national politics, firms sought to pool their political influence by working collectively through the U.S. Chamber of Commerce (USCC) or the National Association of Manufacturers (NAM). State associations, going by names like the Minnesota Employers' Association (MEA), California Chamber of Commerce (CCC), or Illinois Manufacturers' Association (IMA), served much the analogous function in state politics. There were numerous instances when individual businessmen and business associations happily endorsed FEP legislation, but such plaudits were typically forthcoming only *after* an FEP statute had been written into law. As long as a statute had yet to be passed, employers were the most consistent, aggressive, and effective source of resistance.[30]

When at all possible, business lobbyists preferred to keep a low profile and work quietly behind the scenes, writing letters and meeting privately with lawmakers. Still, they did not hesitate to speak out loudly against FEP legislation at legislative hearings, if it suited their purposes. What they said in such instances was telling. Professing a strong belief in the rightness of racial equality, conservatives nonetheless minimized the scope and severity of discrimination; argued that discrimination would wither away if left alone; claimed that existing laws were sufficient to any problem that might have existed; trumpeted the effectiveness of educational and voluntary methods over enforceable legislation; and warned ominously that attempts to achieve tolerance through legislation would actually heighten color-consciousness and lead to preferential treatment in the form of racial and religious quotas.

If the liberal campaign for freedom from discrimination met with the opposition of economic and political elites, it also rankled thousands of ordinary whites who lived in rural and suburban areas outside the South. For them, FEP unleashed a powerful current of racial resentment. Living in sparsely populated communities with little racial or ethnic diversity, rural and suburban whites considered FEP legislation "class" legislation that gave special preferences to racial and religious minorities living in corruption-ridden, big cities. It violated their sense of fair play and their market-oriented conceptions of meritocracy. Ordinary whites did not organize themselves into political associations to defend their perceived interests, but their animosity toward FEP laws is evident in the hundreds of letters they individually sent to their elected officials.

The shrewdest opponents of FEP legislation understood American politics well enough to maintain the appearance of bipartisanship. Yet they turned to big-business, small-government Republicans at the most critical moments in the legislative process. It was a judicious choice.

Most state legislatures were dominated by large Republican majorities for much of the postwar period, and the greater part of their advantage came from the overwhelming electoral success of the GOP in rural districts, where malapportionment meant that residents of rural areas enjoyed a level of electoral representation that was disproportionate to their presence in the population. Among the fiercest critics of FEP in Congress were conservative Republicans like Robert A. Taft of Ohio and Clare Hoffman of Michigan. In both Congress and the states, conservative Republicans rallied against FEP legislation, casting unfavorable committee votes, making critical speeches, introducing voluntary legislation, and executing parliamentary maneuvers that they thought would undermine the prospects of passage.[31]

The sources of opposition were many, but they were clear. If northern Democrats and liberal Republicans found southern Democrats to be the first barrier to civil rights, then organized business, rural and suburban whites in the "North," and conservative Republicans defined the outermost political limits of policy-making. At key moments throughout the 1940s and 1970s, it was the real or imagined opposition of the conservative bloc that delayed the passage of FEP legislation in major states; limited the scope of government authority over discrimination; led to the fragmentation and decentralization of administrative institutions; shifted enforcement to the courts; encouraged private actors to pursue "voluntary" approaches to addressing discrimination; and obstructed legislation that would have created a federal agency with regulatory authority along the lines of the NLRB. In a valuable study that is notably attentive to the conservative role, Paul D. Moreno rightly emphasizes the importance of midwestern Republicans like Taft and Everett M. Dirksen (R-IL), who were able to influence policy because they held the balance of power in the U.S. Senate. They were indeed critical, but they were only the most visible members of the conservative bloc. Other postwar conservatives—House Republicans, organized business, and statehouse Republicans—proved equally adept at exploiting political institutions and the party system to shape policy.[32]

The critical position of the conservative bloc in the politics of civil rights had profound consequences. Over time, successive waves of conservative opposition created a policy legacy that actually facilitated the emergence of affirmative action. By the mid-1960s, when demands for the racial integration of the work force surged, federal officials found themselves bereft of the tools to enforce equal treatment under the law, despite the passage of the Civil Rights Act. At the same time, organized business feared that Congress would eventually be tempted to grant the EEOC administrative enforcement authority. So federal bureaucrats and corporate executives turned to affirmative action instead. Underlying the advent of affirmative action is thus a great, unnoticed irony: Postwar conservatives succeeded in fending off national FEP legislation at the cost of laying the foundations for affirmative action, a policy that their ideological heirs would find even more abhorrent.

Any scholar writing on the emergence of affirmative action policies in employment inescapably touches on a larger, interdisciplinary conversation about the manner in which politics shapes the policy-making process. This conversation has progressed steadily for decades, but it has gone through a period of exceptional ferment in recent years, and it therefore seems appropriate for me to indicate and clarify the main ways in which *The Fifth Freedom* is related to it.

The approach I take to understanding the political development of public policy is quintessentially sociological. Other approaches direct our attention to the preferences of the median voter or the heroic strivings of "great men." I begin with a fundamentally different intuition, one that looks in the first instance to political conflict among different social and economic groups—variously defined—as the motive force behind the emergence, development, and retrenchment of public policy. Drawing on much the same reservoir of ideas as do Jill Quadagno, Peter Baldwin, and Gøsta Esping-Anderson, I see the formation of public policy as deeply rooted in political mobilization of different social and economic groups, who work to promote their collective self-interest by demanding specific types of government action and inaction, or rather, specific types of government policy. My work thus builds on the age-old, sociological insight that public policy "is built on a foundation of concrete demands, made by concrete groups, who clamor for public, that is, governmental, response."[33]

I put a special emphasis on analyzing the political mobilization and political conflict among *elite groups*; namely, groups that are advantageously situated in the larger social, political, and economic structure. Examples of such groups range from the various trade associations that have sprung up to promote the interests of American industry (e.g., manufacturers, planters, merchants, bankers, realtors, and insurers) to the much more loosely organized "Protestant establishment" that dominated the life of the United States throughout much of the twentieth century. To be sure, grass-roots movements can matter a great deal in the policy-making process, and a burgeoning tradition in political sociology rightly focuses on them. The expression of collective grievances through social protest and public demonstrations often corresponds broadly with the emergence of policy. In fact, there is ample historical evidence that social movements can even stimulate political demand for a policy where none previously existed. When the question of policy change is considered from a distance, social movements are often essential to any inclusive analysis. But policies are frequently made, remade, and unmade even after the marching stops, to borrow a felicitous metaphor from Hanes Walton. The mobilization of a social movement is not always a necessary condition of policy-making. Moreover, if the motivating research question involves accounting for the finer-grained but no less vital features of *policy design*—what specific benefit a program offers, what kind of protection it affords, how it is financed, who is eligible for it, and how it is enforced—then students of the policy-making process cannot restrict their analysis to just social movements. What is also required is a careful, close-up look at the preferences, abilities, and strategies of elite groups. Other approaches can offer only partial guides to understanding the critical intricacies of policy design, mainly because a range of policies is often compatible with the sweeping demands of social movements. the subtle pressures of public opinion, or the grand designs of world-historical leaders. To make clear sense of why certain policies win out over plausible alternatives, what is required is a focus on the clash between elite groups.[34]

This elite-centered perspective has obvious affinities with the theoretical tradition of C. Wright Mills and G. William Domhoff, both of whom stress the numerous ways in which politics is biased toward elites and their interests. Like these and other well-known critics of pluralism, I do not think that the players are more or less equal; that the playing field is level; or that the rules treat all the players the same. I am fairly well persuaded by evidence to the contrary. Of course, it is the stuff of sheer fantasy to think that American politics is cannily orchestrated by a unitary, omnipotent elite. There is more than one elite, and none is all-powerful. Yet the policy-making process, particularly in the United States, often seems to favor elite groups. Any complete analysis of policy formation and policy development must therefore begin with them. The impulse to ascribe causal significance to elites is far from original; it has assumed many incarnations over the years, emerging in decades-old debates over the corporate-liberal thesis as well as Peter Swenson's recent galvanizing call to "bring capital back in." But the impulse seems like a valid one, especially in the U.S. setting. In the pages that follow, I focus especially closely on the role played by organized business in the politics of policy-making. With only a few exceptions, its influence has been consistently overlooked in the history of civil rights, partly because it has been obscured by business itself. But there was no single interest group whose opposition had a greater impact on the manner in which the United States regulates job discrimination. Organized business did not always get what it wanted, but even as it settled for what it considered second-best options, it exerted a profound, circumscribing influence on the set of policy alternatives that subsequent generations would confront.[35]

Of course, elites are not the only force in the policy-making process. I hope that readers familiar with recent scholarly debates will recognize the substantial weight that I give to other factors, ranging from political institutions, public opinion, social movements, political parties, and legislator ideology to timing and sequencing. Of these, I place the strongest emphasis on the role of political parties and political institutions, particularly how it is possible for them under certain circumstances to constrain or amplify the power of social groups in the policy-making process. If conservatives imposed the final political limits on the development of anti-discrimination policy in employment, they did not do so because they were always overwhelmingly powerful. In certain instances, it is true that conservatives were strong enough essentially to dictate the outcome. In other instances, they were not quite as strong, yet they were still able to achieve results that were largely consistent with their preferences. This was due mainly to the operation of political institutions and the party system. For example, conservatives and the congressional Republicans who represented them were numerical minorities, but the supermajority vote required to end a Senate filibuster conferred upon them the balance of power. In the states, malapportionment meant that rural conservatives were overrepresented in the state legislature, usually by Republicans. Sheer strength of numbers and party discipline made it a relatively simple matter to keep FEP laws off the books. Even when conservatives were not particularly numerous, a variety of institutional features of American politics—chiefly partisan control of "veto points" in the policy-making process—made it possible for them to get their way much of the time. What resulted from the interplay among conservative mobilization, political parties, and political institutions over time is the contemporary system for regulating job discrimination. In tandem with other factors, conservative resistance to FEP—as it was refracted through the prism of American parties and political institutions—led to affirmative action as we know it today.[36]

My inference about the effect of conservative mobilization, political parties, and political institutions on the emergence of affirmative action is based on what is sometimes called a "counterfactual analysis." This type of analysis aims to explain why an actual outcome of interest (i.e., the factual) prevailed over a range of potential alternatives (i.e., the counterfactuals). A specific outcome can be said to have occurred because other alternatives never came to fruition. Explaining the outcome of interest thus becomes a task in determining why other potential paths were not taken. In developing a counterfactual analysis of affirmative action, I build on a burgeoning trend in the historical social sciences. A cluster of scholars is beginning to recognize the analytical utility of distinguishing between factual and counterfactual outcomes. "All major historical questions," Maurice Zeitlin writes in an early observation, "break down into two others, one 'factual' and one 'counterfactual': what happened in history and what might have happened?" Explaining why the factual prevailed over the counterfactual can provide a strong basis for credible inference in studies involving only a single case. Through the judicious use of counterfactuals, case studies can avoid the sin of "just-so" storytelling, a convenient but unconvincing mode of analysis in which events are said to have worked out just as they had to for the outcome of interest to occur. It is important to note that there is no single type of counterfactual claim. According to Daniel Carpenter, there are at least three. "The outcome [of interest] might not have occurred at all; it might not have occurred when it did; it might not have occurred in the form that it did." *The Fifth Freedom* aims to offer evidence in support of a claim conforming to the third type. Had conservatives not been so successful in opposing FEP legislation, affirmative action might have taken on a vastly different legal and political meaning, and job discrimination might have become regulated through a federal administrative agency that sought only to ensure equal treatment.[37]

Of course, most traditional historians remain leery of counterfactuals and rightfully so in many instances. They prefer looser formulations, writing of alternatives forgotten or paths not taken. To many of them, counterfactual sounds dangerously too much like second-guessing or wild speculation. More insidiously, counterfactuals tempt scholars to make inferences on the basis of alternatives that only they can see, relying on the gift of hindsight. The counterfactual I pose, however, is not theoretical or imaginary. I would call it a historical counterfactual. Manali Desai has argued that a counterfactual analysis should be based on "what was *demonstrably possible*." This is what I would consider the minimal burden that a counterfactually informed analysis should meet. A stronger kind of analysis is based not on possibilities that scholars can identify today in retrospect but on possibilities that people living at the time actually perceived themselves and strove to realize. The strongest kind of counterfactually informed analysis goes even further and makes a compelling case that the alternatives at play in a historical situation were not merely imagined or possible but actually plausible. How strong the analysis is depends on how realistic the alternatives were and how close they came to being actualized. *The Fifth Freedom* does not go so far as to argue that FEP legislation was a likely outcome thwarted by conservative opposition, but it does try to make the case that liberals were perfectly justified in thinking that success was possible, even though they proved unable to win in the end. Whether or not the case that I have assembled is convincing is a determination that readers will have to make themselves.[38]

This book presents a varied assortment of archival and statistical evidence, much of it drawn from untapped sources, in support of the argument that conservative resistance to FEP led over time to the unexpected emergence of affirmative action. The analysis is developed in chronological and thematic fashion, and it ranges across multiple levels of the federal system. Each chapter of the book focuses on a different episode in the larger struggle to regulate job discrimination.

The story I tell begins at outset of the Second World War. Chapter 2 examines the precarious life of the wartime FEPC and traces the complex pattern of influence that it exerted on the politics of civil rights and the development of national policy. Among the most far-reaching effects of the FEPC was the role it played in launching a decades-long campaign for strong and comprehensive FEP legislation. This campaign was spearheaded by a newly formed bloc of liberal groups for which fair employment practices were the raison d'être. Postwar liberals had sound reasons to believe that congressional action was within their reach, particularly when their prospects peaked during Truman's second term. But they would never realize their early aim to reconstitute the wartime FEPC. By the Kennedy years, what had emerged instead was a series of executive orders that covered only narrow segments of the labor market. There were many reasons why liberals failed to win legislation. Among the most obvious and important was the divided character of public opinion. Also crucial was the implacable opposition of southern Democrats, who exploited a range of institutional "veto points" in Congress to obstruct FEP proposals. But the grip of southern Democrats sometimes proved inadequate to their ambitions. There were crucial moments when northern Republicans—under the sway of the conservative, Taftite wing of the GOP—held the balance of power, and the fate of the "fifth freedom" rested with them. What they chose to do with their power in such moments was revealing. Though they would have preferred to keep the public spotlight on southern Democrats, conservative Republicans often proved willing to heed the wishes of their rural constituents as well as the business community, obstructing liberal legislation whenever they considered it necessary for them to do so. Even when liberals mounted their strongest efforts, conservatives proved willing to accept only voluntary legislation. The combined opposition of southern Democrats and northern Republicans was simply too much for liberals to overcome. Instead, they sought executive orders to regulate discrimination in federal employment and contracting—areas where government enjoyed the power of the purse and conservatives could muster less persuasive ideological objections. It was a sensible and understandable compromise, and thousands of Americans benefited from the new policies. The turn toward the executive-led regulation, however, did not come without political costs, although these costs would become fully apparent only decades later.

Liberals did not take sole aim at federal policy. Even as they found themselves limited by a conservative bloc during the wartime period, they actively sought out other policy-making venues where the prospect of success seemed better. Chief among these were state legislatures outside the South. During the Truman administration, success in the states actually formed a cornerstone of a larger strategy. By passing and implementing FEP laws in the populous, industrial states of the North, liberals hoped to demonstrate the value of wielding legislation against discrimination, building political momentum for congressional action. Chapter 3 presents a political and legislative history of the first state FEP law, which cleared the New York State legislature in 1945. The passage of Ives-Quinn significantly elevated liberal hopes. In the face of considerable hostility from rank-and-file Republicans as well as the unbridled enmity of their business allies, liberals had managed to prevail in a fight worth winning. The episode was certainly not a total loss for conservatives, who hit upon a powerful, new formula for framing the rhetoric of their opposition. In particular, they learned the value of professing support for the principle of racial equality while simultaneously rejecting any government regulation of job discrimination; they also learned how to talk about racial quotas and insinuate preferential treatment. Nevertheless, liberal groups carried the day, benefiting from the support of urban Democrats and liberal Republicans. The successful passage of Ives-Quinn marked the beginning of a new phase in the liberal campaign for freedom from discrimination. Whether other laboratories of democracy would prove equally willing to experiment with civil rights remained unclear, but liberals and conservatives alike understood the stakes. Nothing less than the meaning of the "fifth freedom" hung in the balance.[39]

After their stunning success with Ives-Quinn, postwar liberals mobilized to press the issue, and a "coordinating committee" for state FEP legislation quickly sprung up in almost every non-southern state across the country. Early success, however, would be frustratingly elusive outside of New York. During the late 1940s, when the passage of state legislation would have yielded the biggest return in national politics, only a few states proved capable of taking action. A handful of smaller states had passed FEP laws by then, but Pennsylvania, Michigan, Ohio, California, Illinois, and other politically significant states had not. Chapter 4 examines why the liberal campaign for state legislation experienced initial success in some states but not others. There were numerous factors at play, including broad differences in public support for a legislative approach to job discrimination, but the most consistent and powerful force in delaying the passage of FEP legislation was the conservative bloc itself. Its influence could only be glimpsed on Capitol Hill, but it was on full display in northern statehouses. Here, too, conservatives held several important advantages, though the source and size of their edge varied from time to time and from state to state. In certain instances, especially in the early postwar period, conservatives were simply too powerful. Due to the malapportionment of state legislatures, which tended to dilute the urban vote, rural voters—most of whom held conservative views on social and economic issues—exerted a disproportionate influence in state politics. The main electoral beneficiaries of the arrangement were Republicans, especially conservative Republicans, who dominated state elections for much of the postwar period. Moreover, organized business was notably stronger in most states than it was in national politics as a whole. Even when their power began to wane in the 1950s, conservatives found that key features of legislative institutions actually magnified their ability to block legislation—far beyond what their raw numbers would suggest. Just as a minority of southern Democrats took advantage of "veto points" to obstruct FEP proposals in Congress, conservative Republicans exploited analogous "veto points" in state legislatures to achieve the same ends. The "Party of Lincoln," as a result, was less an aid than a hindrance to the cause of fair employment practices. Of course, it was impossible for conservatives to hold civil rights at bay indefinitely. By 1961, most states had managed to pass FEP laws, but the legislation of the Eisenhower era was not so much a spur to action as it was a substitute for it. The window of political opportunity for a federated strategy had closed shut, and liberals would have to devote the preponderance of their attention to spotting and seizing their opportunities in national politics.

The second major political opportunity for federal action finally came when the church-led, southern-based civil rights movement reached an inspirational new summit in the mid-1960s. Its mobilization elevated public support for civil rights and laid the political foundations for the passage of the Civil Rights Act of 1964. The new law, however, failed to confer any enforcement authority upon the EEOC, much the less cease-and-desist authority that liberals had long coveted. Liberals steadfastly refused to accept the defect, successfully lobbying Congress in 1972 to take legislative action. Here was the third opportunity that Congress had to pass FEP. It was also the last opportunity, and Congress demurred. When it passed the Equal Employment Opportunity Act of 1972, Congress decided against administrative enforcement in favor of a new, court-based approach, empowering the EEOC to sue on behalf of aggrieved workers in the federal courts. The legislation was undoubtedly a step forward, but it also signaled the final eclipse of fair employment practices. The liberal dream since the New Deal was deferred yet again, this time indefinitely. Chapter 5 traces the causes and consequences of the continuing failure to regulate job discrimination through the establishment of a strong and centralized administrative agency. The same combination of political forces that stood in the way of FEP legislation during the postwar years—conservative Republicans, organized business, and southern Democrats—also blocked the EEOC from obtaining any enforcement authority until 1972. The social and political pressure for reform, however, did not suddenly wither away. Instead, it was channeled into the federal bureaucracy and federal courts, where the most aggressive forms of policy innovation had historically taken place. Liberals had always acquiesced to executive orders and court rulings as alternatives to legislation. Such policies were meant to compensate for the statutory vacuum and indeed provide a stepping stone for future legislative campaigns. Now they became a point of departure for a very different set of policies that went under the name equal employment opportunity—and affirmative action.

A final chapter draws conclusions about the origins of affirmative action and discusses their larger implications. Following the federated campaign for FEP legislation from the 1940s through the 1970s, *The Fifth Freedom* offers a new perspective on scholarly debates in a number of closely related fields. For students of political sociology, it reveals the importance of considering how elite mobilization, political parties, and political institutions interact over time to shape the development of public policy. In particular, it reminds us of how partisan control of "veto points" in the policy-making process of a federal system can not only slow the passage of certain long-sought policies but can also sow the conditions for the rise of altogether new policies that few political actors ever fully anticipate. Political scientists specializing in American politics will recognize the challenge that *The Fifth Freedom* poses to dominant ideas about the electoral realignment that began in the mid-1960s and culminated in the Reagan-Bush years. My findings suggest that substantial fractions of the Republican elite and grassroots tended toward racial conservatism long before the advent of affirmative action. Whether or not public policy had taken a "color-conscious" turn in the late 1960s, any Republican majority would have been racially conservative. For historians of the civil rights movement, *The Fifth Freedom* raises questions about the prevailing "discontinuarian" perspective that continues to pervade popular and historical writing about the subject. By focusing on civil rights and electoral politics in the North before 1964, it joins other recently published studies that uncover a host of political continuities that have until now remained hidden from full view. To political historians of the postwar United States,

The Fifth Freedom contributes to the ongoing historiographical debate that conflicts during the 1940s proved critical to the decline of New Deal liberalism and the rise of the New Right. This was indeed a crucial decade, to borrow Eric F. Goldman's phrase, but not only because liberals either capitalized on or squandered their opportunities. The late 1940s are significant because they were a genuine moment of historical contingency in which conservatives took full advantage of their opportunities, though the profound consequences of their narrow victories would become apparent only in the fullness of time. For better and for worse, Americans concerned about racial inequality and public policy continue to wrestle with the unresolved legacies of battles initially fought more than half a century ago.[40]

2

The Strange Career of Fair Employment Practices in National Politics and Policy, 1941–1960

The year 1941 marks a watershed in U.S. history. It began with President Franklin D. Roosevelt reaffirming his "all-out short-of-war" policy toward the mounting conflict across the Atlantic. Still wary of drawing isolationist criticism, FDR continued to balk at the prospect of sending American soldiers to die on European soil. Instead, he would call upon the United States to transform itself into a "great arsenal of democracy" and supply Great Britain with the munitions it desperately needed to fend off the Axis menace. American industry responded eagerly and came to life. Soon, supply ships loaded with guns, shells, and tanks began steaming across the Atlantic. Yet the United States could stave off direct military involvement only for so long. Escalating violence and bloodshed would dispatch the last sirens of isolationism. By the end of the year, Moscow was under siege, Pearl Harbor lay in shambles, and America had become a central, if reluctant, belligerent in the Second World War. In the history of the home front, 1941 represented the year that the Great Depression finally yielded. In 1940, there had been slight upticks in the standard array of economic indicators, but it was not until 1941 that the economy finally took off, fueled primarily by a spurt of war-related expenditures. Federal military outlays swelled from $1.8 to 6.3 billion, and purchases of goods and services for national defense grew from $2.2 to 13.7 billion, representing more than 10 percent of gross national product. Unemployment plummeted to the lowest levels in the previous ten years, with only 9.9 percent of the civilian labor force unable to find work. America at mid-century was a country in the midst of massive and wrenching changes, but 1941 was a decisive point of inflection.[1]

Not all momentous events during the year garnered front-page headlines. On June 25, 1941, FDR quietly signed Executive Order 8802 into law, one of many orders that he would issue during the wartime period. This one prohibited employment discrimination in the federal government and defense-related industries, and it established a modestly empowered committee to receive and investigate charges of racial and religious discrimination. Anyone could have overlooked the inconspicuous debut of the President's Committee on Fair Employment Practice (FEPC), as it was then called. Even a careful reader of the *New York Times* might have failed to spot a short article on page twelve announcing the executive order, tucked away as it was amidst reports of the German blitz across the Russian steppe and stories of industrial strife. The lack of widespread fanfare seemed justified. Roosevelt's committee would lead a beleaguered existence, harried by a motley crew of political enemies. Its friends put up a vigorous defense, but the committee would not outlast the war. Years later, when scholars would have the time to assess the accomplishments of the wartime FEPC, they would have trouble determining whether it had succeeded in opening up any job opportunities beyond the ones generated by tight wartime labor markets.[2]

But the impact of the FEPC was far from insubstantial. The most far-reaching consequences of the wartime FEPC were not economic but *political* in nature. Few developments better illustrate E. E. Schattshneider's discerning observation that "new policies create new politics." Hugh Davis Graham has rightly stressed how the troubled existence of the committee shaped "virtually all subsequent debate" over civil rights and employment. Yet it also did much more than structure political rhetoric. The fight to save the wartime FEPC served as a catalyst for grass-roots mobilization. It spurred a wider range of liberal interest groups to collaborate more closely with each other—in the name of civil rights—than ever before in the twentieth century. In fact, entirely new organizations were formed to coordinate the resulting whirlwind of political activity, and they and their progeny long outlived the committee itself. Key members of the committee staff parlayed their positions into top posts in the lobbying world, where they presided over the postwar effort to reincarnate the committee. Most of all, what emerged from the wartime experience— what Merl E. Reed has aptly called the "seedtime" of the modern civil rights movement—was a specific regulatory ideal and a concrete legislative program. The tenuous existence of the FEPC gave the liberal bloc a definite campaign. More than one hundred bills were introduced into Congress, most of them outlawing job discrimination and proposing to endow a new FEPC with regulatory powers highly akin to the National Labor Relations Board (NLRB). Over a dozen legislative hearings on fair employment practices (FEP) legislation were held in committees or subcommittees. Scores of liberal groups lent the campaign their money, time, and support. The seemingly insignificant committee had sparked a vast and sustained social and political movement, one that was not without prospect of success.[3]

As the postwar period progressed, however, liberals won only a string of halting, partial victories. The high-water mark of liberal possibility came during the second Truman administration, but Congress ultimately remained unsympathetic to liberal entreaties. Only the House ever saw fit to clear FEP legislation, and even then the approved bill was not the kind that liberals had specifically sought. Indeed, only a handful of FEP bills ever escaped committee, and still fewer went to the floor of the House or Senate for a vote. The liberal campaign for "fair employment practices" found greater success in provoking action on the part of the executive branch. Presidents from both parties issued a series of executive orders of prohibiting discrimination in federal employment and federal contracting. The orders varied in their scope of coverage as well as in the type and strength of enforcement authority that they accorded government officials, but all of them were highly limited interventions in which private employers were regulated lightly, if they were regulated at all. By 1963, federal antidiscrimination policy had acquired a labyrinthine quality. Whether a person was protected against discrimination depended on whether he or she was employed by the private sector, the federal government, or a government contractor; what procedures the federal department or contracting agencies put into place when implementing the executive order; whether the officials in charge wanted to enforce the order; and whether they possessed the regulatory tools that would allow them to administer sanctions or penalties in proportion to whatever violation had demonstrably occurred. It was a highly fragmented and decentralized system of social regulation—one from which the private sector had largely managed to elude inclusion.

What explains the strange career of FEP? This puzzling patchwork of policies, established through a combination and executive action and congressional inaction, cries out for accounting. Any answer must begin with the recognition that the political development of national policy did not merely reflect the ebb and flow of liberal groups. There were many influences. Adverse public opinion, as Paul Burstein has argued, exercised a powerful restraining force on the pace and extent of reform. The structure of political institutions made some office-holders more sensitive than others to liberal demands. The geopolitical imperative to maintain the semblance of racial democracy widened the range of political possibilities, even as a corrosive discourse of red-baiting shrank them. The very idea of guaranteeing equal treatment in the labor market through the passage of legislation provoked a surprisingly wide and often fatal opposition from a variety of opposing groups—some of it open, some of it obscured. Not surprisingly, southern Democrats were among the most visible and effective critics. Paul D. Moreno rightly stresses the key role of "southern irreconcilables who held filibuster power in the Senate and controlled the Rules Committee in the House."[4]

But the virtuoso demagoguery of Sen. Theodore Bilbo (D-SC), Rep. John E. Rankin (D-MS), and their compatriots hid a significant undercurrent of opposition among conservative Republicans. Lawmakers like Sen.

Robert A. Taft (R-OH) and Rep. Clare E. Hoffman (R-MI) did not themselves accept the segregationist or supremacist rationales proudly trumpeted by many southern Democrats, but neither did such conservatives
agree with what they regarded as a liberal nostrum for eradicating discrimination. Conservatives favored what they considered a more soft-
spoken and less intrusive approach, reflecting the preferences of the business community and the rural and suburban whites who elected them.
This vast combination of forces arrayed against liberals proved too much
in the end. In the instances when southern Democrats proved incapable
of nakedly obstructing FEP legislation, conservative Republicans in the
House and the Senate—and indeed the conservative bloc more broadly—
held the balance of power and sided with the South. Though they won
some notable victories, liberals would have to wait twenty years after
the demise of the wartime FEPC before Congress would act against job
discrimination.

The origins of the wartime FEPC can be traced to the handful of years
that marked the fleeting hiatus between depression and war. The broader
economy had begun slowly to revive in 1940, but African Americans were
among the very last to experience relief—partly because their fortunes
had sunk so shockingly low. Heartbreak and deprivation, of course, had
touched Americans of all racial backgrounds in the previous decade.
Plants and factories closed by the hundreds. Men and women of all faiths,
backgrounds, and nationalities were thrown out of work. Cupboards
grew empty, and children went hungry. Renters missed their monthly pay-
ments, homeowners defaulted on their mortgages, and entire families
were cast out of their residences. In the worst of times, thousands of the
most desperate Americans made their homes in clapboard shantytowns—
Hoovervilles as they were mockingly called. Misery touched almost everyone, but blacks were the group of Americans hardest hit. In the rural
South, the falling price of cotton plunged many black sharecroppers from
subsistence farming into outright starvation. Those who fled to southern
cities found little to cheer them. Even the meanest and dirtiest jobs were
no longer on offer. In the urban North and West, what little demand there
had been for their semi-skilled and unskilled labor vanished. Since northern blacks depended on such jobs more heavily than northern whites, they
experienced astonishingly high levels of unemployment—as high as 40 to
50 percent in some northern cities. Times were grim, no matter where in
the country they lived. Nearly 87 percent of all African Americans in 1939
fell below the poverty line, a stupefying figure nearly twice that of whites.
"The depression dealt a staggering blow to blacks," Harvard Sitkoff has
written. "It magnified all their traditional economic liabilities. It created
newer and harsher ones."[5]

For many African Americans, getting on their feet again proved espe-cially challenging because of the difficulty they had finding jobs, notably in the industrial sectors benefiting the most from the influx of war-related dollars. Defense contractors hired few African Americans for skilled or semi-skilled positions. In fact, it was not unusual for employers not to hire any black workers at all. A steel company in Kansas City was not alone when it announced a policy of total exclusion: "We have not had a Negro worker in twenty-five years, and do not plan to start now." When skilled black applicants were fortunate enough to find employment, it was often only at lower pay levels than their experience and ability should have commanded. Union attitudes frequently posed a barrier as well. When blacks lobbied Boeing Aircraft in Seattle for jobs, a representative of Aeronautical Mechanics Local No. 741, International Association of Machinists, notified the company of their position in no uncertain terms: "Labor has been asked to make many sacrifices in the war and has made them gladly, but this sacrifice is too great." Looking for help from employ-ment agencies did not much improve the situation. Whether it was be-cause of out-and-out prejudice on the part of the staff, or because well-intentioned placement officers hoped to shield black applicants from likely disappointment, African Americans were typically encouraged to register only for unskilled positions. The discriminatory practices all added up. As thousands of Americans eagerly snapped up new jobs, Afri-can American participation in the labor market actually fell. Gunnar Myr-dal found that "in October 1940, only 5.4 percent of all Employment Service placements in 20 selected defense industries (airplanes, automo-biles, ships, machinery, iron, steel, chemicals, and so on) were nonwhite, and this proportion had, by April 1941, *declined* to 2.5 percent."[6]

This time African Americans did not greet their predicament with forced smiles and reasoned acceptance. During the First World War, black leaders had urged their followers to suppress their grievances in the inter-est of national unity. For the most part, African Americans heeded the call. But their wartime loyalty had not been rewarded, as many of them had hoped it would be. Now a widespread sense of militancy took hold. Its most public expression emerged in black newspapers. The *Pittsburgh Courier* offered a powerful symbol of the new mood, launching the famed "Double V Campaign" at the outset of the war. As one reader explained, "The first V [stood] for victory over enemies from without, the second V for victory over our enemies from within." For his part, Roy Wilkins, assistant secretary of the National Association for the Advancement of Colored People (NAACP), rarely missed the opportunity to expose racial injustice from his weekly column in the *New York Amsterdam News*. Job discrimination was among his favorite targets. "According to my in-formation," he wrote in a typical prewar column, "every airplane factory is lily white," assigning blame for the situation to both companies and labor unions alike. Not to be outdone, editors at *Chicago Defender* likewise condemned the lack of progress being made. "All efforts toward elimination of bias in the industries that are receiving defense contracts have so far met with a stone wall," they wrote. "Is not the time at hand for us to inquire before the enemy guns begin to thunder over our heads, what sort of democracy is America preparing to defend?" The discontent eventually rose to the attention of the mainstream press in a high-profile article published in the *Saturday Evening Post*, where long-time executive secretary of the NAACP, Walter White, remarked pointedly on the decline of black morale.[7]

White eventually parlayed such concerns into a highly publicized audience with FDR in September 1940, but the meeting amounted to naught in the way of policy change. Though a large delegation of black leaders accompanied the NAACP executive secretary to the White House, African Americans would win their biggest concession from the federal government only after A. Philip Randolph, president of the Brotherhood of Sleeping Car Porters (BSCP), America's first black union, threatened to lead thousands of African Americans in a protest march on Washington, D.C. The charismatic Randolph had spent the past decade of his life organizing the BSCP. When it won recognition from the AFL in 1935 and a contract from the Pullman Corporation two years later, he gained the widespread admiration of whites and blacks alike. Randolph's popularity had secured him a place in the September delegation to the White House, but he found the whole experience disappointing and concluded that high-flying overtures for equality would remain ineffective in the absence of mass mobilization. Months later, while riding on a train through Virginia, Randolph hit upon the idea of a march, and he snapped into action. After drumming up financial and rhetorical support from the NAACP and the Urban League, he formed the March on Washington Movement (MOWM). Halfway into 1941, he won a second conference with Roosevelt. Randolph tirelessly lobbied the president, and his basic intuition eventually proved correct. FDR remained steadfastly unwilling to integrate the armed forces against the express wishes of his defense chiefs, who felt they had already made major concessions and believed they could go no further without seriously jeopardizing military preparedness. The president was also fearful of alienating southern Democrats, who chaired the most powerful committees in Congress and could easily obstruct any legislative initiatives he wished to pursue. But he was less wary of taking action on war-related employment, over which his administration wielded the power of the purse. With some final prodding from Randolph, FDR relented. On June 25, 1941, he issued Executive Order 8802, establishing the president's Committee on Fair Employment Practice.[8]

Roosevelt's order led to more than a few hyperbolic pronouncements. It inspired one enthusiastic observer to declare it the most important government document since the Emancipation Proclamation. The *Chicago Defender* concurred. In their reckoning, Executive Order 8802 was "one of the most significant pronouncements that has been made in the interests of the Negro for more than a century." It all sounded a bit grandiose and exaggerated, but the establishment of the FEPC was indeed noteworthy for a number of reasons. Not since Reconstruction had any branch of the federal government bestirred itself to protect the civil rights of African Americans. Certainly no twentieth-century president had voluntarily chosen to engage the question. It is true that African Americans venerated FDR, but not because they thought he was a champion of civil rights; his relief policies did far more to bring them into the New Deal electoral bloc than his stance on racial issues. The most that Roosevelt had done to advance the race was the appointment of elite African Americans to a handful of mid-level posts in his administration. Mary Betheod McClune, Robert C. Weaver, and William Hastie, and other such appointees formed a "Black Cabinet" for which FDR received important credit from liberals and little opprobrium from conservatives. With the issuance of his executive order, however, he broke from his own precedent, responding to the threat of popular mobilization, making nondiscrimination a formal policy of the United States in limited segments of the labor market, and establishing a whole new federal agency to monitor compliance. Only the most hardened and cynical liberals could totally resist hopeful feelings when they heard the hosannas greeting the establishment of the FEPC.[9]

Yet the economic achievements of the FEPC left something to be desired. While the committee did manage to stage several high-profile hearings, adjust thousands of individual complaints of discrimination, and establish an unparalleled infrastructure within the federal bureaucracy for addressing discrimination, it was ultimately beset by problems too severe and numerous to sustain long-term success. Part of the difficulty lay with the broader structure of American industrial relations. Decentralized hiring practices, for instance, encouraged employers and unions to trade blame for discrimination, making it difficult for the committee to ascertain which party was truly responsible. Other problems had to do with the committee itself. There was precious little continuity in leadership. A succession of able men were appointed to head the committee: Mark Etheridge, editor of the *Louisville Courier-Journal*; Malcolm MacLean, president of the Hampton Institute; Monsignor Francis J. Haas, Dean of the Social Sciences at Catholic University; and Malcolm Ross, a long-time federal official. None of them served long enough, however, to learn the ropes, much less become a major force for reform. The enforcement authority of the committee was legally ambiguous. A young White House attorney, Joseph Rauh, had spent days wrangling with Randolph about the specific language of the first order. Wanting the committee to have "teeth," Randolph returned draft after draft to a frazzled Rauh until it seemed adequate. But the hard truth was that the language of the executive order gave the FEPC little recourse in the face of delay, obstruction, or outright noncooperation by scofflaw employers or unions. It provided the FEPC with scant authority to enforce the law. The committee could not even turn to the federal courts for legal action. The final version of the order reflected the private wishes of Robert P. Patterson and James V. Forrestal, who originally urged FDR to abandon the order altogether. Aware that the president would feel compelled to issue the order, they asked him at the very least to deny the committee the authority to cancel contracts. The historical record does not appear to permit a rigorous assessment of their true motives, but if they had hoped to limit the effectiveness of the committee, then their efforts largely succeeded.[10]

The most serious problems that the FEPC faced were political in nature. Not surprisingly, southern Democrats and their constituents were among the quickest to mobilize against the FEPC. Recognizing that the Second World War could give the administration a convenient pretext for altering their accustomed way of life, southern elites proved a significant and effective source of opposition. The committee's jurisdiction over employment was especially disconcerting to them. Along with black disenfranchisement, job segregation served as the linchpin of racial apartheid in the South. The lack of economic resources made it all the more difficult for blacks to break down the barriers to political participation. Hence, when the committee decided in 1942 to hold a full-scale hearing on the employment practices in Birmingham, public opinion throughout much of the region predictably boiled over. The southern press roundly condemned the hearings. One magazine, *Alabama*, objected to the "race trials" being conducted by the FEPC and urged southerners to "fight this ominous encroachment on the sacred principles of their homeland." The barrage of frenzied objections had their intended effect. Fearing reprisals from southern voters during the midterm elections, FDR hastily transferred the FEPC to the War Manpower Commission (WMC), where the committee was gradually stripped of the ability to call hearings without prior approval by WMC chair, Roosevelt-loyalist Paul McNutt. Scarcely a year after it had been created, Roosevelt's committee had succumbed to political pressure from Dixie.[11]

After the demise of the first committee, Randolph renewed his threat to organize a protest march on the capitol, demanding that the president reinstate the FEPC. By the middle of 1943, Roosevelt was willing to oblige. The midterm elections had concluded none too disastrously for the Democrats, and he issued a second executive order in May that duly reconstituted the committee. Its performance exceeded that of the first committee, owing primarily to the ambition of Malcolm Ross, its last chairman. Yet the second incarnation of the committee did not last much longer than the first, falling victim to a clever rider to the Independent Offices Appropriations Act of 1944. Sen. Richard B. Russell (D-GA) had seen to it that the rider became part of the final bill. Russell's amendment required Congress to appropriate funds expressly for any federal agency that had been established by executive order and had been in existence for more than a year. Targeted primarily at the FEPC, it not only appealed to southern Democrats but also to conservative Republicans who had long worried about the unremitting and ill-advised aggrandizement of executive authority under FDR and the New Deal. The provision worked to perfection. The FEPC survived the appropriations process for only a year. In 1945, Congress set aside limited funds for the FEPC and ordered the committee to end operations the following summer. The committee was unceremoniously liquidated on June 30, 1946.[12]

The performance of the FEPC may have fallen short of liberal expectations, but the committee nonetheless left a profound bequest. Its achievements were not measurable by the number of complaints it received, or by the cases it successfully "adjusted," or even by the acts of discrimination it plausibly deterred. The most enduring legacies of the wartime committee were not economic but political in nature. Its creation ushered in a new era in the politics of civil rights. This sort of "policy feedback" was not entirely unique in the annals of American political history. Policy innovation has often led to "changes in social groups and their political goals and capabilities," in the words of Theda Skocpol. For instance, American veterans became a self-conscious, politically active group only with the introduction and liberalization of Civil War pensions. The social and agricultural policies of the New Deal, to use another well-researched example, encouraged the cross-regional political mobilization of large, export-oriented commercial farmers, who had very little in common with urban, industrial workers—quite in contrast to Sweden, where a different set of policies had the effect of politicizing small farmers and encouraging the formation of a farmer-worker alliance. The result was less political support in the United States for redistributive policies than in Sweden. What distinguishes the FEPC from these previous cases of feedback is that the political reverberations that it set into motion endured long after the committee had faded from existence. The wartime FEPC managed to survive only five years, and for much of the time it languished in political and legal limbo. Yet it profoundly reconfigured and transformed the political character of the struggle for civil rights.[13]

Its most lasting contribution was the occasion it provided for the formation of a new, sprawling bloc of liberal interest groups that campaigned at first to preserve and then to resuscitate the FEPC. The bloc was interracial, interfaith, and truly nationwide in scope. It targeted not just Jim Crow segregation in the South but also employment discrimination all across the country; not just discrimination against African Americans but also discrimination on the basis of religion, ethnicity, or national origin. The breadth of the bloc marked a substantial departure from racial politics in earlier years, when race advancement organizations were the primary lobbies, and when lynching and poll taxes topped their legislative agenda. The campaign for anti-lynching legislation, for instance, was led primarily by the NAACP. The campaign against the poll tax, coordinated by the National Committee to Abolish the Poll Tax, sported a fairly broad base of interest groups, but groups other than the NAACP were involved only on a limited basis. More importantly, poll taxes and anti-lynching legislation were largely sectional problems that gave rise to largely sectional solutions. The politics associated with them were hence organized along sectional lines, pitting northerners against southerners. The politics of fair employment, by contrast, displayed national dimensions. After all, job discrimination was not only prevalent in the South; it was extensive throughout northern labor markets and implicated northern employers and their unions. Labor market discrimination also affected religious and ethnic minorities living in northern cities, not just African Americans in the South. The bloc was by no means a highly disciplined unit but rather a loosely organized alliance of groups whose moments of collective political action were motivated by the shared interests of their members as well as by a common belief that government should take a strong role in protecting racial and religious minorities from job discrimination.[14]

There could be no doubt that self-interest was central to the political involvement of groups whose membership stood to benefit directly from the protection that FEPC offered, even if it was more symbolic than real. In this regard, race advancement organizations perhaps took the strongest interest. The NAACP would work ceaselessly, it once stated, until "skill of the hand" and "sharpness of the mind" became the only factors that determined black employment. It was only natural, since African Americans bore the brunt of the most egregious and damaging forms of discrimination in American life. However, plunging into the political arena to address broad-based socioeconomic concerns represented a departure of sorts for the two main African American civil rights groups. The NAACP had historically focused on dismantling formal barriers to racial equality through recourse to the courts; it had only recently turned to the political process to address the broad socioeconomic concerns of ordinary African Americans. The NAACP's support for the passage of legislation that would establish a permanent FEPC marked a definite point of inflection in its overall orientation. Even as the NAACP continued to pursue its court-based campaign to undo the legal and constitutional basis of segregation, Walter White, Clarence Mitchell, Roy Wilkins, and other top officers of the NAACP appeared regularly at congressional hearings, delivering strong and moving testimony. The active involvement of the National Urban League (NUL) could not have been entirely expected either, and it too reflected a shift in orientation. The NUL still preferred to resolve racial problems through education and conference, as it had done since its founding in the Progressive Era, but younger leaders like Lester Granger and Julian Thomas were more comfortable publicly defending the idea that legislation was necessary, if only because it could ultimately enhance the effectiveness of their traditional approach.[15]

A complex blend of self-interest and moral conviction encouraged a broad spectrum of religious groups to back the liberal bloc. The support they offered, however, was varied from group to group, and within every group there were clear divisions between the clergy, which tended toward liberalism, and rank-and-file congregants, whose views ranged from liberal to reactionary. Jewish groups such as the American Jewish Congress (AJC), American Jewish Committee (AJ Committee), Anti-Defamation League of B'Nai B'rith (ADL), and National Council of Jewish Women were perhaps the most thoroughly supportive. Particularly active among them was the AJC, whose Commission on Law and Social Action served as an important source of ideas, strategy, and experience. Almost all Jewish groups tended to explain their support by invoking traditions of Jewish solidarity with oppressed minorities, and there was little reason to doubt the sincerity of their professions. Also motivating them was a general commitment to pluralist politics. The stubborn persistence of labor market discrimination against Jews, particularly during the 1940s, was, however, one of the biggest drivers of their involvement. Indeed, groups like the AJC saw their defense of other minorities as essential to the protection of Jews. If they stood up for others in their time of need, perhaps others would stand up for them when the tables were turned.[16]

Christian organizations also represented a substantial segment of the national bloc. The most active and consistent group among Christians was the Religious Society of Friends, which operated through the Friends Committee on National Legislation (FCNL). But key numbers of Catholics, as Kevin Schultz shows, were also committed to equality and tolerance, partly out of a new conviction that they themselves deserved equal treatment despite their religious distinctiveness. At the same time, Catholic involvement was also rooted in the concrete experience of labor market discrimination, which was directed largely at Italians, Poles, Irish, and other peoples whose ethnicity or national origin was strongly associated with Catholicism. Perhaps the most politically active Catholic group on civil rights, as revealed in work by Martin Zielinski, was the Catholic Interracial Council (CIC) of New York, which was led for many years by Rev. John LaFarge and eagerly sought to promote "fair play" in the labor market. By contrast, Protestants were much less attached to the bloc. Although leaders of the Federal Council of Churches—and later the National Council of Churches—were as willing as their Jewish and Catholic counterparts to express public support for FEP legislation, they were far less enthusiastic about taking concrete political action.[17]

The threads of self-interest were perhaps less obvious but no less important when it came to the collection of industrial unions that together formed the Congress of Industrial Organizations (CIO). Even after the merger of the CIO with the American Federation of Labor (AFL) in 1955, international unions formerly affiliated with the defunct CIO still exhibited a stronger commitment to racial integration than their AFL counterparts. The main exception among AFL unions was the BSCP, Randolph's all-black outfit. To be sure, CIO words were almost always stronger than their deeds, and the intensity of their commitment varied across internationals and locals as well as different regions of the country. In many cases, union leadership favored FEP more than ordinary workers— but industrial unions like the United Steelworkers of America (USWA), International Ladies Garment Workers Union (ILGWU), and the United Packinghouse Workers of America (UPWA) were nevertheless among the most reliable and generous allies of the FEP cause. In the vanguard of racial liberalism was the United Automobile Workers (UAW), led by the peerless Walter Reuther. Though he was not without his critics, Reuther did more than any single labor leader to push the cause of FEP legislation. Surely he thought the cause was just, but he also saw blacks as a core constituency of the liberal bloc. Equally important were the social realities of the workplace. The UAW, like other industrial unions, organized the entire industry irrespective of skill level. This meant that they could simply not ignore semi-skilled and unskilled workers most of whom were black. If they were intent on generating enough power in the labor market, it would be necessary for them to bring African Americans into the house of labor.[18]

The liberal bloc did not indiscriminately ally with all of their potential friends, however. Echoing the fierce antiradical atmosphere of the Cold War, racial liberals pointedly rejected support from any organization with even the slightest taint of communism. Randolph himself had maintained a staunch anticommunism in his words and actions since his years of organizing the BSCP, and his National Council was no exception. During the National Emergency Civil Rights Mobilization in 1950, no communist-front organizations were invited by organizers to participate, including the Civil Rights Congress, Progressive Party, American Labor Party, and Young Progressives of America. At the request of the CIO, eleven unions on trial for suspected leadership by communists were also left off the list of invitees. To prevent unwanted infiltration, organizers of the mobilization went so far as to require all delegates to provide a letter of introduction on stationery from a top official of their organization. The major casualty of the fratricidal conflict on the American Left was not the communists themselves, who never constituted more than a fraction of the labor movement or the national electorate. As some historians have argued, it was rather the contingent of "independent" leftists who expressly opposed the Soviet regime but also disagreed with the general trajectory of American liberalism and hoped instead to institute a political economy along European lines. Liberals sought the broadest possible bloc to the greatest possible extent, but their staunch anticommunism—most likely a political necessary during the Cold War era—led them to reject a different vision of the political economy, sweeping away all remaining vestiges of hope for the growth of social democracy.[19]

The bloc rallying behind the FEPC nevertheless boasted unprecedented diversity, politically and geographically. The challenge of coordinating the political activities of so many otherwise disparate groups fell initially to the National Council (NC) for a Permanent FEPC, which brought the liberal bloc together under one roof. Administrative acumen had never ranked high among Randolph's considerable talents, and his inattention hobbled the NC with personality conflicts, factional infighting, and lack of adequate funding.[20] The NC did mount several respectable campaigns during and after the war, but it had grown ineffective and moribund by 1949 when the NAACP announced that it would mobilize church groups and labor unions for a massive two-day conference in Washington, D.C. The gathering symbolized the demise of the NC and the rise of a lobbying organization that would soon replace it. The next January four thousand delegates attended National Emergency Civil Rights Mobilization. The passage of FEP legislation was their top priority, and Senate majority leader Scott W. Lucas (D-IL) pledged to bring an FEPC bill to the floor before other all other civil rights measures. The mobilization suffered a catastrophic defeat in 1950, but fifty national organizations rallied again in 1952 and pooled their political and financial resources to form a new lobby, which they called the Leadership Conference on Civil Rights (LCCR). Its most immediate objective was reforming the Senate rules that had stymied Truman's civil rights agenda in previous years, especially the FEP plank. The LCCR, however, would go on to lead the broader charge for civil rights legislation for the remainder of the century, playing a central role in the drive for the Civil Rights Act of 1964 and Voting Rights

Act of 1965. It was almost certainly never Roosevelt's intention in 1941 to spur the formation of the modern civil rights lobby when he reluctantly issued Executive Order 8802, but the establishment of the LCCR more than a decade later was clearly rooted in the eventful summer when FDR reluctantly gave in to Randolph's demands for integration.[21]

The wartime FEPC also functioned as a kind of training ground for many figures who would become central to the broader civil rights movement. The staff of the FEPC gained valuable experience in navigating the world of Washington politics—experience that they leveraged in the postwar years to win top posts with liberal interest groups that were central to the fight for civil rights. Examples abounded. A largely unknown college instructor at Dillard University, Elmer W. Henderson, was hired during the war to lead the FEPC field office in Chicago. After the committee was liquidated, he did not return to his old teaching post. Instead, he went on to serve as director of the National Council for a Permanent FEPC and then the head of the American Council on Human Rights. Henderson also lent his name to a critical Supreme Court ruling that laid the legal groundwork for *Brown v. Board of Education*. Decided in 1950, *Henderson v. United States* held that racial segregation on interstate trains was unconstitutional. Henderson was the plaintiff, and it was his experience on Southern Railway's segregated dining cars in 1943—while he was traveling on business for the FEPC—that formed the basis of his lawsuit. The wartime experience also proved formative for Will Maslow. Before starting with the committee, Maslow had graduated Columbia Law School and had gone on to work for the National Labor Relations Board. In 1945, after a few years as director of field operations for the FEPC, Maslow was hired to lead the Law and Social Action Commission of the American Jewish Congress. From his new post, Maslow and his hand-picked team of attorneys served as the legal architects and political strategists of a federated campaign to pass legislation prohibiting discrimination—not only in employment but also in higher education, housing, and public accommodations. In his capacity as a member of the National Council and the AJC, Maslow helped to draft initial versions of FEP bills that were eventually introduced into Congress. Later in his career, he became executive director of the AJC in 1960 and helped to organize the March on Washington in 1963. The single most influential African American lobbyist in the postwar years, Clarence Mitchell of the NAACP, took a major step forward in his career when he landed a job at the FEPC as a senior fair practice examiner. His experience with the FEPC catapulted him to the position of labor secretary at the NAACP and he was rapidly promoted to the top post at the NAACP's Washington Bureau, where his skill and tact earned him a reputation as the "101st senator."

Through the mid-1970s, Mitchell found himself at the center of every major fight over civil rights in Congress. Like so many other racial liberals—both prominent and anonymous—he had come to prominence through the FEPC.[22]

If the rise and fall of the wartime FEPC provided the basis for the formation and politicization of the postwar civil rights lobby, it also furnished the lobby with a regulatory ideal and a host of supporting arguments. The living apotheosis of their ideal was the NLRB, which, along with the Securities and Exchange Commission (SEC) and the Federal Communications Commission (FCC), constituted one of the signal regulatory achievements of the New Deal. The establishment of all three agencies reflected the ascendancy of a belief among many liberals at the time that their traditional preference regarding government intervention in the economy—based on the idea that the state should step in only intermittently to break up monopolies on the rare occasions when they arose—required modification. A growing number of liberals had begun to believe that conflict was both inherent and rife in a modern capitalist economy, which could flourish only if expert administrators—free from the political pressure faced by the legislators—continuously and actively monitored the economic activity of private interests, stepping in to protect and defend the public interest whenever necessary. This interventionist shift in thinking was clearly manifest in the regulatory design of the NRLB. Congress had established the agency in 1935 through the passage of the National Labor Relations Act, unofficially named the Wagner Act after Sen. Robert F. Wagner (D-NY). The law protected the right of workers to organize their own unions, and it made the NRLB the federal agency responsible for carrying out and enforcing the law. Its specific responsibilities included the formal supervision of the process by which workers could establish a union at their workplace as well as the receipt and investigation of complaints that employers were using unlawful means to discourage unionization. If the agency determined that illegal activity had occurred, it could order the employer to cease and desist—and even order the employer to pay compensatory damages. The NLRB was enormously successful early on, providing important validation for liberal ideas about economic conflict and regulation. Before the agency was weakened by the Taft-Hartley Act of 1947, it successfully shielded workers from the worst abuses of employers and presided over the explosive growth of the labor movement. Many liberals believed that discrimination was rife throughout the American economy. It would not wither away with time, and therefore the FEPC ought to actively protect workers from job discrimination in the same way that the NLRB protected them from unfair labor practices. The most far-sighted liberals also nurtured the hope that the FEPC would serve as a catalyst for the civil rights movement, much as the NLRB had done for the labor movement.[23]

The very idea that something called "discrimination" could and should be the focus of government regulation set liberals apart from their forbearers and peers. To be sure, liberals, moderates, and even conservatives agreed that Swedish sociologist Gunnar Myrdal had correctly identified the taproot of racial inequality in his study, *An American Dilemma*. Published in 1944 to great fanfare, it traced the inferior social and economic position of African Americans to the prejudicial beliefs lodged deeply in the "heart of every American." But liberals for their part did not exploit Myrdal's celebrated diagnosis to conclude that prejudice was the only legitimate target of attack in the assault on racial inequality. Nor did they accept the claim that moral suasion and informal education—aimed at changing prejudicial beliefs—were the best remedies for the problem. Instead, they distinguished between prejudice and discrimination. Ideas, feelings, and beliefs were matters of private conscience, difficult to discern and even more difficult to change by force. Discrimination, however, was behavior that could be observed and regulated through government authority conferred by legislation. Editors at the *Washington Post* put the point evocatively: "Laws forbidding murder make no effort to forbid hatred among men; but they do effectively curtail any homicidal expression of hatred." In a different editorial, they reached toward labor law for a useful analogy: "Nothing so effectively served to bring about the acceptance of collective bargaining in our industrial relations as the force of law."[24]

The shrewdest and most sophisticated liberals made sure to concede that prejudice and discrimination were mutually causative, bound up in a "vicious circle" with one another. They were nonetheless careful to maintain that the two were not identical. According to Maslow and his colleague Joseph Robison at the AJC, "[P]rejudice, a state of mind, seems largely invulnerable to direct attack; [but] discrimination, a form of conduct, can be regulated." Racial liberals were careful not to scoff at informal methods of education and conciliation, but they contended that such methods would be woefully ineffective if discrimination itself was not also subject to coercive government authority. "You may educate," said the UAW's Reuther, "but at the same time you have to pass laws to support this education." Enforcement authority was not intrinsically desirable; it was important primarily because it facilitated education and conciliation. Aggrieved parties were likely to reach mutually satisfactory resolutions of a complaint if the government could sanction them for violating the law. As Sen. Hubert H. Humphrey (D-MN) once noted in his congressional testimony, "With the 'must' it is like this thing you carry in your right-hand pocket. If need be, you have force."[25]

These may seem like reasonable ideas today, but mid-century liberals found themselves constantly on the defensive. This was not only because the idea of regulating job discrimination was so new, but also because critics of the wartime FEPC—not all of them southerners—succeeded in sowing so many disconcerting misconceptions about the committee into public discourse. When Rep. Mary T. Norton (D-NJ) took to the floor of the House in 1945 to demand a fair hearing for an FEP bill that she had introduced, she was forced to spend her time preemptively addressing questions about FEPC rather than making a pitch for it. In fact, she posed and answered more than three dozen questions that she felt merited serious responses. A cursory look at only a few of the questions readily conveys the extent of the misconceptions among the public. "Does the bill require an employer to hire Negroes, Jews, Mexicans, or other minorities?" "Does the bill require an employer to hire a particular percentage or quota of Negroes or of any other minority groups?" "Is there enough discrimination in employment to justify a federal bill?" "Does the bill confer special privileges on minorities?" "Does this bill promote social equality?" "Will such a law cause riots or bloodshed?" As strongly as they believed in their cause, clear-eyed liberals could not doubt for a moment that they were sailing into a strong headwind. Norton spent so much time responding to such questions that she barely had any time left to state a positive case. It was a pattern that would recur for years thereafter.[26]

At times, skepticism about the wisdom of government intervention emanated from the most surprising sources. When the *New York Times* expressed doubt about the "wisdom and efficacy" of an FEP proposal before Congress in 1946, Randolph responded effectively right away. The paper had published a closely reasoned editorial asserting that discrimination was difficult to prove because it involved a question of intent. "You are confusing prejudice with discrimination," Randolph responded. "Prejudice, racial, religious or national, is subjective, and involves intent. It is an emotion or feeling, a state or attitude of mind. It is an inner condition. Not so with discrimination. Discrimination, racial, religious, or what not, is an objective practice which can be seen, heard, and felt." Indeed, appreciating the distinction was essential to understanding the raison d'être of FEP legislation. Randolph gestured to the Wagner Act to bolster his argument. It would be misleading to argue that the NLRB was ineffective because it had failed to eliminate feelings of hostility toward American workers. This missed the whole point of the law. The central purpose of the agency was to rid the workplace of blacklists, yellow-dog contracts, and company unions—that is, observable practices that discriminated against workers. In much the same way, he reasoned, "FEPC is not designed to abolish prejudice but to eliminate discrimination." Randolph concluded his letter with a grimly humorous flourish. "The law cannot compel Protestants to love Jews, but it can stop hoodlums from smearing synagogues with swastikas. Federal legislation may not be able to make Senator Bilbo embrace Representative Adam C. Powell but it can stop mobs from lynching Negroes."[27]

Liberals nevertheless did their best to press a positive, multifaceted case for FEP laws across the United States, publishing their arguments in general liberal periodicals like the *New Republic*, *The Nation*, and *Commentary* as well more specialized in-house periodicals like AJC's *Congress Weekly*, CIC's *Interracial Review*, and the monthly *Report* of the American Council of Race Relations. They also held meetings in churches, union halls, and homes; distributed vast quantities of educational literature; and made appearances on dozens of radio shows. A postwar rally in Madison Square Garden drew more than ten thousand participants, including a massive women's choir that sang a specially composed song about the FEPC: "Some say we fight a losing cause / But God's plan they can't see / For He has power above all laws / And he likes FEPC." Years later, enough public interest remained in the subject of FEP legislation that it was even made the topic of the collegiate National Debate Tournament for the 1952–53 academic year.[28]

Among the most straightforward and consistent arguments that liberals made were appeals to egalitarian ideals and moral principles. "There is nothing more fundamental to a democratic society than equality of economic opportunity," declared the *Washington Post*, one of the earliest and biggest backers of FEP legislation among national newspapers. The passage of a law, according to Rep. Charles M. La Follette, Jr. (R-IN), would mean that the United States was honoring the national promise that "nothing shall interfere with a man's opportunity to occupy any position or hold any job, except his own lack of ability." Such arguments were particularly effective because they resonated with the beliefs of millions of ordinary Americans. When asked to justify FEP legislation, 59 percent of respondents in a Gallup Poll who had heard of such legislation in Congress made a moral case: Everyone "should have equal rights," stated one respondent. Others argued that FEP legislation "gives all an equal chance," that "[a]ll men [are] created equal," and that equal opportunity is "one of [the] basic precepts of our democracy." The struggle against the Axis menace cast such claims into sharp relief. "Racial, religious discrimination in the field of employment is a denial of democracy and is of the essence of fascism," said Rabbi Stephen S. Wise of the AJC. Protesting the postponement of hearings, La Follette asked, "Shall we say to the Negro, the Jew, the Mexican, who survives [the war] and returns from what we are pleased today to call the battlefields of freedom, 'Freedom from discrimination was not among the freedoms you fought for?'"[29]

Liberal rhetoric took a new turn in 1947, when Truman stood before Congress and asked for $400 million in foreign aid to Greece and Turkey to contain the expansionist ambitions of the Soviet Union. "I believe it must be the policy of the United States to support free peoples who are resisting attempted subjugation by armed minorities or by outside pressures," he said. The policy would quickly become known as the Truman Doctrine, and it had profound ramifications not only for American foreign policy but also domestic politics. With geopolitical circumstances greatly altered, liberals began stressing the importance of promoting democracy at home in order to limit Soviet influence abroad, especially in the developing world. Discrimination against racial minorities was morally wrong, but it also made the country look patently hypocritical in the eyes of countries that were contemplating the choice between Western-style democracy and Soviet-inspired communism. "[I]t is high time we stopped this business," wrote the *Cleveland Plain Dealer* after a troubling episode in which a casualty of the Korean War was denied burial in Sioux City because his widow refused to sign a statement certifying that he had "all white blood." The veteran belonged to the Winnebago tribe. "We can't do it," commented the editors, "as decent human beings, and we can't do it as a nation trying to sell democracy to a world full of non-white peoples." In 1950, Sen. Jacob Javits (R-NY) made a typical case for FEP legislation during the Cold War. The passage of FEP legislation, he said, would "demonstrate to the colored peoples of the world the utter falsehood of any effort to impugn the good faith of America's leadership in the fight for freedom and democracy."[30]

Other arguments declined to invoke soaring rhetoric; they belonged to a more practical and utilitarian genre. During the wartime period, it was popular to point out that discrimination sapped black morale and disrupted national unity. Neither condition was desirable in the struggle against fascism. Liberals were also fond of arguing that discrimination undermined the full utilization of the labor force. Detroit was winning the war, and it should run as smoothly as possible. The more sophisticated advocates among liberals understood that FEP legislation could be seen as a benefit to only the groups that it protected, and they couched their arguments accordingly. "I am not 'carrying water' for the minority," protested Hubert H. Humphrey when confronted with the accusation by Louisiana's Allen J. Ellender. "I do not like the term. . . . [T]he sooner we quit talking about minorities in America and the sooner we talk about the American citizen—the American people—the sooner off we are going to be in handling this problem—take out some of the hyphens in the American name." A few liberals even worried out loud that the racial tensions would erupt in the postwar period. "The competition for jobs will become acute, and may very well develop race tension and race riots," said one of them. "It is well to remember that an epidemic of race riots marked the postwar years of 1919 and 1920."[31]

The liberal commitment to FEP, however, consisted of far more than new ideas and impassioned rhetoric. Its most important expression came in the form of a real legislative campaign that was not altogether without chance of success. "Congress is the key," observed Malcolm Ross, who remained a significant presence on the scene for a few years after the demise of the FEPC. Nearly all liberals concurred with his judgment, and more than one hundred FEP proposals were introduced into Congress. The bills naturally varied in the language and content of their specific provisions, but the vast majority of bills were liberal in their proposed scope of coverage as well as in the type of enforcement authority that they conferred to the federal government. The wartime FEPC, it will be recalled, held jurisdiction over a narrow segment of the labor market, primarily federal contractors in defense-related industries; moreover, it had no formal authority to punish infractions of the law and thereby compel compliance. By contrast, liberal proposals for FEP legislation explicitly outlawed racial and religious discrimination in both public *and* private employment—and they established a permanent federal agency with *administrative* powers to enforce the law, in the manner of the NLRB.[32]

Typical liberal proposals looked like H.R. 2232 in the 79th Congress (1945) or S. 984 in the 80th Congress (1947). In addition to outlawing discrimination, these and other bills gave the newly created agency the authority to receive individual complaints of unequal treatment; subpoena witnesses and compel testimony to ascertain the truth or falsity of the charges; and then order offending employers or unions to cease and desist from their discriminatory behavior. Since victims of discrimination often missed out on economic gains that they would have achieved in the absence of illegal behavior, liberal proposals also authorized the agency to order "affirmative action" on the part of the offending parties. This "affirmative action" was a form of administratively ordered redress, and it normally involved ordering the hiring, rehiring, or promotion of someone who had been unfairly treated. It could also involve monetary compensation to the victim, usually in the form of back pay. The NLRB possessed and exercised both types of enforcement authority in cases over which it had proper jurisdiction, and many liberals hoped to secure at least the same kind of power for a permanent FEPC.[33]

In fact, liberals strongly preferred NLRB-style administrative enforcement to judicial enforcement, believing that complaints of job discrimination had no place on the dockets of federal courts. Such complaints tended to arise from a limited range of circumstances, and they involved so many of the same legal and evidentiary considerations that it seemed more efficient to handle them through a carefully tailored and well-streamlined administrative process, rather than through the courts, which were better suited for more complex cases arising under infinitely more varied circumstances. The courts did have a role. In particular, knotty cases would have the right of judicial review, but only if they presented novel or unresolved questions of law. The particular type of administrative enforcement in the typical bill—known as "retail" enforcement because it involved handling complaints on a case-by-case, individual basis—also appealed to liberals because it offered enough flexibility to be practicable. Those who were well versed in the intricacies of administrative law and familiar with the problems of regulatory design correctly understood that any enforcement regime would work if and only if the government could threaten and impose sanctions that were commensurate with the scale of the demonstrated infraction. If the sanctions were too trivial, offenders would continue to discriminate. Small fines would do little to encourage good behavior; recalcitrant employers would simply figure the penalties into the cost of doing business and pass them along to the customer. On the other hand, if the sanctions were too onerous, as they were when contract cancellation was the only enforcement tool available, government officials would be understandably reluctant to impose them. What competent, self-interested bureaucrat would ever truly recommend the cancellation of a major federal contract in order to resolve one, two, or even three complaints of discrimination? "What is needed," Maslow of the AJC noted, "is some sanction more certain of application and hence more likely in practice to be a deterrent." One of the strengths of retail enforcement was that it would give federal officials the authority to tailor their penalty to fit the unique circumstances of every case at hand, raising the likelihood that a painful sanction could be handed down, thereby improving the deterrent potential of the law.[34]

Scores of liberal bills made their way off drafting tables or out of file folders and into the legislative hopper of Congress. Liberals found their most consistent allies in the ranks of northern Democrats, such as Reps. Emanuel Celler (NY), Helen G. Douglas (CA) (see figure 2.1), Augustus Hawkins (CA), Mary T. Norton (NY), and Adam Clayton Powell (NY), as well as Sens. Dennis Chavez (NM), Paul H. Douglas (IL) and Hubert H. Humphrey (MN). They tended to represent urban districts or urban states, where the political demand for FEP ran the highest. Indeed, most liberal bills were sponsored or cosponsored by northern Democrats, who drew heavily on experience and acumen of liberal groups in designing legislation and drafting speeches. The first liberal bill, for instance, was introduced to the House by Rep. Thomas E. Scanlon (D-PA) in 1944. Republicans were not entirely unreliable. The liberals among them introduced enforceable bills as well. But they were decidedly less numerous. During the Truman years, twenty northern Democrats sponsored liberal

Figure 2.1 U.S. Rep. Helen G. Douglas (D-CA) meeting with black union leaders in her Los Angeles home, 1944. Ingrid Winther Scobie, Douglas's biographer, estimates that a quarter of her south-central district in 1945 was black. Along with men like Adam Clayton Powell (D-NY), Douglas was one of dozens of non-southern Democrats in Congress whose racially and religiously diverse constituency demanded freedom from discrimination at mid-century. Courtesy of the Carl Albert Center Congressional Archives, University of Oklahoma.

bills in the House, compared to only twelve Republicans. Moreover, most Republicans who sponsored liberal bills did so during the wartime period—for example, Everett M. Dirksen with H.R. 401 and H.R. 1575 in 1945. Their enthusiasm for "compulsory" enforcement waned noticeably thereafter. The same overall pattern emerged in the Senate, where nineteen northern Democrats sponsored liberal bills, compared to fourteen Republicans. Among the more politically significant bills were H.R. 3986, H.R. 4004, H.R. 4005, and S. 2048 in 1944; H.R. 2232 in 1945; S. 101 and S. 984 in 1947; H.R. 4453 in 1949; and S. 1732 and S. 551 in 1952.[35]

The liberal campaign peaked during the early years of the second Truman administration, when a flood of liberal bills poured into Congress (see figure 2.2). No bill ultimately passed, but for a moment FEP was the undisputed "storm center of the fight" over civil rights, as the *Congressional Digest* observed in 1950. During the 81st Congress (1949–50), when FEP legislation came as close as it ever would to passing, more articles were published on the subject in the *New York Times* and *Washington Post* than were published on either anti-lynching or anti–poll tax

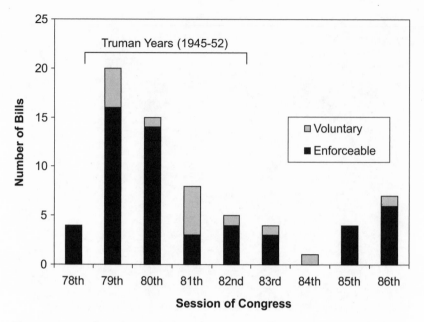

Figure 2.2 Number of Fair Employment Practices Bills Introduced into Congress, 1943–1960. *Note*: This chart tracks both voluntary and enforceable bills, and it shows that the introduction of all types of bills peaked during the Truman administration. *Source*: U.S. Congress, *House and Senate Bills and Resolutions* (Congressional Information Service, various years); *Congressional Record*, various years.

legislation—two perennial favorites of the civil rights bloc (see figure 2.3). Nor did all FEP bills languish anonymously in the legislative hopper after their introduction. Key numbers of legislators from both parties pressed for public hearings, participated in questioning witnesses, provided their own testimony, and cast votes to report FEP proposals to the full chamber. Over a dozen congressional hearings on job discrimination were held through 1964, usually taking place in the House or Senate labor committees and involving scores of witnesses (see table A.2). Many of the hearings were admittedly political theater staged by members keen on appealing to the demands of their urban-industrial constituencies. But the hearings became largely symbolic only during the Eisenhower years. The roster of participants in hearings on FEP legislation during the Truman years was impressively long and read like a who's-who list of the civil rights lobby.[36]

In fact, Congress did take serious action on several bills (see table A.3). No less than five FEP proposals were favorably reported out of committee after hearings. Of these, S. 101 (1945–46) and S. 1728 (1949–50) would

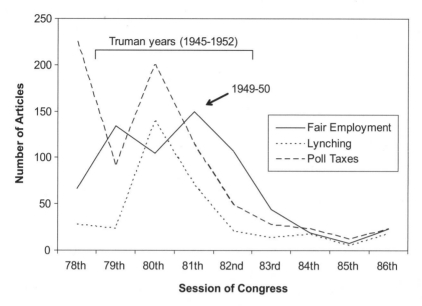

Figure 2.3 Articles on Civil Rights and Congress in the *New York Times* and *Washington Post* by Type of Issue, 1943–1960. *Note*: This chart shows the number of articles mentioning "fair employment," "lynching," or "poll taxes" in conjunction with "Congress" in both newspapers. It indicates that fair employment practices (FEP) legislation was the most widely reported civil rights issue during Truman's second term. *Source*: Author's searches on ProQuest Historical Newspapers.

generate overheated debates in the normally genteel Senate, touching off well-organized southern filibusters that eventually required three separate cloture votes, one in 1946 and two in 1950. In the House, after weeks of parliamentary intrigue in 1950, H.R. 4453 actually came to a roll-call vote and passed—albeit only after it had been stripped of enforcement authority. This was certainly not the result that liberals had wanted, but the politics reached a new zenith of intensity, signaling just how high the stakes had become. On balance, then, liberals made modest but real progress toward their legislative goals. The campaign to secure FEP legislation in Congress was never fully realized, but neither was it a fruitless quest, and postwar liberals at the time could hardly be faulted for nurturing some hope of success.[37]

There were, of course, numerous reasons behind the limited success of the liberal campaign. The divided character of public opinion about civil rights in general, and FEP legislation more specifically, was the most abstract reason of them all. It was also the most challenging to assess, not the least of which was because of the uncertainty of the polling numbers. Despite a justified reputation for increased rigor—survey researchers had come a long way since *Literary Digest* had erroneously predicted a Landon victory over FDR in 1936—opinion polling was still a relatively new field in the postwar period. Its fallibility was nowhere more embarrassingly on display than in the 1948 presidential election, when the celebrated triumvirate of George Gallup, Elmo Roper, and Archibald M. Crossley forecast that Republican contender Thomas E. Dewey would defeat Truman. The president responded to their prognostications with combative skepticism, telling a preelection audience in Queens that there would be many "red-faced pollsters" on Election Day. Time proved Truman correct, and he won the race by more than four percentage points. The episode was not a total debacle. It had been an unusually complicated election, and the mistakes stemmed less from inadequate methodology than the fact that most of the final polls were taken too early, in mid-October. The results were likely accurate, but they missed Truman's last-minute surge of support, a product of the belated momentum he had generated on his rollicking, whistle-stop train tour of the country. The perceived validity of polling nevertheless suffered another grievous blow, and many elective office-holders continued to eschew polling data, relying instead on reading constituent letters, receiving voter delegations, and exploiting other traditional means of ascertaining the prevailing sentiment of their district.[38]

Yet polls could provide a useful snapshot of public opinion for anyone wanting to interpret them with the appropriate amount of care and restraint. What they revealed on the question of FEP legislation was deep national ambivalence. If they had spent any time scrutinizing the numbers, liberals or conservatives could have found reason for cheer. The basic pattern remained unchanged for much of the postwar period. Opponents of the policy appeared slightly to outnumber supporters. A third of the respondents in each of two polls conducted by the Gallup Organization in 1948 and 1949 expressed the belief that the federal government should "go all the way" in "requiring employers to hire people without regard to race, religion, color, or nationality" (see table 2.1). No follow-up questions were asked to clarify what respondents thought "all the way" meant, but it seems safe to interpret their answer as indicative of strong support for FEP legislation of the liberal variant, or perhaps even a stronger version. A somewhat larger fraction of respondents, averaging around 45 percent, preferred that the government "do nothing" about the issue. Two polls by the Gallup Organization in 1952 and 1953 showed the same results (see table 2.1). When asked whether there should be a "national law requiring employers to hire people without regard to color or race," one-third of respondents in each of the two polls agreed. A slightly larger percentage—just under half of all respondents—felt that the states should decide for themselves whether to pass such legislation. Other polls more or less confirmed the Gallup findings, and the pattern remained fairly stable through 1957, when a national survey carried out by the Roper Organization also found a third of respondents supported a federal law against job discrimination. This balance of support and opposition nonetheless made FEP legislation one of the more unpopular items on the civil rights agenda. According to Gallup Polls from the Truman years, two-thirds of Americans consistently supported the abolition of the poll tax in southern states; approximately one-half endorsed the desegregation of interstate travel; and slightly less than half believed that the federal government should have a right to intervene in cases of lynching.[39]

Opposition to FEP legislation and other parts of the civil rights agenda was not evenly spread across the country; it had obvious sectional dimensions. Most southerners did not want the federal government to go "all the way" in mandating nondiscriminatory hiring by employers. Quite to the contrary—only 9 percent of southerners agreed with the statement in a 1948 poll by Gallup. A large majority, 68 percent, believed that the federal government should do nothing. In a 1949 poll, 15 percent agreed that the federal government should "go all the way," but nearly two-thirds of southern respondents still felt that the federal government should go "none of the way" in mandating nondiscriminatory hiring by employers. In a 1952 and a 1953 poll by Gallup, southerners remained implacably opposed to a federal solution. The presidential contest between Adlai Stevenson and Dwight D. Eisenhower had injected the language of states rights into the national discourse on civil rights, and nearly three-quarters of southern respondents felt that states, and not the federal government, should be left to decide the issue of job discrimination on their own.[40]

Of course, southern exceptionalism could be exaggerated. While the South was the section of the country most opposed to national FEP legislation, Americans across all sections of the country differed on the question. In a 1948 Gallup Poll, roughly a third of respondents living outside the South expressed support for strong federal action, but a surprising 42 percent felt that the federal government should "do nothing." A slim plurality of Americans outside of Dixie opposed federal action on FEP legislation. The same pattern emerged when nonsouthern respondents were asked the same question by Gallup in 1949. In 1953, opponents of federal action were evidently in the plurality in nearly every major region of the United States. Respondents residing in the Midwest favored "states' rights" over a national law by a 44–30 margin, respondents in the West by a 36–32 margin, and respondents in the East by a 42–41 margin. The differentials were slim enough that it was difficult to read

TABLE 2.1
Public Support for Federal Action on Fair Employment Practices (FEP): Gallup Poll, 1947–1953

Question	1947	1948	1949	1950	1951	1952	1953
Should go all the way in requiring		32	33				
Federal, not state, should require						32	31
If he is qualified	57						
Employer could not refuse	62						
No person could be denied	70						

Question Wordings and Variants
Should go all the way in requiring (Gallup 414K and 439T): "How far do you yourself think the Federal Government should go in requiring employers to hire people without regard to race, religion, color, or nationality?" (1. All the way, 2. Should do nothing, 3. Depends on type of work, 4. Should leave matters to the states, 5. Don't know).

Federal, not state, should require (Gallup 495 and 510): "Some people say we should have a national law requiring employers to hire people without regard to color or race. Other people say that it should be left up to each state to decide on this for itself. Which side to you, yourself agree?" (1. National, 2. States, 3. Neither, 4. No opinion).

If he is qualified (Gallup 407T): "Do you favor or oppose a Federal law (for all the states) which would require employers to hire a person if he is qualified for the job—regardless of his nationality, religion, race or color?" (1. Favor, 2. Oppose, 3. No opinion).

Employer could not refuse (Gallup 407K): "Would you favor or oppose such a law (a proposed Federal law under which an employer could not refuse to hire any person for a job because of his religion, race, or color) for all states?" (1. Favor, 2. Oppose, 3. No opinion).

No person could be denied Gallup 408K): "A federal law (for all states) has been proposed which says that no person could be denied a job because of his religion, color, or nationality. Would you like to have your Congressman vote for or against this proposed law?" (1. For, 2. Against, 3. No opinion).

Notes: Entries are percentage of respondents giving an answer supporting an FEP law. Gallup 407K was asked only of respondents who had heard of such a federal law.

Sources: iPoll Databank (Roper Center for Public Opinion Research, University of Connecticut), http://www.ropercenter.uconn.edu/ipoll.html; Paul Burstein, *Discrimination, Jobs, and Politics: The Struggle for Equal Employment Opportunity in the United States* (Chicago: University of Chicago Press, 1985), 57.

too much into them. Nevertheless, the substantial lack of support for federal action all across the country—and not just in the South—must have given pause to thoughtful liberals, even as their opponents seized upon the poll numbers to bolster the argument that the United States was not yet ready for FEP legislation.[41]

But several pieces of polling data offered liberals good reason for hope. Of the respondents in a 1947 Gallup Poll who had actually heard that FEP legislation was pending in Congress, 62 percent favored a federal law "under which an employer could not refuse to hire any person for a job because of his religion, race, or color" (see table 2.1). When all respondents in a related Gallup Poll were asked whether they would support a hypothetical federal law that would "require employers to hire a person if he is qualified for the job—regardless of his nationality, religion, race, or color," 57 percent of the respondents in a Gallup Poll said they would (see table 2.1). In a separate survey administered in 1947, Gallup asked a more concrete question that sought to determine whether his respondents wanted their elective representatives actually to act on their policy preferences. "A federal law (for all states) has been proposed which says that no person could be denied a job because of his religion, color, or nationality," read the question. "Would you like to have your Congressman vote for or against this proposed law?" A whopping 70 percent of the respondents reported that they would want their member of Congress to vote for the legislation (table 2.1), while only 20 percent did not. Tellingly, almost all respondents felt "very strongly" or "fairly strongly" about their response, one way or the other. Such poll numbers suggested a brighter outlook for national FEP legislation.[42]

Why the discrepancy of twenty-five to forty percentage points? Perhaps it was shoddy methodology that led to the 1947 numbers. This is certainly a valid concern, given the fledgling state of the field at the time. Nevertheless, it is worth pointing out that the 1947 numbers were consistent across three different questions on two separate surveys. Any oversight must necessarily have been severe enough to generate a massive error, not once but three times. Nor does it seem valid to regard the discrepancy as a reflection of a true decline in public support for FEP legislation from 1947 to 1948. Such a drop does not mesh with a chronology of major events during the period. Both polls in 1947 were taken in November, almost immediately after the release of Truman's famous report on civil rights, *To Secure These Rights*. The poll in 1948 was administered in March, five months later. Even if the report gave civil rights a favorable burst of publicity, nothing occurred in the intervening period that could possibly account for a decline of such magnitude. It is true that Truman, following the advice of advisor Clark Clifford, began adopting a much more aggressive stance on civil rights. The president mentioned the topic in his State of the Union address and then made civil rights the centerpiece of a special address to Congress in February. Perhaps his newfound commitment to civil rights severely alienated key constituencies within the New Deal bloc, notably southerners. But southern reaction did not truly boil over until July, when Humphrey's speech at the Democratic National Convention led to the infamous Dixiecrat revolt. July was also the month when Truman triggered even greater hostility by issuing Executive Order 9980 and desegregating the armed forces. Moreover, much of the reaction was concentrated in the black-belt states, especially Mississippi, Alabama, Louisiana, and South Carolina. Even if there was a slight drop off, it seems that little evidence can be mustered to support the inference that public support for federal action on FEP plunged drastically in the five months from November 1947 to March 1948.[43]

The discrepancy more likely reflects differences in the specific wording of the questions themselves. It should have been unsurprising that only a third of respondents would ever agree with the statement that the federal government should go "all the way" in "requiring employers to hire people without regard to race, religion, color, or nationality." The phrase "requiring employers to hire people" had a strongly coercive ring; it did not seem to preserve much discretion for employers and could be easily understood to mean that they would be forced to hire individuals that they might not have wanted to hire for entirely legitimate reasons. The phrase "all the way" may have also appeared too open-ended to many respondents. Did that mean that the federal government would have the authority to dictate the hiring of certain individuals no matter what objections a particular employer might have? It was when the question about federal action was asked differently that pollsters uncovered a broader reservoir of support. One of the questions from 1947 explicitly noted that the law would protect someone only "if he is qualified for the job," directly dispelling the concern that employers would be compelled to take on unqualified applicants. The other two questions asked whether respondents would want their Congressman to vote for a law that would ensure that "no person could be denied a job" or guarantee that employers "could not refuse to hire a person for a job" simply on the basis of their religion, color, or nationality. This phrasing evoked a situation in which somebody would have been hired—that is, would have been a good fit and would have been qualified for the position—but was denied a job on account of racial, religious, or national-origin discrimination. All three questions explicitly stated or strongly implied that the federal government should not permit employers to reject the employment of someone who otherwise would have been employed of it were not for his or her race, religion, or nationality. When survey questions were worded in such a manner, support for federal action appeared high.[44]

Liberals could also take heart in the apparent malleability of public opinion on the question of civil rights. Support for congressional action fell, but there were also occasions when it rose. A liberalization of public opinion was most visible in the way many ordinary Americans regarded Truman's civil rights program. According to a Gallup Poll conducted in March 1948, 61 percent of respondents had heard of the program. Of these, only 9 percent felt that Congress should pass the program "as a whole." In a poll taken after the November election, fully 42 percent felt that the program should be passed "as a whole" by Congress. Truman had campaigned hard for the black ballot, especially in northern industrial states, but his rhetoric appears to have persuaded a broader slice of the electorate than African Americans.[45]

Looking broadly over the poll results, both liberals and their critics could find reason for optimism. Liberals were surely cheered by the finding that support for FEP legislation depending on the exact way in which survey questions were worded; it was also a good sign for them that public opinion on civil rights could be prodded in a liberal direction. On the other hand, critics of FEP legislation must have been gladdened by the relatively consistent finding that only a third of Americans favored the strongest conceivable form of federal action. There was no clear consensus. Public opinion regarding FEP legislation was ambiguous at worst and ambivalent at best. The persistent inability or unwillingness of Congress to take legislative action could be found closer to earth, in the corridors of Capitol Hill.

The first barrier to Congressional passage of FEP legislation was the determined opposition of southern Democrats. Though they never constituted a majority in either chamber of Congress, they nevertheless exerted a political influence disproportionate to their numbers. Jill Quadagno, Ira Katznelson, Robert C. Lieberman, and Michael Brown have all pointed to the central significance of the South in national politics and policy. Few types of civil rights legislation threatened the foundations of the southern political economy more directly, and still fewer triggered such unrestrained enmity. By and large, southern Democrats succeeded in their resolve to obstruct the passage of enforceable FEP legislation. It was not the first time they had left their mark on the politics of social legislation. Many signature programs of New Deal severely marginalized African Americans by finding creative ways of excluding them from government benefits. The considerable protections conferred by the Wagner Act, for instance, conveniently did not cover agricultural or domestic jobs—segments of the labor market where African Americans were disproportionately concentrated. The same occupational exclusions characterized the Old-Age Insurance program of the Social Security Act. Other programs, such as Aid to Dependent Children, simply left the fate of African Americans to the whim of unsympathetic local officials. Such exclusions led to vast benefit disparities in the South. Even federal officials made concessions to southern pressure. For instance, wage differentials between black and white workers were tacitly condoned by the National Recovery Administration. The handiwork of southern Democrats should have been evident to anyone who cared to look with a dispassionate eye.[46]

There were two well-known institutional features of legislative life in Congress that the modest minority of southern Democrats exploited to their resounding advantage. In the House, it was their dominance of the Rules Committee that enabled them effectively to obstruct FEP legislation. To be sure, southerners were a major force in the most powerful committees in both chambers, largely because the one-party system that prevailed throughout the South ensured the regular reelection of Democratic incumbents, giving them seniority over officials of either party who represented competitive districts. Often, their seniority would translate into a committee chairmanship, giving them agenda-setting power among other things. It was thus not uncommon for bills opposed by southern Democrats to remain mired in their original committee of jurisdiction, usually the House (or Senate) Labor Committee. This was the fate of numerous promising FEP proposals. The influence of southern Democrats on the House Rules Committee was, however, especially significant because all House bills required a rule from the Rules Committee in order to become eligible for any floor action, most crucially a roll-call vote. Hence, even if liberals succeeded in getting a standing committee to report a FEP proposal favorably, it would still require a rule from the Rules Committee to move forward in the legislative process. This represented a second "veto point" over which southern Democrats exercised reliable control. As a result, none of the FEP bills successfully reported by their original committees received the necessary rules for floor consideration. For much of the wartime and postwar period, southern Democrats ruled the Rules Committee; they regularly commanded a sizeable bloc of votes and often chaired the committee as well. One example of their influence came in 1945, during the 78th Congress, when a tie vote in the House Rules Committee effectively denied a floor vote on Rep. Mary T. Norton's (D-NJ) FEP bill, H.R. 2232. Six of the nay votes came from southern Democrats and their border-state allies. In 1950, another tie vote in the Rules Committee bottled up a similar FEP bill, H.R. 4453, which had been submitted on behalf of the Truman administration by Adam Clayton Powell (D-NY). Once again southern Democrats provided the bulk of votes against the issuance of a rule.[47]

The filibuster represented the other institutional device utilized by southern Democrats to block FEP legislation, sometimes spectacularly. House rules limited the amount of speaking time available to individual representatives. There was no such rule in the Senate, where a single senator could speak indefinitely on any topic of his or her choosing—even one that was not germane to the legislation at hand. A determined senator or a minority of senators could simply talk or threaten to talk forever until their colleagues agreed to drop or modify whatever legislation was under consideration. The onset of a filibuster was not necessarily fatal to legislation—at least in theory. Rule 22 in the Standing Rules of the Senate did permit a vote to impose cloture, a cessation of debate, if assent was granted by two-thirds of senators present. Between 1949 and 1959, Rule 22 was changed to make it even more difficult to achieve cloture, requiring yea votes from two-thirds of the entire chamber. In the case of FEP legislation, however, all filibusters mounted by southern Democrats in fact proved fatal. Having honed their tactics in earlier battles over anti-lynching and anti–poll tax legislation, southern Democrats succeeded in defeating cloture votes on three separate occasions. The first came during the 78th Congress (1946) over S. 101, and the other two defeats took place during the 81st Congress (1950) over H.R. 4453. Led in each instance by the able and indefatigable Senator Russell, southern Democrats exhibited impressive solidarity in their voting behavior. In the cloture vote of 1946, liberals fell short of the two-thirds majority it required, and the bulk of the opposing votes came from southern Democrats. The great success of southern Democrats in defeating Truman-era FEP bills through the filibuster meant that the mere threat of a filibuster could deal a grave blow to the political momentum of any civil rights proposal.[48]

Though many of their most inflammatory speeches were given during filibusters, southern Democrats did not require the convenience of a filibuster to inveigh against FEP legislation. Few topics unleashed their oratorical gifts more readily. Throughout the wartime and postwar period, southern Democrats crafted objections of enduring force, drawing upon their rhetorical facility to fuel resentment and stoke outrage. For southern Democrats in general, but especially for ones hailing from the Black Belt states of Mississippi, South Carolina, and Alabama, it often seemed that no claim was too hyperbolic, no metaphor too strained, no argument too incredulous or untenable.

The primary audience for such theater was southern elites, but southern Democrats had a surprising number of sympathizers in the North. Many of them chose to contact Richard B. Russell (D-GA), owning to his national prominence and visible stand on the issue. A resident of Lorraine, Ohio, wrote to him in 1946 to tell him that his stand was more popular than he might have thought:

> You might learn a lot by talking to northern whites. A great majority of them are opposed to this [FEPC] bill. I belong to the UAW CIO but like thousands of other whites up here I do not believe in this bill even thought the CIO is for it. . . . The CIO cannot control the intelligent white vote. If this bill passes, in fifty years the niggers will outvote the whites. They multiply faster than the whites do. A mistake was made when they were given the right to vote.

A woman from Ferndale in Michigan sent Russell a handwritten note to tell him that she had stayed up until 3 a.m. in the morning reading his speech in the Senate against FEPC, despite having to wake up at 6 a.m.

the next day. "How fortunate we are to have a few such courageous Christians in Congress," she wrote. "Our union men are much misinformed" by the "people who control publication of union literature." They used all the "propaganda tricks . . . not for the benefit of the union men but for minorities." Would the good senator kindly send copies of his speech so she might share them with church leaders and union members? A self-identified Democrat from Los Angeles, attorney Thomas R. Lynch, wrote to Russell to explain that he would actually vote for Eisenhower in the 1952 election based primarily on Ike's opposition to a "punitive" FEPC, which Lynch regarded as totally unnecessary and mostly unwanted. "After all, the Jews don't need any kind of FEPC, the Catholics are much too proud to fight for it: only the Negroes demand that Farmer Jones of California be forced to employ newly arrived Texas Negroes instead of his neighbors' sons." Generations later, voters like Lynch would be styled by political observers as Reagan Democrats. Still other northerners transmitted documents and literature from the North that they hoped southern Democrats might find useful in formulating their critique. J. W. Cunningham, a Toledo businessman, sent along a sheaf of material that he had developed as an opponent of state legislation in Ohio. Cunningham, a Republican, reassured Russell that FEP legislation was desired only by a "very small minority of our people and a very small minority of our lawmakers." This tiny vanguard had formulated a clever strategy. "Spark-plugged by highly-organized paid professionals who cleverly enlist the aid of well-meaning but often misled religious and charitable groups, it is made to appear that the whole movement is a Christian and humane thing—and that it is opposed only by a bigoted a[nd] selfish few." But the exact opposite was true, he said. "All the talk and breast-beating about 'civil rights' and 'discrimination' is in fact an attempt to secure preferred treatment for a small minority at the expense of the equally sacred 'civil rights' of the majority." Cunningham hoped that there was something in the material that Russell would "get an idea from." The senator welcomed such consideration from northerners, heaping praise on Cunningham in a charming and flattering response. A man of "vision and courage," Cunningham had hit the nail on the head. The liberal campaign for FEP was a "dramatic illustration of the tail wagging the dog." But the truth is that Russell and other southern lawmakers did not need much help from their northern sympathizers. They were more than capable of fashioning a kaleidoscopic barrage of attacks on their own.[49]

A number of key themes recurred in the rhetoric of southern Democrats, whether they were taking aim at the wartime FEPC or at legislation that would reincarnate it in a liberal visage. The first argument in the southern brief against FEP legislation involved a strategy of denial. There was no race problem in the South, southerners insisted. A federal agency of any sort was unnecessary. This was but one of the reasons why South Carolina's Senator Bilbo lambasted a permanent FEP bill as the "greatest legislative monstrosity in the history of the American Congress." It was a case of governmental overkill, a solution in search of a problem. To be sure, racial segregation did exist, but it was also a practical, effective arrangement that made primordial sense. Segregation, argued Rep. Jamie L. Whitten (D-MS), actually promoted societal stability: "In the South, the only place where the two races have gotten along, we have practiced segregation. The white man is protected in his home and his meeting places from interference. The Negro is protected in his." Furthermore, segregation enjoyed the legitimacy of democratic sanction, since it was "approved by whites and blacks alike," in the words of Georgia's Senator Russell. This was clear to any reasonable person who lived in the South. The only people who claimed otherwise, according to Rep. Malcolm Tarver (D-GA), were "pettifogging and troublemaking busybodies . . . who know nothing about our problems, care nothing about them, and whose sole purpose is to oppress, if possible, destroy the progress of the southern people." Legislation establishing a permanent FEPC was nothing more than a naked tool of sectional persecution.[50]

When stirring up generic resentments against the Yankees did not seem sufficient to their purposes, southern Democrats resorted to the insinuation that the FEPC was a Trojan horse designed to smuggle a most sinister and alien idea into the South; namely, social equality. This term "social equality" might have sounded innocuous to the uninitiated ear, but anyone listening closely would have realized that it was coded language for interracial marriage. As one southern opponent charged, FEPC was not merely concerned with employment, all labels to the contrary. Instead, it was designed to "foist certain ideas of social, not economic, equality . . . upon white people of the country who feel a certain pride in their race, and justly so, and who, while they are willing and anxious that the Negro shall have his economic rights, are not willing, and will never submit, to his being forced upon them as a social equal and bedfellow." African Americans and their friends who claimed no interest in such social equality faced a harsh and accusatory rejoinder. "They lie," Theodore Bilbo (D-MS) once retorted. "Back in the heart of every Negro in America who is behind movements of this kind is the dream of social equality and intermarriage between whites and blacks."[51]

Bilbo's vehemence was unusual. More commonly deployed was a range of arguments about the unintended consequences of the law. Any federal action would have perverse effects; it would only make matters worse. If there were a race problem in the South, it would resolve itself nicely if the federal government would only let things alone. "If the FEPC is abolished and the Negro and white man left alone, racial problems will be solved,"

Representative Whitten predicted. The shrewdest speakers remembered to point to the ironies inherent in a law that would lead to the opposite of what it intended. In a debate over fiscal appropriations for the wartime FEPC, Senator Russell argued that the committee, which had been justified as a vehicle for promoting national unity, had "done more to stir up bitterness and dissension in the South than anything else which has happened there for many years." Russell continued, "Its activities have had the effect of alienating many of the best friends the Negro has ever had and have caused bad feelings between the races." The law, moreover, hurt African Americans when it was supposed to help them. Rep. Ed Gossett (D-TX) related to his colleagues a story about a job ad in a Dallas newspaper that had openly solicited black applicants for a good position in the paper industry. Unbelievably, the FEPC had struck down the ad as unlawful. Gossett pounced: Why should Congress give the committee funding to harm people it was meant to help? "The FEPC promotes unfair practices, it stirs up trouble, it constitutes a menace to democracy," he concluded. Gossett was probably speaking figuratively to make a point. It was not so clear that other southern Democrats were doing the same. For them, the FEPC could potentially rip the country apart when it was supposed to bring the country together. "Let us stop this FEPC," implored Rep. Lucius M. Rivers (D-SC) of his House colleagues. "If we do not, gentlemen, I say with every ounce of sincerity within me that there is going to be bloodshed in my part of the world the like of which has never happened before in the history of this country." Rep. John S. Gibson (D-GA) echoed the prediction in even starker terms, hinting at the possibility of violent insurrection. "[T]here are only two things that are going to save this Nation," he said. "One is ballots and the other is bullets. . . . I ask the people of the United States to think deep enough to save this Nation by their ballots, that it may not have to be saved by bullets."[52]

Apocalyptic pronouncements and thinly veiled threats were the most extreme variant of the basic claim that the FEPC or FEP legislation would backfire. Attempts to associate FEP with the taint of communism or radicalism were far more widespread. Long before the Truman Doctrine became American foreign policy, southern Democrats engaged in aggressive red-baiting. From the days of the wartime FEPC, it ranked among their favorite techniques. If liberals saw in the passage of FEP legislation a blow for democracy in the global struggle against communism, then southern Democrats sought to cast the same legislation as the product of a conspiracy promoted by an unpatriotic fifth column. In 1944, Rep. James O. Eastland (D-MS) branded individual staff members of the FEPC as subversive. On the floor of the House, he called out former FEPC chairman Malcom Ross, the CIO's John Brophy, the AFL's Boris Shiskin, the NAACP's Charles H. Houston, the AJC's Will Maslow, and attorney

Emanuel Bloch by name, tracing their connections to organizations that had been deemed subversive by the Attorney General. Eastland singled out Sidney Hillman for special abuse, mentioning that he was a known associate of Leon Trotsky and leaving the rest to the imagination of his listeners. Eastland's fellow Mississippian, Representative Rankin, went even further; he claimed that FEP legislation was "sponsored by the CIO Political Action Committee, headed by Sidney Hillman, a Russian-born racketeer whom the anticommunist Americans of his own race literally despise, and who is raising money by the shake-down method with which he is now trying to control our elections." Rankin finished the thought with a characteristically bombastic, if somewhat nonsensical, flourish. "He wants to be Hitler of America." Sen. Walter F. George (D-GA) preferred a more understated formulation, but he also saw the FEPC as "one more important step" down a slippery slope toward the Soviet system. When a private "employer cannot say whom he shall employ, whom he shall promote, or how long he wants the employee to work for him"— what could it be but communism? As he took pains to explain, FEP legislation "communizes America by taking away the elemental, primary rights of owners in the management and control of their private property, and vesting that authority in a federal bureau in Washington."[53]

The most damaging argument, however, came in the form of the claim that the campaign for FEP legislation was a flagrant attempt by powerful minority groups to fix the labor market in their favor. Its official legislative moniker, southern lawmakers argued, was fundamentally deceptive. Far from bringing about a truly equal playing field, "fair" employment practices legislation gave unfair preference to minorities, and ordinary white Americans would find themselves thoroughly discriminated against. In the words of Representative Rankin, H.R. 4005 would "force every enterprise to employ Negroes, Japs, or members of any other race, whether they were wanted or not, and promote them over white people, regardless of the trouble that such an arrangement produced." Pointing to the operation of the wartime FEPC, Representative Whitten strongly concurred: "[I]t is not to prevent unfair discrimination against Negroes that this so-called Fair Employees Practice Committee exercises itself. What they wanted, what they have done and are doing is to discriminate in favor of the Negro in an effort to secure the votes of the Negroes that they win the national elections." Rep. Charles E. McKenzie (D-LA) had no doubt what effect the law would eventually have on employment practices. Whether it was forced on them by the committee or preemptively adopted by employers, proportional representation would become the rule of thumb in hiring and employment: "every business and organization would have to employ a proportionate number of every race, creed, and nationality in the community."[54]

This line of argumentation was damaging precisely because it directly contradicted all variants of the liberal claim that the passage of FEP legislation served the interests of every American. Instead, it played to suspicions that the law would benefit racial minorities at the expense of the white majority. Lawmakers like Rep. Samuel F. Hobbs (D-AL) made no mistake in clarifying exactly which group would bear the brunt of discrimination: "It is being fomented and practiced against Caucasians—native-born American citizens, the bulk of our taxpayers." Such arguments enabled southern Democrats to cast themselves as men of principle and courage, willing to stand up against a powerful, unscrupulous minority on behalf of the hard-working white Americans who abided by the law and paid their taxes. These ordinary men and women—most Americans, they never failed to remind their listeners—were too polite or too busy to complain about their predicament, but they were not getting a fair shake from the federal government. It was more interested in pandering to racial and religious minorities, who did not hesitate to throw around their political clout. "The real American people of this Nation," Representative Whitten said in a typical formulation, "are sick and tired of the national political parties catering to, and running after, the racial and political minorities of the country in order to secure their vote. Sometimes it looks like the Democratic Party and Republican Party will do anything to secure the vote of the Negro, the support of the CIO, and other organized minorities in the national election. Both parties seem willing to ignore the rights of the solid white Americans. They are letting the tail wag the dog."[55]

Southerners pointed to the FEPC itself to cinch their case. For anyone who wanted to fathom why minorities would resort to manipulating the federal government for special favors—instead of rolling up their shirtsleeves and getting to work—it was necessary to look no further than the committee itself. "I think it's common knowledge," said one southern Democrat, "that the FEPC has demanded and succeeded in having positions in many or practically all of the Government agencies here in Washington filled with persons who are not qualified to do the work to which they have been assigned, and the appointments are due wholly to the fact they happen to be colored or happen to have a particular creed." Rep. B.B. Hare (D-SC) found such assertions credible, citing testimony from agency heads who publicly complained about the training level of his minority hires. Hare also claimed that somebody else had come forward off the record to report that it took extra time for efficient clerks to correct the mistakes and oversights of FEPC-directed hires. "Now if these witnesses are to be believed," Hare continued, "the only conclusion I can reach is that these people would never have been employed if the

FEPC had not insisted and, in fact, directed that there should be discrimination in favor of appointing these people instead of appointing more capable and efficient white persons in their place." Southerners drew attention to the racial and religious makeup of the FEPC itself to dispel all remaining doubts that it was fair and independent. Quite to the contrary, it had been captured by a politically aggressive, self-interested minority. "It has not hesitated to discriminate against the white race in its own employment policies," noted Senator Russell. "The Negro population of this country is slightly less than 10 percent, but the record discloses that two-thirds of the employees of this agency are Negroes. I mention that fact to show the political nature of this agency." Representative Rankin felt so strongly about the point that he put together tables delineating the racial breakdown of the top staff. Several were eventually published as part of the *Congressional Record*. In some of his speeches, he even took the time to go over his list, mulling over the racial identities of committee staff: "[One] of them who is registered as a white person is merely a clerk-stenographer, and his name is given as Otome Saito—which sounds Oriental to me."[56]

The vehemence of southern rhetoric did not fade away with the war. Nearly the whole litany of southern complaints against FEP legislation was evident in a strongly worded editorial published in 1952 by Senator Russell in the *Aiken Standard and Review*. Russell began by denouncing the bill as grossly "misnamed." It was not fair in any regard. Nor did it provide any employment—"except for a vast army of Federal employees to police American business and American agriculture." The bill should be opposed by right-thinking and honest Americans for any number of reasons. It established a governmental setup in which "the ordinary rules of the law do not apply." The right of a person to "jury trial in his home community" would essentially be nullified, and a single administrative agency would hold the authority of the prosecutor, judge, and jury. The bill threatened to "nationalize all jobs." No wonder "every Communist and every Socialist" is wholeheartedly "supporting this bill," he remarked. Russell took special care to describe how the proposed legislation would trample upon the "rights of the ordinary, everyday, average working American." Unlike some of his compatriots, he was not "particularly prejudiced against aliens"—but, he wrote sarcastically, he was "old-fashioned enough to believe that American citizens should be accorded equal rights with aliens." This principle would be decisively undermined by the bill, which made it possible for "any alien" or "any immigrant" to bring an employer before a "kangaroo court" on charges of discrimination. The "average American" was prevented from doing the same. Such a disparity meant that minorities could potentially "subject the employer to great expense" if denied jobs or promotions, and employers would naturally favor them over American citizens, who did not enjoy the same protection. "This naturally will result in rank discrimination against the rights of the American to the job. It is bound to result in discrimination in favor of aliens and other minority groups."[57]

The parliamentary skill, disciplined organization, and potent rhetoric of southern Democrats were crucial in limiting the legislative progress of FEP proposals. Yet they had the effect of obscuring the existence of any opposition on the part of the GOP. To be sure, some Republicans were stalwart supporters of FEP. Men like Sen. Irving M. Ives (R-NY) and Sen. Wayne Morse (R-OR), both liberals, spearheaded the charge for enforceable legislation in Congress. For much of the postwar period, however, the GOP was divided into two wings. The fading liberal wing to which Ives and Morse belonged, was led by New York's mustachioed governor, Thomas E. Dewey, while the rising conservative wing—which had never accepted the New Deal—was guided by the redoubtable Sen. Robert A. Taft of Ohio. Conservatives such as Taft were certain that Dewey's strategy of outflanking the New Deal was fundamentally misguided. "There is only one way to beat the New Deal," Taft once insisted, "and that is head on. You can't outdeal them." Thus it was understandable that Taft, a Republican, and other conservatives, such as Rep. Hoffman, feared and opposed the passage of FEP legislation, which Republicans like Dewey accepted and even promoted.[58]

This undercurrent of Republican opposition was effectively masked by southern demagoguery, but the bifurcation of the GOP position was also difficult to discern because of the political calculations involved. Lawmakers like Taft and Hoffman were canny strategists. It could not have been lost on them that there was no need for them to publicly take a strident stand on FEP legislation. The hostility of southern Democrats was all but guaranteed, and many of them were only too glad to serve as a lighting rod for liberal opprobrium on civil rights. To be sure, Taft and other conservative Republicans did not shy away from working against FEP bills. For instance, in 1948, Taft voted with southern Democrats against reporting an FEP bill from the Senate Labor Committee. Just as often, however, he and his GOP allies professed limited support, particularly if it had the potential to encourage or deepen internecine conflict between northern and southern Democrats. In 1944, when Republicans had adopted a strong plank in favor of FEP legislation, Taft concurred with a Senate report on a bill granting enforcement authority to a permanent FEPC; but then he did little, if anything, to push the legislative process forward. The next year, as the *Washington Post* noted, he reversed his position. In 1946, he pledged to vote for cloture to end a filibuster on a liberal bill but acknowledged that he would ultimately not vote for the bill.[59]

Liberals themselves understood the political value of fair employment practices to the GOP. Though he was referring to the 79th Congress when he penned the words, Malcolm Ross might just as easily have described any other Truman-era Congress when he noted in *Commentary* that "FEPC was a wedge that threatened to split the Democratic party." Republican members "merely stood amused on the sidelines while northern Democrats unsuccessfully tried to withstand the embattled South." It was not hard to understand why conservative Republicans often hid and sometimes contradicted their true preferences.[60]

Nevertheless, their true preferences could be glimpsed by knowledgeable and perceptive observers of Washington politics. Republicans had long expressed wariness of federal authority, and members of the conservative faction had been dismayed by the growth of the federal government during the New Deal. When it came to FEP legislation, which they closely associated with Roosevelt and the New Deal, their concerns were even more basic and philosophical. It was not that they were unmoved by the blight of racial segregation or the economic plight of African Americans. Whether their professions were truly sincere, conservative Republicans consistently expressed respect for the idea of racial equality—and particularly for the ideal of equal treatment. The problem for them was that regulating discrimination or any other kind of human behavior was not only infeasible but was also outside the realm of possibility. Conservatives took seriously William Graham Sumner's dictum that "stateways cannot change folkways," and no one more so than Taft. "It is just about as difficult to prevent discrimination against Negroes as it is to prevent discrimination against Republicans," Taft once quipped. "We know the latter is impossible."[61]

Even if they accepted liberal distinctions between prejudice and discrimination as valid, and many of them did not, conservatives nevertheless insisted that lasting change in human behavior required more than government coercion. Outward behavior would remain unchanged and people would revert to their old patterns if a fundamental and intentional change in their feeling and consciousness did not come first. The only way to change thoroughly their hearts and minds was not through coercion but their own voluntary action. If people were truly going to change how they acted in the world, they had to decide for themselves what was right and wrong, and then act accordingly. Any kind of external coercion was ill-advised; persuasion and education were the only things than anyone else could do. This was the *Weltanschauung* that gave rise to the conservative refrain that you "cannot legislate tolerance," which was uttered scores of times in debates over FEP legislation. "We have got to break with the corrupting idea that we can legislate prosperity, legislate equality, legislate opportunity," said Taft in a representative remark. "All of these good things came in the past from free Americans freely working out their destiny." Taft himself made the conservative case against FEP legislation no more lucidly than when he asserted that "[p]rogress against discrimination must be made gradually and must be made by voluntary cooperation and education." Imposing FEP bills simply "places the government in the position of trying to regulate the hiring and firing of just about everybody."[62]

Such beliefs formed the central basis of conservative opposition to FEP legislation, but they expressed other serious concerns as well, many of them echoing the favorite arguments of southerners. No segregationist himself, Taft nonetheless must have grasped the affinities that he shared with southern Democrats when he charged in a prominent speech that the passage of FEP legislation would force "every employer to choose his employees approximately in proportion to the division of races and religions in his district, because that would be his best defense to harassing suits." "Race and religion," he intoned, "would enter into every decision. Catholic institutions, for instance, will have to employ Protestants. . . . White waiters and porters could insist upon most of the work in the Pullman sleepers and dining cars." In a letter to a prominent constituent who had urged him to support FEP legislation, Taft's Republican colleague from the Midwest, Clifford R. Hope (R-KS), reiterated his commitment to racial equality but supplied the usual conservative response: "I do not believe that we can legislate against intolerance or prejudice. It may look like a long hard process to get rid of those things by education, but I think that's the only way the job can be done permanently." Hope then went on to make a criticism that would have brought a nod of agreement from Richard Russell, John Rankin, and other southern Democrats who had expressed concerns that an FEPC would lead to discrimination in reverse. Hope did not believe that a regulatory agency with an NLRB-style setup could work impartially to resolve complaints. It was inherently disposed toward favoring the group or groups it was meant to protect. "[T]hese tribunals," Hope wrote, "while sitting in quasi-judicial capacity, do not consider themselves as impartial judicial bodies but rather as special pleaders for the group whose complaints they are called upon to consider."[63]

Personal beliefs were not the sole motivation of conservative Republicans. So were the policy preferences and ideological commitments of their constituents, many of whom did not hesitate to convey their frank views in writing, even if they proved misinformed. In 1946, F. H. Wendell, owner of Wendell Washer Company in Cleveland, told Taft to "enter a vigorous protest against the establishment of a Fedaral [*sic*] Fair Practice

Commission." Wendell made his concern quite clear: "We understand that the passage of this bill will force all employers to hire at least 7% negroes." This was simply not acceptable to him, but he was also careful to clarify that his position did not derive from racial animus but instead from his fidelity to democratic principle. "This protest," he explained, "is not sent with any feeling of malice to the colored race but in the name of justice and the upholding of American ideals." W. P. Purfield, owner of Purfield's Foot Comfort Shop in Detroit, wrote to convey similar thoughts to Rep. Homer Ferguson (R-MI). Purfield had heard that the initial executive order mandated a quota of "7% negroes," but that later it was raised to 15%. Either way, it was unacceptable to him and, in his view, should be unacceptable to anyone. A resident of Lakewood, Ohio, Ruth Meeks, wrote Taft to urge him to repudiate FEP legislation. She had decided not to vote for Truman even if he declared his candidacy, and she was delighted to hear that Taft was willing to run. But she had seen a report in the *Cleveland Plain Dealer* noting Taft's support of an FEP bill. Now she found herself "bewildered" about what to do. In truth, Meeks was mistaken. Taft did not support a liberal FEP bill but a conservative one that was strictly voluntary and educational in nature. It was nonetheless clear what she thought of liberal legislation. "That stand just is *not right*—in fact it is *not democratic* and it is *not Christian*. In *our* land, a person should be judged for his qualifications, ability, and character— and not for the color of his skin."[64]

Polls tended to confirm what Republican lawmakers were hearing from their constituents—particularly their Republican constituents. According to a 1952 California Poll, only 35 percent of self-identified Republicans favored a federal FEPC law. Nearly 40 percent felt that any law would not be a good idea. By contrast, 56 percent of Democrats surveyed supported federal legislation, and only 24 percent wanted no law at all. The partisan difference grew even more pronounced when Californians were asked who they supported for president, Adlai E. Stevenson or Dwight D. Eisenhower. Only 37 percent of Californians intending to vote for Eisenhower expressed support for a federal FEP law. Even fewer, 19 percent, wanted a state law. In fact, most Eisenhower supporters, 39 percent of them, did not want any kind of law at all. The pattern was starkly different among Californians intending to vote for Stevenson. While they did not seem particularly fond of state legislation, it was because 62 percent of them wanted federal legislation. Only 18 percent of Stevenson supporters did not favor a law at all. It is possible to exaggerate the extent of partisan differences. Californians were perhaps more racially conservative than other Americans outside the South, and there was a clear and stark difference in the racial politics of Stevenson and Eisenhower. The former was known for his support of FEPC and would have attracted racial liberals, while the latter was known for his opposition to the "compulsory" method and would have attracted racial conservatives. But even though the time and contest were unique, they were not exceptional. For much of the postwar period, Republican voters in California and other states outside the South bristled at the prospect of a national FEPC law.[65]

Perhaps even more important to conservative Republicans were the views of organized business, one of their most powerful and well-financed constituencies. What organized business actually thought of the issue, however, was notoriously difficult to discern. In the same way that conservative Republicans did not often voice their beliefs regarding FEP, organized business did not often take a visible stand against FEP legislation in Congress. The unbridled hostility of many southern Democrats made it practically unnecessary and politically unwise. Yet most segments of organized business opposed FEP legislation on the grounds that it usurped traditional managerial prerogatives over the hiring and firing of employees. Of course, business was no monolith. In 1950, *Business Week* published a widely circulated article that concluded after interviews with numerous executives that state FEP legislation had not been as disruptive to industrial relations as feared. Nor did business leaders ever fail to speak up on behalf of equal opportunity as a principle. Eric Johnson, president of the U.S. Chamber of Commerce (USCC) and a leading moderate in the business community, boldly denounced bigotry and discrimination: "I repeat intolerance is destructive; prejudice produces no weather; discrimination is a fool's economy." But even he raised doubts that legislation was the right answer to the problem. Indeed, the most powerful and important political associations were unambiguously, if quietly, opposed to legislation that would curtail the autonomy of business. Groups like the USCC, which had been formed upon the recommendation of Taft's father, former president William Howard Taft, kept close track of the issue every year, reporting daily developments in its legislation bulletin, *Governmental Affairs Legislative Daily*. When a young Congressman, Everett M. Dirsken (R-IL) introduced a liberal FEP bill in 1945, it caught the attention of the chamber, which privately worried that the bill could give the federal government "discretionary control over hiring and firing of all employees." Only two years later the board approved a recommendation that the "enactment of fair employment practices legislation by the Congress should be opposed by the Chamber with the same aggressive action as is taken upon other legislation." Larger companies, represented in national politics by the National Association of Manufacturers (NAM), adopted a similar stance. In the postwar period, NAM consistently supported voluntary methods over legislation. Its official policy, announced annually in *Industry Believes*, endorsed not "freedom from discrimination" but the "freedom of opportunity for every individual to work at an available job for which he is qualified." Hence the "[e]mployment of individuals and their assignment to jobs should be determined by matching the individual's skills and qualifications with the requirements of an available position." The government, however, should not interfere with the process through legislation. "These objectives can best be achieved through voluntary methods," NAM concluded.[66]

Small businessmen throughout the country shared the same sentiment. In a characteristic early missive, Clarence Iden, a local wholesale grocer in New Mexico, wrote to Sen. Dennis Chavez, protesting his FEP bill on the grounds that it would "take from the employer his whole control of the affairs of his business" without any valid reason. The wholesaler flatly denied the existence of discrimination: "I do not know of any employer who has refused, or been inclined to refuse, employment of a Spanish-American who was qualified for the position for which he has made application." Passing legislation would not only constitute overkill, Iden suggested, but it would also inflict harm on an innocent bystander—business. "[T]o enact a law of this kind would be most destructive to the interests and welfare of every businessman in the country," he asserted. In 1947, L. M. Evans, president of a small company based in Cleveland, did not outright reject the existence of discrimination in a widely circulated address he gave to the tenth-anniversary meeting of the National Small Business Men's Association. But he did object to FEP laws nonetheless. Evans invoked what was by then a litany of classic objections. "Creed" was an entirely fair basis on which to evaluate the character of a potential employee. Discrimination could never truly be proven because it involved a state of mind. The careful selection of employees necessarily entailed discrimination, which should be regarded as a virtue not a vice. The bill would create a bureaucratic monstrosity. It would fail because state ways simply could not change folkways. It would raise consciousness of race and creed rather than suppress it. It was "extremely unfair to the Negro race in America." It would lead to "racketeering and blackmailing." Evans had little doubt about the proper approach to the problem. "If America is to become stronger and our minority groups are to be given their rightful privileges, education, understanding, tolerance and freedom will bring it about—not regimentation." Though they were perhaps unusually vocal, Idens and Evans were not isolated examples. In fact, they were typical. The *Los Angeles Times* reported in 1949 that a poll of the National Federation of Small Businesses (NFSB) indicated that 90 percent of its membership opposed FEP legislation. In fact, opposition to the FEPC was the single issue on which the membership of the NFSB was

most united. Among other reasons, NFSB members rejected FEP legislation because they feared that it may "deprive them of their freedom to
choose employees of their own selection."[67]

Motivated by a mix of reasons, conservative Republicans introduced
several bills into Congress that carved out a limited role for the federal
government in addressing job discrimination. Taft led the way. In 1945,
responding to the Chavez-sponsored S. 101, he introduced S. 459, which
declined to outlaw discrimination but proclaimed instead that discrimination against persons on the basis of race, creed, or color was "contrary to
the principle of freedom and equality of opportunity, is incompatible with
the provisions of the Constitution, foments domestic strife and unrest,
deprives the United States of the fullest utilization of its capacities for
production and defense, and burdens, hinders, and obstructs commerce."
The bill caught the attention of NAM, which duly reported on it in *NAM
News*. Taft's proposal called for the establishment of a Fair Employment
Practice Commission to administer the law. Taft's version of the FEPC,
however, did not possess any enforcement powers. The commission was
given the authority to conduct studies of discrimination, make plans for
eliminating discrimination, publish reports, furnish technical assistance
to businesses and unions seeking to comply with the law, initiate investigations of specific complaints, subpoena witnesses, and hold conciliation
proceedings between antagonistic parties. Nevertheless, Taft's bill, like
others of the same ilk that would follow it, granted not a whit of ability
to coerce compliance or sanction wrongdoing. A discriminatory employer
or union could flaunt the law without suffering so much as a single
stipulated penalty or consequence. When asked by Sen. Dennis Chavez
(D-NM) what he thought of Taft's bill, Bishop G. Bromley Oxnam, President of the Federal Council of Churches, expressed disappointment. "I
cannot believe that a bill which does not actually make discrimination in
employment illegal and which has no enforcement provisions will ade-
quately serve the purpose of securing justice for minority groups." An
editorial in the *Washington Post* was similarly critical, arguing that Taft's
proposal threatened to "nullify" the FEPC altogether. The committee
would represent little more than a "disembodied spirit."[68]

Taft did not fight particularly hard to see his bill become law. More
often, he and his co-partisans spent their time undermining liberal FEP
legislation, preferably during the most opaque moments of the legislative
process. His endorsement of educational FEPC, however, would later
prove useful when he confronted his urban constituencies during reelection (see figure 2.4). It meant that his claim to support FEPC was at least
plausible. In 1948, Taft placed a full-page ad in the *Cleveland Call and
Post*, and it prominently featured his position on FEPC: "I think discrimi-

Figure 2.4 U.S. Sen. Robert A. Taft (R-OH) addressing African American constituents at a YMCA in Dayton, Ohio, 1949. The votes of northern blacks were sought not only by urban Democrats but even at times by Taft and other conservative Republicans running for statewide office. Taft was a staunch opponent of liberal or "enforceable" fair employment practice (FEP) bills, but he would insist that he was a supporter of fair employment—by which he meant to indicate his support for "voluntary" or "educational" FEP legislation that lacked any enforcement provisions. Courtesy of Stanley Kubrick, photographer, *LOOK* Magazine Collection, Library of Congress, Prints and Photographs Division [Reproduction number LC-L9-249-U59, frame 89].

nation in employment makes it very difficult for colored people to make their living in honest ways and causes them to turn to crime." In response to the problem, he supported a federal board that could recommend legislation if necessary. Taft's most ardent supporters understood the value of his stance. A flyer distributed by a Republican volunteer, likely during the 1950 election, warned voters to disregard propaganda about Taft that portrayed him as anti-black and anti-FEPC:

> Don't listen to lies! When people tell you that Taft is anti-Negro, they are lying! Who kept Bilbo from entering the Senate? Bob Taft. Who was the leader of the Republican Congress which *passed* a wartime FEPC bill? Bob Taft. The Democrats have been promising FEPC for years and years. It took a Republican Congress led by Taft to pass an FEPC Bill. A vote for Taft is a vote for FEPC![69]

The strategic maneuvering of the GOP did not escape the attention of liberals, who missed few opportunities to announce that they were tracking the behavior of the GOP contingent in Congress. The *Chicago Defender* said that the GOP had an "alphabetical allergy." In a National Council press release in 1947, Randolph cast the Republican-controlled 80th Congress (1947–48) a "test of the sincerity, cohesiveness, and leadership" of the GOP. Henderson concurred, promising to hold Congress "responsible if it abdicates in the face of filibuster." Any filibuster, he stressed, could be "broken under the existing rules if the Republican majority acts to break it." A confidential analysis of likely Senate votes by the National Council confirmed their premise that the "only hope of enactment of S.984 in an effective form lies in the Republican Party swinging enough of the 15 Republican senators who are opposed in various degrees around to support the bill without weakening amendments." There were other signs as well that the GOP held the balance of power at crucial moments in the politics of FEP legislation. When the Rules Committee bottled up a strong bill through a tie vote in 1950, southern Democrats did cast the majority of votes against reporting the bill to the floor. But they did not have a workable majority on the committee overall, and their success required help from Republicans. GOP legislators quietly rendered what help was needed. "Publicly, the Republicans couldn't admit they wanted to keep the Rules Committee from reporting out the bill," *Newsweek* noted. "Behind closed doors, they were doing everything possible to block it there." One of the first contributions came when Rep Clarence Brown (R-OH) delayed a crucial vote by stating that he would oppose a rule in the absence of Reps. James Wadsworth (R-NY) and Howard Smith (D-VA). "You know that I am for FEPC," he said with a reportedly "sly" smile, but he announced that he would be forced to vote against it if the two other members did not have a fair chance to express their preferences on such a vital piece of legislation. Further help was rendered by the GOP on February 16 when two Republicans with substantial rural constituencies—Reps. Leo E. Allen (R-IL) and Wadsworth (R-NY)—joined with four southern Democrats to defer reporting the bill. There was some partisan finger-pointing in the days afterward, and Rep. Adolph J. Sabath (D-IL) did not shy away from laying blame at the feet of Allen, Wadsworth, and their party. In widely reported comments, Sabath conceded that the "Dixiecrats" were responsible in large measure for the predicament, but he was equally incensed at his GOP colleagues on the Rules Committee. "The country should know that if the Republicans had voted for a rule today, it could have brought the bill to the floor of the House." Editors at the *New York Times* agreed: "[T]here are enough Democratic and Republican members of that committee who disbelieve so strongly in what their own parties stated [in 1948] that they are not even willing to give the House a chance to consider the measure."[70]

If conservative Republicans and southern Democrats worked together to derail FEP legislation, it was not due to collective action of a highly coordinated kind. There was no caucus, no organization, not even joint meetings. Since the 75th Congress (1937–38), when a southern-conservative coalition first came together, it had been a "loose bloc of the moment," to borrow James T. Patterson's phrase. As congressional scholar Eric Schickler has noted, it was essentially a private assemblage. "Our group . . . did not meet publicly," Representative Smith would later recall of the men who controlled the Rules Committee. "The meetings were not formal. Our group met in one building and the conservative Republicans in another. Then Eugene Cox, Bill Colmer, or I would go over to speak with the Republicans, or the Republicans might go come to see us. . . . A bloc did exist in legislation. But . . . [t]here were not join meetings of conservative Republicans and southern Democrats." The bloc nevertheless proved a constant source of frustration for liberals. As perceptive observers of American politics invariably noticed, FEP legislation almost always provided the necessary moment for the "bloc of the moment" to come together. Sen. Herbert H. Lehman (D-NY) minced few words in his analysis: "Republican leaders in Congress have worked in close cooperation with the Dixiecrats against almost every piece of Fair Deal legislation, including civil rights." Charles M. La Follette, then national director of Americans for Democratic Action, concurred. "I am sure you will agree that there is a very real kinship between Northern Republicans and many Southern Democrats," he wrote to a prominent conservative in 1949. "A great number of Republican party leaders are 'Northern men of Southern principles'; scratch a Dixiecrat and you will find a Northern or Eastern special interest. Dixiecrats fume at proposals for guaranteeing civil rights; many Northern chambers of commerce have an equal distaste for FEPC."[71]

Liberals found the cross-party, conservative coalition in Congress a formidable adversary, but they did not succumb without a vigorous fight. In fact, they battled back determinedly on several fronts. In addition to mobilizing their grass-roots constituencies, liberals creatively exploited a variety of parliamentary devices to break the stranglehold of the southern-conservative bloc on institutional features of the legislative process that had proved adverse to FEP legislation. In the House, where the Rules Committee represented the main obstacle, they repeatedly sought to take advantage of the Calendar Wednesday rule, which offered standing committees the chance every Wednesday to bring up any bills under their jurisdiction that were listed on the House or Union calendars. On a number of occasions, they turned to the discharge petition, whereby members could remove a bill from a committee that had not reported it after thirty days of consideration. If the petition contained signatures from a majority of House members, any signatory to the petition could move to discharge the bill, which would be accorded high privilege if the motion carried. At times, liberals managed to institute new rules when the old ones proved too limiting. During the 81st Congress (1949–50), House rules were modified so that chairmen of a legislative committee that had favorably reported a bill could call it up for floor action if it had been pending in the Rules Committee for more than twenty-one days. The filibuster was the main obstacle in the Senate, and liberals tried to reform the cloture rules so as to make it easier to limit debate. They failed and instead made it harder on themselves, but it was not completely unrealistic of them to think that they could win a cloture vote one day. Adding together the Senate seats held by northern Democrats and Republicans, it seemed that there were always enough potential votes for cloture (see table 2.2).[72]

It was not wishful thinking for liberals to nurture hopes of overcoming the southern-conservative coalition. They were, of course, optimistic about how close they were to succeeding, particularly in their public statements and especially in their fundraising solicitations. The headiest pronouncements came during the Truman administration. "If the bill had come to a vote," wrote New Dealer Felix S. Cohen in one breezy assessment, "it would have passed by a large majority—such is the prevailing national sentiment." A headline in *The Crisis* conveyed certainty of passage in far fewer words: "Permanent FEPC Likely." Even the normally level-headed Paul Sifton, who would soon become the long-time legislative representative for the UAW, did not always show his usual restraint. "With proper mobilization of nationwide sentiment for fair employ-

TABLE 2.2

Actual and Potential Votes for Cloture on Civil Rights Legislation in the U.S. Senate, 1938–1964

Date	Issue	Vote	Yeas needed	Yeas shy	GOP seats	Dem. seats	North. Dem.	Potential yeas
Jan. 27, 1938	Anti-lynching	37–51	59	8	16	76	43	59
Feb. 27, 1938	Anti-lynching	42–46	59	17	16	76	43	59
Nov. 23, 1942	Anti-poll tax	37–41	52	15	29	65	31	60
May 15, 1944	Anti-poll tax	36–44	54	18	37	58	27	64
Feb. 9, 1946	FEPC	48–36	56	8	39	56	27	66
Jul. 31, 1946	Anti-poll tax	39–33	48	9	39	56	27	66
May 19, 1950	FEPC	52–32	64	12	42	54	23	65
Jul. 12, 1950	FEPC	55–33	64	9	42	54	23	65
Mar. 10, 1960	Civil Rights Act	42–53	64	22	35	65	36	71
May 9, 1962	Literacy tests	43–53	64	21	36	64	37	73
May 14, 1962	Literacy tests	42–52	63	21	36	64	37	73
June 10, 1964	Civil Rights Act	71–29	67	—	33	67	39	72

Notes: The cloture rule (Rule 22) was adopted by the U.S. Senate in 1917. Through 1964, it was invoked twenty-nine times, a dozen times involving filibusters on civil rights legislation. Imposing cloture from 1949 and 1959 required a two-thirds vote of the membership of the Senate, rather than two-thirds of Senators present. "Potential yeas" are calculated by adding together the number of seats held by Republicans and northern Democrats. This calculation uses a highly restrictive definition of "northern Democrats" that excludes all Senate Democrats from the eleven states of the former Confederacy as well as Kentucky, Oklahoma, Missouri, Maryland, Delaware, and West Virginia. For a useful discussion on the issues involved in defining the South as a region for the purposes of analyzing Congressional politics, see Ira Katznelson, Kim Geiger, and Daniel Kryder, "Limiting Liberalism: The Southern Veto in Congress, 1933–1950," *Political Science Quarterly*, 108 (1993): 283–306, esp. fn 3, p. 284.

Source: Congressional Quarterly, *Congress and the Nation, 1945–1964* (Washington, DC: Congressional Quarterly Service, 1965), 3, 5, 29, 32, 47, 1637, and *Official Congressional Directory*.

ment," he wrote in 1947 to Roy Wilkins, "S. 984 can be made a law within the next twelve months." Such a penchant for embellishment, however, was not unique to the emerging bloc of liberal groups pressing for FEP legislation. What better way was there to mobilize involvement and sustain morale than to project the sense that success was right around the corner? Most importantly, liberals did have their chances, even if they did not ultimately reach their objectives.[73]

The campaign to pass FEP legislation crested twice, and both instances revealed the full dimensions of the political opposition that liberals faced. The first near-miss came during the 79th Congress (1945–46), when the House Labor Committee reported out an FEP bill introduced by Rep. Mary T. Norton (D-NJ). It was immediately referred to the Rules Committee, which refused to take action. Norton sought to have her bill released from the Rules Committee by circulating a discharge petition among members of the House, and her effort got off to a solid start. By the end of 1945, however, only 157 members of the House had signed the petition, sixty-one less than the 218 required. Norton abandoned the petition in the subsequent session of Congress. Instead, she and her allies tried to use the Calendar Wednesday rule to pry the bill, but they failed on four separate occasions, bringing the House campaign to a close. In the Senate, Dennis Chavez succeeded in bringing his FEP bill to the Senate floor at the beginning of 1946, when southern Democrats deployed a clever parliamentary gambit to launch a month-long filibuster. In fact, they achieved the impressive if dubious feat of staging a second filibuster within their first one. A cloture vote was eventually held, but only forty-eight members favored the cessation of debate, fewer than the fifty-six required.[74]

The failure of the legislation campaign in the House and Senate stemmed from myriad reasons, not the least of which was the discipline and organization of southern Democrats. Equally important, however, was a lack of enthusiasm on the part of many Republicans. On the cloture vote in the Senate, twenty-five Republicans, twenty-two Democrats, and one Progressive voted in favor, while twenty-eight Democrats and eight Republicans voted against. Cloture failed by a mere eight votes. While southern Democrats contributed the most negative votes, nay-saying Republicans represented the difference between failure and success. This was indeed the smallest margin on any civil rights question since the attempt to impose cloture on a debate over anti-lynching legislation in 1938. Perhaps it was too much to expect all eight Republicans to have voted for cloture, but it was easy to see why so many liberals ardently believed their campaign might succeed with time.[75]

Even more telling is the partisan breakdown of the signatories on Norton's discharge petition. In late 1945, staffers at the National Council polled members of the House to determine whether they had lent their name to the petition. What they found was what appeared to be a clear partisan difference. Only a quarter of the Republican delegation had signed the petition, compared to more than 40 percent of the Democratic delegation. The historical record does not reveal, as yet, whether GOP reluctance to sign the petition reflected the top-down imposition of party discipline or simply the economic conservatism of individual Republicans. Statistically, it is impossible to make the case either way (see table A.4). What does seem clear is that much of the GOP delegation to the 79th Congress was cut from the same broad, ideological cloth. On average, Republicans were more conservative than their Democratic counterparts on questions of fiscal and regulatory policy. Republicans varied in their commitment to civil rights, but most of them shared a fundamental aversion to the expansion of federal spending and regulation (see figure A.1). This economic conservatism does not mean that Republicans could not have been persuaded to support FEP legislation. Republicans of the same degree of economic conservatism differed in whether they signed the petition; but proportionally fewer Republicans than Democrats signed it, a curious and striking fact for the "Party of Lincoln." Numerous political observers took notice of the development, including editors at the *Washington Post*, who maintained that "Republicans, although piously applauding the FEPC principle, have conspicuously refrained from signing the discharge petition necessary to dislodge it."[76]

The campaign that unfolded the 81st Congress (1949–50) was even more closely contested than the one in 1945–46, and it was even more revealing. During the first session, in 1949, committees in both the House and the Senate held hearings on FEP legislation, and a record number of participants testified. Political momentum grew rapidly. Institutional reforms also contributed to a sense of possibility. While a series of missteps in the Senate had made it more difficult to impose cloture on a filibuster—which now required assent from two-thirds of all senators, and not just two-thirds of the members present—liberals had succeeded in forcing the adoption of the twenty-one-day rule in the House, making it easier to wrest pending bills from the Rules Committee. If a strong bill could be first pushed through the House, it could put enormous pressure on the Senate to act. Such thoughts must have been on the minds of the 4,000 delegates who attended the National Emergency Civil Rights Mobilization, which gathered in Washington, D.C., at the outset of the second session in 1950. When he addressed the delegates, majority leader, Sen. Scott Lucas (D-IL), warned the audience that he could not guarantee the enactment of FEP legislation, but he expressed a hopefulness that others were surely feeling as well. Lucas also expressed optimism in private After a meeting of the Democratic policy committee, he argued in favor of a

House-first strategy. "They really have a chance to pass the FEPC bill over there and that would strengthen our case over here."[77]

Despite the best efforts of House Speaker Sam Rayburn (D-TX) to keep FEP legislation under wraps, liberals on the Education and Labor Committee succeeded in forcing the bill out of the Rules Committee, not through the twenty-one-day rule but rather Calendar Wednesday. To the chagrin of liberals, progress would stall thereafter. When the House transformed itself into a committee of the whole to consider the bill, Rep. Samuel K. McConnell (R-PA) offered a substitute amendment that established the FEPC without enforcement authority. McConnell's substitute was adopted by a fairly close vote (222–178), winning the support of 117 Democrats and 105 Republicans. Most of the Democrats who approved the substitute were predictably from the South, but two-thirds of the Republican delegation voted yea as well, contributing nearly half the eventual total. Among the more prominent Republicans in the southern-conservative coalition were minority leader Joseph W. Martin, Jr. (R-MA), future senator and president Richard Nixon (R-CA), Manhattan attorney Frederic R. Coudert (R-NY), and Charles Halleck (R-IN). A statistical analysis does not provide a basis for determining whether Republican votes reflected the demands of party leadership or the ideological commitments of individual legislators (see table A.5). What is clear is that in the 81st Congress the average Republican member was more wary of fiscal and regulatory expansion than the average Democratic member. It is possible that many rank-and-file Republicans could have been convinced to vote down the McConnell substitute, going against their "natural" ideological preferences. Some of their co-partisans made precisely such a decision, but the majority of them did not.[78]

Despite the disappointing defeat in the House, Senate liberals forged ahead, and majority leader Lucas (D-IL) moved to introduce a strong FEP bill on May 5. A southern filibuster predictably ensued, and two weeks later the first of two failed cloture votes was held. Two-thirds of the chamber, or sixty-four votes, was necessary to shut off debate, but the effort fell twelve votes short, garnering only fifty-two votes. The second vote was held on July 9, and it failed as well. This time, fifty-five voted for cloture and thirty-three against, nine short of the required total. Lucas was convinced of the reason why liberals had failed in the Senate. "I did the best I could in the recent legislative battle," he wrote to Mary McLeod Bethune afterward, "but was beaten down by the coalition of southern Democrats and northern Republicans." In a speech to the Senate, Paul Douglas agreed with his fellow senator from Illinois. "[T]his coalition represents, with certain exceptions, a marriage of the most conservative sections of the Republican Party with the most conservative sections of the Democratic Party. By giving to any thirty senators the power to make it possible to talk any bill to death, it enables the Northern Republicans to let the Southern Democrats stall civil rights."[79]

The fight in the 81st Congress made clear a political logic that the most perceptive observers at the time had already noticed. While southern Democrats almost always proved to be the first barrier to FEP legislation, conservative Republicans set the outermost limits of what was politically viable. A fair employment bill had cleared the House because it was voluntary. Another had failed in the Senate because it was not.

The campaign for "freedom from discrimination" ran fatally aground due to the southern-conservative coalition in Congress. But liberals did not pour all of their political resources into the struggle on Capitol Hill. Grasping the unique policy-making potential of American political institutions—in which a separation of powers gave interest groups several alternate venues for instituting policy—liberals turned elsewhere to win what battles they could, hoping to maintain the political momentum for legislation. As the NAACP's Clarence Mitchell would later recall, liberals specifically sought executive orders, hoping that they would serve as a "bridge between the old wartime executive order and the day we would be successful in getting legislative action in Congress." The orders were far from ends in themselves. "I do not believe that you can accomplish a great deal with executive order," Mitchell said. "I think you really need legislation." But the "overriding value" of executive orders was "keeping the fair employment idea alive and leading to legislation."[80]

Liberals largely succeeded in these more modest aims, convincing both Truman and Eisenhower to issue a limited series of orders protecting workers from job discrimination in restricted segments of the labor market. In 1948, Truman issued Executive Order 9980 prohibiting "discrimination because of race, color, religion, or national origin" in federal employment. It instructed each federal department to appoint a Fair Employment Officer who would be responsible for carrying out the new policy, and it created a seven-member Fair Employment Board (FEB) in the Civil Service Commission (CSC) to coordinate and oversee the fair employment program of the federal government. If a case could not be resolved within a department, the FEB was to serve as a court of last appeal. Although it had no direct enforcement powers, the board was authorized to refer particularly difficult cases to the president for action. In 1951, Truman issued Executive Order 10308, which made the heads of each federal contracting agency responsible for obtaining compliance with the nondiscrimination provisions of government contracts. It established an eleven-person Committee on Governmental Contract Compliance (CGCC) as an advisory body that would work closely with contracting agencies to study their practices and recommend changes to help eliminate discrimination.[81]

Upon assuming office, Eisenhower also demonstrated a concern for fair employment in federal employment and contracting, but he did not extend or expand on Truman's initiatives. If anything, Eisenhower's orders sought to circumscribe the power of the federal government more closely. When he issued Executive Order 10479 in 1953, he disbanded Truman's CGCC and established the Committee on Government Contracts (CGC), giving it mostly the same mandate and powers as the CGCC. Although the CGC broke some new ground in the way that the federal government addressed the issue of racial discrimination in employment, as John D. Skrentny and Timothy N. Thurber argue, it was ultimately ineffective. The committee lacked enforcement authority, so it focused primarily on public education and public relations. In 1955, Eisenhower issued Executive Order 10590, weakening Truman's FEB by taking it out of the CSC and forcing it to depend on the staffs of accused agencies for help when looking into charges of discrimination. The administration made an effort, but a small one.[82]

That postwar presidents were willing to protect civil rights in a limited way through a series of executive orders reflected the growing importance of the black ballot in national elections. As Scott C. James and others have noted, the Electoral College tended to magnify the political importance of the black vote in extremely competitive states. As a result, black voters often held the balance of power in critical northern swing states. This meant that postwar presidential candidates could not choose to remain silent on civil rights. At the very least, they had to offer their rhetorical commitment. At most, they had to consider issuing an executive order. By way of contrast, black ballots varied in their relevance to Congressional elections. African Americans did represent a key constituency for representatives from northern urban districts as well as senators representing states with large numbers of minorities. Many of these legislators, in fact, were the strongest supporters of FEP legislation. These legislators, however, were limited in number—certainly not numerous enough to form a voting bloc that could win FEP legislation without the significant participation of Republicans.[83]

Fortunately for liberals, the political outlook seemed even rosier at lower levels of the federal system; namely, state legislatures outside of the South. By definition, there were no southern Democrats there—none to obstruct FEP legislation, none to control key committees, and none to muster a filibuster. Equally important, Republicans would face unprecedented pressure to live out their reputation as the "Party of Lincoln." It would no longer be possible for them to pawn off blame on the South. During the end of the wartime period and the outset of the postwar period, liberals also saw a grander stratagem in the cards. If it was not possible to win the Congressional legislation outright, perhaps there could be a parallel campaign in the states outside the South. This campaign would not replace but actually complement the congressional campaign. If one state could be convinced to pass an FEP law, then perhaps more states would follow suit. Success would breed success. Allies would be gladdened, critics mollified, and opponents disheartened. Political momentum would begin to cascade, and perhaps Congress would be moved to act. It would not be the first time in American history that frustrated reformers would repair to the formidable redoubt of the states, hoping to gather force for a federal campaign. The gambit had become so familiar by 1932 that Supreme Court Justice Louis Brandeis famously likened the states to the laboratories of democracy. "It is one of the happy incidents of the federal system," he wrote, "that a single courageous state may, if its citizens choose, serve as a laboratory, and try novel social and economic experiments without risk to the rest of the country." Indeed, signature pieces of New Deal legislation were actually conceived and nurtured in the states. Taking the campaign for FEP to the states would indeed constitute a social and political experiment in the great American tradition, and the first test would come in wartime New York.[84]

3

Experimenting with Civil Rights: The Politics of Ives-Quinn in New York State, 1941–1945

The legislative chamber was filled with many more people than usual. Hundreds of observers sat in the audience, and scores of others stood stiffly in the back of the room, two to three rows deep. A civil rights bill outlawing job discrimination had been introduced a few weeks before, igniting one of the fiercest political controversies in recent memory. Critics of the measure had worked patiently for weeks to stage a public hearing, and earlier in the day they had taken advantage of the chance to testify, raising a litany of complaints. Now the time had come for their leader to make a definitive statement. He spoke carefully and expanded on the criticisms that his colleagues had made earlier. It was a strong performance, culminating in the most potent and resonant charge of the day. The law, he prophesied, would essentially impose "quotas" in hiring and promotion. Its passage would spell doom for the free market and meritocracy: "It means the end of honest competition, and the death knell of selection and advancement on the basis of talent."[1]

It is easy to guess that such a scene must have unfolded on Capitol Hill, perhaps in the mid-1960s, when civil rights finally took center stage in national politics. It would seem even easier to guess the identity of the critics. Surely it was southern Democrats, uttering whatever artful rhetoric they thought would help agrarian elites preserve their flagging control over the political and economic life of the South. In fact, historians familiar with the period will correctly recall that Sen. Sam Ervin, a North Carolina Democrat, raised the charge of quotas in the 1963 congressional debate over Title VII of the Civil Rights Act of 1964, eventually compelling Hubert Humphrey, Minnesota's Democratic senator, to deny explicitly that the law would require racial quotas or racial balancing. Neither guess, however, would be correct. The hearing had taken place years earlier, not in Washington, D.C., but in Albany, New York, where lawmakers had been maneuvering around a fair employment practice (FEP) bill for the better part of three weeks. There were obviously no southern Democrats in the packed New York State Assembly Chamber that day. Instead, the opposition was lead by Republican state senator Frederic Bontecou, ringleader of a rank-and-file revolt of GOP legislators, who rose to read aloud a lengthy letter written by Robert Moses—park commissioner, descendant of German Jewish émigrés, and the fabled power broker of New York. At stake was the passage of the Ives-Quinn bill, which mandated equal treatment in public and private employment. In his letter Moses furnished opponents of Ives-Quinn with potent new language in which to frame their criticisms. Others before him had argued that the bill would lead to "proportionate" representation, but Moses was the first to overtly invoke the specter of "quotas." It was February 20, 1945.[2]

With only a handful of exceptions, historians have largely overlooked the battle over Ives-Quinn, mainly because it passed by a bipartisan majority. What little is known comes from Richard N. Smith, Paul D. Moreno, and Martha Biondi, and their work hints at a hard-fought battle involving business groups, conservative columnist Westbrook Pegler, Republican lawmakers from upstate New York, and park commissioner Moses, who expressed fears of quotas. The persistent obscurity of Ives-Quinn also stems partly from the lingering assumption that the postwar struggle over civil rights was simply a matter of shepherding reluctant southerners into a "liberal consensus" about civil rights that prevailed elsewhere in the country. What the wartime confrontation over FEP in New York State reveals, however, is that there was nothing easy or straightforward about extending civil rights to all Americans, even in the liberal, urban North.[3]

The wartime legislature in New York approved Ives-Quinn only after a massive grass-roots mobilization and a public endorsement by liberal Republican governor Thomas E. Dewey. The outcome represented a major triumph for Empire State liberals, who succeeded in fashioning a broad and effective bloc that included the National Association for the Advancement of Colored People (NAACP), American Jewish Congress (AJC), Catholic Interracial Council (CIC), American Civil Liberties Union (ACLU), and numerous unions affiliated with the Congress of Industrial Organizations (CIO). Thurgood Marshall, Rabbi Stephen Wise, and Mike Quill were only a few of the many liberal leaders who ably spoke up on behalf of Ives-Quinn. Equally impressive was the dedicated support it elicited from ordinary men and women, who wrote scores of letters urging lawmakers to pass the bill and turned out en masse to legislative hearings in the dead of winter. The bloc could also boast of bipartisan support from elected leaders, including liberal Republicans like Dewey, Irving M. Ives, Fiorello H. La Guardia, and Alvin S. Johnson, as well as stalwart Democrats like Herbert S. Lehman and Frieda S. Miller. Of course, backers of Ives-Quinn did not always get along perfectly well. There were occasions when members of the bloc expressed misgivings about each other, or about the bill itself. Yet these divisions did not prove not fatal in the end. The coherence and strength of the liberal bloc proved more than sufficient to the challenge of lobbying for civil rights legislation through the normal channels of electoral politics.

The proposed law faced more serious obstacles than liberal disunity. Perhaps the most significant challenge came not from within the liberal bloc but from outside of it. It may have been difficult for Congress-watchers to gauge the full extent of opposition to FEP legislation. Massive political resistance on the part of southern Democrats made it easy for other critics to conceal or downplay their true preferences. There could be no question, however, about the situation in the Empire State, where the strongest and most unified opposition to Ives-Quinn emanated from a conservative bloc of industrial, commercial, legal, and retail interests; rural and, to a lesser extent, suburban whites; and the largely conservative Republican legislators who represented them. This bloc openly waged a campaign against FEP legislation at every step of the legislative process—from the time when job discrimination surfaced on the legislative agenda at the outset of the war to the early months of 1945, when the bloc fomented a major, if short-lived, insurgency against liberal GOP leadership. Conservatives suffered a stinging loss with the passage of Ives-Quinn, but their defeat did not come before they pioneered key elements of a powerfully new stance on resistance to civil rights. Although they professed a belief in the principle of equal treatment, they minimized the extent of discrimination; argued that it would wither away in the absence of government intervention; and warned that attempts to legislate tolerance would actually heighten color-consciousness and lead to preferential treatment in the form of racial and religious quotas.

Still, it was liberals who could take the most inspiration from the victory in Albany. They had successfully scaled the first, crucial summit in their federated campaign for freedom from discrimination. Now there was a legitimate reason to hope that fifth freedom might well flourish elsewhere across the country. At the same time, however, conservatives had no reason to despair. To be sure, they had lost a key battle, but they also gained valuable experience and forged powerful new weapons for the other conflicts that surely lay ahead.

The political impetus for the passage of antidiscrimination legislation in employment did not materialize overnight. The battle over Ives-Quinn was the culmination of a policy sequence that began in early 1941, when the ideological problem posed by the conflict looming overseas was growing increasingly visible. The country might soon be marching against a fascist enemy overseas, but how could it legitimately denounce doctrines of racial supremacy abroad if it countenanced segregation and discrimination at home? The question grew only more pressing as thousands of African Americans began moving to the Empire State, settling in cities such as New York, Buffalo, Albany, and Rochester and seeking work in a resurgent economy fueled by more than $21 billion in defense spending over the course of the war.[4]

At first, it seemed that elected officials in the Empire State would respond to the question with more than symbolism and rhetoric. When three state assemblymen from Harlem introduced legislation in 1941 calling for fair employment, Gov. Herbert H. Lehman established the New York State War Council Committee on Discrimination in Employment (CDE) to handle individual allegations of job bias. Lehman appointed a roster of highly prominent and influential African Americans to the new committee, notably A. Philip Randolph of the Brotherhood of Sleeping Car Porters (BSCP), Lester Granger of the National Urban League (NUL), and Channing Tobias of the Young Men's Christian Association (YMCA). Other local eminences included Beardsley Ruml of the Federal Reserve Bank of New York, David Sarnoff of the Radio Corporation of American, and Rabbi Stephen S. Wise of the AJC. Freida S. Miller, New York's accomplished industrial commissioner, was made chair of the committee. After further lobbying by CIO unions, Lehman then signed the Mahoney antidiscrimination bill, which barred defense contractors from refusing to hire a person on account of his or her race or religion. The bill did not put the CDE on statutory footing, as some observers erroneously surmised, but it gave the committee further momentum and raised hopes that something could and would be done about discrimination.[5]

Lehman's choice of Miller seemed especially sound. Miller was a younger member of the same generation of public-minded women that included Frances Perkins and Eleanor Roosevelt. Joining the Department of Labor in 1929, she was appointed industrial commissioner in 1938, making her the second woman ever to hold the post, after Perkins herself. Miller's two biggest responsibilities included the administration of the workmen's compensation program and the rollout of the state unemployment insurance program, both of which entailed processing thousands of claims and disbursing millions of dollars in benefits. When the CDE was added to her already-sizeable roster of responsibilities in 1941, she had already acquired more than ten years of experience in industrial relations. It would have been difficult to imagine somebody else more properly qualified than she.[6]

At the beginning of her tenure, Miller heavily stressed the educational and conciliatory functions of the committee. It would aim primarily to inform New Yorkers of their rights and responsibilities under the law, and it would also work informally to persuade them to abandon any discriminatory practices, using the "conference method" pioneered by the NUL. Only in "extraordinary cases" would the committee consider taking legal action to enforce the law. Accordingly, several thousand copies of the

Mahoney Act were printed and sent out to defense contractors. Letters were mailed to community leaders asking them to endorse the democratic principles of tolerance for which the committee stood. The committee distributed ten thousand copies of a program manual to schools, clubs, and informal groups interested in promoting better intergroup relations.[7]

The new CDE concentrated especially hard on reaching out to employers. Its campaign reached a zenith in 1942 when the CDE began disseminating a fifty-page handbook, *How Management Can Integrate Negroes in War Industries*. The handbook was every bit the primer that the title suggested. The author, Lincoln University professor John A. Davis, recommended a gradual, strategic approach to the problem—enlisting a supportive supervisor, targeting white-collar jobs first, and hiring a "high type" of African American. Often, he noted, successful companies "start[ed] the program off with the appointment of a neat, efficient, attractive, well-qualified colored girl in the employment office itself." Davis expressed great faith in the effectiveness of conference and education. When a white worker refused to work with a black worker, it was "seldom" necessary to fire or transfer them—"if the situation is clearly explained." Getting management to eliminate discrimination was no more difficult. "When the problem is plainly stated, any competent supervisor will put the national interest ahead of his personal prejudice."[8]

Employers, however, reacted ambivalently to the campaign. Mark A. Daly, vice president of the Associated Industries of New York State (AINYS), seemed impressed with the handbook. No doubt satisfied that it recommended only gradual, voluntary steps, he offered to send out fourteen hundred copies to his membership, which included General Motors, Bethlehem Steel Company, Corning Glass Works, Otis Elevator Company, IBM, and Pfizer. "Your booklet is a most comprehensive statement covering one important phase of a very difficult problem," Daly wrote approvingly to Miller. "I am sure every employer will welcome an opportunity to read it." Other employers expressed interest as well. Within days of its publication, requests for the handbook poured in from eighty cities and twenty-five states, and over twenty-five thousand copies were eventually distributed. But the CDE's efforts did not meet with universal approval. A. E. Crockett, a top official at Rochester's Industrial Management Council, expressed doubt that eliminating discrimination required any special effort by government at all. His personal observation suggested that it was fast receding of its own accord. Crockett cited the example of a local school whose graduates commanded a "premium" among local employers: "[O]ut of 37 men of Italian race in [the] June, 1941 graduating class at Edison Tech, all but three are employed." Of course, pockets of discrimination lingered, but "substantial progress" had been made and would continue to be made: "[A]fter a while it will be nearly gone, if not entirely so."[9]

Crockett's observation was belied by the number of times that the CDE sought to "adjust" complaints of discrimination through informal conference between aggrieved parties and those accused of discrimination—304 cases in 1942 and 435 in 1943. The field staff faced immense difficulties in resolving such complaints, since there was little the committee could do in the face of delay, obstruction, or rank noncompliance. Several committee members expressed growing dissatisfaction with the "painfully slow rate in getting results" and asked Lehman to strengthen the CDE. Within months, he signed additional legislation. Miller quickly announced that she would interpret the new law as a legitimate basis for issuing administrative orders to defense contractors. "If appeal and persuasion should fail to convince holders of war contracts that they should hire an applicant on his merits, regardless of his race, color, creed, or national origin, such employers will be served with a formal order." A CDE report later specified that such an "order may require the submission of monthly or bi-monthly reports of pertinent employment data to the Industrial Commissioner; it may order the employer to cease and desist from the practice of certain discriminations based on race, creed, color or national origin; or it may direct the employer to take affirmative action to correct discriminatory refusals to hire."[10]

Miller's threat to issue administrative orders that proscribed or prescribed action did not require any radical revisionism on her part. As a longtime labor official, she reached for the regulatory tools most familiar to her. Such administrative orders had been commonplace in labor relations since the Wagner Act, which conferred cease-and-desist authority on the National Labor Relations Board (NLRB) as well as the power to order offending companies to take "affirmative action including restitution" to compensate individuals who had been victimized by their unlawful activity. Many state labor boards, including the one in New York, enjoyed the very same powers. Only a few years later, in 1944, Rep. Thomas Scanlon, a Pennsylvania Democrat, introduced a bill that called for the creation of a permanent federal FEPC with NLRB-style powers over job discrimination (including the authority to order "affirmative action"). Hence, when Miller began to invoke analogous administrative powers in late 1942, she was merely extending a regulatory model prevalent in industrial relations to the area of civil rights.[11]

Miller's announcement nonetheless marked the zenith of the committee's fortunes. Miller issued her first order in October 1942 against Brewster Aeronautical Corporation, but whether she had misconstrued her authority would remain an unanswered question as the CDE entered a period of uncertainty. At the end of the year, Lehman's committee fell into disarray. Lehman resigned his office to accept a position as head of the U.S. Office of Foreign Relief and Rehabilitation Operations. When Republican attorney Thomas E. Dewey won the election to replace Lehman, Miller resigned as well. Dewey did not immediately appoint her successor, and suddenly the fate of the committee appeared in limbo. Dewey's hesitation ended only in August of 1943, when Harlem erupted in a race riot that led to six deaths and $5 million in property damage. Only then did he reconstitute the CDE, naming Alvin S. Johnson as chair. The *New York Times* had no illusions about the difficulty of Johnson's assignment. "The Harlem disorders," it wrote, "are just one yardstick of the magnitude of the task" that confronted him. Nonetheless it deemed Johnson a "distinguished" leader who "commands confidence." The perspicacious, bespectacled Johnson was indeed a logical choice to lead the second incarnation of the CDE. As the founder of the University in Exile at the New School, which provided a refuge for Jewish scholars fleeing the shadow of the Third Reich, he had acquired unimpeachable credentials in the defense of racial and religious tolerance. A former editor of the *New Republic*, he was a lively, arresting correspondent, and his missives were full of clever allusions and eloquent turns of phrase. Johnson's experience and skills were among the few reasons to hope that the CDE could recover.[12]

Such hopes were soon dashed. The reorganization of the committee, rather than serving as a source of inspiration, raised a thicket of troubling questions instead. What would happen to the CDE after the war? Had it been effective only because of labor shortages or patriotic fervor? What could it possibly do to ensure the compliance of a company or union determined to flout the law?

Although these questions were apparent to most observers who followed the CDE closely, nobody was more concerned about the limits of the CDE than the new chairman himself. The larger mandate of the committee, Johnson told almost everyone, would obviously vanish with the end of the war, as would the war contracts over which it had specific jurisdiction. Even if the CDE did somehow survive beyond the war, it had no independent authority to enforce the law: "no counsel of its own, no power to hold hearings and subpoena witnesses, no power to launch inquiries and prepare reports." Johnson pointed out, correctly, that he would have to petition the industrial commissioner for enforcement. Such problems tempted him to recommend the abolition of the committee, "[A]s matters stand, we haven't the power to a real job . . . [and] I can't sacrifice my established record of doing a real job when I set out to do one."[13]

Johnson did not recommend abolition. Instead, he worked energetically to convince the committee that new legislation was necessary. By early 1944, he had organized a consensus, and a subcommittee of the CDE set out to make legislative recommendations. Their most substantial proposal—which declared that the "opportunity to obtain employment without discrimination because of race, color, creed, national origin" was a "civil right"—clearly bore the signs of his handiwork. It called for the establishment a permanent, stand-alone commission with centralized jurisdiction over public and private employment as well as independent authority to enforce the law, including the authority to order recalcitrant offenders "to cease and desist from such unfair employment practice and to take such affirmative action, including hiring or reinstatement of persons with or without back pay." The initial idea of borrowing the regulatory framework of the State Labor Board had originated with Miller, but under Johnson it was given further definition. Administrative enforcement was especially important to him. As he would later write, "[L]etting the Attorney General or the district attorneys enforce the law is strongly favored by those who won't want any law against discrimination enforced."[14]

The CDE proposal was introduced into state legislature by Sen. Arthur H. Wicks (R-Kingston), but it would never emerge from committee. Dewey introduced a different bill calling for the creation of the New York State Temporary Commission against Discrimination (TCAD), which would study the problem and make legislative recommendations for the subsequent session. The bill, which the New York Times characterized as an "admitted substitute" for the CDE proposal, passed easily in the Republican-controlled legislature, sparking a range of public responses that ranged from partisan sniping to reasoned patience and feigned outrage. More significantly, Dewey's move fatally split the CDE. Johnson conceded that everyone, including himself, was "bitterly disappointed" in the outcome. If their proposal had become law, it would have made "freedom from discrimination a civil right." Nevertheless, he stayed on board. Eight other members made good on their threat to resign in protest, including Tobias, Granger, and attorney Louis Weiss, who had spent so many hours helping Johnson with the legislation. They argued that the "urgency and gravity of the problems" were so "great" that seeking to study them further was "wholly unjustified." The CDE could not "continue to function without any real power" when most of the public believed it "has and exercises extensive powers to reduce . . . discrimination."[15]

The spate of resignations effectively marked the end of the CDE. The beleaguered committee that had been formed at the outset of the war years had left a mixed legacy. On the one hand, it had not demonstrably improved the economic prospects of racial minorities—not nearly as much as proponents had hoped. A comprehensive 1946 study by Robert C. Weaver, director of the Negro Manpower Service in the War

Manpower Commission, concluded that black wartime gains were "occasioned principally by economic necessity." On the other hand, it represented a major stride forward on the road to the passage of Ives-Quinn. The committee had found ample evidence of discrimination, Miller had imagined a new regulatory setup, and Johnson had given it legislative definition—but was legislation the best way to handle discrimination? The experience of the CDE had thrown the question into high relief. How it would be addressed was a matter for the TCAD to resolve.[16]

Irving M. Ives seemed an unlikely guardian of civil rights. Except for a short tour of duty in France and Germany during the First World War, he had spent most of his life in central New York. In 1930 he was elected to the New York State Assembly as a Republican from his native Chenango County and quickly rose to become majority leader of the Lower House. Ives later won election to the U.S. Senate, where he became known for his consistent liberalism on civil rights. When Ives was elected chairman of the new TCAD on June 19, 1944, however, there was little in his personal background or political record to indicate that he would lend his name to a strong antidiscrimination bill or become the central legislative figure supporting it.[17]

The first meeting of the TCAD went smoothly. Most members of the commission—a bipartisan roster of legislators as well as representatives of business, labor, civil rights, and religious organizations—seemed ready to approach the process in good faith, making a point of ordering copies of Gunnar Myrdal's *An American Dilemma*, published earlier in the year to great fanfare. There were only faint murmurs of discontent. Not surprisingly, Frank S. Columbus of the railroad brotherhoods—long a bastion of racial exclusion—took a strong position against what he called "'must' legislation" (a mandatory law with enforcement mechanisms). It was Mark A. Daly, executive vice president of the AINYS, who made the most unexpected revelation. In 1942 Daly had considered discrimination a "very difficult problem," but in a startling turnabout he now doubted whether it existed. "I cannot conceive of any man discriminating against a Negro if he is skilled." Daly called for the TCAD "to make a preliminary study to distinguish between discrimination and what might be termed sensible, logical selection and placement of employees." Most commissioners, however, repeatedly agreed with Ives that "what is necessary in this state is some form of FEPC." The only disagreement concerned emphasis. What kind of balance should be struck between education and enforcement?[18]

Johnson, who had been elected vice chair, privately pressed Ives to adopt the CDE proposal for a permanent commission with the power to enforce the law. In time, Johnson's vision would prevail. By November the TCAD had decided to recommend the establishment of a new commission with administrative enforcement power. To raise public awareness and solicit public input, Ives and other commissioners embarked on a draining series of hearings across the state. For eleven days after Thanksgiving, often traveling by train at night, they heard testimony from witnesses in Albany, Syracuse, Rochester, Buffalo, and New York City. Each hearing lasted all day. The public response was astounding. More than two hundred political, community, religious, and civic groups sent representatives to give statements and make suggestions. The verbatim transcript of the hearings, printed in three volumes, ran in excess of fifteen hundred pages.[19]

As extensive as they were, however, the TCAD hearings were as politically uneventful as the deliberations of the commissioners themselves, particularly in contrast to the rancorous clash in Congress earlier in the year. There, southern Democrats had wielded their formidable rhetorical talents in a failed bid to consign the federal FEPC to fiscal oblivion. Malcolm C. Tarver, a Democratic representative from Georgia, assailed it as "one tentacle of a devilfish" that created entirely new problems for the country; it "promote[d] disunity where none had existed before." Rep. Jamie L. Whitten, a Mississippi Democrat, noted that 61 of 106 staff persons at the FEPC were black. Such a disparity provided clear evidence to him that the intent of the committee was not to "prevent unfair discrimination against Negroes. . . . What they wanted, what they have done and are doing is to discriminate in favor of the Negro." Rep. Samuel F. Hobbs, an Alabama Democrat, charged the FEPC with racial proportionalism: "[A]ccording to the FEPC, if there are in a community 10 Negroes out of each 100 persons, then 10 percent of those employed in each category of employment must be Negroes." The shrewdest speakers sought to expose unintended ironies. Rep. Ed Gossett, a Texas Democrat, told his colleagues about a job ad in a Dallas newspaper that had openly solicited black applicants for a good position in the paper industry. Unbelievably, the FEPC had struck down the ad as unlawful. Gossett pounced: Why should the committee be given federal funding to harm people it was meant to help?[20]

The hearings over which Ives presided were tame by comparison. To be sure, there was no absence of public disagreement between liberals and spokesmen for the business community. Leaders of CIO-affiliated unions spoke out forcefully on behalf of the bill. Michael J. Quill, president of the Transport Workers Union, warned that if a bill with "teeth" did not pass, "labor will have to organize and see that the Legislature is changed." In contrast, business lobbyists saw no need for enforceable legislation, extolling the virtues of voluntary policies and claiming that if left alone, discrimination would inevitably fade away. Agreeing that discrimination was a moral blight, one employer in Buffalo nonetheless felt "convinced that the best—yes, the only effective—method of combating this evil is through persuasion, education, and good example." Crockett, from the Industrial Management Council in Rochester, sought to minimize the problem as he had two years earlier in his letter to Miller. "I personally know of no discrimination," he said, "and I do know that the spirit of tolerance that was spoken of so frequently at Albany does exist in a larger measure than it ever existed before. We have moved ahead since this war began, and I believe the effects will be lasting."[21]

Notwithstanding the objections of a few thick-skinned business spokesmen, there was a broad consensus about the pervasiveness of discrimination. Scores of witnesses stepped forward to offer their personal testimony. A representative of the Albany branch of the NAACP told TCAD commissioners about the difficulty that African Americans experienced when seeking jobs in the retail and teaching sectors. She hoped that the TCAD proposal would pass before her son came home from serving overseas. "My boy, like the thousands of other Negroes, Jew, and Catholic boys, will expect a better America for which they have sacrificed and fought, when he returns." A rabbi related a firsthand story about a steel mill manager who turned down twenty-two young Jewish men for employment. Members of the Italian Civic League in Rochester reported "many instances" of discrimination against Americans of Italian descent. Thurgood Marshall of the NAACP sought to make certain that the connection between job discrimination and the war effort was not lost on anyone, quoting a passage from Justice Frank Murphy's ruling in the *Hirabayashi* decision. "Distinctions based on a color and ancestry," he intoned, "are utterly inconsistent with our traditions and ideals. They are at variance with the principles for which we are now waging war."[22]

If most participants in the hearings agreed that discrimination was the central problem, they also agreed with the Myrdalian diagnosis that discrimination stemmed largely from prejudices lodged deeply in the "heart of every American." "Let us always bear in mind," Ives constantly reminded his audiences, "that discrimination in itself is not the disease, it is a symptom . . . the disease is prejudice." Few participants, though, believed that discrimination could be ended only—or even most effectively—through educational outreach and moral suasion. That discrimination stemmed from prejudice did not obviate the need for government regulation. "We do not believe education alone can solve the problem," said Louis Hollander, president of the New York State CIO. Education would be effective only if there was a cost to noncompliance. In fact, he explained, participants' knowledge that enforcement action was a real possibility might strengthen informal methods: "If you have no law, education itself will not do it." The only disagreement among supporters of the bill was about whether the TCAD proposal went far enough. Some witnesses worried that the bill did not have enough teeth and would lead to interminable foot dragging by accused parties. Others focused on arcane but important questions of regulatory design, particularly the provision giving judges the authority to try cases appealed from the commission de novo. That "practically invites appeal," said one participant; it could virtually "nullify" the "effective operation" of the proposed commission, suggested another. Still others wondered whether the commission would be more useful if it could initiate investigations without waiting for a complaint.[23]

The TCAD transmitted a final report to the Assembly on January 29, 1945. The centerpiece was a recommendation to create a new regulatory commission whose powers had been anticipated by Miller and given substance by Johnson. The new commission would have a strong educational component, but it would also enforce the law by receiving and handling complaints. Complaints would first be addressed informally by bringing the parties together in a private conference and seeking to reconcile their views through persuasion and mediation. Only if informal methods failed would the commission hold a public hearing to assess the validity of the complaint, subpoenaing witnesses and records if necessary. If it determined that discrimination had occurred, it could direct the offending party to "cease and desist from such unlawful employment practice and to take such affirmative action, including (but not limited to) hiring, reinstatement, or upgrading of employees, with or without back pay, or restoration to membership in any respondent labor organization." To protect the rights of everyone involved, such orders were subject to judicial review.[24]

The next day Ives joined with the Democratic senator Elmer F. Quinn to introduce TCAD's proposal to the legislature. Now, however, dissent was spilling into the open. News reports noted that opposition was brewing upstate. TCAD's final report, indeed, had been sprinkled with irate footnotes. Daly had contributed a lengthy footnote that reiterated his long-standing misgivings about the proposal even as he endorsed the ideal of equal treatment. Like "every other right-thinking citizen" and "every intelligent executive in industry," he was opposed to "any discrimination because of race, creed, color or national origin or ancestry." Nevertheless he was strongly convinced that "there is sufficient law on the books" to address any lingering discrimination that did exist. There was no need for more laws.[25]

Still, supporters could easily find reasons for optimism. The bill had benefited from a lengthy and public gestation, reducing its vulnerability to charges that it was the brainchild of wild-eyed agitators wanting to plunge the state precipitously into a social experiment. Perhaps more important was the unbending determination of the main sponsor to see his bill passed. At the outset, Ives had known "little about the problem and felt that the proper solution must lie largely in a broad program of education." It had become apparent to him over the months, however, that discrimination "not only has existed, but does exist" and constitutes a "fundamental contradiction in our American Way of Life." The experience had opened his eyes to the full scope of the problem and steeled his resolve to find a sensible solution. Ives considered TCAD's legislative proposal, which combined informal methods with administrative enforcement, to be "moderate, reasonable, and workable," and little would dissuade him from trying his utmost to see it become law. "I mean business on this thing," he declared.[26]

The suddenness and ferocity of the public resistance to Ives-Quinn must have surprised almost everyone, Ives most of all. If critics had once sought to frame their concerns in reasonable terms, they now abandoned any pretense of moderation. A bill they opposed had landed on the docket, and it had the potential to pass. It was no slapdash improvisation, but rather the product of careful, consensual, and bipartisan reflection. The time for restraint had come and gone, and harsher language was needed.

The source of the flare-up was no surprise (see figure 3.1). Frank Columbus of the railroad brotherhoods predictably asked legislators to vote against the measure. Organized business, however, unleashed the most damaging line of attack. Diverse segments of the business community—manufacturers, merchants, and the corporate bar—joined to praise the intent of the bill but prophesied that all manner of terrible consequences would erupt if it were adopted. Businesses and jobs would flee the state in droves. The proposed law was "hysterically conceived," in the words of the West Side Association of Commerce in New York City, and it would "intensify rather than eliminate any discrimination which exists." Julian Myrick of the New York State Chamber of Commerce warned legislators that the law would give "disgruntled" employees the leverage to "blackmail" employers by threatening to complain at every possible opportunity. The resultant concern on the part of employers could lead to the "enforced employment of undesirable persons." No comparison seemed too outlandish or out of bounds. The law would fuel a "burning resentment" that would exacerbate intolerance and "tend to foment . . . the possibility of race riots, pogroms, and the evils associated with the Ku Klux Klan." A spokesman for the Commerce and Industry Association said that the law would "work against those whom it was intended to benefit," implying darkly that a kosher butcher would be forced to hire a gentile.[27]

Watch Out!

Figure 3.1 "Watch Out!" *PM*, February 9, 1945. Two of the most important interest groups opposing the passage of Ives-Quinn were the railroad brotherhoods and organized business. The latter included the Associated Industries of New York State, New York Bar Association, New York Board of Trade, New York Chamber of Commerce, and almost every other business group of note. This cartoon shows two bald men, one symbolizing labor and the other symbolizing business, pulling out a chair labeled "Anti-Discrimination Bills" from underneath a stylish woman—"N.Y. State"—who is trying to sit down. Courtesy of the General Research Division, The New York Public Library, Astor, Lenox, and Tilden Foundations.

In the meantime, supporters did not sit on their hands helplessly. Although organized labor could not match the coherence of the business community—with the state Federation of Labor showing decidedly less enthusiasm than CIO-affiliated unions—it rallied to the cause of fair employment, as did the NAACP, the NUL, the AJC, and dozens of other liberal groups. Ives himself spoke out, reiterating his conviction that discrimination was a clear and present threat to American democracy as it sought to repel fascism overseas. The only question for him was whether the state would continue on a path of "drifting and indifference" or declare a fresh start and "establish a new agency to handle the most important phase of the discrimination problem—discrimination in employment." He noted that the proposed agency would be no leviathan; it would stress education and informal methods first, relying on enforcement mechanisms only when absolutely necessary. Ives had apparently struck the right tone. A serviceman overseas wrote to tell Ives that he and his crew mates had read the full text of Ives's speech and had come away impressed: "If this war is against anything, it is a war against racial prejudices, discrimination, and bigotry."[28]

Not all liberals felt as Ives did. A debate that raged across the editorial page of the *New York Times* revealed some doubts. The debate had been shrewdly orchestrated behind the scenes by Charles C. Burlingham—admiralty lawyer, judicial reformer, and "New York's First Citizen." A widely respected, headstrong Democrat, Burlingham quickly concluded that the "remedy [provided by Ives-Quinn was] worse than the disease." The chief problem was the reliance on administrative enforcement. To justify their new jobs, commissioners would face implacable pressure to find discrimination wherever they looked. Only the judiciary could remain independent and impartial. "I prefer the Courts to the Bureaucrats," he pronounced.[29]

Burlingham had launched the debate with the publication in the *New York Times* of a letter signed by notable liberals, including the attorney Whitney North Seymour and the reformer Oswald Garrison Villard. Most of the signers had agreed very reluctantly to lend their names, but the letter criticized Ives-Quinn in no uncertain terms. It lauded the goal of reducing prejudice and discrimination but charged that Ives-Quinn set up a "costly machinery" and "inquisitorial process" that would prove useless, since the true motivations for employment decisions were impossible to discern. Moreover, the law would lead workers to exaggerate the extent of discrimination and management to conceal their prejudices: "[P]rejudice will become a commodity to be bootlegged." The reference to Prohibition, however maladroit and strained, captured the essence of their objection. "It is as impossible to destroy prejudice and discrimination by law," Burlingham's group wrote, "as it is to control opinion or morals. It is far wiser to rely on the force of slow but steadily growing public opinion, guided and developed under the leadership of fair-minded men and women of every race, color, creed, and national origin."[30]

The letter jolted liberals, but only because such views were rare among them. Far more typical were the sentiments expressed by Jack R. McMichael, executive secretary of the Methodist Federation for Social Service. In a rejoinder to Burlingham, McMichael conceded that "racial prejudice cannot be eliminated by legislation alone, since prejudice is largely a matter of emotional attitude." He pointed out, though, that prejudice and discrimination were not identical, and the latter was the appropriate target of government policy. "Discrimination . . . is not primarily a matter of internal unbrotherly feelings but of external unbrotherly actions—the proper and effective sphere for legislation with teeth." The counsel for the ACLU, Osmond K. Fraenkel, questioned the sincerity of critics. "Pious hopes and crocodile tears will accomplish nothing." What was needed was administrative action, which would be more efficient than the courts because commissioners would acquire specialized expertise in handling the cases. Another interfaith group of liberals—including most prominently the attorney Robert S. Benjamin, the jurist Charles B. Sears, and the attorney Charles Evans Hughes, Jr.—published a letter calling public opinion a "weak reed" on which to rest hopes for equal treatment in the postwar period. Only new legislation would suffice.[31]

By contrast, there was near unanimity among conservatives that Ives-Quinn would bring ruinous consequences on the Empire State. The *Wall Street Journal* expressed admiration for the goal of the bill but doubted whether "the evil to which this bill addresses itself can be effectively dealt with by any kind of statute; we are convinced that the bill is too loosely drawn to escape stirring up more friction and bad feeling than it could ever allay." Writing under the pseudonym Henry Stuart Clark, the conservative author and economist Henry Hazlitt lambasted Ives-Quinn. "The so-called anti-discrimination bill now before the Legislature of this state," wrote the future "Business Tides" columnist for *Newsweek*, "seems to me far more likely to stir up racial antagonisms, to encourage blackmail against employers, and to undermine industrial discipline and production, than to solve the problem that it is ostensibly intended to solve." He pointed to the example of the Wagner Act, which he claimed prevented employers from firing incompetent, insubordinate, and troublesome workers. Ives-Quinn was similarly extremist: "[It] represents the method of zealots, who can never think of any way of curing an evil except by coercion. The bill may undo what years of education and tolerance have done and could still do."[32]

As a clash of ideology unfolded on the op-ed pages, Republican legislators, working closely with the business lobby, wasted no time setting out to undermine the bill in the legislature—and with good reason. The GOP controlled the Assembly by a margin of 94–55 and the Senate by 35–21. If public opinion could be inflamed against the bill, it could fall easily to defeat. The same hope fueled Republican and employer demands for a second round of public hearings. When the bill came under consideration by the Senate Finance Committee, Sen. Frederic Coudert, Jr., a Republican from Manhattan (New York County), submitted a petition signed by seven business groups calling for another chance to present their views. The *New York Post* roundly denounced the move as "Republican filibustering," but Coudert claimed that passing such a controversial measure without "objective public consideration" could jeopardize whatever chance of success it might have. Although the board of directors at AINYS had unanimously voted their opposition to Ives-Quinn, and Daly had advised his membership not to testify in 1944, Daly now somewhat disingenuously claimed that employers "did not have enough advance notice at all of the details of the bill" and "could not commit themselves publicly concerning a bill which they had not studied and analyzed."[33]

Coudert's petition touched off what the *New York Times* characterized as a "large-scale revolt against the demand of Republican legislative leaders." Party leaders who held or aspired to statewide office, such as Dewey and Ives, took a liberal stance on fair employment because they needed to compete for minority votes in statewide elections, but most GOP members faced different electoral circumstances. Led by Senator Bontecou, a Republican from Poughkeepsie (Dutchess County), and Assemblyman William M. Stuart, a Republican from Steuben County, February's insurgency took strongest root among rank-and-file Republicans who represented upstate districts where few members of racial or religious minorities resided. Such districts were largely conservative and Republican, and their ideological tenor was clearly reflected in local papers, which consistently expressed doubts about Ives-Quinn. The *Troy Morning Record* dubbed it a "New Volstead Act." "Discrimination . . . is based on prejudice," wrote the *Niagara Falls Gazette* in a passage that borrowed shamelessly from Burlingham's letter, "and it is just as impossible to destroy prejudice as it is to control opinion or morals." Stuart's criticisms of the measure—he considered the bill "in itself discriminatory"—were prominently featured in upstate newspapers. Those objections could reflect poorly on the critics of Ives-Quinn, but a report in the *Watertown Times* sought to distinguish "upstate Republicans" from the "Bourbon Democrats" of the South. Members of the GOP were not "in favor of discrimination as such." "They are, however, hard-headed, sensible, 'up-country' Yankees, proud of their heritage of independence."[34]

The stance of political elites upstate reflected the ideological convictions of their constituents. There was no single grass-roots organization coordinating the dissent of upstate whites, and few constituent letters have survived. But some upstate residents did write individually to GOP officeholders before and after the passage of Ives-Quinn, and the letters expressed a strong opposition to protecting civil rights through legislation. A resident of Elmira worried that the bill would lead to "legalized blackmail" against employers, whom he considered the "Forgotten Men" of American politics. Unscrupulous workers, it was feared, would threaten to file costly, if baseless, complaints in order to extract concessions from their employers. A manufacturer based in Olean thought that Ives-Quinn would "create a great deal of bad feeling and will tend to cause race riots." The employer pointed to his workers as the main source of the problem. During a recent labor shortage, he had wanted to employ black workers, but he claimed that his employees "to a man" threatened to "walk off the job" if African Americans were hired. When he asked his workers why they felt so strongly, he was told that they simply refused to "use the same toilet facilities and locker rooms" as a black man. A self-identified Republican wrote Dewey from the hamlet of Batavia in western New York, denouncing Ives-Quinn as a "lousy piece of work." Though he and his brother had both been enthusiastic supporters of Dewey in the 1944 presidential election, he was "disappointed" to see the governor taking a "page out of Roosevelt's book."[35]

While centered in the villages and hamlets of upstate New York, grass-roots hostility to the bill was not confined to them. Some of the most intense feelings emanated from the suburban areas surrounding New York City and even Manhattan itself. A resident of Freeport, on the suburban fringe of New York City, was angry that racial minorities might succeed in writing racial preferences into the law. "The only unfortunate thing," he wrote,

> is that a lot of us Americans were not lucky enough to be born a member of one of these minority groups, who high pressure you into putting over the Ives bill while our sons were away! These people were only interested in putting themselves in a favored position via kangaroo courts, Soviet style, regardless of their habits or behavior as individuals! There has been less general discrimination here than any place else in the world, the Ives Bill is an insult to all Tolerant Americans the state over!

A self-proclaimed Dewey supporter from Richmond Hill in the New York City borough of Queens could not fathom why the governor would back a law to benefit blacks when "it is the decent young white men who are winning this war for America and Americans, not the disease-infested Negroes." One resident of New Rochelle in Westchester County thought that the law could only have been passed to "intimidate the white people of this state." A resident of Manhattan objected to Ives-Quinn because it would force whites to come into contact with blacks. "I know girls who have had to give up their jobs because they got sick from the smell of them." "Instead of smoothing down the distinctions which promote discrimination," wrote another city dweller, "it accentuates them." Still another thought blacks should pull themselves up by their bootstraps: "If politicians and busy-bodies will only leave the Jews and colored alone they will find their rightful level just as we Irish did."[36]

Dewey tried to tamp down the unrest in his party, publicly throwing his full weight behind the bill. The decision won him kudos from the *New York Herald Tribune*, but the intervention did not decisively settle matters. By mid-February, conservative and upstate Republicans had succeeded in their call for a hearing. They hoped to use the hearings as a high-profile stage to present united opposition from powerful and influential business groups, elevating public concern to a point where party leaders would at least agree to strip the bill of enforcement provisions. The stakes were high for everyone else as well. The Harlem-based *Amsterdam News* saw the hearing as a chance for liberals to demonstrate their support, exhorting readers to "Back [the] Proposed State FEPC!" Victor Bernstein of the New York City daily *PM* agreed, calling for a "march on Albany." Bernstein expressed confidence that his call would be answered. "Coudert wants a hearing," he wrote. "Let him hear." A favorable hearing could actually help a different Republican, Ives, who had been weighing a U.S. Senate run. It would validate the stance he had taken and enable him to present himself as a fair-minded leader in a statewide election. Dewey had the most to lose or gain. If the hearing derailed the bill entirely, it would severely damage his credibility and widen the breach between him and the GOP rank and file; it would also weaken his standing in the national party, forcing him to cede control to Sen. Robert A. Taft of Ohio and the conservative wing. Yet, if the hearing went well, he could further consolidate his control of the state party and claim national leadership on the question of civil rights; it might also boost the overall political fortunes of the Republican ticket in the next presidential election. All eyes turned to Albany.[37]

The hearings could not have disappointed anyone for lack of interest or attendance. Every seat on the floor and gallery of the Assembly chamber was filled. The audience—estimates of its size varied wildly from three hundred to one thousand—was packed two to three rows deep against the walls (figure 3.2). Employers had a perfect chance to make their arguments on the most visible stage they had thus far enjoyed. Gustave Michelson of the New York Board of Trade spoke first. Like most other Americans, he said, employers considered freedom from discrimination a laudable goal, but Ives-Quinn would "unduly emphasize differences" and "pit race against race, color against color, creed against creed." Daly, following Michelson, compared Ives-Quinn to the ineffectual Volstead Act. The only real consequence of the bill would be to put "just one more nail in the coffin of New York business as it continues losing the competitive struggle with other states." When his turn came, Whitney North Seymour of the New York State Bar Association maintained that Ives-Quinn was "bound to create prejudice where it does not now exist" and that it established a new and dubious "civil right" that directly conflicted with the "traditional right of the employer to use his own judgment in selection of his employees."[38]

Figure 3.2 Attorney Charles H. Tuttle of the New York State Temporary Commission against Discrimination (TCAD) endorsing the Ives-Quinn bill before a packed New York State Assembly Chamber, February 20, 1945. One of the main sponsors of the bill, state representative Irving M. Ives (R-Chenango), is sitting in the middle of the front row with his hands clasped in his lap. There were hundreds of observers in attendance, many of them delegates from liberal interest groups. The most sensational moment of the day came when Sen. Frederic H. Bontecou (R-Dutchess) read aloud a letter from park commissioner Robert Moses warning that outlawing discrimination would lead inevitably to racial "quotas." Courtesy of AP/World Wide Photos.

If most critics reiterated familiar themes, the park commissioner Robert Moses made the most original contribution to their rhetorical arsenal in a letter prominently read aloud by Senator Bontecou. Moses had long rejected governmental regulation of discrimination. At the New York Constitutional Convention of 1938, he had railed against a proposal that would have amended the state constitution to outlaw discrimination. "You cannot legislate tolerance by constitutional amendment or statute," he had warned. Now he went even further. Not only was it impossible to protect civil rights through legislation, it also could lead to a perverse and unanticipated outcome: If the bill passed, a logic of proportionalism would guide employment decisions. Other critical voices had made similar arguments on the floor of Congress. Most recently, Senator Taft had charged that a permanent federal FEPC would force "every employer to choose his employees approximately in proportion to the division of races and religion in his district." Moses cast the criticism in new, provocative language, arguing that a legislative assault on discrimination would lead to "quotas."

> The most vicious feature of this proposal is that it will inevitably lead to the establishment of what in European universities and institutions, from the Middle ages to World War II, was known as the "numerous clauses," that is, the quota system under which Jews and other minorities were permitted only up to a fixed number proportionate to their percentage of the total population. . . . An honest employer harassed by the system proposed to be established here will either ask the State Commission against Discrimination to fix the various religious and racial quotas which will satisfy them, or he will be forced to establish quotas of his own based upon the anticipated point of view, the practices and the decisions of the new commission. How can such an outrageous and intolerable situation benefit the members of any minority group? It means the end of honest competition, and the death knell of selection and advancement on the basis of talent.[39]

Moses had a subtle but alarming message to convey. Fearful of administrative scrutiny from the new agency, an employer would either preemptively engineer his work force to reflect the makeup of the local population or ask government officials to dictate the proportions acceptable to them. It did not matter to Moses that Ives-Quinn mandated nondiscrimination. Nor did he point to specific language in the bill that gave rise to his concern about proportional representation. For him and his fellow conservatives, using legislation to guarantee the equal treatment of racial and religious minorities—rather than relying on "education, moral suasion, conference" and other informal means—would itself lead to "quotas" plain and simple.[40]

Moses did not pluck the word "quota" out of thin air. The political discourse of the state had run thick with charges of quotas since the advent of a long-smoldering controversy over attempts to limit Jewish admissions at colleges and universities. As early as the 1910s, Columbia University administrators—years before their more illustrious counterparts at Harvard, Yale, and Princeton—had begun to take steps to reduce the representation of Jewish students, whose presence was seen as driving the sons of New York's Protestant elite to pursue higher education in schools far outside the city limits. By 1921, Columbia had lowered the percentage of Jewish students to 22 percent of the student body (from a high of roughly 40 percent), prompting concerns about quotas.[41]

The controversy was reignited in early 1945 when local newspapers began publishing stories about a private report of the American Dental Association (ADA) that seemed to recommend the imposition of racial and religious quotas in admissions to dental school. The author of the report had allegedly observed that the student body at Columbia's dental school—and other schools in New York—was "made up overwhelmingly of one racial strain" and suggested that the school would enjoy greater influence if it admitted a student body that was a "more balanced picture of the citizenry of the Nation." A minor uproar ensued. There could be little doubt which social group the author had in mind. The phrase "one racial strain . . . means Jewish students," said someone who had read the report. *PM*'s Albert Deutsch blasted the report as a "brazen attempt to impose a racist policy" akin to the "*numerus clausus* policy" that was historically prevalent in "anti-Semitic areas of central Europe." Predictably, school administrators issued strong denials. Though his critics remained doubtful, Willard C. Rappleye, dean of Columbia's dental school, was especially forceful. "We have no quota, never had one, and never intend to have one." The controversy gained national visibility when Rep. Emanuel Celler, a Democrat from New York, spoke out against the ADA report on the floor of the U.S. House of Representatives and found himself in a face-to-face confrontation with a fellow Democrat, Rep. John E. Rankin of Mississippi. Leaping to his feet and shaking his fist, Rankin complained that Celler used the "Jewish question" to badger his colleagues and then went on to defend the prerogatives of the ADA: "Remember that the white Gentiles of this country also have some rights." The very next day a group of educational leaders, including representatives of the National Educational Association, sent a telegram to President Franklin Roosevelt requesting the establishment of a national fair educational practices commission to help eliminate "quotas and other forms of racial and religious discrimination in the nation's colleges." A member of the group, Alonzo F. Myers, chairman of the Department of Higher Education at New York University, denounced quotas as a "Nazi practice." By the time Moses sent his letter to Bontecou, charges and denials of quotas had been garnering headlines for three weeks. Though he was not particularly active in Jewish communal life, Moses surely had not missed the extensive press coverage of the incident.[42]

Moses chose his words well, and he made certain that the indictment of quotas would have national resonance. In addition to providing the letter to Bontecou, Moses personally sent a copy of his letter to Westbrook Pegler, an influential columnist for King Features Syndicate. Pegler had a talent for spotting evocative language, and he immediately seized on "quotas" to excoriate Ives-Quinn. Days after Moses sent his letter, Pegler published a nationally syndicated column studded with angry denunciations. The column even appeared in the *Atlanta Constitution*. After running through the standard criticisms, it ended with a characteristic fulmination: "Far from erasing such taboos," he wrote, "this law would emphasize origin, creed, color and race and result in the Hitlerian rule of quotas by which Jews in schools and the professions were restricted in proportion to their number in the entire population."[43]

Such charges were so potentially damaging that they attracted a preemptive refutation by Mayor Fiorello La Guardia of New York, who sent his aide Reuben Lazarus to the Albany hearings to read a prepared statement. In a display of his keen political instincts, La Guardia reassured anyone listening that Moses had overreached in his criticism. The bill "does not give preference to anyone because of race, creed, color or religion." It required employment or promotion only on a merit basis: "[Ives-Quinn] does not compel an employer to employ quotas or to employ a less efficient person because of race, creed, color, or religion, but it specifically prohibits discrimination solely on these grounds." La Guardia conceded that educational approaches were highly effective, but he remained convinced that guaranteeing the protection of civil rights without "provid[ing] the machinery for its enforcement would be a mere mockery."[44]

La Guardia's ringing endorsement foreshadowed a parade of witnesses who defended Ives-Quinn in the most aggressive terms. While business spokesmen had mounted a unified front and shown great discipline—rarely deviating from the same basic objections—they were overwhelmed by force of sheer numbers. Representatives of more than two hundred groups had braved the winter weather to come forward and testify, and supporters reportedly outnumbered opponents by a margin of 8–1. The strongest witnesses included Thurgood Marshall of the NAACP, B. F. McLaurin of the BSCP, Reginald A. Johnson of the NUL, Stephen S. Wise of the AJC, John F. Brosnan and Stephen S. Jackson of the New York State Catholic Welfare Committee, Rev. Wayne White of the Methodist Federation for Social Service, and Louis Hollander of the New York State CIO. The hearings went on for twelve hours, ending only at two in the morning. Surveying the scene before him, one legislator opposed to Ives-Quinn was reportedly heard muttering, "You can't bust your head out against this stone wall."[45]

His lament proved correct. The hearings backfired against Bontecou, Stuart, Coudert, and the rank-and-file insurgency that they had briefly led. If there had ever been a chance that Dewey, Ives, or other party chieftains might lose their nerve in the face of overwhelming public opposition to the bill, it ended abruptly in Albany on February 20. Precisely the opposite had occurred. Racial conservatives had committed a strategic mistake by misreading the willingness and ability of liberal groups to mobilize a massive and unprecedented show of support for Ives-Quinn. A day after the hearings, Bontecou and Stuart knew they been out-organized, calling their foes a "brilliantly organized minority." It was a backhanded compliment, but they publicly conceded that the bill would probably pass without any weakening amendments. The concession did not stop them from working behind the scenes to attach a rider to Ives-Quinn that would subject it to a public referendum, but none of their attempts succeeded. Within weeks, Ives-Quinn cleared the Assembly by a margin of 109–32 and the Senate by a margin of 49–6.[46]

The votes confirmed patterns that the most perceptive political observers had identified weeks earlier. Every Democratic legislator voted for the bill, but the Republican delegation was divided in both chambers, with the split more pronounced in the Assembly than the Senate. (The former was apportioned according to population, the latter by county.) Naysayers fit a common profile; they had typically won their last election by a healthy margin, and they tended to represent sparsely populated, predominantly rural counties with little industrial activity and few racial or religious minorities. Hardly any of their constituents stood to benefit from the protection that Ives-Quinn offered, certainly not enough to make a difference on Election Day. Not all Republican legislators representing such counties cast ballots against the Ives-Quinn bill—Ives himself was the most prominent example—but the vast majority of opponents of his bill (all Republican) represented such counties (see table 3.1). In aggregate, nonmetropolitan counties were less populous, less dense, more rural, less industrial, and they took in proportionately fewer defense dollars than metropolitan counties. Nonmetropolitan counties were, in aggregate, overwhelmingly represented by Republicans, and most such nonmetropolitan GOP legislators voted against Ives-Quinn. Of the fifty-nine legislators sent by nonmetropolitan counties, only three belonged to the Democratic Party. More than half, or 54 percent, of the Republican delegation from such counties opposed the bill, compared to only 11 percent of the Republican delegation from metropolitan counties. It was no coincidence that Bontecou and Stuart were popular politicians from archetypal nonmetropolitan counties. By contrast, Coudert, despite his key role in building up the revolt, ultimately voted for Ives-Quinn; he had narrowly won election from his Manhattan district in 1944.[47]

The bipartisan majorities might have grossly understated the extent of Republican opposition. "Man after man has told me that he is voting against his convictions," wrote Coudert to Moses, but nothing could be done in "face of terrific minority and executive pressure." No further correspondence about the vote seems to have survived, and it is impossible to know whether other members concurred with Coudert's representa-

TABLE 3.1

Social and Political Characteristics of Counties in New York State by Type of County, c. 1945

	Metropolitan counties	Non-metropolitan counties	New York State
Social and economic characteristics			
Population	11,095,942	2,383,200	13,479,142
Population density	1,226.3	61.3	281.2
Percent white	94.95%	98.5%	95.6%
Percent rural	8.2%	58.7%	17.2%
Value added manufacture per capita	$265	$170	$248
Defense contracts per capita	$1,840	$653	$1,630
Political characteristics			
All legislators	145	59	204
Democratic legislators	73	3	76
Republican legislators	72	56	128
Percent of legislators who were Republican	50%	95%	63%
GOP votes against Ives-Quinn bill	8	30	38
Percent of Republicans voting against Ives-Quinn	11.1%	53.6%	29.7%

Notes: The following eighteen counties belonged to a metropolitan area according to the 1940 U.S. Census: Albany, Bronx, Broome, Erie, Herkimer, Kings, Monroe, Nassau, New York, Niagara, Oneida, Onondaga, Queens, Rensselaer, Richmond, Rockland, Schenectady, and Westchester. New York State comprised sixty-two counties in all. Population density was calculated by dividing population by land area in square miles. Residents were classified as rural by the Census if they did not live in cities or other incorporated places having 2,500 inhabitants or more. Value added by manufacture was defined as the value of products minus the cost of materials, supplies, fuel, and energy. Defense contracts included all war-related supply contracts of more than $50,000 reported by the War Production Board for the period from June 1940 to September 1945. The calculations do not include one Assemblyman affiliated exclusively with the American Labor Party.

Sources: U.S. Census Bureau, *County Data Book* (Washington, DC: U.S. GPO, 1947), 272, 276–77; *New York Red Book: 1945*, 45–46, 106–10, 565–82; *Journal of the New York State Assembly*, 168 sess., February 28, 1945, p. 880; *Journal of the New York State Senate*, 168 sess., March 5, 1945, p. 751.

tion, or whether he was simply trying to console a powerful ally who had cast his lot with the losing side. It is clear how Coudert himself felt. As a member of the U.S. House of Representatives in 1950, he would vote with dozens of southern Democrats in favor of a voluntary FEPC. But his judgment about the underlying causes of the outcome seemed right to most close observers, including the *New York Herald Tribune*, which likewise asserted that the governor's leadership and "exceedingly strong community support" made the crucial difference. Without Dewey's un-equivocal backing and the dramatic show of political force in Albany, it might have taken much longer to pass Ives-Quinn. As it was, Dewey signed Ives-Quinn into law on March 12, 1945, and the entire country was put on notice that it had entered a new phase in the struggle against job discrimination.[48]

Few, if any, of the nightmarish prophecies about Ives-Quinn came true. "The most casual investigation proves that these grim prophecies have not been borne out," wrote Bruce Bliven in the *New Republic*. In the heat of the moment, critics had predicted that the sky would fall, but it did not. Employers did not appear to set any quotas for racial hiring, and there is no evidence that they demanded the New York State Commission against Discrimination (NYSCAD) to set quotas. The economy did not grind to a standstill. Ives-Quinn did not trigger any pogroms or race riots. In fact, the racial character of the labor force across New York State began changing without great discord. Payrolls of public utilities included Jewish names for the first time. Banks and insurance companies began hiring black clerks, and black saleswomen appeared behind the cosmetics counter at the biggest and most fashionable department stores in New York City. Much of the progress happened without the spectacle of public hearings or the drudgery of enforcement proceedings. Some companies, of course, refused to change their practices. A job application at one firm asked prospective workers to account for why their appearance did not match their surname: "If your name is Murphy, and your photograph does not look like Murphy, kindly explain." Many business executives and company owners, however, simply complied with the new law, finding that the law was readily workable. A few could hardly contain their enthusiasm. "Some of the new people I've hired are outstanding," one employer said. "You ought to point out to employers the benefits they get from an increased labor market, where they have access to so many more qualified workers." Other company executives were willing to have their laudatory statements featured in pro-FEP pamphlets circulating in other states.[49]

NYSCAD did not entirely escape criticism. Nor was it without genuine flaws. The sharpest attacks, surprisingly, came from the Left. The agency had held too few hearings; it had needlessly dismissed too many cases; it should not have confined itself to matters of employment. Many of these criticisms, however, were not entirely fair. The cases that NYSCAD chose to handle were strategically selected, often involving large companies that set the pace in their sector of the economy. The paucity of hearings did not stem from a lack of willpower on the part of NYSCAD so much as the desire of employers to avoid the public limelight. When confronted by NYSCAD with a choice between holding a hearing or negotiating a settlement—regardless of whether the complaint had merit—most employers understandably opted for settlement, hoping to avoid bad publicity. The chief defect of the law was that it did not give NYSCAD the authority to launch investigations or inquiries into employment practices without first receiving a complaint about discrimination. This not only meant that individuals had to prove willing to shepherd a complaint through the administrative process, instead of letting NYSCAD take the lead, but also that complaints tended to pile up at the *least* discriminatory companies, where minorities at least applied for a job because they thought they stood a decent chance at getting a fair shake. This feature of the law hence left the worse offenders off the hook.[50]

Nevertheless, liberals in the mid-1940s could look back on Ives-Quinn with a measure of genuine satisfaction. Politically, it was a strong validation of their Brandeisan strategy. New York State was the first laboratory of democracy, and despite the emergence of formidable opposition, it had succeeded in passing FEP legislation. Dozens of states, emboldened by the example of New York, introduced similar bills in the wake of Ives-Quinn. The law itself—as well as the campaign for it—became a nationwide model for others to imitate. "New York's experience, over more than a year, has been distinctly favorable," Irwin Ross noted correctly in the *New York Times Magazine*. "The ball is now passed to the rest of the country." But what would other states do? Would they be willing to run with the ball? Even if other states proved willing, conservatives would surely not go quietly into the night. Even in a state as inhospitable to them as New York, they had put up a creative resistance. Would liberals be strong and smart enough to overcome the opposition that would surely arise in other states? These were the questions on everyone's mind. Would the states truly bear out their reputation as the laboratories of democracy, or would they instead serve as steam valves of reform or incubators of reaction? The fate of the campaign for the fifth freedom hung in the balance.[51]

4

Laboratories of Democracy? The Unsteady March of Fair Employment in the States, 1945–1964

Most liberals must have felt a burst of optimism at the outset of Truman's second term. Harry had given the Republicans hell. Running from behind during the last weeks of the historic 1948 election, he had determinedly gone on the offensive, railing against the GOP-controlled "do nothing" Congress and surging dramatically to victory in the very last days of the campaign. Perhaps the year's most enduring political image was a photograph of a grinning, victorious Truman holding up the morning edition of the *Chicago Tribune*, which had prematurely run a headline reading, "Dewey Beats Truman."[1]

The interfaith, interracial group of men and women who were concerned about fair employment practices (FEP) had better reason than most liberals to think that the moment for genuine, widespread change had arrived. "The recent elections have evoked a great deal of optimism" among Americans concerned about civil rights, wrote Gilbert Gordon, a Chicago-based attorney for the American Jewish Congress (AJC). For much of the fall, Truman had spoken out strongly on behalf of civil rights, motivated primarily by his reelection strategy. One of his most trusted advisors, Clark Clifford, had recognized that African Americans formed a sufficiently large bloc of voters in battleground states—particularly New York, New Jersey, Pennsylvania, Ohio, Michigan, and Illinois—that it would be advisable for the president to take a strong, public stand on civil rights in order to secure their votes. Over the course of the campaign, Truman heeded Clifford's advice, promoting his historic civil rights report in a message to Congress, issuing an executive order that outlawed discrimination in federal employment, and making civil rights part of his October stump speech. Truman barely won the race, of course, and many observers at the time concluded that his slender margin of victory was provided by his dominance over Dewey in the black neighborhoods of Chicago, Cleveland, Detroit, Harlem, Los Angeles, Philadelphia, and St. Louis. Now the president was returning to office after a year of making campaign promises, and Congress had gone over to Democratic hands. Strong rhetoric did not always mean strong action, and progress was no certainty, but change seemed in the cards. Much of the nation seemed poised to take a major step forward on civil rights.[2]

The political situation in the states seemed even more promising in 1949. It had not taken long for other states to follow in the footsteps of New York. Its mid-Atlantic neighbor, New Jersey, passed legislation only months after Ives-Quinn was signed into law. In 1946, Massachusetts became the first FEP state in New England. Liberals had actually sought a law in Massachusetts a year earlier, but they had neglected to cultivate support from legislators outside of the Boston area, and the mistake proved fatal. When they tried again in 1946, liberals found themselves once more opposed by the Associated Industries of Massachusetts, the Boston Chamber of Commerce, the real estate boards, and the conservative legislators allied with them. Conservatives cited a litany of reasons for their opposition. Some wondered, unjustifiably, whether it would stand judicial scrutiny. "Let's send it to the Supreme Court and see if it's constitutional," they suggested. Others professed general support for the FEPC but expressed dislike for "*this* bill." Still others were reduced simply to pleading that their opposition to the bill should not be interpreted as support for intolerance and segregation. "Some of my best friends are Negroes and Jews," pleaded one legislator to the sound of laughter in the chamber.[3]

Massachusetts liberals nevertheless prevailed in 1946, drawing on the same repertoire of tactics that had yielded success in New York. A grassroots bloc of African Americans, Jews, Catholics, and members of the Congress of Industrial Organizations (CIO) rallied behind the bill, working with lawmakers representing urban districts—primarily Democrats but also liberal Republicans. When the bill was under consideration by the lower chamber, three hundred delegates reportedly visited the Massachusetts statehouse, buttonholing uncertain legislators and lobbying the President of the Senate and Speaker of the House, both Republicans. Liberals wrote scores of letters, formed numerous delegations, met with key lawmakers, and packed the galleries at legislative hearings. Lawmakers were sharply divided by party, but opponents began slowly to concede. The bill eventually cleared the house by a vote of 164–59. Weeks later, the Senate voted to pass it 22–11. Democratic governor Maurice Tobin signed the bill on May 23 to great pomp and circumstance, with more than 100 legislators and organizational representatives present at the ceremony. The stirring success in Massachusetts drew accolades from liberals elsewhere, and it would inspire nearby Connecticut to pass an FEP law in the following year. Congress may have proven difficult terrain, but when Truman began his second term, "freedom from discrimination" found itself on the march through the state legislatures of the urban North, Midwest, and West.[4]

If fair employment practices were a focal point for the congressional politics of civil rights in the late 1940s, state legislatures outside the South were a focal point of the struggle for fair employment practices. Political

pragmatism figured prominently behind the choice of venue. With an obstructionist group of southern Democrats and conservative Republicans
showing no sign of letting up in Congress, success seemed easier to achieve
in the states. "Balked in their effort to enact any type of Federal civil rights
law," admitted the AJC's Will Maslow, "proponents of such measures
have been giving increased attention to state legislatures." The move had
clearly paid off in New York State. Yet there was also a larger strategic
vision that many liberals had in mind. The basic institution was simple:
Victory in the states could lead to victory in Congress. In the words of
one official from the National Association for the Advancement of Colored People (NAACP), "Congressmen will be much more kindly inclined
toward a Federal permanent fair employment practices bill if their own
state adopts such a measure." Others agreed with the judgment. "As each
additional state takes such action," wrote one of Adlai Stevenson's associates, "we move ever closer to a nation-wide endorsement of FEPC." A
similar thought occurred to Sen. Irving M. Ives (R-NY), who told delegates to the National Emergency Civil Rights Mobilization in 1950 to
pursue the "fight for FEPC in the states because for every success in the
states we pick up more support in Congress." By 1964, twenty-nine states
had passed FEP bills of one kind or another, and Congress finally moved
to outlaw job discrimination in Title VII of the Civil Rights Act. It would
seem that the federated strategy had succeeded.[5]

In truth, however, the campaign for state legislation proved far from
easy. In his classic study of national policy, Hugh Davis Graham writes
that state FEP laws had "swept the northern half of the country" by 1963.
But the truth is that the states did not all pass FEP laws at once. Sidney
Fine's pioneering chronicle of Michigan's struggle reveals years of determined obstruction by business-friendly GOP legislators who hailed from
rural districts. A similar alliance kept Pennsylvania liberals from quickly
winning a law in the Keystone State, as revealed by Eric L. Smith, Kenneth
C. Wolensky, and James Wolfinger. The states may have been the laboratories of democracy, but not all laboratories proved equally willing to
experiment with FEP legislation. In fact, some of the most populous and
politically important states in the country—among them Pennsylvania,
Ohio, and California—did not pass enforceable FEP laws until many
years after New York (table 4.1). In perhaps the most surprising development, Illinois did not pass an FEP law until 1961, three years before Congress finally passed the Civil Rights Act. It was ironic. African Americans
in the "Land of Lincoln" began to receive serious government protection
from job discrimination only three years before their counterparts in
apartheid Mississippi. The point was not lost on liberals themselves,
though it may have escaped the notice of subsequent historians. As the
Truman years drew to a close, advocates of state FEPC slowly came to
realize that their earliest successes would prove difficult to duplicate right

TABLE 4.1
State FEP Laws, 1945–1964

Year	State(s)	Annual frequency	Cumulative frequency
1945	New York, New Jersey	2	2
1946	Massachusetts	1	3
1947	Connecticut	1	4
1948			
1949	New Mexico, Oregon, Rhode Island, Washington	4	8
1950			
1951			
1952			
1953	Alaska	1	9
1954			
1955	Michigan, Minnesota, Pennsylvania	3	12
1956			
1957	Wisconsin,[a] Colorado	2	14
1958			
1959	California, Ohio	2	16
1960	Delaware[b]	1	17
1961	Idaho,[b] Illinois, Kansas, Missouri	4	21
1962			
1963	Vermont,[b] Indiana,[a] Iowa,[b] Hawaii	4	25
1964			
Total		25	25

[a] preexisting commission given administrative enforcement powers in the form of cease-and-desist authority

[b] civil or penal enforcement

Notes: Following V. O. Key, I define the South as the eleven states once making up the former Confederacy. States altogether failing to pass fair employment practice laws before Congressional passage of the 1964 Civil Rights Act include Arizona, Kentucky, Louisiana, Maine, Maryland, Montana, Nebraska, New Hampshire, North Dakota, South Dakota, Utah, and Wyoming. No southern state (Alabama, Arkansas, Florida, Georgia, Louisiana, Mississippi, North Carolina, South Carolina, Tennessee, Texas, and Virginia) passed an FEP law. States passing nonenforceable FEP laws include Wisconsin in 1945, Indiana in 1961, Nevada in 1961, West Virginia in 1961, and Oklahoma in 1963.

Sources: Civil Rights Act of 1964 (Washington, DC: Bureau of National Affairs, 1964), 57; *State Fair Employment Laws and Their Administration* (Washington, DC: Bureau of National Affairs 1964), 66–67, 93, 257; Duane Lockard, *Toward Equal Opportunity* (New York: Macmillan, 1968), 24.

away. There were no southern Democrats in Springfield, Sacramento, Lansing, Harrisburg, or Columbus, but liberals found themselves unable to extend "freedom from discrimination" just the same.[6]

Observant southerners took eager notice of legislative failures in the North and wasted few opportunities to paint them with the broadest possible brush. When an FEP bill failed the Illinois legislature in 1949, editors at the *Shreveport Times* drew a predictably sweeping conclusion, inter-

preting the defeat as evidence that northerners had come to the same realization about the futility of using laws to promote social change. "It is
not the south alone that realizes that the racial problem cannot be solved
by punitive legislation."[7]

The reasons for the consistent inability of certain states to pass FEP
laws, however, were much more precise, and no single factor was more
consistently important than the opposition of the conservative bloc whose
political influence had only been glimpsed Washington, D.C., and Albany.
The conservative bloc would prove even more visible and influential elsewhere in the country—and particularly in state legislatures outside the
South. At times, it was clear that conservatives enjoyed a dominant position in nearly all aspects of the policy-making process. Especially in the
immediate postwar years, public opinion was often set against the passage
of FEP laws in many states, and legislatures were stacked with Republican
lawmakers, many of them elected from conservative, noncompetitive,
rural, districts. Naturally, liberals found it difficult to move their agenda
forward. For instance, when liberals put an FEP proposal to a statewide referendum in Truman-era California, massive opposition from
Republican voters doomed it to defeat. When liberals turned to the legislative process, they found themselves unable to extract their bills from
Republican-dominated committees. Despite their best efforts, liberal fortunes improved only slowly. Even when public opinion began to tilt in a
more liberal direction in late 1940s, organized business successfully
prevailed upon conservative legislators in many states—most of them
Republicans—to block and obstruct FEP laws. As a result, numerous proposals continued to die in Republican-controlled committees throughout
the 1950s. By the end of the Eisenhower years, liberals found that conservative resistance had effectively short-circuited their federated strategy.
State action had been a virtual impossibility in the South. Elsewhere, it
had not been impossible. It had only been *untimely.* Most states did eventually take legislative action, but too late to generate the broader momentum
that liberals had sought. Liberals put up a valiant fight for FEP legislation
in the states, but despite their early successes, they lost out to a determined
foe that enjoyed major political and institutional advantages at key moments. Freedom from discrimination would have to wait for national action until the 1960s, when the mobilization of the civil rights movement
helped liberals break through the walls of political inertia.[8]

The prospects of a liberal victory, of course, were still very much in flux
during the 1940s, when almost every industrial state witnessed the efflo-
rescence of a broad-based campaign for state FEP legislation. As in national politics, liberals who were active in state politics were a diverse lot,
but they were united primarily by the common conviction that government could and should ensure equal treatment in the labor market

through legislative means. Not surprisingly, liberals were also brought together out of a definite sense of self-interest. Core members of the liberal bloc included many of the racial and religious minorities who had a clear social and economic stake in the passage and successful operation of an FEP law. They were represented in the larger policy-making process by local and state affiliates of such groups as the NAACP and the National Urban League (NUL), as well as affiliates of religious organizations like the AJC and the Catholic Interracial Council (CIC). Also involved, though perhaps to a lesser extent, were the Japanese American Citizens League (JACL) and the Federal Council of Churches (FCC), which would later merge with other groups to form the National Council of Churches (NCC) in 1950. Local unions associated with the CIO formed a vital source of people, ideas, connections, and money in the campaign for state FEP laws. In contrast to the craft-oriented unions associated with the American Federation of Labor (AFL), CIO-affiliated locals—of auto-workers, steelworkers, or meatpackers, for instance—were based primarily in mass-production industries and organized workers at every skill level, including the racial, ethnic, and religious minorities who tended to occupy the least-skilled positions in the labor market. Though there was certainly variation from local to local, CIO unions were more consistently supportive of FEP legislation than AFL unions. A prominent exception to AFL's lukewarm support for FEP was Randolph's AFL-affiliated Brotherhood of Sleeping Car Porters (BSCP). Rounding out the liberal bloc typically were state or local affiliates of the ACLU and Americans for Democratic Action (ADA). It was an enormously diverse group.[9]

To coordinate their efforts, liberals formed an array of umbrella organizations at the statewide level. Financed and staffed by their constituent groups, such committees were essentially the state-level counterparts of the National Council for a Permanent FEPC (NC) in the 1940s and the Leadership Conference on Civil Rights (LCCR) in the 1950s and 1960s. Among the more nationally visible organizations were the California Committee for Fair Employment Practices (CCFEP), the Illinois Fair Employment Practice Committee (IFEPC), the Minnesota Council for Fair Employment on Merit (MCFEM), and the State Council for a Pennsylvania FEPC.

Such committees were extremely active in state politics and deployed a range of tactics in their legislative campaigns, depending on the political circumstances. When it seemed that too few people knew or cared about FEPC, or when it seemed that misunderstanding of the issue was running high, liberal groups focused on raising awareness among voters and lawmakers, as the Colorado Committee for Equal Employment Opportunities (CCEEO) did in 1951. Led by Joseph E. Cook, it launched a massive educational program that included the distribution of more than ten thousand promotional pamphlets, articles, and brochures—some aimed at a general audience and others targeted at special groups such as businessmen, Catholics, and Protestants. When legislators seemed insufficiently impressed by the level of public interest, liberals organized delegations of community leaders for statehouse visits, often timing their trip to coincide with key legislative developments. In 1951 and then again in 1953, California liberals mobilized themselves to pack the galleries during legislature hearings. In 1953, C. L. Dellums and the California Committee for Fair Employment Practices (CCFEP) succeeded in bringing over five hundred delegates to Sacramento in a high-profile, statewide mobilization. The statewide organization in Ohio, though it was perhaps better organized than most groups, was typical in the wide range of tools that it used in its lobbying. Named the Ohio Committee for Fair Employment Practices (OCFEP), it was founded in 1948 by local affiliates of the NAACP, NUL, Community Relations Board, National Council of Jewish Women, and other liberal groups. It ran a highly sophisticated operation under the leadership of Theodore M. Berry, Cincinnati city councilman and NAACP official. The OCFEP tried everything it could to pass an FEP law in Ohio. Like other committees, it developed a program of public education that included the distribution of informational pamphlets and period newsletters with updates on the latest legislative developments in Columbus. It mounted a highly aggressive lobbying operation, encouraging sympathetic voters to write their local representatives and forming delegations to visit with lawmakers. The OCFEP also understood the value of the stick, seeking to unseat legislators who had demonstrated hostility toward FEP proposals. It was not for want of effort or skill that Ohio liberals—or liberals elsewhere—failed in their early efforts to pass FEP laws.[10]

The initial hurdle faced by liberal groups like the OCFEP, particularly at the outset of the postwar period, was the general conservatism of the mass electorate. There were clearly a number of moments when majorities of voters in certain states felt uneasy at the thought of outlawing discrimination and establishing a state agency to enforce the law. If the battle for congressional legislation was constrained at times by the policy preferences of voters active in national politics, then public sentiment also placed limits on the passage of state laws—and restricted the set of strategic options that political elites could consider pursuing. In 1945, when respondents in a Gallup Poll were asked whether they favored or opposed a law in their own state that would "require employers to hire a person if he is qualified for the job regardless of his race or color," only 43 percent said they favored such a law. The opposition was concentrated primarily in the South, but it was not wholly restricted to it. In fact, public sentiment about state FEP laws also varied considerably outside of the South, and there is some elementary evidence that the level of support for FEP legislation in a particular state was associated with how early it passed. When the level of public support for FEP legislation in 1945 is plotted against the eventual year of passage for each state, it yields a clear pattern. States where public opinion was favorable toward state FEP laws in 1945 tended to pass such laws earlier than states where public opinion was less favorable (figure 4.1). For example, New York and Massachusetts were states in which FEP laws were popular during the wartime years, and both of them were pioneers of state legislation. By contrast, wartime support for FEP was lower in Minnesota and Illinois, and they did not pass their FEP laws until 1955 and 1961, respectively. Indeed, few states experienced the early passage of FEP legislation if it seemed that the mass electorate was clearly opposed to it. For instance, California passed an FEP law only in 1959, when a slim majority of the respondents in the California Poll— just 51 percent—concurred with the statement that "[n]o one should be refused a job because of his race, color, or religion—and there should be a law to this effect." As liberals sought to take the campaign for "freedom from discrimination" to other states, they found public opinion to be a definite brake on their progress.[11]

But a favorable climate of public opinion did not guarantee the early passage of FEP legislation. For instance, FEP legislation was not a popular cause in the state of Minnesota through the first months of 1949. Opinion surveys in *Minnesota Tribune's* Minnesota Poll indicated that a majority of residents there did not support the enactment of an FEP law. Over the course of the year, however, Minnesotans began to change their mind in substantial numbers. Governor Luther W. Youngdahl, a liberal Republican in Dewey's mold, campaigned mightily for FEP legislation. Truman's civil rights program made civil rights one of the most salient issues in domestic politics. By 1950, 75 percent of respondents in the Minnesota Poll supported FEP legislation for their state. Public support would remain at the same high level for the next five years, but legislation did not come right away. In fact, it was only in 1955 that Minnesota would pass FEP legislation, years after a clear and sizeable majority had already solidified in support of it. A supportive electorate was not by itself a sufficient condition of passage. It was only a necessary condition.[12]

Why did so many ordinary Americans oppose FEP legislation at the onset of the postwar era? What exactly did they believe? Only the most politically active Americans took the time to convey their policy preferences in writing to their elective representatives, and it is difficult to know whether and what the "average" American thought of FEP laws, but constituent letters are nevertheless enormously revealing. The most common rationale for opposition was a deep-seated skepticism that

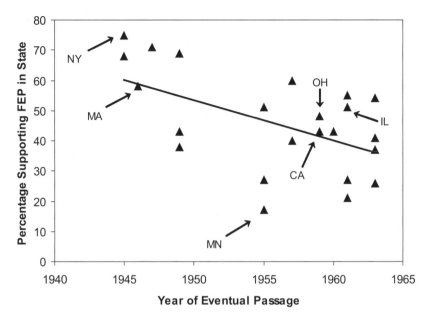

Figure 4.1 Public support in the states for state-level FEP laws (c. 1945) by year of eventual passage. *Note*: Each point on the chart represents a state. The downward-sloping dotted line summarizes the overall pattern of the scatterplot, and it indicates a negative association. In a very rudimentary sense, states where public support was low in 1945 took longer to pass FEP legislation than states where public support was high. *Source*: Gallup Poll, 1945. See the appendix for more.

government intervention could effectively promote social change. Conservatives defined the problem of racial inequality in psychological or moral terms and believed that it was simply impossible for government to do anything of lasting value. "You can't legislate an individual's thinking or feeling," wrote a resident of Rockford, Ill., to his state representative. Individual beliefs were simply beyond the reach of any government policy or program. Only people themselves could change what they believed. A resident of Chicago echoed the same sentiment; it was "impossible to legislate brotherly love." As many of his fellow conservatives were wont to do, he gestured to the Volstead Act as proof by example: "[P]rohibition did the cause of temperance no good." Others argued that passing laws to control social and moral behavior was not impossible but still very difficult. Either it would backfire, or it would be nonsensical. One Rockford resident mocked a provision of a proposed FEP law that excluded agricultural and domestic workers from coverage. It simply made no sense to him. "It is, apparently, permitted for me to advertise for a Swedish or Negro cook or for Mexican or Jewish farm hands, but judged to be bad if I express a preference for a Jewish girl secretary, a Gentile salesman, or a colored janitor."[13]

An equally common objection came in the form of the claim that state FEP laws were merely a tool used by special interests to seize more than their fair share of the economic pie. The average American did not benefit from such laws. The only beneficiaries were corrupt, big-city political interests—unions, ethnics, Catholics, Jews, and blacks—who were brazenly willing to throw around their political clout to win special treatment for themselves. To many conservative letter-writers, it was no accident that FEP attracted the most "vociferous support from do-good organizations, socialists, communists." They were willing to exploit "large numbers of people resentful of their station in life." In contrast, a silent majority of decent Americans did not have the time to shamelessly lobby on their own behalf. The "great majority make little noise," wrote one such person, as "they are too busy working." The law seemed to be motivated by good intentions, and that is why it was popular among some well-meaning segments of the population, but everyone knew that good intentions often led to perverse outcomes. "We are all acquainted with the proverbial road to hell," this same person concluded.[14]

Among key numbers of conservatives, accusations of special treatment appear to have been motivated by various degrees of racial animus. The most prejudiced among them did not even bother to conceal their racism. Wrote one resident of Peoria, "To compel white people to work with and associate with niggers, will [sic] cause an untold amount of trouble." After hearing a radio broadcast in which Adlai Stevenson endorsed FEP legislation, a resident of Chicago and self-proclaimed Democrat wrote him angrily to let him know that "we white people do not want the fair employment bill passed to force us to hire people we do not want." This man saw fit to explain himself. "We do not like negroes is [sic] many reasons." They "steal," they are "noisy," and the "body odor they have is so bad in the hot weather one gets sick working by them." A resident from Los Angeles, complaining that the strongest "fumigation" could not cleanse a house she had rented out to black tenants, argued that a state FEP law could constitute a gross infringement against the freedom of association that rightfully belonged to every white Californian. It violated "[t]heir rights to live and work with people they wish to have in their homes and work shops." Such conservatives claimed that the only reason why their genuine opposition had gone unnoticed by politicians and government officials is that they were too busy doing their jobs, making a living, and supporting their families. "Thousands of people would come to Sacramento to speak against this Bill if they could get away from work," one Californian wrote. Most white Californians were also too decent to plead on their own behalf, preferring to soldier on bravely in the face of adversity rather than look to someone else to solve their problems. Most whites still had their dignity and self-respect. "I know thousands of white folks that are liveing [*sic*] just as poorly [*sic*] now as there [*sic*] negroes or other nationalities. But they figure [*sic*] this wont [*sic*] last and are just putting up with things." Other conservatives couched their objections in concerns about "social equality." A resident of Rockford sought to cast the law as a backdoor attempt to impose social equality. There were plenty of laws on the books already. Let us not, he said, pass additional laws to "enforce on everybody the obligation to accept [everyone] as social equals." There was no plausible basis for such legislation. "[Y]ou should not be required to employ a negro private secretary any more than you would be obliged to take in the same percentage of negro guests in your home that you do of white folks in the course of a year."[15]

Though it was less common than antiblack animus, anti-Semitism fueled the opposition of other conservatives. One resident of North Hollywood wrote to tell Gov. Earl Warren that there was no point to FEP legislation, unless the objective was to harass members of the racial and religious majority. "What can you hope to accomplish? Persecution of majority groups?" The woman had written Warren because Democratic politics had been drifting too far left for her taste, and she felt that only Republicans could be trusted to resist the trend. "It might interest you to know that I am a Democrat who voted for you, and other Republicans because I am sick to death of 'leftish' influences in our party." The woman left no doubt about who she meant. "Jews are Jews first—and Americans second. Do they need special consideration?" A wartime pamphlet circulated in Illinois called for readers to "Help Save America for Americans" and urged the defeat of S.B. 254 and H.B. 353, FEP bills that were "sponsored by Jews and Jewish Organizations." The bills, it said, were an "attempted LEGALIZED JEWISH CONSPIRACY to force employers to employ JEWS and JEW REFUGEES."[16]

The deep sense of aggrievement that FEP laws triggered among some conservatives was tinged with class resentment. In a letter insinuating that an FEP law would lead to "proportionate" representation of racial groups in employment, one resident of Evanston asked Adlai Stevenson to exclude Catholicism as a protected category. "If you persist in agitating for this socialist FEPC legislation," she wrote, "for goodness sake leave us Catholics out of it." She conceded that certain Catholics were prominent backers of FEPC. But she argued that regular Catholics were not. "The only Catholics who favor such legislation are the clergy, who are more religious than practical." Similar feelings infused the observations of another Evanston resident. Most supporters of FEPC lead charmed lives, she suggested. They did not have to bear the brunt of racial integration themselves, and it was easy for them to support social change when no self-sacrifice would be required of them. In her words, "[T]he only people I know who are for FEPC are members of the League of Women Voters who do no have to go out to work for a living, and are not directly affected by it." A resident of Rockford made a similar case. "[T]he committee in this area sponsoring this bill are almost all professional people, few of them having real employment experience or responsibilities. It does seem to me [as] though these lawyers, doctors, ministers, social workers, teachers, and politicians have found a way to exclude their own professions from the bill while fixing compulsion upon other types of employers."[17]

Many politically engaged Americans in the 1940s might have felt uneasy about supporting FEP legislation in the states, even outside the South, but some types of Americans were more apprehensive than others. Perhaps most pertinent to legislative politics were the partisan divisions. A breakdown of the raw data from the Gallup Poll in 1945 indicates that FDR voters were eleven percentage points more likely to support state FEP laws than Dewey voters. A statistical analysis of the data supports the same general inference (see table A.6). On average, Republican voters were less supportive of state FEP laws than Democratic voters. It was not only the Empire State where Republicans felt strongly opposed to the passage of FEP laws. Their counterparts in other states outside the South tended to feel the same way.[18]

Voters had a rare chance to act decisively on their convictions in the general election of 1946, when Californians voted on a statewide referendum known as Proposition 11. As it was worded, Proposition 11 declared it "unlawful to refuse to hire, to discharge, or discriminate in conditions of employment against any person because of race, religion, color, national origin, or ancestry." It also provided for the establishment of a strong state agency to enforce the law. Liberals had decided in early 1946 to put FEP on the ballot after a Republican-controlled committee buried an FEP bill sponsored by Augustus F. Hawkins (D-Los Angeles). The defeat had convinced Hawkins and his allies that the legislature was too deeply in the thrall of "selfish groups" and their "puppets" for fair employment practices to prevail. It was the second time in as many legislative sessions that one of his FEP measures had been quashed. Hoping that the Assembly would pass a law was like believing in Santa Claus, quipped Hawkins. The only option was to take freedom from discrimination to the people themselves, since the legislative process was broken. Still, getting a referendum on the ballot was no sure thing. It took months of grass-roots work to gather enough signatures to qualify Proposition 11 for the ballot. The response was encouraging. Led by numerous branches of the NAACP, a selection of CIO- and AFL-affiliated unions, the League of Women Voters, the Catholic Interracial Council (CIC), the *California Eagle*, and the *Los Angeles Sentinel*, thousands of Californians turned out to lend their support to the drive. At one point, more than one thousand people in San Francisco, San Diego, and Los Angeles were volunteering to collect signatures. By summer, nearly two hundred thousand valid signatures had been obtained. Californians would have a chance to decide the nature of their commitment to civil rights in the most direct manner possible in American democracy.[19]

It was precisely then that the fight over Proposition 11 turned truly ugly. Liberals had demonstrated some ability to realize their convictions, and now the battle would be joined. The rhetoric of the opposition was every bit as harsh and vicious as it had been in New York a year earlier. As revealed by Kevin Allen Leonard in his study of wartime Los Angeles, a mysterious group calling itself the "Committee for Tolerance" spearheaded the charge. According to a CIO periodical, it was financed by the state chamber of commerce, although the committee curiously spent a great deal of time directing its propaganda at workers. One pamphlet prophesied a totalitarian nightmare if Proposition 11 passed: "[Y]ou might lose your job at the whim of appointed commissioners forcing another person into your place." What was worse, according to the pamphlet, is that "anyone believing himself held back by his color, his race, his religion, his national origin, or his ancestry need only complain." The commission could "force him into your job." The committee was far from alone in trying to foment reaction against civil rights among the mass public. It had equally committed allies in the legislature. Two weeks before Election Day, a rabidly anticommunist state senator, Jack B. Tenney, went on a statewide radio broadcast to denounce Proposition 11 as little more than a communist plot. Tenney charged that "minority groups" had been duped by an "atheistic, totalitarian, foreign ideology." As far as he was concerned, backers of Proposition 11 were committing a crime by "raising the flames of hope in innocent and uninformed people" and whipping them into a "rising fury of racial and religious frictions and antagonisms."[20]

The state CIO was admittedly prone to blaming its long-time enemy for almost every conceivable problem, but it was correct to identify business as the primary source of opposition to Proposition 11. Scarcely a month after it had become clear that the referendum would be on the November ballot, representatives of numerous business groups met in Los Angeles to begin planning their opposition. Among the most aggressive and organized was the California Chamber of Commerce (CCC). At a meeting in September, all six Regional Councils of the chamber—plus the statewide Industrial Committee—unanimously recommended opposition to Proposition 11. In justifying their recommendation to the Board of Directors, the committee invoked a range of criticisms that would have been familiar to big-business, small-government conservatives elsewhere across the country. It was "not possible to legislate prejudice and intoler-ance out of people." Proposition 11 was aimed at the "wrong parties—that is, at the employer" rather than the workers "whose prejudices actu-ally cause unfair employment practices." It would lead to the "needless harassment" of employers and the "destruction of certain constitutional rights." Finally, it would have the effect of "increasing rather than de-creasing discrimination." The recommendation was approved by the board—which paused only to applaud educational efforts against dis-crimination—and then operatives of the chamber snapped quickly into action. Frank P. Doherty, a director, was authorized to run the Southern California campaign; he was the main force behind the Committee for Tolerance. Ray Wiser was his counterpart in Northern California. It was customary for the chamber to distribute a list of recommended votes on ballot propositions, but Doherty and Wiser took the additional step of developing and disseminating "special literature against F.E.P.C." It was a massive effort. More than fifty thousand special folders of informational material were assembled and distributed. Billboards were taken out across the state. Endorsements were solicited, and speeches were made at dozens of community meetings. Doherty sent out fifteen thousand copies of a letter warning recipients that Proposition 11 was a communist-inspired proposal. It would create an "unfair law" that "pretends to pro-mote tolerance and good will" but would instead "arouse intolerance, disunity, and hatred." Weeks later, citing the support of farmers, clergy, and twenty-eight chambers of commerce, he would call the proposition "the most dangerous threat to individual rights and the unity of our peo-ple ever placed on the California ballot." It was a suitably hyperbolic charge, but Doherty was hardly the only representative of organized busi-ness to speak out in such exaggerated terms against Proposition 11. The roster of opponents would soon grow to include Employers' Councils in San Jose, Sacramento, and Stockton, as well as the United Employers of Oakland and San Francisco Employers' Council. As the election drew near, other groups that had been content to let Doherty take flak for his public stance came into full view themselves. Directors at the California Retailers' Association voted to oppose Proposition 11 on the grounds that it would "not do the job it is supposed to do" and "will in fact create chaos and discontent." Officials and local affiliates of the California Farm Bureau publicly denied that California farmers ever discriminated against workers on account of race and roundly denounced the initiative. A vice president of the group called it "unwholesome and un-American," a poi-sonous device promoted by the "same professional radicals who agitate day and night for disunity, chaos, and confusion." On the Sunday before Election Day, opponents delivered something akin to a coup de grâce.

Three radio stations in Southern California rebroadcast Tenney's earlier broadside: KNX at 11:15 a.m., KFWB at 7:00 p.m., and KMPC at 7:30 p.m. A prominent ad for the broadcasts was featured in the *Los Angeles Times* amidst other ads for political programs. It would been hard for even the casual reader to miss the screaming headline: "Don't Be Misled! Hear the Facts on Proposition #11."[21]

It was more than coincidence that Tenney and the sponsors of his broadcast would have advertised in the *Los Angeles Times*. Before the early 1960s, when his son Otis began to remake the entire operation, few papers were less impartial and nonpartisan than Norman Chandler's *Times*. It rarely endorsed Democratic candidates for office, and it offered only the skimpiest coverage of their campaigns. True to form, it carried articles that were primarily—and even only—critical of Proposition 11. As the opposition campaign got underway in July, political editor Kyle Palmer, who did little to hide his Republican leanings, unleashed a tirade against the referendum. According to him, nothing imaginable was a bigger threat to free enterprise and the rule of law. Proposition 11 "contemplates a surrender of rights which are basic in the structure of the American system." Its abolition of the jury system, he railed, represents a "calculated step toward totalitarianism." The commission is at once "investigator, jury, and judge," and hearings "would not be bound by usual rules of evidence." The greatest irony, in his mind, was that the sacrifice of so many fundamental American principles would not even bring the desired benefits. "Enactment of the proposed FEPC," Palmer concluded, "would set no man or woman free, but will place shackles on human feelings, emotions, sympathies, susceptibilities, instincts, liberties." Days before the election, Palmer's views were seconded by the editorial board of the *Times*, which ran a piece entitled "Promotion of Race Prejudice." The *Times* was not alone among California newspapers for having misgivings. Voter guides published in the *San Francisco Chronicle*, *Oakland Tribune*, *Fresno Bee*, and *Sacramento Bee* were also advising readers to vote it down. The *Times* editorial, however, was more comprehensive than the rest of them, hitting all the high notes in the conservative chorus of criticism: Compulsory laws would aggravate and not alleviate the problem. Regulating discrimination, as admirable as it might seem, violated the "precious" tradition that permits private employers to hire, promote, and fire whomever they pleased. Trial by jury would be abolished, and blackmail would inevitably follow. "The most probable result of the act in the hands of ordinary human beings would be the accentuation of prejudice and the disruption of productive industry." According to the *Times*, fair-minded Californians had only one choice on Election Day: "Vote 'No' on Nov. 11."[22]

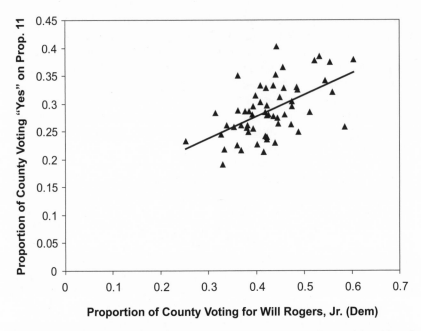

Figure 4.2 California counties by proportion voting "yes" on Proposition 11 and proportion voting for Will Rogers, Jr. (Dem.), in the U.S. Senate election, November 1946. *Note*: Each point represents a county. The upward-sloping line summarizes the overall pattern, and it indicates that counties favoring Rogers were also more likely to support Proposition 11 than counties favoring his opponent, William F. Knowland (Rep.). Source: Anthony S. Chen, Robert Mickey, and Robert Van Houweling, "Backlash Reconsidered: The Political Attitudes and Electoral Behavior of Non-Southern Whites on Civil Rights, 1946–1950," paper presented at the Annual Meetings of the Social Science History Association, Baltimore, Md., 2003. See the appendix for details.

In their most hopeful moments, liberals might have let themselves believe that the criticism was a sign of insecurity on the part of their conservative opponents, but it would have been more accurate to see it as a sign of growing confidence. Retailers and farmers had been reluctant to make their true views known so long as the outcome remained highly uncertain. It was too risky. They could wind up on the record as opposing a new law that would almost be surely wielded against them. That they were growing increasingly willing to speak out publicly in October suggested a shift in their private calculations. Either they had concluded that the contest was close enough that public statements could make a crucial difference. Or they had concluded that Proposition 11 would probably not pass and that there could be no penalty for speaking out. Either way, it did not bode well for liberals.

Siding with employers and other business groups, California voters rejected Proposition 11 by a 2–1 margin. The initiative collected only 675,697 yeas, compared to 1,632,646 nays. Liberals were predictably crushed. Reactions among conservatives were mixed. The *Los Angeles Times* held up the result as a "victory for tolerance, sanity and fair dealing," but the exultant sentiments of one Angeleno, conveyed privately to Earl Warren, seemed to suggest otherwise. His opposition was grounded not only in high-minded ideas about fair play; it was laced with racial prejudice as well. The "overwhelming vote against Proposition 11," he wrote, "means that the people of this state want no action forcing Negroes upon them. It means that the people of California realized overwhelmingly that Negroes simply constitute blight upon an otherwise nearly perfect area."[23]

The enormous margin of victory triggered equally dubious celebrations among other Californians, but what is most notable was the across-the-board opposition that it had attracted among Republican voters. The vote on Proposition 11 was nothing if not highly partisan. Most observers came to the conclusion informally, but their impression is confirmed by a statistical analysis of Proposition 11 (see figure 4.2). In a basic study that estimates the partisan breakdown of the statewide vote for Proposition 11 by using county-level election returns for the proposition and the contest for U.S. Senate, Robert P. Van Houweling, Robert Mickey, and I have calculated that roughly 51 percent of Democrats voted for Proposition 11, compared to 12 percent of Republicans. In a more sophisticated and comprehensive analysis of richer, precinct-level data—utilizing a more robust set of methods—we find evidence supporting the same general inference. Republican voters were much more likely than Democrats to vote against FEP. It is a striking fact. In the one known instance when regular men and women outside the South had a chance to express clearly their own preferences about regulating job discrimination, a large majority of people took a conservative stance, and Republicans led the way.[24]

As the confrontation over California's referendum revealed, conservative voters were not the only group—and certainly not the most powerful group—standing in the way of state FEP laws. When attorney Will Maslow of the AJC surveyed the legislative scene during the war, he did not hesitate to point a finger at the most obvious suspect. "Organized opposition" to state FEP laws, he noted, came primarily from "chambers of commerce and employer associations." A report of the American Council on Race Relations made the same observation five years later: "In state after state, from one year to the next, the focal point of opposition to FEPC has been the organized business and industrial interests."[25]

To be sure, generalizations about business involvement in the policy-making process should be made with caution. The political and legislative organization of business groups varied as much as the makeup and structure of state economies. Some states were thoroughly dominated by a lobby that sought to promote the parochial interests of a single, influential industry or economic sector. Other states witnessed varying degrees of conflict and cooperation among a range of competing lobbies. Most states also played host to a broad, encompassing organization that represented the collective, class-wide interests of all firms involved in private, for-profit enterprise—usually organized around their role as employers. Even these organizations varied in their structure. According to one knowledgeable observer, there were three main types of employers' associations in the postwar period. The two largest associations, located in New Jersey and Pennsylvania, belonged to a category unto themselves. They were heavily member-driven, and each one boasted a roster of over nine thousand companies. The second type was a large, representative association where the executive manager was involved primarily with policy and administrative matters, leaving a substantial staff to carry out recruitment, legislative analysis, lobbying, and other essential affairs. This was the type of organization prevalent in California, Connecticut, Illinois, Indiana, Massachusetts, Missouri, New York, Ohio, and Texas. The third type was the "one-man" association in which there was a central figure in whom the employers of the state placed a high degree of responsibility and trust; he was widely considered their spokesman. All three types of associations were capable of acting effectively, and all of them shared the same goal of creating a favorable "business climate"—by which they meant preventing tax increases, reducing or limiting the growth of regulation, and maximizing government subsidies.[26]

Business groups also varied in their degree of effectiveness, but one characteristic shared by the most consistently successful associations was the ability to keep close and accurate track of legislative developments. They were highly proficient at collecting high-quality political intelligence, especially reliable information on how legislators were planning to cast their votes. They also frequently conducted membership surveys in order to understand what kinds of policies their members preferred and how well their members understood the issues. The most useful findings from the surveys—usually evidence of unanimity—were often trumpeted through press releases. Inconvenient truths about internal divisions were kept quietly confidential. Surveys were also useful because they made it easier to forecast what members would actually do if they were encouraged to become politically active. At the same time that business groups sought to monitor the policy-making process neutrally, they also simultaneously acted as partisans, setting out to influence the policy-making process to maximize benefits and minimize costs for their members. Special reports were commissioned and distributed to educate members about how new or controversial issues might favorably or adversely impact them. The dissemination of periodic legislative advisories not only kept members apprised of key developments in the statehouse, but also provided a useful channel for informing members about recommended courses of action. At key moments, interested members were asked to call or write their local legislators to express their views, and they were encouraged to form delegations if they were especially concerned about a particular issue. Certain legislators were sometimes singled out for special attention because of their unique influence (e.g., committee chair) or uncertainty about which way they would cast their vote. Other legislators were mentioned so that members could thank them for taking agreeable stances. In all of this, members were advised to act privately in order to protect them from unflattering public scrutiny. The facilitation of private political action was, after all, one of the basic motivations behind the establishment of a statewide association. "It is not good public relations for an individual company to appear" at a public hearing, noted one lobbyist. It could put off clients or customers who held different views. Instead, the association should take a public stand, serving as a lighting rod for whatever criticism emerged, while the heads of individual companies could take their case to legislators more quietly, working toward the same end without incurring the same costs.[27]

Despite the variation in their structure of organization and level of effectiveness, most business associations ran a fairly strong lobbying operation. When it came to state FEP legislation, overwhelming numbers of them decided as a matter of policy to throw their clout behind the opposition. To put it simply, organized business was the financial and political nucleus of the conservative bloc. With the exception of right-to-work laws, few other types of legislation evoked so much antipathy during the postwar period. Maslow and other liberals were not exaggerating when they lamented the consistent ferocity of business opposition. In nearly every state, across nearly every sector of the economy, business groups mobilized collectively against state FEP laws, almost always with a formal stamp of approval from their board of directors. In the battle over Ives-Quinn in New York State, organized business was led by Associated Industries of New York State (AINYS), whose membership included affiliates, divisions, or subsidiaries of such blue-chip companies as General Motors, IBM, and Pfizer. Other business opponents of Ives-Quinn also included merchants, banks, retailers, and the corporate bar. The business community in California was led by the self-proclaimed "spokesmen for business," the California Chamber of Commerce (CCC), whose board of directors comprised top executives from powerful companies such as

Bank of America, North American Aviation, Pacific Gas and Electric, Pacific Mutual Life Insurance, Robinson's, S&W Fine Foods, Sunkist Growers, Southern California Edison, Southern Pacific Company, and the Standard Oil Corporation of California. In the years after their defeat of Proposition 11, CCC directors routinely voted to oppose FEP legislation. An archetypal policy was hammered out in 1946, when the board condemned FEP legislation at "all levels of government" on the grounds that it would "accentuate racial prejudice" in industrial relations. The policy formally declared support for the "principle that there should be no discrimination in employment" but insisted that discrimination could only be eradicated through "cooperative educational efforts on the part of labor, management, and the government." Numerous smaller firms joined the CCC in opposition, and their efforts were coordinated by groups such as the Merchants' and Manufacturers' Association, the Associated Farmers, the San Francisco and Oakland Chambers of Commerce, and the San Francisco Retail Council.[28]

The same general pattern of opposition was evident throughout the industrial Midwest as well. Along with the Illinois Chamber of Commerce, two other groups formed the core of opposition forces in Illinois. One was the statewide Illinois Manufacturers' Association (IMA), which represented a spectrum of industrial concerns. Its membership was drawn from throughout the state but included a substantial fraction of the small and medium-sized firms based outside of Chicago. The senior leadership of the IMA included top executives from Armour and Company, Caterpillar Tractor, Morton Salt Company, Pullman Incorporated, Standard Oil of Indiana (Amoco), and U.S. Steel. There could be doubt about their policy preferences. Beginning in 1945, in one legislative session after the other, IMA directors committed their staff to opposing the passage of FEP laws, which they considered "impractical" legislation that would "seriously interfere" with business and "promote unnecessary strife and dissension." In doing so, they set into motion one of the most impressive lobbying operations in state politics. The IMA assiduously tracked the progress of FEP bills through a prosaically entitled weekly bulletin, *State Legislation*. In it, IMA staffers noted the result of roll-call votes, highlighted IMA statements at public hearings, exhorted members to contact their local legislators, and showered them with primers on political action. The other key business group in Illinois ran a smaller lobbying operation but rivaled the IMA in political and economic influence. Formed by top Chicago-based companies, the Chicago Association of Commerce and Industry (CACI) boasted an impressive roster of members, including American Airlines, First National Bank of Chicago, Inland Steel, Marshall Field, Sears, United Airlines, Westinghouse Electric, and Western Union. Its board of directors likewise voted repeatedly to oppose state legislation.

The principle of nondiscrimination deserved commendation, they conceded in 1947, but "morals and ethics cannot be enforced by legislation" and "education and the practice of tolerance offered the best solution."[29]

The political activity of the business community was more centralized in Minnesota, where it was organized largely under the auspices of the Minnesota Employers' Association (MEA), whose political arm was guided for many years by a capable attorney, Otto Christenson. Among the more notable members of the MEA were nationally prominent companies and their affiliates, including General Mills, Northwestern Bell, Coca Cola, and Pillsbury Flour Mill. With the approval of his board in hand, Christenson proved adept year after year at marshalling his limited resources in opposition of state FEP legislation. Through the publication of the *Guidepost*, his biweekly legislative report, he kept MEA members abreast of major developments in St. Paul. Compared to the lawyerly, analytical approach adopted by most legislative advisories, Christenson's *Guidepost* reported on legislative affairs in a personal, plain-spoken style. Throughout the late 1940s and early 1950s, pending FEPC proposals often made the front page, and Christenson exhorted his members to write their legislators. A closing sentence to a 1951 dispatch was typical of his approach: "If it is worth your money to support a Trade Association, if it is worth your money to maintain a state-wide Association of Employers, if it is worth your time to read this letter, then it is worth a few more minutes and a three-cent stamp to let your State Senator hear from you now to urge him to defeat F.E.P.C."[30]

Business groups deployed a variety of tactics in their effort to keep state FEP laws off the books. The most straightforward and public approach entailed sending out a distinguished elder spokesman to speak out against them at legislative hearings. Such spokesmen were always careful to profess their commitment to the principle of racial equality, but only as a prelude to attacking FEPC. The initial criticism was invariably that it was impossible to "legislate tolerance," and the example of Prohibition would usually be offered as supporting evidence. This basic assertion would then be followed by a series of arguments in the alternative. Even if legislating tolerance were possible, discrimination was not very widespread. To the limited extent that discrimination did exist, good progress was being made against discrimination in the absence of a law, and there was every reason to believe that it would soon disappear altogether. Why pass a law when one was simply not necessary? Moreover, success might come at too high a cost. The spokesmen would then usually sketch out a parade of horribles. Further government regulation of employment would undermine the spirit of free enterprise, violate key constitutional and legal rights, destroy the managerial prerogative to hire the most qualified workers, put a crimp on profits, and ultimately encourage companies to go elsewhere in search of more favorable business climates.[31]

In their most imaginative moments, business spokesmen would gesture toward the most terrible consequence of all: Laws against discrimination were counterproductive and could make things horribly worse. Instead of reducing prejudice and discrimination, state FEP laws would exacerbate them. In some cases, such laws might actually create prejudice and discrimination where none previously existed. Christenson made a version of this argument in 1949, when he claimed that an FEP proposal before the Minnesota legislature was "discriminatory in itself." The reason was simple. "It gives the minority special privileges," he wrote, "because only those of the minority will file complaints." A personnel manager at a Minnesota refrigerator company echoed Christenson's line. The law "confers special privileges on special groups." At a 1945 hearing before the Senate Judiciary Committee in Illinois, Charles F. Hough, representing the Associated Employers of Illinois and thirty-seven other business groups, made a similar point. Hough based his opposition on the implication that FEP legislation essentially mandated the preferential treatment of racial and religious minorities. "The point is," he said, "we are all Americans and should be treated equally and should not ask for special privilege because we are representatives or not representatives of any political party, class, religion, creed, race, or color." Not to be outdone, Ray Suter of the Ohio Chamber of Commerce warned at a 1951 hearing in Columbus that a "quota system" would "necessarily eventuate from the passage of FEPC." More than six years after Robert Moses injected the charge of "quotas" into the politics of civil rights, conservatives were still making the same argument in states that had yet to pass FEP legislation.[32]

The public stance of organized business was never fixed. Its rhetoric shifted gradually over time. The harshest language was usually reserved for the time that FEP was still a new issue on the political scene and critical first impressions were still being formed by the mass public. This was the moment when employers would deny or minimize the existence of discrimination and play on the social and economic anxieties of the electorate. It was when employers would predict that an FEP law would trigger a deluge of black migration, incite race riots and pogroms, or wreck the state economy. It was when employers would argue that FEPC would create an uncontrollable government bureaucracy. In the earliest years of the Minnesota campaign, for instance, Christenson took to denouncing FEP legislation as a "police club in the hands of the state." Such a law was a step backward on the slippery slope toward communism. "Any legislation that takes away power from the individual and gives it to the government, instead of taking power away from the government and giving it back to the individual, is a step nearer regimentation or totalitarianism." This was strong stuff. But Christenson moderated his rhetoric over time. By 1955, it was clear from opinion polls that most of the public favored FEPC, and it would do no good to invite any doubts about his credibility by carelessly interjecting hyperbole. In testimony to the Minnesota House Labor Committee, Christenson acknowledged that there are "good arguments on both sides" of the FEP issue. It was a "subject upon which good men differ" with one another. Now he suggested that his main concern was that a state law was simply unnecessary. Minneapolis, St. Paul, and Duluth had all passed municipal FEP ordinances, which covered most of the individuals who were demanding protection from discrimination. Why pass a state law and take an unnecessary risk when municipal laws covered most everyone who required any protection? It was a far cry from his combative, hardball rhetoric from the early years.[33]

Organized business just as willingly worked behind the scenes to influence key votes. One of the clearest instances came in 1953, when business mounted a shrewdly effective campaign against FEP in Ohio. According to Charles P. Lucas, a legislative officer with the OCFEP, things got off to a suspicious start, and liberals should have known that something was up. When a House committee took public testimony on an FEP bill in early April, liberals turned out in substantial numbers to the capitol, and their representatives made a strong presentation. The chairman of the OCFEP, Theodore M. Berry, gave a particularly cogent performance. In a statement packed with well-chosen examples and stylized statistics, he declared that discrimination was "bad business," "bad defense policy," "morally indefensible," and "bad international relations." By contrast, business spokesmen responded with a series of weak statements, quite in contrast to their vitriolic effort in the previous legislative session. When the Ohio Council of Retail Merchants reportedly withdrew their traditional opposition to FEPC, some liberals began to sense the possibility of victory. The shifting-around in the business community was vaguely reminiscent of what had recently occurred in Cleveland. In 1950, after some initial hesitation, Cleveland's city council had passed a strong municipal FEPC ordinance. What preceded the vote was the decision of the Cleveland Chamber of Commerce to drop their opposition and accept FEPC. Now the merchants were pulling out of the state fight, a development that portended a similarly happy outcome. "There is no question," reported the OCFEP's legislative advisory, *News Bulletin*, "that the withdrawal of the merchants from the opponents' camp makes the prospect of passing an Ohio FEP brighter."[34]

The reason for the anemic testimony of organized business, however, soon became obvious. Both the Ohio Chamber of Commerce (OCC) and Ohio Manufacturers' Association (OMA) had apparently decided to avoid a public fight over the bill because they preferred to kill the bill privately, in committee, away from the bad publicity that a floor vote would inevitably bring. When members of the committee returned to their home districts a few weeks later, they were invited to a series of luncheons and dinners, where OCC and OMA representatives tried to convince them that FEP would damage Ohio business. This process of quiet persuasion continued when committee members returned to Columbus. According to the OCFEP's Lucas, on the eve of the vote to report the bill out of committee, all lobbyists of any note—"all the big boys"—were out in force, "doing their job." They "bombarded the members of the committee, talking with them personally, urging their disapproval of all FEP bills." In fact, "right up to the last moment" on the morning of the vote, lobbyists were there "on the scene." They almost got their way. The committee voted to report the bill to the House, but the margin of victory was narrow. A vote that should have turned out 12–2—or 11–4 at the worst—instead squeaked through, 8–7. Of the members voting to report the bill, four were Democrats and four were Republicans. All seven members declining to report the bill were Republicans. Two years earlier, five of them had actually supported a very similar bill, but, as Lucas noted, they "got off the reservation" right before the vote. Even though the vote turned out favorably for his side, Lucas gave his opponents credit for their skill and dedication. "From all of my years in Columbus," he acknowledged, "I want to say that business did one of the most spectacular jobs I have ever seen." The episode foreshadowed the difficulty that FEPC would have for the remainder of the session. The bill passed the House 75–52, just as the OCC and OMA feared it would, but the Senate Commerce and Labor Committee voted against bringing the bill to the floor. It is not entirely clear from the archival record whether the OCC and OMA mounted the same full-court press behind the scenes as they had in the House, but it is hard to imagine that they sat politely on the sidelines. The liberal-leaning *Cleveland Press* certainly did not hesitate to offer an explanation for the adverse decision of the Senate committee: "They voted . . . the way the Ohio Chamber of Commerce and Ohio Manufacturers' Association wanted them to."[35]

Organized business proved politically shrewd in other ways. Understanding the soft spot that most legislators had in their hearts for mom-and-pop businesses, large companies sometimes tried to frame their political associations as the grass-roots organizations of small businessmen. That is what Gilbert Gordon of the AJC suspected at any rate. During the 1945 and 1947 sessions in the Illinois legislature, what was represented as a bottom-up association of small retailers was actually a lobbying operation bankrolled by large Chicago department stories. "The employers used the retailers association as a 'front,'" he insisted. The retailers constantly played up the "burdens [that an FEP law] would place upon the overburdened 'small businessmen.'" But the whole line was disingenuous. "The fact that the retailers association is financed almost totally by the multimillion dollar department store industry centering on State Street in Chicago was never disclosed."[36]

Even the constituent letters that showed up in the mailboxes of elected officials were not always the spontaneous expression of genuine sentiment. Sometimes they had been directly solicited by business groups. This seems to have been the case in 1949, when the Illinois State Chamber of Commerce (ISCC) published and distributed a detailed, twenty-eight page pamphlet that was sent to every member of the chamber as well as to Governor Adlai Stevenson. The pamphlet reported that an FEP bill had been favorably reported to the House, and it importuned members to communicate with their local officials. It offered many reasons to take immediate action, including the fact that the Communist Party might be involved in the promotion of FEPC. A more important reason, however, was the way in which the bill would interfere with the prerogative of employers to hire, promote, and fire whomever they pleased, based on what they thought was best for their business. Any employer, the ISCC went on to say, should be "permitted to hire all Irishmen, all Poles, all Englishmen, all Jews, all Negroes, all Protestants, all Catholics, or all Mennonites, if he wishes to do so." Worse still, legislation could create an overbearing commission such as the one in New York, where the absence of any minority employees at an establishment was regarded as "prima facie" evidence of discrimination, even if no discrimination had ever occurred. This was effectively a quota, insinuated the ISCC. Commissioners in New York strongly rejected quotas, but this inconvenient fact did not stop the ISCC from railing against them: Quotas ran fundamentally against American notions of meritocracy. African Americans should be entitled to as many jobs in a field as they were qualified to hold. Quoting an article in *Life*, authors of the pamphlet asserted that the United States was "almost by definition the land of the individual, not the land of class enclaves or percentage categories." Laws such as FEPC, which promoted the "minority group idea," were decidedly "un-American." FEPC encouraged "organized minorities" to believe "they can receive special consideration from government or from our economic system if they are well enough organized and if they will make enough noise." This was bad enough, but FEP laws threatened the survival of free enterprise itself. "Business is bending under the weight of regulations issued by government bureaus," claimed the ISCC, "and it is so severely handicapped by government interference that businessmen have had great difficulty in performing their main function of creating jobs and producing goods and services." Intolerance and bigotry were definite problems, and "everything possible" should be done to eliminate them. Yet legislating tolerance was simply not possible, for all the reasons that the ISCC had taken great pains to elaborate. Education was the best and only approach.[37]

Some employers apparently took the cue, and the arguments that appeared in their letters paralleled many of the ones made in the ISCC pamphlet. The president of a joint manufacturer in Rockford wrote to Stevenson in April, only a few weeks after the publication of the ISCC pamphlet. Although he blamed the "attitude of the worker" for the problem, he conceded the existence of discrimination and agreed that it was fundamentally wrong. "No fair minded person can quarrel with the elimination of discriminatory practices." The problem with the pending legislation, however, is that it would interfere with the ability of the employer to "judge men to determine which of several potential employees is most capable." This was something that a state or federal agency could never do. Discrimination was "best eliminated by education—through the cooperation and understanding on the part of all concerned, instead of through the medium of force and legislative mandates." A works manager at a machinery and tool manufacturer, also based in Rockford, expressed his "sympathy" with the goal of "eliminating prejudice," but disagreed with legislative method. Though the pending legislation did not force employers to hire anyone, his criticisms were based on the assumption that it did. "You cannot improve the situation by forcing industry to hire, for instance, colored people and instructing it to put these people to work alongside white people where they will use the same rest room facilities and lunch rooms." The problem was that some workers would simply not go along with integration. A potentially bigger problem was that passage of FEP legislation would validate the unrealistic, "do-gooder" idea that "colored people" could and should take the whole issue into their own hands. The manager went on to describe a recent near-riot as evidence of the trouble that such ideas were already causing in his community. The incident began when a "colored couple" that had "gotten out of hand" was asked several times by a police officer to "move along in order to avoid a disturbance." The couple resisted, which led to the "colored woman's jumping on the police officer, clawing and kicking." Several fights broke out, and of course fights were the "very thing that starts riots." FEPC and other civil rights measures were at the root of the problem. "Practically all of the serious race riots in this country have been in the North, and usually they have been the result of some so-called 'do-gooders' planting the seeds in the minds of the colored people that they should rebel." It is ultimately impossible to prove that either Rockford executive wrote to Stevenson directly as a result of the ISCC's urging, but it seems equally impossible to deny the larger point. Not infrequently, business groups played an active role in generating the constituent letters that were held up as proof of what small businessmen themselves wanted.[38]

At the same time, many letters were surely the authentic expression of what ordinary employers truly believed, and other letters expressed views that were no less genuinely held for having been solicited. One employer in California wrote that "the hireing [sic] of employee[s] is entirely a matter for the employer to decide. . . . It is the employers['] right to exercise his own personal judgment as to how he shall operate his business. The proposed FEP law is an infringement on personal liberty." The head of a Minnesota mercantile company explained that prejudice could not be corrected through legislation, and employers should not be punished for whatever discrimination did exist. Expecting employers to "control the prejudices of their customers and workers is too much." A manufacturer of pressure tubing in Evanston worried that FEP laws represented a "complete abandonment of legal procedure" and ran "contrary to our entire judicial system." The Rockford Chamber of Commerce was concerned that the "minute we tell the American people that they must do something, or we try to legislate brotherly love, we will hurt the progress that has been made rather than make any contribution toward improvement." A car dealer in LaSalle, Ill., thought it was obvious that the bill was politically motivated. It would create another huge bureaucracy that would provide jobs for voters without accomplishing anything constructive. An owner of a box manufacturing company in Rockford wrote to "go on the record as being utterly opposed" to FEPC. He took pains to explain that his stance did not reflect any bigotry on his part. In fact, he felt "sympathy for some of the objectives" of the bill, but he remained convinced that "greater progress and accomplishment can be had through education and voluntary methods than through the legislative process."[39]

As with their official spokesmen, individual employers reached for the insinuation of special treatment and racial quotas when the going got tough. The secretary-treasurer of Saint Paul Structure Steel, C. E. Comfort, detested the way that such a law would compromise what he thought were rightfully his prerogatives. Comfort saw the law as forcing employers to choose between rejecting a clearly unqualified worker and exposing themselves to charges of discrimination, or hiring a clearly unqualified worker and lowering the overall productivity of the work force and their standard of living. "Thus," he concluded, "this type of law which seeks to aid the minority, damages the majority, and should not be enacted." One executive at a Los Angeles sign company, who hoped to vote for Warren if he chose to run for president, considered FEP bills the "most un-American bill[s] ever presented to voters through Communist inspired sources hoping to stimulate race hatred of the worst sort." The worse thing was that it would set up "another Government snooping bureau to force employers to hire a certain percentage of Negroes, Japs, Hindus, etc. [sic]." A contractor in Chicago made a similar charge in a letter to Governor Adlai Stevenson. "Do you think that the employers of Illinois will enjoy being told whom they must employ, that for a certain number of employees they must employ, on a racial basis, 5 Negroes, 3 Jews, 1 Atheist, and 2 Agnostics?" FEP legislation, he said, was "alien to the American concept of freedom," and it represented a clear "attempt of minorities to rule the majority."[40]

It was not only the most politically active and interested employers who expressed critical views. A survey of Illinois managers, for instance, largely confirmed that most employers were uneasy with FEP legislation. The survey was carried out in 1950 by the FEPC Study Group of the Illinois State Chamber of Commerce, and it was based on interviews with roughly three hundred managers across the state, representing a broad cross-section of the economy. Only half of the respondents reported employing African Americans. When they were asked what Illinois "industry" should do "to solve this problem of integrating minority group employees into their workforces," an overwhelming 78 percent of those surveyed said "support education and hiring." None chose legislation. It is a striking figure, but it is one that should be taken with a grain of salt, since respondents were given a choice of only three responses to the question: 1) "education and hiring," 2) "nothing," or 3) "don't know." Someone wanting to endorse FEP legislation would not have been able to answer the question! In fact, not a single question on the survey directly asked respondents what they thought of state FEP legislation. It would have been hard to design a survey less likely to detect support for FEPC. Obviously, it is impossible to know whether the design flaw was a result of intention, incompetence, or accident, but the effect was all but certain. It minimized the chance that any support for FEPC might be uncovered. Still, despite the obvious problems with the survey, the truth might not have been too badly distorted. In 1950, more than three-quarters of Illinois employers—when given the following choice of answers: education, nothing, and uncertainty—were perfectly comfortable endorsing education as the solution to the problem of job discrimination.[41]

Not all employers preferred education to FEP laws. Statements by executives supportive of FEPC were frequently circulated by liberals hoping to convince skeptics that some businessmen saw value in it—or at least did not find FEP as encumbering as they initially thought. A *Business Week* article with the title "Does State FEPC Hamper You?" was especially popular. Copiously reprinted and widely distributed by the Community Relations Service, it matter-of-factly concluded that "[e]mployers agree that FEP laws haven't caused nearly the fuss that opponents predicted." The article included a barrage of endorsements from managers

and executives. Many statewide organizations put together their own materials as well. A pamphlet entitled "Businessmen with Experience Favor
FEP Laws" was published in 1955 by the CCFEP. It was filled with inspirational testimonials under the heading, "Former Foes—Now Friends."
One story was related by the New York Board of Trade's M. D. Griffith,
one of the most vociferous opponents of Ives-Quinn. "I am one of those
who was against the antidiscrimination law when it was first introduced,"
he confessed. He could not deny, however, that "progress has been
achieved" under Ives-Quinn. There was nothing to fear. "On the contrary,
I think that they would discover in such a law—a very good friend."[42]

But such professions were somewhat dubious. Many employers who
publicly expressed support for FEPC were *already* covered by an FEP law,
and their statements had no certain value. This seems the case with the
businessmen whose favorable views on the subject were included in an
educational pamphlet published in 1949 by the Pennsylvania State Council for a Pennsylvania FEPC. The pamphlet prominently featured their
endorsement of FEPC, and it would have been easy for anyone to walk
away impressed. Such statements were so rare. A careful reader, however,
would have realized that the majority of the companies or lobbies were
based in New York, Connecticut, and New Jersey—states that had passed
FEP laws several years earlier. Hence the endorsements came from businessmen or organizations representing companies that were already under
the watchful eye of state regulators. They may have been perfectly sincere
in their statements, but it also seems hard to imagine that they would
have publicly denounced the law, even if they truly disliked it. Why run
the risk of angering their regulators when they could easily ingratiate
themselves instead? Moreover, since they were themselves subject to regulation, they would do well to make sure everyone else around the country
was subject to regulation as well. Even if the law were not onerous, it was
only sensible to make sure that the playing field was level across the states.
Critical views of the law surely existed among some employers in New
York and Connecticut, but they probably did not have a good chance
of making it into the pamphlet. Liberals would have only approached
employers who were favorably disposed toward the law, and critical statements would probably not have been included lest they cast the state law
in a poor light. Employers in FEP states thus had strong incentives to
speak highly of the law, and liberals had equally strong incentives to make
sure that only the most favorable endorsements received publicity.[43]

Similar divisions among employers surfaced in Minnesota. In educational materials distributed by the League of Women Voters, several
businessmen were credited with supporting a strong FEP bill in 1951.
Among them were Donald C. Dayton, President of the Dayton Company;
Harris A. Bullis, Chairman of the Board for General Mills; and Bradshaw

Mintener, General Counsel of Pillsbury Mills. Mintener's sincerity seemed real; he had sent out letters to three thousand employers in 1949, urging them to consider supporting FEPC. There is no reason to think that Dayton, Bullis, and other businessmen were not equally sincere. It should be pointed out, however, that many of these companies had major operations in Minneapolis, which had been operating an FEP ordinance since 1947. Few of their hiring practices would have to change if a state FEP law were to pass. The passage of a statewide law, if anything, would force everyone in the state to compete on the same terms that they faced everyday. Moreover, if their firms ever ran afoul of the Minneapolis ordinance, it could only help that they were on record in support of state legislation. What is most ironic is that Dayton, Bullis, and Mintener were affiliated with companies that remained dues-paying members of the Minnesota Employers' Association, at least through 1954. Such companies, in a sense, were having it both ways. Certain of their executives were winning them plaudits for racial enlightenment, but at the same time they were contributing membership dues to a political organization that was aggressively obstructing precisely the type of legislation that they were receiving credit for supporting.[44]

The cunning of employers paid rich dividends over time. In many states, they repeatedly came out on the winning side of close votes in committee or on the floor. Nobody understood their influence better than the lobbyists themselves. A recruitment brochure for the MEA boasted about the hard work it put in "day after day" to "block each ill-advised bill affecting business as it came up" during the 1953 session. "In many cases," it insisted, "the decision against passage of legislation adverse to industry was made by a margin of only one or two votes in committee or a handful of votes on the floor of either House." The end result was that "[n]ot one bill opposed by the Association was enacted into law." MEA boasts were not wholly baseless, particularly when it came to FEP legislation. A tie vote on an FEP measure before the House Labor Committee in 1947 doomed it to remain there. The deciding vote was cast by the chair of the committee, John J. Kinzer, a representative from Cold Spring. A member of the conservative caucus and a well-known ally of the MEA—he approvingly observed that the MEA was "recognized by the legislature as the spokesman for statewide management interests"—Kinzer did not normally vote, but a member of his committee had passed away, and Kinzer's participation was necessary to force a tie. In 1953, liberals passed a strong bill by a 39–22 margin in the Senate, but the bill was referred to the House Appropriations Committee, which refused to report it. A vote to release the bill from committee failed to achieve the two-thirds majority that it required, failing by a seven-vote margin, 81–44. Of course, MEA opposition was only one among many factors that prevented Minnesota from becoming an FEP state, but the close votes surely magnified any influence it may have possessed. Though the CCC was operating miles away in California and featured a very different style of organization, it was similarly boastful about the role it had played in bringing down Proposition 11 and keeping all subsequent FEP proposals bottled up in committee. "A major accomplishment of this organization," it claimed in a 1952 promotional brochure, "has been in successfully fighting off so-called race and religious discrimination measures. Its uncompromising stand in 1946 was a factor in defeating Proposition Number Eleven, which would have established a Fair Employment Practices Commission in California. The Chamber and other agencies fought off this serious threat again last year when FEPC proposals were defeated in the Legislature."[45]

The critical importance of employer opposition to FEP legislation was clearly evident in New Jersey, where the business community was genuinely divided. For most of 1945, the State Chamber of Commerce tried to work behind the scenes to derail an FEP law modeled directly on Ives-Quinn. Its effort failed, and New Jersey became the second state behind New York to pass a law. According to Earl Warren's trusted advisor, Walter A. Gordon, who personally traveled to New York and New Jersey late in the year to study the new FEP laws there, New Jersey was able to pass legislation because former Democratic governor Charles Edison had taken a personal interest in the issue and convinced many of the most important businessmen in the state that discrimination was a severe drag on economic efficiency. The only Democrat in his family—his father was the famous inventor—Edison was the rare businessman who supported the New Deal and served in Roosevelt's cabinet on the premise that it took "courage to try new things." He would later become disillusioned with the Democratic Party and even rejected Eisenhower as too liberal, but in 1945 he still retained some commitment to his earlier ideals. Clearly, he proved persuasive to enough of his fellow businessmen to neutralize them as a political force. A similar division within organized business surfaced in Illinois during the 1961 legislative session. Directors of the IMA remained implacably opposed to FEPC and voted unanimously to oppose it. In a dramatic break from precedent, CACI adopted a new position. After privately surveying employers in FEP states, it found that most of them agreed that the "laws haven't turned out to be as onerous as had been expected." In fact, 74 percent had "recommended that Illinois employers 'work to get a law they can live with.'" The size of the majority was too substantial to doubt, and CACI shifted directions. The board unanimously resolved that "employment in every field should be open to all persons without regard to race . . . creed or color," and it committed itself to "bringing about a workable FEPC Law in the State of Illinois." The fraying consensus among Illinois employers was just as consequential as it had been in New Jersey. That year, Illinois passed an FEP law.[46]

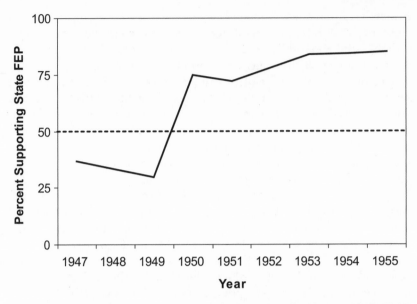

Figure 4.3 Public support in Minnesota for state FEP legislation, 1947–1955. *Note*: This graph presents the percentage of respondents in the Minnesota poll expressing support for the passage of a state law against job discrimination. Some data points are linearly interpolated for visual convenience. Note that a majority of respondents began supporting such a law in 1950, but a law did not pass until 1955. *Source*: See the appendix for details.

Perhaps the best illustration of the decisive way in which the character of business opposition shaped the political fortunes of FEP legislation came in Minnesota, where a law was passed in the mid-1950s. A large majority of the state had favored a state law since 1949 (see figure 4.3), but liberals proved unable to win passage of a law until 1955, when the liberal caucus gained control of the lower house of the legislature, and Orville F. Freeman (Democratic-Farmer-Labor) was elected governor. But the session was also distinguished by a major shift in the stance of employers toward FEPC. After years of speaking publicly against FEP on behalf of the MEA, Christenson found himself without the authorization to do so. His board had decided to remain officially silent on the issue; he could speak about FEPC only as a private citizen. The change in official policy had stemmed from a serious and irreconcilable difference of opinion that had opened up in the association. Most members of the MEA had historically been opposed to FEP legislation, but key numbers had begun to arrive at the same conclusions as Judson Bemis, a vice president of a Minneapolis-based bag company. Bemis had come around to supporting FEPC. Speaking before the Minnesota Senate Judiciary Committee in 1955, he confessed that he had not always been so supportive. "If anyone had told me, ten years ago, that I would ever be testifying before a legislative committee on behalf of an FEPC bill, I would have said they were crazy." Bemis offered three reasons for his change of heart. First, he had personally witnessed the operation of the Minneapolis FEPC and had concluded that it operated in a responsible, constructive manner. Cries of "totalitarianism" seemed highly overblown to him. Second, while he still believed that tolerance could never be legislated, legislative "nudging" could not hurt. He recalled the example of his young son, who declared that he disliked any new food his parents wanted to feed him. "But when the gentle yet firm had of parental authority gets the spoon into his mount, 99 times out of a hundred he finds it's O.K. after all." The third reason occurred to Bemis on a recent trip he had taken to India, which made him fully appreciate the fact that "there are many under-developed countries where people are black or yellow or red." In the Cold War, it could only hurt the geopolitical interests of the United States to remain inactive against discrimination. "Can we afford to substantiate the Communist propaganda to these people that democracy and discrimination go hand in hand?"[47]

His testimony decisively shaped the outcome of the deliberations. The *St. Paul Recorder* reported that Bemis in particular had a "tremendous effect on the committee" and "neutralized the effectiveness of the chief opponent," the MEA's Christenson. Bemis also gave liberals the final round of ammunition that they needed. Fighting off last-minute, dilatory motions from conservatives, liberal Republican Elmer L. Anderson gave an impassioned speech in which he pointed to the public support for FEP in the Minnesota Poll and repeatedly invoked Bemis's testimony. Some long-time observers praised it as "his most effective speech since he has been in the Senate." Before long, Minnesota joined Michigan as the first state in the Midwest to pass FEP legislation. No single state perfectly exemplifies the political influence of business, but Minnesota comes close. In the Gopher State, as elsewhere outside the South, business groups worked successfully to keep FEP laws off the books, long after public opinion had swung massively in favor of the liberal view—until divisions in their ranks rendered it impossible for them to act as a unified political force.[48]

If the leaders of organized business were opposed to FEP legislation, they understood American politics well enough to maintain the plausible appearance of bipartisanship. They nonetheless turned to Republican office-holders at the most critical moments in the legislative process.[49] This had been the case, it will be recalled, when AINYS belatedly realized that Ives-Quinn was politically viable. It then tapped powerful Republican Sen. Frederic Coudert, Jr., for assistance. In his study of civil rights in postwar Michigan, Sidney Alan Fine notes that GOP legislators had strong sympathies for the legislative priorities of the Michigan Manufacturers' Association and the automobile industry. A similar alliance was evident in California politics. "The real powers in the Republican party," observed the *California Eagle*, a statewide black newspaper, were not only the "big industrialists" but also the "large-scale farmers." Both groups had lobbying arms that were working to exert "every possible pressure" on Republican legislators so as to keep FEP proposals "bottled up in committee." Otto Christenson of the MEA had no illusions about the identity of his closest allies in the legislature. When an FEP bill was killed off in 1949, he wrote approvingly to his membership: "Republicans took the leading role in defeating the bill. Not all, but almost all, of the senators who talked against the bill, or who voted against the bill, were Republicans."[50]

The responsiveness of Republican office-holders to the political demands of business interests was perhaps revealed most indelibly in Ohio's titanic clash in 1953. A committee in the upper house had voted 5–4 against reporting the bill to the floor, with all five votes in the majority coming from Republicans. The vote killed any remaining chance of passage, and the margin of victory was provided by a GOP senator who reneged on his earlier pledge to vote for FEP, much to the frustration of liberals. The only significant opposition to FEP had come from the OCC and the OMA, and liberals feared that the GOP office-holders were simply doing the bidding of their business backers. After the legislative session, OCFEP officials met with the state GOP leadership to discuss why the party had proven incapable of making good on its 1952 campaign pledge to support FEP. The conversation grew heated, and the GOP brass conceded under persistent questioning that liberal suspicions were correct. "Gentlemen," said one of them, "you know who picks up the tab for our work, and those who pay the piper call the tune."[51]

The politics of FEP legislation evinced strong partisan dimensions, with Republican officeholders—partly motivated by the need to appear responsive to the political demands of a central constituency—displaying a far greater degree of racial conservatism than Democratic officeholders. Their opposition to state FEP laws, however, derived from their own ideological commitments as well. Republican office-holders themselves were hardly shy about making their sentiments public, and their rhetoric bore striking resemblances to the discourse of "conservative egalitarianism" allegedly inaugurated by Goldwater and perfected by Reagan. Like their business allies, Republican office-holders professed their allegiance to the ideal of racial equality, and they passed up few opportunities to denounce the evil of racial discrimination. Yet their denunciations did not prevent many of them from opposing FEP in the name of merit-based competition in the marketplace. For instance, one California Republican justified his opposition to FEP by claiming that it was "intended to take care of people who are not qualified." Another argued that it would "aggravate and cause more turmoil than it's going to alleviate." A third claimed that it would "discriminate in favor of members of [the] minority race." A young assemblyman from Southern California, Casper Weinberger, voiced a common GOP complaint about FEP legislation—that it was a form of "compulsion," "state control," and "interference" that would simply exacerbate the problem at a moment when "progress is being made against discrimination" through private, voluntary action. Weinberger would have agreed with the equally critical sentiments expressed by his co-partisan, George E. Drach, assistant majority leader of the Illinois Senate. According to Drach, FEP legislation was simply too onerous and intrusive. In bending over backward to protect the illusory rights of some Americans, it violated a fundamental to which every American was rightly entitled. "I'm not convinced that FEPC would be good for anybody," he said. "We keep hearing about freedoms from this and that, but don't hear enough about the freedom to be let alone, as enunciated by the late Justice Brandeis of the U.S. Supreme Court."[52]

Republicans could be just as shrewd as their business allies when dealing with the political process. In moments when they sensed that pressure for reform had reached a critical threshold, they were not above introducing "educational" or "voluntary" legislation as a steam valve, just as Taft had done in Congress. This type of legislation was consistent with their ideological commitments, but its introduction invariably complicated the political dynamics at play—primarily to the advantage of the GOP. Republicans could begin to claim, plausibly, that they too supported FEPC legislation. Democrats would suddenly have to expend political capital suppressing another proposal while promoting one of their own. The public could grow tired of the distinction or confused about what it really meant. If a voluntary bill came to a floor vote, Democrats would be put in the difficult position of having to decide whether to vote for a type of legislation that most of them found manifestly inadequate, or reject it and risk the damaging charge that they were an insincere majority or an obstructionist minority. If the bill actually became law, liberals would have to remain vigilant, keeping track of its performance and preparing to strengthen it if it proved unsatisfactory.

Such were precisely the possibilities that were set into motion in Colorado when majority leader of the Republican-controlled Senate, Frank Gill, sprang his voluntary bill on the well-meaning liberals at the beginning of the 1951 session. The CCEEO had followed the liberal playbook carefully at the beginning of the session. They carefully cultivated bipartisan interest in a bill. They built a broad-based coalition of racial, religious, and labor groups to shield themselves from certain charges of radicalism. They flew out Henry Spitz of the New York State Commission against Discrimination (NYSCAD) to brief lawmakers and businessmen. The message he conveyed should have appealed to most of his audience. Conciliation and education can settle most every problem, "but not unless the law is back by legal penalties which may be imposed upon violation." Gill's bill came as a total surprise. Liberals had been soliciting bipartisan sponsorship of their bill for weeks only to be told by Republican lawmakers that legislative action should wait until Spitz had concluded his visit. Perhaps liberals had interpreted the suggestion as a sign that Republicans were trying to stay open-minded. In any case, the last thing that liberals expected was that they would be preempted. They reacted to Gill's move with scorn, calling his bill a "subterfuge" and a "sham." A liberal bill was quickly introduced in the House by a bipartisan group of sponsors, and the CCEEO launched a massive lobbying effort. Two delegations were formed and visited the capitol. Democrats tried to amend Gill's measure to their liking but failed every time on straight, party-line votes. When the question was finally called, Democrats held their noses and voted for the bill. In the words of the minority leader, Sam Taylor, "half a loaf is better than none at all." Of course, half a loaf was decidedly not what Colorado liberals had hoped to achieve at the outset of the session. They had wanted the whole thing. Gill's gambit paid off handsomely for conservatives, and a whole loaf would not come until 1957.[53]

Republican office-holders did not monolithically oppose FEP, just as northern Democrats did not unanimously support it. FEPC enjoyed backers on either side of the aisle—but it was a lopsided bipartisanship. This was clear in the partisan distribution of public endorsements, bill sponsors, committee votes, and floor votes. It was also evident in electoral politics, and nowhere was it more obvious than in Colorado during the 1950 primaries. Members of the Denver Unity Council interviewed all of the candidates running in order to determine their views on the desirability of a "strong, workable" FEP law. What the council found paralleled what was happening in almost every state outside the South. Democrats vastly outnumbered Republicans on the list of candidates supporting strong legislation. Both of the Democrats running for U.S. Congress pledged to support FEP. Neither of the Republicans did. Eight of the Democratic candidates running for state senator endorsed FEPC, compared to only one Republican. Twenty of the Democratic candidates running for state representative supported FEPC—and only five Republicans.[54]

A favorable view of FEPC was the exception to the rule in the GOP. Racially liberal Republicans were limited in number; they tended either to occupy or covet statewide office, which made it necessary for them (if they wished to win votes in urban areas) to assume the mantle of racial liberalism. Republican lawmakers representing urban districts also tended to reject FEP on ideological grounds, but at times they could be persuaded to change their minds in the face of a mobilized and informed electorate. Only a handful of Republican lawmakers supported FEP in the absence of pressure. The majority of them consistently and categorically rejected FEP, ensconced as they were in noncompetitive, rural (and to a lesser extent suburban) districts where few of their constituents would actually benefit from the passage of the law, and most of them would resent it. John J. Kinzer, majority leader of the Minnesota House, summed up the frustrations of many rural Republicans when he reiterated his opposition to FEPC in 1953: "[O]ur business people in the country are getting along very well without this legislation. If the cities want it, let them pass an ordinance. Leave us alone."[55]

Not surprisingly, liberals were among the quickest to recognize the full dimensions of the fight (see figure 4.4). A CCEEO analysis of the 1951 fight in Colorado over a voluntary bill noted that "all the negative votes are all by legislators from rural districts." In 1953, editors of the *California Eagle* pointed to the "rural-minded and Republican-controlled" California Senate as one of the biggest barriers to the passage of FEP, calling for a "March on Sacramento" in protest. In a subsequent interview, W. Byron Rumford would agree that rural, Republican legislators—particularly in the Senate—were among the biggest roadblocks to FEP in the Golden State: "Yes, you see those fellows didn't have any black constituents to amount to anything." This was a barrier with which most liberals were familiar; it was a topic that preoccupied them. At a meeting of the OCFEP in 1955, much of the discussion focused on how to break the stranglehold of "rural Republican elements" on the state legislature. W. O. Walker of the *Cleveland Call and Post* argued that it was impossible for racial minorities, who lived primarily in urban areas, to do anything. They simply did not pose an electoral threat. The only solution was to encourage church groups and other allies with influence in rural districts to support FEPC-friendly Republicans in the primaries. Someone else at the meeting disagreed with Walker, pointing out that urban Republicans could be targeted by minority voters. This threat, in turn, could force GOP leaders to lean on their rural co-partisans.[56]

The rural, agrarian locus of Republican opposition to FEP legislation, while real, should not be permitted to obscure the raw partisanship that defined the issue. To be sure, when compared to office-holders from urban

Figure 4.4 "Take Down the Barrier: Republican Legislators," *Cleveland Press*, March 20, 1951. This editorial cartoon shows a door labeled "Employment Opportunities for All" blocked shut by a wooden plank labeled "Republican Legislators." Though the *Press* was a Democratic-leaning paper, it correctly identified GOP legislators as the major obstacle to fair employment practices (FEP) legislation in Ohio. Republican opposition to FEP legislation was a decisive political force there as well as in California, Illinois, Michigan, Minnesota, Pennsylvania, and other electorally crucial states. Courtesy of the Western Reserve Historical Society, Cleveland, Ohio.

or suburban districts, rural office-holders of both parties held more conservative positions on FEP and other social issues, reflecting the conservative preferences of their constituents. But partisanship mattered decisively, even in the most rural and underdeveloped areas. In 1957, when California's Senate Labor Committee voted 5–4 to table an FEP that the Assembly had already passed, all five Republicans on the committee voted in the affirmative. All of them represented primarily rural and agrarian counties:

Sonoma, Orange, Tehama, Glenn, and Colusa, Tulare, and Marin; but two Democrats representing similar counties—Nevada, Sierra, Placer, and Kings—voted in the negative, along with their urban co-partisans. The same pattern appeared in Colorado. When the Senate voted to pass a voluntary bill, 25–10, liberal Democrats agonized over the decision. Should they accept a "slice or two of ersatz bread," or should they reject it altogether? Most of them ultimately decided to approve the bill. Republicans from urban districts did not hesitate to vote in the affirmative; they cast their votes to portray themselves as friends of civil rights in their next election. The naysayers were primarily rural Republicans who represented jurisdictions such as Cheyenne County on the eastern plains of Colorado or San Juan County in the middle of the Rockies. Several crucial Democrats from equally rural jurisdictions—Alamosa and Eagle counties—nevertheless voted for the proposal along with their co-partisans. In his analysis of two roll calls in Ohio's lower chamber, Duane Lockard notes a strong rural-urban split, but the division softens when the rural-urban split is cross-tabulated by party. Much of the rural opposition came from Republicans. For their part, rural Democrats were much more likely to support FEPC. In most states outside the South, partisanship was not the only factor shaping the politics of state FEP legislation, but it often vastly outweighed other considerations.[57]

But how did Republican office-holders translate their policy preferences into active and successful opposition? In a striking inversion of the obstructionist pattern that prevailed in the Congressional politics of civil rights, where *southern Democrats* wielded control over the powerful Rules Committee in the House and the threat of a filibuster in the Senate, *Republican* control over "veto points" in state legislatures seems to have delayed the passage of FEP laws. Whenever the GOP enjoyed formal or informal authority over a stage of the legislative process when legislation could be potentially derailed, they rarely failed to take advantage of the situation.[58]

This occurred in numerous ways. In some cases, GOP control over veto points was quite literal. When governor Goodwin Knight of California threatened to exercise his constitutionally conferred gubernatorial veto over any FEP bill that passed the legislature during his tenure in the late 1950s, it could not but help to cloud the prospects for forward progress. Unenthusiastic or hesitant legislators could easily vote against any viable proposal and pass off the blame on Knight, explaining to interested onlookers that they were reluctant to waste their votes on a lost cause. In other cases, GOP control over veto points was less literal but no less effective, unfolding as it did through the committee system. Although the norms and rules governing committee assignments varied considerably across states, it was almost always true that the majority party in either house of the legislature enjoyed a commanding position in deciding the makeup and leadership of legislative committees. Hence the dominance of the GOP in postwar statehouses meant that the most powerful committees were often ruled by Republican majorities and chairmen. This combination worked to devastating effect. Once an FEP bill was introduced, usually in the lower chamber, it was invariably assigned to a Republican-controlled committee for initial analysis and consideration. Here the low political profile of most committees made it fairly simple for Republicans to work toward tabling the bill indefinitely, or schedule it for a public hearing late in the session, when the legislative agenda would surely be tied up with other urgent matters. Even if a public hearing was somehow held early, it was still relatively easy for Republicans to persuade the GOP majority on the committee to decline reporting the bill to the chamber as a whole. Such a vote in committee might anger liberal activists, but it would seldom make front page news and result in damaging repercussions at the ballot box. If the initial committee actually reported an FEP proposal favorably, there were still additional opportunities for obstruction. Since the substance of most FEP proposals spanned the formal jurisdiction of several committees, it was unproblematic to refer any successful proposals to a second Republican-controlled committee, where they would face similarly daunting obstacles. Not surprisingly, these proposals often failed to emerge from the second committee. In the rare event that a bill was successfully reported to the floor of the lower chamber, it would have to garner enough votes to pass—and then it would go to the upper chamber, where it would have to navigate another set of analogous barriers before going to the governor for his signature. If the presence of multiple veto points in American statehouses presented a pervasive structural bias against the adoption of new legislation, Republican control of such veto points also made it easy for Republicans to purposefully throw up high barriers to the passage of FEP laws for much of the postwar period.[59]

The critical importance of Republican control over veto points can be seen in the legislative history of FEP laws in very late-adopting states. Illinois offers a clear example (table A.8). There, it was the Senate that was the major barrier. As early as 1943, liberals succeeded in getting an FEP bill approved by the more liberal House, which passed it 86–19 only to have it bottled up by the Senate Committee on Industrial Affairs, ruled 8–6 by Republicans. Other bills were passed by the House in 1949, 1953, 1955, 1957, and 1959, usually by substantial margins, and each one of them failed to emerge from the same Senate Committee, which was almost invariably controlled by a Republican majority. In 1961, the IFEPC launched a "Past Due!" campaign, and it correctly laid the blame for the failure of FEP legislation at the feet of the GOP: "This year, again,

Republican members hold the key." Its pronouncement was vindicated when the committee, where the GOP constituted a smaller majority than in previous years, released a bill to the Senate. It was quickly approved, and naturally the House followed suit. Illinois had finally passed an FEP law, nearly twenty years after it had been initially introduced in Springfield and three years before Congress passed the Civil Rights Act.[60]

Republican use of veto points was perhaps even more visible in California (table A.9). The first FEP bill was introduced into the California Assembly by Democrat Augustus F. Hawkins (South-Central Los Angeles) in 1945. For more than a decade afterward, Hawkins would take turns sponsoring FEP proposals with another black Democratic Assemblyman, W. Byron Rumford (Berkeley-Oakland). In spite of their best efforts, however, California would pass an FEP law only in 1959, mainly because of the difficulty that Hawkins and Rumford faced in extracting their proposals from Republican-controlled committees in the Assembly. From 1945 to 1953, either the Committee on Governmental Efficiency and Economy (CGEE) or the Committee on Ways and Means (CWM) succeeded in stymieing every single FEP proposal that came before them, almost always by party-line votes. The lower house finally passed a bill in 1955 when it voted to withdraw the bill from the CWM. Tellingly, fewer than half of all participating Republicans voted for withdrawal. But a new obstacle soon appeared in the form of the Senate Labor Committee, where a party-line vote doomed the proposal. That same committee also quashed the bill in 1957 in yet another party-line vote. Only in 1959, after Democrats won majorities in both houses and Edmund "Pat" Brown won the gubernatorial race, did FEP legislation finally pass. It was no accident that the year marked the first time that Democrats controlled both branches of state government in the postwar period, leaving the GOP without authority over a "veto point" for the first time since FEP surfaced on the legislative agenda.[61]

Of course, Proposition 11 was a major setback for California liberals, and perhaps Republicans were emboldened in their obstruction by the strong signal that the vote conveyed about the underlying preferences of the California electorate. The same pattern, though, is evident in other states that did not have a referendum, most importantly Ohio (see table A.10). There, too, FEP legislation passed immediately following a transition to a Democratic government in 1959. FEP bills had been first introduced into the legislature as early as 1945, and the House began to pass enforceable FEP bills starting in 1949. But the bills invariably faced extreme Republican hostility in the Senate, where they lost a series of close committee and floor votes. By the mid-1950s, Ohio liberals had grown irate, denouncing the GOP leadership for their reactionary stance. Nevertheless, no amount of criticism led GOP lawmakers to back down. Ohio passed a law only in 1959, when Democratic governor Michael V. DiSalle entered office with an overwhelming Democratic majority in both chambers of the legislature.[62]

How party control of state government figured in the passage of FEP laws was a matter of enormous controversy, and both sides pelted each other with contradictory claims. As early as 1945, *Business Week* was reporting that liberals and labor were blaming "Republican bloc voting" for the failure of FEP bills in Massachusetts and Pennsylvania. Over time, liberals grew increasingly frustrated with the snail's pace of progress in certain states, and they became more and more willing to make Republican lawmakers the central target of their criticisms. In 1953, after the Commerce and Labor Committee had refused to recommend the bill to the Ohio Senate in a 5–4 vote, Theodore Berry roundly condemned the "Party of Lincoln." All five refusals had come from Republicans. Berry blasted the legislators as "little men" for their "obstruction" and charged the GOP with hypocrisy, pointing out how it had pledged in 1952 to support FEP. A press release from the OCFEP went even further, lambasting the "top leadership of the Republican party" for "carefully and deliberately" orchestrating a "political murder" of the bill. "We know the criminals," it concluded. "If no change occurs, we must plan together in the coming election to insure they do not go unpunished." Two years later in California, one newspaper editorial claimed, correctly, that FEP had been bottled up by a "tiny majority of five men" in the Senate Labor Committee. All five were Republicans "and out of the reach of liberal wrath, elected as they are from rural areas, notorious for their opposition to social change and their exploitation of migratory workers, usually of minority racial backgrounds." It was not the first time that such a failure had occurred in the Golden State. Once again, Republicans posed the main barrier to civil rights, and unless "radical changes" were made to the legislature, subsequent campaigns for FEP might be "doomed to the same finish." The editorial urged voters to hold Republicans "accountable for the failure of its standard bearer to redeem the party's pledges to its people." Nothing less was warranted. "For far too long, Republicans have hoodwinked minorities on the subject of civil rights . . . there has been much ambiguity, plus a tendency to let them slip by in the shadow of the glory that was Abraham Lincoln." The bipartisan comity of the early postwar years, however strategic it may have been, had obviously melted away.[63]

   Republicans naturally objected to liberal attacks and sought to make the case that their party had actually been responsible for the passage of state FEP legislation. In 1963, when it became clear that Kennedy's civil rights proposal was going to receive serious consideration in Congress, strategists at the Republican National Committee (RNC) would advise GOP lawmakers to point out the historical role of their party in the passage of state FEP legislation. RNC strategists noted that such laws had passed more frequently under Republican than Democratic majorities. In addition, they pointed out that states that had "pioneered" FEP laws in the late 1940s were more likely to have Republican rather than Democratic governors.[64]

Which side appears to have been correct? Republican claims were not entirely off base, but they do not go very far in helping us to decide whether Republican control of veto points improved or worsened the prospect that a state would pass an FEP law. This requires more than just looking at patterns of party control during the legislative sessions in which state FEP laws were enacted. Such information tells us only that Republicans were more likely to have legislative majorities or hold the governorship in sessions when FEP legislation passed. Since we do not know whether Republicans had many or few chances to pass FEP laws, it is difficult to interpret the significance of the differential. Is it evidence that Republicans were true friends of FEPC? More specifically, did it mean that Republicans eagerly took advantage of the few opportunities that came their way? Or did it mean instead that they sat on FEP proposals for years before reluctantly acquiescing to them? It is equally important to have information on the passage rate of FEP laws under other configurations of party control. Then it would be possible to determine whether GOP control of veto points was better or worse than the alternatives. The evidence seems fairly convincing in the case of Illinois, California, and Ohio, but what about across the full set of northern states?

A crucial complication in identifying the independent effect of party control is that party control is not the only plausible factor influencing the passage of state FEP laws. It is obviously only one of many factors. A substantial literature on state politics suggests that economic and political modernization is commonly associated with the passage of state legislation. In general, states that are wealthy, industrialized, and urbanized tend to adopt policy innovations such as FEPC sooner than their poorer, rural, and agricultural counterparts. The same tendency for innovation is characteristic of electorally competitive states whose legislatures create apportionment schemes that accord proportionate weight to cities relative to rural areas. Also relevant is a generic tendency of states to influence their neighbors. States are more likely to adopt a law if their neighbors have already done so. As for factors specific to the political history of FEPC, it seems fairly likely that states with large populations of African Americans, Catholics, Jews, and union members were earlier adopters than other states, while states with strong employers were slower adopters than other states. Lastly, it seems plausible that states with a more favorable climate of public opinion toward FEPC may have passed such laws earlier than other states. The sheer number of possibilities raises an obvious question. How can anybody be certain that GOP control of veto points is independently responsible for the delayed passage of state FEP legislation? Many other things could have been going on.[65]

A first look at the evidence bears out many possibilities (table 4.2).[66] In the two decades from the end of the Second World War to the passage of the Civil Rights Act, there were roughly five-hundred legislative sessions in which nonsouthern states might have passed FEP laws. Enforceable legislation was passed twenty-three times (not including Alaska and Hawaii). Thus the overall passage rate was approximately 5 percent. There is evidence that Republican control of "veto points" depressed the chances that a state would pass FEPC. When the GOP controlled as few as one veto point (that is, one chamber of the legislature or the governor's office), states had about a 4 percent chance of passing a law. By contrast, when Republicans had control over no veto points, states had roughly a 6 percent chance of passing a law, well above the average overall rate. Other state characteristics, however, seem strongly associated with the passage of legislation as well. As the literature on state politics suggests, there are a several factors that seem positively correlated with passage, including per capita income, industrialization, and urbanization. When the states are divided into quartiles on these characteristics, states in higher quartiles have a higher passage rate than states in lower quartiles. Malapportionment does not seem to exhibit a linear relationship with passage, but electoral competition shows a positive correlation with higher passage rates, as does the passage of an FEP law in a neighboring state. As for state characteristics associated with the politics of FEP, states with higher proportions of Jews, Catholics, unions, and NAACP members have higher passage rates than states with lower proportions of such populations. States with stronger employers, as measured by the presence of a right-to-work law, were less likely to pass FEP laws. Furthermore, states with higher levels of public support for state FEPC—as measured by the statewide distribution of responses to a question on the Gallup Poll in 1945—passed such laws at higher rates than states with lower levels of public support for state FEPC. This overall pattern of associations makes it entirely plausible that Republican control of veto points per se was not responsible for temporal variation in the passage of FEP legislation. Too many other factors were related, making it difficult to disentangle and identify the separate effect of Republican control.[67]

Through a statistical technique called event-history analysis, however, it is possible to simultaneously weigh the independent influence of all the variables for which there are data. Briefly put, event-history analysis is a method of regression analysis that is used to identify the factors associated

TABLE 4.2
Passage Rate of State FEP Legislation by State Characteristics, 1941–1964

	For binary variables			
	Yes	No		
GOP control of veto points	4.2%	6.0%		
Public opinion favorable	5.0	4.0		
Employer strength (RTW law)	1.9	5.8		
	For continuous variables by quartiles			
	Highest	Second	Third	Bottom
Income (1964 dollars)	9.6%	6.4%	1.6%	0.8%
Industrialization (1964 cents)	10.3	3.2	3.2	1.6
Urbanization	9.5	4.0	4.0	0.8
Electoral competition	6.4	6.2	5.0	0.8
Malapportionment (RTV Index)	2.6	6.3	6.5	2.9
Percentage black	5.6	3.2	8.0	1.6
Percentage Jewish	7.9	4.0	3.0	3.2
Percentage Catholic	7.9	4.8	3.2	2.4
NAACP membership	6.3	6.5	5.6	0.0
Union density	7.9	4.0	4.0	2.4
Bordering states with FEP (%)	11.7	7.6	0.5	0.5

Notes: Each entry is the percentage of legislative sessions in which an FEP law passed in a state that previously did not have a strong FEP law. This figure is calculated for the period from 1945 to 1964, during which there were a total of 502 legislative sessions. The raw passage rate for the period is 5 percent (23 events/502 sessions). All monetary variables are expressed in 1964 dollars or cents. For a discussion of measurement and data, see the appendix.

with a decrease or increase in the likelihood that a particular "event" of interest will occur. This method permits us to determine with a fair degree of confidence whether Republican control of veto points is associated with a reduction in the probability that a state would pass an FEP law, even when taking into account other relevant variables. When event-history analysis is applied to the wide range of relevant variables that are correlated with the passage of FEP legislation, it strongly confirms what is evident in the legislative history of FEPC in Illinois, California, and Ohio (see table A.11). The loss of GOP control over all veto points in a given state, all other things being equal, increases the chance that the state will pass FEP legislation by about four percentage points. This effect is a large one, given that the average passage rate is 5 percent.[68]

This finding is instructive, and it is consistent with the initial evidence. Yet there is one remaining problem: Republican control of a veto point was not randomly assigned to the states. If it were possible to assign Republican control randomly to some states, in the manner of a clinical trial, then determining its effect would be a simple matter of comparing the passage rate in "treated" states with the passage rate in the "placebo" states. In actuality, states chose their pattern of party control. This complicates the task of identifying the separate effect of Republican control because states that chose to give Republicans the ability to exercise a de facto veto against legislation were probably very different from states that chose to give Democrats full control over state government. Of special concern is whether the states where voters opposed FEP laws also had a tendency to elect Republicans to office in sufficient numbers to give the GOP control over at least one veto point. This is a problem because it suggests that Republican control was "self-selected" by states whose voters did not want FEP legislation, perhaps because of their racial conservatism. If such self-selection were the case, then it would not be possible to assert that parties had an independent role in the politics of state FEPC. When elected to office, Republicans and Democrats were simply carrying out the will of the people—not the preferences of their parties. The event-history analysis so far guards against self-selection to a limited extent because it includes data on public opinion about state FEP laws, but the data are not of high quality. If the statistical analysis is based on data that do not capture the key dimension motivating voters to give Republicans control over a veto point, then the basic problem remains.

One final step in the analysis provides evidence against self-selection. By looking to see whether the effect of Republican control persists over all levels of electoral competition, it is possible to assess whether the observed association between Republican control and FEP passage is illusory. This approach is based on the assumption that electorally competitive states—states in which the two parties are nearly equivalently represented in state government—are states in which voter sentiment about FEP legislation is also evenly distributed. The basic intuition is quite simple. As the parties in the states approach perfect competition, party assignment is "as good as" random. Under this assumption, if Republican control of veto points truly reduced the chances that a state would pass FEP legislation, then the effect of Republican control should persist even in the most electorally competitive states. This assumption seems eminently reasonable. If it is true that states where voters opposed FEP laws tended to elect Republicans to office, and if it is also true that states where voters favored FEP laws tended to elect Democrats to office, then it seems only reasonable to assume that voter sentiment about FEP laws is the most evenly distributed in the set of states where the Republicans and Democrats hold office in the roughly equivalent proportions.[69]

A reassuring pattern is evident in the data. When the states are partitioned into quartiles by their level of electoral competition, it is clear that

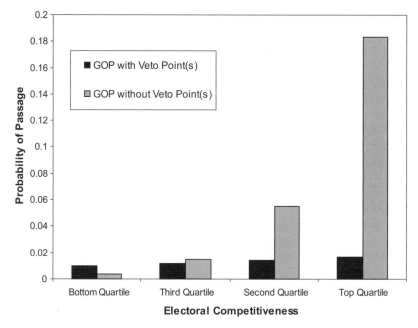

Figure 4.5 Predicted likelihood of passage by GOP control of veto point(s) and electoral competition. *Note*: This chart presents the probability that a state would pass an FEP law in a given session, depending on whether the GOP controlled a veto point and depending on the overall level of electoral competition. It shows that the differential probability of passage between GOP and non-GOP states was greatest in the most electorally competitive states. *Source*: Author's calculations as described in the appendix.

the negative effect of Republican control not only persists in the most competitive quartile but also actually grows (see figure 4.5). The most electorally competitive states were the states in which Republican control had the largest effect. States in the two least competitive quartiles exhibit low passage rates whether or not Republicans controlled a veto point. Passage rates are higher in the second most competitive quartile, but Republican control lowered them by about four percentage points. In the most competitive quartile of states, passage rates are above average, but Republican control lowered them by more than seventeen percentage points. The effect of Republican control is hence very robust; it can be seen even in the set of states where public sentiment about FEP is most evenly distributed.[70]

The statistical evidence taken as a whole weighs in convincingly on the side of liberals. When they blamed Republican lawmakers for obstructing FEP legislation, it was not a cheap political shot. Other factors surely mattered as well, but if the GOP controlled a veto point in the legislative process, it significantly clouded the prospects that a state would pass a law. The political circumstances in a state could all be highly conducive to success—public opinion could be favorable, liberals could be well-organized—but "freedom from discrimination" was marching uphill as long as Republicans had a sufficient presence in state government.

The difficulty that liberals faced in winning state FEP legislation was not without larger consequence. In fact, it undercut their broader strategy to use the states as a means of generating political momentum for the broader fight in Congress. Perhaps the biggest liability was the failed campaign for Proposition 11, which reverberated not only in California but also beyond. The disastrous outcome gave conservatives a talking point for years. As late as 1957, California conservatives were still justifying their opposition to state FEP legislation by pointing to the results of the referendum as evidence of the popular will. The people had spoken, argued one of them. The judgment was clear—no compulsory FEPC for California. "Yet some legislators," he continued sarcastically, "apparently believe the people do not know what they want or need, and so they take it upon themselves to provide laws for them." In 1948, California attorney Zach Lamar Cobb wrote to Gov. Fielding L. Wright of Mississippi to inform him of the final tally on Proposition 11, in case he should find the information useful. The same year, Franklin Hitchborn of Santa Clara wrote a similar letter to Sen. Richard B. Russell (D-GA), taking care to break down the vote in selected counties. Congressional conservatives certainly knew what to do with the results. In the climactic 1950 House fight over the McConnell substitute, Rep. Donald L. Jackson (R-CA) took great pains to remind his colleagues that "1,682,664 of 2,358,343 citizens of California voted 'no' and 675,697 votes 'yes' on FEPC." According to Jackson, it had gone down to "unqualified defeat" for a morally unobjectionable reason. The "voters of California did not want to delegate to the State government some of the constitutional rights which reside with the individual, and are a matter of personal conscience and responsibility." California voters had answered a "resounding 'no' to a compulsory and penalty-providing FEPC," and he considered the referendum a plebiscitary "mandate" that he could not shirk in good conscience. "I may be required to tell 24,814 voters why I voted against compulsion on this measure, but I can also tell 99,549 voters who opposed FEP in my district that I have followed the explicit instructions given me in this connection."[71]

Trying to contain the cloud of reaction that her state had incubated, Helen Gahagan Douglas (D-CA) responded as best she could to Jackson, arguing that the electorate had been grossly deceived by a massive propaganda campaign. In her reckoning, "There were billboards from one side of the State to the other—screaming that this was a communistic program." She insisted that people for whom the law was designed to help actually misunderstood what it was for. "Many thousands of dollars were spent to misrepresent the issue," she said. "[W]ild statements were made and deliberately misled voters." Nevertheless, it was a tough case to make. It did not matter to enough people that Douglas was correct in the general thrust of her charges. The historical record amply supports her claim that business groups spent thousands of dollars on their opposition campaign, running their political operations against Proposition 11 through groups with misleading names such as the "Committee for Tolerance." Nobody liked to think that thousands of grown men and women could be so easily duped in America.[72]

The defeat of Proposition 11 left California liberals shell-shocked, disorganized, and slow to recover. The California Committee on Civic Unity (CCCU) carried on gamely, but conditions were challenging. No strong effort was mounted in 1947, and financial problems prevented it from relaunching the state campaign in 1949, though it did hold a conference that attracted over 2,000 delegates who agreed to make state FEPC a top priority. In 1951, liberals were able to organize themselves effectively enough to pack the seats at a public hearing on an FEP bill in Sacramento, and the legislative session in 1953 witnessed an even stronger attempt, partly because the NAACP threw itself entirely behind the campaign. Research on prevalence of discrimination was carried out, and legislative pamphlets were published and disseminated. In March, a massive delegation of activists descended on Sacramento, holding meetings at the Native Sons Hall and Westminster Presbyterian Church. Political circumstances seemed more favorable as well. In the private estimation of Irving S. Rosenblatt, president of the CCCU, the potential for legislative action was greater in 1953 "than ever before in the history of this legislation." Rosenblatt specifically pointed out that Earl Warren (who had been silent on FEP since 1946) and the Republican State Central Committee were both reportedly urging the legislature to enact FEPC. One observer wrote to Tarea Hall Pittman of the NAACP Western Regional Council to share his sense that victory was "at least within striking distance." By 1955, California liberals were well organized enough to stage a massive rally in Sacramento. In 1959, they would finally free themselves from the long shadow cast by Proposition 11. Yet their surge came at a distinctly inopportune moment. By the end of the Eisenhower years, fair employment practices had fallen down far on the list of congressional priorities. The innovation of the omnibus approach to legislation meant that employment discrimination would have to compete with provisions aimed at poll taxes, segregated schools, and other bulwarks of Jim Crow. The campaign for "freedom from discrimination" had been truly national in scope, but much of the nation's attention had begun to focus on bus boycotts and school desegregation in Dixie.[73]

Still, liberals had their chances in the early postwar years. California was not yet the electoral plum and cultural bellwether that it would later become. Many other states were more electorally and politically significant. The federated strategy that liberals had devised was not without prospect of success, and their best opportunities came during the second Truman administration. The state campaign peaked in 1949 and 1950, precisely the years when the 81st Congress gave FEP legislation the most serious look it had ever received on Capitol Hill. Northern state legislatures were getting flooded with a deluge of civil rights proposals. "The legislative sessions of 1949," observed the American Council on Race Relations, "were notable for the many measures introduced in the state legislatures" that addressed "racial and intergroup relations." In fact, eighteen states outside the South were specifically contemplating FEP legislation, including Arizona, Colorado, Illinois, Indiana, Iowa, Michigan, Minnesota, Missouri, Montana, Nebraska, New Mexico, North Dakota, Ohio, Oregon, Pennsylvania, Rhode Island, Utah, and Washington. Gilbert Gordon of the AJC pointed with keen optimism to a set of "northern industrial states" where political circumstances seemed especially congenial because of strong leadership. Democratic governors in Illinois, Ohio, Wisconsin, and Michigan had specifically pledged to support Truman's civil rights program. On the other side of the aisle, Republicans from Dewey's wing of the GOP held the governor's office in Minnesota, California, and Pennsylvania. It could be a big year for liberals.[74]

Of all the states contemplating FEP legislation in 1949, perhaps it was Illinois that seemed best prepared to follow the template laid out by New York. A *Special Report on Employment Opportunities in Illinois* had been published late in the previous year by the Illinois Interracial Commission. The commission presented ample evidence of job bias and went on to recommend the passage of an FEP statute. A liberal bill was introduced into the House by fifty-seven state representatives. A similar bill was introduced in the Senate and boasted ten sponsors. The House acted first, passing its bill by a vote of 81–43–3. All signs pointed toward the Senate quickly following suit. After extensive political intelligence-gathering, legislative analysts at the Illinois Fair Employment Practice Committee had concluded that there was a 28–19 majority in the Senate favoring FEPC, with the bulk of the opposition coming from outside Cook County. The *Chicago Defender* reported in early June that the Republican majority would not oppose the House-passed bill, because "they fear a negative reaction in next year's elections." The prospect of passage seemed so strong that long-time president of the Julius Rosenwald Fund, Edwin Rogers Embree, privately wrote to Governor Stevenson to tell him that his "last information was that it seemed likely that such an ACT would be passed by this year's legislature" and advised him to begin drawing up a list of potential appointees and noting that the success of other commissions had depended on the "caliber" of the appointees. Stevenson readied himself and contacted Chester Bowles, Democratic governor of Connecticut, which had enacted a FEP law in 1947. "It seems not unlikely that the FEPC will pass the Senate," Stevenson wrote. How should he go about negotiating the delicate politics of appointing commissioners?[75]

Other states were also seriously contemplating an FEP law in 1949, and several of them seemed well poised to make legislative breakthroughs in the early months of the year. Among the most politically relevant states was Robert Taft's native Ohio. The question of FEP legislation was not new to Ohio. As a senator, Taft, of course, had been a strong critic of the "compulsory" approach in congressional debates during the mid-1940s. In fact, Paul Sifton, then a legislative analyst with the NC, strongly suspected that Taft's uncompromising stance had been heavily influenced by the staunch opposition of Ohio business groups to state FEP legislation. In a 1947 letter to a fellow liberal, Sifton suggested that the "material put out by the Ohio Chamber of Commerce attacking the state FEPC bill . . . may, in a degree, explain Senator Taft's reluctance to support the bill we proposed." Prospects for the passage of a state law in Ohio looked far better in 1949, as Republican governor Thomas J. Herbert had been unseated by Democrat Frank Lausche in the preceding elections. The issue came to a head quickly. FEP bills were introduced in both chambers of the Democratic-controlled legislature, and the House Committee on Industry and Labor reported a strong bill that subsequently cleared the entire chamber, 90–83. Largely at the behest of OCC lobbyists, the Senate passed a voluntary bill. It was an unexpected setback. Charles Lucas of the Cleveland NAACP and OCFEP angrily reported to the *Cleveland Call and Post* that he had seen a "Chamber of Commerce representative whispering" in a key senator's ear, and "he was nodding in assent. And before that, C. of C. lobbyists had passed out this watered-down version to Senators as they filed in[to] the chamber." Nevertheless, liberals like Lucas still hoped that enough political leverage could be mustered later on so that the conference committee would deliver a compromise along liberal lines. If they succeeded, Taft would be under much greater pressure to support enforceable legislation in 1950. Elsewhere around the country, liberals were pressing forward with equal determination. With the support of Democratic governor G. Mennen Williams, Michigan liberals successfully staged a public hearing in March, and a "highly diversified army" of delegates to the capitol "stormed the legislative ramparts" to cheer on the supportive testimony of union, religious, and African American leaders.

Seven bills had been introduced into the Pennsylvania legislature, including several by Republicans. Republican governor James Duff seemed independent-minded enough to resist any opposition posed by the powerful Grundy-Martin-Owlet wing of the Pennsylvania GOP, which had long been dominated by industrial interests. It seemed highly likely that a bill would reach a vote. Westward, across the Great Lakes, Minnesota was also building momentum toward a state law, hoping to capitalize on the success that Minneapolis was having with the municipal FEP ordinance that it had passed a few years earlier. Luther W. Youngdahl threw his political clout behind a state FEP bill, making it a central plank of his legislative programs and taking to the airwaves to promote it. The governor even went so far as to twist arms very publicly to ensure that his bill would be reported favorably to the Senate. Public hearings were held in February to "overflow crowds," and a young Whitney Young was among those speaking on behalf of the proposed law.[76]

It was just as well that the interest in FEPC was reaching a crescendo. The stakes were enormous for everyone involved. Success would most directly benefit the hundreds of thousands of Americans who would enjoy new protection from employment discrimination. Politically, passage of FEP legislation in Ohio, Illinois, Pennsylvania, and other populous, industrial states would validate the liberal strategy and promote the cause of fair employment practices in the state and national arena. States that had shown less enthusiasm for FEP laws, such as California, might feel compelled to follow suit, and liberals might prove capable of generating enough political pressure on nonsouthern legislators to break the inevitable Senate filibuster. Certain key Democrats would likely enjoy a political boost. The majority leader of the Senate, Scott Lucas (D-IL), was running for reelection, and the passage of Illinois legislation might embolden him to push harder for Congressional legislation. It certainly would make it more difficult than before for anyone to charge that the senator was out of touch with the prevailing sentiment in his state. Representative Douglas (D-CA) was readying herself for a Senate run, and passage of FEP laws in the sensible Midwest may have given her a stronger defense against conservative efforts to tar her reputation with the red-baiting label, "Pink Lady."

Perhaps the biggest stakes involved the fate of the GOP. Taft would be running for reelection in 1950, and it would put enormous pressure on him if his home state had seen fit to pass legislation that he himself had consistently opposed. In fact, passage of FEP laws would in all likelihood signal the continued viability of liberal Republicanism, which had suffered a grievous blow with Dewey's shocking defeat in 1948. Republican governors such as Youngdahl and Duff—along with Ives, Javits, and other GOP liberals in Congress—might leap to greater prominence, and the liberal wing of the party could continue to pursue its strategy of measured accommodation with the New Deal. At the very least, it would deepen the internal debate within the GOP about how to deal with the general issue of civil rights and the specific question of FEPC. A front-page article in the *Chicago Defender*, entitled "Civil Rights Issue Splits Republicans," captured the possibilities that were in play at the end of 1949. Republican governor Alfred E. Driscoll of New Jersey had won a landslide election over Democratic candidate Elmer H. Wene in late 1949, partly on the strength of Driscoll's popularity among black voters, who admired his role in passing strong civil rights legislation. As a result of the election, some fellow party members had begun to argue that Republicans should "trump the Democratic hand on FEPC" by "marshalling every Republican vote possible for cloture" and then "take credit" for the achievement. Such voices would surely be amplified if key states decided in 1949 to pass FEP legislation.[77]

The state campaign, however, failed to gain significant ground in 1949, and such voices could draw upon only a few examples of how racial liberalism might pay off for the GOP. Only four of the eighteen states where legislation had been introduced—New Mexico, Oregon, Rhode Island, and Washington—actually mustered the political will to pass FEP laws. The states were functioning less as laboratories of democracy and more as steam valves for reform. In a postmortem on the 1950 unsuccessful fight for FEP legislation in Congress, *Newsweek* columnist Ernest K. Lindley argued that it was just as well that it had failed, noting pointedly that only a handful of states had seen fit to pass "compulsory" laws.[78]

Liberals must have been especially frustrated that the margin of defeat in other states was exceedingly narrow in most cases. Republican opposition was usually the deciding factor. The party was divided in almost every state between a liberal and conservative wing, but when it came time to cast decisive votes in 1949, Republicans had few problems closing ranks and relying on their superior numbers or their control of legislative institutions to win. If southern Democrats took advantage of legislative institutions to obstruct FEP proposals in Congress, conservative Republicans made use of similar leverage in northern state legislatures to derail FEP bills. The Minnesota Senate, meeting as a Committee of the Whole, refused to pass Youngdahl's bill, 29–34 and then indefinitely postponed it, 33–28. There is no official tally of how each lawmaker voted, but Christenson's staff at the MEA "kept careful track of the vote," and he declared in the *Guidepost* that "Republicans generally opposed the bill" and "took the leading role in defeating the bill." When liberal Democrats tried to pry an FEP bill free from the House Labor committee in the Pennsylvania legislature, they lost a party-line vote, 109–89. In a strikingly similar scenario, Democratic legislators in Michigan tried to have a Democratic bill discharged from the House State Affairs Committee, but lost a party-line vote, 57–39. In neighboring Illinois, liberals fought to push their House-passed bill through the Senate, where prospects had momentarily improved. In mid-June, liberals counted 25 votes in support of their bill—only one short of the necessary majority. But the length of the deliberations took their toll. Just enough senators lost their nerve and defected at the last minute, and the Senate failed to pass the bill by the narrowest of margins, 23–25. Weeks later, Ohio's Senate followed suit, rejecting the conference report, 13–17. Democrats did control the chamber, but their edge was too narrow—nineteen to fourteen—and Republican discipline was too strong. There was little margin for error. A greater margin might have made a difference. Not a single Republican cast a vote for the conference bill, and the defection of a handful of key Democrats led to yet another setback for liberal hopes.[79]

In the aftermath of hard defeats came hard consequences. Among the most significant of them was the loss of key allies. Democrats gave up more than a dozen seats in the House after the 1950 elections, but most visible concessions were in the Senate, where Republicans nearly retook the chamber. Scott Lucas lost a hotly contested race to Everett Dirksen, and Helen Gahagan Douglas to Richard M. Nixon. Leader of the conservative wing, Robert A. Taft, was reelected to the Senate. Not a single one of these incoming or returning Republicans hailed from an FEP state. None would have to do any fast talking if an FEP bill came to a vote in Congress. While the electoral outcomes were determined by far more than just civil rights, there was a certain symbolism in the moment. The strongest friends of the FEP ideal had been ushered off the political stage. Its most vehement enemies had won or reclaimed elective office. The handful of key states that represented the balance of power in national elections and set the political agenda of the postwar order had narrowly rejected a swift commitment to "freedom from discrimination." Liberals fought for their cause valiantly, but their foes were stronger or better advantaged. Liberal sentiment was simply not widespread enough for FEP laws to prevail in some states. In other states, where it was broad based, it was checked by GOP control of veto points in the legislative process. Had more states adopted FEP legislation by 1949, such victories might have made a critical difference on Capitol Hill, especially during the second session of the 81st Congress. It was not to be, however, and the opportunity for a broader victory slipped away.

To be sure, liberals remained undaunted by the slow pace of progress, and they would eventually succeed in passing FEP laws in most states outside the South. By 1961, even Illinois had passed such a law. A black clerk sobbed quietly in the Senate cloakroom when the bill cleared the Senate. Tears were also reportedly shed by state Sen. Marshall Korshak

(D-IL), long-time sponsor of FEPC. These men were shedding tears of joy. But they may as well have been shedding tears of grief for what might have been. By the end of the Eisenhower years, there had been a profound shift in the underlying rationale for state FEP laws. Such laws were no longer meant to be a spur to congressional action. They were instead a substitute for congressional inaction.[80]

With time, of course, Congress did eventually bestir itself to legislate against job discrimination. To great fanfare and acclaim, Congress passed the Civil Rights Act in 1964, including a provision that covered employment. It marked the first time in the twentieth century that "freedom from discrimination" had been given statutory backing by the federal government. The new law, though, was not quite like the one that liberals had demanded for so many years. Nor was it like the laws that most states had passed. It was incomplete, and it invited years of additional conflict. As liberals and conservatives took up their battle positions on Capitol Hill after 1964, knowledgeable observers of American politics experienced a strong sense of déjà vu. Many of the sectional and partisan patterns that were clearly visible had first surfaced in the Truman era, and now they were playing out again—though there was nothing farcical about it. As they had done so many years ago, liberals and conservatives fought to a standstill during much of the Kennedy, Johnson, and Nixon administrations. Yet something was critically different as well. In the shadow of continuing congressional inaction—indeed, because of congressional inaction—a new and controversial policy was emerging, through a combination of executive orders and court rulings. It was something that nobody had ever truly wanted or clearly foreseen, and it was called affirmative action.

5

I Have a Dream Deferred: The Fall of Fair Employment and the Rise of Affirmative Action

As late afternoon turned into dusk on July 2, 1964, Lyndon B. Johnson must have felt a keen sense of exultation as he strode into the East Room of the White House. It was the zenith of his short tenure as president. After clearing a path through the treacherous political thickets of the 88th Congress and enduring one of the longest and most acrimonious filibusters in the history of the Senate, Johnson and his administration had managed to secure safe passage for the Civil Rights Act of 1964. Parts of the bill had been greatly weakened by the political compromises that made it possible, but it was nonetheless an unparalleled legislative achievement. Congress had not passed a comprehensive civil rights bill of such latitude since Reconstruction, nearly a century earlier. Today, only five hours after the House voted to accept the Senate's version of the bill, Johnson would sign the bill into law. Standing around Johnson during the ceremony was a bipartisan group of congressmen whose support had been critical. In the past three months he had drawn on his legendary political skills to flatter, cajole, implore, and bully Sen. Everett Dirksen (R-IL), Rep. Emanuel Celler (D-NY), Rep. William McCulloch (R-OH), and Sen. Hubert Humphrey (D-MN). Now they took their places next to him as a burst of flash bulbs illuminated their visages for the triumphant, front-page photographs that would appear the next day in newspapers across the country.[1]

Arrayed beyond the congressmen were many of the men—but few of the women—who had led a decades-long struggle to make the federal government the final guarantor of civil rights. The group included the venerable A. Philip Randolph, president of the Brotherhood of Sleeping Car Porters (BSCP); Roy Wilkins, long-time official and now executive director of the National Association for the Advancement of Colored People (NAACP); Whitney Young, director of the National Urban League (NUL); and Clarence Mitchell, chief lobbyist for the NAACP. Hovering close by was the Reverend Martin Luther King, Jr., head of the Southern Christian Leadership Conference (SCLC) and representative of a more confrontational generation of black leadership, whose campaign of non-violent direct action against segregation dramatized the dimensions of the moral dilemma that sociologist Gunnar Myrdal had so eloquently delineated two decades earlier. The significance of the day was not lost on Johnson, who used over seventy-five pens to sign the bill, giving them away as mementos of the occasion. It was indeed a time of celebration and commemoration.[2]

Yet the high spirits hid the fact that key liberal demands had gone unheeded by Congress. Of these, one of the most important was a provision for the establishment of a robust agency akin to the National Labor Relations Board (NLRB), with the regulatory scope and authority to eradicate job discrimination root and branch. Title VII of the Civil Rights Act covered employment discrimination, but it provided for a rather different system. Its centerpiece was the frail Equal Employment Opportunity Commission (EEOC). Unlike the agency that liberals had sought and conservatives had feared, the EEOC did not wield any direct administrative enforcement powers. If mandatory conciliation proceedings between the aggrieved parties failed, it could only direct workers to federal district court, where they would be forced to pursue their claims against employers or unions through costly, time-consuming litigation. In the years that followed, liberals tried hard to remedy what they viewed as the inherent deficiencies of the legislation. Through the first Nixon administration, they proposed numerous bills that would have turned the EEOC into a regulatory agency in the mold of the NLRB. Such proposals were not without prospects of success. Yet none of them passed in full form. Once in 1966 and then again in 1970, legislation aimed at strengthening the enforcement powers of the EEOC passed one house of Congress only to perish in the other. In 1972, Congress finally did respond with legislation, passing the Equal Employment Opportunity Act. But the new law made only incremental adjustments to the law and left the court-based regulatory model largely intact.

In the absence of a strong and centralized federal agency with statutory authority, antidiscrimination policy issued forth from varying and sometimes contradictory institutional sources. Indeed, equal employment opportunity (EEO) policy came to consist of a Byzantine concatenation of statutory provisions, executive orders, and administrative rules and regulations—in addition to federal court decisions that defined the constitutional legitimacy of such policies and set limits on their interpretation. The means for enforcing compliance with civil rights policies varied as considerably as their sources. Behind the regulations governing federal contractors there was the vague but less-than-credible threat of coercion. While government contracts could theoretically be withheld or even cancelled, it had rarely ever happened, partly because it was such a drastic step. Behind other policies there was little more than the irritating possibility that workers and attorneys would decide to go through with court action. Behind still others there was the threat that the failure of business or labor to regulate themselves effectively would strengthen arguments for more substantial government intervention into their affairs.[3]

Most strikingly of all, EEO policies differed greatly in the degree to which they encouraged or discouraged attentiveness to race. For instance, Section 703(a) of Title VII banned the consideration of race, color, religion, sex, or national origin by employers and unions. Section 703(j) took pains to invalidate any subsequent interpretation of Title VII that would "require" any employer or union to "grant preferential treatment to any individual or to any group because of the race, color, religion, sex, or national origin of such individual or group." By contrast, regulations issued in 1961 by the President's Committee on Equal Employment Opportunity (PCEEO) required federal contractors to begin annually enumerating the racial makeup of their work force by filing out Standard Form 40, which had been expressly created for the purpose. The advent of something called "affirmative action" made racial attentiveness even more directly an aspect of federal policy. Beginning in 1968 with the Johnson administration, regulations issued under Executive Order 11246 required federal contractors to take affirmative action by establishing "goals" and "targets" for integrating minorities into their work force. The regulations became caught up in bureaucratic infighting, but a year later officials at Nixon's labor department announced the controversial establishment of the Philadelphia Plan, which required all bidders for government construction contracts to formulate a pre-bid "affirmative action program" that specified concrete "goals" and "targets" for the utilization of minority workers in each trade. In 1970, similar regulations were extended to all government contractors through the labor department's issuance of Revised Order No. 4. At the same time, major American corporations affiliated with a federal program called Plans for Progress (PfP) were also voluntarily taking affirmative action—that is to say, analyzing the racial composition of their work force and setting overt employment and promotion goals for minorities. The federal courts were not standing in anyone's way. Affirmative action had been little more than vague phrase in the early 1960s. By the end of the decade, it had emerged as the most politically explosive tool for racial integration in the employment programs of both the public and private sectors.[4]

What explains the emergence of a fragmented, court-based system of regulating job discrimination? Why did it remain weak and decentralized despite efforts to remedy the situation? Why was the focus on achieving compliance with regulations as much as on enforcing the law? Most intriguingly, why did a small but controversial cluster of policies called affirmative action arise? This chapter traces the limits of Congressional action on job discrimination in the 1960s and early 1970s to the same combination of political forces that obstructed FEP legislation in earlier decades. A coalition of southern Democrats and conservative Republicans stood in the way of all legislative initiatives that would have conferred administrative enforcement authority on the EEOC. Just as in years past, conservative Republicans—lobbied aggressively by organized business— held the balance of power at key moments, due to well-known institutional features of the legislative process. From the time that Title VII became part of the Civil Rights Act, to the eventual passage of the Equal Employment Opportunity Act of 1972, these Republicans consistently exploited their serendipitous position to thwart the liberal campaign and gradually shift the locus of regulation toward the courts. Freedom from discrimination remained a constant object of liberal dreams from Kennedy to Nixon, but it remained a dream deferred. The result was a regulatory vacuum that left federal officials saddled with the responsibility of upholding the law without the enforcement tools to do the job. As grassroots demand for government action against job discrimination swelled during the 1960s, federal officials realized the political and administrative value of launching a compliance-based affirmative action program in the continuing absence of statutory authority for administrative enforcement. At the same time, voluntary affirmative action programs began to emerge among major American companies, who initiated them partly to ward off the threat of further legislation by Congress. Capping off the process, federal judges issued a series of rulings that upheld the legality and constitutionality of the new programs as they had developed. For years, FEP legislation had languished in the legislative branch of the federal government, despite the best efforts of the liberal bloc. Now something called affirmative action was unfolding in the executive and judicial branches.

Few pieces of legislation enjoy more widespread approval than the Civil Rights Act of 1964. Scholars of otherwise divergent views concur on the political significance of the legislation and the grand scope of the social changes that it is said to have wrought. In his history of affirmative action, Hugh Davis Graham calls the Civil Rights Act, not unreasonably, a "spectacular achievement." Along with the Voting Rights Act of 1965, he sees it as the legislative apotheosis of "liberalism's core command against discrimination." Fellow historian Allen Matusow has characterized the bill as "the great liberal achievement of the decade." The sociologist Nathan Glazer boldly argues that it marked the "beginning of a new stage in race relations" that "drove discrimination out of public life." In a volume dedicated to assessing the legacies of the act, political scientist Bernard Grofman echoes Glazer's sentiment: "If ever any piece of legislation showed the power of the central government to change deeply entrenched patterns of behavior, it is the Civil Rights Act of 1964."[5]

The impulse of many present-day scholars to view the passage of the Civil Rights Act as a watershed moment in what has been called the Second Reconstruction is readily understandable. Virtually all participants and observers at the time felt that the country was on the verge of crossing a moral and political threshold. As the prospect for cloture in the Senate grew ever more certain in May 1964, Senator Dirksen, whose efforts were instrumental in solidifying the Republican vote, offered a memorable peroration about racial equality. Paraphrasing the French writer Victor Hugo, he pronounced that "no army can withstand the strength of an idea whose time has come."[6]

Many northern liberals considered progress on the civil rights bill as a vindication of their conceit that Americans had finally been permitted to follow the better angels of their nature, overcoming the machinations of a backward region that had too long held hostage the country as a whole. The "nation's objective," wrote Harvard Law Professor Mark DeWolf Howe, had finally been achieved against efforts to "preserve the ugly customs of a stubborn people." By contrast, other liberals acknowledged that white opposition to civil rights was widespread across the country. It was hard to ignore that Governor George Wallace of Alabama, then a rabid segregationist who had stood in the doorway to block the enrollment of black students at the University of Alabama, had garnered a high number of votes in the Wisconsin and Indiana primaries. Sunbelt conservative Barry Goldwater, the governor of Arizona and an outspoken critic of the Civil Rights bill, was advancing in his bid for the presidency as well. Yet these liberals, too, were exultant, declaring cloture a "triumphant, historic act." They claimed that it revealed "more about the true spirit of the country than the minority vote piled up by Governor Wallace this spring, and more also than Senator Goldwater's progress toward the Republican nomination." Similarly, editorial writers at the *New York Times* concluded that the "overwhelming" support for the bill "testified that the great majority of this nation's people and of their representatives in Washington understood . . . that the time had come to put the full weight of the law behind what is morally right."[7]

Eager to claim and dispense credit for a job well done, civil rights leaders heaped encomiums on the legislation as well as the Congressmen whose votes had made it possible. There was a great deal of sincerity in their celebratory rhetoric, but it was also good politics. In the afterglow of success, embellishing the significance of the legislation could only enhance the reputation of anyone associated with helping it to pass. At the same time, applauding the effort of allies might incline them to lend their support again in the future. An old hand at Washington politics, NAACP Executive Director Roy Wilkins carried out the routine with great aplomb. Wilkins called the Civil Rights Act the "culmination of decades

of efforts by the NAACP and many other organizations and individuals,"
and he went on to claim, somewhat hyperbolically, that it constituted
nothing less than a "Magna Carta of Human Rights." In letters to senators who voted to invoke cloture—twenty-seven Republicans, forty-four
Democrats—he offered the thanks of the NAACP as well as "the general
Negro public and the millions of friends of the civil rights issue." Wilkins
acknowledged contributions from both parties. Just as Republicans "once
more echoed Abraham Lincoln," Democrats "upheld the finest tradition
of their party." He took special care to credit Dirksen, telling the senator
that the successful results of the vote "tended mightily" to "reinforce your
judgment and to vindicate your procedure." The compliment was not
entirely strategic. Dirksen's maneuvers had, in truth, delivered the margin
of victory. Nonetheless, he would remain the dean of the Republican establishment for the foreseeable future, and his influence might prove necessary again. Wilkins would do well to curry favor with him now.[8]

Of course, denouncing the Civil Rights Act was good politics for others
as well. Segregationists like Wallace used it as fodder for incendiary campaign speeches about the depredations of integration. Others grounded
their objections in more philosophical and ideological concerns. Writing
in 1963 from his post at Yale Law School, Robert Bork expressed the
common conservative dismay that the bill would run roughshod over
the principle of individual liberty. The most pressing question when it
came to civil rights legislation was not "whether racial prejudice or preference is a good thing but whether individual men ought to be free to deal
and associate with whom they please for whatever reasons appeal to
them." Bork's considered opinion was unambiguous. Simply because "I
find your behavior ugly by my standards" did not necessarily mean that
"I am justified in having the state coerce you into more righteous paths.
That is itself a principle of unsurpassed ugliness." If his criticisms were
sincere then, it is hard to imagine Bork toasting the enactment of the Civil
Rights Act in 1964.[9]

Strong convictions were not confined to editorial writers or Ivy League
law school professors. Few pieces of legislation in American history have
stirred the passions of ordinary Americans more intensely. The most mur-
derous response came from self-professed vigilantes in southern states.
On June 11, 1963, President John F. Kennedy delivered a televised speech
announcing that his administration and its allies would pursue civil rights
legislation in Congress. Only one day later, NAACP field secretary
Medgar Evers was assassinated. Evers was shot by a sniper as he got out
of his car in the driveway of his own home in Jackson, Mississippi. Bleed-
ing badly, he tried to reach the house for help, but his wounds were too
severe for him to live much longer. Within moments, he died.[10]

Many black voters outside the South saw fit to write their elected representatives to profess their support for the Civil Rights Act. A black mother living in south-central Los Angeles, Mary L. Mitchell, wrote to Congressman Augustus Hawkins (D-CA) the same day that Evers was gunned down. In a hand-written letter, she informed Hawkins that "discrimination is just as prevalent in California as it is in Alabama." She recounted her own early encounter with discrimination. "In 1942, I was denied the privilege of attending the Muscatel Grammar School in Rosemead, California." The exclusion had greatly diminished her opportunities. "I know what this has done to my life," she wrote plainly. More than anything else, she hoped to protect her child from suffering the same fate. She told Hawkins that she had long ago promised to "do anything within my power" to ensure that the same experience of exclusion "doesn't happen to my child." Mitchell urged Hawkins to do "anything within [his] power" to ensure the passage of "meaningful civil rights legislation."[11]

The ringing endorsements of contemporary scholars, the waves of high emotion sweeping the country at the time, the plaudits of civil rights leaders eager to claim and dispense credit for a major victory, and the truly historic dimensions of the legislation itself—all make it difficult to resist a triumphalist narrative.

At the time, however, the bill was enormously unpopular among many Americans—and not only southerners. Northerners living in rural, sparsely populated areas also strongly opposed legislation. A resident of Girard, Ill., writing to Paul Douglas when the civil rights bill was sent over to the Senate in 1964, voiced a common litany of complaints. "I do not feel we need more laws," she began. There were plenty of existing constitutional safeguards against discrimination, specifically the Fourteenth Amendment. Anything more would constitute the active promotion of integration. Moreover, trying to coerce behavior through legislation could actually create new problems to compound the old ones. "Prohibition was a failure," she wrote. "It was forced." Even more dangerous was the tendency of civil rights laws to accord special treatment to African Americans. "If you set up special laws for Negroes you infringe on us all." What was needed were laws that promoted equal rights. "All should have voting rights without poll tax. *All races* [have the] same rights to join unions. Fair job rights *for all*, not *black all*. No preferential, no limits, *no quotas*" (emphasis in original).[12]

It is also easy to overlook that it was highly uneven from provision to provision. It is easy to presume that the bill was all it was ever hoped to be—and it is easy to forget that even as the bill opened up new possibilities it just as surely represented the foreclosure of certain alternatives. To be certain, the Civil Rights Act of 1964 was a major legislative landmark. Omnibus civil rights legislation had not been enacted since Reconstruction a century earlier. It is perhaps the single-most significant political development in the history of the struggle against Jim Crow segregation. Yet the Civil Rights Act was decidedly not of a piece. Comprising eleven distinct titles, it covered vast swaths of social, political, and economic life in the United States—voting, public accommodations and facilities, public education, federally assisted programs, and employment, to name a few. Yet it was not uniformly strong across titles. Its myriad aims, however noble and lofty, were not all equally realized by the design and substance of the provisions themselves. Nor did each title come to have the same degree of effectiveness.

Thoughtful observers at the time recognized that the legislative outcome of Kennedy's belated initiative would only imperfectly embody the ideals that had given rise to it. Reporting on the administration's proposal, Alexander M. Bickel of the *New Republic* anticipated, correctly, that "not all of its words are likely to become law, and not all of its provisions which do get enacted will be equally important or effective." Critical to the impact of the legislation would be enforcement tools that Congress saw fit to authorize. Court-based methods of enforcement seemed problematic to Bickel. "Even at the hands of sympathetic courts," he wrote, "the proposal will suffer from the limitations that naturally attach to all judicially enforced law." While it was not entirely devoid of problems itself, administrative enforcement appeared the stronger alternative. Like dozens of other liberals, Bickel believed that "a full-scale administrative agency, like the National Labor Relations Board, say, or the Security and Exchange Commission, might be capable of having a more immediate, wider, and a more uniform impact."[13]

Eventually, because the Civil Rights Act relied primarily on court enforcement, it would become clear that segregation and discrimination were most effectively challenged in areas where the federal courts quickly and unambiguously signaled their resolve to enforce the law. This was certainly the case with the title covering public accommodations. Only six months after passage of the Civil Rights Act, Title II was unanimously upheld as constitutional in the Supreme Court's *Heart of Atlanta Motel* decision. Desegregation quietly ensued. In areas such as voting, however, so many crippling concessions had been exacted over the course of congressional deliberations that a new piece of legislation altogether was needed. As the provision was written, no amount of resolve on the part of the federal courts could rescue it from inadequacy. The civil rights bloc quickly recognized the flaws of Title I, and the next year—sustained by Johnson's massive Democratic majorities—the Voting Rights Act of 1965 was delivered by the 89th Congress.[14]

Title VII, covering private employment, was neither as sturdy as the public accommodations provision nor as insubstantial as the voting provision. Falling somewhere in between Title I and Title II, it answered the demands of neither liberals nor conservatives. Liberal groups associated with the Leadership Conference on Civil Rights (LCCR) demanded the establishment of a fair employment agency with administrative enforcement powers. Opposing them was the familiar tandem of southern Democrats and conservative Republicans, with the latter raising their customary objection that the bill would unduly extend federal authority over private economic activity. They preferred no legislation at best and educational legislation at worst.[15]

In 1963, the prospects for achieving fair employment legislation were more fluid than they had been in years, even if liberals did not always correctly perceive their chances. A handful of knowledgeable participants, including much of the Kennedy administration, felt certain that such a provision remained unattainable. While vice president Lyndon B. Johnson considered fair employment the "most important" title in the bill, he remained convinced that passing a civil rights bill with it intact would be "absolutely politically impossible."[16] Others outside the administration felt that fair employment faced long odds. Recalling the demise of numerous earlier bills, editors at the *Chicago Defender* were not as pessimistic as Johnson, rating its prospects as "dim." Still, there was surprisingly widespread recognition of the possibility that fair employment might well clear Congress. "It is too early to say whether the proposal will become law," observed *U.S. News and World Report*, "but it now appears to be nearer passage than in many years."[17]

Neither liberals nor conservatives had their way at the end. In what surely must have been a surprising development for liberals in the Kennedy and Johnson administrations, a fair employment provision did, in fact, remain part of the Civil Rights Act of 1964. Eventually covering all firms and unions with twenty-five or more people, Title VII expressly prohibited private employers and labor organizations (along with employment agencies) from discriminating against individuals on the basis of their "race, color, religion, sex, or national origin." Section 703 went on to specify various employment practices that were to be considered illegal. These included a range of discriminatory practices at all stages of the employment cycle—from hiring and promotion to firing. For purposes of enforcement, the bill created a five-person federal agency called the Equal Employment Opportunity Commission. The EEOC would be led by a chairman and vice chairman, and the president had the power to appoint all five positions.[18]

If the EEOC was truly intended to enforce the law, it was paradoxically denied any direct enforcement powers. Instead of having the authority to issue cease-and-desist orders and mandate various forms of restitution—as the EEOC would have had under numerous liberal proposals—it was given a range of lesser powers. For instance, it had statutory authority to make "technical studies" and furnish "technical assistance" to private employers and unions. Yet if employers or unions simply refused to follow the law, the EEOC could do nothing itself to force compliance. Its central thrust was rather to encourage voluntary compliance. As such, it was given the power to receive and investigate written allegations of discrimination from workers. In the course of their investigation, EEOC officials were permitted to subpoena relevant witnesses and documents. In the event that the EEOC determined the charges to be true, however, the commission could not act straightaway to enforce the law. It was first required to encourage the aggrieved parties to settle matters on their own. In the words of Section 706(a), it would first have to "eliminate any such alleged unlawful employment practice by informal methods of conference, conciliation, and persuasion." Of course, lacking any enforcement powers or punitive sanctions of their own, EEOC officials faced understandably long odds when trying to elicit voluntary compliance from employers or unions who were determined to evade the law.[19]

Only if the EEOC failed to secure voluntary compliance—which could take months—would enforcement proceedings begin. Even then, the EEOC performed a sharply circumscribed role. For instance, it was not the commission itself that would enforce the law. That task fell by design to the federal courts. If enforcement action proved necessary, the EEOC was permitted only to direct aggrieved workers to the appropriate federal court, where they could sue the alleged offender by filing a private civil action. This lawsuit could not draw on any evidence gathered by the EEOC when it was trying to determine whether there was a reasonable basis to believe that the allegations were true. In fact, Section 706(a) explicitly barred any such information from being "used as evidence in a subsequent proceeding." The court would hence be responsible for both establishing the facts of the case as well as interpreting the application of the law. If, on the basis of its own independent inquiry, the court ultimately concluded that an unlawful employment practice had occurred in violation of Title VII, then it would be the court—and not the EEOC— that would have the statutory obligation to "order such affirmative action as may be appropriate" to achieve compliance and compensate workers for the harms they may have incurred.[20]

This model of regulation was a far cry from the sword that liberals had sought or the leviathan that conservatives had feared. By defining and prohibiting various unlawful practices in private sector employment, Title VII did greatly extend federal regulatory authority over job discrimination. In keeping with conservative wishes, however, Title VII stressed voluntary rather than enforced compliance. While the EEOC was given the authority to investigate allegations of discrimination, it could not itself

force offending employers or unions to comply with the law—no matter
how egregious or self-evident their violation. At the same time, Title VII
did not lack teeth entirely. In conservative proposals of yesteryear, it remained unclear whether even legal action would be permitted. By contrast, Title VII unambiguously stipulated a court-based procedure in
which the federal courts held the power to enjoin respondents from committing further discriminatory acts or to offer restitution to aggrieved
workers. Hence the EEOC possessed highly limited and indirect enforcement power—in the sense that it was a key participant in a two-tiered
regulatory process that could possibly culminate in the exposure of guilty
parties to legal action and hence potential damages.[21]

What explains the particular features of the regulatory compromise embodied in Title VII? That the passage of a civil rights bill was conceivable
in 1963 owed largely to an epic confrontation that unfolded over several
weeks in Birmingham, Ala., one of the most segregated cities in the country. In the spring of that year, thousands of African Americans took to
Birmingham lunch counters and streets to protest the segregation of public facilities and accommodations. Led by the Reverend Dr. Martin Luther
King's SCLC, hundreds of demonstrators were met by Eugene "Bull"
Connor's police force, which promptly arrested and jailed them. King
himself was arrested on Good Friday, April 12. Behind bars, he penned
his celebrated "Letter from Birmingham Jail" on bits of smuggled scrap
paper. The showdown between King and Connor came to a head on May
3, when more than a thousand black children assembled at the Sixteenth
Street Baptist Church to participate in a march. Wanting to break up the
march before it took place, Connor unleashed his men on the children
and hapless bystanders. Connor's repression succeeded in averting the
march, but it also yielded a collection of indelible, sickening images—
fearsome police dogs jumping at protesters, streams of water savagely
blasting children down the street and pinning them against building walls,
and police officers wielding their billy clubs with reckless abandon. The
protests had been held in the nonviolent tradition that King espoused, but
the brutalization of their friends, brothers, and sisters proved too much
for some blacks to take. Some black residents let go of their restraint and
began to throw rocks at the police. Non-violence was breaking down.[22]

Largely as a result of the repression on display in Alabama, Kennedy
reversed his administration's stance on civil rights. Since the day of his
inauguration, he had been determined to defer action on civil rights legislation. Like presidents before him, he knew that his broader legislative
program would stagnate if he offended powerful southern Congressmen
by pressing too hard or fast on civil rights. One liberal noted in July that
a mere "two months ago" the possibility of omnibus legislation "would
have been thought laughable." It was the confrontation at Birmingham

that forced a drastic revision of Kennedy's political calculus. With the civil rights movement gaining momentum, further episodes of insurgency were sure to come. More worrisome, it was no longer certain that African Americans would continue to abide by the methods of nonviolent direct action favored by King's SCLC. This heightened white fears that doing nothing on civil rights now would only strengthen the hand of radicals like Malcolm X and ensure that there would be, in the words of James Baldwin, a "fire next time." Under such circumstances, Kennedy grew concerned about the political price of inaction. If he failed to act decisively, voters would surely take their dissatisfaction with his irresolute leadership to the ballot box. At the same time, political conditions in Congress looked more favorable for civil rights than ever before. If he accepted the risk and soldiered ahead, he stood a good chance of succeeding. The administration's bill, H.R. 7152, was sent to Congress on June 19, 1963, just a little over two months after King penned his historic jailhouse missive.[23]

Cold War politics also figured into Kennedy's decision-making, as the tremors from the South generated discomfiting levels of negative publicity overseas. China and the Soviet Union both gave the crisis prominent coverage in their broadcasts and news publications. A story from China charged that "democracy and freedom" were "hollow slogans." The official Soviet news organ, *Pravda*, condemned the "Monstrous Crimes of Racists in the U.S.A." At a conference of independent African nations in Addis Ababa, Ethiopia, in late May, delegates expressed shock at the treatment of the protesters and spent considerable time formulating a formal response. Later, Secretary of State Dean Rusk sent a notice to all U.S. diplomatic and consular offices, reassuring them that the federal government intended to take "decisive action" well before the crisis began to "impinge even more seriously upon our policies and objectives." It had never been more important, exhorted Rusk, to "defend the United States against the global convulsion of bad publicity about race relations."[24]

Kennedy's newfound commitment to seeing civil rights legislation through Congress was not the only, nor ever perhaps the most important, force ushering the Civil Rights Act toward passage. Over the hot summer, civil rights activists escalated their demands for action, reflecting the venerable A. Philip Randolph's conviction that "Congress will not act on any meaningful civil rights legislation unless it is made to act by pressure." The civil rights movement reached a dramatic summit on August 28, when, fulfilling Randolph's vision from twenty years earlier, more than 250,000 people descended on the nation's capitol in a March on Washington for "Jobs and Freedom." Marchers were treated to performances by singers Joan Baez and Mahalia Jackson, appearances by movie stars Sidney Poitier, Charlton Heston, and Marlon Brando, and speeches by

Walter Ruether; but the unquestioned highlight of the day came when King stepped to the podium to deliver his now-beloved speech, "I Have a Dream." The pressure generated by such demonstrations was put to effective use by a cadre of experienced civil rights lobbyists, whose activities were coordinated on Capitol Hill by the LCCR. The core of experienced lobbyists included Joseph Rauh of Americans for Democratic Action (ADA), Andrew Biemiller of the American Federation of Labor-Congress of Industrial Organizations (AFL-CIO), Jack Conway of the AFL-CIO Industrial Union Department, Rev. Walter Fauntroy of the SCLC, and the NAACP's Clarence Mitchell.[25]

Kennedy's assassination brought to the presidency a man possessed of consummate legislative talents and ample willingness to exercise them. Lyndon B. Johnson had spent six terms as representative and three terms as senator—including seven years as the youngest Democratic leader in the history of the Senate—honing his legendary skills of persuasion. Upon assuming office, he applied them assiduously. Years later, Mitchell would call Johnson's influence the "deciding factor" in securing the Civil Rights Act.[26]

The racial conflagration in Birmingham, ongoing social and political pressure from the civil rights movement, Kennedy's tragic martyrdom, Johnson's consummate ability and determination as president—each of these factors may be considered essential prerequisites, even necessary conditions, for the passage of meaningful omnibus civil rights legislation, which would have been inestimably more difficult to achieve in their absence. Whether singly or jointly, however, they far from dictated the final structure of the statute as a whole. Nor did they come close to dictating the provisions of any single title. Explaining why the Civil Rights Act contained the range of titles it did—and why Title VII called for a court-based system of enforcement centered on the threat of private civil action—calls for a closer look at enduring partisan and ideological divisions in Congress, particularly the overlooked importance of conservative Republicans and their loathing for government regulation of economic and social behavior.[27]

There can be little doubt concerning the base of support for civil rights. Any omnibus bill could count on the votes of northern Democrats like Emanuel Celler (D-NY) in the House and Hubert H. Humphrey (D-MN) in the Senate. In addition to the qualified support of moderate Republicans like Representative McCulloch, it could also depend on liberal Republicans such as Rep. John V. Lindsay (R-NY) or Sen. Thomas Kuchel (R-CA). With just as much certainty, however, it could expect to attract the wily obstructionist stratagems of southern Democrats, who continued to chair more than half the committees in the House and two-thirds of the committees in the Senate. Accordingly, the bill would have to run a gauntlet of daunting and familiar hurdles. Even if the bill somehow eluded the grasp of the Rep. Howard "Judge" Smith (D-VA), who controlled the all-powerful House Rules Committee, it still might fall into the hands of the Senate Judiciary Committee, chaired by Sen. James O. Eastland (D-MS).[28]

In the event that their control of the committee system in either chamber failed them, southern Democrats could always resort to the time-honored weapon of the Senate filibuster, whose real or threatened deployment had succeeded in gutting civil rights bills twice, once in 1957 and 1960. If southerners did not tire of speaking, civil rights supporters could only end debate by invoking cloture, which at the time required the votes of sixty-seven senators. Led, as always, by Richard B. Russell, Jr. (D-GA), southerners held twenty-one seats in the Senate. The civil rights bloc could count on roughly sixty votes, perhaps a bit more, from northern Democrats as well as liberal and moderate Republicans. The remaining votes belonged to Republicans, and of the thirty-three Republicans in the Senate, it would be eight or nine conservative Republicans who would play the most decisive role in the passage of any civil rights bill.[29]

Without the participation of Republicans in both houses of Congress—particularly that of the conservative faction of the GOP—it would be wholly impossible to form a bipartisan coalition robust enough to shepherd the civil rights bill past certain danger. The bill's destiny, and its substance, rested largely with them. Editors at the *Chicago Defender* instantly recognized the political arithmetic of the upcoming battle in Congress. "The administration cannot hope to pass the legislation without substantial GOP help." While "it was not yet clear how it could be used," Republicans held the "balance of power." Magnifying the leverage of conservative Republicans were reasonable doubts that they or their party stood to gain anything from supporting civil rights. In the past, Republicans had strongly supported most types of civil rights legislation—theirs had been the "Party of Lincoln." Yet the electoral payoff for siding with the civil rights bloc remained uncertain. In contrast to many Democrats, most Republicans did not hold office in districts or states with a sizable black electorate, and their northern white constituents began to express wariness about the actual social and economic changes that a commitment to racial desegregation would necessarily entail. "The hope for passing a civil rights bill this year, or next, is receding," warned the *New Republic*. "Republicans from more-or-less lily-white states or districts (and that means the majority of Republicans) are beginning to sense that their constituents, although all for equality in principle, do not want to compete with Negroes for jobs or live next door to them." At the same time, Democrats needed the civil rights bill more than Republicans did.

Kennedy's reelection campaign would begin shortly, and he would come under certain attack if he did not do something to diminish the racial tension in the country. On the other hand, standing up for civil rights involved considerable political risks. If conservative Republicans pledged their support incautiously, it might invite Democrats to press for a bill that had absolutely no chance of passing in order to blame Republicans for its inevitable failure.[30]

Republicans such as Sen. Barry Goldwater (R-AZ) and Sen. Everett M. Dirksen (R-IL), like Robert A. Taft (R-OH) before them, possessed a special aversion to legislation that would expand federal regulation of private social and economic activity (figure 5.1). Like key numbers of other conservative Republicans, they were chary about granting the federal government coercive powers or sanctions to ensure compliance with the law. They supported fair employment practices (FEP) and equal employment opportunity in principle, but could not be more strongly opposed to NLRB-style enforcement. Indeed, they were predisposed to oppose almost any other kind of enforcement mechanism as well. Dirsken's conservative views on regulation were well known to most observers at the time, and Goldwater would come out strongly against the Civil Rights Bill, ultimately voting against it because he considered racial inequality a "problem of the heart and mind" that was beyond the reach of legislation. In an irony that has gone overlooked, it seems that Dirksen himself had introduced two "enforceable" FEP bills into Congress in the 1940s as a young U.S. representative. He had certainly changed his mind by 1963.[31]

The stance of conservative Republicans reflected the political and economic interests of the employers and companies whose interests they tended to represent. In the words of *New Republic*'s Murray Kempton, conservative Republicans shared ideological affinities with "businessmen who dislike fair employment practice laws if only because they mean keeping even more records and entertaining even more federal agents." Liberal views pervaded Kempton's magazine, but he correctly noticed the extent to which conservative Republicans, foremost among them Dirksen, had become aligned with the business community. "Dirsken is the Senator most trusted to represent the American businessman in his distaste for any visitor from government who does not come bearing subsidy. There are no less than a dozen Republican Senators whose inclinations to sympathy, like Dirksen's, are vulnerable to no appeal so much as the one which comes from a chamber of commerce." And business groups did appeal to Congress. The president of the U.S. Chamber of Commerce (USCC), Walter Carey, wrote senators in May 1964 to express the concerns of the chamber about several provisions. A representative of the Illinois Chamber of Commerce, James B. O'Shaughnessy, would later note that his organization had lobbied Congress intensively during the

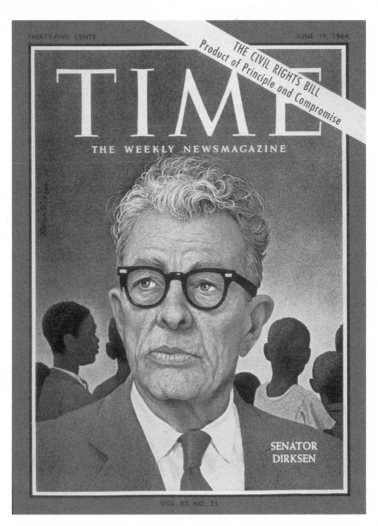

Figure 5.1 U.S. Sen. Everett M. Dirksen (R-IL) on the cover of *Time*, June 19, 1964. There was a widespread understanding that the Civil Rights Act of 1964 was a product of "principle and compromise," in the words of the banner on this *Time* magazine cover. As the top Republican in the Senate, Dirksen was given most of the credit for brokering the compromise between the southern and northern wings of the Democratic Party. What often went overlooked was what the minority leader refused to concede. In 1964 and then again in 1966, Dirksen's implacable opposition to cease-and-desist authority left the Equal Employment Opportunity Commission bereft of any enforcement power until 1972. Courtesy of Time Life Pictures/Getty Images.

deliberations over the Civil Rights Act, likely visiting Dirksen himself on several occasions: "We like to feel that we had a small role to play in the drafting of the final version of Title VII, for after four delegation trips to Washington and numerous conferences of our labor relations committee, we developed sixteen pages of suggested amendments to the section, and many of them found their way into the statute."[32]

If it was not clear at the outset of the legislative process how Republicans would exercise their leverage, it soon became evident that they would expend the bulk of it scaling back both the scope and the enforcement provisions of most titles. Yet it would hardly be necessary for conservative Republicans to lift a finger. Others would do much of the work for them. A fateful moment for Title VII came after Emanuel Celler's (D-NY) Subcommittee No. 5 reported the bill to the House Judiciary Committee on October 2, 1963. Much to the chagrin of the Kennedy administration—which had been making a concerted effort to craft a bipartisan bill with Republicans—liberal Democrats had relied on their majority in the subcommittee to push through a very strong bill, one that the administration feared would ruin their strategy. This bill included a title on the FEPC that provided for administrative enforcement. Introduced as an amendment by Peter W. Rodino (D-NJ), it was based in its entirety on liberal Democrat James Roosevelt's (D-CA) H.R. 405, which had been approved earlier in the year by the House Education and Labor Committee. The architects of Kennedy's original bill had left out an FEP provision at the last minute for fear that it would too severely antagonize Republicans, and now its reappearance spelled obvious trouble.[33]

The subcommittee's inclusion of a fair employment title had been no honest accident. Celler had planned to report a muscular bill in order to have something to trade away in the full Judiciary Committee, which he also chaired. The approach, however, did pose some risks by raising strong feelings on all sides and complicating the political dynamics. Celler's bill elated civil rights leaders. Earlier, they had reluctantly followed the counsel to ask for "one-half of a loaf" and expect only "one-quarter of a loaf." Now, at last, circumstances seemed appropriate to fight for a "whole loaf" and to expect one. Not surprisingly, the bill angered House Republicans, most of all McCulloch, ranking minority member on both committees. McCulloch had been working closely with the administration to craft a bipartisan bill, and he considered the subcommittee version a grand betrayal, since it could place Republicans in the uncomfortable position of having to prune back the bill. This would put the Democrats in perfect position to blame the GOP again for the demise of civil rights. Kennedy also considered the bill a betrayal, and he privately expressed frustration at the civil rights lobby. "Can Clarence Mitchell and the Leadership group deliver three Republicans on the Rules

Committee and sixty Republicans on the House floor?" he asked. The subcommittee bill shattered the fragile bipartisan comity that Kennedy had sought to nurture.[34]

From mid- to late October, as the bill faced the scrutiny of the full Judiciary Committee, Celler, McCulloch, and Justice Department officials worked cautiously and quietly to avert crisis and revive bipartisan cooperation. A new compromise bill to satisfy Republicans was delicately worked out over the course of several weeks. The destiny of the fair employment provision was sealed at morning meeting on October 28 at the Congressional Hotel. At 10am, Deputy Attorney General Nicholas deB. Katzenbach and civil rights chief Burke Marshall met with McCulloch and two Republican aides, William Copenhaver and Robert Kimball. It was during the meeting that both sides agreed to do away with the subcommittee version of Title VII, sensing that it would not withstand the scrutiny of conservative Republicans. In a subsequent congressional fight over EEO policy, Joe Rauh would later charge that Dirksen's support for the Civil Rights Act made it necessary to compromise on Title VII by denying the EEOC cease-and-desist authority. It is not clear from the archival record whether Dirksen himself ever *directly* intervened in the McCulloch–Department of Justice (DOJ) negotiations. Yet it would be unwarranted to discount Rauh's argument as pure advocacy, for it was ultimately the known hostility of conservative Republicans (and particularly Dirksen in the Senate) to administrative regulation that dictated the specific terms of the compromise on Title VII.[35]

At the same time, the compromise bill did not abandon the fair employment title altogether, which would have enraged liberals. Instead, it replaced the liberal title with a court-centered proposal by Robert Griffin (R-MI), Charles Goodell (R-NY), and Albert Quie (R-MN). This trio of younger Republicans considered administrative regulation to be as one-sided and coercive as did their conservative elders. Yet they had a greater appreciation of the importance of granting the federal government a modicum of enforcement powers—so long as business and labor would be given a fair chance to plead their case in federal court. The essence of the Griffin-Goodell-Quie proposal, in fact, was that it called for court-based enforcement of job discrimination. If informal conciliation proved inadequate to forcing compliance on the part of employers or unions, the EEOC could file a lawsuit on behalf of a complainant in federal district court.[36]

The change garnered little sustained attention at the time. When the bipartisan bill was eventually accepted by the House Judiciary Committee on October 29, *Time* briskly noted that a "national equal opportunities commission is set up to outlaw discrimination in industry—establishments employing twenty-five or more people and engaged in interstate commerce. The commission can sue for enforcement in federal court." In a lengthy article summarizing the cascade of developments that week, *Newsweek* breezily reported that "FEPC stayed on as a concession to the liberals, but, instead of deciding cases of job discrimination, the agency would have to prove them in Federal court." Yet the introduction of a court-enforcement system was the most decisive alteration in the substance of Title VII. No single concession more vividly symbolizes the costs of bipartisanship. Nowhere is the price of Republican support—and the overlooked significance of conservative Republicans in shaping civil rights policy—more concretely captured than in the nature of the quiet compromise reached in the waning days of October.[37]

Liberals did enjoy at least one stroke of good luck along the final path to the Senate. In a meeting that took place immediately before the House Judiciary Committee was set to vote, House Republican leader Charles Halleck (R-IN) told Kennedy flatly that he could not support the FEPC provision. Knowing that Halleck's support was critical, Kennedy instantly yielded: "Well, Charlie, it's late; you'd better get over there, and we'll vote it out." After the congressman left the room, Kennedy turned to Katzenbach and complained: "I thought you said he was on board the FEPC provision." Katzenbach reassured the doubtful president that McCulloch had told him that Halleck would accept Title VII. This was a mistaken assurance, but it would be a year later before Katzenbach would realize that his otherwise reliable memory had failed him. Reviewing notes from his meetings, he belatedly realized that McCulloch had made a point of telling him the Halleck would *not* support FEPC. Liberals were fortunate that Halleck did not make a fuss. Although he could have ordered Republicans to scuttle the committee vote over the fair employment title, he decided to support Title VII anyway. By a vote of 20–14, the bipartisan bill was accepted by the Judiciary Committee for consideration; it was successfully reported out of committee two days before Kennedy's assassination. On February 10, 1964, when it overwhelmingly passed the full House by a vote of 290–130, Title VII remained largely as it had been left in McColloch-DOJ agreement.[38]

When the bill reached the Senate later in 1964, it did not fall into the clutches of Eastland's feared Judiciary Committee. Instead, it was successfully sent to the entire Senate and therefore placed directly into Dirksen's purview. This would prove the other major test of the bill. If conservative Republicans derived their influence from holding the balance of power, then it was Dirksen who controlled their votes. Dirksen commanded the respect of his GOP colleagues because of his lengthy tenure in the Senate, his reputation for compromise, and his superb oratorical skills. But his centrality in the passage of the Civil Rights Act was also a function of Democratic strategy. Senator Humphrey, Kennedy's floor leader in the

Senate, deliberately made Dirksen the linchpin of Senate deliberations, hoping to flatter his sense of self-importance. The high point of Dirksen's leverage might well have been the early weeks of April 1964, when it became clear that Humphrey and Kuchel had cobbled together a bloc of fifty-nine votes for the civil rights bill. One of the most active members of the administration on the bill, no less a figure than Robert F. Kennedy, then Attorney General, clearly understood Dirsken's political relevance. As he would later recall, on the nervous occasions when his brother and Vice President Johnson demanded to know who was going to supply enough votes to carry the administration's bill, there was a clear answer. "[I]n the last analysis . . . [it] was Dirksen." Kempton of the *New Republic* made a similar observation. Cloture would be within reach if Johnson's "black arts" could conjure up another four votes from the Democratic side. Then only four more GOP votes would be needed to reach the sixty-seven required. But "everyone that is possible is also a Dirksenite." This made Dirksen the "last hope of the resistance." It also gave him tremendous power to dictate the terms of his consent to the bill.[39]

If he held the power to eviscerate the bill, particularly Title II (Public Accommodations) or Title VII (Employment), which he personally opposed, Dirksen did not wield it with total abandon. "He must, of course, extract some price for turning over the citadel," wrote Kempton. "But [t]he changes in the law which he demanded," Kempton went on to note, "were almost daily less of substance and more of form." Kempton was only partially right when it came to Title VII. Some interventions, of course, were insignificant. But several of Dirksen's amendments would touch on precisely the issues that were central to subsequent litigation. Dirksen added the word "intentionally" in Section 703(g), and he excluded bone fide seniority systems from Title VII coverage.[40]

Perhaps the most important of Dirksen's amendments involved the enforcement authority of the EEOC. The shift from an administrative to court-based enforcement had already occurred in the House leadership compromise the previous October. Yet it remained unclear throughout the Senate debate exactly what system of legal enforcement would be established. Would it be one in which the EEOC had a limited but still meaningful capacity to propose broad principles and policy to the federal courts by selectively filing lawsuits that implicated key legal or constitutional issues? Or would it be a fragmented, decentralized system whose development would be driven largely by aggrieved individuals pursuing private litigation in disparate venues across the country? Dirksen's proposed amendment No. 511 was unambiguous on the question; it sought altogether to deny the EEOC the power to file suit. According to a legal analysis by the LCCR, Dirksen's amendment would have a devastating impact, "devitalizing the already weak enforcement provisions of Title

VII." It would effectively nullify the deterrent effect of the law. Anyone tempted to violate the law would know that the EEOC was toothless and that the onus of enforcement fell primarily upon the victims of discrimination and their attorneys. Dirksen faced enormous bipartisan pressure to relent—including overtures from Robert Kennedy, Nicholas Katzenbach, Burke Marshall, Mansfield (D-MT), Hubert Humphrey, Clifford Case (R-NJ), and Thomas Kuchel (R-CA)—but the long-term senator from Illinois never budged, knowing full well the extent of the leverage he possessed. Kuchel was privately disgusted by Dirksen's obstinacy. A compromise in May eventually broke the impasse. Facilitated by the ever-pragmatic Robert Kennedy, it surely met with Dirksen's satisfaction. As the title was amended, nobody could complain that the law could not be enforced. If there was preliminary evidence that a person or a group of people at a particular employer or in a certain union seemed engaged in pervasive and systematic discrimination, then the Attorney General was authorized to file a "pattern or practice" lawsuit. On the other hand, individual victims themselves retained the right to initiate a private civil action. It was the EEOC itself that was left without any statutory authority whatsoever to enforce the law. Its function was strictly advisory. It could recommend that the DOJ or aggrieved individuals bring suit, but it was otherwise helpless.[41]

It was only a matter of time before Title VII would become the focus of political conflict. For all of the panegyric rhetoric that they showered on the Civil Rights Act in 1964, liberals were keenly aware of the regulatory difficulties created by the provision, and they had no intention of letting the problems go unabated. As the date on which the law would take effect drew near, civil rights groups began to voice the private misgivings that many of them had muted in the previous year. Head of the NAACP Legal Defense Fund Jack Greenberg called the EEOC "weak, cumbersome, [and] probably unworkable." Greenberg sought to flood the agency with complaints. It would be unable to handle its workload, and liberals would have another reason to call for reform. "We think the best way to get it amended," he said, "is to show that it doesn't work." Just a day after Title VII became law, James Farmer, national director of the Congress on Racial Equality (CORE), declared that the "present administrative structure of Title VII involves too much red tape [and] is too cumbersome." Farmer demanded that the provision be immediately amended to improve administrative efficiency and increase the penalties assessed for infractions of the law. Demands for regulatory reform were nearly unanimous among liberal groups.[42]

Evidence compiled by the Democratic Study Group confirmed the weakness of the new agency. By 1971, it had received more than 52,000 charges of discrimination. Of these, 35,445 were investigated, and 63 percent of the investigated cases turned up reasonable cause to believe that discrimination had occurred. Yet only half of the investigated cases led to a total or partial conciliation agreement. It was a fairly dismal record by any reasonable standard.[43]

It was unsurprising that civil rights organizations such as the NAACP, CORE, and LCCR found Title VII and the EEOC wanting. Criticisms of the agency, however, were far from self-serving obsessions of the civil rights community. In fact, they were widespread and mainstream. The black press led the way, as it had in the postwar struggle for FEP legislation. Criticisms also surfaced as a major topic of news coverage and editorial comment in the major dailies. Editorial pages of several papers repeatedly called for Congress to grant the EEOC cease-and-desist authority. The editorial page of the *New York Times* was perhaps the most consistently supportive out of all the national newspapers. "It has long been evident," it wrote in 1971, "that more effective enforcement of the bias ban depends on giving the EEOC the power to issue cease-and-desist orders on its own." News reports of legislative developments noted matter-of-factly that the EEOC lacked enforcement authority and had to rely on voluntary compliance by unions and employers. As the *Los Angeles Times* observed in a typical report, "The EEOC has no power to force compliance with the law; it can only use conciliation to get the accused employer to hire the complaining applicant."[44]

The deepest criticisms were fashioned by top legal scholars. In a well-received study published by the Twentieth Century Fund in 1966, Columbia Law School professor Michael I. Sovern offered a thorough and balanced critique of Title VII and the EEOC. Sovern was indisputably one of the most brilliant legal minds in the country. At the tender age of twenty-eight, he had become the youngest full professor at Columbia in living memory; he would soon become dean. Unlike the most ideologically motivated critics of Title VII, however, he conceded that his analysis might be premature. The EEOC had yet to develop a track record of enforcement. If it turned out that noncompliant employers and unions were yielding gently to conciliation proceedings, then "Title VII's procedures will not seem so misshapen as they do today." Yet even the temperate Sovern, who had devoted four years to preparing his study, could not resist concluding that the EEOC was a "poor, enfeebled thing." The regulatory solution he proposed to strengthen the commission was the same one echoed by numerous other critics. In addition to having broader coverage, it should be given the power to "institute administrative enforcement proceedings, including a fair hearing and eventuating in a judicially enforceable cease-and-desist order."[45]

All manner of state and federal officials belonged to the swelling chorus of consensus about the necessity of administrative enforcement authority—without which their duties, they believed, were virtually impossible to fulfill. In testimony before a congressional subcommittee in 1965, George H. Fowler head of the New York State Commission for Human Rights, unambiguously called on Congress to give the EEOC the authority that his own agency had wielded for two decades. "Our experience in New York leads me to believe that an agency operating under the present Title VII of the Civil Rights Act of 1964, without administrative enforcement machinery, will not and cannot be as effective as one which has the power to issue an enforceable order after a hearing." The contrast with the EEOC could not be starker. "We're out to kill an elephant with a fly gun," one EEOC chairman said colorfully. Indeed, nearly every chair of the EEOC, beginning with Franklin D. Roosevelt, Jr., called for administrative enforcement authority. Steven M. Schulman, who took over Roosevelt's post, put a fine point on the matter in 1967, explaining that he did not need a battering ram against discrimination. Cease-and-desist authority would be useful because it would facilitate successful conciliation proceedings between aggrieved parties. Speaking before an audience at Pepperdine University, he highlighted the example of the Pennsylvania Human Relations Commission, where "[t]he mere existence of the cease and desist provision has lent weight to [their] deliberations and has led . . . [to a] large number of successful adjustments." Schulman added, "By the same token, I believe that cease and desist powers for the EEOC will result in successful conciliation." The subsequent EEOC chairman, Clifford L. Alexander, Jr., would join Roosevelt and Schulman in calling for administrative enforcement, as would William H. Brown III in the first few months of his term as Nixon's appointee to the post.[46]

Federal and state commissioners were joined in their demands by the U.S. Civil Rights Commission (USCRC). In the late 1960s, under the leadership of Notre Dame president Rev. Theodore M. Hesburgh, the USCRC began to make periodic, comprehensive studies of federal civil rights enforcement. Its voluminous 1970 report, running more than one-thousand pages, found a "number of inadequacies common to nearly all Federal departments and agencies—inadequacies in agency recognition of the nature and scope of their civil rights responsibilities, in the methods used to determine civil rights compliance, and in the use of enforcement techniques to eliminate noncompliance." The report addressed the state of civil rights in housing and federally assisted programs, but one of the longest and complex sections took aim at private employment. Staff researchers found that the EEOC had a "meager budget and staff" with which to handle the mass of complaints it was expected to process. Most important, while the EEOC enjoyed fairly "wide jurisdiction" over job discrimination, it possessed only "limited means to enforce" the statutory provisions of Title VII. The key reform was clear. While the USCRC recommended that EEOC Commissioners act more aggressively to initiate industry-wide compliance and to streamline the complaint procedures, it placed enforcement powers at the top of the list. "Congress should amend Title VII of the Civil Rights Act of 1964 to authorize the Equal Employment Opportunity Commission (EEOC) to issue cease and desist orders to eliminate discriminatory practices through administrative action." This finding and recommendation were also featured in a short follow-up report issued seven months later, and they were reiterated in a full-scale report issued in 1971.[47]

Reformist sentiment emanated as well from the highest circles of policymaking in the Johnson administration, where top-ranking officials seriously contemplated supporting legislation in every session of Congress after the passage of the Civil Rights Act. Many of them agreed with Katzenbach that Title VII was simply a "very poor provision." Ramsey Clark, who would take over Katzenbach's role at the Department of Justice (DOJ), reached to similar conclusions. "There appears to be no doubt as to the benefits that would accrue were the EEOC given cease and desist powers," he wrote. Most comparable federal agencies, like the NLRB, Federal Trade Commission (FTC), or Securities and Exchange Commission (SEC), wielded such powers. In fact, these were precisely the powers proposed by H.R. 10065, "which passed the House and was endorsed by the Administration." A report by the DOJ in 1968 found that the EEOC had been "severely hampered" by its lack of enforcement authority. "Largely because it has no power to issue binding orders," it surmised, "EEOC's efforts to conciliate are often unsuccessful." This crippled any chance that the law would be enforced. "If EEOC is unable to achieve successful conciliation, the only available remedy for a person complaining of the violation is time-consuming private litigation, which would be an additional burden on the already overburdened federal courts." Only individuals with the time and money to pursue a case for years would see justice served. The DOJ recommended the conferral of cease-and-desist authority upon the EEOC, which won strong support from the Bureau of the Budget. It agreed that the "EEOC's efforts to conciliate are often unsuccessful because it lacks enforcement power such as the cease and desist authority would provide." It deemed the proposed legislation "necessary" and suggested that it "should be transmitted to Congress."[48]

There was naturally opposition to reform in Congress, and southern reactionaries were among the loudest and most sensational critics. Equally outspoken, however, was the business community in every section of the country. Its rationale for opposition shifted over time, and so was the type of policy it was willing to accept. Nevertheless, it was continuously opposed to any kind of strengthening legislation that would give administrative enforcement authority to the EEOC. Initially, business groups adopted a public posture of restrained opposition, urging Congress to let the existing arrangement have a chance to work before making any modifications. A spokesman for the Illinois Chamber of Commerce, which claimed a membership of 20,000 individuals and 8,000 companies, testified at length against a bill under consideration in 1965. The chamber had been a long-time opponent of state FEP legislation in Illinois, and James B. O'Shaughnessy, representing the chamber, frankly acknowledged as much. Yet he claimed that the chamber supported "equal employment for all"—as long as it was achieved through voluntary means. The proposed legislation before Congress was thus simply "untimely and inappropriate." At minimum, he argued, two years should be given to develop a track record before any further legislation should be contemplated. The testimony of the U.S. Chamber of Commerce (USCC) contained similar views. With the full backing of their board, which had voted in March to oppose the bill, lobbyists for the chamber pointed out that the law had been in operation for less than two weeks and asserted that any changes were "premature." Voluntary compliance was already widespread, and conciliation proceedings were working well. It was not the right time to contemplate reform.[49]

Two years later, in 1967, it became clear that there would never a good time to grant the EEOC administrative authority, at least in the eyes of the business community. Liberals once again pressed for cease-and-desist authority, as they had in the two previous sessions. Among those testifying in favor of strengthening legislation were Sen. Edward W. Kennedy, Ramsey Clark, Steven Shulman, Jack Greenberg, Whitney Young, Clarence Mitchell, Joseph Rauh, Jr., and Roy Wilkins. It was an impressive roster of liberal leaders, all of them with impeccable credentials, and they energetically invoked the full range of arguments that they had developed over the years. James W. Hunt, head of labor relations for the USCC, took the lead in responding on behalf of business groups. The board of the chamber had voted again in 1966 to oppose the extension of cease-and-desist authority, and it remained opposed in 1967. This time the chamber declined to advance the argument that reform was premature. Hunt did not attempt to make the case that reform was untimely. Instead, he argued that the bill would "virtually destroy the conciliatory approach," which he insisted was meeting with "great success" and should therefore remain the main tool of federal policy. Legislating further authority for the EEOC was the "worst possible course of action" because it would actually "frustrate the objective of Title VII." Mandating an administrative procedure would simply create a lengthy, legalistic process that would prevent individuals from obtaining a speedy resolution to their complaints. As evidence, Hunt pointed to a finding that the average case before the NLRB took twelve months to resolve, while the EEOC was required to resolve charges within sixty days. "What the individual needs is a job," he argued in his written testimony, "not a lawsuit."[50]

Most segments of organized business would eventually drop their hard-line opposition and began to accept the necessity of somehow strengthening the EEOC. This recognition crystallized during the Nixon administration, when the regulatory weakness of the EEOC had become obvious to almost all reasonable observers. "Just about everybody," according to a 1971 piece in the *Wall Street Journal*, "thinks the Equal Employment Opportunity Commission needs more teeth." The only question that remained unresolved was the kind of teeth it should be given. Most liberals remained loyal to the idea of administrative enforcement, though a handful had begun to make the case that other options might be worth considering. Business groups, though, continued to regard cease-and-desist authority as a nonstarter. Testifying quietly but firmly against such proposals during Nixon's first term were the American Retail Federation, Aerospace Industries Association, National Association of Manufacturers (NAM), Associated General Contractors of America, and USCC. In their private correspondence, business leaders were less politic but no less clear about their feelings. In the words of a NAM in-house attorney, granting cease-and-desist authority to the EEOC was a proposal to which the association took "violent exception."[51]

What business groups were ultimately willing to accept by 1971, ironically, was essentially the same legal enforcement system implied by the House-passed version of the Civil Rights Act. Hunt may have mocked the use of lawsuits as an enforcement tool in 1967, but now that some kind of legislative action seemed all but inevitable, giving the EEOC the power to file suit after the failure of conciliation proceedings was precisely the change that organized business thought was necessary. NAM's position was fairly typical. In written testimony to Congress in 1971, it condemned cease-and-desist authority as "particularly dangerous" because it violated "fundamental concepts of our constitutional system" and would be "unnecessarily disruptive of industry." The association hastened to note that it strongly supported the "freedom of opportunity for every individual to work at an available job for which he is qualified." Yet this freedom would be severely compromised by giving the EEOC cease-and-desist authority. It would be far preferable—"speedier and more equitable"—to handle disputes over job discrimination by lodging complaints in U.S. district courts. As such, NAM recommended a court-based proposal that it claimed would provide adequate, due-process safeguards for complainants and respondents alike. The USCC took much the same position. It similarly endorsed the principle of equal employment opportunity, but warned that the NLRB model would violate due process as well as a right to a fair and impartial hearing of a case. It would do so because the EEOC would effectively become transformed into the "policeman, prosecutor, judge, and jury" in all cases of job discrimination brought under Title VII. "A greater guarantee of fairness," according to the prepared testimony of the USCC, "lies in the 'district court' approach to enforcement." In the span of five years, business groups had gone from decrying lawsuits to recommending them.[52]

The conflict over enforcement was never purely rhetorical or symbolic. It was, in fact, fought out fiercely and repeatedly in Congress. Numerous bills proposing to strengthen the EEOC were introduced between the passage of the Civil Rights Act in 1964 and the Equal Employment Opportunity Act in 1972. Full-scale hearings, replete with impassioned testimony, were held several times over the same period. The fights seldom made front-page headlines, partly because news editors understandably favored more sensational tales of uncontrollable rioting and black power. In the rarer instances when coverage of the civil rights legislation did take place, it tended to focus on new initiatives in areas such as housing rather than proposals to augment existing laws. Nevertheless, the struggle over the EEOC in Congress did not go entirely unnoticed; it found itself relegated to the less popular parts of newspapers and magazines. A story in the *Los Angeles Times* characterized the situation aptly, noting that the "classic liberal-conservative battle over the power of regulatory agencies" was rife with weighty questions but nonetheless remained "quiet" and "little-noticed."[53]

The liberals leading the charge in the House were Adam Clayton Powell, Jr. (D-NY) and Augustus F. Hawkins (D-CA) (figure 5.2). Both had long-standing interests in FEP and equal employment opportunity. Powell had been Harlem's representative to the House since 1945, and he had introduced fair employment legislation in nearly every session of Congress. Hawkins represented south-central Los Angeles; he had entered Congress in 1965 after serving for thirty years in the California Assembly, where he had worked closely with W. Byron Rumford to pass enforceable FEP and fair housing legislation. Joining the two from across the aisle were liberal Republicans, among them Ogden R. Reid (R-NY) and Charles E. Goodell (R-NY). Prior to entering office in 1963, Reid had chaired the New York Commission on Human Rights, and during his tenure as a Republican representative he testified in favor of administrative enforcement and introduced several such bills, among them H.R. 8999 and H.R. 2704 in 1969. Goodell was one of the three primary architects of the compromise bill that became Title VII in 1964, but he had

Figure 5.2 U.S. Rep. Augustus F. Hawkins (D-CA) giving a speech during the California primaries, 1966. Hawkins had spearheaded a fifteen-year campaign for a state FEP law as a long-time state legislator in California. After leaving the California Assembly for Congress in 1963, he repeatedly pressed for national legislation along similar lines. His ambitions, however, were continually frustrated by a coalition of conservative Republicans, organized business, and southern Democrats. In 1966, one of his bills passed the House only to find itself indefinitely tabled by minority leader Everett M. Dirksen (R-IL) in the Senate. Courtesy of Special Collections, Young Research Library, University of California, Los Angeles.

become a convert to cease-and-desist authority in 1966, when he voted for the Hawkins bill. In the Senate, liberals could count, of course, on liberal Democrats like Hubert Humphrey and Edward Kennedy, but they also depended consistently on the leadership of Jacob Javits (R-NY), who essentially reprised the role of Irving M. Ives (R-NY) in the post-war years.[54]

Congressional liberals were just as deeply critical of the EEOC and Title VII as were their allies outside of Congress. They were well aware that Title VII could be enforced through private civil action in the federal courts, but they felt that the procedure placed too heavy of a burden on the victim. In the words of one reformer, most would-be litigants were "individuals who possess extremely modest financial resources" were "intimidated by the prospect of becoming participants in a lawsuit which they themselves are responsible for conducting to a conclusion." At the same time, liberals made it clear that they did not desire administrative enforcement for its own sake. They insisted, to the contrary, that the mere existence of substantial sanctions would promote compliance and help to fulfill the best, original purpose of Title VII—conciliation between aggrieved parties. "Intelligent and earnest conciliation," said one of them, "is absolutely vital to the achievement of equal employment. . . . But methods of polite persuasion are inadequate standing alone. Divorcing conciliation from enforcement is like separating business agreements from the law of contracts." The principal purpose of granting the EEOC administrative enforcement powers—along with other strengthening provisions, such as those consolidating jurisdiction over contract compliance and federal employment in the hands of the EEOC—was to establish a strong, centralized regulatory framework that would give equal treatment a real chance at succeeding.[55]

An exchange between Augustus Hawkins and Charles E. Goodell in 1966 was particularly revealing of the broad kind of regulatory framework that liberals intended to establish. In the midst of a floor debate, Goodell argued insistently that it was not the "intention of the Congress that the Commission shall be able to go into an area and set quotas for hiring." Nor was it the intention of Congress to permit the EEOC to infer discrimination from the "imbalance" of minorities at a company or union in comparison to the "total number or percentage of persons" of minority backgrounds "in the available work force in any community." Hawkins concurred, noting that such a thing is "already prohibited by law." The EEOC would "not look at patterns and other situations in the community or in the plant," continued Goodell, "but it will look at the facts that are applied and which are applicable to" individual cases. This focus on aggressively addressing individual complaints was key to securing the support of Goodell and other Republican liberals. Strengthening legislation would "set up a system here that has great power, so they [EEOC Commissioners] can go into matters of this kind and correct injustices." Central to the ability of the EEOC to "correct injustices" was the authority to order offending employers and unions to cease and desist from their discriminatory behavior—and the authority to order offending parties to take "affirmative action" (such as back pay or reinstatement) to compensate victims for the harms that they had suffered.[56]

Opposing northern Democrats and liberal Republicans were not only southern Democrats but key numbers of conservative Republicans, most of whom felt a deep wariness about aggrandizing the federal role in regulating discrimination. Of these, the minority leader of the Senate, Dirsken, was again the most influential and visible, as he continued to hold the balance of power on civil rights legislation. Only he could break the back of a southern filibuster; but he strongly disliked the EEOC—even when it was powerless. In 1969, for instance, he had threatened to oust one of the EEOC's chairmen, Alexander, Jr., for "harassing" employers. On another occasion, he threatened to launch a filibuster himself if a cease-and-desist provision was not removed from pending legislation. Some liberals sought to demonize Dirksen and pinned responsibility for regulatory failure almost entirely on him. In the view of the LCCR's indefatigable Joseph Rauh, it was Dirksen's demands that made it necessary to accept a crippled EEOC in 1964: "Senator Dirksen said in plain English, bluntly, either give up the cease-and-desist powers, or there will be no title VII, maybe no bill." Rauh similarly argued that it was Dirksen who was responsible for Nixon's eventual opposition to administrative enforcement of Title VII: "[I]t was perfectly clear that Senator Dirksen still opposed cease-and-desist powers [in early 1969] and it was equally clear that the administration yielded at that point to Senator Dirksen and adopted this judicial device rather than cease-and-desist powers." It is possible that Rauh's claim is correct, but it is not entirely clear from the historical record. Hugh David Graham finds that there were multiple voices inside the administration urging the president's opinion in the same direction. In particular, Assistant Attorney General William Rehnquist and senior aide Arthur Burns argued strongly against administrative enforcement in the early months of Nixon's first term. Although he conceded that the existing framework was problematic, Rehnquist had leaned especially heavily on the argument that administrative agencies tended to favor "one or another of the groups whose interests are protected by their statute." What is clear, however, is that it would be a mistake to single out Dirsken as the only or even the primary Republican opponent of administrative enforcement in Congress. Many other congressional Republicans shared Dirksen's ideological convictions; he was no lone wolf. When Representative Robert P. Griffith (R-MI) worried that a strengthened EEOC would inescapably "function as investigator, conciliator, prosecutor, judge, and jury," his comments reflected a larger, conservative uneasiness with administrative regulation. Moreover, since southern Democrats were sure to filibuster any civil rights legislation, all Republicans exercised a certain degree of power. If any one of them had wanted to raise a roadblock in the Senate by threatening to filibuster or withhold his vote, it would not have been difficult to pull off. The full extent and significance of GOP opposition became apparent when Dirksen passed away in late 1969. Even after his death, other similarly minded GOP legislators, such as Sen. Paul Fannin (R-AZ) continued to work in his stead against liberal proposals, and they succeeded much of the time. Perhaps the most notable and effective among them were Sen. Peter H. Dominick (R-CO) and Rep. John N. Erlenborn (R-IL), both of whom were highly active and effective on the issue.[57]

In fact, critics of administrative enforcement held the upper hand for years. The unhappy destiny of two particular bills vividly demarcates the bipartisan character of the political barriers to passing strengthening legislation. The first of these was contemplated during the famously Democratic 89th Congress (1965–66). Events had begun auspiciously in the first session. Adam Clayton Powell's (D-NY) Committee on Education and Labor favorably reported H.R. 10065 on August 3, 1965. The bill had been introduced by Augustus F. Hawkins (D-CA). Powell's committee had held intensive hearings on related bills in July, and it issued a strong report endorsing the Hawkins bill, which was designed essentially to repeal and replace Title VII. In addition to expanding the jurisdiction of the EEOC to include firms with eight or more employees, H.R. 10065 proposed to give the agency strong administrative enforcement powers. After it was reported, however, Howard "Judge" Smith's (D-VA) Rules Committee predictably refused to issue the Hawkins bill a rule, forcing civil rights liberals to invoke the twenty-one day rule, which had been adopted only at the beginning of the session. (The rule permitted a majority of the House to withdraw a bill from the Rules Committee after twenty-one days.) Forcing twenty-two exhausting roll calls, seven more than the record at the time, Republicans fought tenaciously to keep the bill in committee. Speaker John W. McCormack (D-MA) charged that Republicans and southern Democrats were conspiring to put on a "limited filibuster." But northern Democrats and liberal Republicans eventually prevailed after a "marathon session" lasting twelve-and-a-half hours.[58]

House floor action on the bill was postponed for the remainder of the first session, but *Congressional Quarterly* sensed a favorable political climate at the beginning of the second session and gave the bill a "good chance of passage." It was a prescient assessment. Despite the round condemnation of the House Republican policy committee, which argued (not inaccurately) that the bill would "transform the Equal Employment Opportunity Commission into an agency that would rival the old National Labor Relations Board under the Wagner Act," H.R. 10065 passed the committee of the whole House on April 27, 1966, by a landslide vote of 299–94. One day later, in his message to Congress, President Johnson endorsed the essence of the Hawkins bill, though he did not identify it by name or number. "The first year's experience of the Equal Employment Opportunity Commission," Johnson said, "suggests that it should be endowed with enforcement power and that its coverage should be broadened." Despite the obvious endorsement, however, the Hawkins bill would founder that very day. After it was referred to the Senate on April 28, it was quietly tabled by inveterate FEPC opponent Dirksen—never to be revived again.[59]

For entirely different reasons, a second strengthening bill failed in the 91st Congress (1969–70). During the first session, in 1969, several bills on equal employment opportunity were introduced. In the House, Hawkins introduced H.R. 6228, which he would later revise and resubmit as H.R. 17555. It essentially recapitulated the terms of his previous FEP proposals. William H. Ayers (R-OH) and other Republicans submitted the Nixon administration bill, H.R. 13517, which authorized the EEOC to initiate legal proceedings in federal courts against intractable offenders. In the Senate, S. 2453, introduced by Harrison A. Williams, Jr. (D-NJ) on June 19, 1969, proposed to give the EEOC administrative authority; it was opposed by the Nixon administration, which preferred instead Winston L. Prouty's (R-VT) court-based bill, S. 2806. Subcommittee hearings were held in both the House and Senate, and the full labor committees of the two houses reported out both bills in the fall of 1970. This time, however, it was the Senate that acted first. Dirsken had passed away the previous fall, shortly after surgery to remove a tumor in his right lung. Dirsken's allies made a strenuous effort to carry on his legacy, but lacking the stature and influence of their recently deceased leader, they ultimately proved unsuccessful. On October 1, 1970, the Senate approved S. 2453 by a surprisingly lopsided roll-call vote of 47–24. The bill granted cease-and-desist authority to the EEOC, despite the efforts of Peter Dominick (R-CO) to amend the enforcement provisions to conform to his court-based proposal, S. 2806.[60]

The focus of the battle then shifted to the House, where the Hawkins bill had passed easily in 1966. There would be no speedy victory in 1970. Fearful that there would be more than enough affirmative votes, House Rules Committee chairman William M. Colmer (D-MS) carried on in the tradition of his predecessor, from whom he inherited the chairmanship. Smith had lost his 1966 reelection campaign, but Colmer shared his views on civil rights and refused to issue a rule that would permit House consideration of the bill. Liberals recognized their predicament. "The problem is a familiar one," wrote Arnold Aronson of the LCCR. The bill was a "major piece of legislation," he continued, and it could come to a proper vote only if members of the Rules Committee would break with the wishes of their chair or if enough signatures could be collected on a discharge petition. Hawkins and Ogden Reid (R-NY) tried to persuade Colmer directly—at very least so they could pin the blame on him if it failed. In a joint missive, they pleaded with him to release the bill: "If your committee does not grant H.R. 17666 a rule in sufficient time to permit Floor action by the House before adjournment, this important measure will once again die as it did in 1966." A scathing editorial by the *Wall Street Journal* denounced Colmer and the Rules Committee for going on a "Rampage Again." No amount of pressure, however, would change his mind; he had "given notice" to all interested participants that the bill would be "quietly smothered." Hawkins, Reid, and civil rights liberals would not have their rule, and strengthening legislation would expire in the 91st Congress.[61]

The defeats of 1966 and 1970 aptly symbolize the combination of political forces that prevented the statutory authorization of cease-and-desist power for the EEOC. A group of southern Democrats and conservative Republicans formed a conservative coalition during the Johnson and Nixon years and prevented the EEOC from gaining administrative authority. In 1966, H.R. 10065 had escaped Smith's Rules Committee in the House only to be tabled by Dirksen in the Senate. By 1970, Dirsken had passed away, and S. 2453 cleared the Senate with relative ease, robust enough even to elude the designs of Dominick. Yet when the bill reached the House, it was unable to escape the graveyard of the Rules Committee. Smith had lost his seat, but a Mississippian with equally thick political skin had taken his place. If a coalition of conservative Republicans and southern Democrats had joined forces to prevent the establishment of an NLRB-style FEPC before 1964, then after 1964 both groups continued to take turns preventing the EEOC from becoming the agency that civil rights liberals had always hoped it would be.

The struggle over enforcement reached a fever pitch during the 92nd Congress (1971–1972). Many close observers felt almost certain that legislation of one kind or another would clear Congress. Liberals tried as best they could to move quickly and take advantage of the obvious opportunity, and they made solid progress through the first half of the 1971 session. Subcommittee hearings were held in the House, reams of testimony were taken, and a Democratic-sponsored bill, H.R. 1746, was sent to the full labor committee in a party line vote. Even the public statements of William H. Brown, III, Nixon-appointed chairman of the EEOC, seemed to portend that the administration might not prove able to present a united front. Brown had been admonished by the administration in early 1969 when he spoke out stridently in favor of cease-and-desist authority for the EEOC but quickly reversed course under the influence of John Ehrlichman and Nixon's other senior advisors. By 1971, however, he once again broke ranks, indicating with only some ambiguity that he favored the administrative approach.[62]

Led by Illinois representative Erlenborn, Republicans sought to replace the subcommittee-approved measure with H.R. 9247, a restrictive, court-based proposal backed by the Nixon administration, the American Retail Federation, USCC, and NAM. Erlenborn's substitute would grant the EEOC the authority to file suit in district court, but it also limited the amount of back pay and prohibited the class actions that had begun to appear. Among the more ingenious arguments mustered by the most aggressive proponents of the substitute was that court enforcement was actually more efficient than administrative enforcement. They claimed that it would take, on average, ten months to obtain relief from the courts, while the experience of the NLRB suggested that three to four years would elapse before relief would be forthcoming under the approach embodied in H.R. 1746. Liberals responded by pointing out that court action could occur only after conciliation failed; moreover, they noted that the time for court action cited by Erlenborn backers referred to the median for all court cases, which included a large fraction of simple, straightforward matters. It was liberals who ultimately prevailed in committee. The committee included virtually no southern Democrats, and it was simply packed with too many liberal, northern Democrats for Republicans to overcome. The GOP maneuver failed by a near party-line vote, 14–19. One member of the GOP voted against the substitute, while one Democrat voted for the substitute. What the full committee eventually reported was a bill that not only granted cease-and-desist authority to the EEOC, but also transferred to the EEOC the responsibilities of the Office of Federal Contract Compliance (OFCC) along with the authority of the Attorney General to file "pattern or practice" suits. The bill moreover eliminated the exemption of state and local government from Title VII, and it expanded coverage to include companies with as few as eight employees. It was a strong effort. There were plenty of different provisions to bargain away in subsequent negotiations, and perhaps enforcement authority would survive the process. Liberal prospects had reached a high point.[63]

But moderate and conservative Republicans—along with the Nixon administration—were simply biding their time. Their failed gambit in the labor committee was only a first act. They enjoyed a stronger position in the full House. The key to their strategy was what A. H. Raskin of the *New York Times* saw fit to report as a "White House-inspired" plan to renew their occasional, cross-party alliance with southern Democrats.

The hostility of southern Democrats to civil rights measures remained undiminished, but they had long been willing to join forces with the GOP at moments when political momentum for change was the greatest. In such instances, they accepted the need to support—or at least not oppose—watered-down, symbolic legislation in order to circumvent even less desirable possibilities. Moreover, if the legislation eventually came to a vote, it would place liberals in a difficult dilemma and could potentially divide them. Should they support legislation they regarded as inferior and inadequate, perhaps in the hopes of using it later as a stepping stone, or should they leave Congress empty-handed? If the legislation were made undesirable enough, it might lose liberal support altogether and fail. More or less the same scenario had unfolded twenty years earlier, when the McConnell amendment creating a "voluntary" FEPC was passed in the House with the votes of southern Democrats and conservative Republicans. Perhaps an analogous scenario could be engineered with a court-enforcement bill. If, on the one hand, liberals eventually acquiesced themselves to the bill, Republicans could claim credit for their leadership for helping to pass a civil rights law, albeit one that fit their ideological preferences. On the other hand, if liberals found the bill simply unacceptable, then Republicans could still take satisfaction in having thwarted the growth of New Deal-style regulation.[64]

The administration strategy came to life in September, when the legislative struggle reached a climax. Knowing that reform sentiment had reached the point of no return, organized business abandoned its earlier opposition to any change and was campaigning heavily in favor of the Erlenborn substitute. In August, NAM had issued a strongly worded legislative advisory to members warning that H.R. 1746 would make the EEOC into a nightmarish "super National Labor Relations Board." Among the many features of the bill that it singled out for disapprobation was the one that would authorize the EEOC to issue "back pay and affirmative action orders." Erlenborn's bill was far preferable. By giving the EEOC only the authority to take a case into district court, it achieved a reasonable "balance" between the rights of complainants and respondents. NAM appealed to its members to act in no uncertain terms: "As there is substantial bi-partisan support in Congress for giving enforcement powers to the EEOC, you should write or wire your Congressman immediately urging him to support H.R. 9247 as a substitute for H.R. 1746" (underlining in original).[65]

The stakes were high for organized business, which expressed confidence that the "grass-roots pressure" that it had generated from individual businessmen was going to pay off. "Going into this week's fight," noted one article in the *Wall Street Journal*, "business lobbyists say a months-long lobbying has won them enough votes to pass a court-enforcement bill." One survey taken by the USCC estimated a ninety-vote edge. It was unclear whether business lobbyists were trying to create a self-fulfilling prophecy of success, but some of them felt that they needed to win by a substantial margin because the Senate was more inclined than the House to pass a liberal bill. "If we win big in the House," said one of them, "then even if the Senate passes a cease-and-desist bill we will have leverage in the (House-Senate) conference committee." Labor and civil rights groups, however, were in the midst of their own aggressive campaign as well. Its focal point was a coordinated effort to convince liberal and moderate Republicans to back cease-and-desist authority. The main strategy centered on leveraging John Anderson's (R-IL) influence as a Republican leader to convince three or four dozen of his GOP colleagues to support the liberal option. As a legislative aide for Senator Harrison A. Williams (D-NJ) noted, LCCR strategists believed that Anderson's personal support for cease-and-desist authority—which he publicly announced in early September—could potentially help liberals pick up "between 30 and 40 votes and will also lead to a close vote or even possibly victory for cease and desist." The stakes of the confrontation were just as high for liberals as they were for the administration and organized business. If it was true that the Senate was more willing to accept cease-and-desist authority than the House, then a victory in the latter chamber spelled almost certain success in the former.[66]

As it turned out, too few of Anderson's co-partisans eventually chose to side with him in the full House. The coalition of southern Democrats and conservative Republicans held firm, and the House passed a court-enforcement bill that also banned class actions. Yet their victory was exceedingly narrow. The key vote came on September 16, when the House voted 202–197 to adopt the Erlenborn substitute in place of the committee-reported bill (table 5.1). It was a remarkable development, with 133 Republicans and 69 Democrats voting for the substitute and 168 Democrats and 29 Republicans voting against it. Few votes pitted liberals against the conservative coalition more starkly. More than 90 percent of northern Democrats opposed the substitute, while 80 percent of southern Democrats and Republicans supported it. Conservatives were "jubilant" with the outcome, while liberal critics said that it was "worse than nothing." The NAACP's Clarence Mitchell tried to salvage something from the obvious defeat, gamely calling the substitution a "slap in the face but not a knockout punch." In a certain sense, he was right. The vote was incredibly close, shocking the smooth lobbyists who had so confidently predicted success weeks earlier. A "white-faced" representative of the [Chamber of Commerce] rushed out of the gallery after the final action, exclaiming, "Whee, that was a close one. I thought we'd win by at least 30 votes."[67]

TABLE 5.1
Selected Congressional Votes on the Equal Employment Opportunity Act of 1972

Date	Issue	All members		Northern Democrats		Southern Democrats		Republicans		Party vote	CC vote
		Yes	No	Yes	No	Yes	No	Yes	No		
1971											
	H.R. 1746 (Hawkins)										
Sept. 16	Erlenborn substitute	202	197	10	155	59	13	133	29	Yes	Yes
Sept. 16	Final passage in House	285	106	130	32	25	47	130	27	No	No
1972											
	S. 2515 (Williams bill)										
Jan. 24	Dominick substitute	41	43	3	30	15	0	22	13	Yes	Yes
Jan. 26	Dominick substitute	46	48	3	31	16	0	26	17	Yes	Yes
Feb. 1	Cloture	48	37	23	4	1	14	24	17	No	Yes
Feb. 3	Cloture	53	35	28	2	1	15	24	16	No	Yes
Feb. 15	Dominick substitute	45	39	4	26	14	0	25	13	Yes	Yes
Feb. 22	Cloture	73	21	35	1	4	11	33	8	No	No
Feb. 22	Final bill in Senate	73	16	33	0	5	9	34	6	No	No

Notes: Following the classification offered by Schickler, I define a "party vote" as occurring when a majority of Democrats opposes a voting majority of Republicans. I define a "conservative coalition vote" as occurring when a voting majority of nonsouthern Democrats opposes a voting majority of southern Democrats and a voting majority of Republicans. See Eric Schickler, *Disjointed Pluralism: Institutional Innovation and the Development of the U.S. Congress* (Princeton: Princeton University Press, 2001). I define the South as the eleven states once making up the former Confederacy. Schickler includes Oklahoma in his definition of the South. This tends to soften regional differences, as Democrats in states such as Oklahoma, Kentucky, and Maryland are counted as nonsouthern Democrats when their views tend to resemble those of southern Democrats. James Buckley of New York and Harry F. Byrd, Jr., of Virginia are listed by Voteview as belonging to other parties.

Source: Author's tabulations based on data retrieved from Keith T. Poole, Howard Rosenthal, and Boris T. Shor, *Voteview for Windows v 3.0.3: Roll Call Displays of the U.S. Congress, 1789–2000* (accessible at voteview.com).

As in the past, legislators tended to cast their ballots according to their underlying, ideological convictions. Social and economic conservatives favored the court-enforcement option, while liberals favored the administrative option. The partisan and sectional pattern of the votes does suggest, however, that a cross-party, conservative coalition had actively mobilized to oppose civil rights legislation (table 5.1). The vast majority of Democrats, of course, had voted against the substitute. Of the Democrats supporting the substitute, however, more than 80 percent hailed from the South. They were joined in their support by more than 80 percent of all voting Republicans. A statistical analysis of the vote provides additional evidence of collective action (table A.12). The analysis is somewhat technically problematic due to the extremely polarized nature of the vote, but it does seem that if a legislator belonged to the conservative coalition—that is, if he or she was either a Republican or southern Democrat—then he or she was more likely to have voted for the Erlenborn substitute than was a northern Democrat, even when taking into account the fact that the average member of the conservative coalition was more socially and economically conservative than the average northern Democrat. Republicans and southern Democrats were not merely voting as individuals; they seem to have been acting collectively as well. Yet the cooperation was only momentary. The final tally on the bill, 285–106, showed a different pattern (table 5.1). A large majority of Republicans voted with the administration, as did a majority of Democrats, who were betting that the Senate could be encouraged to pass a liberal bill, one that would hopefully survive the conference committee. Naysayers were a combination of southern diehards and stalwart conservatives. Almost everyone reverted to voting their ideological preferences, and there is no evidence that the southern-conservative coalition was active on the vote. But there was no need for it to rouse itself again. Its work had already been done.[68]

A similar choice between court and administrative enforcement emerged the same year in the Senate, where two bills marked the terrain of debate. S. 2515 was introduced by Harrison A. Williams (D-NJ), and it resembled the original Hawkins-Reid bill in most major respects. It had the support of the liberal bloc and was unanimously reported to the Senate by the labor committee. Pete Dominick (R-CO) sponsored S. 2617, which recapitulated the terms of the Erlenborn substitute and gave the EEOC the right to sue in federal district court.[69]

The fight began encouragingly for Senate liberals. Only a month after their narrow loss in the House, S. 2515 was reported out of subcommittee and cleared the Senate labor committee unanimously, 17–0. In an embarrassing rebuke to the administration, all seven Republican members of the committee sided with their Democratic colleagues in the committee vote. Dominick had tried to substitute his bill instead, but the committee beat him back resoundingly, 15–2. The remainder of the year saw little action on EEO issues, but the confrontation augured well. Perhaps it would be possible to win in the Senate what had been denied in the House.[70]

When the next session began in early 1972, there was no doubt which bill business groups preferred. Lobbyists for the National Association of Manufacturers (NAM), American Retail Federation, and U.S. Chamber of Commerce (USCC) mobilized aggressively in favor of court enforcement. In a typical legislative advisory, analysts for the USCC objected to the Williams bill on the grounds that it would give the "EEOC Czar-like powers of policeman, prosecutor, judge, and jury." The court-based regime, they noted, had "never been acceptable to old-timers in the civil rights ranks, who have always insisted that the law should be enforced through an administrative agency like the NLRB." Nevertheless, the chamber continued to stress, along with Dominick himself, that administrative enforcement would encourage partisan wrangling, undermine due process, and prove less expeditious and efficient than court enforcement. A few weeks later, the NAM president, W. P. Gullander, made a similar plea to association members, urging them to support the Dominick bill, now Senate Amendment 611. It was clear that some type of enforcement power would likely be given to the EEOC, but the district-court approach was far more acceptable than William's S. 2515, which would make the EEOC a kind of "super power agency furnishing its own judicial functions." Gullander exhorted his membership to take action: "I urge you to immediately write or wire both of your senators urging support of the Amendment 611 to S. 2515 and at the same time expressing opposition to S. 2515 as it is now written."[71]

In the face of unrelenting pressure from organized business, Senate liberals put up a valiant fight for the Williams bill. It quickly became clear that a definite majority of the chamber supported the cease-and-desist approach. Twice, liberals succeeded in fending off attempts in the full Senate to substitute the Dominick bill. In each case, they handed a defeat to a coalition of southern Democrats and Republicans (table 5.1)—but their margin of victory was razor thin. Each time, they won by only two votes, the first time 41–43 and the second time 46–48. The roll calls were so closely contested that the Nixon administration sent Spiro Agnew to the Senate for the second, in case he was needed to break a tie. Such narrow margins doomed the administrative option. When the inevitable southern filibuster began, this time led by Sam Ervin (D-NC), it proved impossible to impose cloture. Not enough Republicans were willing to end debate. Liberals pushed for cloture twice, and each time they failed. If liberals had bested the southern-conservative coalition in twice defeating the Dominick substitute, now they found themselves incapable of winning a cloture vote. Here the southern-conservative coalition found itself on institutionally friendlier ground. The required majority for cloture—two-thirds of the senators voting—was prohibitively high. It was only after the Senate accepted the Dominick substitute by a 45–39 vote that cloture succeeded. A statistical analysis of the three key votes on the Dominick substitute reveals that party discipline was most likely responsible for the voting pattern (table A.13). Even when the underlying ideology of individual legislators is taken into account, Republicans were still more likely to support the administration's position than Democrats. With the Dominick substitute completed, more than a sufficient number of Republicans swung over to the yea column on the next cloture vote. The Senate debate ended, and the final bill easily cleared the chamber by a vote of 73–16.[72]

Nixon signed the Equal Employment Opportunity Act of 1972 into law a few weeks later. It had moved rapidly through conference committee. The categorical ban on class actions, one of most severe provisions in the House-passed bill, quickly disintegrated in conference when Albert H. Quie (R-MN), one of the original architects of court enforcement, moved against Erlenborn to oppose it. The revised bill then won strong votes from both chambers. Casual observers of the legislative end-game might have seen the enactment as a heart-warming triumph of bipartisanship over southern intransigence, but appearances were deceiving. To be sure, there could be little doubt that the law was a worthwhile improvement on Title VII. It gave the EEOC the authority to initiate a private lawsuit on behalf of employees if conciliation proceedings failed. It expanded the jurisdiction of the EEOC to cover public and local government, educational institutions, and a wider swath of small employers. The law also clarified the responsibility of the federal government to uphold nondiscrimination. After the passage of the Senate bill, the NAACP's Mitchell pronounced himself "completely satisfied" to David Rosenbaum at the *New York Times*, saying he was "especially pleased" with the new coverage of state and local employees. Yet the EEOC remained a far cry from the agency that liberals had been envisioning for decades. There could be no denying, as Rosenbaum dutifully reported in the same article, that "lobbyists for the various civil rights and women's organizations had hoped Congress would give the commission even more power—the authority to order employers and unions to stop discriminating." While he might have been satisfied with the bill on balance, Mitchell surely could not have been pleased by the loss of cease-and-desist authority. The EEOC was once again denied such powers. In fact, it would never acquire them. After 1972, liberals effectively ended their decades-long quest for "fair employment practices" and "freedom from discrimination." The conservative bloc in 1972 had won a final victory. There would never be a national FEPC. Small numbers of Republicans in Congress might have thrown their weight behind a liberal bill, and it would have made a major difference. Some of them did in fact cast their votes in such a fashion, but most of them chose court-enforcement instead. It was a lasting defeat for liberals. In the years and decades thereafter, they would never again mount a comparable effort in Congress. Instead, something called affirmative action, which had been taking uncertain shape in the executive and judicial branches, would begin to fill the void.[73]

The term "affirmative action" entered into the discourse of civil rights gingerly and ambiguously. It had first appeared in the Wagner Act of 1935, which gave the NLRB the power to order offending employers "to cease and desist from such unfair labor practice, and to take such affirmative action, including reinstatement of employees with or without back pay, as will effectuate the policies of this Act." During the Second World War and the two decades thereafter, liberals interested in civil rights borrowed the phrase from the field of industrial relations and featured it in scores of "mandatory" fair employment bills that they introduced into state legislatures and Congress. There, the phrase "affirmative action" was used to describe a key enforcement power that would be wielded by a potential FEPC; namely, the ability to order discriminatory employers or unions to compensate their victims for any harm they may have suffered. It did not yet have any legal status, but it was a phrase that many knowledgeable liberals would almost have recognized and associated with FEPC.[74]

By 1960, liberals had already begun to inch toward invoking "affirmative" in a slightly different context, with talk of "positive efforts" and "affirmative programs" edging into their discussion of job discrimination. The decisive change came in 1961, when the phrase "affirmative action" appeared in President John F. Kennedy's Executive Order 10925, which significantly reorganized the federal government's existing effort to address job discrimination. Instead of responding to growing demands for racial equality by pushing for civil rights legislation early in his administration, Kennedy issued an executive order, just as his three predecessors had done before him. Indeed, Kennedy's order consolidated Eisenhower's old Government Contracting Committee (GCC) and his old President's Committee on Government Employment Policy (CGEP) into a single President's Committee on Equal Employment Opportunity (PCEEO). Kennedy's new committee had varying degrees of responsibility for achieving nondiscrimination in three main areas of employment. Job discrimination occurring under federal contracts was the responsibility of the Government Contract Employment Division of the PCEEO, while job discrimination by federal employers was handled by the Government Employment

Division. A third program, called Plans for Progress (PfP), bore a somewhat more tenuous formal connection to the committee. Led initially by Atlanta attorney and businessman Robert B. Troutman, Jr., PfP sought to encourage large, private employers (many of whom in the early years were actually government contractors) to integrate their work forces voluntarily. Overseeing the entire PCEEO operation during the Kennedy years was Vice President Johnson, who, like Nixon before him, served as the public face of the federal government's response to discrimination.[75]

A key author of Kennedy's groundbreaking order—indeed the man specifically responsible for incorporating the phrase affirmative action—was Hobart Taylor, Jr., a black Texas-born attorney with a master's degree in economics from Howard University and a law degree from the University of Michigan Law School. Taylor would first become special counsel for the PCEEO and then later Executive Vice Chairman. When Vice President Johnson asked him to rework a draft of the executive order in early 1961, it was Taylor who inserted the word "affirmative" into a section on government contracting requiring federal contractors to "take affirmative action to ensure that employees are employed, and that employees are treated during employment, without regard to their race, creed, color, or national origin." Taylor wanted a phrase that was "broader in concept" than any of the alternatives that were in circulation at the time. To some observers, it might have seemed like a minor, semantic tweak—Taylor himself liked the alliterative feel of affirmative action—but change proved anything but semantic.[76]

Indeed, it was under the auspices of the PCEEO and the bureaucratic penumbra of Kennedy's executive order that the modern meaning of affirmative action first began slowly to take shape. While the meaning of the term was not perfectly clear at first, there can be little doubt that many federal officials construed the main mission of the PCEEO explicitly in terms of affirmative action. The purpose of the committee, as federal officials announced at a meeting of community leaders, was to promote "affirmative action in government employment" and to implement "a broad program to achieve broad affirmative actions in government contract compliance." What they meant by affirmative action was the active and immediate implementation of nondiscrimination and equal treatment in employment. In fact, Johnson could not have made one of the central goals of the PCEEO any clearer than he did in a 1962 letter to the *New York Times*, where he wrote that "the objective of the committee is to insure equal employment opportunity for all of our citizens without regard to race, creed, color, or national origin." Johnson's letter ended with the firm assertion that the time for equality had indubitably arrived. "People are entitled to fair play and equal treatment now."[77]

But delivering equal treatment meant more than simply vowing to treat everyone equally now and henceforth. It meant taking strong, immediate, and proactive steps to make sure that equal employment opportunity was actually being extended to all Americans. This was also what affirmative action signified to many of those centrally involved with PCEEO.

According to the language of the PCEEO in a report on a 1962 conference of community leaders held in Washington, D.C., "affirmative action in government employment" referred to policies in which "special effort was necessary to make sure that all employees were being given equal opportunity." This might take the form of designating a "high-ranking official, usually at the assistant secretary level" to serve as an equal employment opportunity officer. In the area of contract compliance, "affirmative action" referred to "steps over and beyond the requirements of the executive order" to guarantee "equal employment opportunity." Here an affirmative action program could mean assigning "skilled personnel to administer the equal employment opportunity program"—frequently individuals with prior training in "intergroup relations work."[78]

Under PfP, private employers worked under a similar definition of affirmative action in the early 1960s, volunteering "to take steps over and beyond the requirements of the executive order in guaranteeing equal employment opportunity for all." PfP had began operations in May 1961, when fifty of the largest defense contractors in the country voluntarily agreed to join the group. The program grew rapidly and triggered a proliferation of activity. By 1963, there were 117 companies that had signed up for PfP, and nineteen executives from the largest and most powerful corporations decided to form a PfP Advisory Council. The council included officials from Texas Instruments, Lockheed, Chrysler, General Electric, AT&T, and IBM. The same year, local and regional activity surged. Companies in Massachusetts voluntarily gathered under the sponsorship of the Boston Chamber of Commerce and the Associated Industries of Massachusetts (AIM) to form the Massachusetts Plan for Equal Employment Opportunity, which included twenty-two firms employing 108,665 workers. Twenty-three firms in Rhode Island joined to form the Rhode Island Employment Plan to "assure" the "full utilization" of "Negroes." Leaders of thirty-one firms in Milwaukee drew up plans for the Milwaukee Voluntary Employment Opportunity Council. By early 1964, PfP comprised 192 corporations. A national conference in the summer of 1964 brought them together in Washington, D.C. It was attended by more than 500 corporate officials, who listened to speeches by Whitney M. Young, Jr., and Hobart Taylor. The attendees took in panel presentations on compliance programs and EEO implementation before breaking up into smaller groups to discuss particular issues in greater detail. The national membership of PfP continued to grow substantially, and remained active in the field until 1969, when Nixon folded it into the National Alliance of Businessmen, a separate business group focused specifically on assisting the "hard-core" unemployed.[79]

Many corporate executives affiliated with PfP were surely sincere in their commitment to racial equality. But they were not wholly motivated by a concern for social justice. By appearing active on the issue and voluntarily implementing EEO and affirmative action programs, corporate leaders participating in PfP understood that they could potentially stave off the onset of further federal regulation. This motive was only thinly veiled at times. At a 1966 meeting of the ad hoc PfP committee on public relations—which included representatives from General Motors, General Electric, AT&T, Lever Brothers, Lockheed, and DuPont—one participant made the connection utterly explicit. "The Hawkins Bill is now up for passage in the House and probably will be passed in eight months," he correctly predicted. In response, the PfP, in his view, should step up communications efforts to the press, employers, government officials, and civil rights leaders. Everyone should know about what has been accomplished by PfP. Such a campaign could provide "enough evidence that would relieve protests for further legislation in the area of equal employment opportunity." A more artful and diplomatic expression of the voluntarist ethos motivating PfP came from Hobart Taylor, who worked closely with the Advisory Council: "Plans for Progress proves . . . that intelligent business leadership supported by clear-cut communication can eliminate grave social problems, open up new opportunity for millions of Americans and substantially increase sales—all with a minimum of governmental activity."[80]

A similar underlying motivation surely drove a major advertising campaign sponsored by PfP under the slogan "Things Are Changing in Job Opportunities." The purpose of the campaign was to convince African Americans, especially young African Americans, that they stood a better and better chance of being treated fairly when they went looking for a job. Its centerpiece, organized by the Advertising Council, was "Things Are Changing," a pop song written by Phil Spector and performed in various versions by Diana Ross and the Supremes, the Blossoms, Jay and the Americans, and Julio Angel and Lucecita. The production of the song was financed by the Rockefeller Foundation to the tune of a quarter million dollars, and by January 1, 1966, almost three hundred radio stations across the country were playing it regularly. A television commercial was also produced as part of the campaign, and it achieved nearly 330 million "home impressions" on television in 1966, even eliciting mention by Walter Cronkite on "CBS Nightly News." Only the least sophisticated observers could miss the obvious point of the whole campaign: There would be less demand for reform the more that African Americans believed that things were already starting to change for the better.[81]

The typical affirmative action program implemented by a PfP company was motivated partly by the same reason. If corporations were widely seen as taking strong, voluntary measures to combat job discrimination—if they were seen as complying with their own, tough regulations—perhaps it would lessen the perception that Congress needed to pass new legislation. Critics derided PfP as mere public relations, but more than a few companies implemented the "Model Plan" promulgated by PfP, which involved adopting a host of "affirmative action" policies aimed at aggressively and immediately implementing nondiscrimination and equal treatment. Such companies were encouraged to advertise their "interest in actively and affirmatively providing equal employment opportunity"; to change their employment practices to "insure that layoffs, terminations, and downgrading practices are made without regard to race, creed, color, or national origin"; to strive for the inclusion of a "nondiscrimination provision in all collective bargaining agreements into which it enters"; and to centralize responsibility of implementing EEO policy in the hands of every divisional head in the company. Just as it did for federal contractors and the federal government itself, taking affirmative action among PfP companies meant working right away to come up with new and effective ways of making equal treatment a manifest reality.[82]

In sum, officials and personnel involved with the PCEEO in the early 1960s used affirmative action to describe the whole gamut of *race-neutral* programs meant to promote the realization of equal employment opportunity. To them, it meant taking active steps toward the attainment of equal treatment, rather than merely announcing a policy of nondiscrimination and expecting it magically to transform existing social practices. This was the meaning of the policy most readily comprehended by the majority of the individuals responsible for executing it. As H. W. Wittenborn, vice president of Cook Electric Company, observed at a regional conference of community leaders held in Chicago, "It must be thoroughly understood that the policy is not a wait and see policy, but an affirmative action policy."[83]

Even in the early to mid-1960s, however, federal officials in the executive branch began using "affirmative action" in a less apparent but no less significant sense. If "affirmative action" meant in the first instance any "special effort" to achieve equal opportunity, then it was also paradoxically used to signify the special treatment of minorities. To be more precise, it referred to policies in which individuals belonging to protected categories were treated differently than everyone else. Under the 1962 Model Plan of Plans for Progress, for instance, employers were encouraged to give minorities special attention and consideration by pledging to recognize "that the effective practice of a policy of merit employment involves more than the nondiscriminatory hiring and promotion of minority group persons." Employers were asked to carry out a comprehensive "review of the records of minority group employees to determine whether their skills and capabilities may be more fully utilized at high job levels, or would warrant their transfer to other types of jobs more readily leading to advancement." They were encouraged to develop an "active program for the appraisal and counseling of minority group employees who appear to have potential for advancement into supervisory and management positions." Cook Electric's Wittenborn understood his responsibility for affirmative action in terms of special outreach and recruitment programs: "Company management should launch affirmative recruiting drives to secure qualified candidates for potential sources of skill. The passive awaiting of applicants is an insufficient response in this program. Sources such as the talent bank of the Urban League should be fully explored and utilized." White employees would not be granted such treatment. There would be no second looks for any of them who might have been unfairly passed over, there would be no extra programs to cull their ranks for potential supervisors or managers, and there would be no special recruitment programs to expand the pool of qualified white applicants. Such programs were reserved exclusively for racial minorities.[84]

In 1964, affirmative action began to refer not only to programs that actively sought to cast a wider net for qualified minorities but also to policies that compensated racial minorities (but not non-minorities similarly situated) for the present effects of past discrimination. This meaning emerged with particular clarity in a speech given by Johnson's labor secretary, W. Williard Wirtz, to a conference of northeastern community leaders in Philadelphia, one month before the enactment of the Civil Rights Act. Wirtz began with a typical shot of liberal rhetoric: "I suggest that the right to work, in the sense that there is a job available, is an essential right, and so is the right to be ready for the jobs that are and will be available." Simply endorsing such rights, however, represented an empty gesture. "An affirmative action program is required if these rights are to be meaningful," he insisted. For minorities, this meant special programs to make up for a long and sorry legacy of racial discrimination. "If an employer or union has in the past discriminated against applicants for jobs or membership on the basis of their race, it's not enough for that employer or union now just to stop discriminating. There is an affirmative responsibility to counteract the effects of the previous policy." No doubt aware that he was employing language that would make him vulnerable to racial demagoguery, Wirtz took pains to distinguish what he meant from hard quotas. "This does not mean hiring or admitting unqualified applicants," he clarified. "It does mean making it clear that equal opportunity does exist, participating in the preparation and training of people who would have been ready if it had not been for that discrimination and accepting, when they are ready, those who would have been accepted earlier, if here had not been a discriminatory policy."[85]

Wirtz echoed the same compensatory sentiments in remarks he delivered at a PfP meeting a few weeks later. It was essential to take a more targeted, aggressive approach to equal employment opportunity, he argued. What was needed, quite simply, was affirmative action. The previous year, when he and other federal officials had carried out a comprehensive review of young men who had been rejected as unfit for military service—many of them racial minorities—they were shocked to learn the depth of the disadvantage that some Americans youths faced. "Over 80 percent of them are the sons of fathers who did not finish high school," he noted. "A great many of them . . . come from broken families. A high percentage come from families than are larger than the means which are available." Surely it was obvious to anyone that more had to be done for these young men than simply extending equal opportunity; they were ill-prepared to compete effectively in the free market. In making such a suggestion, he did not mean to endorse a "job preference idea." "I want to dismiss that thought completely and shove it entirely aside," he said. "[A]ny talk or thought about a quota kind of employment . . . would be terribly, terribly misguided." But a new and different effort was warranted. "[I]f there is one place where something more than equality seems justified, it is in neutralizing the effects of discouragement which have lead to a deadening of motivation, a lack of education, a lack of confidence, a lack of qualifications." This is precisely what he meant when he promoted the idea of affirmative action. "[T]he essential part of the affirmative action program," he said, "is to make up for the lack of training, including the lack of motivation." Affirmative action could not just meant proactively extending equal opportunity; it had to mean compensating individuals for the accumulated disadvantages that had been thrust upon them by accident of birth.[86]

At a White House Conference on Equal Opportunity in 1965, affirmative action was used in a similarly robust sense. The conference attracted a roster of prominent Americans active in the field, and it featured panels on the growing list of crucial issues: patterns of discrimination, federal-state-local relationships, sex discrimination, record-keeping, and apprenticeship. Herman Edelsberg, then an official with the EEOC, presided over a panel on affirmative action. An excerpt from the conference program offers a glimpse of how Edelsberg and other panelists would talk about affirmative action. The concept meant to them much more than the simple provision of equal opportunity, and it also appeared to mean much more than the proactive pursuit of equality of opportunity:

The employer, the labor union, the community and the government have responsibilities beyond the letter of the law, to provide not only equal employment opportunity but the opportunity to be equal. This requires creative cooperation among these institutions to eliminate existing handicaps and obstacles to minority achievement and the creation of a climate of welcome to minority workers.

In this reckoning, affirmative action referred to programs that gave racial minorities the "opportunity to be equal," making up for any handicaps that they may already have been saddled with. This specific emphasis, like the emphasis Wirtz had put on the term earlier, implied a compensatory dimension that was missing in the earliest uses of the term. It was reminiscent of the powerful metaphor that President Johnson used to describe affirmative action in his widely quoted speech at Howard University the same year. "Freedom is not enough," he said memorably. "You do not take a person who, for years, has been hobbled by chains and liberate him, bring him up to the starting line of a race and then say, 'You are free to compete with all the others,' and still justly believe that you have been completely fair." Employers, unions, and others should work to overcome any handicaps or obstacles that had prevented minority achievement in the past, so that if equality opportunity were extended, racial minorities would be able to compete with others on the same footing.[87]

A year later, Vice President Humphrey drove home the point when he spoke to the NAACP National Convention. Millions of African Americans had been denied equal opportunity in both the recent and distant past. A declaration of equal opportunity today would do little to help them; they were simply not in a position to compete on the same basis as other Americans, who had almost always been afforded their fair share of opportunities to develop and grow. More was needed, he argued. "We must take vigorous affirmative action through skillfully designed training programs to help compensate persons who have been denied all opportunity to prepare themselves for today's market." Humphrey's declaration would have drawn murmurs of agreement from some business leaders. As a PfP report argued in 1967, "Members of minority groups who have been disadvantaged in their environment and education are frequently unprepared to enter the world of business after the gates have suddenly opened. Furthermore, generations of rejection have made them suspicious of even the most sincere open-arms policy. Consequently business and industry must prove what they say through programs of motivation and training."[88]

Even as federal officials and corporate executives began to expand the meaning of "affirmative action" to include a compensatory dimension, they began to promote racial attentiveness in other ways—notably in the expansion of federal efforts to map out the racial makeup of the work force in federal employment, federal contracting, and private employment. It was during the Eisenhower administration that federal contractors had first been required to enumerate their workers by race, but interest in such tools took a quantum leap forward during the Kennedy years. Initially carried out in 1961, a census of federal employment enabled the PCEEO to form for the first time a broad "picture of minority employment in the federal establishment as a whole." In 1961, PfP requested that participating private employers file Form EEO-10 so that the PCEEO might begin to collect data on racial patterns in their employment practices.[89]

Officials at the PCEEO's Government Contract Employment Division developed the most elaborate and comprehensive reporting system. As a condition of their compliance, government contractors were required annually to file a racial census of their work force on Standard Form 40, which was drafted shortly after issuance of Executive Order 10925 and approved by the Bureau of the Budget in late 1961. The PCEEO was only exaggerating slightly when it claimed in a report published the subsequent year that the development of a compliance reporting system for government contractors might well prove to be "among the most significant steps taken in twenty years of federal antidiscrimination effort." It conceded that the nondiscrimination clause had been a regular feature of federal contracts since the Second World War, but went on to claim that the establishment of the compliance-reporting program by the PCEEO represented the first time that federal contractors were required to file periodic reports as a "condition of [their] performance." What was more, no previous program had ever tried to "systematically" document the effects of the nondiscrimination clause. This would soon be possible with the compliance-reporting program in place. The report also argued that the program would make it possible for contractors themselves to determine whether any changes in their employment practices were increasing their rates of minority utilization. No such information had ever been available to them before. The PCEEO thus sought to frame itself as breaking important new ground and taking a more "affirmative approach" to eliminating job discrimination.[90]

There was some basis to the assertion. A 1963 *Report to the President* contained fairly detailed information on the racial composition of the contractor workforce. More than 10,000 compliance reports had been filed by contractors employing about 4.2 million workers, and the overall patterns were illuminating, if unsurprising. Roughly six percent of all workers were African American, and they were underrepresented in almost every sector, industry, region, occupation, and city. But perhaps the real value of the system was that it permitted the identification of areas where affirmative action might be encouraged. The employment census gave federal officials an additional tool to force compliance—without re-sorting to the regulatory bomb of contract cancellation. "Through the compliance reports, for the first time, the Committee and agency contract officials will be able to determine those companies, those areas, those industries in which additional affirmative action must be taken to ensure equal employment opportunity."[91]

Though it was a substantial improvement over Eisenhower's commit-tees, it is true that the PCEEO was somewhat less of a force for social change than its own promotional materials made it out to be. It never cancelled a contract, and John D. Skrentny is entirely correct to assert that "it is not clear what the program officials did with the information [obtained from compliance reports], if anything." But the significance of compliance reporting cannot and should not be defined solely in terms of the impact it had on the number of minority workers hired or promoted or the number of discriminatory acts prevented. In a larger sense, compli-ance reporting was a harbinger of a subtle but fundamental shift in the overall approach that the federal government was beginning to take in the struggle against job discrimination. The state of compliance in con-tract law, as Hugh Davis Graham observantly points out, is not the same as a presumed state of innocence in criminal or civil law. This distinction is at the heart of the regulatory transformation that began to take root in earnest after nearly two decades of congressional inaction. Liberal-designed FEP legislation contemplated the establishment of a regulatory system in which a federal commission would pursue a fairly robust en-forcement program—determining, when necessary, whether individual unions or employers were innocent or guilty of violating the law. The commission would have been authorized to investigate complaints by workers, and if it determined that the complaint was valid, it was respon-sible for trying to reconcile the aggrieved parties. If the conciliation pro-ceedings failed, the commission would then hold hearings to collect evi-dence and testimony. Unions or employers would naturally be granted a presumption of innocence, but the evidence would eventually go before the FEPC for judgment. If the commission deemed that the worker had met his or her burden of proof, then it could find the union or employer guilty of an unlawful employment practice and order it to cease and de-sist—and possibly make amends to the victim (take "affirmative action") for any harms that he or she had incurred as a result of the unlawful action. It was a straightforward idea. The law prohibited discrimination against individuals on account of their race, and a federal agency would actively enforce the law if someone was guilty of violating it. By contrast, compliance with government regulations implied an altogether different regulatory framework. Guilt and innocence were not the operative legal and regulatory categories. Government contractors and private compa-nies could either be compliant or noncompliant, and the burden of proof fell on them—rather than a complainant—to establish their regulatory status. Moreover, as Graham notes, compliance was generally not determined after the occurrence of an alleged infraction but *beforehand*. Contractors and companies had to demonstrate compliance with federal regulations if they wished to bid on (or continue to hold) government contracts. Alternatively, private companies had a strong incentive to comply with ambitious, self-defined goals or programs if they wanted to make the case that legislative action was unnecessary. The difference between the two regulatory models was easy to miss for anyone without legal training or extensive experience in the field of intergroup relations. Yet the Kennedy administration's substantial expansion of compliance reporting and voluntary action significantly shifted the emphasis of federal policy away from administrative enforcement of the law and toward regulatory compliance, whether the regulations were issued by executive agencies or set by companies eager to demonstrate their ability to change on their own.[92]

The shift only deepened during the Johnson administration with the issuance of Executive Order 11246 in 1965. With it, Johnson's order recapitulated Kennedy's ban on discrimination in federal employment and contracting, specifically calling on contractors to "take affirmative action to ensure that applicants are employed, and that employees are treated during employment without regard to their race, creed, color, or national origin." To enforce the contracting provisions of the order, Johnson established the Office of Federal Contract Compliance (OFCC) within the Department of Labor (DOL).[93]

But even the second major appearance of "affirmative action" in the *Federal Register* left the meaning of the term ambiguous. Though officials denied that it meant "preferential treatment," it was unclear precisely what the term did mean. As late as 1967, Edward C. Sylvester, Jr., then head of the OFCC, conceded as much: "There is not fixed and firm definition of affirmative action." Numerous contractors remained bewildered through 1968. Indeed, it was not truly until 1969, with the establishment of the Philadelphia Plan, that the meaning of the term publicly crystallized. The *contretemps* over the Philadelphia Plan is well known by now. The impetus for the policy came from the top down as well as from the bottom up. The program technically began under the Johnson administration in late 1967, when labor officials drafted new regulations that required federal construction contractors to submit detailed, pre-award "manning tables" outlining their minority hiring goals in all phases of their work under contract. The order specifically targeted Philadelphia, but, as Thomas J. Sugrue reveals, it came on the heels of massive protests by civil rights activists at federal job sites in St. Louis, San Francisco, and Cleveland. A year later, however, Comptroller Elmer Staats ruled the plan illegal because it did not stipulate a detailed set of minimum requirements prior to the award of a contract, as required by law. After the Staats ruling, it seemed only natural that the plan would die a lonely death in the quiet recesses of the federal bureaucracy, especially after Nixon's election. But it did not. It was actually revived by the Nixon administration in 1969, after federal officials were warned by Philadelphia civil rights activists that riots might engulf the city if strong action were not taken. Shortly thereafter, Labor Secretary George Shultz and Assistant Secretary Arthur Fletcher presided over the issuance of regulations that required federal contractors to submit pre-award "goals and timetables" toward the integration of their work force. The goals were expressed in terms of percentage ranges, which were based on the availability of minority workers in the local area. Contractors were not required to meet a quota, but they would be judged on whether they had made a good faith effort to achieve their goals. A heated controversy over quotas nevertheless erupted and spilled into Congress, led by Sen. Samuel Ervin (D-NC) and quietly fanned by NAM. The conflict must have pleased administration officials, who hoped to use the Philadelphia Plan to drive a wedge between organized labor and the civil rights movement. In 1970, Shultz's Department of Labor (DOL) went even further than the year before, issuing Revised Order No. 4, which extended the basic framework of the Philadelphia Plan to all federal contractors. Despite the political tempest it had triggered, affirmative action now meant something clear after years of ambiguity. When it came to the realm of government contracting, it referred to the "goals and timetables" for integration that federal contractors were required to specify in order to qualify and be retained as bidders.[94]

What made Fletcher and other federal officials turn to such a strong formulation of affirmative action in contracting was not just the pressure of civil rights activism but also the regulatory inadequacy of earlier policies, which had simply yielded too little change in the employment practices of unions. Title VII had been written in such a way that EEOC had jurisdiction over unions but no enforcement power. Hence, if the government genuinely wanted to take strong action against union discrimination—as Attorney General John N. Mitchell pointed out in a letter to Shultz—it would be necessary to work through federal contractors, who were subject to the power of the purse. Moreover, it would be necessary to hold them as accountable as possible. Indeed, Fletcher was utterly convinced that setting "goals and timetables" was the only effective method of achieving real results. Following what John D. Skrentny calls a logic of administrative pragmatism, Fletcher embraced the setting of numerical goals: "I did this because my study and experience had convinced me that such targets were essential if we are to measure results in terms of increased minority employment. Without such targets, the paper compliance and the interminable ineffectiveness of the government programs would go on. I had not come to Washington to preside over a continuation of the ineffective programs of the past."[95]

The "goals and timetables" formulation of affirmative action did not remain confined to the DOL for long. It would be eagerly seized upon by the toothless EEOC, which took the opportunity to promulgate its opinions at an industry-government meeting sponsored by NAM and PfP in 1968. "There is no difference" between the "EEOC and the OFCC concepts of affirmative action," it stated. "The EEOC considers that the same concepts apply under both Title VII and the Executive Order." Although the commission never officially issued any binding regulations about affirmative action, it urged companies to act nonetheless. "Every employer should adopt a program of affirmative action without waiting for its affirmative action obligations to be precisely defined in judicial or administrative enforcement proceedings." It pointedly noted that many employers had taken the advice: "This has been recognized by employers who have voluntarily established their own equal employment opportunity programs and have joined in cooperative programs such as those of Plans for Progress—a voluntary association of more than four hundred of the Nation's largest industrial employers—and the National Alliance of Businessmen."[96]

Indeed, many PfP companies—not all of whom were federal contractors—were developing strongly analogous forms of affirmative action at roughly the same time as the DOL itself. As the controversy over the Philadelphia Plan played out through early 1970, OFCC Director John Wilks announced somewhat defensively that Revised Order No. 4, which extended affirmative action to all federal contractors, "contains basically the same guidelines that were formerly part of the Voluntary Plans for Progress affirmative-action hiring program." Wilks was speaking knowledgeably and candidly. Many PfP companies were taking aggressive affirmative action well before federal contractors were made to take it and well before the EEOC had asked private employers to take it. In a 1969 report, PfP noted that it had successfully solicited the participation of more than one-hundred major American companies that employed roughly a third of the workers covered by the Civil Rights Act. Moreover, it claimed that two out of the seven of the 1.4 jobs million jobs added to their payrolls in the past four years had been minority placements. The numbers were undoubtedly imprecise and exaggerated, but there could be far less doubt about the source of whatever actual progress they had made. It came from affirmative action. "The statistical growth in minority employment," noted the report "has been largely the result of many affirmative action programs of member companies. Many of the most successful and inventive minds in business and industry have been released from other pursuits to concentrate on preparing minority workers for employment, on seeking them out, identifying their job problems, qualifying them to be hired, and up-grading and promoting them to better jobs." Little more than the fear of legislative action—and perhaps a politic desire to adopt a cooperative attitude with federal officials—was pushing American industry to take affirmative action, but it was a pioneer of affirmative action just the same.[97]

A pamphlet developed and distributed by PfP —entitled "Affirmative Action Guidelines"—suggests the scope and nature of the affirmative action programs that many participating companies may have been voluntarily implementing by the late 1960s. The pamphlet had been prepared in 1968 by members of the PfP staff as a "service to industry," and it was distributed in October of that year at a series of joint NAM/PfP Equal Opportunity Conferences held in Chicago, Houston, Los Angeles, and New York. The pamphlet began by defining affirmative action as "specific and individual *results oriented* programs designed to materially increase the utilization of minorities at all levels and in all segments of the workforce" (italics in original). Examples of such programs included more than simply reaffirming a company-wide commitment to equal employment opportunity and more than just making sure that the responsibility for achieving nondiscrimination was assigned to specific personnel. It also meant the "Identification of Problem Areas" and the "Establishment of Company Goals and Objectives by Division, Location and Job Classification," including "target completion dates." To identify problem areas, PfP staff recommended that companies analyze the "racial mix of their work force" and "applicant flow," noting cases in which there were "no minorities in specific work classifications" or cases in which the "ratio of minority applicants [was] below [the] ratio of [the] minority applicant community." The pamphlet also urged companies to examine any "selection process [that] eliminates a high[er] percentage of minorities than non-minorities," including but not limited to "position descriptions" that were unrelated to actual job duties and "test norms not validated by location, work performance and inclusion of minorities in [the test] sample." When problem areas were successfully identified, companies were encouraged to set hiring or promotion goals, including a timetable if at all possible. The pamphlet offered several examples of what such goals might look like:

—Completely desegregate facilities by October 1, 1968.
—Increase flow of minority applicants for sales positions by at least 35 percent by December 1, 1968.
—New York office plans to hire 20 sales representatives by June 1, 1969. Ten of the twenty will be minorities. Six of the ten will be Negro.
—Fifteen percent of employees promoted into supervisory positions in 1969 will be minorities.

The guidelines formulated by PfP were nowhere near identical to the Philadelphia Plan or Revised Order No. 4—if anything, PfP guidelines were far more aggressive and explicit—but it appears that many large American companies were at least contemplating various forms of racially attentive affirmative action in the late 1960s, perhaps even before the federal government began ordering federal contractors to set "goals and timetables."[98]

Some companies surely did little or nothing to change their employment practices, and others did not go as far as PfP staff would have wished, but the PfP pamphlets did not all languish in the filing cabinets of well-meaning personnel directors. There is evidence that certain PfP companies did actually take racially attentive forms of affirmative action in the late 1960s, though the specific details of the program varied from firm to firm. In 1967, for instance, First Pennsylvania Bank and Trust Company launched Project 35. At the suggestion of the mayor, First Pennsylvania identified and hired thirty-five minority employees who had been members of the "hardcore" unemployed. For ten to fifteen weeks, they were assigned as extra workers to all departments of the bank. Each person received training for specific jobs, and all were asked to attend weekly, evening sessions for special instruction and further skill-building. Project 35 was not intended purely for public relations. For the right men and women, it would eventually yield a job. There is no surviving record of whether the bank actually did hire any of thirty-five participants, but the intention was clear. As one bank official stated, "[w]e seek to develop their skills, where needed, to orient them to bank employment and to motivate them for future development. Those who succeed will become permanent employees of the bank." In 1968, Goodyear Tire of Akron reported to PfP that it had "made a very substantial increase in the number of Negroes in supervis[ory], professional and technical capacities." Among the newer initiatives at Goodyear included a "six-month program of intensified pre-vocational training" for twenty men that would lead to the successful completion of an apprenticeship program. The company had also provided a group of women "special training currently for ultimate placement as stenographers and secretaries." Also in 1968, the Hartford County Manufacturers Association and the Greater Hartford Chamber of Commerce established the United Aircraft Training Center in East Hartford. Through the Training Center, local employers sponsored individual trainees, helping them to obtain basic education and occupational training in such work as machine operation, assembling sheet metal working, materials handling, and tool-crib attending. For trainees interested in nonindustrial employment, training was offered to qualify them for work as a typist, file clerk, cashier, stock clerk, or mail clerk. Sponsors paid each trainee during their training session, which varied in length depending on his or her level of prior education, and a job was guaranteed after graduation.[99]

The setup in Hartford was not particularly unique. Many other companies took affirmative action in the same manner in the late 1960s. A PfP report noted that regional and local employment councils affiliated with PfP more than tripled in 1966, growing from seventeen to fifty-two, and many of the councils worked closely with "retraining and upgrading programs undertaken by social agencies" in their area. Such cooperation with government and the nonprofit sector often took the "form of job slots for program graduates." PfP companies in Cleveland led the establishment of a program, Project AIM-JOBS, which sought to place 2,000 "hard-core unemployed." The program entailed a two-week orientation period, after which participants who lacked minimum qualifications would be offered remedial education and placement assistance. PfP companies in nearby Dayton, including Coca-Cola, IBM, General Motors, Standard Oil, and Xerox, made a similar pledge, promising to "exercise affirmative action in seeking out members of minority groups in whatever part of our society they exist to provide them with meaningful job opportunities. . . . We will provide training, to the extent possible, to assist all applicants and employees alike in meeting requirements for better jobs." Just as congressional inaction had encouraged federal bureaucrats to implement racially attentive forms of affirmative action, corporate officials found themselves motivated for different reasons to voluntarily pursue similar initiatives.[100]

The federal courts did not sit still as a flurry of activity emanated from the executive branch and corporate sectors. A lawsuit was filed by the Contractors Association of Eastern Pennsylvania against the Philadelphia Plan, charging that it violated the Civil Rights Act and the Fourteenth Amendment. Both the trial court and the appeals court moved to uphold the legality and constitutionality of the plan, with the appeals court ruling in 1971 that the plan was a "valid executive action" because it was designed to "remedy the perceived evil that minority tradesmen have not been included in the labor pool available for performance of construction projects in which the Federal Government has a cost and performance interest." The case was not granted certiorari by the Supreme Court, and the place of government-mandated, racially attentive affirmative action in contracting was assured in federal law for the time being.[101]

A different case in 1971 was granted certiorari by the Supreme Court, and it signaled the judicial legitimation of yet another form of racially attentive policy. *Griggs v. Duke Power Company* started as a class action by a group of black workers at the company's Dan River Station in North Carolina. The company had required that all employees hold high school diplomas and attain acceptable scores on aptitude tests in order to obtain employment, promotions, and transfers. This might have seemed eminently reasonable under most circumstances, but African Americans in North Carolina—having lived their whole lives under Jim Crow segregation—graduated from high school at a much lower rate than whites and also failed the aptitude tests at a much higher rate than whites, making it impossible for them to obtain employment and move out of the undesirable jobs and departments to which they were usually relegated. The plaintiffs decided to sue Duke, arguing that the job requirements violated Title VII. Both the trial court and appeals court ruled against the plaintiffs, holding that Duke had not intentionally meant to discriminate when setting the requirements. The plaintiffs then appealed to the Supreme Court, which took the case and ruled surprisingly in their favor. One of the crucial issues on which the decision turned was that the requirements that Duke established were not designed to predict the ability of workers to perform certain types of jobs or categories of jobs. This ran afoul of EEOC guidelines in 1966 permitting only job-related tests. The *Griggs* court ruled that the EEOC deserved "great deference" from the judiciary in issuing such guidelines, which, based on the legislative history of the Civil Rights Act, should be construed as expressing the will of Congress. "What Congress has commanded," Chief Justice Warren Burger wrote in the majority opinion, "is that any tests used must measure the person for the job and not the person in the abstract." The broader legal and historical significance of *Griggs* was that it carved out a place for disparate-impact doctrine in American anti-discrimination law. For years thereafter, *Griggs* would be interpreted by the federal courts—not uncontroversially—as holding that the language of Section 703(a)(2) of the Civil Rights Act made it unlawful for employers to "limit, segregate, or classify" their employees in ways that led to a disparate impact on the employment opportunities of racial minorities, regardless of employer intent. As noted by Richard Primus, the EEOC had been arguing in the years leading up to *Griggs* that Title VII prohibited employment practices that led to a disparate impact. Several lower courts seemed to agree. *Griggs* settled the matter for some time. "What is required by Congress," Burger wrote, "is the removal of artificial, arbitrary, and unnecessary barriers to employment when the barriers operate invidiously to discriminate on the basis of racial or other impermissible classification." Legislation strengthening the EEOC may have been stuck in the middle of a difficult battle in Congress, but racial attentiveness had made another important inroad through a combination of bureaucratic and judicial action.[102]

By the time that the Burger court was contemplating *Griggs*, affirmative action had come a long way. Its meaning had been fundamentally unclear when it first appeared in Kennedy's executive order. In the years thereafter, it was used in a dual sense by government officials and corporate executives, referring both to race-neutral programs meant to proactively establish equal employment opportunity as well as racially attentive programs that accorded racial minorities varying degrees of differential treatment. By 1972, on the eve of the long-awaited moment when Congress would finally grant the EEOC enforcement some kind of authority, it had grown fairly clear what affirmative action meant. It was part of a rapidly developing cluster of racially attentive public policies—including racial surveys of employment and disparate impact doctrine—that had found ample room to grow in the executive and judicial branches of the federal government because Congress had proven unwilling to assert itself by establishing a federal agency with reasonable authority to enforce a law against job discrimination. For both federal contractors and private companies, affirmative action referred to setting "goals and timetables" for achieving the racial integration of their work forces. The policy had become a key component of a regulatory framework that leaned heavily on compliance with mandatory or voluntary regulations, rather than on the aggressive enforcement of equal treatment. With the passage of the Equal Employment Opportunity Act of 1972, which permanently anchored the locus of regulation in the courts, there was no going back to fair employment practices and the program that it envisioned. Affirmative action and a whole host of other racially attentive policies were here to stay for at least the next two decades.

There can be little doubt that the Civil Rights Act represents a major watershed in American history. But it did not come without a price. To form a bipartisan coalition broad enough to clear the numerous legislative hurdles that would culminate in the inevitable Senate filibuster by southern Democrats, liberals had to win the cooperation of conservative Republicans, who therefore enjoyed the balance of power in the politics of civil rights. Indeed, conservative views were uppermost in the minds of the Kennedy administration and Republican congressional leaders when they met in 1963 to craft a bill and a fair employment provision that would not be condemned to certain death. Rightly concerned with the deep antipathy of conservative Republicans toward administrative forms of enforcement, they agreed to set aside the strong liberal version of Title VII endorsed by the House Judiciary subcommittee, replacing it with a proposal by young Republican moderates to restrict the enforcement power of the EEOC to filing lawsuits in federal district court. This compromise formed the basis of a court-centered enforcement bill that cleared the whole House. When the House bill went over to the Senate, Republican Everett M. Dirsken used his leverage to strip the EEOC of even this modest power, leaving the agency a "poor, enfeebled thing." No other phrase from the era more evokes the costs of bipartisanship more powerfully.

But the struggle for administrative enforcement did not end in 1964. Even though the Civil Rights Act had established the EEOC to regulate employment discrimination, liberals and conservatives found themselves continually clashing over the question of enforcement authority. Ultimately, northern Democrats and a handful of liberal Republicans simply could not muster the necessary political strength in either chamber to overcome a coalition of southern Democrats and conservative Republicans. Buoyed by the aggressive lobbying of organized business, the southern-conservative coalition proved capable of mustering a slim majority on some occasions and benefiting from political institutions such as the Senate filibuster on other occasions. In either case, it was the party discipline of Republicans that made southern-conservative success possible.

Had any such strengthening proposal actually passed Congress, even at this late hour, the political and legal development of affirmative action might have looked strikingly different. There might have emerged a coherent, primarily "color-blind" policy framework anchored by a regulatory agency whose operations would have been governed by a ramified body of administrative laws and federal court decisions. That agency would not only have wielded cease-and-desist authority, but it would also have been empowered to order that "affirmative action" be taken by offending employers and unions to compensate victimized workers, a power that would eventually come to be wielded by the federal courts. Perhaps affirmative action might not have come to describe a legally embattled set of racially attentive policies that continue to be associated with quotas and preferential treatment. In a 1971 debate over the Equal Employment Opportunity Act, Shirley A. Chisholm (D-NY), the first black woman to serve in Congress, could not have rendered the counterfactual any clearer (figure 5.3). "Would the gentleman agree," she asked rhetorically, "that if the EEOC had the right and opportunity to issue cease-and-desist orders, then it would have to naturally follow that perhaps we would not have to be speaking this afternoon in terms of preferential quotas?"[103]

Of course, the EEOC was never given the authority to issue cease-and-desist orders, and its ongoing regulatory weakness, a direct legacy of conservative resistance, furnished the institutional and political space for the emergence of affirmative action and other racially attentive policies. This development was almost wholly unanticipated by most liberals or conservatives. What liberals sought in the 1960s and early 1970s—indeed, what they had sought since the Second World War—was an FEPC or EEOC with the power to protect Americans from employment discrimination and the authority to compensate them for the wrongs each of them may have demonstrably suffered. What they ultimately received in exchange for their efforts was something else entirely: a court- and compliance-based system of regulating job discrimination in which affirmative action was a small but controversial part. This decentralized and hybrid system would grow more powerful over time, opening up numerous job opportu-

Figure 5.3 U.S. Rep. Shirley Chisholm (D-NY) speaking at a press conference, 1971. The first black woman elected to Congress, Chisholm took a vocal role in supporting legislation that would have granted the Equal Employment Opportunity Commission (EEOC) administrative enforcement authority. In a 1971 debate, she pointedly asked whether Congress would be wrangling over quotas if the EEOC possessed cease-and-desist power. A year later, Congress decisively embraced a court-based system instead, marking the final eclipse of fair employment practices and the rise of equal employment opportunity and affirmative action. Courtesy of Library of Congress, Prints and Photographs Division, U.S. News and World Report Magazine Collection, reproduction number LC-U9-24470, frame 17A/18.

nities that had been closed off in years past. It would do so through the aggressive enforcement of federal officials such as William H. Brown III, legal pressure from civil rights organizations and ordinary workers, and judicial deference to bureaucratic rule-making and corporate initiative. But only a handful of liberals, among them Alfred W. Blumrosen, had glimpsed its potential. The system that ultimately developed, including affirmative action, was never the imagined endpoint of the liberal campaign against job discrimination that began during the Second World War. It was rather the unintended consequence of permanently deferring the dream of fair employment.[104]

6

Conclusions and Implications

Studies of political development are their most compelling when it can be shown why politics and policies took the particular directions they did—and not other directions they plausibly might have. Without due consideration of historically grounded counterfactuals, arguments about the origins and development of particular policies can skirt dangerously close to tautology. As political scientist Margaret Weir notes in her study of employment policy in the United States, "[P]olicy decisions are, most obviously, choices among alternatives." The analytical challenge is explaining why some choices were made and others were not. In their research on community colleges, sociologists Steven Brint and Jerome Karabel make a similar point, explaining the critical importance of understanding why "particular kinds of [organizational] forms are chosen over possible alternatives, and why organizational forms change over time in particular directions."[1]

The scholarship on the origins of affirmative action has made enormous strides in recent years, but it has still not completely grappled with the whole range of policy alternatives that were in play during the long-standing struggle against job discrimination. While arguments that stress the unique role of urban riots, union racism, regulatory capture, and political institutions during the Johnson and Nixon administrations constitute major contributions, they do not fully account for the particular kind of regulatory system that had emerged by 1972. More specifically, they are hard pressed to explain the emergence of a fragmented, court-centered framework for regulating job discrimination—one in which the maintenance of racially attentive "goals and timetables" by federal contractors and private corporations became understood as signals of compliance with the law. *The Fifth Freedom* offers evidence that affirmative action arose as the unexpected by-product of the failed struggle for a different regulatory framework, that of fair employment practices (FEP). The struggle for FEP legislation and "freedom from discrimination" had begun in 1941 when A. Philip Randolph's March on Washington Movement forced Roosevelt's unexpected establishment of the wartime FEPC. While the committee did not outlast the war, it did set a decades-long policy feedback into motion, bringing into existence a new political bloc that sought a framework akin to that of the National Labor Relations

Board (NLRB) for regulating job discrimination. Beginning in the mid-1940s, groups like the National Association for the Advancement of Colored Peoples (NAACP) and Leadership Conference on Civil Rights (LCCR), industrial unions like the United Automobile Workers (UAW), religious organizations like the American Jewish Congress (AJC), and liberal lobbies like the Americans for Democratic Action (ADA) made common cause. This liberal bloc of groups was not entirely without prospects for success. Working together, they pinned their highest hopes on legislation establishing a federal regulatory agency with expansive jurisdiction over job discrimination and powers of administrative enforcement—which included not only cease-and-desist authority, but also the power to order offending companies or unions to take "affirmative action" to compensate individuals against whom they had discriminated. Among the most avid congressional sponsors of such legislation were liberal Republicans and northern Democrats. If liberals and their congressional allies had gotten their way, then affirmative action would have taken on a vastly different political and legal significance than it has today. This possibility, which was very real, provides the counterfactual missing in previous studies of affirmative action.

Much to their dismay, liberals never achieved a full measure of success. The most infamous enemies of civil rights were racial reactionaries and their representatives in Congress—wily, hard-nosed southern Democrats. Yet it was a bloc of conservative Republicans, organized business, and rural and suburban whites outside the South who held the balance of power in national politics and controlled the machinery of statehouse politics for so much of the postwar period. This conservative bloc played a critical but overlooked role in shaping the precise character of the regulatory regime that would eventually emerge. At key moments of the postwar period, it was the real or imagined opposition of the conservative bloc that obstructed the passage of FEP legislation in Congress, delayed the passage of state FEP legislation, encouraged a succession of presidents to substitute executive action for legislative leadership, hamstrung the Equal Employment Opportunity Commission (EEOC) in 1964, shifted the locus of regulation to the courts, prevented the EEOC from being strengthened in subsequent years, made it necessary for the federal government to mandate "goals and timetables" on the part of contractors, and motivated private companies to pursue voluntary measures along the same lines. The initial limits on "freedom from discrimination" may have been set by southern Democrats and their constituencies, but the outermost limits of political possibility were set by conservatives, who enjoyed remarkable success in exploiting political institutions and the party system to their lasting advantage. What ultimately resulted was a regulatory vacuum that encouraged the emergence of affirmative action and other racially attentive programs. Paul Frymer has argued that the federal courts played a significant and independent role in the racial integration of labor unions, partly because elected officials failed to act. In much the same way, affirmative action in employment enjoyed the political and institutional space to grow, because Congress refused to legislate against discrimination for so long—and then did not pass strong enough legislation when it finally did act. It was too little too late, and the consequence was affirmative action.[2]

Of course, it is impossible to say with total confidence what really would have happened if liberals had managed to win NLRB-style enforcement authority for the federal agency responsible for upholding the law against employment discrimination. It seems perfectly reasonable, though, to think that federal policy would have embarked on a vastly different regulatory trajectory and that affirmative action would not have taken on the same legal and political meaning as it has today. This is not the same as claiming that an NLRB-style FEPC or EEOC would have been more effective at eradicating racial inequality than the compliance- and court-based system that actually evolved. It is often said that the United States has a "weak" state, but work by Frank Dobbin, John Skrentny, Robin Stryker, Robert Lieberman, William Novak, and Sean Farhang suggests that the weak American state is actually quite strong in many instances, not in the least because of the power and reach that the federal courts sometimes have. Indeed, when it comes to the specific question of civil rights, Paul Frymer, Nancy MacLean, Timothy Minchin and others have turned up compelling evidence that the enforcement of Title VII by the federal courts—prodded by a grassroots mobilization of black workers and civil rights groups—eventually contributed to the significant reduction of racial inequalities in employment, especially in the South.[3]

Nevertheless, if liberals had gotten their way, it seems reasonable to believe that a different regulatory structure would have taken root and that affirmative action would have come to describe neither the "goals and timetables" set by contractors and private employers, nor even to aggressive, court-ordered consent decrees of the kind that have remade police and fire departments across the country. Instead, it would have referred to administrative orders that were meant to make whole a person who had suffered demonstrable harm. Job discrimination would not have become regulated by a compliance- and court-based regime consisting of both racially neutral and racially attentive policies. Responsibility for regulating job discrimination would have been fairly well centralized in the hands of a single administrative agency with broad jurisdiction over job discrimination, and the agency would have embarked on a regulatory program that emphasized enforcement. A body of administrative law would have developed to govern the entire process, and the federal courts would have intervened only occasionally to define and clarify any statutory ambiguities that remained. The regulatory approach of the agency would have been to do whatever it could within the bounds of the authorizing legislation (and consistent with the political will of the commissioners) to ensure that individuals were treated equally in the labor market regardless of their race, religion, or national origin. It would have ordered the cessation of discrimination whenever it was discovered, and it would have ordered offending parties to make amends. "Color-blindness" would have been the regulatory order of the day. There would have been less room for racially attentive policies—much less policies of the kind that today go under the name "affirmative action."[4]

On the other hand, if liberals had gotten their way, many of the thorniest issues that have bedeviled antidiscrimination law in the past quarter-century would still probably have surfaced anyway. Job discrimination was a pervasive problem in American labor markets, and no federal agency would have been able to eradicate it instantly. The slow pace of progress would have fueled charges of underperformance and led to demands for stronger policies. There would have been a vigorous argument over the definition of discrimination. What exactly was discrimination? What kind of evidence would be required to sustain a charge? Could discrimination be inferred only by the racially disparate impact of certain employment practices, or would it require evidence of intentionality or state of mind? There would have been difficult questions to resolve about how to redress the problem of discrimination in a time-bound society. What should happen to white workers whose promotions and career advancement, through no fault of their own, had been based on separate lines of racial seniority? Strongly analogous debates would have emerged on any number of relevant questions.

This makes it tempting to think that many racially attentive policies as we know them today, including affirmative action, would have arisen *even if* liberals had gotten their way. What should be appreciated, however, is that the political and policy environment would have been dominated by the existence of a federal agency with statutory authority to receive, appraise, and redress individual complaints of job discrimination. Any dissatisfaction with the performance of the agency would probably have been initially channeled toward demanding or legislating additional authority for the agency. In fact, numerous regulatory options aimed at strengthening the ability of the agency to enforce the law would have been considered first before it would have become politically feasible and intellectual defensible to call for racially attentive policies. For instance, there probably would have been a debate about giving the agency authority to initiate investigations without having to wait for a complaint first.

There may have also been a debate about the possibility of granting the agency the authority to issue binding, industry-wide orders as other federal agencies are authorized to do.

The history of state commissions can give us a telling glimpse of how national politics and policy-making may have unfolded if Congress had ever passed enforceable FEP legislation. It can provide an instructive basis for contemplating how a national FEPC may have negotiated what Paul D. Moreno has called the "vexing antimony" between the pursuit of equal treatment and the temptation of disparate impact and racial proportionalism. In their research on the New York State Commission against Discrimination (NYSCAD), which wielded the powers that liberals were seeking for a federal agency, Moreno and Martha Biondi find that civil rights leaders and community groups did indeed express strong dissatisfaction with the pace of social change during the late 1940s. Through organizations like the Committee to Support the Ives-Quinn Law, they pushed for faster processing of complaints, asked the commission to launch industry-wide investigations in the absence of individual complaints, and suggested the use of statistical disparities between racial groups to infer the existence of discrimination. Other critics called for quotas. By 1963, even Stanley Lowell, chairman of the New York City Commission on Human Rights, was suggesting the use of preferential treatment to compensate blacks for the legacy of discrimination. But demands for quotas and preference were repudiated by NYSCAD through the early 1960s. It did launch industry-wide investigations into the airlines, banks, and railroads in the mid-1950s under chairman Charles Abrams, but it otherwise held firm to the original vision of Ives-Quinn—that is, to facilitate conciliation between aggrieved parties where possible and to right individual wrongs when necessary. Biondi convincingly argues that civil rights organizations learned how to make the legal and political case for affirmative action by criticizing the limits of NYSCAD, but it is important to remember that the commission itself never took affirmative action of any sort. The case of the Empire State hence provides some validation of the counterfactual scenario. If affirmative action emerged at the national level in the 1960s when federal policies were unquestionably weak, it does not appear to have emerged when policies were stronger, as they were in postwar New York.[5]

This alternate path is not a theoretical or fictional possibility in national politics either. It is grounded in historical precedent there as well. For example, Congress moved to strengthen the federal law against housing discrimination in 1988. To remedy the inadequacies inherent in the Fair Housing Act of 1968, it passed the Fair Housing Amendments Act, permitting aggrieved parties to resolve their differences through the administrative process instead of through the courts and giving the Department of Housing and Urban Development (HUD) the authority to initiate investigations in the absence of a complaint. Such changes may have come too late to make much of a dent in the familiar pattern of metropolitan segregation, but they are precisely the kind of changes that liberals would have sought had they begun to question the regulatory adequacy of a national FEPC.[6]

Even if it eventually proved impossible to resist calls for the establishment of racially attentive programs, whether or not they were dubbed "affirmative action," such policies would have gone through some degree of legislative scrutiny, acquiring a different political significance along the way. Affirmative action would not have been pieced together through a politically vulnerable patchwork of executive orders, administrative regulations, and court decisions. Any racially attentive policy operating with the force of law would have had to clear the hurdle of the legislative process in order to reap the political benefits of statutory sanction. This possibility, too, has ample precedent in civil rights. It is often forgotten that the landmark Voting Rights Act of 1965 was preceded by several ineffectual laws, including the Civil Rights Act of 1957 and the Civil Rights Act of 1960. Neither law had a significant impact on the enfranchisement of blacks in the South. This sorry precedent had a number of important political ramifications, one of the most important of which is that it gave liberals and the Johnson administration a credible basis for arguing that previous approaches had been tried and stronger medicine was unfortunately necessary. Partly as a result, the Voting Rights Act was one of the strongest and most radical pieces of legislation in American history. The original Voting Rights Act belonged to a wholly different genre of legislation than the Civil Rights Act of 1964 or the Fair Housing Act of 1968. It did not merely articulate a generic prohibition against discrimination and establish mild provisions for enforcement. It suspended specific voting practices, such as literacy tests. It directed the federal government to challenge the use of other specific voting practices, such as poll taxes. One section of the law spelled out a two-pronged triggering formula for determining whether the harshest provision, known as Section 5, would apply to a state or subdivision of a state. This triggering formula included, among other things, specific dates and numerical thresholds that were historically grounded and meant to single out particular jurisdictions widely acknowledged as problematic and recalcitrant. A jurisdiction might be covered if fewer than 50 percent of voting age people were registered to vote on November 1, 1964, or if fewer than 50 percent of voting age people actually voted in the 1964 presidential election. When the whole formula was applied, it was no accident that Alabama, Georgia, Louisiana, Mississippi, South Carolina, and Virginia (along with Alaska) were the states that deemed as covered in their entirety by Section 5. This meant that they would be required to obtain permission from the DC District Court or the Department of Justice (DOJ) before making any changes to their election laws. Implicitly acknowledging the depth and intrusiveness of the intervention that Section 5 represented, Congress set time limits on its applicability. The act would later be engulfed in even more controversy when Section 5 came up for renewal, but only die-hard southern rejectionists would argue that the provisions as they were originally written were totally illegitimate. Thus, even if affirmative action and other racially attentive policies were inevitable, they would probably not have arisen through a combination of executive and judicial action. If a bona fide regulatory agency in the mold of the NLRB had actually existed and if racially attentive policies were seriously contemplated by policymakers, they would have probably been sought through the legislative process, and any resulting policies would have been initially shielded from the damaging insinuation that they were the product of a bureaucratic and judicial end-run around the democratic process. For a time, affirmative action might have enjoyed sounder political footing than it does today.[7]

The analysis presented in the *The Fifth Freedom* is not only relevant to the debate about the origins of affirmative action in employment. It is also pertinent to broader scholarly conversations across a number of fields. Sociologists interested in the politics of the policy-making process in the United States may recognize that it joins work by Edwin Amenta, John Skrentny, and others in the emphasis that it places on the crucial role played by elites. More specifically, it demonstrates how paying attention to the political mobilization of economic elites may help us comprehend why particular policy alternatives emerge over time and why policy change takes one trajectory of development over another. Indeed, what the thirty-year struggle over "freedom from discrimination" reveals is the central significance of organized business to American political development and policy-making. Social movements, public opinion, and other forces furnish the broad, essential preconditions for policy change, but comprehending the particular type of change that occurs requires a look at the hopes and fears of economic elites such as organized business—and their collective mobilization in politics. The political impetus for policy change flows from many sources, but the demands and mobilization of elites are indispensable to understanding key features in the design of the policies that ultimately emerge out of the political crucible of the policy-making process.[8]

At the same time, what the postwar struggle against job discrimination underlines is the crucial relevance of political institutions and political parties to the outcome of struggles over policy. Elites are not always powerful enough to get what they want right away, and they do not always wield their power brusquely and directly. In many instances, they set out to exert their influence and achieve their objectives by exploiting political institutions and the party system over time. Throughout the wartime and postwar period, organized business fought FEP legislation by forging an alliance with the conservative faction in the GOP, and it was GOP influence at key "veto points" in the policy-making process that proved essential. In particular, it was the super-majority required to impose cloture in the Senate that gave the conservative bloc the balance of power, which in turn enabled it to obstruct FEP legislation or dictate the terms of passage. The end result was that job discrimination was left unregulated or weakly regulated for more than three decades. The same point is illustrated in a different manner by the politics of state FEP legislation. Here organized business also forged long-term alliances with the GOP in many states, and it was once again GOP control of veto points in the policy-making process—particularly key committees in state legislatures—that delayed the passage of state FEP laws and short-circuited the federated strategy that liberals had devised. Even when conservatives were in the minority, as long as the GOP controlled a single veto point, states without FEP legislation were less likely to enact it.

The importance of veto points in the policy-making process—specifically the number of veto points available to opponents of policy innovation—has been well established in the literature on comparative politics, particularly in the work of Ellen Immergut, Evelyne Huber, and John D. Stephens. In research on various aspects of American politics and policy, other political sociologists have pointed convincingly to the crucial role of political parties, including Edwin Amenta, Sarah Soule, and Yvonne Zylan. What the circuitous path from fair employment practices to affirmative action reveals is the value of blending the two insights together. In the national and state politics of FEP legislation, it was the *partisan control of veto points* that was essential in shaping the scope and tempo of policy innovation. What matters is neither the number of veto points that are present in the legislative process nor the raw percentage of lawmakers in the legislature belonging to one party versus another. What matters is whether a particular party controls a veto point along the way to the enactment of a policy. More importantly, partisan control of veto points in the policy-making process of a federal system can actually create the political conditions for the advent of novel policies that few political actors ever fully envision. Robert Lieberman and Isaac W. Martin have observed that the decentralized structure of political institutions in the United States has both a restrictive *and* a generative impact on policy-making. The political history of affirmative action is consistent with the same argument. In successfully obstructing the passage of strong FEP legislation for so long, conservatives unknowingly prepared the political and institutional terrain for the rise of affirmative action, something the ideological heirs would ironically profess to find even more abhorrent.[9]

The story related in the *The Fifth Freedom* also closely intersects with debates among American historians about the political trajectory and the ideological content of liberalism after the Second World War. This debate is oriented around a cluster of related questions. How could liberalism, once a badge of ideological honor for so many Americans, fallen so low in public esteem? What explains the exhaustion and collapse of more muscular and ambitious forms of liberalism that existed in earlier decades? When and why did liberalism turn away from a broad-based critique of industrial capitalism and take on the more limited, rights-based formulation that it still exhibits today?

As historian Gary Gerstle perceptively notes, one influential strand of thought begins with Eric F. Goldman's contention that the ten-year period after the Second World War was the "crucial decade" in the fate of the liberal order. It was then that major questions about the economic and political organization of the postwar period were finally settled. It was then that a "liberal consensus" triumphantly took root. There was neither a massive rededication of the New Deal, nor a gross regression to the status quo ante. But most Americans accepted the legitimacy of a mixed economy, repudiated the easy complacency of isolationism, and acquiesced to the necessary evil of interest-group pluralism. Only on the question of civil rights did consensus prove elusive. This would quickly change, however. By 1963, when the racial crisis in Birmingham pricked the conscience of the nation, support for civil rights had become part of the liberal consensus as well. Nearly everyone outside the South rejected racial segregation and discrimination, and there was high confidence that the South would eventually join the rest of the country. Liberalism seemed poised to scale new heights, and there was a palpable sense that it might prove capable of remedying the defects of industrial capitalism. But the liberal consensus would not outlast the 1960s. Urban riots, black power, antiwar protests, and white backlash against policies like busing and affirmative action did irreparable harm to liberalism, and it unraveled in short order.[10]

A newer, revisionist perspective rejects the centrality of the 1960s to the fate of liberalism. It was not the 1960s but the 1940s when American liberalism—weakened by failures of will and judgment—lost the opportunity to reconfigure the political economy along European lines. A fratricidal conflict on the Left, culminating in the purge of most radicals from the labor movement, undercut a potential left-liberal alliance and undermined any prospect of social democracy. The civil rights movement as well chose to accept the basic structure of American capitalism, turning away from anticolonial and anticapitalist movements overseas. As a result, what emerged from the decade was a "shrunken liberalism"—to borrow a phrase from Gerstle—that was more concerned with protecting the legal rights of individuals and groups to participate in a consumption-oriented society than a liberalism that was concerned about fundamentally reforming and restructuring the economy.[11]

Recent studies of racial inequality in the urban North bolster aspects of the revisionist view. Probing the postwar history of cities like Chicago, Oakland, New York, and Detroit, historians such as Arnold R. Hirsch, Robert O. Self, Chris Rhomberg, Martha Biondi, and Thomas J. Sugrue find evidence of racial tensions within the New Deal bloc—notably between white, working-class ethnics and African Americans—that long antedated the unraveling of liberalism in the late 1960s. Sugrue's work on Detroit illustrates with exceptional clarity and acuity how a "grass-roots rebellion against liberalism" during the 1940s and 1950s "from within the New Deal bloc itself." The resistance of northern, working-class ethnics to the racial integration of their neighborhoods and workplaces during these years suggests that the "'silent majority' did not emerge *de novo* from the alleged failures of liberalism in the 1960s; it was not the unique product of the white rejection of the Great Society." Rather, this backlash was the "culmination" of "simmering white discontent" that had begun decades earlier. The devastation and destruction wrought by the Detroit riot of 1967 should not be regarded as the appalling consequence of liberal excess in the 1960s but the tragic endpoint of the liberal failure to overcome racial inequality in earlier decades.[12]

Such divisions on the Left—between radicals and liberals, working-class ethnics and African Americans—are also evident in the political history of FEP legislation. But a different perspective on the fortunes of liberalism emerges from the legislative transcripts, government publications, local newspapers, constituent letters, and private correspondence that inform *The Fifth Freedom*. The most unified and significant opposition to government regulation of job discrimination came not from within the liberal bloc, but from without. It sprung from a conservative bloc of business interests; rural and, to a lesser extent, suburban whites; and the conservative Republican legislators who represented them. No love was lost for the New Deal among these constituencies, which rejected liberalism of most kinds, if not all kinds: Government had no legitimate role in regulating the economy or promoting social change. "You cannot legislate equality," it was said over and over again. All across the country—from the corridors of Capitol Hill to dozens of statehouses outside the South—conservatives professed support for the goal of racial equality but aggressively repudiated liberal approaches to guaranteeing freedom from discrimination.

Conservative mobilization proved hugely decisive to the fate of liberalism and civil rights, never more so than during the 1940s. This was a crucial decade, but not because liberals either seized or squandered their opportunities. It was crucial because conservatives took full advantage of *their* opportunities and stemmed the tide of liberalism in the many forms it took during the period. Even as a limited variant of liberalism made inroads in national politics and policies, conservatives won key victories at the national level (e.g., Taft-Hartley, defeat of FEPC) and otherwise repaired to the states, where they would cannily piece together more successes and await the opportunity to strike back more broadly. The states were not quite laboratories of democracy; they served more as incubators of conservatism and pressure valves for reform, and conservatives would use them to nurse their strength in the states over the years before returning to the national scene in dramatic fashion during the Reagan-Bush years.

The broad debate among historians over the political fortunes and ideological content of postwar liberalism is closely linked to a conversation among political scientists about the forces responsible for the racial alignment of the two major parties in contemporary American politics. How and why do most African Americans and racial liberals tend to vote Democratic, while most racial conservatives—largely whites—tend to vote Republican? To what extent is affirmative action responsible for this electoral alignment?[13]

The prevailing view, first proposed by Edward Carmines and James Stimson, is that "the struggle over race . . . permanently rearranged the American party system" through an elite-led process of "issue evolution." More specifically, Carmines and Stimson argue that the critical juncture came in 1964 during the presidential contest between incumbent Lyndon B. Johnson and Sen. Barry Goldwater (R-AZ). In the wake of the confrontation in Birmingham and the March on Washington, public demand for government action was peaking, and Congress was in the midst of deliberating over the Civil Rights Act. Each candidate made a deliberate, strategic choice about how to position himself and by extension his party. LBJ threw himself wholeheartedly behind the bill, embracing the liberal idea that the government could and should play a major role in addressing racial inequality, while Goldwater chose to oppose it, eventually becoming one of only eight nonsouthern senators casting a vote against its passage.[14]

This bifurcation of party elites on race and civil rights represented a historic shift, according to Carmines and Stimson. From the New Deal to the Great Society, "issues of race were not partisan issues." There was no Republican view, no Democratic view. "Before 1964 the two sides of the racial debate were progressivism and racism." *Both* Republicans and northern Democrats exhibited liberalism on the question of civil rights, and their main opposition consisted of southern Democrats, many of whom were motivated by racist, segregationist convictions. "Advocates of racial liberalism," write Carmines and Stimson, "were to be found equally among northern Democrats and Republicans. Hostility to the aspirations of black Americans was almost exclusively the province of the southern wing of the Democratic party."[15]

If the divergent choices of party elites in the mid-1960s were unprecedented, they were also enormously consequential. By supporting the Civil Rights Act, Johnson committed his party to the black freedom struggle, significantly reshaping the composition of the Democratic coalition. Southern blacks gained franchise and would soon begin casting Democratic ballots, but southern whites started to drift toward the GOP. The party might have recovered its footing with time, but a new challenge presented itself after 1964 when there was a radical "change in the civil rights agenda itself." That agenda, in the words of Thomas and Mary Edsall, "shifted away from an initial, pre-1964 focus on government guarantees of fundamental citizenship rights (such as the right to vote and the right to equal opportunity), and shifted toward a post-1964 focus on broader goals emphasizing equal outcomes or results for blacks, often achieved through racial preferences." Democratic elites ultimately chose to embrace the shift, but the choice came at a high price. Their support for policies like affirmative action and busing triggered a nationwide, white backlash against civil rights, not only severing any remaining ties that southern whites may have had with the party but also newly alienating white ethnics in the urban North. The coalition that had been in place since the New Deal began slowly to disintegrate.[16]

The choices of Republican elites were equally decisive. Goldwater's opposition to the Civil Rights Act signaled the invention of what Carmines and Stimson call "racial conservatism"—that is, the belief that government could not and should not regulate acts of discrimination, which were essentially private in nature. "Barry Goldwater was not a racist, nor was his band of ideological followers," they are careful to note. Instead, he and his allies mounted a distinctively "ideological opposition" to the "new civil rights initiatives" of the era, claiming that such initiatives "undermined free-market capitalism, constrained individual freedoms, and led to inefficient overpowerful government." This innovation enabled Republicans to oppose civil rights without seeming terribly bigoted, giving them a politically effective way of appealing to disaffected elements of the Democratic coalition. The advent of affirmative action only played into

Republican hands. Indeed, such programs made the ideal target for racial conservatism. Over time, Goldwater's formula proved immensely appealing to racially resentful whites, who gravitated toward the GOP in ever greater numbers. By 1980, Ronald Reagan had perfected the approach, using a language of what the Edsalls call "conservative egalitarianism" to profess his commitment to racial equality—even as he castigated affirmative action as a blatant affront to color-blind, merit-based, market competition. Reagan's triumph over Carter and his landslide defeat of Mondale completed the dissolution of the Democratic order, heralding the rise of a new Republican majority that had been forged out of the broken shards of Roosevelt's class-based coalition.[17]

This elite-led perspective on electoral realignment has now become a part of the standard narrative about recent American politics. It is hard to avoid encountering some variation on the theme that the embrace of racial liberalism by the Democratic party, particularly its support for affirmative action, contributed decisively to the emergence of a new party system. It seems equally difficult to avoid encountering some variation of the argument that Goldwater's path-breaking choice to oppose the Civil Rights Act on ideological grounds made it possible for future Republicans to position themselves in a way so as to benefit from the growing racial resentment of white voters. An article in *The Economist* published the week after Reagan's death in 2004 typifies the conventional wisdom. The article rightly observed that Reagan presided over "one of the great realignments in American politics," one in which "southerners, westerners, and blue-collar workers . . . abandoned the Democrats for the Republicans." Others had attempted to pull off the same alchemy before him and did not succeed. Goldwater failed miserably and Nixon had only "half-tried" to assemble a "conservative governing coalition." "How did Mr. Reagan manage to pull off what many people regarded as impossible?" asked the authors. "The underlying reason was the implosion of liberal America," and much of the blame for the implosion could be pinned on one factor in particular: "The Democratic Party's embrace of affirmative action . . . [which] stirred up a mighty backlash among whites." Goldwater had first envisioned the ideological contours of a new Republican majority, Democrats committed a series of strategic errors, and Reagan brought Goldwater's vision to fruition by taking full advantage of the political deck that he was handed.[18]

The Fifth Freedom challenges numerous facets of the conventional wisdom, starting with the presumption that rank-and-file Republicans and their leaders tended toward racial liberalism before Goldwater's run for the presidency in 1964. In their study of state party platforms, Brian Feinstein and Eric Schickler find that Democrats in northern states were becoming racially liberal as early as the 1940s, largely in response to the demands of grassroots constituencies. *The Fifth Freedom* reveals a streak of racial conservatism among GOP elites in the 1940s and 1950s. It was evident at times in national politics but it was most prevalent in the states, where Republican lawmakers led the charge against FEP legislation using the same obstructionist tactics that have become commonly associated with southern Democrats in Congress. This racial conservatism among Republican elites reflected the racial conservatism of their base. The partisan sentiment powerfully manifested in the vote on Proposition 11 was not confined to California. The average white Republican in the 1940s and 1950s was significantly more racially conservative that the average northern Democrat. Hence it does not seem reasonable to think that realignment was set into motion because Goldwater staked out a new ideological position around which a new Republican majority then coalesced. It seems far more consistent with the evidence to believe that his opposition to the Civil Rights Act simply brought to national promi-nence a stance that was familiar to a majority of Republicans, high and low. Goldwater did very little to lead Republican voters. Rather, he was among the first nationally prominent Republicans to sense correctly where voters were trying to lead him, something that many Republicans in state politics already knew well. There was no point in trying to build a Republican majority around racial liberalism. The only viable electoral strategy for the GOP in national politics tilted in the direction of racial conservatism, and another Republican politician would have eventually and correctly drawn the same conclusion if Goldwater had not done it first. To be sure, elites remained crucial to many aspects of *policy-making*, but their influence on other partisan political processes such as realign-ment—as Taeku Lee and David Karol conclude in other work—did not go entirely unchecked.[19]

In contrast to the conventional wisdom, Republicans did not invent the rhetoric of conservative egalitarianism during Goldwater's presidential run and then perfect it during the Reagan-Bush years. It had actually been invented and perfected decades earlier. The day after the climactic hearing on the Ives-Quinn bill in wartime Albany, Robert Lane wrote his friend Robert Moses to express his hopes for the future of civil rights. "If this bill passes," he wrote, "my guess is that in his mellow fifties my son, if he is the man I hope he will be, will look back on the arguments advanced against it in his young manhood with a tolerant, understanding, forgiving, even if slightly incredulous eye, and wonder how people could ever have thought like that." Lane's guess was not borne out. In the decades after the passage of Ives-Quinn, despite progress toward the achievement of formal equality, his son would have noticed the deployment of strikingly similar rhetoric. Critics of fair employment practices continued to profess a belief in racial tolerance but also continued to oppose FEP legislation on the grounds that it would promote preferential treatment, lead to racial quotas, undermine healthy competition based on merit, and hence exacerbate rather than reduce racial divisions. Such cries did not simply slide into political obscurity. Throughout the 1940s and 1950s, conservatives uttered them repeatedly in battles over FEP legislation.[20]

If conservative egalitarianism did not originate in the 1960s, neither was it triggered solely by southern discontent with racial integration. Matthew Lassiter, Kevin Kruse, Joseph Crespino, and Joseph Lowndes trace the origins of modern conservatism to racial conflict in the postwar South, and they are surely correct to do so, but the history of the struggle over FEP laws suggests that the torrent of racial resentment that fed the growth of modern conservatism had many tributaries. Martha Biondi has briefly noted the rhetorical parallels in criticisms of FEP and affirmative action in her study of postwar New York City, but what has not been fully apparent is just how deep and widespread the parallels are. *The Fifth Freedom* reveals that important elements of conservative egalitarianism—and indeed the larger language of "white backlash"—were pioneered in the 1940s and 1950s by northern chambers of commerce, rural and suburban whites, and the conservative Republicans who allied with them. This conservative bloc claimed to oppose discrimination but nevertheless sought to portray enforceable laws against job discrimination as a thinly veiled attempt to secure the votes of powerful, urban minorities, who were unfairly exploiting their political clout to win special treatment for themselves at the expense of honest, taxpaying citizens.[21]

The substance of the conservative challenge to FEP legislation in the 1940s and 1950s lends further credence to Sugrue's argument that the "chain reaction" of rights, race, and taxes—so keenly anatomized by Edsall and Edsall—was not suddenly triggered by conflicts over the Great Society and affirmative action in the 1960s. The reaction had begun years earlier in northern states and cities, and the major liberal initiatives of the decade simply lent a national focus to racial resentments that had been simmering for years. This implies that affirmative action and other "color-conscious" policies were not uniquely responsible for fanning the flames of "white backlash" and providing Republican elites with the ideal racial wedge issue to shatter the New Deal coalition. To be sure, strategists like Kevin Phillips correctly recognized the extent to which racial resentment had become a substantial force in national politics by the late 1960s. But color-conscious policies bear no special blame. As early as the 1940s and 1950s, congressional Republicans were already using civil rights as a wedge issue, and statehouse Republicans and their constituents were fighting against state FEP legislation, casting their opposition in free-market, antiregulatory rhetoric. If the GOP had not recognized the political utility of affirmative action when it burst into the spotlight in the late

1960s, it would have surely made use of a different civil rights policy—whether color conscious or color blind—to accomplish the same ends. Theories of electoral realignment should begin somewhere other than the advent of affirmative action.[22]

The broadest significance of the fight over FEP legislation in the 1940s is that it challenges the premise that the 1960s was a decisive moment for the politics of electoral realignment. The 1940s did not merely prefigure the shape of things to come. It gave rise to fundamental aspects of racial politics that are mistakenly regarded as emerging *de novo* decades later. Well before the emergence of affirmative action, business groups, Republican legislators, and rural whites had joined forces to oppose color-blind laws that would have promoted equal treatment in the labor market. They did so using a powerful new language of conservative egalitarianism. Subsequent battles over FEP laws in other northern states were quickly overshadowed by bus boycotts and sit-ins in the South. But battles over state FEP laws would also keep the new language alive in northern politics until the late 1960s, when it would be grafted neatly onto partisan conflicts over affirmative action. When northern, working-class ethnics began to search in the late 1960s for words to express their disgruntlement with affirmative action, when Republican presidents such as Richard Nixon and Ronald Reagan sought to capitalize on such feelings to build and consolidate their electoral majorities, there was no need to invent a new lexicon of racial resentment. Nor was it necessary to reach toward Dixie, though Dixie had been busy. The words had already been invented. They were strangely familiar, and they were close at hand.

The story presented in *The Fifth Freedom* also encourages us to reconsider well-worn and popular narratives about the history of civil rights. Many writers, often of widely divergent political commitments, continue to endorse the idea that there was a sharp historical break in the mid-1960s. The period is seen as marking an epochal transformation of politics and society, and the most common narrative convention is based on a stylized contrast between two different countries.

America before 1964–65 is portrayed as a country preparing itself to respond at last to the heroic entreaties of the civil rights movement. For decades, African Americans had waged a humble campaign to dismantle the system of racial apartheid that made them second-class citizens in a nation-state whose founding proclamation held that all men were created equal. In the face of the countless indignities and privations visited upon them by Jim Crow, thousands of ordinary African Americans rallied themselves courageously. They took to the courts. They took to elementary schools and public universities. They took to buses and lunch counters. They took to the streets—old and young, rich and poor, famous and anonymous. They marched mostly alone at first, but in time they were joined by legions of white allies—many Gentiles but especially Jews. Slowly but surely, stories of their bravery and sacrifice in Little Rock, Montgomery, Greensboro, and Birmingham galvanized the conscience of a nation. America was prepared at last to shed the racism of a backward region and deliver the promise of a dream deferred. No moment more aptly symbolized or clearly defined the swelling moral consensus for civil rights than when the Rev. Martin Luther King, Jr., strode to the podium at the foot of the Lincoln Memorial in 1963 to tell the country of his dream. That dream, in his most eloquent and rapturous peroration, was a dream of a society utterly blind to race—where his children would not be "judged by the color of their skin but by the content of their character." King's audience on that day, familiar with his rousing style of call-and-response oratory, heartily shouted out their approbation. And yet his words had struck a chord that would resonate far beyond earshot of the marchers gathered around him. Americans across the country were moved to tears, and many fervently embraced his dream as their own. Even one of his fiercest critics, James Baldwin, admitted that on "that day, for a moment, it almost seemed that we stood on a height, and could see our inheritance; perhaps we could make the kingdom real, perhaps the beloved community would not forever remain that dream one dreamed in agony." Only perpetually mistrustful black nationalists like Malcolm X did not share Baldwin's sense of hope and optimism, worrying that "this dream of King's is going to be a nightmare before it's over."[23]

America after 1964–65 is depicted as a very different country, one that had plunged into a nightmare indeed. Here was a nation that had witnessed the shocking and tragic assassinations of King and Robert Kennedy, whose deaths seemed to symbolize the premature end to the promise of the "beloved community." Here was a nation that had been torn apart by an unprecedented paroxysm of urban rioting in which the luminous hopes of yesteryear had been replaced by the fearsome slogans of black power. Expressions of faith that "We shall overcome" had been brusquely swept aside by militant, nihilistic cries of "Burn, baby, burn" and "Look out, whitey! Black power's gon' get your mama!" Here was a nation rife with Glazer's "ethnic dilemmas," with Americans only gradually coming to grasp the deep irony in the spread of federal policies like busing and affirmative action, which had been foisted upon it by a radicalized civil rights movement that claimed King's legacy as its own, even as it veered precipitously away from the ideals that had guided him. Such policies are framed as directly contradicting the principles of color-blindness that had recently commanded the widespread enthusiasm of the American people. Brought into existence by a combination of administrative, executive, and judicial action—rather than by legislation—they are said to be nothing if not an example of color-consciousness, alienating the majority of Americans and prompting a massive and fatal backlash against civil rights.[24]

A typical, if unusually sophisticated, expression of the discontinuarian perspective is exhibited in Stephan and Abigail Thernstrom's voluminous study, *America in Black and White*. In the course of documenting the thesis that in a "relatively short time . . . we have by many measures come a very long way" in American race relations, the study reveals all the characteristic features of the dominant historiography. The horrors and inequities of African American life under Jim Crow are recounted in exacting detail. The civil rights movement is described in glowing terms. Its leaders are venerated for their political shrewdness and tactical brilliance. The chief villains, die-hard segregationists like Orval Faubus, George Wallace, and Bull Connors, are appropriately reviled, along with their apologists and defenders in Congress. Milestones of the struggle are acknowledged in tones of breathless admiration—*Brown*, the Montgomery bus boycott, Central High, the Greensboro sit-ins, Freedom Rides, James Meredith and Ole Miss, Birmingham.[25]

Most crucially, a dividing line is drawn through the decade with the passage of the Civil Rights Act of 1964 and the Voting Rights Act of 1965. "The great civil rights statutes of the mid-1960s were an amazing triumph," write Thernstrom and Thernstrom. This legislation ignited "a revolution whose swift outcome was unimaginable in 1955 when Rosa Parks was told to move from her seat on a bus." Yet it also marked the end of another era, for at the very moment the civil rights movement had successfully beseeched Congress to act decisively, "things took a dramatic turn for the worse." Riots erupted, and chants of black power began to echo across American cities. The turning point came in the year 1968, which the Thernstroms identify as the "beginning of the affirmative action era." The authors, like most other writers in the same tradition, reach for the trope of irony to characterize apparent and sudden turns of events. "Ironically, just at the point at which the majority of white Americans had decided that enough was enough in the way of social engineering on the racial front, the White House, executive agencies, and the Supreme Court banded together to institute more racial engineering of a new and radical sort." In sharp contrast to congressional legislation, which sought only to guarantee equal treatment, the resultant policies sought to impose "proportional representation of the races in schools, jobs, and political office." In the span of a few short years, all promise and hope for a color-blind society was being precipitously abandoned and the least democratic branches of the federal government were leading the way.[26]

If the idea of a radical break pervades writing on the postwar period, then Hugh Davis Graham mounts the sharpest discussion and most explicit defense of the discontinuarian perspective in his meticulously researched study of affirmative action, *The Civil Rights Era*. Graham contrasts himself with historians such as Mary Frances Berry and John Blassingame, cautioning against seeing too much continuity in the history of race relations. Drawing inspiration from C. Vann Woodward, who, in his book *Thinking Back*, was critical of the tendency to treat the past as a long and continuous chain of events, Graham questions the "presentist and gloomy" notion that the civil rights reforms of the 1960s did little more than to right formal wrongs while leaving the structures of substantive inequality intact. The decade can only be seen as marking a remarkable break from the past, symbolizing human freedom from the inevitabilities of history. "The black mobilization for civil rights," he writes, "was a revolutionary social movement that utterly destroyed the biracial caste system in the South." It ranks as nothing less than a "rare and stunning achievement of liberation."[27]

Few scholars would disagree with the idea that the civil rights movement was revolutionary in many respects. Still fewer would deny that it deserves generous, if not primary, credit for the role it played in dismantling segregation in the South. Nevertheless, it is worth reflecting on Graham's clear skepticism toward "pessimistic" interpretations of the civil rights era. In cautioning against the temptations of continuarianism, Woodward was addressing a recurrent and stubborn impulse in southern history, manifest in not one but two generations of historiography, to see the New South as a straightforward extension of the Old South. It is not likely that in criticizing a tendency of southern history Woodward meant to hold up discontinuity as a tenet of correct historiographical practice. Indeed, the emphasis on change and continuity, he writes, should "derive from substance not theory." The enduring problems of history are "not about absolute but about relative matters, not about the existence but about the degree or extent of the phenomenon in question."[28]

The cycle of historical scholarship on the postwar politics of civil rights has not progressed far enough to permit anyone to carry out the kind of close, critical assessment that Woodward saw as the sine qua non of historical reasoning. Many writers take discontinuity far granted, but the time for pronouncing a definitive verdict on the matter has not yet arrived. Indeed, what is problematic about the discontinuarian perspective is not that it is factually wrong or interpretively overambitious but that it rests on a highly uneven foundation of scholarship. This imbalance exists along two dimensions. The first is geographical. There is a veritable mountain of prize-winning monographs on the struggle of the civil rights movement against Jim Crow segregation in the South. Taylor Branch's *Parting the Waters*, Richard Kluger's *Simple Justice*, or Diane McWhorter's *Carry Me Home* all come readily to mind. It is not as easy to think of comparably significant books on the non-South precisely because there are fewer of them by comparison. The second is temporal. Studies of developments in the South tend to cover the period before the riots, while studies of developments outside the South tend to cover the period after the riots. The situation is slowly changing, with a spate of powerful new studies on postwar Chicago, Oakland, Los Angeles, Philadelphia, and New York City, and it seems worth waiting for the wheel of scholarship to revolve one more time before assuming the case on discontinuity is closed.[29]

The Fifth Freedom offers still more reasons for rethinking the discontinuarian view. Rather than regarding civil rights exclusively as a matter of Jim Crow segregation in the South, it follows Nancy MacLean in focusing on employment, tracing the politics of civil rights along the seam of a single issue that cuts cleanly across sectional divisions. Moreover, it picks up the storyline during the Second World War and carries it well across any presumed historical divide, ending only in 1972. At the same time, it breaks from the tendency of previous research to focus on the pre-1965 South or the post-1965 North and West. Instead, it delves into the politics of fair employment in the *pre*-1965 North and West.[30]

What it finds as a result are fewer radical ruptures and more threads of continuity than previously acknowledged. The civil rights movement in the late 1960s did not experience total apostasy at the hands of young black radicals. Notwithstanding the perceptions of even its closest observers, legions of movement activists did not suddenly reject the policy priorities they had claimed to hold dear during the "early" phase of the movement. Writing for *The Public Interest* in 1971, Harvard sociologist Nathan Glazer thought he sensed a change in the goals of the civil rights movement. By moving from "*equal opportunity*" to the attempt to "ensure a *full equality* of achievement for minority groups," he wrote, "we are not simply continuing an old civil rights effort; we have become involved in something entirely new."[31] Glazer's perceptions were not wholly inaccurate, but like others who would follow in his footsteps, he overlooked the ongoing fight in Congress over the regulatory framework for job discrimination. The old guard in the civil rights movement continued to push for the kind of strong enforcement powers and a degree of regulatory centralization that they had sought since the 1940s. They also happened to be the members of the movement with the greatest influence in the policy-making process. The sayings and doings of black radicals made for great headlines, but they wielded nowhere near the political clout that the old guard did, even in their final days. If anything, it was conservatives who had begun to shift their position in the late 1960s, accommodating themselves to the fragmented system of court enforcement that they had been instrumental in creating. This, of course, is not the same as claiming that there were no changes in the civil rights movement at all. Black nationalism was admittedly a political force of some significance, and liberals like Roy Wilkins had indeed lost a measure of their former influence. Nonetheless, it is easy to exaggerate the extent of the break.

It is also easy to think that the civil rights movement turned North for the first time in the late 1960s. The history of FEP laws, however, reveals a vibrant and active civil rights movement outside the South during the 1940s and 1950s. The civil rights movement is said to have turned its attention northward for the first time in 1966, when the Rev. Martin Luther King, Jr., took to the streets of Chicago. King was reportedly shocked, bewildered, and depressed at the reaction he drew. He would have been far less surprised, however, if he had realized that a different civil rights movement had already been operating there and had proven capable on occasion of overcoming such hostility. If the storied southern wing of the civil rights movement was led by a bloc of religious and student groups, chief among them the Southern Christian Leadership Conference (SCLC) and Student Nonviolent Coordinating Committee (SNCC), then the "other" civil rights movement—anchored geographically in states outside the South—comprised an interracial, interfaith bloc of interest groups that sought to win racial equality through the normal channels of electoral politics.[32] Its defining conflicts did not involve education or voting rights. Nor did its modus operandi consist of the carefully crafted lawsuit or direct action against Jim Crow. African Americans outside the South could and did vote, and the Second Great Migration increased their numbers and electoral clout over the postwar period. Hence the "other" civil rights movement worked in tandem with other groups sharing the same interest, and it worked to win civil rights legislation from reluctant city halls and state legislatures.

Further research is needed before it is possible to properly weigh the balance of change and continuity, but some preliminary guesses may be hazarded about the directions in which future scholarship may point. If the civil rights legislation of the mid-1960s continues to be seen as the reflection of a moral consensus on civil rights, it may be recognized as a fragile and shallow consensus that had been achieved with great reluctance. If the white backlash of the 1970s continues to stimulate historical inquiry, it may be seen less an acute response to black power and affirmative action than as a continuous extension of white resentment against civil rights policies—"color-blind" or "color-conscious." If the roots of a partisan realignment are still traced to the 1960s, it may not seem as complete and abrupt, particularly for Republicans involved in state and local politics. Whatever discontinuities hold up to the test of further research, they may well appear less sharp then they do today, and they may well be bound by far more historical continuities than it is possible to discern now.

Near the end of his second term as president, Ronald Reagan nominated Anthony M. Kennedy to the Supreme Court. Kennedy was confirmed in the Senate without political incident. The occasion might have led some liberals to breathe a collective sigh of relief. Reagan's first choice for the post, ultraconservative Robert H. Bork, a prominent critic of the Civil Rights Act, had touched off one of the most contentious and bruising nomination battles in Senate history. Liberals mobilized intensively to defeat Bork's nomination, and their success led to the eventual appointment of the moderately conservative Kennedy. Perhaps they had dodged a bullet by getting him instead. In truth, Kennedy's appointment did little to prevent the consolidation of racial conservatism on the Rehnquist court, especially when it came to questions of civil rights. Indeed, along with Reagan's other appointees—Sandra Day O'Connor, Antonin Scalia, and William H. Rehnquist (as chief justice)—Kennedy formed the nucleus of a newly assertive conservative opposition to affirmative action, disparate-impact doctrine, and other racially attentive policies.[33]

The magnitude of the shift that was taking place on the Rehnquist court became apparent almost immediately after Kennedy's appointment. To be certain, support on the court for affirmative action had already been waning somewhat. In *Wygant* (1986), decided months before Rehnquist became chief justice, a plurality of four justices had held that any public policy invoking racial classifications must prove capable of withstanding the highest level of judicial review—strict scrutiny—in order to avoid violating the Equal Protection Clause of the Fourteenth Amendment. The plurality argued that such a policy must be "narrowly tailored" to serve a "compelling state interest." Remedying "societal discrimination" did not constitute such a purpose. A more "particularized" finding of discrimination—"some showing of prior discrimination by the government unit involved"—was necessary. Kennedy's arrival in 1988 decisively solidified the racial conservatism of the court. A five-justice majority in *Croson* (1989), including Kennedy, confirmed that the Fourteenth Amendment required strict scrutiny of a state and local policy that classified individuals by their racial background. The majority indicated that such a policy would meet strict scrutiny only if it were based on a "factual predicate" of "identified discrimination"—and only if the proposed remedy (that is, affirmative action program) was narrowly tailored to the precise scope of the injury suffered. George H. W. Bush's 1991 appointment of Clarence Thomas, who replaced the retiring Thurgood Marshall, simply completed a transformation that had been well under way for years, and shortly thereafter a majority on the Rehnquist court announced in *Adarand* (1995) that any race-based federal policy would also be subject to strict scrutiny. If the constitutional fate of affirmative action was unclear before Kennedy's appointment, then there could be little doubt about it post-*Adarand*. In just under a decade, affirmative action had lost significant ground. The policy was not unconstitutional per se, but it was permissible only under the most stringent conditions. Critics of the Rehnquist court protested that strict scrutiny was "strict in theory but fatal in fact," and they seemed correct for a time. It would take nearly a decade for the court to prove them wrong.[34]

It is ironic that it was Rehnquist who presided over a Supreme Court that pronounced affirmative action a constitutionally permissible remedy only when it was possible to identify instances of past discrimination with a clear scope of injury and only when such action was specifically tailored to address the injury sustained. In their struggle for FEP legislation, generations of liberals had sought to establish a regulatory system that embodied similar principles—one that targeted discrimination against *individuals* and provided for "affirmative action" to compensate them for specific harms they had demonstrably suffered at the hands of particular unions or employers. This was also the regulatory aspiration behind proposals that would have granted the EEOC cease-and-desist authority. Rehnquist had argued against such a proposal as assistant attorney general in the Nixon administration, but now his court seemed to declare permissible what he had personally viewed with a skeptical eye.

The irony was perhaps even more apparent in Scalia's concurrence in *Croson*. Scalia wrote that it was entirely permissible for government to "undo the effects of past discrimination" by "giving the identified victim of state discrimination that which it wrongfully denied him—for example, giving to a previously rejected black applicant the job that, by reason of discrimination, had been awarded to a white applicant, even if this means terminating the latter's employment." This might seem like a case of impermissible, race-based action, but it was "worlds apart" from the racial quota at issue in *Croson*. "In such a [hypothetical] context," Scalia explained, "the white jobholder is not being selected for disadvantageous treatment because of his race, but because he was wrongfully awarded a job to which another is entitled." It is admittedly true that *Croson* concerned a municipal contracting scheme, while the crux of the dispute over FEP laws revolved around private employment. So the parallels can go only so far. But it is hard to imagine that Augustus F. Hawkins (D-CA), who was serving his last term in the U.S. House of Representatives in 1989, could have resisted shaking his head and flashing a wry grin if he had read Scalia's concurrence. A racial conservative on the nation's highest court appeared to have bestowed his judicial blessing on the broad outlines of a regulatory framework that his ideological forerunners had struggled mightily to keep in check.[35]

Irony is a favorite trope of authors writing about affirmative action, and critics of policy have been the most adept at identifying its ironic dimensions. The questions are nothing if not familiar. Is it not ironic that a policy aimed at promoting racial equality treats people unequally based on their race? Is it not ironic that a policy meant to facilitate the realization of racial democracy was instituted through the scheming machinations of unelected judges and bureaucrats? Is it not ironic that nobody marched in the streets for a policy that is justified in the name of the masses? Is it not ironic that a policy embraced by Democrats was actually instituted under a Republican president?

These questions may or may not point to genuine ironies. But the forgotten history of the postwar struggle for "freedom from discrimination" suggests that some of the deepest ironies about affirmative action may have gone overlooked. It is ironic that Everett M. Dirksen, one of the staunchest opponents of granting the EEOC administrative enforcement authority, introduced an enforceable FEP bill as a young Congressman from Illinois. It is ironic that the "Party of Lincoln" was largely responsible for making the "Land of Lincoln" one of the last states outside the South to guarantee equal treatment in employment. It is ironic that, in debates over affirmative action, cries of quotas, preferential treatment, and group rights sprang forth so easily from the mouths of critics whose ideological ancestors used the very same language to denounce race-neutral civil rights policies like FEP laws. It is ironic that employers are among the most ardent backers of affirmative action today, when in the recent past they belonged to the leading edge of opposition to civil rights. It is ironic that affirmative action is often cited as an example of bureaucratic and judicial activism, when it was the Rehnquist Court that was largely responsible for incarnating the intentionalist, individualist approach to antidiscrimination law that Congress (often at the behest of conservatives) repeatedly rejected when it took the form of FEP legislation. Most of all, it is ironic that conservative opposition to FEP legislation led to the advent of affirmative action, a policy that many conservatives found even more odious.[36]

Yet perhaps irony is not the correct trope for a story of forgotten alternatives and roads not taken. In fact, there is something distinctly tragic in the fall of fair employment practices and the rise of affirmative action. The fifth freedom—freedom from discrimination—was never meant to be an end in itself. It was sought because it would make the Four Freedoms a meaningful reality for all Americans, not only those fortunate enough to be born into the racial majority. It does seem tragic, then, that at the very moment the federal government had begun to pry open labor markets with the strongest antidiscrimination tools it had ever wielded, good jobs of all kinds began to disappear from the American economy. With them vanished the grand expectations of equality and security that were encouraged but never fulfilled by the postwar order.

Appendix _____

Wanting to broaden the audience for *The Fifth Freedom*, I decided to limit the amount of methodological discussion in the main text. What follows is a specialized appendix aimed at readers who would like to learn more about the evidence on which I base major claims in the body of the book. This appendix offers a detailed discussion of the data, variables, and models that I used to generate the statistics and figures that are presented in the main text and tables. The ideological scales (NOMINATE scores) and votes used in all of the roll-call analyses were extracted from Keith T. Poole, Howard Rosenthal, and Boris T. Shor, *VoteView for Windows v. 3.0.3: Roll Call Displays of the U.S. Congress, 1789–2000* (accessible at voteview.com). The construction of these scales, and their application to various issues and periods in American political history, including postwar civil rights, are described in Keith T. Poole and Howard Rosenthal, *Congress: A Political-Economic History of Roll Call Voting* (New York: Oxford University Press, 1997), esp. 44. The statistics and graphics were done with Stata or Microsoft Excel. All publicly shareable datasets may be found online for downloading at http://www.tonychen.org.

Chapter 1

I calculated the entries on earnings in table A.1 from data presented in Katz, Stern, and Fader, and their calculations, in turn, are based on a sample extracted from the Integrated Public Use Microdata Series, Version 3.0. For the figures on unemployment, I rely on data reported by Fairles and Sundstrom, who in turn draw from the Census Public Microdata Samples.[1]

Chapter 2

Committee Hearings and Roll-Call Votes on Fair Employment Practices and Equal Employment Opportunity Legislation in Congress

Table A.2 lists committee hearings on fair employment practice bills and equal employment opportunity bills from 1944 to 1972. As the table indicates, numerous hearings were held over the three decades. Although many of the hearings held in the 1950s were symbolic, they had been

TABLE A.1
Black-White Disparities in Labor Market Outcomes for Men, 1940–1970

Outcome	1940	1950	1960	1970
B-W unemployment ratios	1.13	1.77	1.98	1.97
B-W earnings ratios for less than high school	0.75	0.76	0.68	0.76
B-W earnings ratios for high school graduate	0.62	0.76	0.71	0.81
B-W earnings ratios for college graduate	0.52	0.67	0.60	0.72

Sources: Robert W. Fairlie and William A. Sundstrom, "The Emergence, Persistence, and Recent Widening of the Racial Employment Gap," *Industrial and Labor Relations Review* 52 (January 1999): 252–70, esp. 255; Michael B. Katz, Mark J. Stern, and Jamie J. Fader, "The New African American Inequality," *Journal of American History* 92 (June 2005): 75–108, esp. 102.

fierce contests in the 1940s and the 1970s. The table indicates the committee or subcommittee in which the hearing was held, along with the session of Congress, dates of the hearing, and bills under discussion. These hearings and their associated reports are important primary sources for scholars wanting to characterize the postwar rhetoric of civil rights.

Table A.3 tabulates select Congressional votes on FEP legislation (1944–51) according to party and region. I define the South as the eleven states of the former Confederacy. This tends to soften regional differences, as Democrats in states such as Oklahoma, Kentucky, and Maryland are counted as nonsouthern Democrats when their views tend to resemble those of southern Democrats. Following the classification offered by Schickler, I define a "party vote" as occurring when a majority of voting Democrats opposes a majority of voting Republicans. I define a "conservative coalition vote" as occurring when a majority of nonsouthern Democrats opposes a majority of southern Democrats and a majority of Republicans. This table also helps to support the claim in the main text that the conservative coalition in Congress mobilized on key occasions to bloc the passage of FEPC legislation and that collective participation of the GOP was essential to the success of the conservative coalition. This is most evident in votes that are classified both as a "party vote" and a "conservative coalition vote."[2]

A Statistical and Graphical Analysis of a House Discharge Petition and a House Vote in the 79th and 81st Congresses

In the main text, I argue that it is difficult to determine whether Republican members declined to sign the Norton petition because of their economic conservatism or party discipline. This claim is based on the results of a logit analysis summarized in table A.4, which presents the estimated coefficients and standard errors for two models of signatories to the peti-

TABLE A.2

Committee Hearings on FEP and Equal Employment Opportunity Bills: U.S. Congress, 1944–1971

Committee and/or subcommittee	Session	Date	Bills
House Labor Committee	78–2	Jun. 1–Nov. 16, 1944	H.R. 3986, 4004, 4005
Senate Committee on Education and Labor	78–2	Aug. 30–Sep. 8, 1944	S. 2048
House Rules Committee	79–1	Mar. 8–Apr. 26, 1945	H.R. 2232
Senate Committee on Education and Labor	79–1	Mar. 12–14, 1945	S. 101, 459
Senate Subcommittee on Antidiscrimination (Labor and Public Welfare)	80–1	Jun. 11–Jul. 18, 1947	S. 984
House Special Committee on Fair Employment Standards Act (Education and Labor)	81–1	May 10–26, 1949	H.R. 4453
Senate Committee on Labor and Labor-Management Relations (Labor and Public Welfare)	82–2	Apr. 7–May 6, 1952	S. 1732, 551
Senate Committee on Labor and Public Welfare	83–2	Feb. 23–Mar. 3, 1954	S. 692
House Subcommittee No. 2 (Judiciary)	84–1	Jul. 13–27, 1955	H.R. 389*
Senate Committee on Judiciary	84–2	Apr. 24–Jul. 13, 1956	S. 3415*
House Committee on Judiciary	85–1	Feb. 4–26, 1957	Numerous*
House Subcommittee No. 5 (Judiciary)	86–1	Mar. 4–May 1, 1959	H.R. 300*
House Special Subcommittee on Labor (Education and Labor)	87–1	Oct. 23–Nov. 4, 1961	H.R. 262
House Special Subcommittee on Labor (Education and Labor)	87–2	Jan. 15–24, 1962	H.R. 262
Senate Subcommittee on Employment and Manpower (Labor and Public Welfare)	88–1	July 24–31, Aug. 2, 20, 1963	S. 773, S. 1210, S. 1211, S. 1937
House Subcommittee on Labor (Education and Labor)	88–1	Apr. 22, 30, May 3, 7, 21, 24, 27–29, June 6, 1963	H.R. 405, H.R. 2999, H.R. 4031
House Subcommittee on Labor (Education and Labor)	89–1	June 15, July 19–21, 1965	H.R. 8998, H.R. 8999, H.R. 10065
Senate Subcommittee on Employment, Manpower, and Poverty (Labor and Public Welfare)	90–1	May 4, 5, 1967	S. 1308, S. 1667
Senate Subcommittee on Labor (Labor and Public Welfare)	90–2	Aug. 11, 12, Sept. 10, 16, 1968	S. 2806, S. 2453
House Subcommittee on Labor (Education and Labor)	91–1/2	Dec. 1, 2, 1969; Apr. 7–10, 1970	H.R. 6228, H.R. 13517
House Subcommittee on Labor (Education and Labor)	92–1	Mar. 3, 4, 18, 1971	H.R. 1746
Senate Subcommittee on Labor (Labor and Public Welfare)	92–1	Oct. 4, 6, 7, 1971	S. 2515, S. 2617, H.R. 1746

* indicates that the bill was considered as part of a larger omnibus proposal encompassing voting, education, housing, and public accommodations.

Sources: Author's search on *Congressional Universe;* Edwin Timbers, "Labor Unions and Fair Employment Practices Legislation," Ph.D. diss., University of Michigan, 1953, pp. 313–37; Paul Burstein, *Discrimination, Jobs, and Politics* (Chicago: University of Chicago Press, 1985), 200.

TABLE A.3
Selected Congressional Votes on FEP Legislation, 1944–1951

Date	Issue [Roll-Call No.]	All members		Northern Democrats		Southern Democrats		Republicans		Party vote	CC vote
		Yes	No	Yes	No	Yes	No	Yes	No		
3/24/44	Retain FEPC funding [168]	36	22	11	6	0	14	24	2	Yes	No
6/20/44	Strike FEPC funding [192]	21	39	1	22	13	1	7	16	Yes	Yes
6/20/44	Limit black FEPC jobs [195]	15	37	0	21	14	1	1	15	No	No
6/30/45	Retain FEPC funding [57]	42	26	22	0	0	19	19	7	No	Yes
2/9/46	Cloture on S. 101 [113]	48	36	22	9	0	19	25	8	Yes	Yes
1/3/49	21-day rule [11]	275	143	153	2	72	29	49	112	Yes	Yes
1/20/50	Cox resolution to rescind [125]	183	236	4	151	81	19	98	64	Yes	Yes
2/22/50	McConnell substitute [146]	222	178	24	126	93	2	105	48	Yes	Yes
2/22/50	Passage of H.R. 4453 [148]	240	177	115	36	0	98	124	42	Yes	Yes
5/19/50	Cloture [334]	52	32	19	6	0	20	33	6	Yes	No
7/12/50	Cloture [369]	55	33	22	6	0	21	33	6	Yes	No
1/3/51	21-day rule [3]	244	179	10	117	82	19	152	42	Yes	Yes

Sources: Author's tabulations are based on data retrieved from Keith T. Poole, Howard Rosenthal, and Boris T. Shor, *Voteview for Windows v3.0.3: Roll Call Displays of the U.S. Congress, 1789–2000* (accessible at voteview.com). The votes on the 21-day rule are also reported in Eric Schickler, *Disjointed Pluralism: Institutional Innovation and the Development of the U.S. Congress* (Princeton: Princeton University Press, 2001), 287.

TABLE A.4

Logit Analysis of Support for FEP Legislation in Congress:
House Discharge Petition, 1945

Variable	(1)	(2)
GOP	−2.146**	−0.285
	(0.254)	(−0.94)
South	−4.435**	−1.072
	(0.546)	(−0.684)
Economic conservatism	—	−4.048**
	—	(1.312)
Social conservatism	—	−3.324**
	—	(0.525)
Constant	1.174**	−0.462
	(0.196)	(−0.434)
Pseudo-R^2	.29	.54
Model χ^2	172.27	320.58
Degrees of freedom	2	4
Observations	447	447

* $p < .05$ ** $p < .01$

Notes: Entries are logit coefficients, with standard errors in parentheses.

Sources: National Council for a Permanent FEPC, "Estimate of Representatives Who Have Not Signed Discharge Petition No. 4," Folder: FEPC, 1944–50, Box 6, Series G, Friends Committee on National Legislation (DG57), Swarthmore Peace Collection, Swarthmore College, Philadelphia, PA; Keith T. Poole, Howard Rosenthal, and Boris T. Shor, *Voteview for Windows v3.0.3: Roll Call Displays of the U.S. Congress, 1789–2000* (accessible at voteview.com).

tion. The unit of analysis is the individual House member. The dependent variable is binary, and it is set to 1 if a member signed the discharge petition and 0 if not. "South" indicates whether a member represents a district located in one of the eleven states of the former Confederacy. "GOP" indicates whether the member is a Republican. "Economic conservatism" is measured on a scale (first-dimension NOMINATE) that ranges from −1.12 to 1.04. "Social conservatism" is measured on a scale (second-dimension NOMINATE) from −1.74 to 1.26. On both scales, negative values indicate liberalism while positive values indicate conservatism. Model 1 is a specification that includes GOP membership and southern residence. The negative and significant coefficient on GOP membership indicates that Republicans were less likely to sign the petition than Democrats in a specification controlling for region. The coefficient for GOP membership becomes insignificant when individual-level ideological controls are added to the specification, as they are in model 2. Here the coefficient for economic conservatism is signed correctly and statistically sig-

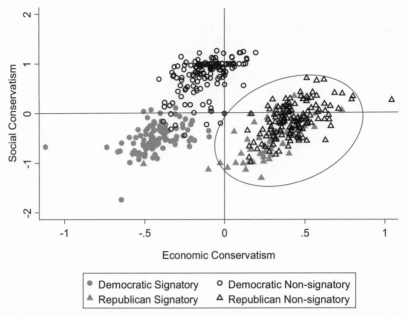

Figure A.1 Scatterplot of legislators by economic and social ideology: House Discharge Petition, 1945. *Note*: Each symbol represents a House member, and the location of each symbol indicates the position of each member in two-dimensional, ideological space. Circles represent Democrats, while triangles represent Republicans. A symbol is empty if a member did not sign a petition and filled in if he or she did sign it. *Source*: National Council for a Permanent FEPC, "Estimate of Representatives Who Have Not Signed Discharge Petition No. 4," Folder: FEPC, 1944–50, Box 6, Series G, Friends Committee on National Legislation (DG57), Swarthmore Peace Collection, Swarthmore College, Philadelphia, PA. Roll-call data and ideological indices are extracted from Keith T. Poole, Howard Rosenthal, and Boris T. Shor, *Voteview for Windows v 3.0.3: Roll Call Displays of the U.S. Congress, 1789–2000* (accessible at voteview.com).

nificant. There is evidence of multicollinearity, however, between GOP membership and economic conservatism. The correlation coefficient between them is extremely high at .86. This correlation is the primary basis of the claim that it is difficult to determine whether House members were declining to sign the petition because of their party identification or their economic beliefs.

Figure A.1 is a scatterplot that depicts the distribution of House members in two-dimensional, ideological space. Democrats are symbolized by circles and Republicans by triangles. As a broad inspection of the figure should make fairly clear, Republicans are far more economically conservative (clustering in two, right-hand quadrants) than Democrats, who are on the whole economically liberal (clustering in the two, left-hand quadrants). But close inspection actually reveals three distinct groupings. Most southern Democrats are located in the top, left quadrant of the scatterplot; they are moderate liberals on economic issues but strong conservatives on social issues. Most other Democrats are located in the bottom, left quadrant, as they are both economically and socially liberal. Republicans are located primarily in the two, right-hand quadrants. Most of them are economically conservative but vary in their degree of social conservatism.

The figure also illustrates whether a member signed the Norton petition. Each symbol is filled in if a member signed the petition and empty if he or she did not. The scatterplot can thus be easily interpreted as a visual illustration of multicollinearity. Since most Republicans are economically conservative, and most Republicans did not sign the discharge petition, it is difficult to tell whether their decision was driven by their individual economic ideology or by collective, party action. Either cause is consistent with the pattern displayed in the scatterplot. Crucially, however, some Republicans did sign the discharge petition. At nearly every level of observed economic conservatism (and observed social conservatism), there are some Republicans who were signatories. To see this, simply visualize a vertical line running through the cluster of Republican members on the right-hand side of the graph. Regardless of where the line is drawn, it is not too hard (except on the far right) to find a Republican signatory somewhere along the line. This implies that it was not unreasonable on the part of liberals to imagine that additional Republicans (at most levels of economic conservatism) might be induced to sign the petition. This scatterplot is thus the basis of the claim in the main text about the difficult of determining why most Republicans did not sign the discharge petition. It is also the basis of the claim that the liberal strategy was not totally implausible.

In the main text, I argue that a statistical analysis does not provide a basis for determining whether Republican votes on the McConnell substitute reflected the demands of party leadership or the ideological commitments of individual legislators. This claim is based on a logit analysis summarized in table A.5, which presents the estimated coefficients and standard errors for two models of the House vote on the McConnell substitute (Roll-Call No. 146). The unit of analysis is the individual House member. The dependent variable is binary, and it is set to 1 if a member voted for the substitute (that is, voted for a voluntary FEPC), and 0 if not. The analysis excludes any member not voting for or against it. "South" indicates whether a member represents a district located in one of the

TABLE A.5
Logit Analysis of the House Vote on the McConnell Substitute, 1950

Variable	(1)	(2)
GOP	2.438**	0.416
	(0.283)	(1.133)
South	5.516**	1.163
	(0.758)	(0.880)
Economic conservatism	—	6.219**
	—	(1.624)
Social conservatism	—	3.710**
	—	(0.627)
Constant	−1.674**	0.238
	(0.222)	(0.549)
Pseudo-R^2	.38	.62
Model χ^2	208.84	340.82
Degrees of freedom	2	4
Observations	400	400

* $p < .05$ ** $p < .01$

Note: Entries are logit coefficients with standard errors in parentheses.

Source: Roll-call data and ideological indices are extracted from Keith T. Poole, Howard Rosenthal, and Boris T. Shor, *Voteview for Windows v 3.0.3: Roll Call Displays of the U.S. Congress, 1789–2000* (accessible at voteview.com).

eleven states of the former Confederacy. "GOP" indicates whether the member is a Republican. "Economic conservatism" is measured on a scale (first-dimension NOMINATE) that ranges from −1.039 to .755. "Social conservatism" is measure on a scale (second-dimension NOMINATE) from −1.192 to 1.317. On both scales, negative values indicate liberalism while positive values indicate conservatism. Model 1 is a specification that includes GOP membership and southern residence. The positive and significant coefficient on GOP membership indicates that Republicans were more likely to vote for the McConnell substitute than Democrats when controlling for region. This coefficient becomes insignificant, however, when individual-level ideological controls are added to the specification—as they are in model 2. The coefficient for economic conservatism is signed correctly and statistically significant. As with the discharge petition, there is evidence of multicollinearity between GOP membership and economic conservatism. The correlation coefficient between the two variables is extremely high at .82. This high correlation is the basis of the claim that it is difficult to determine whether House members were voting because of their party demands or their economic beliefs.

Chapter 4

Figure 4.1

Figure 4.1 reports the percentage of respondents in each state favoring state FEP laws when asked the following question: "Do you favor or oppose a law in your state that would require employers to hire a person if he is qualified for the job regardless of his race or color?" The figures are based on the author's calculations using data from a national, public opinion poll conducted by the Gallup Organization from June 14–June 19, 1945 (AIPO No. 1945-0349, Form K, N = 1,589), Roper Center for Public Opinion Research, University of Connecticut. The downward-sloping line is a least-squares line fitted using the "Add Trendline" tool (linear option) in Microsoft Excel.

This figure is strictly meant to give a visual image of the rough, bivariate association between public opinion and time of passage. The association is not precise. In addition to the problems associated with the quota-control sampling method that Gallup used at the time (a more thorough discussion follows), it should also be mentioned that the underlying data are drawn from a national survey (rather than fifty individual state surveys), and the sample sizes are very small for some states. Not much more information can be extracted from the data.

A Statistical Analysis of Gallup Poll Data from 1945

The main text reports that Dewey voters were less likely to support the passage of state FEP legislation than were FDR voters. This claim is based on a statistical analysis of a national, public opinion survey conducted by the Gallup Organization from June 14–June 19, 1945 (AIPO No. 1945-0349, Form K, N = 1,589).[3] In an earlier version of the manuscript, my analysis was based on a dataset that I obtained from the Roper Center through the good offices of JoAnn Dionne at the University of Michigan. With extensive help from my research assistants, I partially reconstructed the dataset for limited use. Recently, Adam Berinsky generously made available a clean dataset that his research team has expertly and comprehensively reconstructed under the auspices of a project financed by the National Science Foundation. In collaboration with Eric Schickler, Berinsky is in the midst of rehabilitating a range of opinion polls from the 1930s and 1940s. These polls will undoubtedly prove a gold mine for future researchers interested in the period. The findings reported here are based on the Berinsky-Schickler dataset, but the results from both datasets are broadly consistent.[4]

It is important to mention up front that the use of early public opinion for individual-level analysis is problematic for a variety of reasons. Perhaps the most worrisome is that early nongovernmental survey researchers did not rely upon probability sampling. As noted by Berinsky, they instead employed quota-controlled sampling, a statistically dubious method in which pollsters sought to interview demographically "predetermined proportions of people from particular segments of the population." To limit the bias in coefficient estimation that is introduced by the quota-control method of sampling, I include the quota-control categories, as Berinsky and others recommend. More specifically, I control for gender (for which Gallup had a hard quota) along with age, economic class, and occupation (for which Gallup had a soft quota) as well as region and city size (by which Gallup stratified the sample). In some models, I also include variables that are plausibly correlated with support for state FEP legislation and are also potentially associated with sample selection. It is notable that the main results reported here are substantially similar even if the analyses are rerun with the preferred weights (weight_edu) included in the Berinsky-Schickler dataset. It remains unclear how quota-control sampling affects the estimation of standard errors in multivariate regression, and so assertions of statistical significance should be weighed carefully.[5]

In the empirical analysis that follows, I model support for the passage of an FEP law as a function of multiple independent variables, including information on party identification. This model can be specified as a logistic regression of the functional form:

$$\log(P_i / (1 - P_i)) = \alpha + \beta x_i,$$

where P_i is the probability of passage for respondent i, x_i is a vector of covariates for respondent i, β is a vector of associated coefficients, and α is a constant.

My empirical strategy is straightforward. I begin with a simple model of support for state FEP legislation that includes only party identification. I then add a group of variables that is associated with the quota-control sampling used by Gallup. A final model adds other available variables that are plausibly associated with support and may also be correlated with the probability of sample selection. Each successive model is more richly specified than the previous model. If a negative association between voting for Dewey and support for FEP legislation remains consistent across all three models, I infer that Republicans were less likely to support such legislation compared to Democrats, controlling for the available observables.[6]

My dependent variable is the answer that respondents gave to the following question on Form K: "Do you favor or oppose a law in your state that would require employers to hire a person if he is qualified for the job regardless of his race or color?" This variable is set to 1 if the respondent gave the "favor" response, and 0 if he or she gave the "oppose" response. Nonresponses are excluded from the analysis, and missing data are handled through list-wise deletion.[7]

The first model includes only the key independent variable—that is, "Party Identification." This variable is measured using responses to a question about a respondent's vote in the 1944 presidential election. I operationalize the variable as a series of dummies indicating whether a respondent voted for Democrat Franklin Delano Roosevelt, voted for Republican Thomas E. Dewey, or belonged to a third category. The third category includes respondents who voted for other candidates, who did not vote, or who voted for an unspecified candidate. I use FDR voters as the reference category. One fortuitous advantage of using the 1944 presidential contest between FDR and Dewey as a measure of party identification is that the latter candidate was a liberal Republican whose racial views were similar to those of FDR. This variable may therefore be construed as a cautious measure of party identification. It limits (though probably does not eliminate) the potential that any observed partisan effect is due to self-selection on ideology or policy preferences by the respondents.

The second model adds a group of independent variables that were used in Gallup's quota-controlled sampling procedure, including gender, age, economic class, occupation, region, and city size. "Gender" indicates whether the respondent is male or female. "Age" is measured as an interval variable. "Class" is entered as a series of six dummy variables indicating whether the respondent is wealthy, above average, average, poor, on old-age assistance, or on relief. The variables are based on the interviewer's assessments, not the self-assessment of the respondent. The reference category is wealthy. "Occupational controls" is a series of dummy variables that indicate the self-identified occupation of the respondent. Occupational categories include business executive, white collar, skilled labor, semi-skilled labor, unskilled labor, domestic worker, small businessman, professional, and semi-professional. The reference category is farmer. "Region" is entered as a series of seven dummy variables indicating the region of the country in which the respondent resides. Maine, New Hampshire, Vermont, Massachusetts, Rhode Island, and Connecticut make up the New England region. New York, New Jersey, Pennsylvania, Maryland, Delaware, and West Virginia form the Midatlantic region. Ohio, Michigan, Indiana, and Illinois belong to the East Central region. Wisconsin, Minnesota, Iowa, Missouri, North Dakota, South Dakota, Nebraska, and Kansas constitute the West Central region. The region of the South includes North Carolina, South Carolina, Virginia, Georgia, Alabama, Arkansas, Florida, Kentucky, Louisiana, Mississippi, Oklahoma, Tennessee, and Texas. Montana, Arizona, Colorado, Idaho, Wyoming, Utah, Nevada, and New Mexico form the Rocky Mountain region. California, Oregon, and Washington make up the Pacific Coast region. The reference category is New England. "City size" is entered as an ordinal variable that measures whether the respondent lives on a farm, in a town with fewer than 2,500 residents, in a town with 2,500 to 10,000 residents, in a city with 10,000 to 100,000 residents, in a city with 100,000 to 500,000 residents, or in a city with over 500,000 residents.

The third and final model adds two variables, both of which are plausibly correlated with support for state FEP legislation as well as the probability of sample selection. "Education" is measured as a series of four dummy variables, including grade school, some high school, high school graduate, or some college or higher. Grade school is the reference category. "Black" indicates whether a respondent is African American.

Table A.6 presents the results of the multivariate analysis. Model 1 is the baseline model. The coefficient for Dewey voter is negative and significant, implying that Dewey voters were less likely than FDR voters to support state FEP legislation. A calculation using SPost indicates that FDR voters were eleven percentage points more likely to support state FEP legislation than Dewey voters (that is, a predicted probability of .51 for FDR voters versus .40 for Dewey voters). This difference is identical to the difference indicated in the basic cross-tabulation. Model 2 is a model that adds a set of variables associated with quota-control sampling. Here the coefficient for Dewey voter is also negative and significant. In fact, it appears even larger than it does in the baseline model. This is confirmed when predicted probabilities are calculated. When all other variables in this model are held at their sample means, FDR voters are fourteen percentage points more likely to support state FEP legislation than Dewey voters (that is, a predicted probability of .52 for FDR voters versus .38 for Dewey voters). Model 3 adds two other variables, education and black. It is the richest specification of the three. Again the coefficient for Dewey voter is also negative and significant, and once again it is larger than it is in less fully specified models. When all other variables in this model are held at their sample means, FDR voters are fifteen percentage points more likely to support state FEP legislation than Dewey voters (that is, a predicted probability of .57 for FDR voters versus .42 for Dewey voters). Hence the negative association of Dewey voters with support for state FEP legislation (relative to FDR voters) is consistently large and statistically significant, and it actually increases as the model specification grows more extensive.[8]

Further analysis (available upon request) indicates that the basic result is fairly robust to different ways of coding party identification. When all respondents in the third category (who voted for other candidates, who did not vote, or who voted for an unspecified candidate) are recoded as Dewey voters and the analyses are rerun, the first two models do not show a strong or significant partisan difference in support. This should be expected, because respondents in the third category are more racially liberal than Dewey voters, according to a cross-tabulation of support for state FEP legislation and party identification. However, a strong and significant partisan difference emerges in the third, most highly specified model, which includes race and education. On the other hand, if all respondents in the third category are recoded as FDR voters and the analyses are rerun, then all three models show the same strong and significant partisan difference. These findings are important because they offer some reassurance that the basic inference about a partisan difference is supported even if respondents not voting for FDR or Dewey (for whatever reason) are systematically different on the unobservables than respondents who did cast a vote for one of the two major candidates.

The totality of the foregoing analysis is the basis of the claim in the main text that respondents who reported voting for Thomas E. Dewey have a significantly lower likelihood of supporting state FEP legislation than individuals who reported voting for FDR, even when controlling for the available observables. I cannot completely rule out omitted variables bias or other kinds of selection bias, but it is heartening that the observed negative association of party identification with public support is evident in almost all models, that it is substantively large, and that it actually increases as the model includes more and more variables.

A Statistical Analysis of Partisan Voting for California's Proposition 11 in 1946: County-Level Ecological Estimates

In the main text, I report that 51 percent of Democrats voted to approve Proposition 11, while only 12 percent of Republicans did so. These figures derive from early estimates that Robert P. Van Houweling, Robert Mickey, and I calculated using county-level data (N = 58) from the 1946 California elections.[9]

Our estimates are based on the fact that the fraction of "Yes" votes on Proposition 11 in any given county may be written as the identity $Y = \beta_d T_d + \beta_r T_r$, where Y is the proportion of "Yes" votes on Proposition 11, β_d is the proportion of Democrats voting "Yes," β_r is the proportion of Republicans voting "No," T_d is Democratic share of total turnout, and T_r is the Republican share of total turnout. We use Will Roger, Jr.'s (Dem.) share of ballots cast for senator as a proxy for Democratic share of turnout, and we use William F. Knowland's (Rep.) share of the ballots cast for senator as a proxy for Republican share of turnout. Under the assumption that β_d and β_r are constant across counties, it is possible to estimate

TABLE A.6
Logit Analysis of Public Support for State FEP Laws: Gallup Poll, 1945

	(1)	(2)	(3)
VOTE: Dewey voter	−0.457**	−0.556**	−0.611**
	(0.126)	(0.153)	(0.162)
VOTE: Other	0.203	0.233	−0.122
	(0.136)	(0.165)	(0.182)
Female		0.076	0.172
		(0.132)	(0.143)
Age		−0.013**	−0.012*
		(0.005)	(0.006)
CLASS: Above average		1.658*	1.602
		(0.812)	(0.819)
CLASS: Average		1.295	1.155
		(0.815)	(0.823)
CLASS: Poor		1.647*	1.430
		(0.823)	(0.836)
CLASS: Old-age assistance		1.693	1.779
		(0.973)	(0.981)
CLASS: Occupational relief		1.818	1.977
		(1.259)	(1.321)
REGION: Midatlantic		−0.749*	−0.737*
		(0.331)	(0.341)
REGION: East Central		−1.086**	−1.096**
		(0.332)	(0.340)
REGION: West Central		−1.521**	−1.527**
		(0.360)	(0.368)
REGION: South and Southwest		−1.898**	−2.494**
		(0.338)	(0.361)
REGION: Rocky Mountain		−1.154**	−1.098**
		(0.394)	(0.402)
REGION: Pacific Coast		−1.069**	−1.213**
		(0.368)	(0.381)
City size		0.241**	0.209**
		(0.056)	(0.059)
Occupation controls		Yes	Yes
Education controls			Yes
Black			3.580**
			(0.445)
Constant	0.052	−0.362	−0.231
	(0.083)	(0.920)	(0.963)
Pseudo-R^2	.01	.13	.20
Model χ^2	23.90	223.07	331.77
Degrees of freedom	2	27	31
Observations	1392	1243	1198

* $p < .05$ ** $p < .01$

Notes: Entries are logit coefficients with standard errors in parentheses. Declining observations across models are due to missing data. Excluded categories include VOTE: FDR, CLASS: Wealthy, REGION: New England.

Source: Author's analysis of Gallup Poll (AIPO No. 1945–0349) rehabilitated by Berinsky and Schickler.

them using an OLS regression of Y on T_d and T_r, suppressing the constant term. Here β_d gives the statewide proportion of Democrats voting for Proposition 11 and β_r gives the statewide proportion of Republicans voting for Proposition 11.[10]

Figure 4.2 shows a scatterplot of counties by the proportion of county voting "yes" on Proposition 11 and the proportion of county voting for Will Rogers, Jr. (Dem.), in the U.S. Senate election in the 1946 California elections. The upward-sloping line is a least-squares line fitted using the "Add Trendline" tool (linear option) in Microsoft Excel.

After calculating our early estimates, Mickey, Van Houweling, and I collected precinct-level data and conducted a battery of more sophisticated analyses. The results using new data and different methods are highly comparable. Using the method of bounds, it is clear that the central elements of the Republican's electoral coalition opposed the initiative, while the central elements of the Democrat's electoral coalition supported the initiative. Diagnostics of the basic Goodman's regression show evidence of aggregation bias, but the results of a quadratic regression and King's ecological inference—each of which is more robust to aggregation bias than Goodman's regression—both point to major partisan differences in voting patterns. At the same time, our analysis of different subsets of the data supports the same conclusion. The estimated gap between the two partisan groups of voters is still larger no matter how the data are stratified, whether by level of urbanization, percentage nonwhite, or value-added manufacturing. Hence the empirical evidence consistently and strongly indicates that Republicans voted for Proposition 11 at a far lower rate than Democrats. Our best estimates indicate that Republican support for Proposition 11 can be pegged somewhere in the low teens, while Democratic support in all likelihood hovered just below 50 percent.[11]

Public Support of FEP Law in Minnesota

Figure 4.3 shows the percentage of respondents in the Minnesota Poll who supported the passage of a government (federal or state) law mandating fair employment practices. For ease of presentation, data points for 1948, 1952, and 1954 are linearly interpolated. Figure 4.3 is based on the results of poll questions list in table A.7, which includes not only the top-line results but also information on the wording and source of the questions.

TABLE A.7
Public Support for State FEP Law in Minnesota: Questions and Sources, 1947–1955

Year	Percent	Question	Source
1947	37%	"It has been suggested that a federal law be passed to prevent employers from refusing to hire qualified workers because of their race, color, or religion. How do you feel about such a law—do you think it SHOULD or SHOULD NOT be passed?"	"Many Would Oppose U.S. Law Requiring No Bias in Hiring," *Minnesota Poll, Minneapolis Sunday Tribune,* October 12, 1947
1949	30%	"Do you think the state should take any action concerning employers who turn down job applicants on account of their race, religion, color, or nationality?"	"Many Think Hiring Bias Exists, But Majority Opposes State Action," *Minnesota Poll, Minneapolis Sunday Tribune,* January 30, 1949
1950	75%	"Some states have laws which say that an employer cannot refuse to hire a qualified worker because of his color or his religion. Those laws are called FEPC, or fair employment practices, laws. Would you be in favor of such a law in Minnesota, or would you be against it?"	"75% of Adults Favor State FEPC Law," *Minnesota Poll, Minneapolis Sunday Tribune,* July 30, 1950
1951	72%	"Some states have laws which say that an employer cannot refuse to hire a qualified worker because of his color or his religion. Those laws are called FEPC, or fair employment practices, laws. Would you be in favor of such a law in Minnesota, or would you be against it?"	"Many Back FEPC Law in Minnesota," *Minnesota Poll, Minneapolis Sunday Tribune,* January 7, 1951
1953	84%	"Some states have laws that guarantee everyone an equal chance to get a job on his own merits, regardless of his color or religion. These laws are called FEPC laws, or fair employment practices, laws. Would you be in favor of such a law in Minnesota, or against it?"	"'Employment on Merit' Proposal Backed by 84%," *Minnesota Poll, Minneapolis Sunday Tribune,* February 22, 1953
1955	85%	"Some states have laws that guarantee everyone an equal chance to get a job on his own merits, regardless of his color or religion. These laws are called FEPC laws, or fair employment practices, laws. Would you be in favor of such a law in Minnesota, or against it?"	"FEPC Law Favored by 85% of State Adults," *Minnesota Poll, Minneapolis Sunday Tribune,* February 6, 1955

Legislative Histories of FEP Legislation in Illinois, California, and Ohio

TABLE A.8

Legislative History of FEP Proposals in the Illinois Legislature, 1943–1961

Year	Proposal and outcome
1943	H.B. 494 passes the House by a vote of 86–19. In the Senate, it fails to clear the Committee on Industrial Affairs, which is controlled 8–6 by Republicans.
1945	H.B. 353 fails the House by a vote of 41–28. Multiple bills are bottled up by the Senate Industrial Affairs and Judiciary committees, which are controlled by Republicans 10–5 and 13–9, respectively.
1947	Multiple bills are killed by the Senate and House Judiciary Committees, which are controlled by Republicans, 15–7 and 19–10, respectively.
1949	H.B. 163 passes the Democratic-controlled House by a vote of 81–43–3. This bill, along with others, is bottled up by the Senate Judiciary Committee, which is controlled by Republicans 14–7.
1951	H.B. 73 fails to clear the House Executive Committee, controlled 14–11 by Republicans. S.B. 67 withers in the Senate Committee on Industrial Affairs, dominated 9–6 by a majority of Republicans.
1953	H.B. 861 passes the House by a vote of 81–31 but then stalls in the Senate Committee on Industrial Affairs, which is controlled by Republicans 14–11. An attempt by two Democrats to rescue the bill from indefinite tabling failed by a vote of 13–29–1.
1955	H.B 27 passes the House 80–35. It is tabled indefinitely by the Senate Committee on Industrial Affairs, controlled by a 10–5 GOP majority. S.B. 251 is stricken by the same committee.
1957	H.B. 185 passes the House by a vote of 111–21–3. It is indefinitely tabled by the Senate Committee on Industrial Affairs, which is controlled by the Republicans 10–5.
1959	Two FEP bills—H.B. 2 and H.B. 495—pass the Democratic-controlled House by votes of 107–28–3 and 105–28–5, respectively. Both bills are referred to Senate committees, where they remain unreported. The upper chamber votes to take the bills out of committee and place them on the floor. H.B. 495 comes to a vote but fails to pass, falling six votes short of the thirty necessary for passage. A substantial majority of Democrats, twenty-two, vote for the bill, and they are joined by only two Republicans.
1961	The Senate Committee on Industrial Affairs, controlled by Republicans by the smaller margin of 7–5, strikes two Senate bills and one passing House bill, but it discharges S.B. 609 to the Senate floor. The bill passes the Senate 31–23 and the House 123–21–1.

Note: Republicans constituted a majority in both chambers in every legislative session save the 66th (1949) and the 71st (1959). Illinois governors included Republican Dwight H. Green (1941–1949), Democrat Adlai E. Stevenson (1949–1953), Republican William G. Stratton (1953–1961), and Democrat Otto Kerner (1961).

Sources: *Legislative Synopsis and Digest*, 63rd General Assembly (Springfield, 1943), 395–96; ibid., 1945, pp. 58, 78, 112, 382; ibid., 1947, pp. 16, 22, 45, 247, 249–50; ibid., 1949, pp. 59, 304; ibid., 1951, pp. 36, 320; ibid., 1953, pp. 623–24, ibid., 1955, pp. 113, 390–91; ibid., 1957, p. 465; ibid., 1959, pp. 109, 507; ibid., 1961, pp. 72, 124, 190; *Blue Book of the State of Illinois* (Springfield, 1943), pp. 355, 357; ibid., 1945, pp. 175, 177; ibid., 1947, pp. 167, 169, 172; ibid, 1949, pp. 125, 127; ibid., 1951, pp. 139, 141, 144; ibid., 1953, pp. 175, 179; ibid., 1955, pp. 19, 195; ibid., 1957, pp. 156, 160; ibid., 1959, pp. 156, 158, 160; ibid., 1961, pp. 182, 186; *Journal of the House of Representatives*, 64th General Assembly (Springfield, 1945), p. 1636; ibid., 1949, p. 935; ibid., 1953, pp. 1803–4; ibid., 1955, p. 1293; ibid., 1957, pp. 1722–23; ibid., 1959, pp. 1390–91; ibid., 1961, pp. 386–87, 3289–90; *Journal of the Senate*, 68th General Assembly (Springfield, 1953), p. 1820; ibid., p. 195; ibid., 1959, p. 1985; ibid., 1961, p. 979; *Chicago Defender*, June 30, 1959, p. 3.

TABLE A.9
Legislative History of FEP Proposals in the California Legislature, 1943–1959

Year	Proposal and outcome
1945	The Assembly Committee on Ways and Means (CWM) votes 13–7 to table A.B. 3. The CWM is controlled 17–8 by the GOP. A motion to consider the proposal without committee approval fails the Assembly 48–29. All but one Democrat (35 of 36) vote in favor of consideration, compared to only 30 percent of all Republicans (12 of 40).
1946	A.B. 11 fails to clear the Republican-controlled Committee on Governmental Efficiency and Economy (CGEE) by a vote of 7–10, with five Democrats and two Republicans recommending the bill and ten Republicans opposing recommendation. It meets a similar fate in the CWM by a vote of 6–10. The GOP controls the CWM by a nine member margin (17–8). The bill appears on the November ballot as Proposition 11, and it is defeated 71–29.
1947	A.B. 2211 is introduced, but no strong effort is mounted.
1949	A.B. 3027 fails to clear the CGEE by a 8–11 vote. The GOP controls the CGEE by a one-member margin (11–10). A vote to withdraw the bill from committee fails the Assembly by a vote of 31–35. All but two Democrats (26 of 28) vote in favor of withdrawal, compared to 13 percent of Republicans (5 of 38). A bill calling for the creation of a "study commission," promoted by Governor Warren, fails to clear the CGEE in a 5–9 party line vote. All five "yes" votes are from Democrats, while all nine naysayers are Republicans.
1951	The CGEE votes 15–3 against A.B. 2251. Warren's milder "study commission" proposal is defeated by a 9–8 vote. The committee is controlled 13–8 by the GOP.
1953	A.B. 900 is rejected 7–6 by the CGEE, which is controlled 9–7 by the GOP.
1955	A.B. 971 passes the Democratic-controlled CGEE by a vote of 8–5. Only one GOP member votes for the bill. The proposal is rejected by the CWM, which is controlled 17–10 by the GOP. A majority in the Assembly votes to withdraw the bill from the CWM and then approves it, 48–27. All but two Democrats (29 of 31) vote for the bill, while only 43 percent (19 of 44) of Republicans do so. In a party-line vote, A.B. 971 dies in the Senate Labor Committee (SLC), controlled 5–2 by the GOP.
1957	A.B. 2000 clears the CGEE and the CWM by a 18–3 vote; it then passes the Assembly 61–15. All but one Democrat vote for the bill, compared to 65 percent of Republicans (26 of 40) who vote in favor. The bill is then referred to the SLC, which tables the bill indefinitely by a party-line vote.
1959	The governorship as well both houses of the Assembly pass into Democratic hands for the first time in the twentieth century. A.B. 91 is approved by the Assembly by a vote of 59–10. All ten members voting "no" are Republicans. S.B. 477 passes the Senate by a vote of 30–5. All but one of the five opposing members are Republicans. Governor Edmund G. Brown signs California's FEP law on April 16, 1957.

Sources: California Assembly, *Journal of the Assembly*, 1945–1959; California Senate, *Journal of the Senate*, 1945–1959; California Legislature, *Assembly Final History*, 1945–1959; *California Eagle*, May 24, 1945; January 20, 1946; June 2, 1955; May 16, 1957; *Los Angeles Times*, February 16, 1945, p. 2; January 17, 1946, p. 2; April 22, 1949, p. 7; May 13, 1949, p. 7; June 6, 1949, p. 8; May 10, 1951, p. 29; April 23, 1953; April 1, 1955, p. 18; May 3, 1955, p. 18; May 12, 1955, p. 23; April 9, 1957, p. 14; April 18, 1957, p. B4; May 14, 1957, p. 18; February 20, 1959, p. 1; March 17, 1959, p. 1; April 9, 1957, p. 1; April 17, 1959, p. 1; Frank Jordan, *State of California Statement of Vote: General Election*, November 4, 1946.

TABLE A.10
Legislative History of FEP Proposals in the Ohio Legislature, 1945–1959

Year	Proposal and outcome
1945	The Republican-dominated Senate Rules Committee votes 6–1 to kill a strong bipartisan bill, S.B. 219. The Republican majority refuses in a party-line vote (16–10) to extricate the bill from the committee. A study bill, S.B. 292, dies in the Rules Committee by a 6–2 vote. A bipartisan bill in the House, H.B. 88, is bottled up by the GOP-dominated House Reference Committee. A discharge petition is circulated, acquiring thirty-eight of the sixty-nine signatures needed, but GOP leaders order members not to sign the petition. All signatures, save one from a black Republican, belong to Democrats. More than 80 percent of the Democratic delegation signs the petition, compared to less then 2 percent of the GOP delegation.
1947	Two strong bills, S.B. 10 and S.B. 90, are introduced in the Senate and become stuck in the Republican-controlled Commerce and Labor Committee. A study bill, S.B. 354, is introduced by a Republican but bottled up by the GOP-dominated Rules Committee. A motion to relieve the committee of the bill fails by a tie vote, 15–15. All four Democrats vote to extricate the bill, but Republicans are deeply split. Roughly a third of the GOP delegation votes with the Democratic minority, half votes against it, and a fifth does not cast a vote. Two bills are introduced into the House, and neither makes it out of committee.
1949	Several bills are introduced in both chambers. A strong bill, H.B. 106, is reported by the Industry and Labor Committee and then passes the Democratic-controlled House (90–83). Sixty-one out of sixty-nine Democrats (90 percent) vote for the bill, compared to nine out of sixty-six Republicans (14 percent). The bill goes over to the Democratic-controlled Senate, which substitutes a voluntary bill and then passes it 17–15 on the strength of votes from thirteen Republicans and four Democratic defectors. This bill fails to clear the House, 63–65, with the coalition from the earlier vote (57 Democrats, 8 Republicans) holding fast against the substitute. A conference committee is convened and a strong bill is reached. But it fails the Senate, 13–17. Six Democrats vote against the compromise, along with eleven Republicans. No Republicans vote for it, only Democrats. Three members declined to vote, all of them Republicans.
1951	Several bills are introduced in both chambers. H.B. 15 is referred to the Industry and Labor Committee and overwhelmingly passes the Republican-controlled House (101–19). All nineteen opponents are Republican. The bill goes to the Republican-controlled Senate but dies because a motion to suspend the rules for a third reading fails, 13–13. Six out of seven Democrats (86 percent) vote for the bill, but Republicans are deeply divided. Out of the twenty-six in the Senate, seven (27 percent) vote for the bill, and a dozen do not (46 percent). Crucially, six Republicans (22 percent) do not cast a vote at all.
1953	Several bills are introduced into both chambers. H.B. 23 passes the Democratic-controlled House, 75–52. Thirty-three of thirty-four Democrats (97 percent) vote for the bill, compared to forty-two of 102 Republicans (41 percent). The bill is transmitted to the Republican-controlled Senate, and specifically to the Senate Commerce and Labor Committee, which declines to report it, 4–5. All five members voting "nay" are Republicans. An attempt to pry the bill away from the committee is tabled by the Senate, 19–13. All nineteen votes to table the motion come from Republicans (out of twenty-three from the GOP delegation).

TABLE A.10 *(continued)*

Year	Proposal and outcome
1955	S.B. 13, S.B. 45, S.B. 92, and S.B. 282 are introduced into the Republican-controlled Senate. H.B. 95 and H.B. 176 are introduced into the House. Republicans outnumber Democrats, 5–2, on the Senate Commerce and Labor Committee, which refuses to report FEP bills, several by a 3–2 vote.
1957	Both chambers are controlled by Republicans. Several bills are introduced, but there is no action of note.
1959	S.B. 10 passes the Democratic-controlled Senate with a bipartisan majority, 25–6. All six nays come from Republicans. The bill goes to the Democratic-controlled House, and after some amendments, it passes with a bipartisan majority, 98–31. Very nearly all Democrats support the bill, and a sizeable minority of Republicans. All who oppose it are Republican, save one.

Notes: Governors of Ohio included Democrat Frank J. Lausche (1945–47), Republican Thomas J. Herbert (1947–49), Democrat Frank J. Lausche (1949–57), and Republican C. William O'Neill (1957–59), and Michael V. DiSalle (1959–63).

Sources: Journal of the Senate of the State of Ohio (Zanesville, Ohio), 96th General Assembly, 1945, pp. 659, 1168; 97th General Assembly, 1947, pp. 66, 114, 73, 123, 839, 866–67; 98th General Assembly, 1949, pp. 445, 494; 792; 99th General Assembly, 1951, p. 1063; 100th General Assembly, 1953, p. 674; 101st General Assembly, 1955; 103rd General Assembly, 1959, p. 191; *Journal of the House of the State of Ohio* (Zanesville, Ohio), 96th General Assembly, 1947, pp. 1328, 1340; 97th General Assembly, 1947; 98th General Assembly, 1949, pp. 368, 547, 930, 1855–56; 99th General Assembly, 1951, p. 1551; 100th General Assembly, 1953, p. 960; 101st General Assembly, 1955; 103rd General Assembly, 1959, p. 570; *Cleveland Call and Post*, June 16, 1945; June 23, 1945; June 30, 1945; May 14, 1949; OCFEP, *News Bulletin*, No. 15, May 13, 1953; ibid., No. 18, June 11, 1953; ibid., May 28, 1955; ibid., No. 10, February 19, 1959.

A Statistical Analysis of the Passage of State FEP Laws: An Event-History Analysis of an Original Dataset

In the main text, I claim that Republican control of "veto points" depressed the likelihood that a state would pass FEP legislation. This claim is based on a discrete-time, event-history analysis of an original dataset. In particular, I model the likelihood of passage as a logistic regression of the functional form:

$$\log \left(P_{it} / (1 - P_{it}) \right) = \alpha + \beta_1 x_i + \beta_2 z_{it},$$

in which P_{it} is the probability that state i passes an FEP law at time t provided that it has not yet done so; α is a constant; x_i is a time-constant vector of covariates for state i; z_{it} is a vector of time-varying covariates for state i at time t, including Republican control of veto points; and β_1 and β_2 are vectors of effects associated with x_i and z_{it}, respectively. Time itself is modeled as a linear trend that is included in the vector of covariates z_{it}.[12]

This model is applied to an original dataset that contains information on the social, political, economic, and institutional characteristics of thirty-seven "northern" states during the period 1941–64. I constructed such a dataset from cross-sectional data on the states that I collected from a wide range of published and unpublished sources, including government reports, private publications, and archival records. Whenever possible, I sought annual data, which permitted me to construct time-varying variables. In some instances when annual data were not available, I collected as much data as possible and then generated time-varying variables through linear interpolation. In other instances, I used the data to generate time-constant variables.[13]

My dataset is organized in the standard unit-time format required by discrete-time, event-history models. Here the unit of observation is a state-year. The first year for which I record observations is 1941. I continue to record observations on all thirty-seven states for each subsequent year in which their legislatures met in regular or special sessions, as reported by *Book of the States*. Once a state passes FEP legislation, it is excluded from the dataset. The last year for which I observe a state that has not yet passed an FEP law is 1964. This procedure translates into a dataset or "risk set" of 502 state-year observations.[14]

My periodization of the risk set rests on a straightforward rationale. I define 1941 as the first year in the risk set because states initially became at risk for passing FEP legislation as a result of Roosevelt's wartime FEPC in 1941. Its establishment touched off a cascade of state-level political developments that culminated in formal campaigns for state FEP laws. The political landscape changed in 1964, when Congress passed the Civil Rights Act. Title VII essentially declared that states without FEP laws on the books would relinquish their right to investigate complaints first through a procedure of their design. This gave states that had not yet passed FEP legislation a strong incentive to do so. Thus I define 1964 as the final year in the risk set.

My dependent variable is the passage of a state FEP law. This time-varying, indicator variable is set to 1 if a state adopted a nominally enforceable FEP law in a given year, and set to 0 if it did not.[15]

My key independent variable is party control—more precisely, "Republican control" of legislative veto points. I specifically operationalize Republican control as a time-varying, binary variable indicating whether Republicans in a given state-year held control over a veto point in the legislative process—that is, a point at which it was possible for Republicans to block legislation. I set the variable to 1 if Republicans in a given year held a majority of seats in the lower house, a majority of seats in the upper house, the governorship, or any combination of the three. The variable is set to 0 when Democrats in a given state-year held unified control of state government.[16]

The passage of legislation is obviously correlated with a number of other factors, and I control for variables that have been demonstrated to influence either the adoption of state civil rights legislation or the pace of policy innovation more generally.[17]

Some of the earliest studies show that economic modernization is very strongly correlated with policy innovation, and the finding has held up over time. I control for economic modernization using three variables. The first is a time-varying variable for "Income," measured by a state's personal income per capita. The second is a time-varying variable for "Industrialization," measured by the value-added in manufacturing per capita. Both amounts are adjusted for inflation using the Consumer Price Index for urban consumers (CPI-U). "Urbanization" is a third time-varying variable, which I measure as the percentage of individuals living in urban areas of the state.[18]

Various aspects of electoral politics also matter. Among them, electoral competition is one of the most relevant. In an electorally competitive environment, where the electoral strength of the parties is comparable, partisan legislators make broader appeals than they would otherwise, thereby improving the chances of policy innovation. I control for electoral competition through a modified version of a time-varying measure initially developed by Skocpol and her co-authors. My measure of "Electoral Competition" is constructed by averaging three fractions: the margin of victory for the sitting governor in the previous election expressed as a fraction of the total votes cast for governor, the seat margin of the majority party in the upper house expressed as a fraction of the total number of seats in the upper house, and the seat margin of the majority party in the lower house expressed as a fraction of the total number of seats in the lower house. I multiply the average of the three fractions by 100 and then subtract the resulting number from 100. This yields a variable for electoral competition that is measured independently of party control. A score of 100 indicates a highly competitive state, while a score of 0 indicates a grossly noncompetitive state.[19]

In order to plausibly identify the effect of Republican control, it is essential to control for public opinion. Failing to control for political opinion in the empirical analysis of policy outcomes can greatly exaggerate the role of party organizations. While the general climate of public opinion appears relevant, it seems even more important to focus on the specific issue of state FEP laws because, in the words of Philip E. Converse, "mass belief systems show little internal consistency." This specific focus is all the more important because the most extensive studies of congressional action on equal employment opportunity legislation suggest the importance of public attitudes regarding civil rights. I control for across-state differences in public opinion on state FEP laws by using data from a Gallup poll (N = 1,581) taken in 1945. From the raw Gallup poll data I calculate the percentage of respondents in each state answering yes to the following question: "Do you favor or oppose a state law which would require employers to hire a person if he is qualified for the job, regardless of his race or color?" (Question 7, Form K, Gallup Organization 1945). This variable is admittedly measured with error since it disaggregates data from what is meant to be a nationally representative sample, but the results do have face validity, according with generally held conceptions of racial liberalism in the states. For instance, New York (75 percent) was among the most supportive of state FEP legislation; Michigan (51 percent) was moderately supportive; while Missouri (21 percent) was least supportive. I retrieve this information by recoding it as a binary variable, which is coarse enough to ensure that a "favorable" state is not misclassified as "opposed," and vice versa. I thus specify the variable "Public Opinion" as a time-constant dummy variable set to 1 if the percentage of residents in a state expressing support for an FEP law is higher than the mean level of support for all thirty-seven states in the risk set; and 0 if it is lower than the mean.[20]

The malapportionment of state legislatures—whereby rural areas enjoyed disproportionate representation relative to urban areas—has been shown to shape certain policy outcomes. Ansolabehere, Gerber, and Snyder find that malapportionment influences the distribution of public expenditures by state governments. I control for malapportionment using the time-constant Right-To-Vote (RTV) index developed by Ansolabehere, Gerber, and Snyder. This variable, "Malapportionment," varies from 1.07 (New Hampshire) to 3.54 (California), where a score of 1 indicates a well-apportioned legislature in 1960 under the one-person, one-vote rule and where higher scores indicate overrepresentation.[21]

I also control for variation in the strength of interest groups involved in the battle over state FEP. As the primary sources show, organized business mounted the most aggressive campaign against state FEP legislation. Organized business, however, is also a group whose political strength is among the most difficult to measure. I use employer-friendly legislation as a proxy measure of business strength on the assumption that states with employer-friendly laws are also states with politically powerful and successful employers. This strategy admittedly warrants caution. Laws beneficial to employers may have passed for reasons that were unrelated to their political strength. Also, employers may view certain laws as serving (or not harming) their interests only ex post. Before such laws passed, employers may have opposed them. Thus, it is crucial to select laws that enjoyed clear, ex ante support from employers and whose passage appears to have been a consequence of employer mobilization. Of the many possibilities, state "right-to-work" (RTW) laws, which banned union shops, seem most attractive. RTW laws began spreading quickly across the states after 1947, when Congress enacted the Taft-Hartley Act over President Truman's veto. Taft-Hartley outlawed the closed shop and gave states the authority to decide whether to outlaw the union shop. Many states chose to do so. By 1964, nearly two-thirds of the states had passed RTW laws prohibiting union shops. Few types of state legislation addressed employer interests more squarely or inspired their political involvement more effectively. For these reasons, I use state RTW laws as a proxy measure of the variable "Business Strength." I code the measure as a time-constant dummy variable 1 if a state passed a right-to-work law by 1964, and 0 if it did not. This measure is extremely coarse, and it measures business power with error. Nonetheless, it is broadly consistent with the assumption that states that had passed RTW laws by 1964 were states in which employers were politically powerful enough to secure and defend their passage.[22]

Organized business was obviously not the only interest group with a stake in fair employment legislation. Many others—including the National Association for the Advancement of Colored People (NAACP), American Jewish Congress (AJC), Catholic Interracial Council (CIC), and a range of international and local unions—proved aggressive advocates as well. In his study of state FEP legislation, Collins finds that the strength of Jewish groups, civil rights organizations, and unions—as well as the size of the Catholic population—were positively related to passage. I control for the electoral and political significance of these groups by including variables on the "Percentage black," "Percentage Jewish," and "Percentage Catholic" for each state-year. I control for union strength by including a variable, "Union Density," that is the percentage of the nonagricultural work force in a union in each state-year. I control for the strength of civil rights organizations by including a measure of the percentage of African Americans with "NAACP membership" for each state year.[23]

A different theory predicts that the electoral importance of social groups standing to benefit from legislation might actually depress the likelihood of passage. Specifically, "racial competition" or "racial threat" theory predicts that passage varies inversely with the size of the black, Jewish, and Catholic population. This is because racial, ethnic, and religious groups are thought to compete against one another for scarce economic resources and white Protestants viewed blacks, Jews, and Catholics as a threat to their dominant position. Since theory gives contradictory predictions regarding the directionality of these three variables, I treat it as a strictly empirical question, following Collins.[24]

Previous studies find a complex series of diffusion effects associated with policy innovation.[25] Analysts have posited a variety of different mechanisms through which the effect occurs, but the most robust and consistent finding is that the adoption of legislation in a neighboring state raises the likelihood that a non-adopter will pass similar legislation. I remain agnostic about the causal mechanisms underling the finding, but I control for diffusion by including a variable ("Neighboring states with FEP") that measures the percentage of neighboring states that have adopted FEP legislation.

Table A.11 presents the estimated logit coefficients and standard errors from five different specifications of an event-history analysis of state FEP legislation.[26] Model 1 is a fully specified model. The estimated coefficient for Republican control is large, negative, and statistically significant, indicating that Republican control lowers the likelihood of a state passing an FEP law, even when controlling for a wide range of observable covariates. In order to guard against the possibility that the estimates in model 1 are inaccurate due to an excessively small event-per-variable (EPV) ratio, models 2 and 3 present the estimates from trimmed specifications. The main result in both models remains highly comparable to the main result in model 1.

Models 4 and 5 present the estimates from a main and interactive model to rule out the possibility that unobserved differences in public opinion or public sentiment are behind the observed effect of Republican control. As discussed in the main text, to the extent that the effect of Republican control persists or grows in highly competitive electoral states, then the estimated coefficients can be validly interpreted as a "party control" effect rather than a "public opinion" effect. This is because public opinion, racial climate, or other directly unobservable characteristics of the states are, in principle, evenly distributed in the most electorally competitive states. Since Republican control depends on the GOP having a majority of legislators in either chamber of the legislature or winning a majority of votes in the previous gubernatorial election, such thresholds provide a set of discontinuities (albeit a fuzzy one) that can be exploited to identify the effect of Republican control. This intuition is the basis of regression-discontinuity research designs, though I apply it in a different setting with far less data. The key result is the estimated coefficient on the interaction term in model 5. The interaction term is a binary variable indicating that a state belonged in the highest quartile of electoral competition and that Republicans also controlled a veto point. The coefficient associated with the term is negative and statistically significant, supporting the claim that the effect of Republican control is independent of underlying public sentiment. At the highest levels of electoral competition, when underlying public sentiment about FEP and other unobservable characteristics are most evenly distributed, Republican control had a strong negative effect on the likelihood of passage. This pattern is also evident in a basic cross-tabulation as well as separate lines for party control (GOP versus non-

TABLE A.11
Selected Event-History Models of State FEP Legislation, 1945–1964

	Model 1	Model 2	Model 3	Model 4	Model 5
Republican control of veto points	−2.443**	−2.718**	−2.099**	−1.273†	2.098
	(0.864)	(0.836)	(0.744)	(0.656)	(1.866)
Income (1964 dollars)	0.002	0.003**	0.003**	0.002*	0.002**
	(0.001)	(0.001)	(0.001)	(0.001)	(0.001)
Industrialization (1964 cents)	0.006				
	(0.011)				
Urbanization	−0.001				
	(0.038)				
Electoral competition	0.038	0.036	0.045*		
	(0.023)	(0.020)	(0.019)		
Electoral competition (quartiles)				0.563*	1.355**
				(0.248)	(0.490)
Public opinion (Favorable = 1)	1.304	1.404*			
	(0.810)	(0.693)			
Malapportionment (RTV Index)	−0.603				
	(0.587)				
Employer strength (RTW Law = 1)	−1.795	−1.898*	−2.437**	−1.548*	−1.807*
	(1.052)	(0.840)	(0.823)	(0.696)	(0.739)
Percentage black	−0.245*	−0.229*	−0.173*		
	(0.124)	(0.099)	(0.084)		
Percentage Jewish	0.159				
	(0.130)				
Percentage Catholic	−0.032				
	(0.046)				
NAACP membership	0.125				
	(0.094)				
Union density	0.092*	0.096*			
	(0.044)	(0.038)			
Neighboring states with FEP	0.052**	0.051**	0.043**	0.047**	0.048**
	(0.014)	(0.012)	(0.011)	(0.011)	(0.010)
Time	0.081	0.001	0.015	−0.001	−0.005
	(0.079)	(0.062)	(0.059)	(0.061)	(0.062)
Interaction (Rep. * Elect. Comp.)					−1.173*
					(0.567)
Constant	−12.47**	−13.16**	−10.61**	−7.79**	−10.55**
	(2.684)	(2.387)	(1.995)	(1.420)	(2.198)
Pseudo-R²	.37	.34	.30	.25	.28
Model χ²	68.86	63.97	56.65	46.90	51.82
Degrees of freedom	15	9	7	6	7

* p < .05   ** p < .01

Note: Entries are logit coefficients with standard errors in parentheses. N = 502.

Source: Anthony S. Chen, "The Party of Lincoln and the Politics of State Fair Employment Practices Legislation in the North, 1945–64," *American Journal of Sociology* 112, no. 6: 1713–74, tables 4 and 5.

GOP) fitted to a scatterplot of predicted probabilities derived from either models 1, 2, or 3.[27]

Figure 4.5 presents a bar chart of predicted probabilities derived from the specification reported as model 5. It visually depicts how the effect of Republican control is the strongest in highly competitive states. The states are partitioned in their level of electoral competition by quartile. Simple inspection of the chart reveals how the gap between states under GOP control and states not under GOP control widens as electoral competition increases. The predicted probabilities for the chart were generated using the SPost Suite, with all variables other than GOP control, electoral competition, and their interaction held at their sample means.[28]

Chapter 5

A Statistical and Graphical Analysis of House and Senate Votes in the 92nd Congress

Table A.12 presents the estimated coefficients and standard errors for two logit models of two different votes in the House in 1971. The unit of analysis is the individual House member. The dependent variable is binary for each model, and it is set to 1 for a yea vote and 0 for a nay vote. Columns 1 and 2 are models of House votes on the Erlenborn substitute (i.e., court-enforcement), while columns 3 and 4 are models of the House vote on passage of H.R. 1746 (amended version). "South" is a binary variable indicating whether a member represents a district located in one of the eleven states of the former Confederacy. "Economic conservatism" is measured on a scale (first-dimension NOMINATE) that ranges from −.82 to 1.351. "Social conservatism" is measure on a scale (second-dimension NOMINATE) from −1.185 to 1.326. On both scales, negative values indicate liberalism while positive values indicate conservatism. "Conservative coalition" is a binary variable set to 1 if a member is a Republican or a southern Democrat, and 0 if not.

Taken together, models 1 and 2 indicate that the vote on the Erlenborn substitute may have been strongly influenced by collective action on the part of the southern-conservative coalition. Model 1 shows that individual-level ideological variables are highly predictive of the vote, as expected. But when "Conservative Coalition" is added to the specification, as it is in model 2, its associated coefficient is large and statistically significant, indicating that belonging to the southern-conservative coalition raised the likelihood that a House member would vote for the substitute—above and beyond the influence of his or her ideological commitments.

Models 3 and 4 indicate that the effect of the southern-conservative coalition disappeared on the final vote for the bill. Model 3 shows that the

TABLE A.12
Logit Analysis of Key House Votes on Equal Employment Opportunity
Legislation, 1971

	(1)	(2)	(3)	(4)
Economic conservatism	14.39**	12.47**	−1.956**	−2.662**
	(1.556)	(1.685)	(0.438)	(0.680)
Social conservatism	2.142**	2.191**	−2.910**	−2.986**
	(0.404)	(0.409)	(0.327)	(0.339)
Conservative coalition		1.438*		0.635
		(0.651)		(0.449)
Constant	0.400	−0.720	1.657**	1.290**
	(0.219)	(0.561)	(0.179)	(0.313)
Pseudo-R^2	.74	.75	.32	.32
Model χ^2	408.79	413.71	144.68	146.74
Degrees of freedom	2	3	2	3
Observations	399	399	391	391

* $p < .05$ ** $p < .01$

Note: Entries are logit coefficients, with standard errors in parentheses.

Source: Roll-call data and ideological indices are extracted from Keith T. Poole,
Howard Rosenthal, and Boris T. Shor, *Voteview for Windows v 3.0.3: Roll Call Displays
of the U.S. Congress, 1789–2000* (accessible at voteview.com).

vote is largely driven by legislator ideology. Model 4 adds "Conservative
Coalition," but the estimated coefficient is not statistically significant.

In order to illustrate visually the contours of the conservative coalition
in ideological space, figure A.2 presents a scatterplot of U.S. House members by their level of economic and social conservatism, as measured by
their NOMINATE scores. This scatterplot draws on the same data used
to calculate the estimates reported in models 1 and 2. Democrats are symbolized by circles, while Republicans are symbolized by triangles. Circles
and triangles are filled in when a member voted with the Nixon administration (i.e., voted for the Erlenborn substitute), and they are empty when
he or she did not vote with the administration. As close inspection of
the scatterplot indicates, member ideology is strongly correlated with
voting. This is easiest to see in the case of economic conservatism, where
most members with a first-dimension NOMINATE score that is higher
than 0 (i.e., economically conservative members) appear to have voted
with the administration. It is also apparent, though less obviously, in the
case of social conservatism. The vast majority of members with a second-
dimension NOMINATE score close to 1 (i.e., very socially conservative
members) voted for the substitute. By comparison, proportionally fewer
members with second-dimension NOMINATE scores in the −1 range (i.e.,
very socially liberal members) voted for the substitute. But the scatterplot
also provides some visual reassurance that the conservative coalition was
actually active on the vote. The two groups of members that formed the

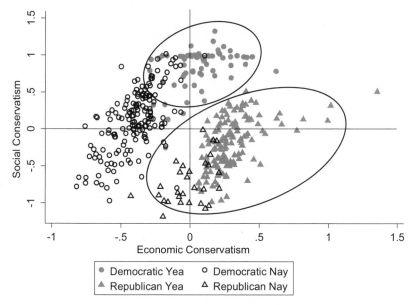

Figure A.2 Scatterplot of legislators by economic and social ideology: House Roll-Call Vote, 1971. *Note*: Each symbol represents a House member, and the location of each symbol indicates the position of each member in two-dimensional, ideological space. Circles represent Democrats, while triangles represent Republicans. A symbol is empty if a member did not vote for the Erlenborn substitute and filled in if he or she did vote for it. *Source*: Roll-call data and ideological indices are extracted from Keith T. Poole, Howard Rosenthal, and Boris T. Shor, *Voteview for Windows v 3.0.3: Roll Call Displays of the U.S. Congress, 1789–2000* (accessible at voteview.com).

conservative coalition—namely, Republicans and southern Democrats—are encircled by two separate ellipses in figure A.2. These two groups of members clearly occupy very different positions in two-dimensional ideological space. The bottom ellipsis contains Republicans, who were nearly all economically conservative but varied greatly in their social conservativism. The top ellipsis contains southern Democrats, who were nearly all socially conservative but varied somewhat in their economic ideology. Yet inspection reveals that the vast majority of members within both ellipses voted for the Erlenborn substitute. Only the most economically liberal members (within each group) did not. That such different groups behaved similarly may be taken as further evidence that the conservative coalition was collectively mobilized on the vote.

Table A.13 is the basis of the claim that selected votes on equal employment opportunity in the 1972 Senate were highly partisan in nature. It presents the estimated coefficients and standard errors for ordinary least squares (OLS) models of three Senate votes on the Dominick substitute

TABLE A.13
OLS Models of Key Senate Votes on the Equal Employment Opportunity
Legislation, 1972

	(1)	(2)	(3)
GOP	1.023**	0.761†	
	(0.216)	(0.389)	
South	2.200**	0.686*	
	(0.260)	(0.272)	
Conservative coalition			0.801**
			(0.235)
Economic conservatism		2.230**	2.344**
		(0.441)	(0.358)
Social conservatism		0.987**	0.974**
		(0.279)	(0.130)
Constant	0.386*	1.043**	1.055**
	(0.160)	(0.209)	(0.177)
R^2	0.45	0.64	0.69
Observations	100	100	100

† $p \approx .05$ * $p < .05$ ** $p < .01$

Notes: Entries are logit coefficients, with standard errors in parentheses.

Sources: Roll-call data and ideological indices are extracted from Keith T. Poole, Howard
Rosenthal, and Boris T. Shor, *Voteview for Windows v 3.0.3: Roll Call Displays of the U.S.
Congress, 1789–2000* (accessible at voteview.com).

(court enforcement). The votes took place on January 24, January 26,
and February 15. The dependent variable is the number of votes cast by
individual senators in support of the position of the Nixon administration
(favoring court enforcement). A yea vote is a vote for the administration's
position, and the dependent variable ranges between 0 and 3, with 3 being
the most consistent with the administration. "South" indicates whether a
member represents a district located in one of the eleven states of the
former Confederacy. "GOP" indicates whether the member is a Republican. "Economic conservatism" is measured on a scale (first-dimension
NOMINATE) that ranges from −.606 to .613. "Social conservatism" is
measure on a scale (second-dimension NOMINATE) from −1.059 to
1.457. On both scales, negative values indicate liberalism while positive
values indicate conservatism.

Model 1 indicates that "GOP" and "South" both predict support for
the administration position. The coefficients associated with each variable
are positive and statistically significant. Model 2 adds individual-level controls for economic and social ideology to the first specification. Though
the result is somewhat sensitive to sample variation—after all, there are
only one hundred data points—"South" and "GOP" remain more or less
statistically significant in the same direction, indicating that membership
in the GOP and representing a southern state are positively associated with

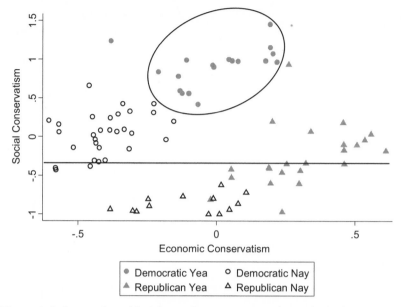

Figure A.3 Scatterplot of legislators by economic and social ideology: Senate Roll-Call Vote, 1972. *Note*: Each symbol represents a House member, and the location of each symbol indicates the position of each member in two-dimensional, ideological space. Circles represent Democrats, while triangles represent Republicans. A symbol is empty if a member did not vote with the Nixon administration and is filled in if he or she did. *Source*: Roll-call data and ideological indices are extracted from Keith T. Poole, Howard Rosenthal, and Boris T. Shor, *Voteview for Windows v 3.0.3: Roll Call Displays of the U.S. Congress, 1789–2000* (accessible at voteview.com).

voting for the administration position—independent of legislator ideology. Model 3 collapses "South" and "GOP" into a single variable: "Conservative coalition." The large, positive, and statistically significant coefficient suggests that a conservative coalition was active in the three votes on the Dominick substitute, also independent of legislator ideology. This pattern of results is consistent with the argument that the conservative coalition mobilized collectively to defend and promote the Dominick substitute, and it is also supports the claim that the conservative coalition was able to come together not only because southern Democrats exerted their well-known discipline but also because the *GOP* exerted *party* discipline. The conservative coalition succeeded in stopping administrative enforcement one last time because Republicans proved cohesive enough in the end to exploit the balance of power to their advantage.

Figure A.3 provides a visual illustration of the statistical relationships summarized by models 1 and 2. The figure is a scatterplot of the Senate vote on January 24. Democrats are symbolized by circles, Republicans by triangles. Each symbol is filled in if a member voted with the administration, and it is empty if a member voted against the administration. It is obvious from inspection that Democrats and Republicans were both internally divided, but it should also be clear that proportionally more Republicans voted with the administration than did Democrats. When region is "controlled for," it is visually equivalent to taking the southern Democrats out of the scatterplot. For convenience, an ellipsis is drawn around southern Democrats in figure A.3. If these members are simply ignored when the graph is inspected, it becomes readily apparent that Republicans were far more likely than Democrats, on average, to support the administration position. Almost all nonsouthern Democrats voted *against* the administration, while more than half of the Republican delegation voted with it. The statistical models indicate that this conclusion holds up even when members' social ideology is controlled. Visually, this can be confirmed by drawing an imaginary horizontal line across the scatterplot at any level of social conservatism between roughly .25 and −.5. When this imaginary line is followed from left to right, it should be clear that the Democrats along the line tend to vote against the administration, while Republicans on the same line tend to vote with it. A sample line is drawn on the scatterplot for illustrative purposes.

Abbreviations in the Notes

AIM Records	Associated Industries of Massachusetts, W.E.B. Du Bois Library, University of Massachusetts, Amherst, MA
AINYS Records	Records of the Associated Industries of New York State, Grenander Department of Special Collections and Archives, University at Albany, State University of New York, Albany
Burlingham Papers	Charles Culp Burlingham Papers, Harvard Law School Library, Harvard University, Cambridge, MA
CACI Records	Records of the Chicago Association of Commerce and Industry, Chicago Historical Society, Chicago, IL
Catherwood Library	Catherwood Library, Cornell University, Ithaca, NY
CCC Records	Records of the California Chamber of Commerce, California State Library, Sacramento, CA
Chavez Papers	*Dennis Chavez Papers, 1917–1963* (microfilm, 1993), Benson Latin American Collection, University of Texas, Austin, TX
Celler Papers	Emanuel Celler Papers, Library of Congress, Washington, DC
CFCU Records	Records of the California Federation for Civic Unity, 1945–1956, Bancroft Library, University of California, Berkeley, CA
CD	*Chicago Defender*
CT	*Chicago Tribune*
Cleary Collection	Cleary Collection, Bancroft Library, University of California, Berkeley, CA
COD Records	Records of the New York State War Council Committee on Discrimination, New York State Archives, Albany, NY
CR	*Congressional Record*
Dewey Papers	Thomas E. Dewey Papers, Rare Books, Special Collections, and Preservation, University of Rochester, Rochester, NY
Dewey Scrapbooks	Thomas E. Dewey, *Scrapbooks, 1935-1954*, Rhees Library, University of Rochester, Rochester, NY
Dirksen Papers	Everett M. Dirksen Papers, The Dirksen Congressional Center, Pekin, IL
Douglas (Paul) Papers	Paul H. Douglas Papers, Chicago Historical Society, Chicago, IL

Douglas (Helen) Papers   Helen Gahagan Douglas Collection, Congressional
Archives, Carl Albert Center, University of
Oklahoma, Norman, OK

FDRL   Franklin Delano Roosevelt Presidential Library,
Hyde Park, NY

GPC   General Pamphlet Collection, Urban Archives, Temple
University, Philadelphia, PA

Hawkins Papers   Augustus F. Hawkins Papers, Young Research Library,
University of California, Los Angeles, CA

Horn Log   Congressional Archives, Carl Albert Center, University
of Oklahoma, Norman, OK

IMA Records   Records of the Illinois Manufacturers' Association,
Chicago Historical Society, Chicago, IL

ISHL   Illinois State Historical Library, Springfield, IL

Ives Papers   Irving M. Ives Papers, Carl A. Kroch Library, Cornell
University, Ithaca, NY

JFKL   John F. Kennedy Presidential Library and Museum,
Boston, MA

Johnson Papers   Archives and Special Collections, University of
Nebraska, Lincoln, NE

Katzenbach Papers   Nicholas deB. Katzenbach Papers, John F. Kennedy
Presidential Library, Boston, MA

Kerner Papers   Otto Kerner Papers, Illinois State Historical Library,
Springfield, IL

LAT   *Los Angeles Times*

LBJL   Lyndon Baines Johnson Presidential Library,
Austin, TX

Lehman Papers   Herbert H. Lehman Papers, Rare Book and
Manuscript Library, Columbia University, NY

Lucas Papers   Scott W. Lucas Papers, Illinois State Historical Library,
Springfield, IL

MACI Records   Records of the Minnesota Associated of Commerce
and Industry, Minnesota Historical Society,
St. Paul, MN

McLaurin Papers   B. F. McLaurin Papers, Schomburg Center for Research
in Black Culture, New York Public Library,
New York, NY

Marshall Papers   Burke Marshall Papers, John F. Kennedy Presidential
Library, Boston, MA

MCFEP Records   Record of the Minnesota Council for Fair Employment
Practices and Merit, Minnesota Historical Society,
St. Paul, MN

Miller Papers   Frieda S. Miller Papers, Schlesinger Library, Harvard
University, Cambridge, MA

Morse Papers   Wayne Morse Papers, Knight Library, University of
Oregon, Eugene, OR

Moses Papers	Robert Moses Papers, Manuscripts and Archives Division, New York Public Library, New York, NY
MSCAD	Records of the Minnesota State Commission against Discrimination, Minnesota Historical Society, St. Paul, MN
NAACP-WC Records	Records of the National Associated for the Advancement of Colored People, Region I, Bancroft Library, University of California, Berkeley, CA
NAM Records	Records of the National Association of Manufacturers, Hagley Museum and Library, Wilmington, DE
NYT	*New York Times*
NYSL	New York State Library, Albany, NY
OCFEP Records	Ohio Committee for Fair Employment Practices Legislation, Western Reserve Historical Society, Cleveland, OH
Peace Collection	Swarthmore Peace Collection, Swarthmore College Library, Swarthmore College, Swarthmore, PA
Pittman Papers	Tarea Hall Pittman Papers, Bancroft Library, University of California, Berkeley, CA
Pittman Papers II	Tarea Hall Pittman Papers, California State Library, Sacramento, CA
Reid Papers	Ogden Reid Papers, Manuscripts and Archives, Yale University, New Haven, CT
RFK Papers	Robert F. Kennedy Papers, John F. Kennedy Presidential Library, Boston, MA
Rumford Papers	W. Byron Rumford Papers, Bancroft Library, University of California, Berkeley, CA
Russell Papers	Richard B. Russell, Jr., Papers, Richard B. Russell Library for Political Research and Studies, University of Georgia, Athens, GA
Stevenson Papers	Adlai E. Stevenson Papers, Illinois State Historical Library, Springfield, IL
Taft Papers	Robert A. Taft Papers, Library of Congress, Washington, DC
Taylor Papers	Hobart Taylor Papers, Bentley Historical Library, University of Michigan, Ann Arbor, MI
USCC Records	Records of the U.S. Chamber of Commerce, Hagley Museum and Library, Wilmington, DE
Vertical File	Vertical File, California State Library, Sacramento, CA
Warren Papers	Earl Warren Papers, California State Archives, Sacramento, CA
WP	*Washington Post*
WHCF	White House Central Files
Williams Papers	Aubrey Williams Papers, Franklin Delano Roosevelt Presidential Library, Hyde Park, NY

H. A. Williams Papers   Harrison A. Williams Papers, Special Collections and
                         University Archives, Rutgers University Libraries,
                         Newark, NJ
WSJ   *Wall Street Journal*

Notes

Preface and Acknowledgments

1. C. Vann Woodward, introduction to *Grand Expectations: The United States, 1945–1974*, by James T. Patterson (New York: Oxford University Press, 1996), xvii; Thomas L. Haskell, "Objectivity Is Not Neutrality: Rhetoric vs. Practice in Peter Novick's *That Noble Dream*," *History and Theory*, 32 (May 1993): 129–57, esp. 133 and 135. See also Thomas L. Haskell, *Objectivity Is Not Neutrality: Explanatory Schemes in History* (Baltimore, MD: Johns Hopkins University Press, 1998).

Chapter One

1. David M. Kennedy, *Freedom from Fear: The American People in Depression and War, 1929–1945* (New York: Oxford University Press, 1999), 469–70; Suzanne Mettler, *Soldiers to Citizens:The G.I. Bill and the Making of the Greatest Generation* (New York: Oxford University Press, 2005); Kenneth T. Jackson, *Crabcrass Frontier: The Suburbanization of the United States* (New York: Oxford University Press, 1985); Jennifer Klein, *For All These Rights: Business, Labor, and the Shaping of America's Public-Private Welfare State* (Princeton: Princeton University Press, 2003); Meg Jacobs, *Pocketbook Politics: Economic Citizenship in Twentieth-Century America* (Princeton: Princeton University Press, 2005); Lizabeth Cohen, *A Consumers' Republic: The Politics of Mass Consumption in Postwar America* (New York: Alfred A. Knopf, 2003), 112–65; Frank R. Dobbin, "The Origins of Private Social Insurance: Public Policy and Fringe Benefits in America, 1920–1950," *American Journal of Sociology* 97 (1992): 1416–50; James T. Patterson, *Grand Expectations: The United States, 1945–1974* (New York: Oxford University Press, 1996), 4, 8–9. At the heart of all grand expectations during the postwar era was the notion of security. At home, security meant protection from the vicissitudes and vulnerabilities inherent in modern industrial life—sickness, injury, unemployment, and old age. This security was to be conferred by the successful operation of a demand-driven consumer economy that was managed primarily through "automatic" counter-cyclical deficit-spending by the federal government—a kind of "commercial" as opposed to "social" Keynesianism, to borrow a distinction from Margaret Weir and Theda Skocpol. See Margaret Weir and Theda Skocpol, "State Structures and the Possibilities for 'Keynesian' Responses to the Great Depression in Sweden, Britain, and the United States," in *Bringing the State Back In*, edited by Peter Evans, Dietrich Rueschemeyer, and Theda Skocpol (New York: Cambridge University Press, 1985), 107–63. Linked to macroeconomic policy was a system of industrial relations that provided economic security for workers through private collective bargaining, which was aimed at securing high wages and stable, lifetime employment with

solid "fringe" benefits such as medical care and private pensions. Economic security in the postwar period was thus tied to the wide availability of, and fair access
to, well-paying, stable jobs in unionized sectors of the labor market, particularly
those in the core manufacturing concerns of the industrial economy, such as steel,
cars, and aviation. On the defining features of postwar political economy, see the
introduction as well as the essays (especially Lichtenstein) in Steven Fraser and
Gary Gerstle, eds., *The Rise and Fall of the New Deal Order, 1930–1980* (Princeton: Princeton University Press, 1989).

   2. Mildred H. Mahoney, "Massachusetts FEPC Succeeds," *Interracial Review*
(August 1948): 118; F. L. Osborne to Earl Warren, June 11, 1946, F3540:3677,
Administrative Files, Public Works-Race Relations, Negro, 1945–46, Earl Warren
Papers, California State Archives (hereafter Warren Papers); *CD*, June 23, 1945,
p. 12. For a letter to Warren similar to the one by Osborne, see Jane Perry to
Earl Warren, November 8, 1945, F3640:3677, Series 317, Earl Warren Papers,
California State Archives (hereafter Warren Papers). Perry had been searching for
a job for three months since moving to California in the early fall, and she was
repeatedly told that there were no jobs for the "colored." The constituent files of
northern legislators—particularly Democrats and liberal Republicans—are filled
with other examples of African Americans turning to the political process for
protection from job discrimination. For example, see Emmitt Luster Stovall, July
18, 1960, Folder: Government Contracts 1960, Box 78, Paul H. Douglas Papers,
Chicago Historical Society (hereafter Douglas (Paul) Papers); or David Bryant to
Otto Kerner, August 11, 1961, Folder: FEPC, 1961–1963, Box 544, Otto Kerner
Papers, Illinois State Historical Library (hereafter Kerner Papers). On the politics
of employment policy during the postwar period, see Margaret Weir, *Politics and
Jobs: The Boundaries of Employment Policy in the United States* (Princeton:
Princeton University Press, 1992). For discussions of black life in postwar north-
ern California, see Albert S. Broussard, *Black San Francisco: The Struggle for
Racial Equality in the West, 1900–1954* (Lawrence: University Press of Kansas,
1993); Robert O. Self, *American Babylon: Race and the Struggle for Postwar
Oakland* (Princeton: Princeton University Press, 2003); Quintard Taylor, *In
Search of the Racial Frontier, 1528–1990* (New York: Norton, 1998); Mark Brilliant, *Color Lines: Civil Rights Struggles on America's 'Racial Frontier,' 1945–
1975* (New York: Oxford University Press, forthcoming). It was no accident that
it was the wife of a veteran who was writing a letter to one of her elected officials.
Military involvement had a hugely galvanizing effect on the political participation
and political beliefs of African Americans. Veterans were among the most active
members of the black cohort that formed the bulwark of the civil rights movement. For a ground-breaking study of the subject, see Christopher Parker, *Fighting
for Democracy* (Princeton: Princeton University Press, forthcoming). On the
broad impact of war on racial inequality, see Philip Klinkner and Rogers M.
Smith, *The Unsteady March: The Rise and Decline of Racial Equality in America*
(Chicago: University of Chicago Press, 1999) and Daniel Kryder, *Divided Arsenal:
Race and the American State during World War II* (New York: Cambridge University Press). The authors stress the critical importance of war to improvements in
black opportunities. For the impact of the Cold War in particular, see Mary Dudziak, *Cold War Civil Rights: Race and the Image of American Democracy* (Prince-

ton: Princeton University Press, 2000) and John D. Skrentny, "The Effect of the Cold War on African-American Civil Rights: America and the World Audience, 1945–1968," *Theory and Society* 27 (1998): 237–85.

3. The literature on the southern civil rights movement is vast. A useful, brief history is Harvard Sitkoff, *The Struggle for Black Equality, 1954–1992* (New York: Hill & Wang, 1993). See as well the relevant chapters of John Hope Franklin and Alfred A. Moss, Jr., *From Slavery to Freedom: A History of African Americans*, 8th ed. (New York: Knopf, 2000), esp. 444–561. Key sociological accounts include Doug McAdam, *Political Process and Black Insurgency, 1930–1970* (Chicago: University of Chicago Press, 1982) and Aldon Morris, *Origins of the Civil Rights Movement: Black Communities Organizing for Change* (New York: Free Press, 1984). Taylor Branch's trilogy uses King's life as a lens for focusing the history of the southern-based, church-led civil rights movement and tracing the broad, ramifying influence it exerted on numerous facets of American politics and society. It is a model of the dominant genre. See the following works by Taylor Branch: *Parting the Waters: American in the King Years, 1954–1964* (New York: Simon and Schuster, 1989); *Pillar of Fire: America in the King Years, 1963–1965* (New York: Simon and Schuster, 1998); and *At Canaan's Edge: America in the King Years, 1965–68* (New York: Simon and Schuster, 2006). See also David Garrow, *Bearing the Cross: Martin Luther King, Jr., and the Southern Christian Leadership Conference* (New York: William Morrow, 1986). For a perceptive essay that identifies many of the major historiographical and political issues at stake, see Jacquelyn Dowd Hall, "The Long Civil Rights Movement and the Political Uses of the Past," *Journal of American History* 91 (March 2005): 1233–63. See also Steven F. Lawson, "Freedom Then, Freedom Now: The Historiography of the Civil Rights Movement," *American Historical Review* 96 (April 1991): 456–71. For other important sociological perspectives, see Kenneth T. Andrews, *Freedom Is a Constant Struggle* (Chicago: University of Chicago Press, 2004); Francesca Polletta, *Freedom Is an Endless Meeting* (Chicago: University of Chicago Press, 2002). The history of civil rights in the North is a subject that is increasingly receiving more attention. See Thomas J. Sugrue, *The Origins of the Urban Crisis: Race and Inequality in Postwar Detroit* (Princeton: Princeton University Press, 1997); Thomas J. Sugrue, *Sweet Land of Liberty* (New York: Random House, forthcoming); Jeanne F. Theoharis and Komozi Woodard, eds., *Freedom North: Black Freedom Struggles outside the South, 1940–1980* (New York: Palgrave Macmillan, 2003); Martha Biondi, *To Stand and Fight: The Struggle for Civil Rights in Postwar New York City* (Cambridge, MA: Harvard University Press, 2003); Matthew Countryman, *Up South: Civil Rights and Black Power in Philadelphia* (Philadelphia: University of Pennsylvania Press, 2005).

4. Patterson, *Grand Expectations*, 642, 723–24, 659–63, 685.

5. Hugh Davis Graham, *The Civil Rights Era: Origins and Development of National Policy* (New York: Oxford University Press, 1990), 343, 469; Jill S. Quadagno, *The Color of Welfare: How Racism Undermined the War on Poverty* (New York: Oxford University Press, 1994), 64, 75, 85; Thomas J. Sugrue, "Affirmative Action from Below: Civil Rights, the Building Trades, and the Politics of Racial Equality in the Urban North, 1945–1969," *Journal of American History* 91 (June 2004): 145–73, esp. 173; Biondi, *To Stand and Fight*; Nancy MacLean,

Freedom Is Not Enough: The Opening of the American Workplace (New York: Russell Sage Foundation; and Cambridge, MA: Harvard University Press, 2006); John D. Skrentny, *The Ironies of Affirmative Action: Politics, Culture, and Justice in America* (Chicago: University of Chicago Press, 1996), 222–25; Nicholas Pedriana, "The Historical Foundations of Affirmative Action, 1961–1971," *Research in Social Stratification and Mobility* 17 (1999): 3–32; Robin Stryker and Nicholas Pedriana, "Political Culture Wars 1960s Style: Equal Employment Opportunity, Affirmative Action Law, and the Philadelphia Plan," *American Journal of Sociology* 103 (1997): 633–91; Robin Stryker and Nicholas Pedriana, "The Strength of a Weak Agency: Early Enforcement of Title VII of the 1964 Civil Rights Act and the Expansion of State Capacity," *American Journal of Sociology* 110 (2004): 709–60; Robert C. Lieberman, *Shaping Race Policy: The United States in Comparative Perspective* (Princeton: Princeton University Press, 2005); Paul Frymer, *Black and Blue* (Princeton: Princeton University Press, 2007). For other important work, see also Paul D. Moreno, *From Direct Action to Affirmative Action: Fair Employment Law and Policy in America, 1933–1972* (Baton Rouge: Louisiana State University, 1997); Terry H. Anderson, *The Pursuit of Fairness: A History of Affirmative Action* (New York: Oxford University Press, 2004); Robert J. Weiss, *"We Want Jobs": A History of Affirmative Action* (New York: Garland,1997). Key unpublished contributions are Stacy K. Sewell, "Contracting Racial Equality: Affirmative Action Policy and Practice in the United States, 1945–1970," Ph.D. diss., Rutgers University, 1999; and Konrad M. Hamilton, "From Equal Opportunity to Affirmative Action: A History of the Equal Employment Opportunity Commission, 1965–1980," Ph.D. diss., Stanford University, 1998. See also Anthony S. Chen, "From Fair Employment to Equal Employment Opportunity and Beyond: Affirmative Action and the Politics of Civil Rights in the New Deal Order, 1941–1972," Ph.D. diss., University of California, Berkeley, 2002.

6. On the politics of state FEP legislation, see Duane Lockard, *Toward Equal Opportunity: A Study of State and Local Antidiscrimination Law* (New York: Macmillan, 1968) as well as Sidney Alan Fine, *"Expanding the Frontiers of Civil Rights": Michigan, 1948–1968* (Detroit: Wayne State University Press, 2000). See also David F. Engstrom, "The Lost Origins of American Fair Employment Law: State Fair Employment Practices Bureaus and the Politics of Regulatory Design," Ph.D. diss., Yale University, 2005. Other important exceptions to the emphasis on the 1960s include Thomas J. Sugrue, *Sweet Land of Liberty*; Maclean, *Freedom Is Not Enough*; Biondi, *To Stand and Fight*; Risa Goluboff, *The Lost Origins of Modern Civil Rights* (Cambridge, MA: Harvard University Press, 2007); " 'Let Economic Equality Take Care of Itself': The NAACP, Labor Litigation, and the Making of Civil Rights in the 1940s," 52 *UCLA Law Review* 1393 (2005); Ira Katznelson, *When Affirmative Action Was White: An Untold History of Racial Inequality in Twentieth-Century America* (New York: Norton, 2005); Biondi, *To Stand and Fight*. On the centrality of the 1940s to the subsequent politics of civil rights, see Richard M. Dalfiume, "The 'Forgotten' Years of the Negro Revolution," *Journal of American History* 55 (June 1968), 90–106; Harvard Sitkoff, "Racial Militancy and Interracial Violence in the Second World War," *Journal of American History* 58 (December 1971): 661–81; Robert Korstad and Nelson Lichtenstein, "Opportunities Found and Lost: Labor, Radicals, and the Early Civil

Rights Movement," *Journal of American History* 75 (December 1988): 786–811; William C. Berman, *The Politics of Civil Rights during the Truman Administration* (Columbus: Ohio State University Press, 1970); Donald R. McCoy and Richard T. Ruetten, *Quest and Response: Minority Rights and the Truman Administration* (Lawrence: University Press of Kansas, 1973); Merl E. Reed, *Seedtime for the Modern Civil Rights Movement* (Baton Rouge: Louisiana State University Press, 1991); Denton L. Watson, *Lion in the Lobby: Clarence Mitchell, Jr.'s Struggle for the Passage of Civil Rights Laws* (New York: William Morrow, 1990); . Also valuable are Paul Burstein, *Discrimination, Jobs, and Politics: The Struggle for Equal Employment Opportunity in the United States since the New Deal* (Chicago: University of Chicago Press, 1985); and Moreno, *From Direct Action to Affirmative Action.* Anderson traces affirmative action to the 1930s, but the bulk of his narrative concerns the 1960s. See, Anderson, *The Pursuit of Fairness.*

7. This book adopts a broad perspective on history, politics, and society. Its central explanatory task, however, is fairly narrow. How and why racial discrimination in employment come to be regulated in the ways that it did, and not in other ways it might have? This question necessitates a focus on African Americans and white ethnics, largely due to the historical period covered by the analysis. These were the main groups involved in the struggle. *The Fifth Freedom* does not trace how women—and people of color other than African Americans—also made vital contributions to the struggle, especially starting in the late 1960s and early 1970s. This is a crucial story, and various aspects of the tale are powerfully recounted and reconstructed in Nancy MacLean, *Freedom Is Not Enough,* but also in Cynthia Harrison, *On Account of Sex: The Politics of Women's Issues, 1945–1968* (Berkeley: University of California Press, 1988); John D. Skrentny, *The Minority Rights Revolution* (Cambridge, MA: Belknap Press, 2002); Hugh Davis Graham, *Collision Course: The Strange Convergence of Affirmative Action and Immigration Policy in America* (New York: Oxford University Press, 2002); Zaragosa Vargas, *Labor Rights Are Civil Rights: Mexican American Workers in the Twentieth Century* (Princeton: Princeton University Press, 2005). A broad history of affirmative action in higher education remains unwritten. For a fascinating look at the origins of affirmative action policies at the institutional pinnacle of American higher education, see Jerome Karabel, *The Chosen: The Hidden History of Admission and Exclusion at Harvard, Yale, and Princeton* (New York: Houghton Mifflin, 2005), 378–409. See as well Joseph Soares, *The Power of Privilege: Yale and American's Elite Colleges* (Palo Alto, CA: Stanford University Press, 2007); John A. Douglass, *The Conditions for Admission: Access, Equity, and the Social Contract of Public Universities* (Palo Alto, CA: Stanford University Press, 2007); Anthony S. Chen and Lisa M. Stulberg, "Beyond Disruption: The Forgotten Origins of Affirmative Action in College and University Admissions, 1961–1969," working paper 2007–01, Gerald R. Ford School of Public Policy, University of Michigan.

8. Goluboff, *Lost Origins of Civil Rights*; Dalfiume, "The 'Forgotten' Years of the Negro Revolution"; Katznelson, *When Affirmative Action Was White*; Victoria Hattam, *In the Shadow of Race: Jews, Latinos, and Immigrant Politics in the United States* (Chicago: University of Chicago Press, 2007), 121; Denton Watson, *Lion in the Lobby: Clarence Mitchell's Struggle for the Passage of Civil Rights*

Laws (New York: William Morrow, 1990); Korstad and Lichtenstein, "Opportunities Found and Lost," 786–811; Sugrue, *The Origins of the Urban Crisis*; Biondi, *To Stand and Fight*. For recent political histories that place a renewed focus on Congress, see Julian C. Zelizer, *Taxing America: Wilbur D. Mills, Congress, and the State, 1945–1975* (New York: Cambridge University Press, 1998); Julian C. Zelizer, *On Capital Hill: The Struggle to Reform Congress and Its Consequences, 1948–2000* (New York: Cambridge University Press, 2004); Paul C. Milazzo, *Unlikely Environmentalists: Congress and Clean Water, 1945–1972* (Lawrence: University Kansas Press, 2006). See also Eric Schickler, *Disjointed Pluralism: Institutional Innovation and the Development of the U.S. Congress* (Princeton: Princeton University Press, 2001). On the crucial importance of looking to state politics for insight into the dynamics of national policy-making, particularly with respect to debates about the rise and fall of the political order inaugurated by the New Deal, see Margaret Weir, "States, Race, and the Decline of New Deal Liberalism," *Studies in American Political Development* 19 (2005): 157–72. See also James T. Patterson, *The New Deal and the States: Federalism in Transition* (Princeton: Princeton University Press, 1969); and Isaac William Martin, *The Permanent Tax Revolt: How the Property Tax Transformed American Politics* (Palo Alto: Stanford University Press, 2008).

9. For excellent older studies of the politics of fair employment practices, see Louis Coleridge Kesselman, *The Social Politics of FEPC: A Study in Reform Pressure Movements* (Chapel Hill: University of North Carolina Press, 1948); Will Maslow and Joseph Robison, "Civil Rights Legislation and the Fight for Equality, 1862–1952," *University of Chicago Law Review* 20 (Spring 1953): 363–413; Louis Ruchames, *Race, Jobs, and Politics* (New York: Columbia University Press, 1953); Lockard, *Toward Equal Opportunity*. A more recent and equally instructive study is Sidney Fine, *"Expanding the Frontiers of Civil Rights": Michigan, 1948–1968* (Detroit: Wayne State University Press, 2000).

10. Ruchames, *Race, Jobs, and Politics*, 165–80; Kesselman, *The Social Politics of FEPC*; Maslow and Robinson, "Civil Rights Legislation and the Fight for Equality"; Graham, *The Civil Rights Era*, 20–21, 33; Moreno, *From Direct Action to Affirmative Action*, 163–65; Burstein, *Jobs, Politics, and Civil Rights*, 27.

11. On the fragmented implementation of Title VII and especially Title VI of the Civil Rights Act, see Hanes Walton, *When the Marching Stopped: The Politics of Civil Rights Regulatory Agencies* (Albany: State University of New York Press, 1988).

12. How the private sector has negotiated the adoption and implementation of affirmative action plans is the subject of considerable investigation by sociologists. See especially Frank Dobbin, *Inventing Equal Opportunity*, (Princeton University Press, forthcoming). Lauren Edelman, "Legal Ambiguity and Symbolic Structures: Organizational Mediation of Civil Rights Law," *American Journal of Sociology* 97 (1992): 1531–576; and Frank Dobbin and John R. Sutton, "The Strength of a Weak State: The Rights Revolution and the Rise of Human Resources Management Divisions," *American Journal of Sociology* 104 (1998): 441–76. See also Lauren B. Edelman, Howard S. Erlanger, and John Lande, "Internal Dispute Resolution: The Transformation of Civil Rights in the Workplace," *Law and Society Review* 27 (1993): 497–534; Lauren B. Edelman, Sally Riggs

Fuller, and Iona Mara-Drita, "Diversity Rhetoric and the Managerialization of the Law," *American Journal of Sociology* 106 (2001): 1589–941. For a thoughtful discussion of politics and neoinstitutionalism, see Elisabeth S. Clemens, "Politics and Institutionalism: Explaining Durability and Change." *Annual Review of Sociology* 25 (1999): 441–66.

13. On the ideological content of liberalism in the mid-century United States, see Brinkley, *End of Reform*. For an example of how liberals used phrases like "freedom from discrimination," see League of Women Voters, "Fair Employment Practice in Legislation in Colorado" (Denver, 1950), 3, Folder 40, Box 3, Records of the Ohio Committee for Fair Employment Practices Legislation (hereafter OCFEP Records), Western Reserve Historical Society. Columnist William O. Walker of the *Cleveland Call and Post* wrote that the "real purpose of FEPC legislation is to proclaim universal civil freedom, not freedom from prejudice but freedom from discrimination based on race." See *Cleveland Call and Post*, May 14, 1949, 4-B. In 1964, as the fight over the Civil Rights Act was peaking, Hubert H. Humphrey called for a fifth freedom, which he called "Freedom of Dignity." Press Release, March 16, 1964, Folder: Bipartisan Civil rights Newsletter, March 13–April 19, 1964, Box 27, Burke Marshall Papers, John F. Kennedy Presidential Library (hereafter Marshall Papers).

14. Gunnar Myrdal, *An American Dilemma* (New York: Harper and Row, 1944), xlvii. For examples of a liberal reasoning on social regulation, see Will Maslow and Joseph B. Robison, "Legislating against Discrimination," *Social Action* 15 (January 15, 1949): 6; Will Maslow and Joseph B. Robison, "Civil Rights Legislation and the Fight for Equality, 1862–1952," *University of Chicago Law Review* 20 (Spring 1953); League of Women Voters, "Fair Employment Practice in Legislation in Colorado"; "The Case for an Effective FEPC Law," *Denver Post*, February 4, 1951.

15. U.S. Department of Commerce, *Historical Statistics of the United States, Colonial Times to 1970*, part 1 (Washington, D.C.: U.S. Department of Commerce, 1975), Series A 73–81, 12; Series A, 172–194, 22; U.S. Department of Commerce, *Sixteenth Census of the United States: Reports on Population*, vol. 2 (Washington, D.C.: U.S. Department of Commerce, 1943), table 3, 8–16; U.S. Department of Commerce, *Special Reports: Nativity and Parentage* (Washington, D.C.: U.S. Department of Commerce, 1954), table 2, 3B-16; U.S. Department of Commerce, *Subject Report: Nonwhite Population by Race* (Washington, D.C.: U.S. Department of Commerce, 1963), Table 1, 1; U.S. Department of Commerce, *Subject Reports: Negro Population*, (Washington, D.C.: U.S. Department of Commerce, 1973), table 1, 1. Anecdotes of discrimination are abundant; they can be easily found in the records of the NAACP and NUL, particularly their labor departments. The records of state FEP agencies are also extremely valuable. For instance, see Massachusetts Fair Employment Practice Commission, "Four Typical Case Histories," n.d., Box 35, B. F. McLaurin Papers, Schomburg Center for Research in Black Culture, New York Public Library (hereafter McLaurin Papers); Joseph L. Bustard, "A Brief Presenting of the Administrative Experiences of the Division against Discrimintion of the New Jersey Department of Education," 1947; Box 35, McLaurin Papers; New Jersey Department of Education Division against Discrimination, *Annual Report, 1947–1948* (Newark, 1948), Box 35,

McLaurin Papers. Other sources of anecdotes include the records of elected officials, especially those representing urban districts or urbanized states, as well as black newspapers. The indexed *Tuskegee Institute News Clippings File* (Sanford, NC: Microfilming Corporation of America, 1976) provides especially useful coverage of the latter for a selection of newspapers across the country.

16. Stanley Lieberson, *A Piece of the Pie: Blacks and Immigrants Since 1880* (Berkeley: University of California Press, 1980); Michael B. Katz, Mark J. Stern, and Jamie J. Fader, "The New African American Inequality," *Journal of American History* 92 (June 2005): 75–108; Robert W. Fairlie and William Sundstrom, "The Emergence, Persistence, and Recent Widening of the Racial Unemployment Gap," *Industrial and Labor Relations Review* 52 (January 1999): 252–70; Stewart E. Tolnay, "Trends in the Relative Occupational Status of African Americans and Immigrants in Northern Cities, 1880–1970," *Social Science Research* 32 (December 2003): 603–32; Gary Gerstle, *American Crucible: Race and Nation in the Twentieth Century* (Princeton: Princeton University Press, 2001); *NYT*, October 6, 1947, p. 15.

17. Carlos E. Castañeda to Will Maslow, February 9, 1945, Frame 240447, Roll 8 [Folder 12, Box 78], *Dennis Chavez Papers, 1917–1963* (microfilm, 1993), Benson Latin American Collection, University of Texas (hereafter Chavez Papers); Statement of United Packinghouse Workers of America before Senate Subcommittee on Education and Labor, March 13, 1945, Frame 240633, Roll 8 [Folder 16, Box 78], Chavez Papers; Raul F. Magana and Jaime Gonzalez to Dear Sir [probably Dennis Chavez], n.d. (probably 1945), Frame 240469, Roll 8 [Folder 12, Box 78], Chavez Papers; Dennis Chavez to Joe Montoya, January 2, 1945, Frame 240233, Roll 8 [Folder 10, Box 78], Chavez Papers; Montoya to Chavez, January 8, 1945, Frame 240211, Roll 8 [Folder 10, Box 78], Chavez Papers; Chavez to Montoya, January 13, 1945, Frame 240199, Roll 8 [Folder 10, Box 78], Chavez Papers; Peter Gonzales, C. S. Garcia, L. C. Homan, H. V. Pain, and Emrigillo Romera to Dennis Chavez, January 23, 1945, Frame 240360, Roll 8 [Folder 11, Box 78], Chavez Papers; Peter Gonzales to Dennis Chavez, January 30, 1945, 240316, Roll 8 [Folder 11, Box 78], Chavez Papers. Castañeda was a historian and librarian at the University of Texas, and he served as a regional director of the wartime FEPC. For other examples of organized political participation by Mexican Americans, see also Isaac Sandoval to Dennis Chavez, March 16, 1945, Frame 240752, Roll 8 [Folder 19, Box 78], Chavez Papers. Frank Paz testified before a Senate Committee in 1945 on behalf of the Spanish-Speaking Peoples Council of Chicago. See Senate Committee on Education and Labor, Fair Employment Practice Act, 79th Cong., 1 sess., 1945, pp. 140–42. More generally, see Vargas, *Labor Rights Are Civil Rights*. For a brilliant analysis of what might be called the "assimilationist" strand of the Mexican American civil rights struggle, see Thomas A. Guglielmo, "Fighting for Caucasian Rights: Mexicans, Mexican Americans, and the Transnational Struggle for Civil Rights in World War II Texas," *Journal of American History* 92 (March 2006): 1212–37.

18. Scott Kurashige, *The Shifting Grounds of Race: Black and Japanese Americans in the Making of Multiethnic Los Angeles* (Princeton: Princeton University Press, 2008), 186–204; Mike Masaoka with Bill Hosokawa, *They Call me Moses Masaoka: An American Saga* (New York: William Morrow, 1987), 192; Bill Hoso-

kawa, *JACL in Quest of Justice* (New York: William Morrow, 1982), 276. For examples of Masaoka's testimony, see Senate Committee on Labor and Public Welfare, *Antidiscrimination in Employment*, 80th Cong., 1 sess., 1947, 195–210; House Committee on Education and Labor, *Federal Fair Employment Act*, 81st Cong., 1 sess., 1949, 134–45; Senate Committee on Labor and Public Welfare, Discrimination and Full Utilization of Manpower Resources, 82nd Cong., 2nd sess., 1952, 320; Senate Committee on Labor and Public Welfare, Antidiscrimination in Employment, 83rd Cong., 2nd sess., 1954, 358.

19. The classic statistical study is Lieberson's *A Piece of the Pie*, but multivariate analysis of IPUMS data on northern cities indicates that the "new" immigrants may have begun to overcome their occupational disadvantage vis-à-vis native-born whites of native parentage (as well as "old" immigrants) starting in the 1940s. For a detailed discussion, see Tolnay, "Trends in the Relative Occupational Status," 619, 623; Reed Ueda, *Postwar Immigrant America: A Social History* (Boston: Bedford Books of St. Martin's Press, 1994); Desmond King, *Making Americans: Immigration, Race, and the Origins of Diverse Democracy* (Cambridge: Harvard University Press, 2000); Mae M. Ngai, *Impossible Subjects: Illegal Aliens and the Making of Modern America* (Princeton: Princeton University Press, 2004); Aristide R. Zolberg, *A Nation by Design: Immigration Policy in the Fashioning of America* (New York: Russell Sage Foundation, and Cambridge, MA: Harvard University Press, 2006); Thomas A. Guglielmo, *White on Arrival: Italians, Race, Color, and Power in Chicago, 1890–1945* (New York: Oxford University Press, 2003); Cybelle Fox, "Race, Immigration, and the American Welfare State, 1900–1950," Ph.D. diss. Harvard University, forthcoming. One example of preferential treatment in favor of white ethnics was the case of court attendants, which were largely "Irish Catholic jobs" in New York City. See MacLean, *Freedom Is Not Enough*, 55. For a critical contribution to our understanding of the relationship between race and ethnicity, see Hattam, *In the Shadow of Race*. The subject of panethnicity has received important attention from sociologists. For instance, see Yen Le Espiritu, *Asian American Panethnicity: Bridging Institutions and Identities* (Philadelphia: Temple University Press, 1992) and Dina Okamoto, "Toward a Theory of Panethnicity: Explaining Asian American Collective Action," *American Sociological Review* (December 2003): 811–42; as well as Dina Okamoto, "Institutional Panethnicity: Boundary Formation in Asian-American Organizing," *Social Forces* 85 (September 2006): 1–25. By contrast, interracialism remains seriously understudied by sociologists. For a path-breaking work on the topic, see Moon-Kie Jung, *Reworking Race: The Making of Hawaii's Interracial Labor Movement* (New York: Columbia University Press, 2006); and Moon-Kie Jung, "Interracialism: The Ideological Transformation of Hawaii's Working Class," *American Sociological Review* 68 (June 2003): 373–400.

20. Wayne A. Santoro aptly distinguishes between "dramatic events" and "conventional politics" in a time-series analysis of black protest, public opinion, and the passage of civil rights legislation. Santoro finds evidence that the "first wave" of breakthrough laws (e.g., the Civil Rights Act of 1964) was associated with black protest and segregationist violence. The passage of such laws, however, led to the demobilization of the civil rights movement, diminishing the importance of dramatic events and heightening the impact of conventional politics on

the "second wave" of legislation (e.g., the Equal Employment Opportunity Act of 1972), especially the role of public opinion. See Wayne A. Santoro, "The Civil Rights Movement's Struggles for Fair Employment: 'A Dramatic Events-Conventional Politics' Model," *Social Forces* 81 (September 2002): 177–206. I argue that a prior wave of FEP legislation actually happened in the states, where the importance of conventional politics vastly outweighed the importance of dramatic events. I also find that conventional politics and dramatic events both dynamically shaped the emergence of first-wave national legislation. For a look at the politics of implementation, see Walton, *When the Marching Stopped*.

21. Kesselman, *The Social Politics of the FEPC*; Ruchames; *Race, Jobs, and Politics*; Lockard, *Toward Equal Opportunity*, 29–43; University of Chicago Committee on Education Training and Research in Race Relations, *Dynamics of State Campaigns for Fair Employment Legislation* (Chicago: American Council on Race Relations, 1950); Chen, "From Fair Employment to Equal Employment Opportunity and Beyond," 85–86; and especially Kevin M. Schultz, "The FEPC and the Legacy of the Labor-Based Civil Rights Movement of the 1940s," *Labor History* 49 (2008): 71–92. See also Cheryl Lynn Greenberg, *Troubling the Waters: Black-Jewish Relations in the American Century* (Princeton: Princeton University Press, 2006).

22. Arnold R. Hirsch, *Making the Second Ghetto: Race and Housing in Chicago, 1940–1960* (New York: Cambridge University Press, 1983); Sugrue, *The Origins of the Urban Crisis*, 101, 231–58; Gary Gerstle, "Race and the Myth of the Liberal Consensus," *Journal of American History* 82 (September 1995): 579–86; Nancy J. Weiss, *Farewell to the Party of Lincoln: Black Politics in the Age of FDR* (Princeton: Princeton University Press, 1983); Paul Frymer, *Uneasy Alliances: Race and Party Competition in America* (Princeton: Princeton University Press, 1999); Kevin Boyle, "The Kiss: Racial and Gender Conflict in a 1950s Automobile Factory," *Journal of American History* 84 (September 1997): 496–523; Judith Stein, *Running Steel, Running America: Race, Economic Policy, and the Decline of Liberalism* (Chapel Hill: University of North Carolina Press, 1998).

23. See Sugrue, *Origins of the Urban Crisis*, 91–178. On how the tension between black and white workers played out in politics and law, see Frymer, *Black and Blue*. It is important to note that racial discrimination against African Americans took no single form. To be sure, many employers, labor unions, and employment offices refused to hire, refer, or promote black workers out of blatantly racist beliefs. Some labor unions and employers even made it a matter of formal policy. In 1946, for instance, nine international unions constitutionally forbade membership for nonwhites. A variety of other social and institutional forces, some more intractable than others, also worked to disadvantage black workers. If hired, black workers were often assigned to the least lucrative jobs. As historian Thomas J. Sugrue has written, in a postwar economy that was divided into a primary sector dominated by large-scale, capital-intensive firms, and a secondary sector consisting of smaller, capital-poor firms, "black workers were disproportionately concentrated in poor-paying secondary sector jobs (in service work, for example) or in the worst 'subordinate' jobs in the primary sector (unskilled janitorial, and assembly work)." Pervasive neighborhood and community segregation in cities throughout the United States meant that whites and blacks did not belong to the same social networks. Since many firms "relied primarily on personal refer-

ences, kinship networks, and church and neighborhood connections," blacks often missed out on the employment opportunities that many whites took for granted. Although their exclusion and marginalization varied enormously across industry and region, different forms of discrimination consistently worked together to confine black workers as a group to the most insecure, poorest paying, and most taxing forms of employment. Sugrue, *The Origins of the Urban Crisis*, 92; Sugrue, "The Tangled Roots," 889. See also Sugrue's essay (chapter 4) in *The Origins of the Urban Crisis*, "'The Meanest and the Dirtiest Jobs': The Structures of Employment Discrimination"; and Sugrue, "The Structures of Urban Poverty: The Reorganization of Space and Work in Three Periods of American History," in *The "Underclass Debate": Perspectives from History*, edited by Michael B. Katz (Princeton: Princeton University Press, 1993); Michael Goldfield, "Race and the CIO: Possibilities for Racial Egalitarianism during the 1930s and 1940s," *International Labor and Working-Class History* 44 (1993): 1–32; and the assorted responses by other labor historians in the same issue.

24. Nicol C. Rae, *The Decline and Fall of the Liberal Republicans: From 1952 to the Present* (New York: Oxford University Press, 1989); Timothy N. Thurber, *The Politics of Equality: Hubert H. Humphrey and the African American Freedom Struggle* (New York: Columbia University Press, 1999); Jennifer A. Delton, *Making Minnesota Liberal: Civil Rights and the Transformation of the Democratic Party* (Minneapolis: University of Minnesota Press, 2002), 112–18; Berman, *The Politics of Civil Rights during the Truman Administration*; McCoy and Ruetten, *Quest and Response*; Carl M. Brauer, *John F. Kennedy and the Second Reconstruction* (New York: Columbia University Press, 1977); Dean J. Kotlowski, *Nixon's Civil Rights: Politics, Principle, and Policy* (Cambridge, MA: Harvard University Press, 2001); Fine, *"Expanding the Frontiers of Civil Rights,"* 34–36. For sociological research on the importance of parties, partisanship, and political competition in the political development of public policy, particularly social policy, see variously Edwin Amenta and Drew Halfmann, "Wage Wars: Institutional Politics, WPA Wages, and the Struggle for U.S. Policy," *American Sociological Review* 65 (August 2000): 506–28; Edwin Amenta, *Bold Relief: Institutional Politics and the Origins of American Social Policy* (Princeton: Princeton University Press, 1998); Edwin Amenta and Jane D. Poulsen, "Social Politics in Context: The Institutional Politics Theory and Social Spending at the End of the New Deal," *Social Forces* 75 (September 1996): 33–60; Ann Orloff, *The Politics of Pensions: A Comparative Analysis of Britain, Canada, and the United States* (Madison: University of Wisconsin, 1993). Classic sociological perspectives on political parties include Seymour Martin Lipset and Robert Michels. In a different vein of scholarship, see work in the "party system" tradition, including Steven Fraser and Gary Gerstle, eds., *The Rise and Fall of the New Deal Order, 1930–1980* (Princeton: Princeton University Press, 1989); Arthur M. Schlesinger, Jr., ed., *The Coming to Power: Critical Presidential Elections in American History* (New York: Chelsea House, 1972); James L. Sundquist, *Dynamics of the Party System: Alignment and Realignment of Political Parties in the United States* (Washington, DC: Brookings Institution, 1983); Walter Dean Burnham, *Critical Elections and the Mainspring of American Politics* (New York: Norton, 1970).

25. On the weakness of state FEP agencies, see Herbert Hill, "Twenty Years of State Fair Employment Practice Commissions: A Critical Analysis with Recom-

mendations," *Buffalo Law Review*, 14 (Fall 1964): 22–69; Biondi, *To Stand and Fight*; Sugrue, *The Origins of the Urban Crisis*. A contemporaneous analysis of state FEP legislation was more positive about their effects. See Irwin Ross, "Tolerance by Law?" *Harper's Magazine*, November 1947. For the most sophisticated econometric analysis, see William J. Collins, "The Labor Market Impact of State-Level Anti-Discrimination Laws, 1940–1960," *Industrial and Labor Relations Review* 56 (January 2003): 244–72. Collins finds that laws passed in the 1940s were more effective than those passed in the 1950s. For a discussion of how state politics figured into national politics during the New Deal, see Edwin Amenta, Elisabeth S. Clemens, Jefren Olsen, Sunita Parikh, and Theda Skocpol, "The Political Origins of Unemployment Insurance in Five American States," *Studies in American Political Development* 2 (1987): 137–82; Theda Skocpol, *Protecting Soldiers and Mothers* (Cambridge: Belknap, 1992), 58–59.

26. Alan Brinkley, *The End of Reform* (New York: Knopf, 1995), 5; Boyle, *The UAW and the Heyday of American Liberalism*; Sugrue, *The Origins of the Urban Crisis*; Biondi, *To Stand and Fight*; David Plotke, *Building a Democratic Political Order: Reshaping American Liberalism in the 1930s and 1940s* (New York: Cambridge University Press, 1996); Steven Fraser and Gary Gerstle, "Introduction" in *The Rise and Fall of the New Deal Order, 1930–1980*, edited by Steven Fraser and Gary Gerstle (Princeton: Princeton University Press, 1989); Nelson Lichtenstein, "From Corporatism to Collective Bargaining: Organized Labor and the Eclipse of Social Democracy in the United States," ibid., 122–52; Ira Katznelson, "Was the Great Society a Lost Opportunity?" ibid.; Steven Fraser, *Labor Will Rule: Sidney Hillman and the Rise of American Labor* (New York: Free Press, 1991); Nelson Lichtenstein, *The Most Dangerous Man in Detroit: Walter Reuther and the Fate of American Labor* (New York: Basic Books, 1995).

27. Biondi, *To Stand and Fight*, 147; Rick Halpern, *Down on the Killing Floor: Black and White Workers in Chicago's Packinghouses, 1904–1954* (Urbana: University of Illinois Press, 1997); Michael K. Honey, *Southern Labor and Black Civil Rights: Organizing Memphis Workers* (Urbana: University of Illinois Press, 1993); Roger Horowitz, *Negro and White, Unite and Fight! A Social History of Industrial Unionism in Meatpacking, 1930–1990* (Urbana: University of Illinois Press, 1997); Alex Lichtenstein, "Exclusion, Fair Employment, or Interracial Unionism: Race Relations in Florida's Shipyards during World War II," in *Labor in the Modern South*, edited by Glen T. Askew (Athens: University of Georgia Press, 2002), 135–57; Robin D. G. Kelley, *Hammer and Hoe: Alabama Communists during the Great Depression* (Chapel Hill: University of North Carolina Press, 1990); Korstad and Lichstenstein, "Opportunities Found and Lost"; Robert R. Korstad, *Civil Rights Unionism: Tobacco Workers and the Struggle for Democracy in the Mid-Twentieth Century South* (Chapel Hill: University of North Carolina Press, 2003); Judith Stepan-Norris and Maurice Zeitlin, *Left Out: Reds and America's Industrial Unions* (Cambridge: Cambridge University Press, 2003); Maurice Zeitlin and L. Frank Weyher, "'Black and White, Unite and Fight': Interracial Working-Class Solidarity and Racial Employment Equality," *American Journal of Sociology* 107 (September 2001): 430–67; Michael J. Honey, *Southern Labor and Black Civil Rights: Organizing Memphis Workers* (Urbana: University of Illinois Press, 1993); Dennis C. Dickerson, *Out of the Crucible: Black Steelworkers in Western Pennsylvania, 1875–1980* (Albany: State University of New York Press,

1986). For an incisive discussion of these questions, see Frymer, *Black and Blue*. On the dilemmas of electoral capture, see Frymer, *Uneasy Alliances*. Martha Biondi has imaginatively reconstructed the hidden history of radicalism in the struggle for racial equality in New York City. See Biondi, *To Stand and Fight*. Biondi's study is regarded by some historians as perhaps too imaginative. See specifically Eric Arnesen, "Passion and Politics: Race and the Writing of Working-Class History," *Journal of the Historical Society* 6 (Fall 2006): 323–56. A broader critique of how the subject of race and communism has been handled in revisionist historiography, see Eric Arnesen, "No 'Graver Danger': Black Anticommunism, the Communist Party, and the Race Question," *Labor: Studies in the Working-Class History of the Americas* 3 (Winter 2006): 13–52. Arnesen's essays should be read in conjunction with the reactions to it that were published in the same issue, including essays by John Earl Haynes, Carole Anderson, Kenneth R. Janken, and Martha Biondi.

28. Ira Katznelson, *When Affirmative Action Was White*; Robert C. Lieberman, *Shifting the Color Line: Race and the American Welfare State* (Cambridge, MA: Harvard University Press, 1998); Ira Katznelson, Kim Geiger, and Daniel Kryder, "Limiting Liberalism: The Southern Veto in Congress, 1933–1950," *Political Science Quarterly* 108 (Summer 1993): 283–306; Desmond S. King and Rogers M. Smith, "Racial Orders in American Political Development," *American Political Science Review* 99 (February 2005): 75–92; Joseph E. Lowndes, *From the New Deal to the New Right: Race and the Southern Origins of Modern Conservatism* (New Have: Yale University Press, 2008); Michael K. Brown, *Race, Money, and the American Welfare State* (Ithaca: Cornell University Press, 1999). See also Nicol C. Rae, *Southern Democrats* (New York: Oxford University Press, 1994); Gilbert C. Fite, *Richard B. Russell, Jr., Senator from Georgia* (Chapel Hill: University of North Carolina Press, 1991); Kenneth W. Vickers, "John Rankin: Democrat and Demagogue," M.A. thesis, Mississippi State University, 1993; John H. Barnhill, "Politician, Social Reformer, and Religious Leader: The Public Career of Brooks Hays," Ph.D. diss., Oklahoma State University, 1981; Brooks Hays, *A Southern Moderate Speaks* (Chapter Hill: University of North Carolina Press, 1959); Bruce J. Dierenfeld, *Keeper of the Rules: Congressman Howard W. Smith of Virginia* (Charlottesville: University Press of Virginia, 1987). On attempts to reform Congress and reduce the power of southern Democrats, see Zelizer, *On Capitol Hill*.

29. *LAT*, June 19, 1941, p. A4; November 2, 1941, p. 5; August 4, 1943, p. A4; *NYT*, September 26, 1943, p. 9; *CT*, December 10, 1943, p. 4. An editorial in the *Christian Science Monitor*, entitled "When Rights Conflict," aptly identified the ideological and political clash at the heart of the struggle over FEPC. See "When Rights Conflict," *Christian Science Monitor*, January 26, 1950. The literature on the rise of the conservative movement is growing rapidly, but see especially Steven Teles, *The Rise of the Conservative Legal Movement* (Princeton: Princeton University Press, 2008); and Thomas Medvetz, "Merchants of Expertise: Think Tanks and Intellectuals in the U.S. Field of Power," Ph.D. diss., Department of Sociology, University of California, Berkeley, 2007, especially chapter 3.

30. For discussions of organized business in the politics of FEP legislation, see Lockard, *Toward Equal Opportunity*, 55; Biondi, *To Stand and Fight*, 19. Among others, Nelson Lichtenstein has written about the critical importance of business

political mobilization in the postwar period. See his "From Corporatism to Collective Bargaining" and Kim Phillips-Fein, "Top-Down Revolution: Businessmen, Intellectuals, and Politicians against the New Deal," Ph.D. diss., Department of History, Columbia University, 2005; Colin Gordon, *New Deals: Business, Labor, and Politics in America, 1920–1935* (New York: Cambridge University Press, 1994); Elizabeth Fones-Wolf, *Selling Free Enterprise: The Business Assault on Labor and Liberalism, 1945–1960* (Urbana: University of Illinois Press, 1994); Peter Swenson, *Capitalists against Markets: The Making of Labor Markets and Welfare States in the United States and Sweden* (New York: Oxford University Press, 2002). There is a robust economic and sociological literature on how firms responded to developments in antidiscrimination law. See Kenneth Y. Chay, "The Impact of Federal Civil Rights Policy on Black Economic Progress: Evidence from the Equal Employment Opportunity Act of 1972," *Industrial and Labor Relations Review* 51 (July 1998): 608–32; John J. Donohue and James Heckman, "Continuous Versus Episodic Change: The Impact of Affirmative Action and Civil Rights Policy on the Economic Status of Blacks," 29 *Journal of Economic Literature* (December 1991): 1603–44; Dobbin and Sutton, "The Strength of a Weak State"; Frank Dobbin, John R. Sutton, John W. Meyer, and Richard Scott, "Equal Opportunity Law and the Construction of Internal Labor Markets," *American Journal of Sociology* 99 (September 1993): 396–427; Dobbin, *Inventing Equal Opportunity*. For the best empirical study on the impact of judicially mandated affirmative action, see Justin McCrary, "The Effect of Court-Ordered Hiring Quotas on the Composition and Quality of Police," *American Economic Review* 97 (March 2007): 318–353.

31. On state politics, FEP, and the GOP, see Lockard, *Toward Equal Opportunity*, 46–57; Fine, "*Expanding the Frontiers of Civil Rights*," 35–62. On malapportionment and representation, see Stephen Ansolabehere and James M. Snyder, Jr., "Reapportionment and Party Realignment in the American States," unpublished manuscript.

32. Moreno, *From Direct Action to Affirmative Action*, 219. See also Henry Lee Moon, *Balance of Power* (Garden City, NY: Double Day, 1948).

33. Lawrence M. Friedman, *A History of American Law*, 2nd ed. (New York: Simon & Schuster, 1985), 657. Exemplars of the "social interpretation" of social and economic policy, include Quadagno, *Color of Welfare*; Jill Quadagno, *One Nation, Uninsured* (New York: Oxford University Press, 2005); Jill Quadagno, *The Transformation of Old Age Security: Class and Politics in the American Welfare State* (Chicago: University of Chicago Press, 1988); Peter Baldwin, *The Politics of Social Solidarity: Class Bases in the European Welfare State, 1875–1975* (New York: Cambridge University Press, 1990); Gøsta Esping-Anderson, *Three Worlds of Welfare Capitalism* (Princeton: Princeton University Press, 1990); Walter Korpi, "Power, Politics, and State Autonomy in the Development of Social Citizenship," *American Sociological Review* 54 (June 1989): 309–28; Gøsta Esping-Anderson, *Politics against Markets: The Social Democratic Road to Power* (Princeton: Princeton University Press, 1985); Walter Korpi, *The Democratic Class Struggle* (London: Routledge, 1983); Walter Korpi, *The Working Class in Welfare Capitalism* (London: Routledge, 1978). Despite their appeal, sociological perspectives have attracted strong criticism, and not entirely without

justification. Their crudest variants are certainly deserving of searching criticism. Policy is seen as a broad reflection of structure or economic forces, serving simply as a tool or instrument used by various social groups to win, consolidate, and preserve their advantage. These groups are unrealistically depicted as historically invariant monoliths, devoid of internal conflicts and impervious to change over time. Moreover, it is often assumed, rather than demonstrated, that policy development is driven by the groups that stand to benefit from them. Inferences about the causes of policy are based more on wish or faith than evidence. Indeed, "interest" is treated naïvely in many cases, with scholars simply assuming that ex post acceptance of a policy by groups can be taken as evidence of their ex ante support for it. Lastly, sociological accounts can easily lapse into teleology and thereby take on a mechanical and impersonal quality. There is little room in them for politics or people and even less room for so many of the things that so obviously pervade human life—luck and accident, cunning and ingenuity, unintended consequences and avoidable mistakes. The individual and collective choices of human beings become obscured. Instead, policies seem to rise and fall at the hour ordained by their historical destiny or theoretical necessity. All of these problems are admittedly evident in past scholarship, to a greater and lesser degree. It is important, however, to remain mindful of the fact that they are not inherent to sociological approaches. They stem from flaws in the application of the approach, not the approach itself.

34. The median voter theorem is famously worked out in Anthony Downs, *An Economic Theory of Democracy* (New York: Harper and Row, 1957). On the Protestant establishment, see E. Digby Baltzell, *The Protestant Establishment* (New York: Random House, 1964); Karabel, *The Chosen*; Peter Schrag, *The Decline of the WASP* (New York: Simon and Schuster, 1970); Richard L. Zweigenhaft and G. William Domhoff, *Jews in the Protestant Establishment* (New York: Praeger, 1982); Richard L. Zweigenhaft and G. William Domhoff, *Blacks in the White Establishment? A Study of Race and Class in America* (New Haven: Yale University Press, 1991); James D. Davidson, Ralph E. Pyle, and David V. Reyes, "Persistence and Change in the Protestant Establishment, 1930–1992," *Social Forces* 74, no.1 (September 1995): 157–75. On the impact of social movements, see Chris Rhomberg, *No There There: Race, Class, and Political Community in Oakland* (Berkeley: University of California Press, 2004); Edwin Amenta, *When Movements Matter: The Townsend Plan and the Rise of Social Security* (Princeton: Princeton University Press, 2006); Kenneth T. Andrews, *Freedom Is a Constant Struggle* (Chicago: University of Chicago Press, 2004); Sarah Soule and Brayden King, "The Impact of Social Movements at Stages of the Policy Process and the Equal Rights Amendment, 1972–1982," *American Journal of Sociology* 111 (2006): 1871–909. For a compelling analysis of how the civil rights movement stimulated the shifts in public opinion that paved the way for the passage of civil rights legislation, see Taeku Lee, *Mobilizing Public Opinion: Black Insurgency and Racial Attitudes in the Civil Rights Era* (Chicago: University of Chicago Press, 2002). In an important study, Hanes Walton offers a vitally important look at the fragmented and largely ineffectual implementation of civil rights legislation. See Walton, *When the Marching Stopped*.

35. C. Wright Mills, *The Power Elite* (New York: Oxford University Press, 1956); G. William Domhoff, *Who Rules America?* (Englewood Cliffs, NJ: Prentice-Hall, 1967). Among works by other sociologists, that of John D. Skrentny emphasizes culture, but it also puts elites—particular policy elites—at the center of analysis. See especially John D. Skrentny, "Policy-Elite Perceptions and Social Movement Success: Understanding Variations in Group Inclusion in Affirmative Action," *American Journal of Sociology* 111 (May 2006): 1762–815, but also his *Ironies of Affirmative Action* and *Minority Rights Revolution* (Cambridge: Belknap Press, 2002). Prominent studies in the pluralist tradition include Robert Dahl, *Who Governs? Power and Democracy in an American City* (New Haven: Yale University Press, 1961); David Truman, *The Governmental Process: Political Interests and Public Opinion* (New York: Knopf, 1953); Nelson Polsby, *Community Power and Political Theory* (New Haven: Yale University Press, 1963). Criticisms of pluralism in political science may be found in Grant McConnell, *Private Power and American Democracy* (New York: Knopf, 1966); Theodore Lowi, *The End of Liberalism: Ideology, Policy, and the Crisis of Public Authority* (New York: Norton, 1969); Charles E. Lindblom, *Politics and Markets: The World's Political Economic Systems* (New York: Basic Books, 1977). Marxist critics include Ralph Miliband, *The State in Capitalist Society* (New York: Basic Books, 1969); Claus Offe, "The Theory of the Capitalist State and the Problem of Policy Formation," in *Stress and Contradiction in Modern Capitalism*, edited by Leon Lindberg et al. (Lexington, MA: D. C. Health, 1975): 125–45. In a narrower sense, Alan Brinkley also privileges the role of elites in his political and intellectual history of the New Deal, *The End of Reform*. On the corporate-liberal thesis, see Gabriel Kolko, *The Triumph of Conservatism: A Reinterpretation of American History, 1900–1916* (New York: Free Press, 1963); James Weinstein, *The Corporate Ideal in the Liberal State, 1900–1918* (Boston: Beacon, 1968); Barton J. Bernstein, "The New Deal: The Conservative Achivements of Liberal Reform," in Barton J. Bernstein, ed., *Toward a New Past: Dissenting Essays in American History* (New York: Pantheon, 1968). A forceful critique of corporate-liberalism is Fred Block, "Beyond Corporate Liberalism," *Social Problems* 24 (February 1977): 352–61. Peter Swenson has sought to make the case that organized business should be at the center of any compelling analysis of industrial relations or social policy. See Peter Swenson, "Bringing Capital Back In, or Social Democracy Reconsidered: Employer Power, Cross-Class Alliances, and Centralization of Industrial Relations in Denmark and Sweden," *World Politics* 43 (July 1991): 513–44; *Capitalists against Markets* (New York: Oxford University Press, 2002); Swenson, *Capitalists against Markets*. On the role of business, see as well Klein, *For All These Rights*; Mark Mizruchi, *The Structure of Corporate Political Action: Interfirm Relations and Their Consequences* (Cambridge: Harvard University Press, 1992); Mark Dixon, "Limiting Labor: Business Political Mobilization and Union Setback in the States," *Journal of Policy History* 19, no. 3 (2007): 313–44; Cathi Jo Martin, *Stuck in Neutral: Business and the Politics of Human Capital Investment Policy* (Princeton: Princeton University Press, 2000); Elizabeth Fones-Wolf, *Selling Free Enterprise: The Business Assault on Labor and Liberalism, 1945–1960* (Urbana: University of Illinois, 1994); Howell John Harris, *The Right to Manage: Industrial Relations Policies of American Business in the 1940s* (Madison: University of Wisconsin Press, 1982); Linda Bergthold, *Purchasing Power in Health: Business,*

the State, and Health Care Politics (New Brunswick, NJ: Rutgers University Press, 1990). For important empirical assessments of business power, see Mark S. Mizruchi, *The Structure of Corporate Political Action: Interfirm Relations and Their Consequences* (Cambridge, MA: Harvard University Press, 1991); Mark A. Smith, *American Business and Political Power: Public Opinion, Elections, and Democracy* (Chicago: University of Chicago Press, 2000). Martha Biondi is a notable exception and emphasizes the role of employers in the racial politics of postwar New York City, but it bears pointing out that she does not provide much primary evidence from employers themselves. See Biondi, *To Stand and Fight.*

36. For a thorough and pioneering consideration of how public opinion shaped the political development of civil rights, see Burstein, *Discrimination, Jobs, and Politics* as well as Taeku Lee, *Mobilizing Public Opinion.* On the effects of public opinion in other areas, see Jeff Manza, Fay Lomax Cook, Benjamin I. Page, *Navigating Public Opinion: Polls, Policy, and the Future of American Democracy* (New York: Oxford University Press, 2002); and Clem Brooks and Jeff Manza, *Why Welfare States Persist: The Importance of Public Opinion* (Chicago: University of Chicago Press, 2007). For work that stresses political culture, see Seymour Martin Lipset, *American Exceptionalism: A Double-Edged Sword* (New York: Norton, 1996); Skrentny, *Ironies of Affirmative Action*; Stryker and Pedriana, "Political Culture Wars 1960s Style"; Frank Dobbin, *Forging Industrial Policy: The United States, Britain, and France in the Railway Age* (New York: Cambridge University Press, 1994). On timing and sequencing, see Andrew Abbott, *Time Matters: On Theory and Method* (Chicago: University of Chicago Press, 2001); Paul Pierson, *Politics in Time: History, Institutions, and Social Analysis* (Princeton: Princeton University Press, 2004); James Mahoney, "The Uses of Path Dependency in Historical Sociology," *Theory & Society* 29 (August 2002): 507–48; Ruth Berins Collier and David Collier, *Shaping the Political Arena: Critical Junctures, the Labor Movement, and Labor Regime Dynamics in Latin America* (Princeton: Princeton University Press, 1991). Key work in the historical-institutional tradition includes Weir, *Politics and Jobs*; Skocpol, *Protecting Soliders and Mothers*; Amenta, *Bold Politics*; Lieberman, *Shaping Race Policy*; Frymer, *Black and Blue*; Sven Steinmo, Kathleen Thelen, and Frank Longstreth, *Structuring Politics: Historical Institutionalism in Comparative Analysis* (New York: Cambridge University Press, 1992); Ellen M. Immergut, *Health Politics: Interests and Institutions in Western Europe* (New York: Cambridge University Press, 1992); Ellen Immergut, "The Theoretical Core of the New Institutionalism," *Politics & Society* 26 (1998): 5–34; Peter B. Evans, Dietrich Rueschemeyer, and Theda Skocpol, *Bringing the State Back In* (New York: Cambridge University Press, 1985); Jacob Hacker, *The Divided Welfare State: The Battle over Public and Private Social Benefits in the United States* (New York: Cambridge University Press, 2002).

37. Maurice Zeitlin, *The Civil Wars in Chile, or, The Bourgeois Revolutions That Never Were* (Princeton: Princeton University Press, 1984), 18; Daniel P. Carpenter, *The Forging of Bureaucratic Autonomy: Reputations, Networks, and Policy Innovation in Executive Agencies, 1892–1928* (Princeton: Princeton University Press, 2001), 35. See also James Fearon, "Counterfactuals and Hypotheses Testing in Political Science," *World Politics* 43 (January 1991): 169–195; John Elster, *Logic and Society: Contradictions and Possible Worlds* (New York: Wiley, 1978).

38. Manali Desai, "The Autonomy of Party Practices in Kerala, 1934–1940," *American Journal of Sociology* 108, no. 3 (November 2002): 626. For a penetrating critique of how case studies and small-N comparisons have historically been conceptualized in sociology, see George Steinmetz, "Odious Comparisons: Incommensurability, the Case Study, and 'Small Ns' in Sociology," *Sociological Theory* 22 (September 2004): 371–400. Steinmetz builds a sophisticated case for what he calls a "critical realist" approach to comparative research, which involves comparisons across theoretical mechanisms and observable events. For a prominent historian who takes a heterodox position on counterfactuals, see Niall Ferguson, ed., *Virtual History: Alternatives and Counterfactuals* (London: Papermac, 1997); Niall Ferguson, *The Pity of War: Explaining World War I* (New York: Basic Books, 1999); Niall Ferguson, *Paper and Iron: Hamburg Business and German Politics in the Era of Inflation, 1897–1927* (New York: Cambridge University Press, 1995).

39. On municipal FEP ordinances, see W. Brooke Graves, *Fair Employment Practices Legislation in the United States: Federal-State-Municipal* (Washington, DC: Legislative Reference Service, 1951); U.S. Congress, Committee on Labor and Public Relations, *State and Municipal Fair Employment Legislation* (Washington, DC: U.S. Government Printing Office, 1952).

40. For a thoughtful discussion and powerful illustration of how "veto points" can inhibit and generate innovation in the policy-making process, see Martin, *The Permanent Tax Revolt*, esp. 19–21. For the leading perspective on racial politics and electoral realignment, see Edward Carmines and James Stimson, *Issue Evolution: Race and the Transformation of American Politics* (Princeton: Princeton University Press, 1989). An excellent example of the burgeoning critique of the conventional wisdom is Brian Feinstein and Eric Shickler, "Platforms and Parties: The Civil Rights Realignment Reconsidered," *Studies in American Political Development* 22 (2008): 1–31. See also Anthony S. Chen, Robert Mickey, and Robert P. Van Houweling, "Explaining the Contemporary Alignment of Race and Party: Evidence from California's 1946 Ballot Initiative on Fair Employment," *Studies in American Political Development* 22 (Fall 2008): 204–28. The phrase "crucial decade" comes from Eric F. Goldman, *The Crucial Decade, 1945–1955* (New York: Knopf, 1956). Thanks to Gary Gerstle for his stimulating comments on the historiographical implications of my work; his comments pushed me to think about my contributions in terms of Goldman's arguments. See Gary Gerstle, "The Crucial Decade: The 1940s and Beyond," *Journal of American History*, 92 (March 2006).

Chapter Two

1. Kennedy, *Freedom from Fear*, 468–69; Harold G. Vatter, *The U.S. Economy in World War II* (New York: Columbia University Pres, 1985), 8–9; U.S. Department of Commerce, *Historical Statistics of the United States, Bicentennial Edition, Part I* (Washington, DC: U.S. Government Printing Office, 1975), 126; *NYT*, December 30, 1940, p. 6; *NYT*, January 5, 1941, RP1; *NYT*, January 5, 1941, p. 1; *NYT*, March 12, 1941, p. 1. See also Richard Polenberg, *War and Society: The United States, 1941–1945* (Westport, CT: Greenwood, 1972), 5–36.

2. "President Orders an Even Break For Minorities in Defense Jobs," *NYT,* June 26, 1941; Weaver, *Negro Labor.* For the most sophisticated econometric assessment, see William J. Collins, "Race, Roosevelt, and Wartime Production," *American Economic Review,* 91 (March 2001): 272–86. For an assessment of how the FEPC impacted employment practices in the Midwest, see Andrew Edmund Kersten, *Race, Jobs, and the War: FEPC in the Midwest, 1941–1946* (Urbana and Chicago: University of Illinois Press, 2000).

3. E. E. Schattschneider, *Politics, Pressures, and the Tariff* (New York: Prentice-Hall, 1935), 288, quoted in Paul Pierson, "When Effect Becomes Cause: Policy Feedback and Political Change," *World Politics* 45 (July 1993): 595–628, esp. 585; Graham, *The Civil Rights Era,* 14; Denton L. Watson, *Lion in the Lobby: Clarence Mitchell, Jr.'s Struggle for the Passage of Civil Rights Laws* (New York: Morrow, 1990), 131. Though their perspectives are now only beginning to influence mainstream narratives of the civil rights movement, many other scholars have stressed the importance of the Second World War, especially Louis Ruchames, *Race, Jobs, and Politics: The Story of the FEPC* (New York: Columbia University Press, 1953); Richard Dalfiume, "The 'Forgotten' Years of the Negro Revolution," *Journal of American History* 55 (June 1968): 90–91; Sitkoff, "Racial Militancy and Interracial Violence in the Second World War," 661–82; Korstad and Lichtenstein, "Opportunities Found and Lost," 786–87; Merl E. Reed, *Seedtime for the Modern Civil Rights Movement: The President's Committee on Fair Employment Practice* (Baton Rouge: Louisiana State University Press, 1991), 345–57; Biondi, *To Stand and Fight;* Anderson, *The Pursuit of Fairness;* Risa L. Goluboff, "The Thirteenth Amendment and the Lost Origins of Civil Rights," *Duke Law Journal* 50 (April 2001): 1609–86; Goluboff, " 'Let Economic Equality Take Care of Itself": The NAACP, Labor Litigation, and the Making of Civil Rights in the 1940s," *UCLA Law Review* 52 (June 2005): 1395–486. For earlier versions of the argument that the establishment of the wartime FEPC fed back decisively into the postwar politics of civil rights, see Chen, "From Fair Employment to Equal Employment Opportunity and Beyond," 47–115; Chen, "The Party of Lincoln and the Politics of State Fair Employment Practices Legislation, 1945–1964," 1717. Kevin Schultz develops a similar point in his fascinating and important study of how struggles over FEP led directly to the creation of the LCCR. See Schultz, "The FEPC and the Legacy of the Labor-Based Civil Rights Movement of the 1940s," *Labor History* 49 (February 2008): 71–92.

4. Burstein, *Discrimination, Jobs, and Politics;* Lieberman, *Shaping Race Policy;* Frymer, *Black and Blue;* Klinkner and Smith, *Unsteady March;* Dudziak, *Cold War Civil Rights.* Moreno's analysis is attentive to the role of conservatives like Taft, but key failures to enact legislation are attributed to southern Democrats. See Moreno, *From Direct Action to Affirmative Action,* 170, 176.

5. Kennedy, *Freedom from Fear,* 38–39; William E. Leuchtenberg, *Franklin D. Roosevelt and the New Deal* (New York: Harper and Row, 1963), 1–3; Klinkner and Smith, *The Unsteady March,* 125; Harvard Sitkoff, *A New Deal for Blacks: The Emergence of Civil Rights as a National Issue* (New York: Oxford University Press, 1978), 34–39; Jaynes and Williams, Jr., eds., *A Common Destiny,* 271.

6. Robert C. Weaver, *Negro Labor*, 15, 19–20, 146–47; employers and unions quoted in Kennedy, *Freedom from Fear*, 765; Myrdal, *An American Dilemma*, 2:412, quoted in Louis Ruchames, *Race, Jobs, and Politics*, 12.

7. Sitkoff, "Racial Militancy and Interracial Violence in the Second World War"; *Pittsburgh Courier*, January 31, 1942, 3; Wilkins quoted in Bracey, Jr., and Meier, "Allies or Adversaries? The NAACP, A. Philip Randolph and the 1941 March on Washington," *Georgia Historical Quarterly* 75 (Spring 1991): 4–6; *CD*, January 25, 1941, 14; Walter White, "It's Our Country, Too," *Saturday Evening Post*, December 14, 1940; Herbert Garfinkel, *When Negroes March: The March on Washington Movement in the Organizational Politics for FEPC* (Glencoe, IL: Free Press, 1959), 33.

8. Ruchames, *Race, Jobs, and Politics*, 17–21; Garfinkel, *When Negroes March*; Richard M. Dalfiume, *Desegregation of the U.S. Armed Forces* (Columbia: University of Missouri Press, 1969), 37–43; Jervis Anderson, *A. Philip Randolph: A Biographical Portrait* (New York: Harcourt, Brace, Jovanovich, 1972), 247–60; A. Philip Randolph to Aubrey Williams, June 16, 1941, Folder: March on Washington, Box 3, Aubrey Williams Papers (hereafter Williams Papers), Franklin Delano Roosevelt Presidential Library (hereafter FDRL); Robert P. Patterson to General Watson, June 3, 1941, Official File 391, Folder: March on Washington, 1937–45, Williams Papers. See also Klinkner and Smith, *The Unsteady March*, 151–160; Beth Tompkins Bates, *Pullman Porters and the Rise of Protest Politics in Black America, 1925–1945* (Chapel Hill: University of North Carolina Press, 2000); Eric Arnesen, *Brotherhoods of Color: Black Railroad Workers and the Struggle for Equality* (Cambridge, MA: Harvard University Press, 2002). No matter how pressing the need for recruitment, military officials remained deeply reluctant to integrate the armed forces. Instead, they promoted the patriotism of black heroes like Joe Louis, hoping, in the words of Lauren Rebecca Sklaroff, that "the use of black cultural symbols could reconcile the escalating 'Negro problem' with official pronouncements of American egalitarianism." See Lauren Rebecca Sklaroff, "Constructing G.I. Joe Louis: Cultural Solutions to the 'Negro Problem' during World War II," *Journal of American History* 89 (December 2002): 958–83. For a fascinating look at the American tradition of marching on Washington, see Lucy Barber, *Marching on Washington: The Forging of an American Tradition* (Berkeley: University of California Press, 2004).

9. *CD*, July 12, 1941, p. 14; Klinkner and Smith, *The Unsteady March*, 160; Weiss, *Farewell to the Party of Lincoln*.

10. Reed, *Seedtime for the Modern Civil Rights Movement*; Anderson, *A. Philip Randolph*, 258; Memorandum from Robert P. Patterson and James V. Forrestal to FDR, June 24, 1941, President's Official File 93, Folder: Colored Matters (Negroes), June-July 1941, FDRL. For different perspectives on the impact of the FEPC, see Kersten, *Race, Jobs, and the War*; Reed, *Seedtime of the Modern Civil Rights Movement*; Cletus E. Daniel, *Chicano Workers and the Politics of Fairness, 1941–1945* (Austin: University of Texas Press, 1991); James Wolfinger, "'An Equal Opportunity to Make a Living—and a Life': The FEPC and Postwar Black Politics," *Labor* 4 (2007): 65–94; Kryder, *Divided Arsenal*; Klinkner and Smith, *The Unsteady March*. For statistical evidence, see Collins, "Race, Roosevelt, and Wartime Production."

11. Reed, *Seedtime of the Modern Civil Rights Movement*, 72–73, 75.

12. *NYT*, February 12, 1944, p. 12; *NYT*, February 29, 1944, p. 34; *NYT*, March 25, 1944, p. 1; *NYT*, May 25, 1944, p. 7; *NYT*, June 11, 1944, p. 5; *NYT*, June 17, 1944, p. 26; Fite, *Richard B. Russell*; Reed, *Seedtime for the Modern Civil Rights Movement*, 157; Ruchames, *Race, Jobs, and Politics*, 131–32; Kryder, *Divided Arsenal*; Kersten, *Race, Jobs, and the War.* Kersten especially emphasizes the role of the "conservative coalition" in the demise of the FEPC.

13. Skocpol, *Protecting Soldiers and Mothers*, 58–59; Margaret Weir and Theda Skocpol, "State Structures and the Possibilities for 'Keynesian' Responses to the Great Depression in Sweden, Britain, and the United States," in Peter Evans, Dietrich Rueschmeyer, and Theda Skocpol, *Bringing the State Back In* (New York: Cambridge University Press, 1985), 107–49; Weir, *Politics and Jobs*, 19. My discussion of policy feedbacks draws heavily on Paul Pierson, "When Effect Becomes Cause: Policy Feedback and Political Chance," *World Politics* 45 (July 1991): 595–628. For other arguments about the specific importance of the FEPC to the formation of the modern civil rights movement, see Watson, *Lion in the Lobby*, 131; Chen, "From Fair Employment to Equal Employment Opportunity and Beyond," 84–86; Schultz, "The FEPC and the Legacy of the Labor-Based Civil Rights Movement of the 1940s." On the impact of interest groups on public policy, see Dobbin, "The Origins of Private Social Insurance." See also Paul Pierson, *Politics in Time: History, Institutions, and Social Analysis* (Princeton: Princeton University Press, 2004); James Mahoney and Dietrich Rueschemeyer, *Comparative Historical Analysis in the Social Sciences* (New York: Cambridge University Press, 2003). For a thoughtful consideration of how social movements that fail to achieve their objectives can nevertheless influence subsequent politics and policy, see Amenta, *When Movements Matter.*

14. Robert L. Zangrando, *The NAACP Crusade against Lynching, 1909–1950* (Philadelphia: Temple University Press, 1980); George C. Rable, "The South and the Politics of Anti-Lynching Legislation, 1920–1940," *Journal of Southern History* 51 (May 1985); Steven F. Lawson, *Black Ballots: Voting Rights in the South, 1944–1969* (New York: Columbia University Press, 1976), 58–85, esp. 62. The catalyzing effect of the FEPC is also noted by Morroe Berger in his review of Louis Kesselman's study of the National Council. Berger writes that lobbying Congress "required a rapid redirection of the main efforts of reform groups," which had until then been dedicated primarily to publishing circulars and presenting " 'interfaith' awards after heavy meals in elegant banquet halls." See Morroe Berger, "The Failure of FEPC," *NYT*, April 24, 1949, p. BR23. See also Patricia Sullivan, *Race and Democracy in the New Deal Era* (Chapel Hill: University of North Carolina Press, 1996).

15. *NYT*, October 6, 1947, p. 15; Kesselman, *The Social Politics of FEPC*, 87–100; August Meier and John H. Bracey, Jr., "The NAACP as a Reform Movement, 1909–1965," *Journal of Southern History* 59 (February 1993): 8; Beth Thompkin Bates, "A New Crowd Challenges the Agenda of the Old Guard in the NAACP, 1933–1941," *American Historical Review* 102 (April 1997): 340–77; Nancy J. Weiss, *The National Urban League, 1910–1940* (New York: Oxford University Press, 1974); Goluboff, *The Lost Promise of Civil Rights.*

16. Biondi, *To Stand and Fight*, 99, 106–7; Elliot Tenofsky, "Interest Groups and Litigation: The Commission on Law and Social Action of the American Jewish Congress," Ph.D. diss., Brandeis University, 1979; Morris Frommer, "The American Jewish Congress: A History, 1914–1950," Ph.D. diss., Ohio State University, 1978, 523, 527; For examples of Jewish support of FEP legislation, see *NYT*, June 14, 1944, p. 20.

17. Kesselman, *The Social Politics of FEPC*, 101–42; *NYT*, May 24, 1944, p. 19. For a superb analysis of how Jews and Catholics began to resist assimilation and demand equal treatment during the postwar period, see Kevin M. Schultz, *Tri-Faith America: How Postwar Catholics and Jews Helped America Realize Its Protestant Promise* (Oxford University Press, forthcoming). Catholic involvement in the politics of civil rights is ably analyzed in Martin Adam Zielinski, " 'Doing the Truth': The Catholic Interracial Council of New York, 1945–1965," Ph.D. diss., Catholic University, 1989, 338–84; 385–427; 428–70. On politics, unions, and Catholicism, see Steve Rosswurm, "The Catholic Church and the Left-Led Unions," in *The CIO's Left-Led Unions*, ed. Steve Rosswurm (New Brunswick, NJ: Rutgers University Press, 1992); Joshua B. Freeman, *In Transit: The Transport Workers Union in New York City, 1933–1966* (New York: Oxford University Press, 1989); Ronald W. Schatz, *The Electrical Workers: A History of Labor at General Electric and Westinghouse, 1923–1960* (Urbana: University of Illinois Press, 1982); Gerstle, *Working-Class Americanism*. Also active on FEPC was the National Catholic Welfare Conference and its monthly publication, *Catholic Action*. On the involvement of Protestant organizations, see Neil Charles Lucas, "The Political Activities of the Federal Council of Churches," M.A. thesis, University of California, Berkeley, 1949, 83–84; Elizabeth Fones-Wolf and Ken Fones-Wolf, "Lending a Hand to Labor: James Myers and the Federal Council of Churches, 1926–1947," *Church History* 68 (March 1999): 62–86. For critical remarks on Protestant support, see Anna Hedgman, *The Gift of Chaos: Decades of American Dissent* (New York: Oxford University Press, 1977), 77–78, quoted in James F. Findlay, "Religion and Politics in the Sixties: The Churches and the Civil Rights Act of 1964," *Journal of American History*, 77 (June 1990): 66–92, esp. 67.

18. Robert H. Zieger, *The CIO, 1935–55* (Chapel Hill: University of North Carolina Press, 1995), 83–85, 154–60, 255–56, 346–49; Korstad and Lichtenstein, "Opportunities Found and Lost," 786–811, esp. 787 and 807; Zeitlin and Weyher, "Black and White, Unite and Fight"; Gerstle, *Working-Class Americanism*; Horowitz, "*Negro and White, Unite and Fight!*"; Judith Stein, *Running Steel, Running America: Race, Economic Policy, and the Decline of Liberalism* (Chapel Hill: University of North Carolina Press, 1998); John Hinshaw, *Steel and Steelworkers: Race and Class Struggle in Twentieth-Century Pittsburgh* (Albany: State University of New York Press, 2002); Ronald W. Schatz, *The Electrical Workers: A History of Labor at General Electric and Westinghouse, 1923–1960* (Urbana: University of Illinois Press, 1982); Kevin Boyle, *The UAW and the Heyday of American Liberalism, 1945–1968* (Ithaca: Cornell University Press, 1995); Lichtenstein, *The Most Dangerous Man in Detroit*; Quadagno, *The Color of Welfare*. For a superb study of how the fragmentation of federal efforts to integrate labor unions contributed to the breakup of the New Deal bloc, see Paul Frymer,

"Race, Labor, and the American State," *Politics and Society* 32 (December 2004). On the Pullman Porters, see Beth Tompkins Bates, *Pullman Porters and the Rise of Protest Politics in Black America, 1925–1945* (Chapel Hill: University of North Carolina Press, 2000). On race in the CIO, see Michael Goldfield, "Race and the CIO: Possibilities for Racial Egalitarianism during the 1930s and 1940s," *International Labor and Working-Class History* 44 (1993): 1–32, as well as various responses to it in the same issue by other labor historians.

19. *NYT*, January 14, 1950, p. 6; *WP*, January 14, 1950, p. 1; *NYT*, January 16, 1950, p. 1; *Christian Science Monitor*, October 10, 1950, p. 16; Nelson Lichtenstein, "From Corporatism to Collective Bargaining: Organized Labor and the Eclipse of Social Democracy in the United States," in *The Rise and Fall of the New Deal Order, 1930–1980*, edited by Steven Fraser and Gary Gerstle (Princeton: Princeton University Press, 1989). On the role of liberal anticommunism in shrinking the horizon of postwar political possibilities, see Korstad and Lichtenstein, "Opportunities Found and Lost," 786–811; Penny M. Von Eschen, *Race Against Empire: Black Americans and Anticolonialism, 1937–1957* (Ithaca: Cornell University Press, 1997); Judith Stepan-Norris and Maurice Zeitlin, *Left Out: Reds and America's Industrial Unions* (Cambridge: Cambridge University Press, 2003); Sugrue, *The Origins of the Urban Crisis*; Biondi, *To Stand and Fight*; among many others.

20. See Kesselman, *The Social Politics of the FEPC*, 36–37, 222. Writing in 1948, Kesselman's verdict on Randolph is harsh. Randolph's "personality" and "experience" had not prepared him to lead a coalition of "widely diverse groups." He was "ideologically intransigent." He was "naïve about political techniques." He was a "political butterfly" who lacked focus. Lastly, he was seen by too many people as aloof. Kesselman blames Randolph for the NC's persistent inability to secure federal legislation. This judgment seems too one-sided. While it is true that the NC was not the most effective lobby, its files seem to reveal that it catalyzed a veritable whirlwind of political activity. See the McLaurin Papers. A reassessment seems worthwhile.

21. *NYT*, October 16, 1949, p. 58; *NYT*, January 8, 1950, p. 29; *NYT*, January 15, 1950, p. 6; *WP*, January 14, 1950, p. 1; *WP*, January 16, 1950, p. 1; *NYT*, February 19, 1952, p. 22; Ruchames, *Race, Jobs, and Politics*; Kesselman, *The Social Politics of the FEPC*; Watson, *Lion in the Lobby*, 131; Reed, *Seedtime of the Modern Civil Rights Movement*; Chen, "From Fair Employment to Equal Employment Opportunity and Beyond," 85–86; Schultz, "The FEPC and the Legacy of the Labor-Based Civil Rights Movement of the 1940s."

22. Reed, *Seedtime of the Modern Civil Rights Movement*, 215, 350–57; Andre McKenzie, "Lobbying Congress for Civil Rights: The American Council on Human Rights, 1948–1963," in Tamara L. Brown, Gregory S. Parks, and Clarenda M. Phillips, eds., *African American Fraternities and Sororities: The Legacy and the Vision* (Lexington: University Press of Kentucky, 2005); *NYT*, July 19, 2001, p. B9; James T. Patterson, *Brown v. Board of Education: A Civil Rights Milestone and Its Trouble Legacy* (New York: Oxford University Press, 2001), 5–6; Nathaniel Popper, "Law as Social Action: A Life in Advocacy," *Forward*, January 9, 2004; Will Maslow to Letter to the Editor, March 1, 1947, p. 14; American Jewish Congress Commission on Law and Social Action, *The Work of the CLSA:*

A Bibliography of Representative Publications (New York: American Jewish Congress, 1957); Biondi, *To Stand and Fight*, 106; Paul Sifton, Memorandum, January 20, 1947, Folder: Administrative, McLauren Papers; Minutes of the Legal Committee of the National Council for a Permanent FEPC, November 26, 1946, McLauren Papers; Denton Watson, *Lion in the Lobby: Clarence Mitchell, Jr.'s Struggle for the Passage of Civil Rights Laws* (New York: Morrow, 1990), 134.

23. Alan Brinkley, *The End of Reform* (New York: Knopf, 1995), 62–63; Graham, *The Civil Rights Era*, 11, 14, 19–34. On the history and operation of the NLRB, see Terry Moe, "Control and Feedback in Economic Regulation: The Case of the NLRB," *American Political Science Review* 79 (December 1985): 1095–97; James A. Gross, *The Making of the National Labor Relations Board: A Study in Economics, Politics, and the Law* (Albany: State University of New York Press, 1981); James A. Gross, *Broken Promise: The Subversion of U.S. Labor Relations Policy, 1947–1994* (Philadelphia: Temple University Press, 1996); Christopher L. Tomlins, *The State and the Unions: Labor Relations, Law, and the Organized Labor Movement in America, 1880–1960* (New York: Cambridge University Press, 1985); Frank W. McCulloch and Tim Bornstein, *The National Labor Relations Board* (New York: Praeger, 1974).

24. Myrdal, *An American Dilemma*, xlvii; Walter A. Jackson, *Gunnar Myrdal and America's Conscience: Social Engineering and Racial Liberalism, 1938–1987* (Chapel Hill: University of North Carolina Press, 1990); *WP*, April 29, 1945, p. 8; *WP*, February 11, 1945, p. B4.

25. Will Maslow, "Fair Employment, State by State," *Nation*, April 1945, p. 411; Will Maslow and Joseph B. Robison, "Legislating against Discrimination," *Social Action* 15 (January 15, 1949): 6; Will Maslow and Joseph B. Robison, "Civil Rights Legislation and the Fight for Equality, 1862–1952," *University of Chicago Law Review* 20 (Spring 1953); *NYT*, November 16, 1951, p. 18; Statement of Representative Helen Gahagan Douglas in Support of H.R. 792, May 11, 1949, p.4, Folder 1, Box 53, Douglas (Helen) Papers; U.S. Senate, Subcommittee of the Committee on Labor and Public Welfare, *Antidiscrimination in Employment*, 80 Cong., 1 sess., June 11–13, 18–20, July 16–18, 1947, pp. 433, 442; Statement by U.S. Senator Irving M. Ives on Behalf of S. 1728, May 8, 1950, Folder: S. 1728, Box 214, Irving M. Ives Papers, Carl A. Kroch Library, Cornell University (hereafter Ives Papers). Hubert Humphrey's racial politics are valuably traced in Thurber, *The Politics of Equality* and in Delton, *Making Minnesota Liberal*.

26. Mary T. Norton, "Questions and Answers About A Permanent Fair Employment Practice Commission," April 27, 1945, Folder 12, Box 8c, Douglas (Helen) Papers. A similar structure of exposition was adopted by the National Council for a Permanent FEPC in a promotional pamphlet they distributed the next year. See NC, "Arguments Most Frequently Used For and Against Federal Permanent FEPC Legislation," January 30, 1946, Folder 8c, Box 12, Douglas (Helen) Papers.

27. Editorial, *NYT*, January 24, 1946; A. Philip Randolph to the editor of the *NYT*, January 29, 1946, p. 19.

28. R.G. Martin, "FEP Rally," *New Republic*, March 18, 1946, pp. 379–81; Midwest Debate Bureau, *Debate Handbook: Compulsory Fair Employment Prac-*

tices (Normal, IL: Midwest Debate Bureau, 1952). The topic for the National Debate Tournament in 1952–53, held at West Point, was "RESOLVED: That the Congress of the United States should enact a compulsory fair employment practices law." See also Felix S. Cohen, "The People vs. Discrimination: The FEPC Initiates a New Epoch," *Commentary* (March 1946): 17; Malcolm Ross, "The Outlook for a New FEPC: The 80th Congress and Job Discrimination," *Commentary* (April 1947): 305–6; Robert J. Alexander, "Fair Employment Practices Legislation," *Canadian Forum* (May 1948): 21.

29. *WP*, February 11, 1945, p. B4; *Appendix to the Congressional Record*, 78th Cong., 2 sess., June 15, 1944, p. A3032; iPoll Databank (Roper Center for Public Opinion Research, University of Connecticut), http://www.ropercenter .uconn.edu/ipoll.html (Gallup Poll #408, November 1947, USGALLUP.47-408K.QK10B, accessed July 13, 2006); *Congressional Digest* 24 (June-July 1945): 184; *Congressional Record* (hereafter *CR*), 78th Cong., 2 sess., May 26, 1944, p. 5062; *CR*, 78th Cong., 2 sess., August 28, 1944, p. 7343. For additional examples of such arguments, see U.S. Senate, Subcommittee of the Committee on Labor and Public Welfare, *Antidiscrimination in Employment*, 80th Cong., 1 sess., June 11–13, 18–20; July 16–18, 1947, pp. 429, 433.

30. Truman and editorial quoted in Eric F. Goldman, *The Crucial Decade, 1945–1955* (New York: Knopf, 1956), 60, 182, 294; *NYT*, January 17, 1950, p. 8; Carole Anderson, *Eyes Off the Prize: The United Nations and the African American Struggle for Civil Rights, 1944–1955* (New York: Cambridge University Press, 2003); Dudziak, *Cold War Civil Rights*; Skrentny, "The Effect of the Cold War on African-American Civil Rights."

31. *CR*, 78th Cong., 2 sess., May 26, 1944, pp. 5063, 5058–59; *CR*, 78th Cong., 2 sess., August 24, 1944, p. 7343; Harold Dublirer, "Legislation Outlawing Racial Discrimination in Employment," *Lawyers Guild Review*, 5 (March-April 1945): 104; U.S. Senate, Subcommittee of the Committee on Labor and Public Welfare, *Antidiscrimination in Employment*, 80th Cong., 1 sess., June 11–13, 18–20, July 16–8, 1947, pp. 433, 439.

32. Malcolm Ross, "The Outlook for a New FEPC: The 80th Congress and Job Discrimination," *Commentary* (April 1947): 305–6; Paul Burstein, *Discrimination, Jobs, and Politics*, 15–36; Graham, *The Civil Rights Era*, 13–16. On Congressional politics during the period, see Zelizer, *On Capitol Hill*; Eric Schickler, *Disjointed Pluralism: Institutional Innovation and the Development of the U.S. Congress* (Princeton: Princeton University Press, 2001).

33. On the NLRB-style powers of a liberal FEPC, see Graham, *The Civil Rights Era*, 34; Moreno, *From Direct Action to Affirmative Action*, 163–65. Liberal bills varied in their approach to regulation. Some proposals gave priority to conciliation, while others provided only for enforcement. Some were modeled directly on the NLRB, while others conformed to the Administrative Procedure Act. See Moreno, *From Direct Action to Affirmative Action*, 163–65. But all liberal bills could be administratively enforced. Conservative bills were voluntary.

34. Will Maslow to the editor of the *NYT*, February 8, 1951, p. 32. On the distinction between "retail" and "wholesale" models of enforcement, see Graham, *The Civil Rights Era*, 189.

35. For examples of "northern" Democratic support for FEP, see Ingrid Winther Scobie, *Center Stage: Helen Gahagan Douglas, A Life* (New York: Oxford University Press, 1992), 144, 151; Thurber, *The Politics of Equality*, 73–77; Boyle, *The UAW and the Heyday of American Liberalism*, 110–11; Ruchames, *Race, Jobs, and Politics*; Berman, *The Politics of Civil Rights in the Truman Administration*; Graham, *The Civil Rights Era*. A different, more extensive analysis of sponsorships is Burstein, *Discrimination, Jobs, and Politics*, 15–39. On Dirksen's wartime bills, see NC, *Report to the Nation*, January 20, 1945, 3, Frame 240370, Roll 8 [Box 78, Folder 11], Chavez Papers and Moreno, *From Fair Employment to Affirmative Action*, 219. Liberal groups often fed talking points to liberal legislators. See Arnold Aronson to Frank W. McCulloch, February 26, 1954, Folder: FEPC 1954, Box 1243, Douglas (Paul) Papers; McCullough to Aronson, March 6, 1954, Folder: FEPC 1954, Box 1243, Douglas (Paul) Papers. Many black voters responded with strong enthusiasm to northern Democratic support for FEPC. One of innumerable examples is John W. Allen to Helen G. Douglas, February 10, 1950, Folder 1, Box 53, Douglas (Helen) Papers.

36. *Congressional Digest* 39, no. 2 (February 1950); Graham, *The Civil Rights Era*, 15. In 1947 and 1949, prominent participants in congressional hearings included A. Philip Randolph of the BSCP, Stephen S. Wise of the AJC, Roy Wilkins of the NAACP, Mike Masaoka of the JACL, Julius A. Thomas of the NUL, Walter P. Reuther of the WAU, Charles H. Houston of the Negro Railway Labor Executive Committee, Clarence Mitchell of the NAACP, Will Maslow of the AJC, Herman Edelsberg of the Anti-Defamation League, and Elmer W. Henderson of the American Council of Human Rights. See Senate Committee on Labor and Public Welfare, *Antidiscrimination in Employment*, 80th Cong., 1 sess., 1947; and the House Committee on Education and Labor, *Federal Fair Employment Practice Act*, 81st Cong., 1 sess., 1949.

37. Ruchames, *Race, Jobs, and Politics*, 199–205; Berman, *The Politics of Civil Rights during the Truman Administration*, 173–74.

38. Sarah Igo, *The Averaged American: Surveys, Citizens, and the Making of a Mass Public* (Cambridge, MA: Harvard University Press, 2007); *NYT*, November 4, 1948, p. 8; *NYT*, November 8, 1948, p. E4; *NYT*, October 30, 1948, p. 7; Alonzo Hamby, *A Man of the People: A Life of Harry S. Truman* (New York: Oxford University Press, 1995), 452–66. In his twenty-plus-year career as a U.S. Representative, Joseph W. Martin, Jr., preferred to meet with his constituents at post offices throughout his district, weighing the opinions expressed there much more heavily than the ones contained in his mail. See William Albert Hasenfus, "Managing Partner: Joseph W. Martin, Jr., Republican Leader of the United States House of Representatives, 1939–1959," Ph.D. diss., Department of History, Boston College, 1986, 31.

39. iPoll Databank (Roper Center for Public Opinion Research, University of Connecticut), http://www.ropercenter.uconn.edu/ipoll.html (USGALLUP.072548 .RK101; USGALLUP.439T.QT13B, USGALLUP.081652.RK13, USGALLUP .020753.RK07, accessed July 13, 2006); Burstein, *Discrimination, Jobs, and Politics*, 57. A poll administered by the Gallup Organization in 1949 found that 67 percent of respondents supported the abolition of poll taxes in southern states,

50 percent felt that African Americans should not be required to sit in a segregated area during interstate travel, and 44 percent felt that the federal government should not have the right to take over a case of lynching. For these and the topline results of other survey questions on civil rights asked by the Gallup Organization, see the following polls at iPoll Databank (Roper Center for Public Opinion Research, University of Connecticut), http://www.ropercenter.uconn.edu/ipoll.html (Gallup Poll #439, March 1949, USGALLUP.042949.R13D, USGALLUP .042949.R13C, USGALLUP.042949.R13B, accessed July 13, 2006); (Gallup Poll #407, November 1947, USGALLUP.072548.RK10F, USGALLUP.072548 .RK10H, accessed July 13, 2006); (Gallup Poll #433, November 1948, US GALLUP.JA1749.R11A, accessed July 13, 2006). For the Opinion Research Corporation poll in which a quarter of respondents supported a federal law, see iPoll Databank (Opinion Research Corporation, September, 1952, USORC.52-NOV.R29, accessed July 13, 2006). For the Roper poll, see iPoll Databank (Roper Organization, March 1957, USROPER.CM103.Q08, accessed July 21, 2006).

40. George H. Gallup, *The Gallup Poll: Public Opinion, 1935–1971* (New York: Random House, 1972), 1:748, 810; 2:1082, 1119.

41. Ibid.

42. iPoll Databank (Roper Center for Public Opinion Research, University of Connecticut), http://www.ropercenter.uconn.edu/ipoll.html (Gallup Poll #408, November 1947, USGALLUP.47-408K.QK10D, accessed July 13, 2006); (Gallup Poll #407, November 1947, USGALLUP.47-407.QK12A, accessed July 13, 2006).

43. On the politics of civil rights in the Truman era, see Berman, *The Politics of Civil Rights in the Truman Administration*, 67–100, 111, 124; Dalfiume, *Desegregation of the U.S. Armed Forces*, 174. It should be noted that half of the respondents in a 1948 poll by the Roper Organization agreed with the following statement: "It should be against the law for employers to refuse to hire people because of their race or religion." See iPoll Databank (Roper Center for Public Opinion Research, University of Connecticut), http://www.ropercenter .uconn.edu/ipoll.html (Roper Organization, July 1948, USROPER.48-067.R15G, accessed July 21, 2006). This finding is consistent with the argument that support for FEP legislation was sensitive to question wording. There would appear, however, to be less support in the Roper Poll of 1948 than the Gallup Polls of 1947. At the same time, it is important to note that the Roper question does not ask about *federal* legislation, while all of the Gallup questions do. It is also the case that the Roper question was asked as part of a battery of questions about hypothetical statements that a politician would make in a campaign speech.

44. My interpretation of the 1947 poll results builds directly on Burstein's observation that poll respondents favored antidiscrimination law when questions emphasized that the law prohibited discrimination against those who were qualified for jobs. See Burstein, *Jobs, Discrimination, and Civil Rights*, 56. It bears mentioning, however, that his discussion is not based on questions pertaining to federal legislation but rather on a 1945 and 1947 question about state FEP laws and a 1968 question on FEP laws in general. In contrast, I analyze questions about *federal* legislation, and, as I discussed earlier, I do not find that public support for

federal legislation was evident only when a poll question explicitly highlighted that black applicants were qualified.

45. iPoll Databank (Roper Center for Public Opinion Research, University of Connecticut), http://www.ropercenter.uconn.edu/ipoll.html (Gallup Poll #433, November 1948, USGALLUP.011749.R10B, accessed July 13, 2006). The results discussed in the main text are derived from Form K, but the findings of Form T are highly comparable. See iPoll Databank (Roper Center for Public Opinion Research, University of Connecticut), http://www.ropercenter.uconn.edu/ ipoll.html (Gallup Poll #433, November 1948, USGALLUP.433T.QT10B, accessed July 13, 2006).

46. Katznelson, *When Affirmative Action Was White*; Katznelson, Geiger, and Kryder, "Limiting Liberalism"; Jill Quadagno, *The Transformation of Old Age Security*; Troy Duster, "Individual Fairness, Group Preferences, and the California Strategy," *Representations* 55 (Summer 1996): 41–58; Lieberman, *Shifting the Color Line*; Brown, *Race, Money, and the American Welfare State*; Raymond Wolters, *Negroes and the Great Depression: The Problem of Economics Recovery* (Westport, CT: Greenwood, 1970); Allen F. Kifer, "The Negro under the New Deal," Ph.D. diss., University of Wisconsin, 1961; Desmond S. King, *Separate and Unequal: Black Americans and the U.S. Federal Government* (New York: Oxford University Press, 1995); Klinkner and Smith, *Unsteady March*, 126–29. For an analysis that downplays the importance of race in the passage of New Deal social policy, see Gareth Davies and Martha Derthick, "Race and Social Welfare Policy: The Social Security Act of 1935," *Political Science Quarterly* (Summer 1997): 217–35.

47. *NYT*, June 13, 1945, p. 25; *NYT*, January 25, 1950, p. 1; Ruchames, *Race, Jobs, and Politics*, 200–201; Berman, *The Politics of Civil Rights in the Truman Administration*, 26; Schickler, *Disjointed Pluralism*, 163–68; 174–79; Lewis J. Lapham, "Party Leadership and the House Committee on Rules," Ph.D. diss., Department of Government, Harvard University, 1954; Quadagno, *The Transformation of Old Age Security*. The six nay votes were cast by Eugene E. Cox (D-MS), Howard W. Smith (D-VA), William M. Colmer (D-MS), Jerome B. Clark (D-NC), Joseph B. Bates (D-KY), Roger C. Slaughter (D-MO). On the southern veto, see V. O. Key with Alexander Heard, *Southern Politics in State and Nation* (New York: Knopf, 1949), 9. For a theoretical and conceptual discussion of "veto points" in the political development of social policy, see Ellen M. Immergut, "Institutions, Veto Points, and Policy Results: A Comparative Analysis of Health Care," *Journal of Public Policy* 10 (October–December 1990): 391–416; and *Health Politics: Interests and Institutions in Western Europe* (Cambridge: Cambridge University Press, 1992). Recent research has demonstrated that the so-called southern veto is more complicated that V. O. Key asserted in *Southern Politics*. In contrast to their position in the depression years, southern Congressmen during the war and postwar period opposed not only civil rights but also labor legislation as well. On this point, see Ira Katznelson, Kim Geiger, and Daniel Kryder, "Limiting Liberalism: The Southern Veto in Congress, 1933–1950," *Political Science Quarterly* 108 (Summer 1993): 283–306. See also Zelizer, *On Capitol Hill*. On southern states as authoritarian enclaves transitioning to democracy, see

Robert W. Mickey, *Paths Out of Dixie* (Princeton: Princeton University Press, forthcoming).

48. Congressional Quarterly, *Congress and the Nation, 1945–1964* (Washington, DC: Congressional Quarterly, 1965), 1637, 1964; Ruchames, *Race, Jobs, and Politics*, 199–205.

49. Elizabeth C. Bruce to Richard B. Russell, January 28, 1946; Stella C. Way to Richard B. Russell, January 26, 1946, both Folder: FEPC Correspondence January 1946, Box 113, Series 10, Richard B. Russell, Jr. Papers, Richard B. Russell Library for Political Research and Studies, University of Georgia, Athens, GA (hereafter Russell Papers); J. W. Cunningham to Richard B. Russell, October 19, 1953, Thomas R. Lynch to Richard B. Russell, May 20, 1952, Folder: FEPC Correspondence, Jan. 1–July 1952, Box 105, Series 10; Russell Papers; J. W. Cunningham, "On FEPC Legislation," n.d. (probably April 1952); J. W. Cunningham to Richard B. Russell, October 8, 1953; Richard B. Russell to J. W. Cunningham, October 16, 1953, all four letters in Folder: FEPC Correspondence, March 1953–December 1954, Box 104, Series 10, Russell Papers. See also Anonymous to Richard B. Russell, January 23, 1945, Folder: FEPC Correspondence, March 1953–December 1954, Box 104, Series 10, Russell Papers. See also David W. Wright to RBR, n.d. (probably April or May 1952; Sam B. Morrison (Minneapolis, MN) to Richard B. Russell, August 25, 1951; Rosa M. Farber to Richard B. Russell, October 27, 1951; R. J. Ellinger to Richard B. Russell, May 16, 1950, all four in FEPC Correspondence, Jan. 1–July 1952, Box 105, Series 10, Russell Papers as well as F. A. Gulicz (California) to RBR, n.d. (postmarked Sept. 15, 1951). Folder: FEPC Special File, Box 106, Series 10, Russell Papers; Mrs. Emerald J. Swartz (Santa Barbara, CA) to RBR, August 28, 1950, Folder Folder: FEPC June 3– Sept. 11, 1950, Box 106, Series 10, Russell Papers.

50. *CR*, 79th Cong., 1 sess., 1945, vol. 91, pt. 5, p. 6027; *CR*, 78th Cong., 2 sess., May 26, 1944, p. 5031; *CR*,78th Cong., 2 sess., June 16, 1944, p. 6034; *CR*, 78th Cong., 2 sess., May 26, 1944, pp. 5027, 5029. For a superb discussion of how the South shaped modern conservatism, see Joseph Lowndes, *The Southern Origins of Modern Conservatism* (New Haven: Yale University Press, 2008).

51. *CR*, 78th Congress, 2 sess. May 26, 1944, p. 5028; CR 78th Cong., 2 sess., June 20, 1944, p. 6250. See also *CR*, 78th Congress, 2 sess., May 26, 1944, p. 5043.

52. *CR*, 78th Cong., 2 sess., May 26, 1944, pp. 5031, 5048–49, 5058, 6034. A major, overlooked irony is that southern Democrats would use the *Dallas News* story to make a different point on the same day. The ad apparently read, "Wanted—Colored man to work at night as paper handler. Essential industry." Pointing out that the ban of the ad was overturned by the national head of the FEPC, Luther Johnson condemned the FEPC for discriminating against whites on the same day that a fellow southerner blasted it for discriminating against blacks! See *CR*, 78th Congress, 2 sess. May 26, 1944, pp. 5029, 5040; *CR*, 78th Cong., 2 sess., May 26, 1944, p. 5053; *CR*, 78th Cong., 2 sess., June 16, 1944, p. 6034.

53. *CR*, 78th Cong., 2 sess., June 19, 1944, p. 6151; *CR*, 78th Cong., 2 sess., June 16, 6031; *CR*, 78th Cong., 2 sess., May 26, 1944, p. 5047; *CRecord*, 78th Cong., 2 sess., May 26, 1944, p. 5054; *CR*, 78th Cong., 2 sess., May 26, 1944,

pp. 5053–57; *CR*, 78th Cong., 2 sess., June 20, 1944, p. 6256. A longer version of Rankin's quote appears in Skrentny, *The Ironies of Affirmative Action*, 156.

54. *CR*, 78th Cong., 2 sess., August 24, 1944, p. 7344; *CR*, 78th Cong., 2 sess., May 26, 1944, p. 5030; *CR*, 78th Cong., 2 sess. May 26, 1944, p. 5039; *CR*, 78th Cong., 2 sess. May 26, 1944, p. 5041; *CR*, 78th Cong., 2 sess. May 26, 1944, p. 5043; *CR*, 78th Cong., 2 sess., June 20, 1944, p. 6256; *CR*, 79th Cong., 1st Sess., 1945, vol. 91, pt. 5, p. 6027; *Appendix to the Congressional Record*, 79th Cong., 1 Sess., 1945, vol.9, pt. 12, p. A3083.

55. *CR*, 70th Congress, 2 sess. May 26, 1944, p. 5030; *CR*, 78th Cong., 2 sess. May 26, 1944, p. 5039. This type of argument did not emanate exclusively from legislators. It was common among many of their constituents as well. As an editorial for the *Kinston Daily Free Press* (NC) argued, "[T]he decent and respectable people of the South, whose lineage goes back to the early days of the settlement of this country and who enjoy the best and purest strains of Americans are getting infernally tired of having a lot of mix-breeds call them names all the time and undertaking to ram down their throats obnoxious legislation such as the anti-lynching law and the so-called FEPC. Such attempts are bold efforts to curry favor with minority groups of self-seekers and get votes." See *Kinston Daily Free Press*, February 11, 1946, p. 4.

56. *CR*, 78th Cong., 2 sess., 1944, p. 6033; *NYT*, June 17, 1944, p. 26; *CR*, 78th Cong., 2 sess., June 16, 1944, p. 6033; *CR*, 78th Cong., 2 sess., May 26, 1944, pp. 5055–57. See also *CR*, 78th Cong., 2 sess., May 26, 1944, p. 5030; *CR*, 78th Cong., 2 sess., May 26, 1944, pp. 5045–46; *CR*, 78th Cong., 2 sess., May 26, 1944, p. 5052.

57. "The FEPC—A Fair Label," *Aiken Standard and Review*, September 1, 1952.

58. James T. Patterson, *Mr. Republican: A Biography of Robert A. Taft* (Boston: Houghton Mifflin, 1972), 269; Rae, *The Decline and Fall of the Liberal Republicans*; Goldman, *The Crucial Decade*. Hoffman argued that the FEPC was unconstitutional. See *Governmental Affairs Legislative Daily*, May 10, 1949, Box 16, Series 1, U. S. Chamber of Commerce Records (hereafter USCC Records).

59. *WP*, February 11, 1945, p. B4; *NYT*, 6, 1948, p. 1, quoted in Berman, *The Politics of Civil Rights in the Truman Administration*, 88; Robert A. Taft to Theodore M. Berry, February 1, 1946, Box 874, Robert A. Taft Papers, Library of Congress (hereafter Taft Papers).

60. Malcolm Ross, "The Outlook for a New FEPC: The 80th Congress and Job Discrimination," *Commentary* (April 1947): 304.

61. Goldman, *The Crucial Decade*, 55; Patterson, *Mr. Republican*, 304; *WP*, February 11, 1945, p. B4; *Elmira Advertiser*, November 14, 1947. The phrase "state ways cannot change folk ways" comes from William Graham Sumner, and it is cited in Graham, *The Civil Rights Era*, 118.

62. Goldman, *The Crucial Decade*, 55; *WP*, February 11, 1945, p. B4; Patterson, *Mr. Republican*, 304. Taft's objection was echoed numerous times in many mid-century periodicals. For instance, see "Equality Is Not Created by Laws," *Collier's* January 29, 1949, p. 74.

63. Statement of Robert A. Taft, n.d. [probably February 5, 1945], Box 605, Taft Papers; Letter from Robert A. Taft to Dave Schoenfeld, Box 1110, June 4, 1952; Taft Papers, Letter from Charles Hollman to Robert A. Taft, January 2, 1948, Folder: FEPC 1947, Box 887, Taft Papers. See as well Moreno, *From Direct Action to Affirmative Action*, 170. Attorney Thomas R. Lynch, a self-identified Democrat from Los Angeles, loved to respond to supporters of FEPC with a question: "Should we then have every sixth President a Catholic: every tenth a Negro: every twelfth a Jew?" See Thomas R. Lynch to Richard B. Russell, May 20, 1952, Folder: FEPC Correspondence, Jan. 1–July 1952, Box 105, Series 10; Russell Papers.

64. F. H. Wendell to Tafft [sic], January 28, 1946, Folder: FEPC 1946, Box 605, Taft Papers; W. P. Purfield to Richard B. Russell, July 8, 1945, Folder: FEPC Material January 1946 "From the Senator's Cabinet" Box 113, Series 10, Russell Papers; Meeks to Taft, December 12, 1951, Folder: FEPC 1951, Box 967, Taft Papers.

65. "Poll Discloses State Support for FEPC Law," *Los Angeles Times*, September 4, 1952.

66. Cohen, "The People vs. Discrimination," 17; "Does State FEPC Hinder You?" *Business Week*, February 20, 1950; U.S. Chamber of Commerce, "Industrial Relations: Policy Declarations of the Chamber of Commerce of the United States, May 2, 1946," Box 11, Series 3, Records of the U.S. Chamber of Commerce, Hagley Musem and Library; U.S. Chamber of Commerce, *Governmental Affairs Legislative Daily* 2, no. 251, December 3, 1945, Box 16, Series 1, USCC Records; *National Chamber in Brief* (1957), Box 12, Series 3, USCC Records; U.S. Chamber of Commerce, Board of Directors, Minutes, 229th Meeting, Washington, DC, March 21, 1947, Box 1, Series 1, USCC Records; Industry Believes: Association Policies on Current Problems Adopted by the Board, 1955, Box 216, Series 16, National Association of Manufacturers Records, Hagley Museum and Library (hereafter NAM Records); National Association of Manufacturers, Board of Directors, Minutes of the Meeting, December 2, 1952, Reel 7, Series 13, Box 199, NAM Records. Fones-Wolf, *Selling Free Enterprise*, 28. For Johnston's doubts about the value of legislation, see Allan Knight Chalmers and A. Philip Randolph to the Board of Directors, National Council for a Permanent FEPC, November 20, 1947, 2, Frame 290567, Roll 13 [Folder 26, Box 79], Chavez Papers. Organized business did not often need to make the case against FEPC because others made it for them. A 1950 editorial at the *Los Angeles Times* was one of numerous editorials that defended what it considered a "very basic right in a free country": the "right of every employer to choose his own employees." See *LAT*, February 26, 1950, p. 4. Organized business also reached out to southern Democrats at times. A top official at the Cleveland Chamber of Commerce wrote Richard B. Russell to let him know that the Committee on National Legislation opposed Norton's H.R. 2232 and other mandatory forms of FEP legislation. See Walter I. Beam to Richard B. Russell, June 13, 1945, Folder 6, Box 58, Series 3, Russell Papers. See also Long Beach Chamber of Commerce, "Obtain Fair Employment Practices By Education Rather Than By Legislation," May 24, 1945, Folder 6, Box 58, Series 3, Russell Papers.

67. Clarence Iden to Dennis Chavez, January 26, 1946, Frame 290125, Roll 13 [Folder 13, Box 79], Chavez Papers; L.M. Evans, "Freedom or Regimentation: Fair Employment Practices Act," in *Vital Speeches of the Day* 13 (June 15, 1947), pp. 541–5; *LAT*, March 21, 1949. For other letters from small employers, see Faye G. Bennison to Helen Gahagan Douglas, June 28, 1945, Folder 8b, Box 12, Douglas (Helen) Papers; R. E. Davis to Helen Gahagan Douglas, January 25, 1950, Folder 15, Box 84, Douglas (Helen) Papers; R.W. McKee to Helen Gahagan Douglas, January 17, 1950, Folder 15, Box 84, Douglas (Helen) Papers; and several other letters in the same folder and box. For his part, Bennison hoped that Douglas would "knock this bill into a cocked hat." See as well the extensive material from Toledo businessman J. W. Cunningham in Folder: FEPC Correspondence, March 1953–December 1954, Box 10, Series 10, Russell Papers.

68. S. 459, February 5, 1945, Box 605, Taft Papers; *NYT*, February 6, 1945, p. 23; NAM News, February 10, 1945, 1, Folder: FEPC 1945-6, Box 605, Taft Papers; Press Release from the Office of Sen. Dennis Chavez, March 6, 1945, Frame 240491, Roll 8 [Folder 13, Box 78], Chavez Papers; *WP*, April 19, 1945, p. 8. There is a detailed response to Taft's bills in the Papers of Charles Culp Burlingham, Harvard Law School Library, Harvard University (hereafter Burlingham Papers). For a fascinating look at a hitherto unknown 1946 proposal by Taft, see David F. Engstrom, "The Taft Compromise of 1946 and the (Non-) Making of American Fair Employment Law," *Green Bag* 9 (Winter 2006): 181. It is not clear that Taft's proposal ever had a genuine chance of succeeding because key provisions were targeted primarily at labor unions.

69. *Cleveland Call and Post*, April 17, 1948, p. 4-A, Betsy Brown, Republican Volunteer Headquarters, "DON'T LISTEN TO LIES!," n.d. [probably 1950], Folder 47, Box 2, OCFEP Records.

70. *CD*, January 12, 1946, p. 12; Press Release, National Council for a Permanent FEPC, July 29, 1947, p. 3, Folder: Master File: Press Releases, Box 4, McLaurin Papers; Press Release, National Council for a Permanent FEPC, September 8, 1947, Folder: Master File: Press Releases, Box 4, McLaurin Papers; Memo, National Council for a Permanent FEPC, Folder 42, McLaurin Papers; *Newsweek*, February 6, 1950, p. 22; *NYT*, February 17, 1950, pp. 1, 22. Rules Committee sits on the bill twice, once on January 24 (5-5) and a second time on February 16 (6-6). In favor of releasing the bill: James J. Delaney (D-NY), Ray J. Madden (D-IN), John McSweeney (D-OH), Adolph J. Sabath (D-IL), Christian A. Herter (R-MA), Clarence J. Brown (R-OH). Against releasing the bill were E. E. Cox (D-GA), William E. Colmer (D-MS), John E. Lyle, Jr. (D-TX), Howard W. Smith (D-VA), Leo E. Allen (R-IL), and James W. Wadsworth (R-NY).

71. James T. Patterson, "A Conservative Bloc Forms in Congress, 1933–1939," *Journal of American History*, 52 (March 1966): 768; Smith quoted in Shickler, *Disjointed Pluralism*, 65. See also James T. Patterson, *Congressional Conservatism and the New Deal* (Lexington: University of Kentucky Press, 1967); Joseph W. Martin, *My First Fifty Years in Politics* (New York: McGraw-Hill, 1960); William A. Hasenfus, "Managing Partner: Joseph W. Martin, Jr., Republican Leader of the House of Representatives, 1939–1959," Ph.D. diss., Boston College, 1986; *NYT*, Dec. 7, 1949, 39; Remarks of Herbert H. Lehman in New

York, October 16, 1952, Folder: Statement of Civil Rights, Herbert H. Lehman Papers, Rare Book and Manuscript Library, Columbia University, NY (hereafter Lehman Papers).

72. *Congress and the Nation*, 1945–1964, p.1616; Berman, *The Politics of Civil Rights during the Truman Administration*, 155, 169–70.

73. Felix S. Cohen, "The People vs. Discrimination: The FEPC Fight Initiates a New Epoch," *Commentary* (March 1946): 17; *CD*, January 6, 1945, p. 1; Memorandum from Paul Sifton to Roy Wilkins, June 20, 1947, Box 35, McLaurin Papers; Johnson, "Legislation in the 79th Congress," 9; National Council for a Permanent FEPC, News Releases, November 21, 1947, Folder: Master File: News Releases, Box 4, McLaurin Papers.

74. Ruchames, *Race, Jobs, and Politics*, 199–205; Will Maslow, "FEPC—A Case History in Parliamentary Maneuver," *University of Chicago Law Review*, 13 (1946): 420–21, quoted in Ruchames, *Race, Jobs, and Politics*, 202; Kesselman, *The Social Politics of the FEPC*, 204; Andrew Biemiller, transcript of radio broadcast on National Broadcast System, February 15, 1946, Folder: House Hearings, Box 4, McLaurin Papers.

75. Ruchames, *Race, Jobs, and Politics*, 204; Maslow, "FEPC."

76. *WP*, December 24, 1945, p. 6. National Council for a Permanent FEPC, "Estimate of Representatives Who Have Not Signed Discharge Petition No. 4," Folder: FEPC, 1944–50, Box 6, Series G, Friends Committee on National Legislation (DG57), Swarthmore Peace Collection, Swarthmore College Library, Swarthmore College (hereafter Peace Collection). For more details on the statistical analysis, see the appendix.

77. Berman, *The Politics of Civil Rights in the Truman Administration*, 141–68; *NYT*, January 17, 1950, p. 8; American Council on Race Relations, "Civil Rights Legislation in Congress," *Report 5*, no. 2 (February 1950): 2; *Civil Liberties Bulletin*, No. 7, November 10, 1949, Folder: Civil Liberties Clearing House, Box 37, McLaurin Papers. Legislative analysts at the U.S. Chamber of Commerce's *Governmental Affairs Legislative Daily* report that some Democrats, including John Lesinski (D-MI) and Adolph J. Sabath (D-IL), were expressing optimism that H.R. 4453 would pass both houses of Congress. See *Governmental Affairs Legislative Daily*, January 4, 1950, Box 16, Series 1, USCC Records; *Governmental Affairs Legislative Daily*, January 12, 1950, Box 16, Series 1, USSC Records. Paul Sifton of the UAW was less optimistic. See Boyle, *The UAW and the Heyday of American Liberalism*, 110.

78. Berman, *The Politics of Civil Rights during the Truman Administration*, 171; *WP*, February 24, 1950, p. 1. The *Christian Science Monitor* approved of the McConnell substitute. See "Progress on Civil Rights," *Christian Science Monitor*, February 27, 1950.

79. *NYT*, February 24, 1950, p. 18; Berman, *The Politics of Civil Rights during the Truman Administration*, 173–74; Wherry quoted in National Civil Liberties Clearing House, *Civil Liberties Bulletin* 14 (July 1950): 1, McLaurin Papers; Ruchames, *Race, Jobs, and Politics*, 199; Scott W. Lucas to Mary McLeod Bethune, March 25, 1949, Folder: Cloture, Box 25, Scott Lucas Papers, Illinois State Historical Library (hereafter Lucas Papers); Scott W. Lucas, "How Republican

Senators Blocked Civil Rights," April 13, 1949, Lucas Papers; Scott W. Lucas to Ira H. Latimer, April 13, 1949, Lucas Papers; Scott W. Lucas to Herbert H. Lehman, June 15, 1950, Folder: Scott Lucas, Lehman Papers; Paul Douglas, Speech to the U.S. Senate, March 17, 1949, Folder: No Label, Box 1183, Douglas (Paul) Papers. Observers at the Civil Liberties Clearing House agreed with many aspects of the analysis offered by Lucas and Douglas. See *Civil Liberties Bulletin*, No. 12, May 1950; Civil Liberties Bulletin, No. 14, July 1950; *Civil Liberties Bulletin*, No. 16, November–December 1950, all Folder: *Civil Liberties Bulletin*, Box 37, McLaurin Papers. So did Jacob Friend, writing for *Congress Weekly* and observing that the Republicans, "except for a small minority, are especially guilty." "They have effected a coalition with Dixiecrats by means of which they give tacit support against civil rights measures in exchange for Southern backing against progressive welfare measures and labor legislation." See Jacob Friend, "The Chances for FEPC," *Commentary*, January 1, 1950, pp. 5–6. Ruchames does not include the first session of the 80th Congress as a high point, but I consider it crucial because it directly laid the political foundations for the climactic confrontation in the second session.

80. Transcript, Oral History Interview with Clarence Mitchell, February 9, 1967, by John Stewart for the John F. Kennedy Library, 20-1, JFKL.

81. Berman, *The Politics of Civil Rights during the Truman Administration*, 117, 192–93; Letter from Will Maslow to the editor of the *NYT*, February 8, 1951, p. 32; *WP*, January 19, 1951, p. 3; Executive Order 9980, 13 *Federal Register* 4311 (July 28, 1948); Executive Order 10308, 16 *Federal Register* 12303 (December 6, 1951).

82. Skrentny, *The Minority Rights Revolution*, 101–3; Timothy M. Thurber, Racial Liberalism, Affirmative Action, and the Troubled History of the President's Committee on Government Contracts," *Journal of Policy History* 18 (November 2006): 446–76; Robert F. Burk, *The Eisenhower Administration and Black Civil Rights* (Knoxville, TN: University of Tennessee Press, 1984), 71, 89–108; *NYT*, January 15, 1951, p. 1; Executive Order 10479, 18 *Federal Register* 4899 (August 18, 1953); Executive Order 10590, 20 *Federal Register* 409 (January 19, 1955); Berman, *The Politics of Civil Rights during the Truman Administration*. Even though Eisenhower's CGC appeared weaker than Truman's committee, it nonetheless sparked the outrage of southerners, who charged that it would impose quotas on federal contractors. "Such power in the hands of government . . . could mean that employers would have to hire proportionate numbers from each of the various religions and sects. Other notions that an administration might dream up could be injected to insure that 'all segments of the population should enjoy its benefits.'" "The Power of the Purse Strings," *Charleston News and Courier*, August 25, 1953, p. 24.

83. Berman, *The Politics of Civil Rights during the Truman Administration*, 79–82, 124–27, 129. The importance of the northern black electorate was even more important in subsequent presidential elections. Writing about the 1952 presidential contest between Stevenson and Eisenhower, *NYT* reporter James Reston observed that the "Negroes in the Northern cities have enough votes to hold the balance of power in any close election." "Negro Vote Now a Major

Target in Campaign," *NYT*, August, 10, 1952, p. E3. For a fine-grained analysis emphasizing the importance of the electoral college, Scott C. James, "A Theory of Presidential Commitment and Opportunism: Swing States, Pivotal Groups and Civil Rights under Truman and Clinton," unpublished manuscript. Copy on file with author.

84. *New State Ice Co. v. Liebmann*, 285 U.S. 262, 311 (1932).

Chapter Three

1. *Hearing on Assembly Introductory 883 and Assembly Print 1138 before the Assembly Ways and Means Committee and Senate Finance Committee* (Albany, 1945), 25–26, Catherwood Library, Cornell University (hereafter Catherwood Library); *NYT*, Feb. 21, 1945, pp. 1, 15.

2. *Hearing on Assembly Introductory 883 and Assembly Print 1138*; *NYT*, Feb. 21, 1945, pp. 1, 15. On Robert Moses, see Robert A. Caro, *The Power Broker: Robert Moses and the Fall of New York* (New York: Knopf, 1974). On the congressional clash over Title VII, see Graham, *The Civil Rights Era*, 106–10, 150; Skrentny, *The Ironies of Affirmative Action*; Anderson, *The Pursuit of Fairness*.

3. Richard N. Smith, *Thomas Dewey and His Times* (New York: Simon and Schuster 1982), 443–48, esp. 446; Moreno, *From Direct Action to Affirmative Action*, 111; Jay Anders Higbee, *Development and Administration of the New York State Law against Discrimination* (Tuscaloosa: University of Alabama Press, 1966), 2–12; Biondi, *To Stand and Fight*, 19–20. Smith's short discussion of the episode hints at a hard-fought, divisive, wide-ranging battle that included opposition from the New York State Chamber of Commerce, the conservative columnist Westbrook Pegler, and park commissioner Robert Moses, who expressed fears of quotas. Paul D. Moreno adds the observation that "large numbers of conservative upstate Republicans" defected from the eventual bipartisan majority. Martha Biondi notes the use of the word "quota" and observes the similarity between the arguments used by opponents of Ives-Quinn and subsequent critics of affirmative action. Graham also discusses the Ives-Quinn bill, noting that the resulting commission was based on an NLRB-style model of regulation. See Graham, *The Civil Rights Era*, 19–22. On the controversy over racial quotas in the hiring policies of key New Deal agencies, see Moreno, *From Direct Action to Affirmative Action*. On the controversy over racial quotas in housing, see Mark Santow, *Saul Alinsky and the Dilemma of Race in the Postwar City* (Chicago: University of Chicago Press, forthcoming). My initial research on Ives-Quinn, based primarily on articles in the *NYT*, is reported in Anthony S. Chen, "From Fair Employment to Equal Employment Opportunity and Beyond: Affirmative Action and the Politics of Civil Rights in the New Deal Order, 1941–1972," Ph.D. diss., University of California, Berkeley, 2002, pp. 158–76, 287–92.

4. Dudziak, *Cold War Civil Rights*; Anderson, *Eyes Off the Prize*; Klinkner and Smith, *The Unsteady March*, 136–201; Gerstle, *American Crucible*, 187–237; John Morton Blum, *V Was for Victory: Politics and American Culture during*

World War II (New York: Harcourt Brace Jovanovich, 1976), 147–220; Richard Primus, *The American Language of Rights* (New York: Cambridge University Press, 1999), 177–233; Karl Drew Hartzell, *The Empire State at War: World War II* (Albany: State of New York: 1949), 67, 88.

5. *NYT*, March 30, 1941, p. 39; New York State War Council Committee on Discrimination in Employment, *Report: March 1941 to July 1944* (Albany, 1944), p. 1; John Bracey, Jr., and August Meier, eds., *Papers of the NAACP, Part 13: NAACP and Labor, Series A* (Frederick, MD: University Publications of America, 1992), Reel 1, Frame 161; CDE, Minutes, April 16, 1941, Folder 20, Box 2, Frieda S. Miller Papers, Schlesinger Library, Harvard University (hereafter Miller Papers); *NYT*, May 8, 1942,p. 9; Max Goldfrank to Herbert H. Lehman, April 10, 1941, Bill Jacket Collection, 1941, chapter 478 (New York State Library, Albany); Abraham Schein to Lehman, April 1941, Bill Jacket Collection; Joseph Curran and Saul Mills to Nathan Sobel, April 11, 1941, Bill Jacket Collection; Gustave A. Strebel to Lehman, April 17, 1941, Bill Jacket Collection. At the beginning of March, William T. Andrews, Daniel L. Burrows, and Hulan E. Jack introduced several antidiscrimination bills. See *New York Amsterdam News*, March 1, 1941, pp. 1, 17, as well as March 8, 1941, pp. 1, 24.

6. *Current Biography* (New York, 1945). See Lauren Rebecca Sklaroff, "Constructing G.I. Joe Louis: Cultural Solutions to the 'Negro Problem' during World War II," *Journal of American History* 89 (December 2002): 958–83; Lauren Rebecca Sklaroff, "Ambivalent Inclusion," Ph.D. diss., University of Virginia, 2003.

7. CDE, Minutes, September 10, 1941; Folder 28, Box 2, Miller Papers; CDE, Minutes, September 17, 1941, Folder 28, Box 2, Miller Papers; CDE, Minutes, October 8, 1941, Folder 28, Box 2, Miller Papers; CDE, Minutes, October 22, 1941, Folder 28, Box 2, Miller Papers; Frieda S. Miller to Defense Employers, September 10, 1941, Box 1, Folder 2, Minutes and Investigations Files, 1941–1945, Records of the New York State War Council Committee on Discrimination, New York State Archives (hereafter COD Records); CDE, *Report: March 1941, to July 1944*, pp. 2–15; Karl Drew Hartzell, *The Empire State at War: World War II* (Albany: State of New York, 1949), 67. On the origins of the complaint-adjustment procedure, see Daniel Kryder, *Divided Arsenal: Race and the American State during World War II*, (New York: Cambridge University Press, 2000), 42–45.

8. John A. Davis, *How Management Can Integrate Negroes in War Industries* (Albany: New York State War Council Committee on Discrimination in Employment, 1942), 3–6, 8–9, 16–17, 22; Higbee, *Development and Administration*, 3.

9. Davis, *How Management Can Integrate Negroes in War Industries*; CDE, "Report for the Month of December 1942," Folder 28, Box 2, Miller Papers; *NYT*, Dec. 28, 1942, p. 18; CDE, *Report: March 1941 to July 1944*, 28, in *Papers of the National Association for the Advancement of Colored People*, Part 13, Series A, Reel 1, Frame 186; Associated Industries of New York State, pamphlet [1945], folder 54: Associated Industries of New York State, Box 207, Series 4, Thomas E. Dewey Papers, Rare Books, Special Collections, and Preservation, University of Rochester (hereafter Dewey Papers); A. E. Crockett to Miller, November 1, 1941, Folder 28, Box 2, Miller Papers, SL-HU. For an exemplary study of the

kind of barriers faced by Italian Americans through the Second World War, see Guglielmo, *White on Arrival*.

10. CDE, Minutes, January 13, 1942, Folder 28, Box 2, Miller Papers; CDE, *Report: March 1941 to July 1944*, pp. 22, 49–76; Frieda S. Miller, memorandum [April 1942], Chapter 677, 1942, Bill Jacket Collection; Channing H. Tobias to Lehman, May 7, 1942, Bill Jacket Collection; *NYT*, May 8, 1942, p. 19; Committee on Discrimination in Employment, *Report: March 1941 to July 1944*, p. 24. The figure for complaints investigated in 1942 covers March–December, not the whole year.

11. *NYT*, Feb. 22, 1935, p. 14; *NYT*, May 15, 1937, p. 6; *CR*, 78 Cong., 2 sess., January 17, 1944, p. 297; H.R. 3986, 78 Cong., 2 sess., January 17, 1944 in U.S. Congress, *House and Senate Bills and Resolutions* (Congressional Information Service). The introduction of the term "affirmative action" into national political discourse is usually traced to a 1961 executive order by John F. Kennedy. See Anderson, *Pursuit of Fairness*, 60–61. On the origins of the NLRB model, see Graham, *The Civil Rights Era*, 33–34.

12. *NYT*, October 5, 1942, 14; *NYT*, December 30, 1942, p. 16; CDE, Minutes, November 12, 1942, Folder 28, Box 2, Miller Papers; Takaki, *Double Victory*, 52–56; *NYT*, August 5, 1943, p. 36; *NYT*, August 6, 1943, p. 14; *Current Biography* (1942). On the Harlem riot, see Dominic J. Capeci, Jr., *The Harlem Riot of 1942* (Philadelphia: Temple University Press, 1977).

13. Walter White to Thomas E. Dewey, August 20, 1943, Box 20, Folder 1, Alvin S. Johnson Papers, Archives and Special Collections, University of Nebraska (hereafter Johnson Papers); Alvin S. Johnson to Paul E. Lockwood, August 23, 1943, Box 20, Folder 1, Johnson Papers; Johnson to the editor of *PM*, March 30, 1944, Box 20, Folder 1, Johnson Papers; CDE, Minutes, September 15, 1943, pp. 3–5; CDE Records; Johnson to Edward Schoeneck, September 30, 1943, Box 20, Folder 1, Johnson Papers.

14. CDE, Minutes, January 31, 1944, February 13, 1944, February 23, 1944, Box 1, Folder 1, Records of the CDE; CDE, *Report: March 1941, to July 1944*, pp. 87–98; *NYT*, March 10, 1944, p. 32; Alvin Johnson to Charles C. Burlingham, December 29, 1945, Box 1-3, Burlingham Papers.

15. Senate Introductory 1693, March 8, 1944, Folder: Discrimination–Employment Background Material, Box 181, Ives Papers; *NYT*, March 10, 1944, p. 32; *NYT*, March 18, 1944, p. 1; *NYT*, March 30, 1944, p. 20; *NYT*, March 26, 1944, p. 44, *New York Amsterdam News*, March 25, 1944, p. 8A, *New York PM*, March 19, 1944; Roy Wilkins to Thomas E. Dewey, March 21, 1944, Folder 6: 1945 Discrimination in Employment, Box 220, Series 4, Dewey Papers; Johnson to editor of *PM*, March 30, 1944; Box 20, Folder 1, Dewey Papers; Johnson to Dewey, March 17, 1944, Box 20, Folder 1, Dewey Papers; Higbee, *Development and Administration*, 4.

16. Robert C. Weaver, *Negro Labor* (New York: Harcourt, Brace and Company, 1946), 78–96, esp. 92; New York State Temporary Commission against Discrimination, *Report of the New York State Temporary Commission against Discrimination* (Albany: Williams, 1945), 22. But see William J. Collins, "Race, Roosevelt, and Wartime Production," *American Economic Review*, 91 (March 2001): 272–86.

17. "Ives, Irving McNeil," available at American National Biography Online (accessed July 23, 2008); *NYT*, Feb. 19, 1930, p. 14; *NYT*, Jan. 26, 1940, p. 1.

18. Myrdal, *An American Dilemma*; New York State TCAD, "Minutes," June 19, 1944, pp. 2–5, esp. 4, 5, New York State Library (hereafter NYSL); TCAD, "Minutes,"August 7, 1944, p. 4; TCAD, "Minutes," September 11, 1944; *NYT*, June 20, 1944, 34. On the railroad brotherhoods, see Eric Arnesen, *Brotherhoods of Color: Black Railroad Workers and the Struggle for Equality* (Cambridge, MA: Harvard University Press, 2001).

19. Johnson to Irving M. Ives, July 10, 1944, folder: Discrimination—Employment Background Material, Box 181, Ives Papers; Temporary Commission against Discrimination, *Public Hearings Starting November 27, 1944* (Albany, 1944), NYSL; *NYT*, November 23, 1944, p. 29; *NYT*, November 28, 1944, p. 21; *NYT*, December 4, 1944, p. 15; *NYT*, December 5, 1944, p. 24. The hearings in 1944 are very briefly discussed in Higbee, *Development and Administration*, 8.

20. *CR*, 78 Cong., 2 sess., May 26, 1944, pp. 5027, 5040–41, 5049, and esp. 5027, 5029, 5030, and 5045–46; *NYT*, February 28, 1944, p. 12; *NYT*, February 29, 1944, p. 34; *NYT*, May 25, 1944, p. 7; *NYT*, May 27, 1944, pp. 8, 18; *NYT*, June 11, 1944, p. 5; *NYT*, June 21, 1944, pp. 11, 20; *WP*, February 29, 1944, p. 3; *NYT*, March 7, 1944, p. 8.

21. *NYT*, December 5, 1944, p. 24; New York State TCAD, *Public Hearings Starting November 27, 1944*, 1:442, 288–305, esp. 298.

22. New York State TCAD, *Public Hearings Starting November 27, 1944*, I: 107, 330, 339, III: 1265–83, esp. 1266; *Hirabayashi v. United States*, 320 U.S. 81, 110 (1943).

23. Myrdal, *An American Dilemma*, xlvii; New York State TCAD, *Public Hearings Starting November 27, 1944*, I: 5, 60, 109, 184, 232, 452, II: 656–57; *NYT*, December 4, 1944, p. 15; *NYT*, December 5, 1944, p. 24

24. New York State TCAD, *Report of the New York State Temporary Commission against Discrimination*, 80–81.

25. Assembly Introductory 833, January 30, 1945, Box 182, Ives Papers; *NYT*, January 29, 1945, p. 1; *PM*, January 29, 1945, p. 11; *New York Amsterdam News*, February 3, 1945, p. 1; New York State TCAD, *Report of the New York State Temporary Commission against Discrimination*, 29.

26. Irving M. Ives, "Why I Favor a Permanent State Commission against Discrimination as Recommended by the New York State Temporary Commission against Discrimination," Folder: January 29, 1945 Ives Statement in Chamber, Box 188, Ives Papers; *NYT*, January 29, 1945, p. 1.

27. *NYT*, February 1, 1945, p. 15; *NYT*, February 12, 1945, p. 32; *NYT*, February 15, 1945, p. 17; *PM*, February 12, 1945, p. 9; Chamber of Commerce of the State of New York to Members of the Senate and Assembly, February 10, 1945, Box 1-5, Burlingham Papers.

28. *NYT*, February 7, 1945, p. 19; *NYT*, February 8, 1945, p. 14; *NYT*, February 13, 1945, p. 8; *NYT*, February 14, 1945, p. 15; Charles C. Burlingham to Allen Wardwell, January 9, 1945, Box 1-4, Burlingham Papers; *PM*, February 9,

1945, p. 2; Vernon O'Rourke to Ives, March 16, 1945, Folder: Correspondence: I–P, 1945, Box 175, Ives Papers.

29. *NYT*, Oct. 5, 1937, p. 6; *NYT*, June 8, 1959, p. 1; *WP*, June 10, 1959, p. A16; Burlingham to Wardwell, January 9, 1945, Box 1-4, Burlingham Papers. See also George Martin, *CCB: The Life and Century of Charles C. Burlingham, New York's First Citizen, 1858–1959* (New York: Hill and Wang, 2005).

30. Burlingham to Mr. and Mrs. John Kingbury, February 13, 1945, Box 1-4, Burlingham Papers; *NYT*, February 13, 1945, p. 22. Burlingham initially asked attorney George Alger to "draft a fine letter to the *Times* to be signed by you and Whitney and me, and a Negro and a Jew and a Labor man." Burlingham personally visited Lester Granger to ask for his signature, but Granger refused, and his response badly rattled Alger and prominent Jewish attorney, Bernard Flexner, nearly ending the effort. Burlingham bought time by asking *Times* editor Charles Merz to "go slow" on editorializing about the bill, warning him that it contained major legal defects. Merz agreed to defer to his legal judgment. A week later, unaware that Burlingham had been preparing a draft, Merz invited him to compose a "full-dress letter." This solicitation was all Burlingham needed to overcome the earlier reluctance of his associates. The final missive was signed by Villard, Alger, Flexner, Seymour, and Elinore M. Herrick. Villard's signature was a coup for Burlingham. There was not a single African American signatory, but Villard—descendent of William Lloyd Garrison and founder of the NAACP— was a worthy substitute. "I had hoped for a Negro," Burlingham wrote, "but Oswald is equivalent to a thousand niggers." See Burlingham to Dewey, January 3, 1945, Box 1-4, Burlingham Papers; Burlingham to George Alger, Box 1-4, Burlingham Papers; Lester Granger to Burlingham, Box 1-4, Burlingham Papers; Burlingham to Whitney N. Seymour, January 26, 1956, Box 1-4, Burlingham Papers; Burlingham to Charles Merz, January 29, 1945, Box 1-4, Burlingham Papers; Merz to Burlingham, January 30, 1945, Box 1-4, Burlingham Papers; Merz to Burlingham, February 6, 1945, Box 1-4, Burlingham Papers; Burlingham to Mr. and Mrs. John Kingbury, February 13, 1945, Box 1-4, Burlingham Papers; "Charles Culp Burlingham" available at American National Biography Online (accessed July 23, 2008).

31. *NYT*, February 15, 1945, p. 18; *NYT*, February 20, 1945, p. 18; *NYT*, Febraury 21, 1945, p. 18.

32. *WSJ*, February 9, 1945, p. 6; *NYT*, February 28, 1945, p. 20. The life, career, and writing of Henry Hazlitt have yet to receive the serious attention they deserve from political and cultural historians. Author of *Economics in One Lesson* (1946), an immensely popular primer that celebrated the free market, Hazlitt began his career in the interwar period as a journalist at *WSJ*, switched during the depression to writing economic editorials for the *NYT*, and then became the "Business Tides" columnist for *Newsweek*, a post which he held for two decades.

33. John S. Mearns, ed., *The New York Red Book: 1945* (Albany: Williams, 1945), 46, 110; *NYT*, February 8, 1945, p. 14; *NYT*, February 14, 1945, pp. 1, 15; *PM*, February 14, 1945, p. 12; *PM*, February 18, 1945, p. 12; *New York Herald-Tribune*, February 14, 1945, pp. 1, 16; "Anti-Discrimination Bill Faces Upstate Opposition," *New York Post*, February 7, 1945; *New York Post*, Febru-

ary 13, 1945, p. 5; *New York Post*, February 15, 1945; *Monitor*, January 31, 1945, pp. 6–7, series 7; Records of the Associated Industries of New York State, Grenander Department of Special Collections and Archives, University at Albany, State University of New York, Albany (hereafter AINYS Records); Board of Directors, Associated Industries of New York State, Minutes, Nov. 28, 1945, series 1, AINYS Records.

34. "Let's Proceed Slowly on This Subject," *Niagara Falls Gazette*, February 19, 1945, in Thomas E. Dewey, *Scrapbooks, 1935–1954*, Roll 32, Rhees Library, University of Rochester (hereafter Dewey Scrapbooks); "Upstate G.O.P. May Oppose Racial Bill: Majority Leader Ives Issues Statement Urging Measure— C.I.O. Favors Proposal," *Watertown Times*, February 13, 1945; "Albany Is Stirred by Racial Measure: Upstate Republicans Fighting Bill Resent Dictation on Those They Can Employ," *Watertown Times*, February 16, 1945. See also *Newburgh News*, February 7, 1945; "Discrimination Bill Draws Criticism: G.O.P. Assemblyman Says It Would Create More Hatred," *Schenectady Union Star*, February 10, 1945; "Racial Bill Conference to Be Held: G.O.P. Assemblymen Are Asked to Parley on Ives Plan," *Binghamton Press*, February 10, 1945; "The New Volstead Act," *Troy Morning Record*, February 22, 1945; "Go Slow on This So-Called Anti-Discrimination Law," *Ballston Journal*, February 22, 1945; and "Anti-Discrimination Bill is Clumsy, Dangerous," *Ogdensburg N.Y. Journal*, February 26, 1945. For notable exceptions, see "An Equal Chance to Work," *Stamford Mirror Recorder*, February 22, 1945; and "The Anti-Discrimination Experiment," *Ithaca Journal*, February 26, 1945. On the partisan allegiances of the black electorate, see Nancy J. Weiss, *Farewell to the Party of Lincoln: Black Politics in the Age of FDR* (Princeton: Princeton University Press, 1983); and Frymer, *Uneasy Alliances*.

35. Garth A. Shoemaker to Dewey, June 25, 1945, Folder 3: 1945 Discrimination Commission, Box 200, Series 4, Dewey Papers; W. H. Kieser to Dewey, April 18, 1945, folder 47: Anti-Discrimination Bill, January–June, Box 219, Dewey Papers; Roy M. Mason to Dewey, March 12, 1945, Dewey Papers. See also Marguerite D. Troupe to Ives, February 5, 1945, Folder: Correspondence, I–P 1945, Box 175, Ives Papers, KL-CU.

36. R.L.R. Parker to Dewey, June 25, 1945, Folder 2: 1945 Discrimination Bill, July–December, Box 200, Series 4, Dewey Papers; M. Patterson to Dewey, June 21, 1945, folder 47: Anti-Discrimination Bill, January–June, Box 219, Dewey Papers; Lillian G. Morrisey to Dewey, March 10, 1945, Dewey Papers; New Yorker to Dewey, May 3, 1945, Dewey Papers; E. Kendall Gillett to Dewey, February 19, 1945.

37. Press Release [from Thomas E. Dewey's office], February 16, 1945, Folder 3: 1945 Discrimination Commission, Box 220, Series 4, Dewey Papers; *New York Herald-Tribune*, February 19, 1945, p. 16; *New York Amsterdam News*, February 10, 1945, pp. 1, 12B; *PM*, February 15, 1945, p. 11; *NYT*, February 14, 1945, pp. 1, 15; *NYT*, February 16, 1945, p. 21; *NYT*, February 17, 1945, p. 26; *NYT*, February 18, 1945, sec. IV, p. 10; *New York Post*, February 16, 1945, p. 5. On *PM*, see Paul Milkman, *PM: A New Deal in Journalism, 1940–1948* (New Brunswick: Rutgers University Press, 1997).

38. *New York Amsterdam News*, February 24, 1945, p. 1; *PM*, February 1, 1945; *Albany Times-Union*, February 21, 1945; *Hearing on Assembly Introductory 883 and Assembly Print 1138*, pp. 5–6, 13–14, 35–37.

39. Robert Moses quoted his own 1938 statement in his 1945 letter to Frederic Bontecou. Robert Moses to Frederic Bontecou, February 17, 1945, Folder: Legislation 1945, Box 25, Robert Moses Papers, Manuscripts and Archives Division, New York Public Library (hereafter Moses Papers); *CR*, 79 Cong., 1 sess., February 5, 1945, p. 782; *PM*, February 6, 1945, p. 10; *Hearing on Assembly Introductory 883 and Assembly Print 1138*, pp. 25–26; *NYT*, February 21, 1945, pp. 1, 15; *New York Herald-Tribune*, February 21, 1945, pp. 1, 30. In the wartime debate over appropriations for the Fair Employment Practices Committee (FEPC), Senator Mead of New York pointed out that the FEPC did not impose "quotas." See *CR*, 78th Cong., 2 sess., June 19, 1944, pp. 6169, 6171. After reading through the transcripts of the 1944 debates in the House and Senate, however, I did not find evidence that any critic of FEPC actually used the word "quota" himself, though a number of them did accuse the committee of forcing employers to hire unqualified minorities. See *CR*, 78th Cong., 2 sess., May 26, 1944, pp. 5026–5063; June 16, 1944, 6021–6038; June 19, 1944, 6148–76.

40. Smith, *Thomas E. Dewey and His Times*, 446, 662–63; Biondi, *To Stand and Fight*, 19; Moses to Bontecou, February 17, 1945, Moses Papers. Previous accounts of the climactic confrontation in Albany appear to draw on news reports in the *NYT* and the *New York Herald-Tribune*, but the hearing transcripts as well as the original Moses letter are well worth consulting for their telling detail. Also valuable are the 1944 transcripts.

41. On anti-Jewish quotas at the pinnacle of the Ivy League, see Karabel, *The Chosen*, esp. 87.

42. *NYT*, February 7, 1945, p. 19; *PM*, January 30, 1945, p. 12; *NYT*, February 8, 1945, pp. 21, 17; *NYT*, February 9, 1945, p. 32; *NYT*, February 10, 1945, p. 24; *NYT*, February 11, 1945, p. 31; *NYT*, February 13, 1945, p. 19; *NYT*, February 27, 1945, p. 17; *New York Post*, February 13, 1945, p. 21.

43. Moses to Bontecou, February 17, 1945, Folder: Legislation 1945, Box 25, Moses Papers; Vivian Schatz to Moses, July 26, 1945, Folder: Legislation 1945, Box 25, Moses Papers; William F. Buckley, Jr., "Rabble-Rouser," *New Yorker*, March 1, 2004, pp. 46–53; *New York Amsterdam News*, May 9, 1942; *Albany Times Union*, February 27, 1945; *Troy Times Record*, February 27, 1945; "New York's State FEPC," *Atlanta Constitution*, February 27, 1945. On Pegler, see David Witwer, "Westbrook Pegler and the Anti-Union Movement," *Journal of American History*, 92 (September 2005): 527–52.

44. *Hearing on Assembly Introductory 883 and Assembly Print 1138*, pp. 62–63; *NYT*, February 21, 1945, pp. 1, 15; *New York Amsterdam News*, February 24, 1945, pp. 1, 12B. On Fiorello La Guardia's stance on civil rights, see Dominic J. Capeci, "From Different Liberal Perspectives: Fiorello H. La Guardia, Adam Clayton Powell, Jr., and Civil Rights in New York City, 1941–43," *Journal of Negro History*, 62 (April 1977): 160–73.

45. *Hearing on Assembly Introductory 883 and Assembly Print 1138*, pp. 35–42; *NYT*, February 21, 1945, pp. 1, 15; *PM*, February 21, 1945; *New York*

Herald-Tribune, February 21, 1945, pp. 1, 30; *New York Post*, February 21, 1945, p. 5; Smith, *Thomas E. Dewey and His Times*, 447.

46. *NYT*, February 22, 1945, pp. 1, 24; *NYT*, February 28, 1945, p. 1; *NYT*, March 6, 1945, p. 1; New York State Bar Association to His Excellency, the Governor of the State of New York, and Members of the Legislature, February 26, 1945, Box 1-6, Burlingham Papers; *Journal of the New York State Assembly*, 168 sess., February 28, 1945, p. 880; *Journal of the New York State Senate*, 168 sess., March 5, 1945, p. 751.

47. U.S. Census Bureau, *County Data Book* (Washington, DC: U.S. Census Burueau, 1947), 272, 276–77; Mearns, ed., *New York Red Book: 1945*, 45–46, 106–10, 565–82; *Journal of the New York State Assembly*, 168 sess., February 28, 1945, p. 880; *Journal of the New York State Senate*, 168 sess., March 5, 1945, p. 751.

48. Frederic R. Coudert, Jr., to Moses, February 23, 1945, Folder: Legislation 1945, Box 25, Moses Papers; *New York Herald Tribune*, February 22, 1945, p. 24; *WSJ*, March 13, 1945, p. 6; Smith, *Thomas Dewey and His Times*, 447; "New York's Tough Anti-Bias Law Stirs Up Debate on Prejudice Issue," *Newsweek*, March 19, 1945, pp. 40–41; "Anti-Discrimination," *Survey* 81 (March 1945), p. 82; "Bias Ban Voted," *Newsweek*, March 10, 1945, pp. 100, 102; "New York Law Bans Job Discrimination," *Life*, March 19, 1945, p. 32–33.

49. Bruce Bliven, "There Ought To Be a Law," *New Republic*, September 6, 1947, p. 20. For the other material, see Elmer A. Carter, "Fighting Prejudice with Law," *Journal of Educational Sociology* 20 (January 1946): 299–306; Herbert R. Northrup, "Proving Ground for Fair Employment: Some Lessons from New York State's Experience," *Commentary* (December 1947): 556; Henry C. Turner, "Tolerance in Industry: The Record," *NYT Sunday Magazine*, August 24, 1947, 14; *NYT*, July 9, 1946, p. 20; *NYT*, May 29, 1947, p. 12; Turner, "Tolerance in Industry," 13–15; Irwin Ross, "New York's 'FEPC' Pays Off," *This Week Magazine*, *New York Herald Tribune*, August 25, 1946; State Council for a Pennsylvania Fair Employment Practices Committee, "Business Looks Ahead to Fair Employment Practices" [1949], General Pamphlet Collection, Urban Archives, Temple University (hereafter GPC). For the most econometrically sophisticated estimates of the economic impact of state FEP laws, see Williams C. Collins, "The Labor-Market Impact of State-Level, Antidiscrimination Laws, 1940–1960," *Industrial and Labor Relations Review* 56 (2003): 244–72.

50. *NYT*, April 5, 1946, p. 19; *NYT*, June 28, 1946, p. 28; *NYT*, February 20, 1949, p. 48; Biondi, *To Stand and Fight*; Moreno, *From Direct Action to Affirmative Action*; Northrup, "Proving Ground for Fair Employment," 554; Bliven, "There Ought To Be a Law," 20; Northrup, "Proving Ground for Fair Employment," 552. See also Graham, *The Civil Rights Era*, 118–19.

51. Maslow, "Fair Employment State by State," 410; Dublirer, "Legislation Outlawing Racial Discrimination in Employment," 104; Irwin Ross, "New York's 'FEPC' Pays Off," *This Week Magazine*, *New York Herald Tribune*, August 25, 1946; *NYT*, March 22, 1946, p. 22. For another glowing review of Ives-Quinn, see "'Fair Employment': Working Model," *U.S. News and World Report*, July 30, 1948, pp. 24–25.

Chapter Four

1. Patterson, *Grand Expectations*, 160–61.

2. Gilbert Gordon, "A New Birth of Freedom in Illinois" (Chicago: American Jewish Congress, 1949), appended to Gilbert Gordon to Walter V. Schaefer, November 26, 1948, Folder 3: Legislation—Fair Employment Practices, Box 100, Adlai E. Stevenson Papers, Illinois State Historical Library (hereafter Stevenson Papers); Berman, *The Politics of Civil Rights in the Truman Administration*, 81–82, 117, 126; *NYT*, November 30, 1948, quoted in Berman; Klinkner and Smith, *The Unsteady March*, 223; Skrentny, "The Effect of the Cold War on African-American Civil Rights," 25; Zachary Karabell, *The Last Campaign: How Harry Truman Won the 1948 Election* (New York: Knopf, 2000); Katznelson, *When Affirmative Action Was White*.

3. Henry R. Silberman, "How We Won in Massachusetts," *New Republic*, July 8, 1946, pp. 10–11. For a deeper look at the passage of the Massachusetts law, see Leon H. Mayhew, *Law and Equal Opportunity: A Study of the Massachusetts Commission against Discrimination* (Cambridge, MA: Harvard University Press, 1968), 77–91.

4. *Boston Daily Globe*, May 7, 1946, pp.1, 2; *Boston Daily Globe*, May 21, 1946, pp. 1, 17; *NYT*, May 21, 1946, p. 15; *NYT*, May 24, 1946, p. 3; Associated Industries of Massachusetts, Legislative Bulletin No. 26, June 21, 1945, p. 4, Associated Industries of Massachusetts Newsletters, 1944–1986, MS 155, Records of the Associated Industries of Massachusetts, W.E.B. Du Bois Library, University of Massachusetts (hereafter AIM papers); AIM, Legislative Bulletin No. 17, April 18, 1946, AIM Papers; AIM, Legislative Bulletin No. 21, May 17, 1946, AIM Papers; AIM, Legislative Bulletin No. 22, May 24, 1946, AIM Papers; Lockard, *Toward Equal Opportunity*, 47. For more detail on the lobbying effort by organized business, see Mayhew, *Law and Equal Opportunity*, 84–85. A comparable scene apparently unfolded in Wisconsin during the 1945 session, when a left-led coalition of interest groups (inspired by the New York example) joined forces to testify on behalf of an FEP bill. The only significant opposition came from the Wisconsin State Chamber of Commerce. Yet the bill failed to pass. Hawaii experienced a similar outcome in 1947, when a liberal coalition pressed for FEP legislation only to see it fall to the opposition of the Chamber of Commerce and their Republican allies. See *CT*, March 15, 1945, p. 29; *CD*, March 29, 1947, p. 7.

5. Letter from Will Maslow to the editor of the *NYT*, July 21, 1955, published in the *NYT*, July 26, 1955, p. 24; promotional materials associated with the radio broadcast of "America's Town Meeting," May 24, 1945, p. 23, March 18, 1945, Folder: January 29, 1945 Ives Statement in Chamber, Box 188, Ives Papers; George E. Conley to Adlai Stevenson, April 30, 1951, Stevenson Papers; *NYT*, January 17, 1950, p. 8; Roderick Stephens to Irving M. Ives, April 26, 1949, Folder: Correspondence, L–Z 1949, Box 192, Ives Papers; Gordon, "A New Birth of Freedom in Illinois." On the flood of state proposals in the 1940s, see American Council on Race Relations, "FEPC Drives Underway in 15 States," *Report* 1, no. 11 (February 1947): 1; Bradley, Phillips, *State FEPC: What the People Say* (Chicago: American Council on Race Relations, 1945); University of Chicago Com-

mittee on Education Training and Research in Race Relations, *The Dynamics of State Campaigns for Fair Employment Practices* (Chicago: American Council on Race Relations,1950).

6. Graham, *The Civil Rights Era*, 117; Fine, "*Expanding the Frontiers of Civil Rights*," 35–62; Delton, *Making Minnesota Liberal*; Lockard, *Toward Equal Opportunity*; Peter Siskind, "Struggling for Fair Employment: The Ideology of Racial Liberalism in the Early Postwar Era," unpublished paper, 1997; Eric L. Smith and Kenneth C. Wolensky, "A Novel Public Policy: Pennsylvania's Fair Employment Practices Act of 1955," *Pennsylvania History* 69 (2002): 489–523; James Wolfinger, "'An Equal Opportunity to Make a Living—and a Life.'"

7. *Shreveport Times*, July 16, 1949. At the same time, some politically active northerners went out of their way to report the failure of FEP laws in their states to southern Democrats in Congress. G. F. Rowlette of Cass Lake Minnesota wrote Sen. Richard B. Russell in 1949 to enclose newspaper clippings on the stunning defeat of an FEP bill in the Minnesota legislature. See G. F. Rowlette to Richard R. Russell, March 27, 1949, Folder: FEPC From the Senator's Desk, 1945–1950, Box 113, Series 10, Russell Papers. There was a fairly extensive round of correspondence between Toledo businessman J. W. Cunningham and Russell on the fight for state and municipal legislation in Ohio. Cunningham shared a brief that he had prepared on the topic in 1952. "There may be something in it which you will get an idea from." See J. W. Cunningham to RBR, October 8, 1953; RBR to J. W. Cunningham, October 16, 1953, both in Folder: FEPC Correspondence, March 1953–December 1954, Box 104, Series 10, Russell Papers.

8. On how the opposition to FEPC was normally "hidden" from view, see the observations of Harold Lett and others in OCFEP, Minutes of the Meeting, January 23, 1955, Folder 1, Box 1, OCFEP Records.

9. Lockard, *Toward Equal Opportunity*; Jill Quadagno, "Social Movements and State Transformation: Labor Unions and Racial Conflict in the War on Poverty," *American Sociological Review* 57 (1992): 621–22; Quadagno, *The Color of Welfare*; Zeitlin and Weyher, "'Black and White, Unite and Fight,'" 430–667; Gordon, "A New Birth of Freedom in Illinois."

10. Lockard, *Toward Equal Opportunity*, 44; *Rocky Mountain News*, February 3, 1951; CCEEO, *Taking Stock: A Final Report on the Campaign for a Fair Employment Practices Law for Colorado* (Denver, 1951), Folder 1, Box 1, OCFEP Records, pp. 28–29, 32; *LAT*, May 10, 1951, p. 2; Press Release, CCFEP, March 23, 1953, Folder 8, Box 2206, Tarea Hall Pittman Papers, California State Library (hereafter Pittman Papers II). The educational materials included one thousand copies of the "ABCs of FEPC"; five thousand reprints of a *Business Week* article entitled "Does State FEPC Hamper You?"; five thousand copies of "A Catholic View" and "It's Your Responsibility" (written for Protestants); and two hundred copies of "Fair Employment Practices Legislation in Colorado" by the League of Women Voters. Useful material on the CCFEP can be found in Carton 4, Folder 6-7, and elsewhere in Records of the NAACP, Region I, 1942–1986, Bancroft Library, University of California, Berkeley, Berkeley, CA (hereafter NAACP-WC Records). See also the Records of the California Federation for Civic Unity, 1945–1956, Bancroft Library, University of California, Berkeley (hereafter CFCU Records). Material on the Minnesota Council for Fair Employment Practices and Merit can be found in the Records of the Minnesota State

Commission against Discrimination, Minnesota Historical Society (hereafter MSCAD Records). Some documents from the Illinois Fair Employment Practice Committee survive in the Folder 3: Legislation—Fair Employment Practices, Box 100, Stevenson Papers, including copies of *FEPC News*, its legislative advisory to members. For a discussion of the State Council for a Pennsylvania FEPC, see Smith and Wolensky, "A Novel Public Policy," 489–523. On the various lobbying activities of the OCFEP, see OCFEP, *Campaign Bulletin*, No. 1, January 12, 1951, Folder 1, Box 1; OCFEP, "Committee Hearings on FEPC," Folder 27, Box 1; OCFEP, Stand of Legislative Candidates from Cuyahoga County on Fair Employment Practices Legislation, October 23, 1952, Folder 2, Box 1; OCFEP, Minutes from Meeting of the Executive Board, December 16, 1954, Folder 2, Box 1; OCFEP, Minutes of Meeting, January 23, 1951, Folder 2, Box 1, all OCFEP Records.

11. *Survey by Gallup Organization, June 14–June 19, 1945*, Roper Center for Public Opinion Research, University of Connecticut. For a methodological discussion about the statistical analysis of Gallup Poll data, see the relevant sections of the Appendix. On public opinion and civil rights, see Paul Burstein, *Discrimination, Jobs, and Politics* (Chicago: University of Chicago Press, 1985). An instructive cross-national analysis of public opinion and social policy is Clem Brooks and Jeff Manza, *Why Welfare States Persist: The Importance of Public Opinion in Democracies* (Chicago: University of Chicago Press, 2007). For a more thorough discussion of how the policy preferences of the mass public may have shaped the electoral alignment of race and party, see Chen, Mickey, and Van Houweling, "Explaining the Contemporary Alignment of Race and Party." California Poll, April 8, 1959, Release #265.

12. *Minneapolis Sunday Tribune*, October 12, 1947; January 30, 1949; July 30, 1950; January 7, 1951; February 22, 1953; February 6, 1955. For the politics of state FEP legislation in Michigan, see Fine, "*Expanding the Frontiers of Civil Rights.*"

13. Wm. K. Ford to Charles W. Baker, March 10, 1949, Folder 3: Legislation—Fair Employment Practices, Box 100, Stevenson Papers; Earl Kribben to Adlai E. Stevenson, February 25, 1949, Folder 3: 1951 Legislation—Fair Employment Practices, Box 115, Stevenson Papers; F. Leroy Hill to Adlai E. Stevenson, May 1, 1949, Stevenson Papers.

14. F. Leroy Hill to Adlai E. Stevenson, May 1, 1949, Folder 4, Box 100, Stevenson Papers.

15. R. M. Westcott to Adlai Stevenson, January 5, 1949, Folder 3: Federal Legislation—Fair Employment Practices Commission, 1949–1952, Box 123, Stevenson Papers; James Morgan to Adlai E. Stevenson, July 6, 1950, Folder: 3—Legislation FEPC N-Z 1951, Box 115, Stevenson Papers; Jennie Johnson to Earl Warren, March 25, 1945, Legislative Correspondence File, F3640:7769, Warren Papers; L.C Ringle to Adlai E. Stevenson, February 10, 1949, Folder 3: Legislation—Fair Employment Practices, Box 100, Stevenson Papers. For other examples, see Lila Caulfield to Wayne Morse, June 16, 1945, Folder: Negro, 1945–1954, Box 94, Series A, Wayne Morse Papers (hereafter Morse Papers); Morse to Caufield, June 20, 1945, Morse Papers; Caufield to Morse, June 7, 1945, Morse Papers; William C. Ardery to Earl Warren, July 17, 1946, Folder: Administrative Files, Public Works-Race Relations, Negro, 1945–46, Series 317, Warren Papers.

For another charge of social equality from a resident of Peoria, see R. M. Westcott to James W. Mulroy, July 3, 1949, Folder: 3—Legislation FEPC N-Z 1951, Box 115, Stevenson Papers.

16. Mildred Field to Earl Warren, January 7, 1947, F3640:3657, Administrative Files: Public Works-Race Relations, 1946–48, Warren Papers; Pamphlet, "Help Save American For Americans," [n.d., probably 1945] Folder 5, Box 112, Series 10, Russell Papers.

17. F. Leroy Hill to Adlai E. Stevenson, May 1, 1949; Mrs. E. G. Kirschten to Stevenson, October 26, 1949, Folder 3, Box 100, Stevenson Papers. L. J. Schmidt to Adlai E. Stevenson, March 30, 1949, Folder: 3—Legislation FEPC N-Z 1951, Box 115, Stevenson Papers. See also Earl Kribben to Adlai E. Stevenson, February 25, 1949, Stevenson Papers; Thomas P. Black to Adlai E. Stevenson, May 28, 1949, Folder 3, Box 115, Stevenson Papers; Mrs. E. G. Krischten to Adlai E. Stevenson, February 8, 1949, Folder: 3—Legislation FEPC N-Z 1951, Box 115, Stevenson Papers.

18. These differences are not precise, and it would be misleading to cite them as exact figures. Further analysis of the raw data, however, indicates that the difference between Dewey supporters and FDR supporters is probably statistically significant. So is the difference between rural and urban residents. For more details on the multivariate analysis, see the discussion in the appendix.

19. Kevin Allen Leonard, "Years of Hope, Days of Fear: The Impact of World War II on Race Relations in Los Angeles," Ph.D. diss., Department of History, University of California, Davis, 1992, pp. 327–31; *Proposed Amendments to Constitution: Propositions and Proposed Laws, Together with Arguments—General Election, Tuesday, November 5, 1946* (Sacramento: Secretary of State, California State Printing Office, 1946); "Group Maps Plan for State FEPC Initiative Campaign," *California Eagle*, November 11, 1945; "Veterans' Bills Lead Special Session List," *LAT*, December 30, 1945, p. 2; *Los Angeles Sentinel*, January 31, 1946, p. 1; *Los Angeles Sentinel*, February 21, 1946, p. 21; *Los Angeles Sentinel*, April 4, 1946, p. 5; June 27, 1946, p. A1; Minutes, NAACP West Coast Regional Conference, March 7, 1947, Folder 1, Box 2197, Pittman Papers II. See also Kevin Allen Leonard, *Battle for Los Angeles: Racial Ideology and World War II* (Albuquerque: University of New Mexico Press, 2006); Chen, Mickey, and Van Houweling, "Explaining the Contemporary Alignment of Race and Party." Jack B. Tenney had apparently spoken on October 29, 1946, at 6:15 pm on KECA and the American Broadcasting System. An advertisement for the broadast in the *Los Angeles Times* read, "Don't Be Mislead! Hear the Facts on Proposition #11." See *LAT*, October 29, 1946, p. 7.

20. Committee for Tolerance and Tenney, quoted in Leonard, "Years of Hope, Days of Fear," 328, 330. On Tenney's anticommunism, see Ingrid Winther Scobie, "Jack B. Tenney and the 'Parasitic Menace': Anti-Communist Legislation in California, 1940–949," *Pacific Historical Review* 43 (May 1974), 188–211.

21. California Chamber of Commerce, Board of Directors' Minutes, September 6, 1946, Folder: Board of Directors Meetings, 1943–1951, Box 2243, Records of the California Chamber of Commerce , California State Library (hereafter CCC Records); CCC, Board of Directors' Meeting, October 25, 1946, 3, CCC Records; *LAT*, August 16, 1946, p. A1; *LAT*, October 7, 1946, p. A3; "C. of C. Opposition

Proposition 11,"*LAT*, October 11, 1946, p. 2; *LAT*, October 16, 1946, p. 7; *LAT*, October 20, 1946, p. A3; *LAT*, October 27, 1946, p. A2; "Employers Group Calls for $2000 Contributions in Plot to Defeat FEPC," *California Eagle*, October 24, 1946, p. 20; *LAT*, October 17, 1946, p. 12; *LAT*, October 29, 1946, p. 5; *LAT*, November 3., 1946, p. 13. For other examples of anti-Proposition 11 campaign material, see Women of the Pacific, *Employers! FEPC Is on Your Doorsteps*, n.d. [probably October 1946], F3640:8854, Legislative Files: Governor's Files—acial Matters, 1946–47, Warren Papers. A useful document outlining the mission, structure, and operation of the CCC at mid-century is "Purposes" (California Chamber of Commerce, 1952), Box 2243, CCC Records. Opposition to state FEP was not new to the Associated Farmers. A legislative advisory to membership called a 1945 proposal "vicious beyond description." Analysts argued that the bill "would not only contribute to but would have created racial strife rather than alleviate it." It was "radical legislation, pure and simple." Of course, little joy could come from standing up against A.B. 3, since it was the subject of "many sincere representations" by the "racial groups who appeared at the hearings on the bill." Yet it was "essential" to block the bill, and the Associated Farmers "accepted that responsibility." See Associated Farmers of California, *The Associated Farmer 5*, no. 12, (June 28, 1945), Folder: Legislature 1945, Box 15, Cleary Collection, University of California, Berkeley, Bancroft Library (hereafter Cleary Collection). While the association was happy to brag privately to members about aggressively opposing FEP legislation in 1945 when the issue had a lower profile, it showed less willingness to do so after late October of 1946.

22. *LAT*, August 25, 1946, p. A4; *LAT*, October 21, 1946, p. A4; "L.A. Icon Otis Chandler Dies at 78," *LAT*, February 27, 2006. The *San Francisco Chronicle* made a slew of similar points in recommending that readers vote down the referendum. The proposition would menace certain "basic rights" and unfairly singled out employers. Though it was motivated by good intentions, it was a "bad law" that threatened "judicial safeguards." See *San Francisco Chronicle*, November 1, 1946, p. 1; November 2, 10; *Fresno Bee*, November 3, 1946, p. 4; *Oakland Tribune*, November 5, 1946, p. 3; *Sacramento Bee*, November 1, 1946, p. 1.

23. *State of California Statement of the Vote: General Election: November 5, 1946* (Sacramento: California State Printing Office, 1946); "Political Notes, Comment of California Interest," *Oakland Tribune*, November 4, 1946, p. 7; "FEPC, Dog Racing Defeated," *Oakland Tribune*, November 6, 1946, p. 1; "A Great Republican Sweep," *LAT*, November 6, 1946, p. 4; "Dog Racing and FEPC Beaten by Wide Margins," *LAT*, November 7, 1946, p. 2; J. M. Whitley to Earl Warren, January 8, 1947, F3640:3657, Administrative Files: Public Works-Race Relations, 1946–48, Warren Papers; Melvin H. Harter to Earl Warren, December 9, 1946, F3640:8854, Legislative Files: Governor's Files—Racial Matters, 1946–47, Warren Papers.

24. The basic calculation, based on a Goodman's regression of county-level data, is first reported in Anthony S. Chen, Robert Mickey, Robert P. Van Houweling, "Backlash Reconsidered: The Political Attitudes and Electoral Behavior of Non-Southern Whites on Civil Rights, 1946–1960," paper presented at the Annual Meetings of the Social Science History Association, Baltimore, MD, 2003. This paper is the initial basis of a published study that reports the results of a more

sophisticated and comprehensive analysis that draws on more robust methods and more detailed data. See Chen, Mickey, and Van Houweling, "Explaining the Contemporary Alignment of Race and Party." For a fuller methodological discussion, see the appendix. Michigan quite nearly had a state initiative on FEPC. Over 180,000 signatures were collected for a petition that would have showed up on the April 7, 1947 ballot, but the Michigan Supreme Court invalidated it. Members of the Michigan Committee for Tolerance were elated. See Wm. H. Leininger to Richard B. Russell, August 1, 1947, Folder 3, Box 57, Series 3, Russell Papers.

25. Maslow, "Fair Employment, State by State," 411; American Council on Race Relations, "State FEPC Campaigns," *Report*, 5, no. 4 (April 1950): 2.

26. Maslow, "Fair Employment, State by State," 411; American Council on Race Relations, "State FEPC Campaigns," 2; Otto F. Christenson, Remarks to the National Industrial Council State Associations Group, Gatlinburg, Tennessee, August 26, 1955, Folder: Guidepost and Related 1955, Box 2, Record of the Minnesota Association of Commerce and Industry, Minnesota Historical Society (hereafter MACI Records). See also Illinois Legislative Council, "State 'Educational' Fair Employment Practice Laws," n.d. [probably 1961], Folder: Civil Rights FEPC et cetera, Box 298, Kerner Papers.

27. MEA, Organization, Objectives, Policies (St. Paul, n.d. [probably 1945]), Box 1, MACI Records; Otto F. Christenson, Remarks to the National Industrial Council State Associations Group, Gatlinburg, TN, August 26, 1955, 17–9, Folder: Guidepost and Related 1955, Box 2, MACI Records; Otto F. Christenson to Secretaries of Chambers of Commerce in Minnesota, February 9, 1950, Folder: Guidepost, 1950 and Miscellaneous, Box 2, MACI Records; *Guidepost* 11, no. L-8 (March 15, 1951), Folder: *Guidepost*, 1951, Box 2, MACI Records; *Guidepost: Special Report* (January 27, 1949), 1–4, Folder: *Guidepost*, 1949, Box 2, MACI Records; *Guidepost* 9, no. L-5 (February 20, 1949): 1–2, Folder: Guidepost 1949, Box 2, MACI Records.

28. CCC, Minutes of Board of Directors' Meeting, March 16, 1945, Folder 1944–45, Box 2243, CCC Records; CCC, Minutes of Board of Directors' Meeting, January 11, 1946, Folder 1945–45, CCC Records; CCC, Minutes of Board of Directors' Meeting, February 14, 1947, Folder 1946–47, CCC Records; CCC, Minutes of Board of Directors' Meeting, October 14, 1949, Folder 1947–48, CCC Records; CCC, Minutes of Board of Directors' Meeting, February 2, 1951, CCC Records; CCC, Minutes of Board of Directors' Meeting, Folder: 1950–51, CCC Records; CCC, Minutes of Board of Directors' Meeting, Folder: 1952–53, Box 2244, CCC Records; "Purposes of the California State Chamber of Commerce," September 30, 1952, Box 2243, CCC Records; *San Francisco Chronicle*, May 1, 1953, p. 5; *San Francisco Chronicle*, May 3, 1955, p. 10; *San Francisco Chronicle*, May 2, 1957; *San Francisco Chronicle*, May 14, 1957, p. 9; Press Release, Office of W. Byron Rumford, February 12, 1959, W. Byron Rumford Papers, Bancroft Library, University of California, Berkeley; Office (hereafter Rumford Papers). A recent and informative analysis of right-to-work laws is David Jacobs and Marc Dixon, "The Politics of Labor-Management Relations: Detecting the Conditions that Affect Changes in Right-to-Work Laws," *Social Problems* 53 (2006): 118–37.

29. IMA, Minutes of Board of Directors Meeting, March 9, Box 12, Folder: Board of Directors Minutes, 1945, Records of the Illinois Manufacturers' Association, Chicago Historical Society (hereafter IMA Records); IMA, Minutes of Board of Directors Meeting, February 14, Box 13, Folder: Board of Directors Minutes, 1947, IMA Records; IMA, Minutes of Board of Directors Meeting, March 11, Box 13, Folder: Board of Directors Minutes, 1949, IMA Records; IMA, Minutes of Board of Directors Meeting, June 12, Folder: Board of Directors Minutes, 1953, IMA Records; IMA, Minutes of Board of Directors Meeting, April 12, Box 13, Folder: Board of Directors Minutes, 1957, IMA Records; IMA, Minutes of Board of Directors Meeting, March 13, Box 13, Folder: Board of Directors Minutes, 1959, IMA Records; IMA, Minutes of Board of Directors Meeting, April 14, Box 13, Folder: Board of Directors Minutes, 1961, IMA Records; IMA, "Some Essentials to Effective Political Action by Business Executives" (Chicago, 1958), Box 16, IMA Records; Digest of Minutes, February 7, 1947, Folder: Chicago Association of Commerce and Industry, Box 51, Records of the Chicago Association of Commerce and Industry, Chicago Historical Society (hereafter CACI Records).

30. Minnesota Employers' Association Board of Directors, Minutes, March 5, 1947; April 2, 1947; May 5, 1948; March 9, 1949; February 6, 1951; February 18, 1953; September 22, 1954; all in Folder: Minutes of Meetings, December 1941–1954, Box 2, MACI Records; *Minneapolis Tribune*, February 20, 1953; *Guidepost*, March 31, 1951, Folder: *Guidepost*, 1951, Box 2, MACI Records; Delton, *Making Minnesota Liberal*, 59. In 1947, Christenson approvingly referred his readers to an IMA analysis of "compulsory" FEP legislation in the Illinois legislature. The IMA had made a separate assessment earlier in the year, and he excerpted a lengthy passage that explained how FEP legislation "singles out" employers and "sets upon them the machinery of a most powerful bureaucracy." See *The Guidepost* 7, no. 10, April 6, 1947, Folder: Guidepost, 1947, Box 2, MACI Records; IMA, "Anti-Discrimination Measures: Fair Employment Practices Commission," April 1, 1947, Folder: Circulars 1947 (discrimination), Box 171, IMA Records.

31. For typical examples of business testimony, see "State Employers Hit FEPC, Take Rap at Youngdahl," *St. Paul Pioneer-Press*, February 18, 1949, and March 1, 1949; Floyd E. Thompson, "Address in Opposition to So-Called Fair Employment Practices Commission Bills (S.B. 19 and 38) before the Senate Judiciary Committee," April 15, 1947, Folder 3, Box 115, Stevenson Papers; David R. Clarke, "Anti-Discrimination Measure: FEPC Legislation, H.B. 163," June 1, 1949 (Chicago, 1949), Folder: Circulars 1949, Box 171, Douglas (Paul) Papers.

32. Otto Christenson to Minnesota League of Women Voters, November 21, 1949, Library of the Minnesota Historical Society; OCFEP, "Some Questions and Answers on FEPC" [circa 1950], Folder 1, Container 1, OCFEP Records; *St. Paul Pioneer-Press*, March 1, 1949, p, 1; "Address by Charles F. Hough before the Senate Judiciary Committee," May 8, 1945, Folder 100, Box 100, Stevenson Papers; Charles F. Hough, "Address in Opposition to So-called Fair Employment Practices Commission," March 22, 1949, Stevenson Papers, "Committee Hearings on FEPC," April 18, 1951, Container 2, Folder 27, Stevenson Papers, WHS. See also Illinois State Chamber of Commerce, *Fair Employment Practice Laws*

(Chicago, 1949), Illinois State Library; Thompson, "Address in Opposition to So-Called Fair Employment Practices Commission Bills."

33. *Guidepost* 7, no. 4 (February 23, 1947): 2–3, Folder: *Guidepost*, 1947, Box 2, MACI Records; "State Employers Hit FEPC, Take Rap at Youngdahl," *St. Paul Pioneer-Press*, February 18, 1949; Report on Distribution of the Pamphlet "Fair Employment Practices Act," n.d. [probably 1950], Folder: *Guidepost*, 1950 and Miscellaneous, Box 2, MACI Records; Otto F. Christenson to Member of the Senate Judiciary Committee, February 24, 1953, Folder: *Guidepost* and Miscellaneous, 1953, Box 2, MACI Records; Otto F. Christenson to Member of the Legislator, March 13, 1950, Folder: *Guidepost*, 1950 and Miscellaneous, Box 2, MACI Records; Otto F. Christenson to Member of the Senate Judiciary Committee, February 24, 1953, Folder: Guidepost and Miscellaneous, 1953, Box 2, MACI Records; *Guidepost*, Legislative Report No. 9—1955 Session (March 7, 1955), Folder: *Guidepost* and Miscellaneous, 1955 (part 3), MACI Records; *Guidepost*, n.d. [probably late 1953/early 1954], Folder: *Guidepost* and Miscellaneous, 1953, Box 2, MACI Records. See also *Sacramento Union*, April 23, 1957; Senate Unit Kills State FEP Bill—Issue Dead for Session," *San Francisco Chronicle*, May 14, 1957, p. 9; "Assembly Kills State FEPC Bill," *San Francisco Examiner*, May 14, 1957; *San Francisco Chronicle*, April 5, 1957.

34. Statement of Theodore M. Berry before the Senate Commerce and Labor Committee Hearing on S.B. 6, March 18, 1953, Folder 27, Box 2, OCFEP Records; *News Bulletin*, no. 10, April 3, 1953, Folder 6, Box 1, OCFEP Records; Paul L. Klein, "Highlights of opponents' Testimony before House Committee—8 April 1953," Folder 27, Container 2, OCFEP Records; Committee Hearings on FEPC in the House Industry-Labor Committee, April 18, 1951, Folder 27, Box 2, OCFEP Records.

35. OCFEP, Transcript of State Meeting, April 23, 1953, Box 1, Folder 1, OCFEP Records; *News Bulletin*, no. 15, May 13, 1953, Folder 6, Box 1, OCFEP Records; "Notes on the Final Senate Committee Meeting," June 10, 1953, Folder 27, Box 2, OCFEP Records; "Does Platform Pledge Mean Anything?" *Cleveland Press*, June 11, 1953.

36. Gordon, "A New Birth of Freedom in Illinois." For a persuasive account of Loop interests in the postwar redevelopment of downtown Chicago, see Arnold Hirsch, *Making the Second Ghetto: Race and Housing in Chicago, 1940–1960* (Chicago: University of Chicago Press, 1983), 100–134.

37. Illinois State Chamber of Commerce, *Fair Employment Practice Laws* (Springfield, 1949), Illinois State Library. Moreno describes in detail how the New York State Commission against Discrimination repeatedly opposed quotas. See Moreno, *From Direct Action to Affirmative Action*, 128. See also Fox River Valley Manufacturers' Association, RE: FEPC Legislation, March 16, 1949, Folder 3: Legislation—Fair Employment Practices, Box 100, Stevenson Papers. A legislative advisory from the Associated Employers of Illinois earlier in the year warned members that an FEP would essentially be a "commission or bureau with dictatorial powers of the widest latitude to control not only the employment, but also the promotion of employees, practically taking these functions away from management." The commission would have "unlimited power to make rules and regulations," and there were no provisions for court review or jury trial: "The commis-

sioner is investigator, prosecutor, and judge." Associated Employers of Illinois, "Summary of FAIR EMPLOYMENT PRACTICES COMMISSION BILL S.B. 145 AND H.B. 163," n.d. [definitely 1949], Folder 3: Legislation—Fair Employment Practices, Box 100, Stevenson Papers.

38. G. C. Gridley to Adlai E. Stevenson, April 7, 1949, Folder 3: Legislation, Fair Employment Practices, Box 100, Stevenson Papers; H. F. Collins to Adlai E. Stevenson, April 4, 1949, Folder 4, Box 115, Stevenson Papers. See also Warren S. Smith to Adlai E. Stevenson, April 11, 1949, Folder: 3—Legislation FEPC N-Z 1951, Box 115, Stevenson Papers.

39. Clarence Mark, Jr., to Stevenson, March 21, 1949, Stevenson Papers; Francis C. Spence to Adlai E. Stevenson, March 28, 1949, Folder 3: Legislation— Fair Employment Practices, Box 100, Stevenson Papers; Frank Kooh to Adlai E. Stevenson, March 21, 1949, Folder 3: Legislation—Fair Employment Practices, Box 100, Stevenson Papers (This letter was sent less than a week after the Fox River Valley Manufacturers' Association notified its membership that the bill might pass. See Fox River Valley Manufacturers' Association, "RE: FEPC Legislation."); Clark to Stevenson, March 29, 1949, Folder 3: Legislation—Fair Employment Practices, Box 100, Stevenson Papers. See also Clarence Mark, Jr,. to Stevenson, March 21, 1949 and Frank Kooh to Stevenson, March 21, 1949, both Folder 4, Box 100, Stevenson Papers; Tom O'Brien to Gordon Rosenmeier, January 15, 1951, F: Correspondence, K-Q, January–May 1951, Box 8, Christian and Gordon Rosenmeier Papers, Minnesota Historical Society, St. Paul, MN.

40. C. E. Comfort to Gordon Rosenmeier, March 10, 1947, Folder: Correspondence, D-I, 1947, Box 24, Rosenmeier Papers; F.A. Ferguson to Earl Warren, October 14, 1946, F3640:8854, Legislative Files: Governor's Files—Racial Matters, 1946–47, Warren Papers; "Old Employer" to W. Byron Rumford, May 4, 1955, Folder: FEPC—A.B. 971—1955, Box 3, Rumford Papers; William F. Krahl to Adlai E. Stevenson, February 18, 1949, Folder 3, Box 100, Stevenson Papers.

41. Personnel and Labor Relations Committee, Illinois State Chamber of Commerce, "Confidential Progress Report of FEPC Study Group" (September 28, 1950), Folder 1951 Legislation—Fair Employment Practice Act, Box 115, Stevenson Papers. Tellingly, when asked to explain their collective failure to integrate their work force, managers blamed everyone but themselves. Slightly more than a third of the employers claimed that the main problem was "obtaining acceptance by other employees." Another third pointed to the "lack of training among colored personnel, for example, getting them to accept responsibility and to get the 'chip' off their shoulder."

42. "Does State FEPC Hamper You?" *Business Week*, February 25, 1950; CCFEP, "Businessmen with Experience Favor FEP Laws" (San Francisco, 1955), loose, Box 3, Rumford Papers. See also Pennsylvania State Council for a Pennsylvania Fair Employment Practices Commission, "Business Looks Ahead to Fair Employment Practices," [circa 1949], GPC; Businessmen for FEPC to Gentlemen, n.d. [probably 1949], Folder 3: Legislation—Fair Employment Practices, Box 100, Stevenson Papers. A group of Denver businessmen sponsored the placement of 250 placards on Denver buses, announcing their support of FEPC, though it did not specify whether their support extended to "compulsory" legislation. See CCEEO, *Taking Stock*, 26, Folder 1, Box 1, OCFEP.

342   NOTES TO CHAPTER 4

43. Pennsylvania State Council for a Pennsylvania Fair Employment Practices Commission, "Business Looks Ahead to Fair Employment Practices." Employers already covered by laws included Pitney-Bowes of Stamford, CT; George F. Mand of the New York Chamber of Commerce; and R. T. Barker of Western Electric, NY; and James Kerney, Jr., of the *Trenton Times*, NJ. A similar dilemma confronted several New Jersey employers when they were contacted by representatives of their state FEPC and asked whether the law was posing any "new difficulties or problems." Predictably, they said no. What else could they say if they did not want to invite suspicion? Besides, if they had taken a chance and actually conveyed the existence of any problems, their statements would probably have been kept under wraps, since it would have cast the state FEPC in poor light.

44. League of Women Voters of Minnesota, "How Valid Are the Arguments against Fair Employment Legislation?" Section 5, 2, Folder: How Valid Are the Arguments against Fair Employment Legislation, Box 1, MCFEP Records; MEA, *Membership List: 1954* (St. Paul, 1954), Minnesota Historical Society Pamphlet Collection. On Mintener's racial liberalism, see Delton, *Making Minnesota Liberal*, 59. On the politics of the Minnesota ordinance, see Delton, *Making Minnesota Liberal* and Thurber, *The Politics of Equality*.

45. MEA, *1953 Legislative Service Record* (St. Paul, 1953), Folder: *Guidepost* and Miscellaneous, 1953, Box 2, MACI Records; Minnesota State Federation of Labor, *Legislative Report: Fifty-Fifth Session*, Minnesota State Legislature, 1947, p. 15, Minnesota State Historical Society Library; Minnesota State Federation of Labor, *Legislative Report: Fifty-Sixth Session, Minnesota State Legislature, 1949*, p. 4, Minnesota Historical Society Library; *Guidepost*, 11, no. L-11 (March 31, 1951), 1-2, Folder: *Guidepost*, 1951, Box 2, MACI Records; Minnesota State Federation of Labor, *Legislative Report: Fifty-Eighth Session, Minnesota State Legislature, 1953*, p. 7, Minnesota State Historical Society Library; Minnesota Legislature, *Journal of the House*, 58th sess., April 18, 1953, 2377; *Minnesota Morning Tribune*, April 16, 1953; CCC, *Aims and Purposes*, September 30, 1952, p. 10, Vertical File, California State Library, Sacramento, California.

46. Walter A. Gordon to Earl Warren, November 29, 1945, F3640:8452, Legislative Files: Special Session Legislation—Race Relations, 1945–46, Warren Papers; American Council of Learned Societies, "Charles Edison," *Dictionary of American Biography: Supplement 8, 1966–1970* (New York: Scribner, 1971); IMA, Minutes, Board of Directors Meeting, April 14, 1961, Folder: Minutes April–June 1961, Box 17, IMA Records; Thomas H. Coulter, "Eye on Chicagoland," *Commerce; Chicagoland Voice of Business*, April 1961, p. 5, Chicago Historical Society, Chicago, IL.

47. *Minneapolis Morning Tribune*, February 23, 1953, p. 6; Wilfred C. Leland to Virginia Huebner, August 3, 1955, Folder: Action by House, 1954–1955, Box 1, MCFEP; *Guidepost*, April 27, 1955, Folder: Guidepost and Miscellaneous, 1955 (part 2), Box 2, MACI Records; Judson Bemis, Statement before the Minnesota Senate Judiciary Committee, March 8, 1955, Folder: Bemis Testimony, March 8, 1955, Box 1, MCFEP Records. For a private letter from Bemis confirming his public views, see Judson Bemis to Fred E. King, February 19, 1955, Folder: Correspondence with Business Leaders, Box 1, MCFEP Records; "Employer Acceptance of FEPC Increases," *Minneapolis Tribune*, March 9, 1955; *St. Paul Re-*

corder, April 22, 1955. See also York Langton to Gene Newhall, March 11, 1955, Folder: Correspondence May 1954–September 1955, Box 1, MCFEP Records. I found no evidence that the MEA had decided to concede the fight because public opinion had been going against FEP. Figure 4.3 reports the percentage of respondents in the Minnesota Poll supporting the passage of a government (federal or state) law mandating fair employment practices. For ease of presentation, data points for 1948, 1952, and 1954 are linearly interpolated. Questions administered in 1953 and 1955, though not identical, were worded in substantially similar fashion. Table A.7 contains the precise wording.

48. "Employer Acceptance of FEPC Increases," *Minneapolis Tribune,* March 9, 1955; *St. Paul Recorder,* April 22, 1955, p. 1.

49. The most influential theories on lobbying suggest that interest groups concentrate their attention and resources on critical legislators who are undecided, hoping to win their support; however, new theoretical and empirical work suggests that lobbyists are less involved in persuading the unpersuaded than subsidizing the legislative costs of the already-persuaded. See Richard L. Hall and Alan Deardorff, "Lobbying as Legislative Subsidy," *American Political Science Review* 100 (February 2006): 69–84; Richard L. Hall and Kris Miller, "Interest Group Subsidies to Legislative Overseers," manuscript, Department of Political Science, University of Michigan. This conclusion is consistent with the historical records that I have reviewed in business archives.

50. Chen, "The Hitlerian Rule of Quotas"; *California Eagle,* May 23, 1957; *Guidepost* 9, No. L-10 (March 27, 1949): 1–2, Folder: *Guidepost,* 1949, Box 2, MACI Records. On the role of business in Michigan politics, see Fine, "*Expanding the Frontiers of Civil Rights,*" 36. See W. P. Thorpe to Dennis Chavez, June 9, 1945, Frame 250361, Roll 9 [Folder 25, Box 78], Chavez Papers.

51. OCFEP, Analysis of the 1953 Campaign for FEPC in Ohio, August 3, 1954, Folder 2, Container 1, OCFEP Records.

52. Lockard, *Toward Equal Opportunity,* 46–48; *Los Angeles Examiner,* May 23, 1955; *California Voice,* April 19, 1957; William Becker to W. Byron Rumford, May 4, n.d.[probably 1955], Folder: FEPC—A.B. 971—1955, Box 3, Rumford Papers, BL; *CT,* Feb. 12, 1959, p. B7.

53. CCEEO, *Taking Stock.* The bill cleared the Senate, 25–10, and the House, 57–2.

54. Denver Unity Council, "FEPC in the Primaries, September 12, 1950" (Denver, 1950), Folder 40, Box 3, OCFEP Records.

55. *Minnesota Tribune,* April 16, 1953. On rural GOP opposition, see also Lockard, *Toward Equal Opportunity,* and Fine, "*Expanding the Frontiers of Civil Rights,*" 36.

56. CCEEO, *Taking* Stock, pp. 11–12, OCFEP Records; *California Eagle,* April 14, 1953; William Byron Rumford, *Legislator for Fair Employment, Fair Housing, and Public Health,* interviewed by Joyce A. Henderson, Amelia R. Fry, and Edward France (Berkeley: Regional Oral History Office, Bancroft Library, University of California), 45; OCFEPC, Minutes of Meeting, January 23, 1953, Folder 1, Container 1, OCFEP.

57. *California Eagle*, May 16, 1957; CCEEO, *Taking Stock*, 12. My analysis of committee votes is consistent with Lockard's analysis of two Ohio roll calls in the House. See Lockard, *Toward Equal Opportunity*, 55–58.

58. A few clarifying and orienting remarks are in order. By the phrase "Republican control of veto points," I do not mean to denote the ability of Republicans to guarantee the realization of their preferred outcomes in the legislative process. Nor do I wish to imply that GOP legislators always and everywhere achieved their "control" over veto points through a highly coordinated form of collective action. The level of coordination varied over time and space. With Immergut, I use the term "veto points" to identify moments when a group of elected officials enjoy formal authority to block the passage of legislation. See Immergut, "Institutions, Veto Points, and Policy Results." I highlight the importance of informal authority as well as party affiliation. My findings are consistent with the results of Erikson's analysis of party control and the passage of state civil rights legislation (i.e., employment, housing, plus accommodations). See Robert S. Erikson, "The Relationship between Party Control and Civil Rights Legislation in the American States," *Western Political Quarterly* 24 (March 1971): 178–82.

59. On the veto threat made by Goodwin Knight, see Tarea Hall Pittman, *Tarea Hall Pittman* (Berkeley: Regional Oral History Office, University of California, Berkeley), http://ark.cdlib.org/ark:/13030/kt4h4nb06r, accessed 2001, pp. 111–12.

60. For more details on the legislative and political history of FEP in Illinois, see table A.9. Illinois Committee for Fair Employment Practices, "Past Due! . . . an FEP Law for Illinois," 1961, Folder: Equal Job Opportunity, Box 119, Records of the Illinois State AFL-CIO, Illinois State Historical Society (hereafter IS AFL-CIO Papers).

61. For more details on the legislative and political history of FEP in California, see table A.8. In his study, Lockard observes that California passed an FEP law when a Democratic governor came into power with a Democratic legislature. See Lockard, *Toward Equal Opportunity*, 55. In an oral history interview, Hawkins argued that the election of Edmund G. Brown was the critical factor in the passage of an FEP law in California. "After the initiative failed, we said, 'Well, the only way we can get one through is to get a governor. So that's why some of us supported Pat Brown." Hawkins claimed that both Warren and Knight opposed FEP, forgetting that Warren had supported FEP legislation *before* the failure of Proposition 11. See Augustus F. Hawkins, Oral History Interview, conducted in 1988 by Carlos Vásquez, UCLA Oral History Program, for the California State Archives State Governmental Oral History Program, 133–34.William Byron Rumford recalled that Warren wanted FEP bills out of committee as well. See Rumford, *Legislator for Fair Employment, Fair Housing, and Public Health*, 42.

62. For more details on the legislative and political history of FEP in Ohio, see table A.10. In his study, Lockard observes that Ohio passed an FEP law when a Democratic governor with a Democratic legislature came into power. See Lockard, *Toward Equal Opportunity*, 55.

63. "New York Ready for Bias Ban," *Business Week*, June 30 1945, p. 94; OCFEPC, News Bulletin No. 18, June 11, 1953, Box 1, Folder 6, OCFEP Records; *LAT*, June 3, 1955.

64. Republican National Committee, Research Division. "Some Facts on Civil Rights Legislation" (August 1963): Part 1, Box 465, Folder: "H.R. 7152 (88)," Emanuel Celler Papers, Library of Congress (hereafter Celler Papers).

65. Lockard takes a preliminary stab at answering such questions in his analysis of two roll calls from Ohio. See Lockard, *Toward Equal Opportunity*, 57.

66. A discussion of variable construction and the underlying data is contained in the appendix.

67. In the main text, I use the term "states" in the discussion, but it is more appropriate to use the term "state-year." My bivariate finding on GOP control is consistent with Erikson's analysis. See Erikson, "The Relationship between Party Control and Civil Rights Legislation in the American States."

68. For a more detailed discussion of measurement and data as well as a step-by-step discussion of the modeling procedure, see the appendix.

69. This overall strategy for gauging the validity of my inference about the effect of Republican control is based on the same intuition of "regression-discontinuity" research designs in economics and sociology. See John DiNardo and David Lee, "Economic Impacts of New Unionization on Private Sector Employers, 1984–2001," *Quarterly Journal of Economics* 119 (2004): 1383–442; David Lee, Enrico Moretti, and Matthew J. Butler, "Do Voters Affect or Elect Policies? Evidence from the U.S. House," *Quarterly Journal of Economics* 119 (2004): 807–59.

70. For precise details on how these figures are calculated, see the appendix.

71. "To The People," *Sacramento Union*, April 23, 1957; Zach Lamar Cobb to Fielding L. Wright, February 6, 1948, Folder: Civil Rights FEPC Material, February 1948, Box 109, Series 10, Russell Papers; Franklin Hichborn to Richard B. Russell, February 24, 1948, Folder; FEPC 1949, Box 108, Series 10, Russell Papers; CR, 81st Cong., 2nd sess., February 23, 1950, pp. 2171–238.

72. CR, 81st Cong., 2nd sess., February 22, 1950, pp. 2171–72. Another major statement by Douglas is "Statement of Representative Helen Gahagan Douglas in Support of S. 792," May 11, 1949, Folder 1, Box 1, Douglas (Helen) Papers. On Douglas, see Scobie, *Center Stage*.

73. California Federation for Civic Unity, Board of Directors Minutes, August 13, 1949, Folder: Board of Directors Material, Box 3, Records of the California Federation on Civic Unity, Bancroft Library, University of California, Berkeley; Minutes, California Council for Civic Unity, February 21, 1951, Folder: Fair Employment Practices, Press Releases, Memoranda, Minutes, Agendas, et cetera, 1950–1953, Box 1, Tarea Hall Pittman Papers, Bancroft Library, University of California, Berkeley (hereafter Pittman Papers); *LAT*, May 10, 1951, p. 29; Press Release, NAACP West Coast Region, January 20, 1952, Box 1, Pittman Papers; Press Release, NAACP West Coast Region, December 30, 1952, Pittman Papers; Minutes, FEP Planning Meeting called by the NAACP, January 31, 1953, Folder 2, Box 2206, Pittman Papers II; CCFEP, "The Case for Fair Employment Practices Legislation in 1953," Folder: FEP List for William Becker, Box 36, NAACP-WC Papers; CCFEP, "First Call for FEPC Mobilization!" 1953, Folder: FEPC for California, Box 3, Rumford Papers; Irving S. Rosenblatt to Alex Skolnick, March 30, 1953; Folder: Fair Employment Practices; Correspondence, 1952–1953, Pittman Papers; Edward Howden to Tarea Hall Pittman, April 3, 1953, Folder: Fair Em-

ployment Practices, Press Releases, Memoranda, Minutes, Agendas, et cetera, 1950–1953, Pittman Papers; Pittman to NAACP Branches, n.d. [probably 1953], Pittman Papers; CCFEP, "Call to Mobilization on FEPC," Folder: Publicity FEPC, Box 3, Rumford Papers. A newsletter from the Friends Committee on Legislation outlined the political travails of FEP proposals in the California Assembly through 1951. See *California Newsletter*, February 9, 1952, Rumford Papers.

74. American Council on Race Relations, "Civil Rights Legislation in the States: January 1 to September 1, 1949" (Chicago, 1949), Folder: State Laws, Box 1243, Douglas (Paul) Papers; AJC, "A New Birth of Freedom in Illinois"; CD, February 19, 1949, p. 1; March 19, 1949, p. 1; American Council on Race Relations, "Release No. 42: Evaluation of State FEPC: Experiences and Forecasts," March 14, 1949 (Chicago, 1949), Folder: General Materials, Box 1243, Folder: State Laws, Box 1243, Douglas (Paul) Papers.

75. Illinois Interracial Commission, *Special Report on Employment Opportunities in Illinois* (Springfield, 1948); Illinois Chamber of Commerce Legislative Department, *Fair Employment Practices Laws* (Chicago, 1949), Folder 3: Legislation—Fair Employment Practices, Box 100, Stevenson Papers; CD, Jun 11, 1949, p. 3; Adlai E. Stevenson to Chester Bowles, June 3, 1949, Stevenson Papers; Bowles to Stevenson, June 15, 1949, Stevenson Papers; Edwin Rogers Embree to Stevenson, April 25, 1949, Stevenson Papers; Gordon, "A New Birth of Freedom in Illinois."

76. Paul Sifton to Elizabeth Magee, February 19, 1947, Folder: Sifton, Box 42, McLaurin Papers; CD, July 9, 1949, p. 11; *Cleveland Call and Post*, May 5, 1949, A-1; Fine, *"Expanding the Frontiers of Civil Rights,"* 40; Smith and Wolensky, "A Novel Public Policy," 500, 503; Lockard, *Toward Equal Opportunity*, 52; *St. Paul Pioneer-Press*, January 7, 1949; February 11, 1949; February 23, 1949; March 2, 1949, pp. 1, 3; March 3, 1949, pp. 1, 3; March 4, 1949, pp. 1, 2; *St. Paul Dispatch*, January 20, 1949, p. 1; "Youngdahl Makes New Appeal for FEPC Law," *St. Paul Dispatch*, February 23, 1949; "Youngdahl Charts fight to Preserve FEPC Bill," *St. Paul Dispatch*, March 2, 1949; "For a State FEPC Law?' *Minneapolis Tribune*, February 15. 1949; "One-Vote Shift Advances FEPC," *Minneapolis Tribune*, March 4, 1949.

77. CD, December 17, 1949, pp. 1, 2. *Pittsburgh Courier*, October 15, 1949, pp. 1, 5; October 22, 1949, p. 1. The *Pittsburgh Courier* called Driscoll a "man of destiny" and, of his achievements, it listed notably the "Freeman Bill" of 1949, which banned segregation in public housing that received state funding, outlawed quotas in college admissions, and strengthened the administration of the FEP law. For an instructive analysis of the GOP at mid-century and beyond, see Rae, *The Decline and Fall of the Liberal Republicans*.

78. *Newsweek*, May 29, 1950, p. 16. Rhode Island passed the law over the strenuous objections of the Associated Industries of Rhode Island. See selected materials in Folder: FEPC, January 1948, Box 109, Series 10, Russell Papers.

79. *St. Paul Pioneer-Press*, March 2, 1949, p. 1; "Changes Fail to Save Bill," *St. Paul Pioneer-Press*, March 26, 1949, p. 1; CT, March 26, 1949, p. 1; "Justice Deferred," *St. Paul Dispatch*, March 26, 1949; *Guidepost*, March 27, 1949, pp. 1, 2, Folder: *Guidepost*, 1949, Box 2, MACI Records; Smith and Wolensky, "A Novel Public Policy," 508; Fine, *"Expanding the Frontiers of Civil Rights,"* 41; CT, June 16, 1949, p. 16; CT, June 17, 1949, p. 1; OCFEP, *Campaign Bulletin*,

No. 17, June 25, 1951, Folder 6, Box 1, OCFEP Records; *CD*, July 9, 1949, p. 9; *Blue Book of the State of Illinois* (Springfield, 1949), 125, 127; *Journal of the House of Representatives* (Springfield, 1949), 935; *Legislative Synopsis and Digest* (Springfield, 1949), 59, 304; *Journal of the Senate*, 98th General Assembly of the State of Ohio (1949), 792, 1522. According to Christenson, Republicans speaking out against FEP included Sletvold, Numeier, Johanson, Swanson, Goodue, Dietz, Laureman, Ledin, Lightner, Miller, Mitchell, and Spokely. The main supporters were Democrats such as Millin, Marvin Anderson, and Julkowski, as well as "Farmer-Laborites" such as Vokelich and Hagen. The division was not strictly along party lines, but "it may generally be said that Republicans opposed the bill and Democrats, Farmer-Laborites, and liberals supported the bill, together with a few Republicans." See *Guidepost*, March 27, 1949, p. 2.

80. *CT*, May 25, 1961, p. 1.

Chapter Five

1. According to one estimate, the 1964 filibuster was the longest one ever mustered, going on for a stunning 534 hours and taking up 63,000 some-odd pages in the *Congressional Record*. The previous record was held by a Senate debate in 1846 over "British occupational rights in territorial Oregon." See Taylor Branch, *Pillar of Fire: America in the King Years, 1964–1965* (New York: Simon and Schuster, 1998), 336, 310. See also *NYT*, July 3, 1964, pp. 1, 9.

2. Myrdal, *An American Dilemma*; *WP*, July 3, 1964, pp. 1, 8; *NYT*, July 3, 1964, pp. 1, 9. On the origins and impact of the Myrdal study, see Jackson, *Gunnar Myrdal and America's Conscience*.

3. The most comprehensive analysis of corporate equal employment opportunity programs is surely Frank Dobbin, *Inventing Equal Opportunity* (Princeton University Press, forthcoming).

4. Public Law 88-352; Graham, *The Civil Rights Era*, 53, 60–61, 327, 343; Skrentny, *The Ironies of Affirmative Action*, 193–211; Sugrue, "Affirmative Action from Below," 145–73; Robin Stryker and Nicholas Pedriana, "Political Culture War 1960s Style." Public Law 88-352 reads as follows: "Sec. 703. (a) It shall be an unlawful employment practice for an employer—(1) to fail or refuse to hire or to discharge any individual, or otherwise to discriminate against any individual with respect to his compensation, terms, conditions, or privileges of employment, because of such individual's race, color, religion, sex, or national origin." "Sec. 703. (j) Nothing in this title shall be interpreted to require any employer, employment agency, labor organization, or joint-management committee subject to this title to grant preferential treatment to any individual or to any group because of the race, color, religion, or national origin of such individual."

5. Graham, *The Civil Rights Era*, 152; Allen J. Matusow, *The Unraveling of America: A History of Liberalism in the 1960s* (New York: Harper & Row, 1986), 96; Nathan Glazer, *Ethnic Dilemmas, 1964–1982* (Cambridge: Harvard University Press, 1983), 1–2; Bernard Grofman, introduction to *Legacies of the 1964 Civil Rights Act*, edited by Bernard Grofman (Charlottesville: University Press of Virginia, 2000), 1.

6. *NYT*, June 20, 1964, cited in Patterson, *Grand Expectations*, 546; Graham, *The Civil Rights Era*, 142. The historian Carl Brauer, for instance, calls the mid-1960s the Second Reconstruction. See Carl Brauer, *John F. Kennedy and the Second Reconstruction* (New York: Columbia University Press, 1977), 259–60, quoted in Graham, *The Civil Rights Era*, 74.

7. Robert Bork, "Civil Rights—A Challenge," *New Republic*, August 31, 1963, p. 22; *New Republic*, June 20, 1964, p. 5; *NYT*, July 3, 1964, p. 20.

8. Roy Wilkins, "Statement on New Civil Rights Act," *The Crisis* (August-September 1964): 434.

9. Robert Bork, "Civil Rights," 24, 22.

10. Patterson, *Grand Expectations*, 481; "NAACP Leader Slain in Jackson" and "Racial Assassination," *NYT*, June 13, 1963.

11. Letter from Mary L. Mitchell to Augustus F. Hawkins, June 12, 1963, Folder: "Legislative Judiciary Civil Rights," Box 76, Papers of Augustus F. Hawkins Papers, Young Research Library, University of California, Los Angeles (hereafter Hawkins Papers).

12. Ruth P. Miller to Paul Douglas, January 10, 1964, Folder: Negro Rights—January 1964, Box 718, Douglas (Paul) Papers. Miller had resided in St. Louis, Mo., for thirty-five years before moving to Girard. For similar themes, see also Ivan R. Snyder to Douglas, Douglas (Paul) Papers.

13. Alexander M. Bickel, "Civil Rights Act of 1963," *New Republic*, July 6, 1963, pp. 9, 10. Not everyone at the *New Republic* believed that the FEPC would matter: "Vice President Johnson's committee of business leaders and CORE's demonstrators have done more to increase Negro job opportunities in the past two years than any FEPC law will do." See "Civil Rights Revolt," *New Republic*, November 2, 1963, p. 4. Yet legions of liberal commentators concurred that the administrative model of enforcement enjoyed manifold advantages over judicially enforced laws.

14. *Heart of Atlanta Motel v. United States*, 379 U.S. 241 (1964). On this point, and for a balanced assessment of the Civil Rights Act, see Patterson, *Grand Expectations*, 545–46, 566–67.

15. Charles W. Whalen and Barbara Whalen, *The Longest Debate: A Legislative History of the 1964 Civil Rights Act* (Washington, DC: Seven Locks, 1985), 22.

16. Transcript, Nicholas D. Katzenbach Oral History Interview I, November 12, 1968, by Paige E. Mulhollan, Internet Copy, Lyndon Baines Johnson Presidential Library, Austin, Texas, 14 (hereafter LBJL).

17. *CD*, June 22–28, 1963; *U.S. News and World Report*, November 11, 1963, p. 109.

18. Section 703 (a)–(h) and Section 704 (a)–(b), Public Law 88-352 (1964).

19. Section 706 (a), Public Law 88-352 (1964). See also the exposition in Michael I. Sovern, *Legal Restraints on Racial Discrimination in Employment* (New York: Twentieth Century Fund, 1966), 74.

20. Section 706 (g), *Public Law* 88-352 (1964). See also the exposition in Sovern, *Legal Restraints on Racial Discrimination in Employment*, 75–76.

21. Until then, Plans for Progress—essentially a council of major companies that voluntarily pledged to take "affirmative action" to expand equal employment opportunity—represented the only significant federal attempt to regulate the be-

havior of participants in private labor markets. Plans for Progress was formed by Kennedy's PCEEO, which was chaired by Vice President Johnson. See Graham, *The Civil Rights Era*, 46, 51–59, and Skrentny, *The Ironies of Affirmative Action*, 114–27.

22. Robert Weisbrot, *Freedom Bound* (New York: Norton, 1990), 68–73; Sitkoff, *The Struggle for Black Equality, 1954–1992*, 118–41; Brauer, *John F. Kennedy and the Second Reconstruction*, 230–36; Graham, *The Civil Rights Era*, 74. A compelling account of events in Birmingham during the mid-1960s is Diane McWhorter, *Carry Me Home, Birmingham, Alabama: The Climactic Battle of the Civil Rights Revolution* (New York: Simon and Schuster, 2001).

23. Bickel, "Civil Rights Act of 1963," 10; Filvaroff and Wolfinger, "The Origins and Enactment of the Civil Rights Act of 1964," in *Legacies of the 1964 Civil Rights Act*, edited by Bernard Grofman (Charlottesville: University Press of Virginia, 2000), 11–13; Graham, *The Civil Rights Era*, 74–75; Weisbrot, *Freedom Bound*, 71; Klinkner and Smith, *Unsteady March*, 268; Brauer, *John F. Kennedy and the Second Reconstruction*, 62, 247.

24. Dean Rusk and news stories quoted in Klinkner and Smith, *The Unsteady March*, 265, 267; Rusk also quoted in Dudziak, *Cold War Civil Rights*, 175. See also Anderson, *Eyes Off the Prize*; Jonathan Seth Rosenberg, *How Far the Promised Land? World Affairs and the American Civil Rights Movement from the First World War to Vietnam* (Princeton: Princeton University Press, 2006); Skrentny, "The Effect of the Cold War on African-American Civil Rights," 237–85.

25. Weisbrot, *Freedom Bound*, 76–85; Randolph quoted in Paula E. Pfeffer, *A. Philip Randolph, Pioneer of the Civil Rights Movement* (Baton Rouge: Louisiana State University Press), 244; Whalen and Whalen, *The Longest Debate*, 14.

26. Transcript, Clarence Mitchell Oral History Interview I, April 30, 1969, by Thomas H. Baker, Internet Copy, 20, LBJL. Johnson's legislative legerdemain is engrossingly rendered in Robert A. Caro, *Master of the Senate: The Years of Lyndon Johnson* (New York: Knopf, 2002), the third volume of a four-part study. Importantly, see also Robert Dalleck, *Lone Star Rising: Lyndon Johnson and His Times, 1908–1960* (New York: Oxford University Press, 1991), and Robert Dalleck, *Flawed Giant: Lyndon Johnson and His Times, 1961–1973* (New York: Oxford University Press, 1999).

27. For a good discussion of the political forces undergirding the development of civil rights policy during the Kennedy and Johnson administrations, see Mark Stern, *Calculating Visions: Kennedy, Johnson, and Civil Rights* (New Brunswick: Rutgers University Press, 1992).

28. Whalen and Whalen, *The Longest Debate*, 19; Graham, *The Civil Rights Era*, 125. Howard W. Smith is the subject of an excellent biography. See Bruce J. Dierenfield, *Keeper of the Rules: Congressman Howard W. Smith of Virginia* (Charlottesville: University Press of Virginia, 1987).

29. For an informative biography of Russell, see Gilbert C. Fite, *Richard B. Russell, Jr., Senator from Georgia* (Chapel Hill: University of North Carolina Press, 1991). For the vote projection, see Whalen and Whalen, *The Longest Debate*, 127, 133.

30. *CD*, June 15–21, 1963; *New Republic*, November 2, 1963, p. 4; Filvaroff, "The Origins and Enactment of the Civil Rights Act of 1964," 15–16. Among

several other historians, Moreno also observes that Dirksen held the balance of power. See Moreno, *From Direct Action to Affirmative Action*, 219.

31. Lieberman, *Shaping Race Policy*, 161; Moreno, *From Direct Action to Affirmative Action*, 219; Edward G. Carmines and James A. Stimson, *Issue Evolution: Race and the Transformation of American Politics* (Princeton: Princeton University Press, 1989); *NYT*, May 13, 1964, pp. 1, 22. In addition to Dirksen, Robert Lieberman counts Wallance Bennett (R-UT), Norris Cotton (R-NH), Bourke Hickenlooper (R-IA), and Karl Mundt (R-IN) among the core members of the key group of conservative Republican senators. On the significance of Goldwater in the rise of American conservatism, see Rick Perlstein, *Before the Storm: Barry Goldwater and the Unmaking of the American Consensus* (New York: Hall and Wang, 2001).

32. Murray Kempton, "Dirsken Delivers the Souls," *New Republic*, May 2, 1964, p. 9; Letter from Walter Carey to Senator, May 12, 1964, Box 10, Series II, Records of the U.S. Chamber of Commerce, HM; Statement of James B. O'Shaughnessy, House Committee on Education and Labor, General Subcommittee on Labor, *Equal Employment Opportunity, 1965*, 89th Cong., 1 sess., June 15, 1965, p. 30. There is good reason to believe that O'Shaughnessy was not exaggerating his level of access to Dirsken. He certainly had ample access in the mid-1960s. For example, chamber officials sent him to see Dirksen in 1966 when the chamber was contemplating legal action regarding the EEO-1 Report that the EEOC had begun requiring employers to keep. See Robert M. Perry to Mrs. John Gomien, April 4, 1966; Folder 1307, Box 17; Robert M. Perry to Bernard J. Waters, April 4, 1966; Gomien to O'Shaughnessy, n.d. (probably April 1966); James B. O'Shaughnessy to Bernard J. Waters, April 4, 1966; all of the foregoing are located in Folder 1307, Box 17, Working Papers, Dirksen Papers, The Dirksen Congressional Center, Pekin, IL (hereafter Dirksen Papers). In a memo to key White House aide Joseph Califano, Attorney General Nicholas deB. Katzenbach took particular note of Dirksen's hostility to the establishment of new regulatory agencies with enforcement powers. These agencies came in two main varieties. The first would have the authority to address individual complaints, like the NLRB, on which it was modeled. The second was a "full-blown enforcement agency, giving it powers similar to those of the FTC. This alternative, rather than dealing with an individual employee's grievance, would permit the commission to prescribe general rules and practices having the force of law." Katzenbach had no illusions about the nature or source of opposition to the latter model. "I cannot conceive of Senator Dirksen's going this far." Memo from Nicholas deB. Katzenbach to Joseph Califano, December 13, 1965, White House Central Files (hereafter WHCF), Subject Files: Legislation (LE/HU), Box 65, Folder: LE/HU 2 8/1/64–12/31/66, LBJL. This memo is also quoted in Graham, *The Civil Rights Era*, 257.

33. Whalen and Whalen, *The Longest Debate*, 35; Graham, *The Civil Rights Era*, 82, 97–98, 132; Burke Marshall Oral History Interview by Anthony Lewis, June 20, 1964, 106, JFKL

34. All quotes from Whalen and Whalen, *The Longest Debate*, 36–39.

35. "Halleck and McCulloch," *Newsweek*, November 11, 1963, p. 34; Daily Log, Monday, October 28, 1963, Folder: Telephone Logs, October 1963, Box 11, Marshall Papers; Appointments File, Monday, October 28, 1963, Folder: Appointments File, Box 4, Nicholas deB. Kazenbach Papers, John F. Kennedy Presi-

dential Library (hereafter Katzenbach Papers); Graham, *The Civil Rights Era*, 132; Lieberman, *Shaping Race Policy*, 160. For more detail on the Katzenbach-McCullough showdown at the Congressional Hotel on the morning of October 28, see Whalen and Whalen, *The Longest Debate*, 57. Rauh's charge regarding Dirksen is recorded in "Quiet Battle Rages over Job Agency's Authority," *LAT*, December 3, 1969. As early as June of 1963, Katzenbach and RFK were well aware of the influence that Dirksen would wield in the Senate and his preferences on major sections of the civil rights bill. See Nicholas deB. Katzenbach to Attorney General, Jun 29, 1963, Folder: Congressional Legislation 6/16–6/29/63, Box 11, Attorney General Series, Robert F. Kennedy Papers (hereafter RFK Papers). On this point, see also Graham, *The Civil Rights Era*, 87.

36. Whalen and Whalen, *The Longest Debate*, 58; Brauer, *John F. Kennedy and the Second Reconstruction*, 307; Graham, *The Civil Rights Era*, 129–32. On the shift to court enforcement in the House, see the informative discussion in Sean Farhang, "The Political Development of Job Discrimination Litigation, 1963–1976," Center for the Study of Law and Society Working Papers, Paper 59 (2007), 14–29. The court-based system of enforcement in the Griffin-Goodell-Quie compromise was not entirely novel. Somewhat ironically, a liberal Democrat, James Roosevelt (D-CA), had introduced a similar bill (H.R. 10144) into the House during the 2nd Session (1962) of the 87th Congress. There is some suggestive evidence, however, that Roosevelt had hoped the bill would serve as a statutory beachhead for subsequent efforts to win cease-and-desist authority. Equally ironic, court enforcement had not always been the preferred system for some of the younger Republicans who had sponsored the original bill. Goodell, for instance, had introduced a classically liberal fair employment bill (H.R. 7252) in the 1st Session (1961) of the same Congress; it called for administrative enforcement. Yet the fundamental point remains the same: It was the GOP that set the outermost limits of the bipartisan bill, for without their cooperation no bill could ultimately pass the House or the Senate. Griffin had been calling for court enforcement throughout 1963, most notably in the committee report on H.R. 405. See U.S. House of Representatives Committee on Education and Labor, *Equal Employment Opportunity Act of 1963*, Report No. 570, July 22, 1963, pp. 15–17. Griffin argued that H.R. 405 was a disappointing reversal of the committee's position on H.R. 10144 in the prior session.

37. *Time*, November 8, 1963, p. 22; *Newsweek*, November 11, 1963, p. 34.

38. Transcript, Nicholas deB. Katzenbach Oral History Interview I, November 12, 1968, by Paige E. Mulhollan, Internet copy, LBJL, 15; Robert F. Kennedy Oral History Interview, 563, JFKL; Whalen and Whalen, *The Longest Debate*, 27–121; Graham, *The Civil Rights Era*, 144; MacLean, *Freedom Is Not Enough*, 70–71. In a reprise of the episode after the president's assassination, Johnson asked Katzenbach if Halleck would go along with an employment provision. Katzenbach mistakenly again claimed that Halleck would give his support.

39. Filvaroff and Wolfinger, "The Origin and Enactment of the Civil Rights Act of 1964," 23; *New Republic*, April 4, 1964, p. 6; Graham, *The Civil Rights Era*, 141–45. See also Timothy N. Thurber, *Hubert H. Humphrey and the African American Freedom Struggle* (New York: Columbia University Press, 1999). On Dirksen, see Byron C. Hulsey, *Everett Dirksen and His Presidents: How a Senate Giant Shaped American Politics* (Lawrence: University Press of Kansas, 2000);

Edward L. Shapsmeier and Frederick H. Schapsmeier, *Dirksen of Illinois: Senatorial Statesman* (Urbana: University of Illinois Press, 1985); Neil MacNeil, *Dirksen: Portrait of a Public Man* (New York: World Publishing, 1970).

40. Kempton, "Dirsken Delivers the Souls," 9; Graham, *The Civil Rights Era*, 146. For a liberal analysis of Dirksen's amendments, see "Dirksen Amendments," *New Republic*, June 6, 1964, pp. 3–4.

41. *WP*, April 11, 1964, A2; *WP*, April 15, 1964, A2; *WP*, April 17, 1964, A2; *CR*, 88th Cong., 2nd sess., April 21, 1964, pp. 8330–31; *NYT*, April 22, 1964, p. 30; An Analysis of Senator Dirksen's Proposed Amendment No. 511 to Title VII of H.R. 7152, April 21, 1964, Folder: Legislative Background Papers, Feb.-Apr. 1964, Box 29, Marshall Papers; Periodic Log Maintained during the Discussions Concerning the Passage of the Civil Rights Act of 1964 by Stephen Horn, Legislative Assistant to U.S. Senator Thomas H. Kuchel (R-CA), Stephen Horn Collection, Congressional Archives, Carl Albert Center, University of Oklahoma (hereafter Horn Log), 138, 159; Appointments File, Tuesday, May 5, 1964, Folder: Calls and Callers 1964: 1 Apr.–30 June, Box 5, Katzenbach Papers; *WP*, May 14, 1964, p. 1; Graham, *The Civil Rights Era*, 147–48; Lieberman, *Shaping Race Policy*, 162; Farhang, "The Political Development of Job Discrimination Litigation, 1963–1976," 32–44.

42. *LAT*, May 17, 1965, p. 16; *WSJ*, May 28, 1965; *NYT*, July 3, 1965, p. 6; *NYT*, July 16, 1965, p. 24; *NYT*, September 16, 1965, p. 32; *NYT*, July 3, 1965; Graham, *The Civil Rights Era*, 189–90; Skrentny, *The Ironies of Affirmative Action*, 122. By the end of the year, EEOC chairman FDR, Jr., pointed out that one-third of the complaint workload and backlog consisted of NAACP-sponsored complaints. Officials at the NAACP "promised him better" screening of cases but warned him to "expect an increasing flow of complaints." Memo from Franklin D. Roosevelt, Jr., to Bill Moyers, November 18, 1965, WHCF, Subject Files: FG/RS/PR18, Box 7, Folder: FG/RS/PR18 11/6/65–11/18/65, LBJL.

43. Democratic Study Group, Fact Sheet 92-12, Equal Employment Opportunities Act of 1971, August 16, 1971, Folder 13, Box 359, Harrison A. Williams Papers, Special Collections and University Archives, Rutgers University Libraries (hereafter H. A. Williams Papers).

44. *NYT*, May 27, 1971, p. 38; *LAT*, December 3, 1969. See also *NYT*, April 26, 1968, p. 24; April 10, 1969, p. 46.

45. Michael I. Sovern, *Legal Restraints on Racial Discrimination in Employment* (New York: Twentieth Century Fund, 1966), 102, 205–6; "Curbs on Job Bias Found Hampered," *NYT*, May 16, 1966, p. 18.

46. *WSJ*, 15 September 1971, p. 12; House Committee on Education and Labor, *Equal Employment Opportunity, 1965*, 89th Congress, 1 sess., 1965, p. 14; *NYT*, July 22, 1965, p. 14; Press Release, EEOC, 9 May 1967, Box 31, Folder: Civil Rights 1965–1971, Hawkins Papers; Remarks of Stephen N. Schulman at Pepperdine College, May 9, 1967, Hawkins Papers. Brown would eventually reverse his position on administrative enforcement, infuriating much of the civil rights community. Brown was "roundly castigated" for his apostasy, and his critics called him a "sellout," accusing him of "backtracking" and "surrender." See "Quiet Battle Rages over Job Agency's Authority," *LAT*, December 3, 1969. Brown endorsed Nixon's preference for court-based enforcement in which the

EEOC would litigate cases on behalf of victims. This shift reflected the larger and gradual accommodation of conservatives to what they considered a more desirable form of enforcement than a full-blown regulatory agency.

47. USCCR, *Federal Civil Rights Enforcement Effort: A Report of the U.S. Commission on Civil Rights 1970* (Washington, DC: U.S. Government Printing Office, 1970), ii, 268–69, 1078; USCCR, *The Federal Civil Rights Enforcement Effort: Seven Months Later* (Washington, DC: U.S. Government Printing Office, May 1971), 3; USCCR, *Federal Civil Rights Enforcement Effort: A Report of the U.S. Commission on Civil Rights 1971* (Washington, DC: U.S. Government Printing Office, 1971), 359. In the late 1960s, members of the bipartisan USCCR included Stephen Horn, former assistant to Senator Thomas H. Kuchel (R-CA) and associate at the Brookings Institution; St. Louis attorney Frankie M. Freeman, first black woman appointed to the USCCR; Mexican-American attorney Manuel Ruiz, Jr.; Maurice B. Mitchell, president of the University of Denver; and Robert S. Rankin. A former staff attorney with the Department of Justice (DOJ) during the drafting of the 1964 Civil Rights Act and 1965 Voting Rights Act, Howard A. Glickstein served as Staff Director and General Counsel of the USCCR. Jeffrey M. Miller led the study as Project Director.

48. Transcript, Nicholas deB. Katzenbach Oral History Interview I, November 12, 1968, by Paige E. Mulhollan, Internet Copy, 15, LBJL, Austin, TX; Report of the Civil Rights Task Force: Proposals for Legislative and Executive Action in 1967, November 1966, WHCF, Aides Files: Joseph Califano, Box 68, Folder: Califano—1966 Task Force on Civil Rights; Memo from General Government Management Division (Rensch) to Director of the Budget, November 14, 1968, 3, Box 26, Task Force Reports, WHCF, LBJL; DOJ-Proposed Initiatives for Inclusion in the State of the Union, Budget, and Economic Messages, 1969: Civil Rights, 5-7, Box 26, Task Force Reports, WHCF, LBJL. In general, Graham tends to understate the extent of support in the Johnson administration for administrative enforcement. The adminstration was only "mildly in favor of congressional proposals for cease-and-desist authority at the EEOC," he writes, arguing that "Katzenbach's task force . . . shared the Budget Bureau's belief that the Hawkins bill's two main provisions 'may be controversial and their essentiality has not been established.'" See Graham, *The Civil Rights Era*, 256, 258. Yet there is ample evidence available—including published and archival sources—to challenge Graham's view. I have sought to present some of the most telling evidence in the foregoing paragraph. On the other hand, it is true that the Nixon administration was nowhere near as enthusiastic about cease-and-desist authority as the Johnson administration.

49. *WP*, May 6, 1967, p. A2; Statement of James B. O'Shaughnessy, House Committee on Education and Labor, Subcommittee on Labor, *Equal Employment Opportunity, 1965*, 89th Cong., 1st sess., June 15, 1965, pp. 30–31, 38; *CT*, March 30, 1949, p. 12; *CD*, April 30, 1957, p. 3; Minutes, June 25, 1965, Folder: Board of Directors Meetings, Minutes, 1963–65, Box 1C, Series 1, USCC Records; *Congressional Quarterly Weekly Report*, July 30, 1965, p. 1514. The legislation also proposed to extend coverage to employers with ten or more employees. This also drew opposition from the chamber, which claimed that "there would be great confusion among these smaller employers to the extent that they

might feel that they had to practice the counterdiscrimination, the discrimination in reverse, and go and see a Negro employee to stay out of trouble." Statement of James B. O'Shaughnessy, *Equal Employment Opportunity, 1965*, p. 39.

50. Minutes, November 3–4, 1966, Folder: Board of Directors Meeting Minutes, 1966–69, Box 1C, Series 1, USCC Records; Prepared Statement of James W. Hunt, Senate Committee on Labor and Public Welfare, Subcommittee on Employment, Manpower, and Poverty, *Equal Employment Opportunity*, 90th Cong., 1st sess., May 5, 1967, 149–53, esp. 150; Statement of James W. Hunt, *Equal Employment Opportunity*, 153–57; *WP*, May 6, 1967, p. A2; *NYT*, April 27, 1966, p. 25. Not every employer opposed the extension of administrative authority to the EEOC. Joseph J. Morrow, a vice-president at Pitney-Bowes, came forward in support of strengthening legislation. See Statement of Joseph J. Morrow, *Equal Employment Opportunity*, 157–59. It is also important to note that business groups were not always opposed to cease-and-desist policies. In 1968, there was private talk among business leaders about the possibility of dropping their opposition to cease and desist—in exchange for legislation abolishing the OFCC. See memorandum from William J. Zinke to Harding Williams, January 25, 1968, Folder: Correspondence–EEOC/AFCC 1967–1968, Box 63, Series 5, NAM Records.

51. Elliot Carlson, "How to Best Toughen the EEOC?" *WSJ*, September 15, 1971, p. 12; Prepared Statement of the NAM, Senate Committee on Labor and Public Welfare, Subcommittee on Labor, *Equal Employment Opportunities Enforcement Act*, 91st Cong., 1st sess., September 16, 1969, pp. 240–43; Prepared Statement of the Aerospace Industries Association of American, *Equal Employment Opportunities Enforcement Act*, 238–40; Prepared Statement of the American Retail Federation, *Equal Employment Opportunities Enforcement Act*, 234–38; Prepared Statement of the Associated General Contractors of America, Senate Committee on Labor and Public Welfare, Subcommittee on Labor, *Equal Employment Opportunities Enforcement Act of 1971*, 92nd Cong., 1st sess., October 4–7, 1971, 377–81; Statement of the NAM, ibid., 471–86, esp. 471; Prepared Statement of the U.S. Chamber of Commerce, ibid., 487–99; Richard G. Godown to Fritz Wenzler, September 4, 1970, Folder: Equal Employment Opportunities Act, Box 64, Series 5, NAM Records.

52. Statement of the NAM, *Equal Employment Opportunities Enforcement Act of 1971*, 471–86, esp. 471; Prepared Statement of the U.S. Chamber of Commerce, *Equal Employment Opportunities Enforcement Act of 1971*, 487–99.

53. "Quiet Battle Rages over Job Agency's Authority," *LAT*, December 3, 1969. The pronounced imbalance in the civil rights coverage of most news organizations after 1964 did not escape the notice of older black leaders. Whitney Young of the NUL acerbically noted the editorial tastes of the national press, which seemed so patently obvious that most residents of black neighborhoods recognized them. "It's reached a point where it's a big joke in Harlem how to get on the front page," he told a writer for the *LAT* in 1966. When interviewed by *U.S. News and World Report* in 1968, he made a similar point about Stokely Carmichael, militant leader of the Student Non-Violent Coordinating Committee (SNCC). "When I make a speech about co-operation between whites and Negroes, I'm given about four or five inches of space. . . . When Stokely talks about

'killing whitey,' his whole speech is reprinted and gets television coverage." Quoted in Nancy White, *Whitney M. Young, Jr., and the Struggle for Civil Rights* (Princeton: Princeton University Press, 1989), 210.

54. Other supporters of cease-and-desist authority included John O'Hara, who introduced H.R. 8852 1965. See *CR*, 89th Cong., 1st sess., June 8, 1965. For a copy of Reid's bill, see H.R. 8999 in Reid Papers.

55. U.S. Congress, Committee of the Whole House, *CR*, 89th Cong., 2nd sess., April 27, 1966, pp. 9119, 9120.

56. *CR*, 89th Cong., 2nd sess., April 27, 1966, p. 9129.

57. Statement of Joseph Rauh, Jr., House Committee on Education and Labor, Subcommittee on Labor, *Equal Employment Opportunity Enforcement Procedures*, 91st Cong., 1 and 2 sess., December 2, 1969, p. 109; Rehnquist quoted in Graham, *The Civil Rights Era*, 425; *NYT*, April 10, 1969, p. 1; April 28, 1969, p. 25; February 8, 1968; *CR*, April 27, 1966, pp. 9128, 9131, 9133.

58. *Congressional Quarterly Weekly Report*, July 30, 1965, p. 1514; U.S. Congress, House Committee on Education and Labor, *Equal Employment Opportunity, 1965*, 89th Congress, 1st sess., 1965; U.S. Congress, House of Representatives, Equal Employment Opportunity Act of 1965, H. Rept. No. 718, 89th Cong., 1st sess., August 3, 1965; *NYT*, September 9, 1965, p. 27; *NYT*, September 14, 1965, pp. 1, 19. H.R. 10065 had somewhat complicated origins. It began in early 1965 as H.R. 9222. Its chief sponsor, Powell, had sought to win approval for his bill by threatening to withhold his vote from another bill that would have repealed the "right-to-work" provision of the Taft-Hartley bill. It was a controversial move that left a bitter taste in the mouths of some friends of civil rights, and it was left to Hawkins to introduce a clean bill after tensions subsided.

59. *Congressional Quarterly Almanac*, January 14, 1966, p. 38; Republican Policy Committee Statement on Equal Employment Opportunity Act of 1965, H.R. 10065, Folder: Civil Rights—EEOC—Legislation, Box 66, Series 5, NAM Records; *CR*, 89th Cong., 2nd sess, April 27, 1966, pp. 9153–54,; *Congressional Quarterly*, April 29, 1966, pp. 867, 900–901; "Special Message to the Congress Proposing Further Legislation to Strengthen Civil Rights," April 28, 1966, *Public Papers of the Presidents of the United States: Lyndon B. Johnson, 1966* (Washington, DC: U.S. Government Printing Office, 1967), 461–69; *Congressional Quarterly*, May 6, 1966, p. 945; *CR*, 89th Cong., 2nd sess., April 28, 1966, p. 9298. NAM officials believed that the Hawkins bill perished because of the potential for a protracted filibuster in the Senate. See W. P. Gullander to Lambert H. Miller, July 13, 1967, Folder: Newport News Shipbuilding, Series 5, NAM Records. The board of the USCC also voted in 1970 to oppose strengthening legislation. See USCC Board of Directors, Minutes, February 26, 1970, Folder: Board of Director Meeting Minutes, 1970–1975 (April), Series 1, Box 1C, USCC Records. In his otherwise scrupulously researched study, Graham mistakenly asserts that Johnson's State of the Union address and his special civil rights message to Congress on April 28 were "silent" on employment discrimination. Graham, *The Civil Rights Era*, 258. It is true that Johnson did not explicitly endorse strengthening legislation in his 1966 State of the Union address; he spent most of his time discussing foreign policy, primarily Vietnam. The four paragraphs allotted to civil rights were understandably reserved for passages proposing entirely new legisla-

tion rather than legislation that would enhance laws already on the books. It is not true, however, that Johnson failed to mention strengthening legislation in his April 28 message to Congress. As he said in his speech, "[t]he social and economic toll exacted by discrimination in employment, for example, is felt in all sections. The federal government has worked strenuously to bring leadership to a national effort against such discrimination through the President's Committee on Equal Employment Opportunity, Plans for Progress with industry, and the establishment of the Equal Employment Opportunity Commission through the Civil Rights Act of 1964. Other specific steps can now be taken to bolster this effort. The first year's experience of the EEOC suggests that it should be endowed with enforcement power and that its coverage should be broadened." Graham's oversight is understandable in a work of such breadth and depth, but it is not historiographically insignificant, for it leads him to underestimate greatly the degree of support within the Johnson administration for strengthening legislation like H.R. 10065, circa 1966. Hence the real puzzle that remains unresolved is why the administration did not assign a higher priority to strengthening the EEOC *despite* substantial and broad support for such a move among White House advisors, USCCR commissioners, heads of state FEPCs, EEOC chairmen, and numerous civil rights liberals. Graham argues that H.R. 10065's demise stemmed from Johnson's sudden desire to seek strong legislation against housing discrimination. This seems like a valid possibility, but Graham does not cite any evidence directly supporting the claim. See Graham, *The Civil Rights Era*, 258–61. At the same time, it is equally possible that Johnson's calculations about how to proceed were decisively shaped by Dirksen's well-known opposition to cease-and-desist authority for the EEOC. This possibility is not directly supported by the archival record either, and so the mystery remains to be resolved by future research.

60. *Congressional Quarterly Weekly Report*, September 18, 1971, p. 2251; *Congressional Quarterly Weekly Report*, September 18, 1970, p. 2251; *Congressional Quarterly Weekly Report*, August 28, 1970, p. 2139; House Committee on Education and Labor, *Equal Employment Opportunity Enforcement Procedures*, 91st Congress, 2nd sess., 1970; "Equal Employment Opportunities Enforcement Act of 1970," House Report No. 91-1434, 91st Congress, 2 sess., 1970; Senate Committee on Labor and Public Welfare, *Equal Employment Opportunities Enforcement Act*, 91st Congress, 1st sess., 1969; "Equal Employment Opportunities Enforcement Act," Senate Report No. 91-1137, 91st Congress, 2nd sess., 1970; *Congressional Quarterly*, October 9, 1970, p. 2465; Graham, *The Civil Rights Era*, 432. Co-sponsoring the Ayers bill were Albert H. Quie (R-MN), Alphonzo Bell (R-CA), John R. Dellenback (R-OR), and William A. Steiger (R-WI). Secondary sponsors of S. 2806 included Henry L. Bellmon (R-OK), Robert P. Griffin (R-MI), Richard S. Schweiker (R-PA), and Hugh D. Scott, Jr. (R-PA).

61. Arnold Aronson, Memo: No. 14-70, 30 November 1970, Box 33: Folder: EEOC Statements, Hawkins Papers; Letter from Augustus Hawkins and Ogden Reid to William N. Colmer, November 25, 1970, Box 33, Folder: EEOC Statements, Hawkins Papers; *WP*, December 5, 1970; Graham, *The Civil Rights Era*, 433.

62. Graham, *The Civil Rights Era*, 428; Don Elisburg to unknown (possibly Harrison A. Williams or his staff), October 4, 1971, Folder 13, Box 359, H. A. Williams Papers. For more on Brown, see Kotzlowski, *Nixon's Civil Rights*, 118–22.

63. *WSJ*, April 8, 1971; *NYT*, May 27, 1971; *Congressional Quarterly Weekly Report*, March 19, 1971, p. 610; March 26, 1971, p. 710; June 11, 1971, p. 1271; NAM Industrial Relations Department, *Guidelines for Action*, June 29, 1971, Folder: EEOC/OFCC—Philadelphia Plan—Civil Rights, Box 64, Series 5; NAM Records; U.S. House of Representatives, Committee on Education and Labor, *Equal Employment Opportunities Enforcement Act of 1971*, Report No. 92-238, 92nd Congress, 1st sess. (Washington, DC: U.S. Government Printing Office, 1971); Democratic Study Group, Fact Sheet 92-112, 11; Graham, *The Civil Rights Era*, 434–39. Voting for the Erlenborn substitute were Romano Mazzoli (D-KY), Albert H. Quie (R-MN), Alphonzo Bell (R-CA), John Erlenborn (R-IL), John R. Dellenback (R-OR), Marvin L. Esch (R-MI), Edwin D. Eshleman (R-PA), Steiger (R-WI), Earl F. Landgrebe (R-IN) , Orval H. Hansen (R-ID), Earl B. Ruth (R-NC), Edwin B. Forsythe (R-NJ), Victor V. Veysey (R-CA), and Jack Kemp (R-NY). Voting against it were Carl D. Perkins (D-KY), Frank J. Thompson, Jr. (D-NJ), John H. Dent (D-PA), Roman C. Pucinski (D-IL), Dominick V. Daniels (D-NJ), John Brademas (D-IN), James G. O'Hara (D-MI), Augustus Hawkins (D-CA), William D. Ford (D-MI), Patsy Mink (D-HI), Scheuer (D-NY), Meeds (D-WA), Philip Burton (D-CA), Gaydos (D-PA), Clay (D-MO), Shirley Chisholm (D-NY), Ella T. Grasso (D-CT), Herman Badillo (D-NY), and Peyser (R-NY).

64. *NYT*, June 6, 1971.

65. NAM Legislative Proposal—an analysis, August 20, 1971, attached to Richard D. Godown to Boyd Thomas, September 14, 1971, Folder: EEOC/ OFCC—Philadelphia—Civil Rights, Box 64, Series 5, NAM Records. See also NAM Industrial Relations Department, Guidelines for Action: EEOC Legislation, June 29 1971, Folder: Folder: EEOC/OFCC—Philadelphia Plan—Civil Rights, Box 64, Series 5, NAM Records. In official policy positions taken in 1966 and 1967, NAM reaffirmed its historic commitment to voluntary action against discrimination.

66. *WSJ*, September 13, 1971; September 17, 1971; USCC, Twelve Major Labor Bills before the 92nd Congress: What You Might Expect If These Bills Are Enacted into Law, 1971, Box 27, Series II, USCC Records; U.S. Chamber of Commerce, Congressional Issues: Summaries of Some of the Major Issue That May Receive Attention in the Second Session of the 92nd Congress, Box 28, USCC Records; Gerry Feder to Senator Williams, September 14, 1971, Folder 18, Box 363, H. A. Williams Papers.

67. *NYT*, September 17, 1971; October 22, 1971, 13; *Congressional Quarterly Weekly Report*, September 18, 1971, pp. 1955, 1977; *Congressional Quarterly Weekly Report*, October 16, pp. 1971, 2137; Graham, *The Civil Rights Era*, 436; Lieberman, *Shaping Race Policy*, 184.

68. For a multivariate analysis of the votes, see table A.11 and the associated discussion in the appendix.

69. Harrison A. Williams to Dear Colleague, n.d. (probably September 1971), Folder 11, Box 359, H. A. Williams Papers; Gerry Feder to Harrison A. Williams, October 11, 1971, Folder 11, Box 359, H. A. Williams Papers.

70. *NYT*, October 22, 1971, 13; *Congressional Quarterly Weekly Report*, November 6, 1971, p. 2285.

71. *Congressional Quarterly Weekly Report*, January 1, 1972, p. 9; Minutes, Committee on Labor and Public Welfare: Executive Session, October 21, 1972, Folder 9, Box 359, H. A. Williams Papers; *Congressional Action: A Bulletin for the National Chamber's Congressional Action System*, V16, N1A, January 7, 1972; W. P. Gullander to NAM membership, January 17, 1972, Folder: Civil Rights— EEOC—Legislation, Box 66, Series 5, NAM Records.

72. *NYT*, January 25, 1972, p. 1; January 27, 1972, pp. 1, 17; February 1, 1972, p. 7; February 10, 1972, 43; February 23, 1972, 1; *WSJ*, February 2, 1972, 2; February 9, 1972, 1; February 10, 1972, 1; February 23, 1972, 5; *Congressional Quarterly Weekly Report*, January 29, 1972, pp. 222, 224, 225; February 5, 1972, pp. 259, 260; February 19, 1972, p. 409; February 26, 1972, p. 454. For a multivariate analysis of the Senate votes, see table A.12 and the associated discussion in the appendix.

73. Gary Feder to Senator Williams, February 7, 1972, Folder 11, Box 359, H. A. Williams Papers; Gary Feder to The Chairman, February 24, 1972, Folder 11, Box 359, H. A. Williams Papers; *NYT*, February 27, 1972, p. E3; Graham, *The Civil Rights Era*, 443; House Committee on Labor and Public Welfare, Subcommittee on Labor, *Legislative History of the Equal Employment Opportunity Act of 1972*, 92nd Cong., 2nd sess., 1972.

74. Graham, *The Civil Rights Era*, 25, 33; Brauer, *John F. Kennedy and the Second Reconstruction*. For a typical example of how "affirmative action" was used in a FEP bill, see S. 984, 80th Congress, 1 sess., March 27, 1947 (Washington, DC: Congressional Information Service).

75. Graham, *The Civil Rights Era*, 40–41, 46.

76. 26 *Federal Register* 1977 (March 6, 1961); Graham, *The Civil Rights Era*, 33. Taylor recalled his intervention in a 1969 oral history interview: "I went up to Abe Fortas' office, and I did it, I put the word 'affirmative' in there at that time." Quoted in Graham, *The Civil Rights Era*, 33. Taylor's memory is corroborated by some documentary evidence. When a manager at Polaroid, H. G. Pearson, wrote Taylor in 1965 to ask about how the term "affirmative action" originated, Taylor wrote back to explain that he was the one who thought of including it. "You have asked about how the term 'affirmative action' originated. I happen to be the person who thought of the addition of that adjective 'affirmative' to the language which had appeared in the previous order. I was torn between 'affirmative' and 'positive' and finally decided on 'affirmative' not only because of its alliterative effect, but because it was somewhat broader in concept—or so it seemed to me, but I am not any longer quite so sure." HT to H.G. Pearson, June 25, 1965, Folder: General Correspondence and Memoranda, Box 8, Hobart Taylor Papers, Bentley Historical Library, University of Michigan, Ann Arbor (hereafter Taylor Papers).

77. Conference of Community Leaders on Equal Opportunity, *The American Dream—Equal Opportunity* (Washington, DC: U.S. Government Printing Office,

1962), 11–2; Lyndon B. Johnson, "For Equal Job Opportunity," *NYT*, June 20, 1962. The letter was reprinted and published in *Information from the President's Committee on Equal Employment Opportunity*, Newsletter No. 6, July 1962. On the importance of the PCEEO to affirmative action, see Moreno, *From Direct Action to Affirmative Action*, 191; and Stacey Kinlock Sewell, "Contracting Racial Equality: Affirmative Action Policy and Practice in the United States, 1945–1970," Ph.D. diss., Dept. of History, Rutgers University, 1999, p. 146. Citing the work of Herman Belz and Hugh Davis Graham, Moreno argues that PCEEO "sponsored a program of voluntary program of racial preference," while Sewell argues that PfP constituted Taylor's "most complete expression of affirmative action." See also Dobbin, *Inventing Equal Opportunity*.

78. Conference of Community Leaders on Equal Opportunity, *The American Dream—Equal Opportunity* (Washington, DC: President's Committee on Equal Employment Opportunity, 1962), 11–12; U.S. President's Committee on Equal Employment Opportunity, *The First Nine Months* (Washington, DC: The Committee, 1962).

79. Conference of Community Leaders on Equal Opportunity, *The American Dream—Equal Opportunity* (Washington, DC: President's Committee on Equal Employment Opportunity, 1962), 12; U.S. President's Committee on Equal Employment Opportunity, *Committee Reporter*, N1 (May 1963): 2; U.S. President's Committee on Equal Employment Opportunity, *The First Nine Months* (Washington, DC: The Committee, 1962), 2; U.S. President's Committee on Equal Employment Opportunity, *Report to the President*, 108–14; U.S. President's Committee on Equal Employment Opportunity, *Committee Reporter*, N1 (November 1963): 1; U.S. President's Committee on Equal Employment Opportunity, *Committee Reporter*, N2 (May 1964): 1; U.S. President's Committee on Equal Employment Opportunity, *Committee Reporter*, N1 (May 1964): 5–6; U.S. President's Committee on Equal Employment Opportunity, *Committee Reporter*, N1 (May 1964): 7–8; *NYT*, June 14, 1969, p. 33. The difference between PfP and NAB was summarized as follows by the Administrative Director of PfP: "Plans for Progress is primarily involved in the promotion and conduct of equal employment as a sound management philosophy and business practice. It is a catalyst to affirmative action in all phase of business and industry. NAB, on the other hand, is designed to do a given task, namely recruiting, employment, and training of hard-core unemployed persons—100,000 by June 1969 and 500,000 by June 1971." See Plans for Progress, *Newsletter* 50 (July–August 1968), 4. Skrentny finds evidence that the adoption of racially attentive employment practices by members of the NAB were driven by the riots. See Skrentny, *The Ironies of Affirmative Action*, 90–91.

80. Minutes, Plans for Progress Advisory Council, January 14, 1966, Folder: Advisory Council Meetings, January 14, 1966, Box 9, Taylor Papers; Minutes, Plans for Progress Advisory Council, October 20, 1966, Folder: Advisory Council Meetings: October 20, 1966, Box 9, Taylor Papers; Plans for Progress, *Report: August, 1964–December, 1965* (Washington, DC: U.S. President's Committee on Equal Employment Opportunity, 1965).

81. "Things Are Changing in Job Opportunities," *Washington Afro American*, October 5, 1965; Henry C. Wehde to Executive Staff, May 11, 1967, Folder: Advertising Council (1), Box 9, Taylor Papers; M. H. Oettinger, Jr., to Hobart

Taylor, Jr., June 29, 1967, Folder: Advertising Council (1), Box 9, Taylor Papers; Bruce L. Roberts to Hobart Taylor, Jr., January 8, 1965, Folder: Advertising Council (1), Box 9, Taylor Papers. The campaign was launched after Watts but planning for it had begun before the riot.

82. U.S. President's Committee on Equal Emplyoment Opportunity, *Report to the President*, 112–13. For one example of a pledge made to PfP, see Pledge of First Pennsylvania Bank to the President of the United States as a Participant in Plans for Progress (Philadelphia, PA, 1967), attached to Charles W. Books to Eugene F. Rowan, October 18, 1967, Folder: Administrative Director, Box 8, Taylor Papers.

83. Chicago Regional Community Leaders' Conference, *Chicago Regional Community Leaders' Conference* (Washington, DC: U.S. President's Committee on Equal Employment Opportunity, 1964).

84. U.S. President's Committee for Equal Employment Opportunity, *Report to the President*, 111–12; Chicago Regional Community Leaders' Conference, *Chicago Regional Community Leaders' Conference* (Washington, DC: U.S. President's Committee on Equal Employment Opportunity, 1964).

85. W. Willard Wirtz, "Program of Civil Responsibilities," *Eastern Region Community Leaders' Conference* (Washington, DC: U.S. President's Committee on Equal Employment Opportunity, 1964).

86. Willard Wirtz, Remarks, pp. 6–40, Folder: Administrative Records (2), Box 8, Taylor Papers.

87. White House Conference on Equal Employment Opportunity Provisional Program, Folder: PCEEO Printed Materials, Box 8, Taylor Papers; "Remarks of the President at Howard University," Washington, DC, June 4, 1965, quoted in MacLean, *Freedom Is Not Enough*, 185. See also President Lyndon B. Johnson's Commencement Address at Howard University: "To Fulfill These Rights," June 4, 1965 (*http://www.lbjlib.utexas.edu/johnson/archives.hom/speeches.hom/650604 .asp*, accessed August 21, 2008).

88. Remarks of HHH to the NAACP National Convention, July 6, 1966, p. 6, Folder: Speeches, Publications, Newspaper Clippings, Box 11, Taylor Papers; Plans for Progress, *Report: January 1966–August 1967* (Washington, DC, 1967).

89. Skrentny, *The Minority Rights Revolution*; Timothy M. Thurber, "Racial Liberalism, Affirmative Action, and the Troubled History of the President's Committee on Government Contracts," *Journal of Policy History* 18 (November 2006): 446–76; Graham, *The Civil Rights Era*, 59; U.S. President's Committee on Equal Employment Opportunity, *Report to the President*, 28, 34–35; U.S. President's Committee on Equal Employment Opportunity, *Report to the President* (Washington, DC: U.S. Government Printing Office, 1963), 109, 112.

90. U.S. President's Committee on Equal Employment Opportunity, *The First Nine Months*, 41–45. A separate form, Standard Form 41, was developed for construction contractors. See also *Information from the President's Committee on Equal Employment Opportunity*, Newsletter No. 4 (January 1962): 2. See also *Guide for Investigations and Compliance Reviews in Equal Employment Opportunity* (Washington, DC: U.S. President's Committee on Equal Employment Opportunity, 1961). See also U.S. President's Committee on Equal Employment Opportunity, *Rules and Regulations* (Washington, DC: U.S. Government Printing

Office 1961). *Rules and Regulations* were amended three times after their initial promulgation on July 22, 1961—once on November 23, 1962, a second time on June 10, 1963, and a final time on September 3, 1963. The changes of September 1963 were the most extensive, reflecting the issuance of E. O. 11114. Discussions of Standard Form 40 include Graham, *The Civil Rights Era*, 53; Skrentny, *Minority Rights Revolution*, 103.

91. U.S. President's Committee on Equal Employment Opportunity, *Report to the President*, 28; Conference of Community Leaders on Equal Opportunity, *The American Dream—Equal Opportunity*, 11–12; U.S. President's Committee on Equal Employment Opporunity, *The First Nine Months*, 3. The NAM Legal Department pointed out that a major difference between the Eisenhower committee and Kennedy committee is that the former only had the power to "advise and recommend," whereas the latter in principle had the power to prescribe government procedures as well as the power to terminate contracts or debar contractors. NAM Law Department Memo, March 23, 1961, p. 8, Folder: EEOC 1965, Box 135, Series 7 NAM Records.

92. Skrentny, *Minority Rights Revolution*, 103–4; Graham, *The Civil Rights Era*, 42; Sewell, "Contracting Racial Equality."

93. Graham, *The Civil Rights Era*, 282–84; Skrentny, *The Ironies of Affirmative Action*, 134.

94. Sylvester quoted in Skrentny, *The Ironies of Affirmative Action*, 135; Robert C. Landon to Edward C. Sylvester, March 14, 1968, Folder: EEOC/OFCC—Philadelphia Plan—Civil Rights, Box 64, Series 5, NAM Records; Graham, *The Civil Rights Era*, 322–45; Sugrue, "Affirmative Action from Below"; Skrentny, *Ironies of Affirmative Action*; Stryker and Pedriana, "Political Culture Wars 1960s Style"; MacLean, *Freedom Is Not Enough*, 95–102; Moreno, *From Direct Action to Affirmative Action*, 262–66; Department of Labor (DOL) Press Release, 10-527, June 27, 1969, Folder: 1969—Civil Rights—OFCC Philadelphia Plan, Box 64, Series 5, NAM Records; DOL Press Release, 10-696, September 23, 1969, Folder: Philadelphia Plan, Box 10, Taylor Papers. On the position taken by NAM on the Philadelphia Plan, see Lambert Miller to Samuel J. Ervin, Jr., October 24, 1969; W.P. Gullander to Leo V. Bodine, January 28, 1970, both in Folder: EEOC/OFCC—Philadelphia Plan—Civil Rights, Box 64, Series 5, NAM Records. Gullander wrote, "Senator Ervin's position is well argued and his principal points (1) the Order sets illegal hiring quotas, and (2) the Congress was misled by administration assurances that no quotas were required . . . seem irrefutable." Though they acknowledged that great progress had been made, NAM officials claimed well through 1969 that they remained highly uncertain about the meaning of affirmative action. "Certainly the fact that industry has many extreme problems in effecting compliance, the fact that regulations are being misinterpreted on both sides, the fact that the government has great need to clarify its position especially what is meant by 'affirmative action,' were made abundantly clear." See R. D. Godown to L.H. Miller, October 4, 1969, Folder: Plans for Progress, Box 64, Series 5, NAM Records.

95. John Mitchell to George P. Schultz, September 22, 1969, Folder: 1969—Civil Rights—OFCC Philadelphia Plan, Box 64, Series V, NAM Records; Arthur Fletcher, *The Silent Sell-Out: Government Betrayal of Blacks to the Craft*

Unions (New York: Third Press, 1974), 65. For more on the role played by Fletcher and administrative pragmatism, see Skrentny, *The Ironies of Affirmative Action*, 139; Graham, *The Civil Rights Era*, 326–29.

96. USCCR, *Equal Employment Opportunity under Federal Law: A Guide to Federal Law Prohibiting Discrimination on Account of Race, Religion, or National Origins in Private and Public Employment*, Clearinghouse Publication No. 17 (Washington, DC: U.S. Government Printing Office, August 1969), 23–27. See also PfP, *Newsletter 50* (July–August 1968), 1; PfP, *Newsletter 52* (October 1968). Useful material on the National Alliance of Businessmen may be found in Folder: National Alliance of Businessmen, Box 10, Taylor Papers. PfP organized a similar question and answer session between the EEOC, OFCC, PfP companies, and non-PfP companies in 1968.

97. *WSJ*, January 16. 1970, 15; DOL, Press Release, February 3, 1970, Folder: EEOC/OFCC—Philadelphia Plan—Civil Rights, Box 64, Series 5, NAM Records; Plans for Progress, *A Summary of Activities and Accomplishments, 1965–1968* (Washington, DC, 1969), Folder: Summary of Activities and Accomplishments, 1965–1968, Box 8, Taylor Papers. In a draft letter to *Business Week*, Lambert M. Miller confirmed that Wilks was correct in asserting that Order No. 4 was based on affirmative action guidelines first promulgated by PfP in 1968. See W. P. Gullander to *Business Week*, January 26, 1970, attached to Lambert M. Miller to W. P. Gullander, January 26, 1970, Folder: Folder: EEOC/OFCC—Philadelphia Plan—Civil, Box 64, Series 5, NAM Records.

98. PfP, "Affirmative Action Guidelines" (Washington, DC, n.d. [probably 1968]), Folder: Speeches, Box 11, Taylor Papers. My assertion that "Affirmative Action Guidelines" was published in 1968 is based on a letter in which the president of NAM, W. P. Gullander, explicitly notes that the "guidelines Mr. Wilks referred to [in 1970] were prepared and initially published by "Plans for Progress" and were included with other reference material distributed to all attendees at the co-sponsored NAM/PfP Equal Employment Opportunity Conferences held across the country in 1968. These guidelines were subsequently included in a join NAM/PfP publication: *Equal Employment Opportunity: Compliance and Affirmative Action*." See W. P. Gullander to *Business Week*, January 26, 1970, attached to Lambert M. Miller to W. P. Gullander, January 26, 1970, Folder: Folder: EEOC/OFCC—Philadelphia Plan—Civil, Box 64, Series 5, NAM Records. Gullander had asked that his general counsel draft the letter because *Business Week* had erroneously reported that NAM was the original author of Order No. 4 in an article entitled, "The Unhappy Parent of New Hiring Rules," which appeared in the January 25, 1970 issue. See also NAM Law Department Memo, February 12, 1970, p. 3, Folder: EEOC/OFCC—Philadelphia Plan—Civil, Box 64, Series 5, NAM Records. For a recounting of the meetings, see PfP, *Newsletter 52* (October 1968).

99. Charles W. Books to Eugene F. Rowan, October 18, 1967, Folder: Administrative Director, Box 8, Taylor Papers; PfP, *Newsletter 50* (July–August 1968), 11.

100. PfP, *Report: January 1966–August 1967* (Washington, DC, 1967); PfP, *Information News Letter* 43 (June–July 1967), 3; PfP, *Newsletter 50* (July–August 1968), 9. PfP staff members held fourteen "affirmative action conferences" with PfP companies in fourteen cities in September and October of 1968. The purpose

of the conference was to review ongoing PfP programs and analyze the progress made by PfP companies. See PfP, *Newsletter* 50 (July–August 1968), 1.

101. *Contractors Association of Eastern Pennsylvania v. Secretary of Labor*, 442 F.2d 159 (3rd Cir., 1971) cert. denied 404 U.S. 854 (1971); Graham, *The Civil Rights Era*, 341, 437; *CT*, January 7, 1970, p. 5; *NYT*, March 15, 1970, p. 30; *NYT*, April 24, 1971, p. 36.

102. Graham, *The Civil Rights Era*, 383–89; *Griggs v. Duke Power Co.*, 401 U.S. 424 (1971); EEOC Guidelines on Employee Selection Procedures, 29 C.F.R. Section 1607.3 (1970); *Parham v. Southwestern Bell Tel. Co.*, 433 F.2d 421, 426-27 (8th Cir. 1970); Local 189, *United Papermakers v. United States*, 416 F.2d 980, 982-83 (5th Cir. 1969); Richard A. Primus, "Equal Protection and Disparate Impact: Round Three," *Harvard Law Review* 117 (December 2003): 506. For a broader, illuminating analysis of the evolving relationship of equal protection and disparate impact, see Primus, "Equal Protection and Disparate Impact." For a variety of views on *Griggs*, see Skrentny, *The Ironies of Affirmative Action*, 166–71; Moreno, *From Direct Action to Affirmative Action*, 267–82; MacLean, *Freedom Is Not Enough*, 109.

103. House Committee on Labor and Public Welfare, *Legislative History of the Equal Employment Opportunity Act of 1972* (Washington, DC: U.S. Government Printing Office, 1972), 261.

104. Kotzlowski, *Nixon's Civil Rights*, 118–21; Nancy MacLean, *Freedom Is Not Enough*; Frymer, *Black and Blue*; Moreno, *From Direct Action to Affirmative Action*; Dobbin, *Inventing Equal Opportunity*.

Chapter Six

1. Weir, *Politics and Jobs*, 163; Steven Brint and Jerome Karabel, "Institutional Origins and Transformations: The Case of American Community Colleges," in *The New Institutionalism in Organizational Analysis*, edited by Walter W. Powell and Paul J. DiMaggio (Chicago: University of Chicago Press, 1991), 343.

2. See Paul Frymer, "Acting When Elected Officials Won't: Federal Courts and Civil Rights Enforcement in U.S. Labor Unions, 1935–1985," *American Political Science Review* 97 (August 2003): 483–99; Frymer, *Black and Blue*.

3. Dobbin and Sutton, "The Strength of a Weak State"; Dobbin, *Inventing Equal Opportunity*; John D. Skrentny, "Law and the American State," *Annual Review of Sociology* 32 (2006): 213–44; Robin Stryker, "Half Empty, Half Full or Neither: Law, Inequality, and Social Change in Capitalist Democracies," *Annual Review of Law and Social Science* 3 (2008): 69–97; Lieberman, *Shaping Race Policy*; William Novak, "The Myth of the 'Weak' American State," *American Historical Review* 113 (June 2008): 752–72; Sean Farhang, "The Litigation State: Public Regulation and Private Lawsuits in the American Separation of Powers System," Ph.D. diss., Columbia University, 2005; Frymer, *Black and Blue*; MacLean, *Freedom Is Not Enough*; Timothy J. Minchin, *The Color of Work: The Struggle for Civil Rights in the Southern Paper Industry, 1945–1980* (Chapel Hill: University of North Carolina Press, 2001); Timothy J. Minchin, *Hiring the Black Worker: The Racial Integration of the Southern Textile Industry, 1960–1980*

(Chapel Hill: University of North Carolina Press, 1999). On the role of the South, see James J. Heckman, "The Central Role of the South in Account for the Economic Progress of Black Americans," *American Economic Review* 80 (May 1990): 242–46;

4. On the effect of court-ordered affirmative action on police departments, see Justin McCrary, "The Effect of Court-Ordered Hiring Quotas on the Composition and Quality of Policy," *American Economic Review* 97 (March 2007): 318–53.

5. Biondi, *To Stand and Fight*, 98–111; Moreno, *From Direct Action to Affirmative Action*, 2, 107–61.

6. On the history of fair housing law, see Douglas Massey and Nancy Denton, *American Apartheid* (Cambridge: Harvard University Press, 1988), 187–212. On the failure of federal efforts to achieve metropolitan desegregation, see Chris Bonastia, *Knocking on the Door: The Federal Government's Attempt to Desegregate the Suburbs* (Princeton: Princeton University Press, 2006). The claim that affirmative action would have taken root despite the passage of FEP legislation is the most powerful criticism of the argument that I make. Almost all counterfactual arguments take the form of the following proposition: "If it had not been for a decisive choice, critical mistake, or fateful accident, then events would have turned out differently, rather than the way they actually did." Causality of a limited sort is ascribed to the choice, mistake, or accident. If, however, a critic can convincingly argue that the actual outcome would have occurred despite the "decisive" choice, "critical" mistake, or "fateful" accident—in other words, if he or she can make the case that the outcome was inevitable—then the counterfactual argument fails. The posited cause is obviously irrelevant to the observed effect. This criticism is why I spend so much time trying to imagine the counterfactual scenario. Doing so—with as much fidelity to actual historical circumstances as possible—permits readers to weigh and assess the validity of the argument for themselves.

7. For an introduction to the history of the Voting Rights Act and the longer history of the African American enfranchisement, see Steven F. Lawson, *Black Ballots: Voting Rights in the South, 1944–1969* (New York: Columbia University Press, 1976). See also Chandler Davidson and Bernard Grofman, "The Voting Rights Act and the Second Reconstruction," in *Quiet Revolution in the South: The Impact of the Voting Rights Act, 1965–1990*, edited by Chandler Davidson and Bernard Grofman (Princeton: Princeton University Press, 1994).

8. See Amenta, *Bold Relief*; John D. Skrentny, "Policy-Elite Beliefs and Social Movement Success: Understanding Group Variation in Inclusion in Affirmative Action," *American Journal of Sociology* 111 (May 2006): 1762–815.

9. Immergut, "Institutions, Veto Points, and Policy Results; Immergut, *Health Politics*; Evelyne Huber and John D. Stephens, "Partisan Governance, Women's Employment, and the Social Democratic Service State," *American Sociological Review* 65 (June 2000): 323–42; Evelyne Huber, Charles Ragin, and John D. Stephens, "Social Democracy, Christian Democracy, Constitutional Structure, and the Welfare State," *American Journal of Sociology* 99 (November 1993): 711–49; Amenta, *Bold Relief*; Amenta, *When Movements Matter*; Sarah A. Soule and Yvonne Zylan, "Runaway Train? The Diffusion of State-Level Reform in ADC/AFDC Eligibility Requirements, 1950–1967," *American Journal of Sociology* 103

(November 1997): 751; Lieberman, *Making Race Policy*; Isaac William Martin, *The Permanent Tax Revolt: How the Property Tax Transformed American Politics* (Palo Alto: Stanford University Press, 2008). For a game-game theoretic application of the veto points concept, see George Tsebelis, *Veto Players: How Political Institutions Work* (Princeton: Princeton University Press, 2002);

10. Gary Gerstle, "The Crucial Decade: The 1940s and Beyond," *Journal of American History*, 92 (March 2006): 1292; Goldman, *The Crucial Decade*, 292–93; Gerstle, "Race and the Myth of the Liberal Consensus," 579–86; Matusow, *The Unraveling of America*

11. Gerstle, "The Crucial Decade: The 1940s and Beyond," 1292; Lichtenstein, "From Corporatism to Collective Bargaining: Organized Labor and the Eclipse of Social Democracy in the United States," 122–52; Ira Katznelson, "Was the Great Society a Lost Opportunity?"; Korstad and Lichtenstein, "Opportunities Found and Lost," 786–811; Von Eschen, *Race against Empire*; Biondi, *To Stand and Fight*; John Higham, "The Cult of the 'American Consensus': Homogenizing Our History," *Commentary* 27 (January 1959): 93–100; Godfrey Hodgson, *America in Our Time* (New York: Vintage Books, 1978), 67–98. See as well Risa Goluboff, *The Lost Promise of Civil Rights* (Cambridge: Harvard University Press, 2007).

12. Hirsch, *Making the Second Ghetto*; Self, *American Babylon*; MacLean, *Freedom Is Not Enough*; Rhomberg, *No There There*; Biondi, *To Stand and Fight*; Thomas J. Sugrue, "Crabgrass-Roots Politics: Race, Rights, and the Reaction against Liberalism," *Journal of American History* 82 (September 1995): esp. 551–52; Sugrue, *The Origins of the Urban Crisis*, esp. 268. See also Sugrue, "Affirmative Action from Below," 145–73.

13. The material in the current section draws on ideas originally presented in Anthony S. Chen, Robert Mickey, and Robert Van Houweling, "Explaining the Contemporary Alignment of Race and Party: Evidence from California's 1946 Ballot Initiative on Fair Employment," *Studies in American Political Development* 22 (Fall 2008): 204–28, as well as Anthony S. Chen, "The Party of Lincoln and the Politics of State Fair Employment Practices Legislation in the North, 1945–1964," *American Journal of Sociology* 112 (2007): 1713–74, and Anthony S. Chen, "'The Hitlerian Rule of Quotas': Racial Conservatism and Fair Employment Practices Legislation in New York State, 1941–1945," *Journal of American History* 92 (March 2006): 1238–64.

14. Edward G. Carmines and James A. Stimson, *Issue Evolution* (Princeton: Princeton University Press, 1990), xi–xii, 42, 45, 47, 141, 154, 160.

15. Carmines and Stimson, *Issue Evolution*, 184–85, 190.

16. Thomas B. Edsall and Mary D. Edsall, *Chain Reaction: The Impact of Race, Rights, and Taxes on American Politics* (New York: Norton, 1989), 7, 178; Carmines and Stimson, *Issue Evolution*, 44, 190.

17. Carmines and Stimson, *Issue Evolution*, 188, 190; Edsall and Edsall, *Chain Reaction*, 7, 178.

18. "He Led a Revolution. Will It Survive?" *The Economist*, June 12, 2004, p. 25.

19. Brian Feinstein and Eric Schickler, "Platforms and Parties: The Civil Rights Realignment Reconsidered," *Studies in American Political Development* 22

(Spring 2008): 1–31; Taeku Lee, *Mobilizing Public Opinion: Black Insurgency and Racial Attitudes in the Civil Rights Era* (Chicago: University of Chicago Press, 2002); David Karol, *Explaining Party Position Change in American Politics: Coalition Management* (New York: Cambridge University Press, forthcoming).

20. Robert P. Lane to Burlingham, Feb. 21, 1945, Box 1-6, Burlingham Papers, HLS-HU; Otto F. Christenson to Minnesota League of Women Voters, November 21, 1949, Minnesota Historical Society, St. Paul, MN; OCFEP, "Some Questions and Answers on FEPC" [1950], folder 1, container 1, OCFEP Records, Western Reserve Historical Society; "Committee Hearings on FEPC," April 18, 1951, folder 27, container 2, OCFEP Records.

21. Matthew Lassiter, *The Silent Majority: Suburban Politics in the Sunbelt South* (Princeton: Princeton University Press, 2006); Kevin Kruse, *White Flight: Atlanta and the Making of Modern Conservatism* (Princeton: Princeton University Press, 2005); Joseph Crespino, *In Search of Another Country: Mississippi and the Conservative Counterrevolution* (Princeton: Princeton University Press, 2007); Joseph Lowndes, *The Southern Origins of Modern Conservatism* (New Haven: Yale University Press, forthcoming); Biondi, *To Stand and Fight*, 19. It may be tempting to think that conservative critics of FEP laws in the 1940s and 1950s were justified in forecasting that passing a law against discrimination would lead to quotas and preferential treatment. Perhaps they were prescient in light of the controversies that would later arise in connection with affirmative action. Such concerns, however, proved overblown. In the weeks before Ives-Quinn passed, business groups and their sympathizers openly foretold that the law could lead to riots and ruination, over and against the reassurances of liberals. Yet the darkest prophecies of conservatives never came to pass. Anxiety over quotas in wartime New York seem especially misplaced. As noted by Hugh Davis Graham, when Sen. Sam Erwin (D-NC) raised the charge of quotas at a hearing on what would become Title VII of the Civil Rights Act, he pointed to the language of specific hiring regulations issued by the Army Corps of Engineers and the Federal Housing and Home Finance Agency. Whether his reading distorted their intent is a question worth asking, but neither Robert Moses nor Westbrook Pegler pointed to anything comparable when making the same allegation two decades earlier. That is because they could not. No such language existed. Their concern was that the passage of legislation mandating equal treatment would—in and of itself—lead employers to impose quotas preemptively in their hiring practices or to ask for quotas so as to set a clear standard for compliance. What conservatives foresaw is not what happened. In states that passed FEP laws, there is little evidence that employers set quotas and no evidence that employers asked state FEP commissions to set quotas. Moreover, when the charge of quotas arose in the 1960s and the decades thereafter, it did not emerge for the same reasons as it did in the 1940s. This time, critics of affirmative action were concerned about specific policies that invoked racial distinctions and that they regarded as functional quotas—and they said so. Ironically, they would probably have readily accepted the policy that Moses and Pegler used the same language to reject. Charges of quotas thus seem less a clear-eyed prediction of a genuine danger than a device of political rhetoric.

22. Sugrue, *The Origins of the Urban Crisis*; Kevin Phillips, *The Emerging Republican Majority* (New Rochelle, NY: Arlington House, 1969).

23. James Baldwin and Malcolm X quoted in Weisbrot, *Freedom Bound*, 83.

24. Standing squarely between the two periods is a wave of urban riots and the rise of black power. This makes it tempting to accept the *post hoc ergo propter hoc* reasoning that is implicit in the discontinuarian perspective—that is, since affirmative action, busing, identity politics, and the breakup of the New Deal bloc happened *after* the riots and black power, it happened *because* of the riots and black power.

25. The following passage about social change typifies their substance and tone: "If so, the change can be traced directly back to the dedication of those who risked their lives in a conscious effort to transform the nation. They made demands that, by 1964, the nation could not refuse. German shepherds, fire houses, and cattle prods: the violent resistance of the white South—in marked contrast to the nonviolence of those who marched and sang—tipped the scales. Nineteen hundred sixty-four was the year the great Civil Rights Act was passed; a year later the Voting Rights Act was enacted. These historic measures committed the full power of the federal government to the task of wiping out Jim Crow and securing equal rights for black Americans." Abigail and Stephen Thernstrom, *America in Black and White: One Nation, Indivisible* (New York: Simon and Schuster, 1997), 122, 544.

26. Ibid., 148, 158, 179–80. The discontinuarian perspective is not confined to writers sharing the same political commitments as the Thernstroms. Many self-identified liberals attribute the demise of the New Deal bloc to policies like affirmative action and busing, which is said to have fatally alienated the white working class. In *Twilight of Common Dreams*, former Students for a Democratic Society (SDS) president Todd Gitlin goes a step further and traces the rise of identity politics as well as the fall of liberalism and the New Left to developments in the late 1960s, when the "principle of separate organization on behalf of distinct interests" began to replace earlier desires for "solidarity and community." Gitlin does concede smartly that "there is no golden past to recover." His concession is belied, however, by a pervasive adherence to the unstated premise that a sharp historical break divides the sixties. The book incessantly refers to the "universalist tradition of the Left" and betrays a discernible nostalgia for a time when "civil rights activists spoke unabashedly of the 'beloved community,' as did their student radical allies in the largely white New Left." There is a continuous, if largely furtive, distinction made between the "early New Left politics of universalist hope" and the "late New Left politics of separatist rage." Without question, affirmative action is a child of the latter politics. "That most contentious program, affirmative action," he writes, "has a root in the Declaration of Independence's commitment to equality from birth, minorities and women having generalized the principle of *one person, one vote* to *one group member, one job*" (italics in the original). See Todd Gitlin, *The Twilight of Common Dreams: Why America Is Wracked by Culture Wars* (New York: Metropolitan, 1995), 16, 43, 96–97, 100, 103, 146.

27. Graham, *The Civil Rights Era*, 451–52.

28. C. Vann Woodward, *Thinking Back: The Perils of Writing History* (Baton Rouge: Louisiana State University Press, 1986), 79.

29. Sugrue, *The Origins of the Urban Crisis*; Self, *American Babylon*; Rhomberg, *No There There*; Kurashige, *The Shifting Grounds of Race*; Josh Sides, *L.A. City Limits: African American Los Angeles from the Great Depression to the Present* (Berkeley: University of California Press, 2003); Biondi, *To Stand and Fight*; Matthew Countryman, *Up South: Civil Rights and Black Power in Philadelphia* (Philadelphia: University of Pennsylvania Press, 2006); James Wolfinger, *Philadelphia Divided: Race and Politics in the City of Brotherly Love* (Chapel Hill: University of North Carolina Press, 2007); Santow, *Saul Alinsky and the Dilemma of Race in the Postwar City*. The publication of Sugrue's forthcoming book is likely to rectify the imbalance significantly. See Thomas J. Sugrue, *Sweet Land of Liberty* (New York: Random House, 2008).

30. MacLean, *Freedom Is Not Enough*.

31. Nathan Glazer, "A Breakdown in Civil Rights Enforcement?" *Public Interest* 23 (Spring 1971): 109; emphasis in original.

32. Thanks to Margaret Weir for first suggesting the phrase to me.

33. Alan Freeman, "Antidiscrimination Law: The View from 1989," in *The Politics of Law: A Progressive Critique*, rev. ed., edited by David Kairys (New York: Pantheon, 1990), 121–50.

34. *Wygant v. Jackson Board of Education*, 476 U.S. 267 (1986); *City of Richmond v. J.A. Croson*, 488 U.S. 469 (1989); *Adarand Constructors v. Pena*, 515 U.S. 200 (1995).

35. *City of Richmond v. J.A. Croson*, 488 U.S. 469 (1989). In his concurrence to *Adarand*, Scalia reiterated his argument about the constitutional legitimacy of compensating individual victims of discrimination: "Individuals who have been wronged by unlawful racial discrimination should be made whole; but under our Constitution there can be no such thing as either a creditor or a debtor race. That concept is alien to the Constitution's focus upon the individual." See *Adarand Constructors v. Pena*, 515 U.S. 200 (1995).

36. H.R. 401,79th Congress, 1 Session, January 3, 1945; CR, 79th Cong., 1 sess., July 12, 1945, pp. 7486. For illuminating reflections on equal protection law, see Richard A. Primus, "Equal Protection and Disparate Impact: Round Three," *Harvard Law Review* 117 (December 2003): 494–587. See also Laura Beth Nielsen and Robert L. Nelson, *The Legal Construction of Discrimination: A Sociological Model of Employment Discrimination Law* (Chicago: American Bar Foundation, 2003).

Appendix

1. Michael B. Katz, Mark J. Stern, and Jamie J. Fader, "The New African American Inequality," *Journal of American History* 92 (June 2005): 75–108, esp. 102; Robert W. Fairlies and William A. Sundstrom, "The Emergence, Persistence, and Recent Widening of the Racial Employment Gap," *Industrial and Labor Relations Review* 52 (January 1999): 252–70, esp. 255.

2. Schickler, *Disjointed Pluralism*,. Note that Schickler includes Oklahoma in his definition of the South.

3. Gallup Organization, Gallup Poll #349: "aipo0349.por" [computer file]. Lincoln, NE: Gallup Organization [producer], 1945. Storrs, CT: The Roper Center, University of Connecticut [distributor], 2003.

4. The Berinsky-Schickler dataset is only one of dozens of datasets that are part of *The American Mass Public in the 1930s and 1940s Project*, Adam Berinsky and Eric Schickler, PIs; supported under National Science Foundation Political Science Program Grant SES-0550431. I am extremely grateful to Adam Berinsky for making this data available to me.

5. Adam Berinsky, "American Public Opinion in the 1930s and 1940s: The Analysis of Quota-Controlled Sample Survey Data," *Public Opinion Quarterly* 71 (Winter 2006): 499–529, esp. 502, 504.

6. Ibid.

7. Roughly half of the sample (N = 1,587) in 1945 was administered this question, which was located on Form K. Approximately half of the sample (N = 1,548) in the 1945 Gallup Poll was given a slightly different survey (Form T) with the question, "Would you favor or oppose a state law that would require employees to work alongside persons of any race or color?" This question merits separate analysis because it suggests a stronger and more indiscriminate form of government intervention than the policy described by the question on Form K. The question on Form K explicitly stipulates that prospective hires are qualified for the job, while the question on Form T leaves open the possibility that a prospective hire might be unqualified. The question on Form T, moreover, seems to imply that the law would require employers to make sure that their employees are working alongside persons of any race or color; it has a slightly more coercive ring than the question on Form K. A separate, preliminary analysis of the data yields results that are broadly consistent with the main analysis. The one exception is that the effect of voting for Dewey in 1944 becomes statistically indistinguishable from zero if controls for political ideology are included in the model. I do not consider the results of the analysis to be strong evidence against the effect of party identification, mainly because the question posed on Form T appears to ask about a much more extensive form of government intervention into labor markets than the question posed on Form K. The severity of the policy could wash out partisan effects (especially after controlling for political ideology), rendering the question too *conservative* a test of partisan differences. I would argue that the analysis presented in the main text is a more appropriate test.

8. J. Scott Long and Jeremy Freese, *Regression Models for Categorical Dependent Variables Using Stata*, 2nd ed. (College Station: StataCorp LP, 2006).

9. Anthony S. Chen, Robert Mickey, and Robert P. Van Houweling, "Backlash Reconsidered: The Political Attitudes and Electoral Behavior of Non-Southern Whites on Civil Rights, 1946–1960," paper presented at the Annual Meetings of the Social Science History Association, Baltimore, MD, 2003.

10. Ibid. The classic specification of the ecological regression is Goodman's, which may be written as $Y = \alpha + \beta_d T_d + \varepsilon$, where Y is the fraction of "Yes" votes on Proposition 11, α is the fraction of Republicans voting "Yes," β_d is the fraction of Democrats voting "Yes," T_d is Democratic turnout, and ε is a stochastic error term. For more details, see Leo Goodman, *American Sociological Review* 18 (1953): 663–66.

11. For specific details and findings, see Anthony S. Chen, Robert Mickey, and Robert P. Van Houweling, "Explaining the Contemporary Alignment of Race and Party: Evidence from California's 1946 Ballot Initiative on Fair Employment," *Studies in American Political Development* 22 (Fall 2008): 204–28.

12. Paul Allison, *Event History Analysis* (Newbury Park, CA: Sage, 1982); Trond Peterson, "The Statistical Analysis of Event Histories." *Sociological Methods and Research* 19 (1991): 270–323; Kazuo Yamaguchi, *Event History Analysis* (Newbury Park, CA: Sage, 1991). I do not report robust standard errors clustered on the state level because states are clearly not independent of one another. See Frances Stokes Berry and William D. Berry, "State Lottery Adoptions as Policy Innovations," *American Political Science Review* 84 (1990): 395–415; "Tax Innovation in the States: Capitalizing on Political Opportunity," *American Journal of Political Science* 36 (1992): 715–42. The reported estimates, however, are highly comparable to those obtained with robust (but non-clustered) standard errors. Results are available upon request. For a more detailed discussion of the event-history analysis, see the relevant sections of Anthony S. Chen, "The Party of Lincoln and the Politics of State Fair Employment Practices Legislation in the North, 1945–1964," *American Journal of Sociology* 112 (2007): 1713–74.

13. I exclude thirteen states altogether, eleven states from the South, as well as Alaska and Hawaii, following the convention in studies of state economic performance.

14. Council of State Governments, *Book of the States* (Chicago: Council of State Governments, 1943–1964). The decision to include only years in which state legislatures met in regular or special sessions represents a compromise between two approaches of contrasting rigor. The least exacting approach, which would severely understate the hazard rate, would be to include all of the years in the period 1945–64. The most exacting (but prohibitively time-consuming) approach would be to include all of the years in which it is definitely known that a legislator introduced a fair employment bill.

15. Indiana and Wisconsin passed *non-enforceable* laws in 1945 and 1961, and *enforceable* laws in 1957 and 1963, respectively. I consider only the passage of enforceable laws; hence, I code Indiana and Wisconsin as having passed FEP laws in 1957 and 1963, respectively. To see if this affects the results, I estimate the trimmed models in table A.4 excluding all observations from both Indiana and Wisconsin. The results, which are highly comparable, are available upon request.

16. Council of State Governments, *Book of the States* (Chicago: Council of State Governments, 1943–64). My coding scheme raises three potential concerns. First, it is possible to classify only state legislatures controlled by a Democratic supermajority (i.e., a veto-proof majority) as "Democratic control" (that is, set to 0). This circumstance, however, was extremely rare outside the South. Moreover, I am not aware of any case in which a Democratic or Republican governor actually vetoed an FEP bill. Republican governors very occasionally threatened a veto, but these cases are correctly coded as Republican control. Second, using a dummy variable discards potentially valuable information about the magnitude of party control as well as information about various configurations of party control that add up to "Republican control of veto points." This is true, but I am less interested in whether the passage of FEP laws is a continuous function of Republican

strength and more interested in whether the passage of FEP legislation is a step function of Republican control—that is, I am more concerned about identifying the difference between a state where Republicans control a veto point and a state where they do not than I am in identifying the difference between a weakly Republican-controlled government and a strongly Republican-controlled government. To gauge the impact of an alternate coding of party control, I estimate the restricted specifications in table A.4 with a more finely differentiated measure of party control; namely, six dummies indicating unified Republican control, Republican governor and divided legislature, Republican governor and Democratic legislature, Democratic governor and Republican legislature, Democratic governor and divided legislature, and unified Democratic control. I use unified Democratic control as the reference category. The results are substantially similar. Thirdly, Minnesota and Nebraska hold nonpartisan elections for the legislature. For these states, I code Republican control based on the party of the governor. To determine if this decision drives the results, I reestimate the restricted models in table A.4 excluding all observations from Minnesota and Nebraska. The coefficient for Republican control is robust to the exclusions.

17. Timothy Besley and Anne Case, "Political Institutions and Policy Choices: Evidence from the United States," *Journal of Economic Literature* 41 (2003): 7–43. I choose *not* to control for innovative propensity using Walker's score, as other researchers have done for reasons that are sound to their purposes. For example, see Sarah Soule and Yvonne Zylan, "Runaway Train? The Diffusion of State-Level Reform in ADC/AFDC Eligibility Requirements, 1950–1967," *American Journal of Sociology* 103 (1997): 751. Ranging from 0 to 1, Walker's score is constructed from data on eighty-eight different programs that had been enacted in at least twenty states by 1965. See Jack Walker, "The Diffusion of Innovations among the American States," *American Political Science Review* 63 (September 1969): 882. The first state to enact a particular program is given a score of 0, while the last state to enact a program is given a 1. States enacting programs in the interim are given a score that corresponds to the proportion of time elapsed between the enactment of the first and last program. Scores for each program are then averaged by state. This score is the *dependent* variable in Walker's study, but it may be inappropriate for use as an *independent* variable in the present study. Not only does it use up a scarce degree of freedom, it is also unclear what the score measures. Using it would only tell us *that* innovative states tend to innovate—that they have a propensity to innovate—but not necessarily *why* they tend to innovate. In results available upon request, I estimate the restricted models in table A.4 using Walker's score as an additional time-constant covariate. The coefficient for Republican control remains negative, large, and statistically significant in all specifications.

18. Thomas R. Dye, "Inequality and Civil-Rights Policy in the States," *Journal of Politics* 31 (1969): 1080–97; Walker, "The Diffusion of Innovations among the American States"; Virginia Gray, "Innovation in the States," *American Political Science Review* 67 (1973): 1174–85; U.S. Bureau of the Census (various years). For CPI-U figures, see the Bureau of Labor Statistics website (ftp://ftp.bls.gov/pub/special.requests/cpi/cpiai.txt, accessed November 9, 2006). It is worth pointing out that Erikson, Wright, and McIver find evidence that income and other demo-

graphic variables influence policy primarily "because income is correlated with the degree of liberal sentiment of state public opinion." See Robert S. Erikson, Gerald C. Wright, and John P. McIver, *Statehouse Democracy: Public Opinion and Public Policy in the American States* (New York: Cambridge University Press, 1993), 86–87. Hence controlling for income partially controls for the ideological character of the state electorate.

19. Walker, "The Diffusion of Innovations among the American States"; Theda Skocpol, Marjorie Abend-Wein, Christopher Howard, and Susan Goodrich Lehmann, "Women's Associations and the Enactment of Mothers' Pensions in the United States," *American Political Science Review* 87 (1993): 686–701; Thomas M. Holbrook and Van Dunk, "Electoral Competition in the American States," *American Political Science Review* 87 (1993): 955–62; Charles Barrileaux, Thomas Holbrook, and Laura Langer, "Electoral Competition, Legislative Balance, and American State Welfare Policy," *American Journal of Political Science* 46 (2002): 415–27; Council of State Governments, *Book of the States, 1945–1964*; Congressional Quarterly, *Congressional Quarterly's Guide to U.S. Elections*, 3rd ed. (Washington, DC: Congressional Quarterly, 1994).

20. Paul Burstein, *Discrimination, Jobs, and Politics* (Chicago: University of Chicago Press, 1985); "Should Sociologists Consider the Impact of Public Opinion on Public Policy?" *Social Forces* 77 (1988): 27–62; Paul Burstein and April Linton, "The Impact of Political Parties, Interest Groups, and Social Movement Organizations on Public Policy," *Social Forces* 81 (2002): 381–408; Wayne A. Santoro, "The Civil Rights Movement's Struggle for Fair Employment: A "Dramatic Events–Conventional Politics Model," *Social Forces* 81 (2002): 177–206; Taeku Lee, *Mobilizing Public Opinion* (Chicago: University of Chicago Press, 2002); Jeff Manza, Fay Lomax Cook, and Benjamin I. Page, editors, *Navigating Public Opinion: Polls, Policy, and the Future of American Democracy* (New York: Oxford University Press, 2002); Clem Brooks and Jeff Manza, *Why Welfare States Persist: The Importance of Public Opinion in Democracies* (Chicago: University of Chicago Press, 2007); Gerald C. Wright, Robert S. Erikson, and John P. McIver, "Measuring State Partisanship and Ideology with Survey Data," *Journal of Politics* 47 (1985): 469–89; Erikson, Wright, and McIver, *Statehouse Democracy*. Converse is quoted in Paul Brace, Kellie Sims-Butler, Kevin Arceneaux, and Martin Johnson, "Public Opinion in the American States: New Perspectives Using National Survey Data," *American Journal of Political Science* 46 (2002): 174. The distribution of the raw variable closely approximates the normal standard distribution. I used the sample mean of the thirty-seven states to replace missing data that were not available for Oregon, New Mexico, Delaware, and North Dakota. This is admittedly a crude control, but it is the best one presently available, and it partially addresses the total absence of public opinion from prior models. I also tried using the raw state percentages from the Gallup poll. When substituted for the dummy variable, it does not yield a statistically significant coefficient. Nor does it affect the main result. I control for public opinion using additional variables. In results available upon request, I use three different measures to control for the ideological character of mass opinion in the states. The first is a score of citizen ideology developed by Berry and his collaborators from data on Congressional roll-call votes and other sources. See William D. Berry, Evan J. Ringquist,

Richard C. Fording, and Russell L. Hanson, "Measuring Citizen and Government Ideology in the American States, 1960–93," *American Journal of Political Science* 42 (1998): 327–48. Although scores are now available annually for the period 1960–2002, I use only the average of the scores from 1960 to 1964 as a time-constant covariate. The averaged score ranges from a low (conservative) of 28.83112 for Nebraska and a high (liberal) of 78.90062 for Rhode Island. When substituted for the main measure of public opinion, it does not yield a statistically significant coefficient. Nor does it affect the main result. The second variable is a survey-based, time-constant measure of state opinion developed by Wright, Erikson, and McIver from pooled (1974–82) CBS/*NYT* surveys. See Wright, Erikson, and McIver, "Measuring State Partisanship and Ideology with Survey Data," 476–79. I use the unweighted version of their measure, which is thought to reflect the distribution of opinion for the "active" electorate. The unweighted measure ranges from a low (liberal) of −.053 for Nevada to a high (conservative) of .333 for Utah. When substituted for the main measure of public opinion, it does not yield a statistically significant coefficient in any of the relevant specifications reported in table A.4. Nor does it affect the main result. (The authors note that the weighted and unweighted measures are highly correlated and generally yield identical results.) Using a third time-constant variable developed by Brace and his collaborators from pooled data (1974–98) in the General Social Survey, I control for mass opinion about racial integration. See Brace et al., "Public Opinion in the American States: New Perspectives Using National Survey Data." The variable ranges from a low of .5 for West Virginia to a high of .88 for Rhode Island. I used the sample mean (.75) to replace missing data for five states. When substituted for the main measure of public opinion, it does not yield a statistically significant coefficient. Nor does it affect the main result.

21. Stephen Ansolabehere, Alan Gerber, and James Snyder, Jr., 2000. "Equal Votes, Equal Money: Court-Ordered Redistricting and Public Expenditures," *American Political Science Review* (December 2002): 767–77.

22. A "closed shop" is a company that will employ only union workers. A "union shop" is a company that does not require union membership as a condition of hiring but requires it for continued employment after a specific period of time. A so-called open shop is a company that does not require union membership for either hiring or continued employment. According to Lumsden and Peterson, states that had passed a Right to Work (RTW) law by 1964 include Arizona (1946), Nebraska (1946), South Dakota (1946), Iowa (1947), North Dakota (1947), Nevada (1951), Utah (1955), Indiana (1957), Kansas (1958), and Wyoming (1963). Indiana repealed its law in 1965. See Keith Lumsden and Craig Peterson, "The Effect of Right-to-Work Laws on Unionization in the United States," *Journal of Political Economy* 83 (1975): 1242. See also David Jacobs and Marc Dixon, "The Politics of Labor-Management Relations: Detecting the Conditions that Affect Changes in Right-to-Work Laws," *Social Problems* 53 (2006): 118–37. It might be tempting to view the successful adoption of an RTW law as proof that labor was unconcerned about the issue or failed to mobilize a counter-offensive. This does not seem historically justifiable, however. Many states that did pass RTW laws did so over the strenuous objections of organized labor. For instance, Indiana passed an RTW law in 1957, but not until after orga-

nized labor mounted a robust response, hosting dinners for undecided business-men and distributing legislative advisories (*NYT,* February 11, 1957, p. 29). When the law eventually passed, ten thousand angry union members—prominently among them the steelworkers of Hammond, Gary, and East Chicago—marched on the statehouse, demanding that governor Harold W. Handley repeal the bill (*NYT,* March 3, 1957, p. 46; *LAT,* March 3, 1957, p. 3).

23. Lockard, *Toward Equal Opportunity,* 29–43; William J. Collins, "The Political Economy of State-Level Fair Employment Laws, 1940–1964," *Explorations in Economic History* 40 (2003): 24–25; U.S. Census Bureau, *Historical Statistics of the United States, Part I* (Washington, DC: U.S. Government Printing Office, 1975); AJC, *American Jewish Yearbook* (New York: American Jewish Committee, various years); *Official Catholic Directory,* various years; NAACP, various years; Leo Troy and Neil Sheflin, *U.S. Union Sourcebook: Membership, Finances, Structure, Directory* (West Orange, NJ: Industrial Relations Data and Information Services, 1985), p. 7-3. The NAACP data were collected from the Records of the NAACP in the Library of Congress. For a full accounting of their whereabouts, please see Anthony S. Chen, "From Fair Employment to Equal Employment Opportunity and Beyond: Affirmative Action and the Politics of Civil Rights in the New Deal Order," Ph.D. diss., Department of Sociology, University of California, Berkeley, 2002, pp. 310–12. Data on Catholic residents by state was graciously provided by Mary Gautier at the Center for Applied Research in the Apostolate at Georgetown University. To identify potential nonlinear relationships, I substituted logged measures of the black, Jewish, and Catholic population, as well as NAACP membership in the full specification. The results differ slightly for the control variables. While the coefficients for Republican control, income, employer strength, and percentage of neighboring states with an FEP law remain similar, the coefficients for Jewish population (ln), Catholic population (ln), and NAACP membership (ln) become statistically significant, and the coefficient for black population (ln) becomes statistically insignificant. All the logged variables are highly multicollinear, however. This is clear when the full specification with logged measures is estimated using OLS regression, and a Variance Inflation Factor (VIF) is calculated for each coefficient. Jewish population (ln), black population (ln), Catholic population (ln), and NAACP membership (ln), all exhibit high VIF scores. Since the main results do not change, and since the interpretation of the percentage measures is more straightforward, I retain use of the percentage measures.

24. Susan Olzak, *The Dynamics of Ethnic Competition and Conflict* (Palo Alto: Stanford University Press, 1992); Angela Behrens, Christopher Uggen, and Jeff Manza, "Ballot Manipulation and the 'Menace of Negro Domination,'" *American Journal of Sociology* 109 (2003): 559–605; Collins, "The Political Economy of State-Level Fair Employment Laws, 1940–1964."

25. See Berry and Berry, "State Lottery Adoptions as Policy Innovations"; Berry and Berry, "Tax Innovation in the States: Capitalizing on Political Opportunity"; David Strang and Nancy Brandon Tuma, "Spatial and Temporal Heterogeneity in Diffusion." *American Journal of Sociology* 99 (1993): 614–39; Yvonne Zylan and Sarah A. Soule, "Ending Welfare As We Know It (Again): Welfare State Retrenchment, 1989–1995." *Social Forces* 79 (2000): 623–52.

26. Models 1, 2, and 3 correspond to models 1, 2, and 5, respectively, in table A.4 of Chen, "The Party of Lincoln and the Politics of State Fair Employment Practices Legislation in the North, 1945–1964." Models 4 and 5 correspond to models 1 and 2, respectively, in table 5 of the published article.

27. On regression-discontinuity, see John DiNardo and David Lee, "Economic Impacts of New Unionization on Private Sector Employers, 1984–2001," *Quarterly Journal of Economics* 119 (2004): 1383–442; David Lee, Enrico Moretti, and Matthew J. Butler, "Do Voters Affect or Elect Policies? Evidence from the U.S. House," *Quarterly Journal of Economics* 119 (2004): 807–59.

28. Long and Freese, *Regression Models for Categorical Dependent Variables Using Stata.*

Index

Abrams, Charles, 234
Advertising Council, 213
Aeronautical Mechanics Local No. 741, International Association of Machinists, 36
Aerospace Industries Association, 195
affirmative action: and administrative enforcement, 4, 17; as administrative orders for federal contractors, 7; alternative development of, 232–33, 235; alternative enforcement powers for, 233–34; and civil rights history, 247; as color-blind, 233; and compensation, 210, 215–18; and conservatives, 25, 26–27; and counterfactual analysis, 25–27, 364n6; and courts, 4, 233; development of, 231–32; and enforcement powers, 231; and Equal Employment Opportunity Act of 1972, 227; and Executive Order 10925, 210; and Executive Order 11246, 172; and federal contractors, 7, 230; and federal fair employment legislation, 51; foundations for, 22–23, 25, 26–27; goals and timetables for, 3, 7, 221–22, 223–24, 227, 230, 231, 232; and Johnson administration, 220; meaning of, 7, 172, 210, 226–27; and Nixon administration, 172; and Philadelphia Plan, 220–22; and Plans for Progress, 172, 212, 214, 216, 222, 223–25; and policy alternatives, 230; as preferential treatment, 220; and President's Committee on Equal Employment Opportunity, 211, 214; and private business, 7, 230; and quotas/proportional representation, 215–16, 228, 247; and race attentive programs, 227, 235; and race neutral programs, 226–27; and Rehnquist Court, 252; and Republicans, 241–42; scholarly accounts of, 3–5, 230; and special treatment of minorities, 214–15, 228; voluntary programs for, 173, 213–14, 223–25, 231
African Americans: and affirmative action, 217; and California fair employment legislation, 131; and Civil Rights Act of 1964, 176; and Committee on Discrimination in Employment, 91; and Democrats, 241; discrimination as demoralizing, 50; and discrimination in North vs. South, 9–10; educational levels of, 10; electoral importance of, 86, 115, 324n83; employment rate of, 2, 10, 256; fair employment legislation as harming, 66; and federal fair employment legislation, 41, 43; and history of civil rights movement, 245–51; and housing, 13; and Ives-Quinn Act, 90–91, 113; and job hierarchy, 14, 36, 43; and liberal bloc, 9–10, 12; and marriage, 65; and Massachusetts fair employment legislation, 116; and military, 59, 310n8; and New Deal legislation, 61; Northern, 35; and Plans for Progress, 213–14; poverty levels among, 35; preferential treatment of, 67; and Republicans, 183; and Roosevelt, 37, 38; and Second Great Migration, 9, 13; and state fair employment legislation, 124, 140, 157, 158, 159; support for Truman, 60–61; and Taft, 78; and unions, 17, 18; wages of, 36, 61; wartime gains of, 96; wartime militancy of, 36; in wartime South, 35; and white ethnics, 13–14; and white workers, 300n23. *See also* minorities
Agnew, Spiro, 208
Alabama, public opinion in, 59–60. *See also* Birmingham, Ala.
Alaska, fair employment legislation in, 118
Alexander, Clifford L., Jr., 192, 199
Amenta, Edwin, 236, 237
American Airlines, 134
American Civil Liberties Union (ACLU), 13, 20, 89, 102, 120
American Council of Race Relations, 49
American Council on Human Rights, 45
American Dental Association (ADA), 109
American Federation of Labor (AFL), 37, 43, 120, 126

The Power of Separation: American Constitutionalism and the Myth of the Legislative Veto by Jessica Korn

Why Movements Succeed or Fail: Opportunity, Culture, and the Struggle for Woman Suffrage by Lee Ann Banaszak

Kindred Strangers: The Uneasy Relationship between Politics and Business in America by David Vogel

From the Outside In: World War II and the American State by Bartholomew H. Sparrow

Classifying by Race edited by Paul E. Peterson

Facing Up to the American Dream: Race, Class, and the Soul of the Nation by Jennifer L. Hochschild

Political Organizations by James Q. Wilson

Social Policy in the United States: Future Possibilities in Historical Perspective by Theda Skocpol

Experts and Politicians: Reform Challenges to Machine Politics in New York, Cleveland, and Chicago by Kenneth Finegold

Bound by Our Constitution: Women, Workers, and the Minimum Wage by Vivien Hart

Prisoners of Myth: The Leadership of the Tennessee Valley Authority, 1933–1990 by Erwin C. Hargrove

Political Parties and the State: The American Historical Experience by Martin Shefter

Politics and Industrialism: Early Railroads in the United States and Prussia by Colleen A. Dunlavy

The Lincoln Persuasion: Remaking American Liberalism by David Greenstone

Labor Visions and State Power: The Origins of Business Unionism in the United States by Victoria C. Hattam